D0292755

TENNESSEE

SUSANNA HENIGHAN POTTER

Contents

▶ **Discover Tennessee** **8**
  Planning Your Trip 10
  Explore Tennessee 14
  • Downtown and the Delta: Memphis
    and West Tennessee 14
  • Into the Heartland: Nashville and
    Middle Tennessee 16
  • Tennessee's Best Parks 18
  • From the Smokies to Scenic City:
    East Tennessee 19
  • From Bluegrass to the Blues:
    A Musical Journey 21
  • Tennessee's Top Festivals 23

▶ **Memphis** **25**
  Sights 29
  Entertainment 48
  Sports and Recreation 57
  Accommodations 61
  Food 64
  Information and Services 72
  Getting There and Around 73

▶ **Western Plains** **76**
  The Delta 79
  Reelfoot Lake 86
  Kentucky Lake 91
  Land Between the Lakes 100

  Jackson 105
  South Along the Tennessee 111
  Southwestern Tennessee 116

▶ **Nashville** **119**
  Sights 124
  Entertainment 147
  Sports and Recreation 163
  Accommodations 168
  Food 174
  Information and Services 183
  Getting There and Around 185

▶ **The Heartland** **187**
  Clarksville 190
  Along the Cumberland 197
  West of Nashville 204
  Franklin 207
  The Natchez Trace 216
  Walking Horse Country 231
  The Southern Heartland 238
  Murfreesboro 256

▶ **Cumberland Plateau** **261**
  The Upper Plateau 264
  The Middle Plateau 278
  The Lower Plateau 287

► **Chattanooga and
the Overhill Country** **298**
Chattanooga 301
The Ocoee. 317
The Hiwassee. 328
The Tellico. 332

► **Knoxville** **337**
Sights. 340
Sports and Recreation. 352
Entertainment 354
Accommodations 359
Food. 360
Information and Services 363
Getting There and Around. 364
Around Knoxville. 365

► **Great Smoky Mountains** **375**
Sights. 383
Driving Tours 389
Hiking. 390
Other Recreation. 394
Practicalities 397
Gateways to the Smokies. 399

► **The First Frontier**. **415**
The Tri-Cities 418
Northern Cherokee
National Forest 432

Ridges and Valleys 442

► **Background**. **453**
The Land. 453
History. 460
Government and Economy 475
People and Culture. 477

► **Essentials** **481**
Getting There and Around. 481
Recreation 483
Accommodations 485
Food. 486
Tips for Travelers 487
Health and Safety 490
Information and Services 492

► **Resources** **495**
Suggested Reading. 495
Internet Resources. 500

► **Index**. **502**

► **Map Index** **516**

Discover Tennessee

It was thanks to my brother-in-law that I first really saw Tennessee from the sky. An amateur pilot, Charlie took me along on a flight over the eastern foothills a few years ago. From 3,500 feet, I could see Sevierville's Victorian courthouse tower and could even spot the 1920s farmhouse where I grew up. The lake near our house surprised me with its size and amoebic shape; fingers of water seemed to stretch out in every direction.

From the sky, East Tennessee is cascading mountains: Ridgelines plunge down into valleys and up to peaks shrouded in clouds. As you head west, the mountains turn to foothills and eventually into the rolling landscape of Middle Tennessee. From above, the patchwork — forests, fields, narrow roads, and fence lines — is more beautiful than any crazy quilt.

Across the Tennessee River and into West Tennessee the landscape becomes flatter still. Plains stretch as far as the eye can see. And then there's the mighty Mississippi River, a wide channel flowing slowly southward through this fertile land, towards Memphis.

Ever since taking this flight, I have asked for a window seat whenever I'm flying to or from Tennessee. What I see is a place that defies expectations. Tennessee is not just Nashville and Graceland. It's not just the Smoky Mountains. It is a land of rivers, fast and slow, of cold mountain streams and rich wetlands, but it is also so much more than you think.

Tennessee is the original home of the Cherokee Indians, whose language lives on in place names like Tuckaleechee, Chattanooga, and even Tennessee itself.

Tennessee has nurtured Nobel laureates, Pulitzer Prize-winners, and statesmen. It's the birthplace of country music and the home of the blues; music seems to flow in the rivers and in the veins of Tennesseans.

Tennessee's people include the generous and independent folk of the eastern mountains, from whose hills and hollers came the sound of shape-note singing and the wail of a fiddle.

Its people too are the smart ones who turned a small city called Nashville into the Athens of the South, and later, Music City USA. They are the imaginative ones who envisioned a new future for the old industrial city of Chattanooga, its downtown reborn.

Out west, in the Delta country and Memphis, the land and the city nurtured bluesmen and rock 'n' roll pioneers. People here are resilient and brave; their city has returned from devastation more than once.

From the sky, you can see Tennessee's beauty, but you have to be on the ground to see the beauty of its people.

Planning Your Trip

▶ WHERE TO GO

Tennessee is long. From tip to tip, the Volunteer State stretches some 432 miles—eight hours on the interstate highway. Cultural and historical differences exaggerate the state's three basic geographical regions: East, Middle, and West Tennessee. These so-called Grand Divisions are each a destination capable of standing alone.

Memphis

Memphis may owe its existence to the mighty Mississippi, but it is music that gives this city its soul. The blues were born in Memphis, and they still live here—in nightclubs on Beale Street and juke joints around the city. But Memphis isn't just the blues. It's gospel, Elvis Presley, Soulsville, Rev. Al Green, Isaac Hayes, and Sun Records. And it's more than music. Memphis is a sophisticated city with fine dining, parks, and art museums. It is a city of the South, where you can unwind at the Peabody Hotel bar, or fuel up with a plate of barbecue.

Western Plains

The Tennessee delta is a spare landscape of cotton fields and farmhouses that spreads between the Tennessee and Mississippi Rivers. It is a landscape that nurtured blues legend "Sleepy" John Estes, writer Alex Haley, and rock icon Tina Turner. Look for bald eagles and wild turkeys amid the knob-kneed cypress trees at Reelfoot Lake. Hike and camp along the shores of Kentucky Lake at the Land Between the Lakes. Along the Tennessee

fans of Elvis Presley paying tribute to the King during Elvis Week, in Memphis

IF YOU HAVE . . .

- **A WEEKEND:** Visit Memphis or Nashville.
- **ONE WEEK:** From Memphis add the Western Plains; from Nashville add the Heartland.
- **TWO WEEKS:** Add Knoxville and the Great Smoky Mountains.
- **A MONTH:** Add the First Frontier, Chattanooga, and the Cumberland Plateau.

a fast-moving stream in the Great Smoky Mountains

River is the state's only pearl farm, the charming river town of Savannah, and Shiloh, the site of an epic Civil War battle.

Nashville

Nashville is the epicenter of country music. It is home of the Grand Ole Opry, the Country Music Hall of Fame, and dozens of recording studios. It is the place where thousands of musicians and songwriters come to make it, and the city's nightlife is all the richer for it. But Nashville is more than cowboy boots and country music. Grand antebellum homes, fine arts, and excellent dining appeal to sophisticates. Museums, historic sites, and the grand Tennessee capitol recall the city's history. And expansive parks invite recreation in this leafy, livable city.

The Heartland

Tennessee's midsection is a road trip waiting to happen. The landscape is rural and relaxing. This is Walking Horse Country, where picturesque horse farms dot the landscape and Tennessee sipping whiskey is made. In Amish Country black buggies and old-fashioned homesteads litter the back roads. The Natchez Trace is a scenic highway that marks one of the oldest overland routes between New Orleans and Nashville. Explore the Heartland in search of perfectly fried chicken, exciting summertime festivals, and the world's longest yard sale.

Cumberland Plateau

The Cumberland Plateau is a dynamic landscape of caves, waterfalls, gorges, and mountains. It is home to some of the state's best parks: the Big South Fork and Pickett State Park in the north; Fall Creek Falls State Park in the center; and Savage Gulf in the south. Come here for outdoor recreation, including hiking, biking, horseback riding, camping, and kayaking. The Plateau offers destinations with fascinating history: the lost English colony of Rugby, the idealistic experiment of Cumberland Homesteads, and the Children's Holocaust Memorial at Whitwell.

Chattanooga and the Overhill Country

Set in a bend of the Tennessee River and surrounded by the Cumberland Plateau and foothills of the Appalachian Mountains, Chattanooga is not called the Scenic City for nothing. It is a great city for families, thanks to its excellent aquarium, children's museum, parks, zoo, caves, and other novel attractions. East of the city lies the southern Cherokee

Forest and the Ocoee River—a destination for whitewater enthusiasts. No other region offers a better glimpse at the legacy of the Cherokee Indians, who once populated the hills and valleys of this Overhill land.

Knoxville

Unlikely destination city Knoxville is emerging as a center for live music and the arts. Famously unknown for decades, that-other-Tennessee-city is coming into its own. Galleries, restaurants, nightclubs, and theaters on Gay Street, Market Square, and the Old City are funky, unpretentious, and fun. Sports fans have been coming to Knoxville for years to watch the University of Tennessee Volunteers play football and basketball, and to tour the Women's Basketball Hall of Fame. New attractions such as the East Tennessee History Center and the re-opened gold-plated Sunsphere add to the city's draw.

Great Smoky Mountains

Tennessee's most lovely wilderness is the Smoky Mountains. It is the vistas that first attract you: the soft-edged peaks, enveloped by wispy white "smoke"; touched by brilliant red and orange at sunset; crowned by crisp white snow in winter. Hike through old-growth forest and mysterious mountain balds. Camp next to a mountain stream. Hunt for wild-flowers. Bicycle the Cades Cove loop to see historic cabins and churches. Outside the boundary of the park are gateway communities offering everything from the Dollywood theme park to quiet rural retreats.

The First Frontier

It was to the eastern mountains of northeast Tennessee that early settlers moved in the 1770s. Some 150 years later the descendants of these mountain folks brought forth modern country music during the Bristol Sessions. This region of Tennessee is more closely linked to Appalachia than any other; this is a landscape of hills and hollers, small towns, and traditional ways. Jonesborough is the first city of storytelling and the Tri-Cities draw race fans to Bristol Motor Speedway.

Cades Cove, in the Great Smoky Mountains

► WHEN TO GO

Summer is the peak travel season for Tennessee. This is the season of hot weather and crowds at many popular sites. Spring and fall are the best times to explore Tennessee. During spring, the weather is mild and you can enjoy springtime festivals. During the fall, the trees change color and temperatures drop.

Visitors in winter may encounter cold weather and snow. Some attractions close or cut back hours from November to February, but the cool months can also be a nice time to tour as you'll have many attractions to yourself.

► BEFORE YOU GO

Transportation

A car is essential if you are traveling in Tennessee. While visitors making a getaway to Memphis or Nashville may be able to subsist on public transportation and taxis, all others will need wheels to see this state. If it's practical, bring your own car. If you're flying in, arrange a rental car ahead of time to save money and ease hassles. It's also a good idea to get a good road map before you set out.

If you are flying to Tennessee, your destination airport will depend on your destination in general. Nashville and Memphis have international airports and generally the best airfare deals. Knoxville, Chattanooga, and the Tri-Cities regional airports are convenient if you're headed to East Tennessee.

What to Take

Take a calling card that will work at pay phones and hotels, especially if you are likely to get off the interstate and out of the range of cell phone signals.

Since your trip is likely to include a fair amount of driving, pack some tunes. Depending on your destination, pick up some classic country, bluegrass, blues, or Elvis albums to get you in the mood. And I never get on the road without a small cooler and some

hiking in the Smoky Mountains

lunch supplies, especially if I may be on the back roads for awhile.

If you're planning on spending time in the Great Smoky Mountains, be sure to pack rain gear and several layers of clothes, including a jacket or sweater—even in the summer. If you think you may do some hiking, bring good boots, a backpack, and a trails map.

Explore Tennessee

▶ **DOWNTOWN AND THE DELTA: MEMPHIS AND WEST TENNESSEE**

The blues, the plains, and the unsung landscape of the Tennessee River. Follow in the footsteps of Elvis, eat real Memphis barbecue, and explore the Delta landscape that gave rise to the blues. Travel along the Tennessee River, stopping at pearl farms, river towns, and the site of one of the bloodiest Civil War battles in Tennessee.

Day 1

Fly to Memphis and check into a downtown hotel, like the Peabody or Talbot Heirs. Dine at E. P. Delta Kitchen and stroll down to Beale Street in the evening.

Day 2

Take the Beale Street Walking Tour in the morning, stopping at the W. C. Handy Home and Museum. Take your picture with the Elvis statue, and go treasure-hunting at A. Schwab. Eat lunch at the Little Tea Shop

Stax Museum of American Soul Music, in Memphis

Alex Haley House Museum, in Henning

downtown, and then head over to Mud Island for the afternoon. Explore the Mississippi River Museum and the River Walk. Eat dinner in Harbor Town on Mud Island.

Day 3

Go to the National Civil Rights Museum in the morning, eat lunch along South Main, and then go to the Stax Museum of American Soul Music in the afternoon. Head to the Cozy Corner for a barbecue dinner.

Day 4

Make it Elvis Day. Start early at Graceland to avoid the crowds and then visit Sun Studio, where Elvis recorded his first hit. Eat a burger at Dyers on Beale Street in memory of the King.

Day 5

Start out at Elmwood Cemetery with the audio tour, and then drive east. Visit the Memphis Brooks Museum of Art and lounge in Overton Park. Tour The Dixon and eat dinner in Cooper-Young.

Day 6

Leave Memphis, driving northeast along Highway 70. Stop in Mason to pick up some of Gus's World Famous Fried Chicken for the road. Visit the Alex Haley House Museum in Henning, and the push on to Reelfoot Lake. Check into the Airpark Inn.

Day 7

Explore Reelfoot Lake State Park. Take a boat cruise or hike along the lakeshore. Eat fried catfish at Boyette's.

Day 8

Drive east to Land Between the Lakes. Visit The Homeplace to see frontier life re-created, and watch a celestial show at the Golden Pond Visitor Center and Planetarium. Overnight at the Riverfront Plantation Inn in Dover.

Day 9

Drive south to Nathan Bedford Forrest State Park to tour the Tennessee River Folklife Center. Press south to Savannah for your overnight.

Day 10

Walk around historic Savannah and then tour the Shiloh National Military Park. Take the audio tour or hike to the Shiloh Indian Mounds. Overnight at the hotel at Pickwick Landing State Resort Park, and eat dinner at the Broken Spoke.

Day 11

Go to Pinson Mounds State Archaeological Park to stretch your legs and tour mysterious Indian mounds. Eat lunch in Jackson at Dixie Castle, and then take the interstate back to Memphis.

cannons at rest at Shiloh National Military Park

▶ INTO THE HEARTLAND: NASHVILLE AND MIDDLE TENNESSEE

Start out in Music City and then strike out through Tennessee's heartland, to old railroad towns and quiet parks. See the stars on the Grand Ole Opry and make a pilgrimage to Lynchburg, home of that most famous Tennessee whiskey. Tour the sites of Civil War battles, and hear the stories of those who fought.

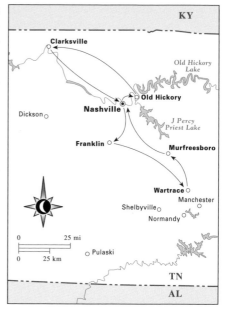

Day 1

Arrive in Nashville. Check into a downtown hotel, such as the Hermitage or Union Station. Eat dinner at the Mad Platter or Jimmy Kelly's, and stroll Lower Broadway and the District on your first night in town.

Day 2

Visit the Country Music Hall of Fame in the morning and the Ryman Auditorium in the afternoon. Have lunch at Jack's Bar-b-que on Broadway and grab an afternoon drink at Tootsie's Orchid Lounge. See the Grand Ole Opry in the evening.

Day 3

Head towards West Nashville. Drive through Music Row on your way to Centennial Park and The Parthenon. Eat lunch at Martha's at the Plantation at Belle Meade, and then spend the afternoon checking out the museum and gardens at Cheekwood. Eat dinner at F. Scott's in Green Hills.

Day 4

Go uptown to the Tennessee State Capitol and the Civil Rights Room at the Nashville Public Library. Then head west along Jefferson to eat soul food at Swett's and visit Fisk University in the afternoon. Catch the show at the Bluebird Cafe over dinner.

Day 5

Drive east to Old Hickory and spend the day at The Hermitage. Explore the home and the grounds of this estate belonging to Andrew Jackson. Grab take-out from Prince's Hot Chicken Shack on your way home and enjoy a quiet night in.

Cheekwood, in West Nashville

Cave in the afternoon. Return to Nashville for the night.

Day 6

Take a day trip to Clarksville. Tour the RiverWalk park along the Cumberland and find the statue of Wilma Rudolph. Eat lunch at Silke's Old World Breads and explore Dunbar

Day 7

Depart Nashville. Drive south to Franklin and visit the Carnton Plantation, epicenter of the Battle of Franklin. Eat lunch at Monell's, and then spend the afternoon shopping downtown

downtown Nashville, on the west bank of the Cumberland River

TENNESSEE'S BEST PARKS

From the majesty of the Great Smoky Mountains in the east to the mystery of Reelfoot Lake in the west, Tennessee is a land of unusual beauty. Wherever you are in Tennessee, look for these exceptional places to experience the outdoors.

Bays Mountain Park (Johnson City): Acres of woodland, a quiet lake, and an educational nature center make this a well-loved and popular park in the Tri-Cities.

Great Smoky Mountains National Park (Gatlinburg): The most-visited national park in the United States offers lovely mountain vistas, miles of hiking trails, and hundreds of campsites.

Reelfoot Lake State Park (Tiptonville): Formed during a massive earthquake, Reelfoot Lake is a surprising landscape of knob-kneed cypress trees and flowering lily pads.

Roan Mountain State Park (Roan Mountain): Tucked high in the northern Cherokee National Forest, Roan Mountain is the site of rhododendron gardens.

Savage Gulf State Natural Area (Beersheba Springs): A river gorge set in the Cumberland Plateau, this wilderness area is a favorite destination for hikers and backpackers.

Savage Gulf State Natural Area, in the Cumberland Plateau

the Tennessee Walking Horse, a champion show horse

and at the Factory. Eat dinner at Saffire and overnight in Franklin.

Day 8

Drive to Normandy and visit the George Dickel Distillery. Eat dinner at the Bell Buckle Cafe and overnight at the Walking Horse Hotel in Wartrace. This can be your home base for three nights.

Day 9

Drive to Shelbyville for the Tennessee Walking Horse National Celebration and eat lunch at Pope's. If it's not celebration season, then head to Lynchburg to tour the Tennessee Walking Horse Museum and the Jack Daniel's Distillery.

Day 10

Drive to Manchester and hike at the Old Stone Fort State Archaeological Park. Tour the museum and then head to Tullahoma for dinner.

Day 11

Drive back to Nashville, stopping in Murfreesboro to visit Stones River National Battlefield on the way.

► FROM THE SMOKIES TO SCENIC CITY: EAST TENNESSEE

Knoxville's Sunsphere, a leftover from the 1982 World's Fair

Start in Knoxville and then head to the wild Smoky Mountains. Explore the rural reaches of the Cumberland Plateau and find the tallest waterfall east of the Rockies. Wind up in Chattanooga to tour the state's best aquarium and see Rock City, the South's most iconic attraction.

Day 1

Fly to Knoxville, and check into the Hotel St. Oliver downtown. Stroll Gay Street and browse at the Mast General Store and Yee Haw Industries. Eat dinner at La Costa in Market Square or the Crown & Goose in the Old City.

Day 2

Visit the East Tennessee History Center. Grab lunch to go from the Tomato Head, and listen to live music at the WDVX Blue Plate Special over the lunch hour. Visit the World's Fair Park and climb to the top of the Sunsphere. Eat dinner in South Knoxville at King Tut Grill.

Gay Street in the epicenter of Knoxville's downtown

Day 3

Head to the Smoky Mountains. Drive to Gatlinburg and check into the Buckhorn Lodge or the Gatlinburg Inn. Drive to the top of Newfound Gap and enjoy the mountain views and cool air.

Day 4

Get up early and take a picnic lunch to Cades Cove before the crowds strike. Look at old farmhouses and churches, and spy deer and cottontails. Hike to Abram's Falls.

Day 5

Head north to the Cherokee National Forest and drive to the top of Roan Mountain. Take a stroll along the Appalachian Trail and look for the wild rhododendron. Overnight in Erwin.

Day 6

Drive to Historic Rugby on the Cumberland Plateau, and tour the Victorian English village. Stay in one of the historic bed and breakfasts and dine on authentic English fare at Rugby's restaurant.

Day 7

Drive south to Fall Creek Falls State Park and hike to the falls, the tallest east of the Rockies. Visit the nature center and stay overnight in the park inn.

Day 8

Drive down the Sequatchie Valley, stopping in Dayton to see the site of the Scopes Monkey Trial and Whitwell to visit the Children's Holocaust Memorial. Press on to Chattanooga and check into the Stone Fort Inn, or another downtown lodging.

Tennessee Aquarium, in Chattanooga

Day 9

Visit the Tennessee Aquarium in the morning. If the weather is nice, drive to Lookout Mountain and tour Rock City and Point Park. Watch the sun set over Chattanooga. If it is raining, visit the Hunter Museum of American Art. Eat dinner at the Back Inn Café.

Day 10

Take a day trip to the Ocoee River in the southern Cherokee National Forest. If you're up for it, raft the white water. Otherwise, take a scenic drive and stop at the Ocoee Whitewater Center. Return to Chattanooga for your final night.

Day 11

Make your way back to Knoxville, stopping in Vonore on the way to tour a replica of the British Fort Loudoun and visit the Sequoyah Birthplace Museum.

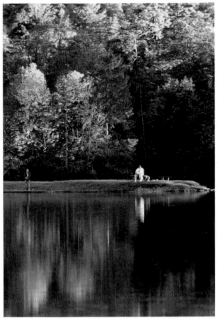

Indian Boundary, one of the most popular destinations in the southern Cherokee National Forest

▶ FROM BLUEGRASS TO THE BLUES: A MUSICAL JOURNEY

Music is what many visitors want to experience more than anything else.

Despite the broad spectrum of musical genres present in Tennessee—bluegrass to the blues—music fans should not just stick to what they know and love. Take a gander on something different and you might just discover a new favorite. At the very least, you will come to see the connections that exist between even the most varied musical forms.

Memphis

Beale Street is still the place to start if you want to find the birthplace of the blues. Visit the W. C. Handy Home and Museum to see where the father of the blues lived while

he was in Memphis. After dark, stroll Beale Street to find live blues and jazz at clubs like the King's Palace and B. B. King's.

The single best musical museum in Memphis is the Stax Museum of American Soul Music. Here you will learn not only about the remarkable story of Stax, but also the soul's musical roots in gospel and country music.

No place in Memphis is more important to American musical history than Graceland, home of Elvis Presley. Here the King lived with his parents, wife, extended family, and his buddies, the Memphis Mafia. See his remarkable taste in decor and pay your respects over his grave in the meditation garden.

W. C. Handy Home and Museum, on Beale Street in Memphis

Sun Studio is where early blues records were made, where Elvis recorded his first hit, and where the likes of Jerry Lee Lewis and Johnny Cash laid down tracks. It's hallowed ground in musical history.

One of Memphis's best-loved juke joints, Wild Bill's, is found in midtown Memphis. It gets kicking late on Friday and Saturday nights.

Western Plains

It was the landscape and hardship of country living that really gave birth to the blues. Drive the rural routes in Haywood County to breath in the Delta air. Stop in Nutbush, the childhood home of Tina Turner. Then stop in Brownsville at the West Tennessee Delta Heritage Center for exhibits about the music and culture of this region.

The International Rock-a-Billy Hall of Fame in Jackson has exhibits and tours, but the best deal is to come on Monday or Saturday nights for the live music and dancing lessons. Rock-a-billy never sounded so good!

Nashville

No part of Nashville says country music quite like Lower Broadway. Colorful honky-tonks offer live music beginning at 10 A.M. every day, and the Wildhorse Saloon is where pretty cowgirls and handsome cowboys go to have fun. For the more serious of mind, start at the Country Music Hall of Fame for an introduction to all things country. Visit the Ryman Auditorium; buy your new boots at one of the half-dozen clothiers on Lower Broadway; and stock up on CDs at Ernest Tubb's. Admire the hardware at

Bluebird Cafe, in Nashville

In a state with more than 800 festivals a year, how do you choose? One strategy: Start with these four outstanding gatherings and then dig in to the rest.

National Cornbread Festival (South Pittsburg, in April): A celebration of the iconic bread of the Southern table includes bluegrass music, taste-offs, and lots and lots of corn bread.

Bonnaroo (Manchester, in June): What started as a jam-band festival on a Tennessee farm has grown into one of the most diverse and well-organized summertime music festivals in the United States.

Elvis Week (Memphis, in August): Elvis mania reaches fever pitch during the annual August remembrance of the King's untimely death.

National Storytelling Festival (Jonesborough, in October): Tellers from around the world spin yarns in Tennessee's oldest town.

Gruhn Guitars, and buy a retro-print poster at Hatch Show Print.

Then for something completely different, don your best duds and enjoy a night at the Nashville Symphony Orchestra. The delightful sounds of one of the South's best symphonies will ease the mind and cleanse the musical palate.

Explore wax museums, souvenir shops, and the Opryland Hotel by day in Music Valley. Spend your evening at the Grand Ole Opry, and your late-night at Ernest Tubb's Midnite Jamboree, still going strong.

Sandwiched between downtown and Hillsboro Village is Music Row, the business center of Nashville. While you're unlikely to see a star, it's still worth the gamble. Take a stroll and then grab a table at the Sunset Grill for more star-watching. At night check out the Bluebird Cafe for the next big thing.

National Storytelling Festival

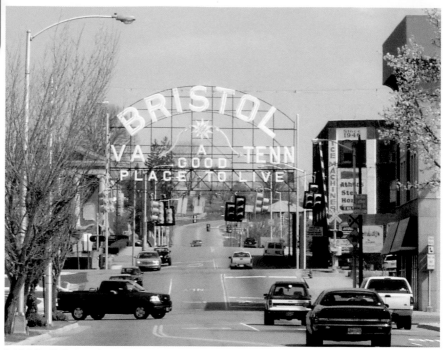

Bristol, the Birthplace of Country Music

Knoxville

Listen to live music over lunch at the WDVX Blue Plate Special and take a foot tour of Knoxville's musical history. See the site of the last hotel where Hank Williams ever slept. Catch a live band in the Old City or on Market Square, or a concert in the historic Tennessee Theatre. Listen to modern roots music at the Laurel Theater in historic Fort Sanders.

Head out to Clinton and the Museum of Appalachia to tour its music room, with exhibits about Uncle Dave Macon and Roy Acuff.

Great Smoky Mountains

Experience the kitschy side of music in Pigeon Forge. Visit Dollywood, a theme park owned and designed by Tennessee native Dolly Parton. Get a ticket to the Dixie Stampede for a night of over-the-top entertainment, or catch an Elvis tribute show.

The First Frontier

Visit Bristol, the Birthplace of Country Music, the site of the historic Bristol Sessions. Visit the Mountain Music Museum and the home of "Tennessee" Ernie Ford. Head to the Carter Fold for a Saturday night concert.

In Johnson City, check in at the Down Home for bluegrass, folk, and country music. This venerable club has been nurturing music fans in upper East Tennessee for more than 25 years.

MEMPHIS

Take away its music, and Memphis would lose its soul. Memphis may owe its existence to the Mississippi River, but it is music that has defined this Southern metropolis. Memphis music started with the spirituals and work songs of poor Mississippi Delta cotton farmers who came to Memphis and created a new sound: the Memphis blues. The blues spawned its own offspring: soul, R&B, country, and, of course, rock 'n' roll as sung by a poor truck driver from Tupelo, Mississippi, named Elvis Presley.

On any given weekend you can still find juke joints where the music flows as freely as the booze, and sitting still is not an option. On Beale Street, music wafts from inside smoky bars out onto the street, inviting you to come inside for a spell. And on Sundays,

the sounds of old-fashioned spirituals and new gospel music can be heard at churches throughout the city.

Memphis music is the backbeat of any visit to the city, but by no means the only reason to come. For as rich as Memphis's history is, this is a city that does not live in its past. The past two decades have been ones of rebirth for Memphis, giving new life to the city as a tourist destination. An NBA franchise arrived, the National Civil Rights Museum opened on the grounds of the Lorraine Motel, a fantastic AAA baseball field opened, and Memphis made its mark with films such as *Hustle & Flow, Forty Shades of Blue,* and *Black Snake Moan.* In 2008, more than 9 million people visited Memphis.

While you're here, sustain yourself on the city's world-famous barbecue, its fried chicken

MEMPHIS

HIGHLIGHTS

◖ Beale Street: The street that gave birth to the Memphis blues celebrates the legacy of this soulful music every night of the week (page 29).

◖ National Civil Rights Museum: For years the Lorraine Motel represented the tragic assassination of Martin Luther King Jr. Today, it tells the story of the African-American struggle for civil rights, from before the Civil War to the present day (page 34).

◖ Stax Museum of American Soul Music: Irresistible soul music is what made Stax famous in the 1960s, and it is what makes the Stax museum sweet today. Exhibits bring to life the work of Otis Redding, the Staple Singers, Isaac Hayes, and more (page 41).

◖ Graceland: The Elvis phenomenon is alive and well. Presley's south Memphis mansion is a testament not only to the King's music, but his fans as well (page 41).

◖ Elmwood Cemetery: The most surprising attraction in Memphis, Elmwood is the final resting place of dozens of Memphis characters: madames, blues singers, mayors, and pioneers of all types (page 44).

◖ Barbecue: Tangy, juicy, and just a little sweet, Memphis barbecue at places like the **Cozy Corner** is the stuff of dreams (page 68).

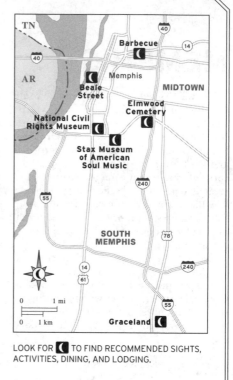

LOOK FOR ◖ TO FIND RECOMMENDED SIGHTS, ACTIVITIES, DINING, AND LODGING.

and catfish, and its homemade plate lunches. Eating may not be why you come, but it will be why you stay.

Memphis is a city of the South. More than just the largest city in Tennessee, Memphis is the hub city for the entire Mid-South, which stretches from West Tennessee all the way down into Mississippi and Arkansas. As such, the city is a melting pot of cultural, musical, culinary, and economic influences from the entire Mississippi River delta.

PLANNING YOUR TIME

You can knock out Memphis's main attractions in a weekend, but it takes a bit longer to soak up the city's special mojo of music, food, and laid-back attitude. In fact, if you want more than just a taste of Memphis's famous blues, its legendary barbecue, or its rich history, plan to stay a week or longer.

Choose downtown Memphis as your home base. The city center is home to the best bars, restaurants, sports venues, live music clubs, and, of course, Beale Street. Downtown is also the liveliest, and one of the safest, parts of Memphis after the sun sets.

While a lot of Memphis's attractions are downtown, others are located in the eastern and southern stretches of the city. A free shuttle is available to Graceland and Sun Studio

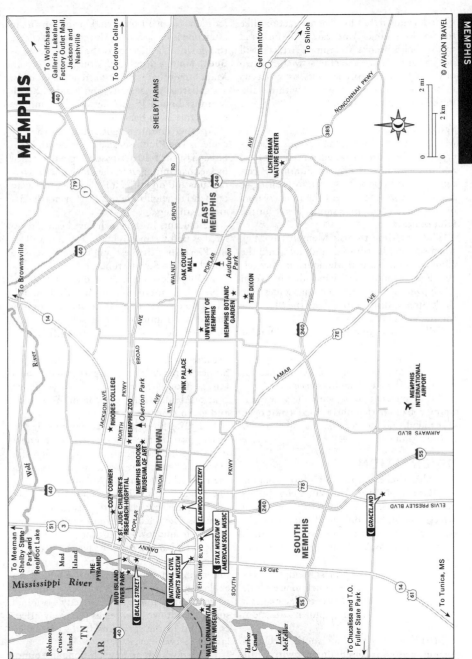

MEMPHIS

To Wolfchase
Galleria, Lakeland
Factory Outlet Mall,
Jackson and
Nashville

To Cordova Cellars →

To Brownsville

To Meeman
Shelby State
Park and
Reelfoot Lake

Germantown

To Shiloh

© AVALON TRAVEL

NONCONNAH PKWY

LICHTERMAN
NATURE CENTER

SHELBY FARMS

EAST
MEMPHIS

OAK COURT
MALL

Audubon
Park

THE DIXON

UNIVERSITY OF
MEMPHIS

MEMPHIS BOTANIC
GARDEN

PINK PALACE

WALNUT

GROVE

POPLAR

RD

AVE

AVE

AVE

BROAD

PKWY

NORTH

JACKSON AVE

RHODES COLLEGE

MEMPHIS ZOO

Overton Park

MEMPHIS
INTERNATIONAL
AIRPORT

LAMAR

AIRWAYS BLVD

Wolf

River

Mud
Island

THE
PYRAMID

MUD ISLAND
RIVER PARK

Mississippi River

Robinson
Crusoe
Island

TN
AR

BEALE STREET

NATIONAL CIVIL
RIGHTS MUSEUM

NATL ORNAMENTAL
METAL MUSEUM

COZY CORNER

ST. JUDE CHILDREN'S
RESEARCH HOSPITAL

MEMPHIS BROOKS
MUSEUM OF ART

MIDTOWN

UNION

POPLAR

DANNY

EH CRUMP BLVD

3RD ST

SOUTH

ELMWOOD CEMETERY

STAX MUSEUM OF
AMERICAN SOUL MUSIC

SOUTH
MEMPHIS

GRACELAND

ELVIS PRESLEY BLVD

PKWY

Harbor
Canal

Lake
McKellar

To Chucalissa and T.O.
Fuller State Park

To Tunica, MS

2 mi

2 km

0

0

from downtown, but for other attractions like the Stax Museum of American Soul Music and the Memphis Brooks Museum of Art, you will need a car or taxi. Take note as well that two of the city's best barbecue joints, as well as its most famous juke joints, are not within walking distance of downtown.

When to Go

Memphis is a city with four seasons. The average temperature in January is 41 degrees, and in July it hits 81 degrees. Summer is certainly the most popular season for visiting— Elvis Week in August sees the most visitors of all—but a Memphis summer is not for the faint of heart.

The best time to visit Memphis is May, when summer is still fresh and mild, and the city puts on its annual Memphis in May celebration. Memphis in May includes the World Championship Barbeque Cooking Contest, the Beale Street Music Festival, and the Memphis International Festival.

Fall is also a good choice. The Memphis Music and Heritage Festival held over Labor Day weekend is a great reason to come to Memphis, and probably the best choice for fans of traditional Memphis music.

But if you can't come when the weather is warm, don't fret. Memphis attractions are open year-round, and the city continues to rock, day in and day out.

ORIENTATION

Memphis perches atop a low bluff overlooking the Mississippi River. The center city district lies, roughly speaking, along the river. Main Street, a pedestrian-only mall (except for the trolleys) runs north–south, while Union, Madison, and Poplar Avenues are main east–west thoroughfares.

While not compact, central Memphis is entirely walkable for people willing to use a little shoe leather. The Main Street trolley makes it easy to see downtown and uptown attractions without a car.

In this book, locations south of Union Avenue are considered **downtown,** while

locations north are **uptown.** Downtown's main attraction is Beale Street. Also contained within the downtown district is the area known as **South Main,** a three-block strip along southern Main Street that is home to trendy boutiques, art galleries, restaurants, and condos. South Main is about a 15-minute walk or 5-minute trolley ride from Beale Street.

Another unique neighborhood in the city center is **The Pinch,** located along North Main Street past the I-40 overpass. Originally settled by German immigrants, the Pinch now has restaurants and nightlife. It is also the gateway to residential neighborhoods farther north that are gentrifying.

Restaurants in the Pinch have been categorized as uptown in this book. You can walk to the Pinch, but the best way to get there is to ride the Main Street Trolley.

In 1989, developers created **Harbor Town,** a New Urban community on Mud Island. The concept was to create a city community that offered amenities like schools, gyms, entertainment, and restaurants all within walking distance of each other. It was also designed to promote a sense of community; homes were built close together with short fences, front porches, and small yards, so that residents would use community parks and green spaces.

In 2007, a boutique hotel opened in Harbor Town, putting the area on the accommodations map for the first time. A major draw for Harbor Town is that it is located right across the river from downtown Memphis, but feels like a tight-knit residential community.

Memphis sprawls south, east, and north from the river. Head east from downtown, and you are in **midtown,** a district of strip malls, aging suburbs, and the city's best park and art museum. Poplar Avenue is the main artery of midtown, and a good point of reference when exploring by car (which is really the only way to get around midtown). The city's original suburb, midtown now seems positively urban compared to the sprawling burbs that creep farther eastward every year.

Located within midtown is **Cooper-Young,**

a re-developing residential and commercial neighborhood that lies around the intersection of Cooper Street and Young Avenue. Since the 1970s, residents of this neighborhood have fought the tide of urban decay by encouraging investment, good schools, and amenities like parks and restaurants, and generally fostering a sense of pride in the area. The result is a neighborhood where you'll find lots of restaurants, a great used bookstore, record shops, and other attractions that draw the city's young and young-at-heart.

East Memphis is where you will find large shopping malls, major hospitals, the University of Memphis, and lots of traffic jams. There are also a few attractions out here: the Dixon and the Memphis Botanic Gardens among them.

Generally speaking, **north and south Memphis** are the most economically depressed areas of the city. Visitors beat a path to attractions like Graceland and Stax in southern Memphis during the day, but you would be wise to avoid these areas at night unless you are with a local who knows the way around.

Sights

DOWNTOWN

Downtown refers to the area south of Union Avenue in the city center. It is the heart of Memphis's tourist district.

◖ Beale Street

If you want to delve into the history and character of Memphis music, look no farther for a starting point than Beale Street, home of the blues.

A combination of forces led Beale Street to its place in musical history and popular culture. Named in the 1840s after a war hero, Beale Street was originally part of South Memphis, a separate city that rivaled Memphis during the 1840s.

Beginning in the 1850s, and continuing in greater numbers during and after the Civil War, African Americans began to settle along the western part of Beale Street. By the 1880s and 1890s, a middle class of black professionals began to emerge, and Beale Street became the center of commerce, entertainment, and life for many of them. Together with black-owned businesses on Beale Street there were also immigrants from Eastern Europe, Ireland, China, Greece, and Germany who operated laundries, bars, restaurants, pawn shops, and more.

From the 1880s until the 1960s, Beale Street was the epicenter of African-American life, not just for Memphians but also for the entire Mid-South region. It was here that blacks felt free from many of society's restrictions.

Beale Street's decline began in the mid-20th century and by the 1970s, it was a shadow of its former self. Investment during the 1980s and '90s led to the street's rebirth as a destination for tourists and source of pride for residents, who could now show off the street that gave birth to the blues.

Today, Beale Street has two distinct personalities. During the day it is a laid-back place for families or adults to stroll, buy souvenirs, and eat. You can also stop at one of several museums and attractions located on the street. At night, Beale Street is a strip of nightclubs and restaurants, a great place to people-watch, and the best place to catch live blues seven nights a week.

W. C. Handy Home and Museum

The story of Beale Street cannot be told without mentioning William Christopher Handy, whose Memphis home sits at the corner of Beale Street and 4th Avenue. The building was originally located at 659 Jeanette Street, but was moved to Beale Street in 1985. Now the W. C. Handy Home and Museum (352 Beale St., 901/527-3427, summer Tues.–Sat. 10 A.M.–5 P.M., winter Tues.–Sat.

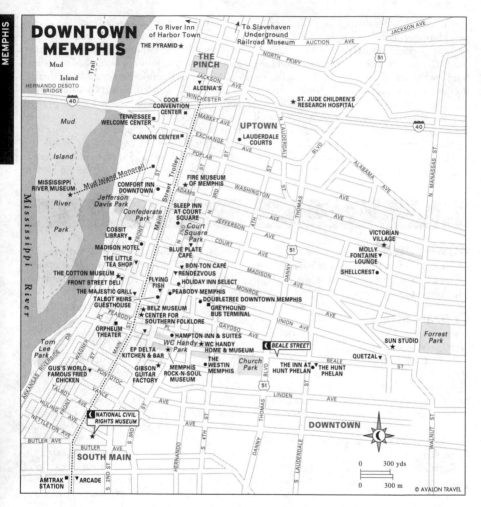

DOWNTOWN MEMPHIS

To River Inn of Harbor Town
To Slavehaven Underground Railroad Museum

THE PYRAMID ★

Mud Island

Trail

HERNANDO DESOTO BRIDGE

THE PINCH

JACKSON AVE

AUCTION   AVE

JACKSON AVE

NORTH   PKWY

51

ALCENIA'S

WINCHESTER

COOK CONVENTION CENTER ■

JACKSON   AVE

ST. JUDE CHILDREN'S RESEARCH HOSPITAL

TENNESSEE WELCOME CENTER ■

MARKET AVE

Mud

CANNON CENTER ■

EXCHANGE   AVE

UPTOWN

LAUDERDALE COURTS ■

N. LAUDERDALE   BLVD

Island

POPLAR   ST

MISSISSIPPI RIVER MUSEUM ★

Mud Island Monorail

COMFORT INN DOWNTOWN ●

FIRE MUSEUM ★ OF MEMPHIS

WASHINGTON   ST

3RD

ALABAMA   AVE

N. MANASSAS   ST

40

River

Jefferson Davis Park

ADAMS

THOMAS   ST

AVE

Park

Confederate Park

SLEEP INN AT COURT SQUARE ■

JEFFERSON   AVE

4TH

AVE

COSSIT LIBRARY ■

FRONT

Court Square Park

MADISON HOTEL ■

COURT   AVE

51

VICTORIAN VILLAGE

THE LITTLE TEA SHOP ▼

BLUE PLATE CAFÉ ▼

AVE

MOLLY FONTAINE ▼ LOUNGE

THE COTTON MUSEUM ★

BON-TON CAFÉ ▼

MADISON   AVE

SHELLCREST ●

FRONT STREET DELI ▼

RENDEZVOUS ▼

DANNY   AVE

THE MAJESTIC GRILL ▼

FLYING FISH ▼

HOLIDAY INN SELECT ●

MONROE   AVE

TALBOT HEIRS GUESTHOUSE ■

PEABODY-MEMPHIS ●

DOUBLETREE DOWNTOWN MEMPHIS ●

PEABODY   PL

BELZ MUSEUM ★ CENTER FOR SOUTHERN FOLKLORE ★

GREYHOUND BUS TERMINAL ■

UNION   AVE

ORPHEUM THEATER ★

GAYOSO   AVE

HAMPTON INN & SUITES ●

BEALE   AVE

BEALE STREET ◄

SUN STUDIO ★

Forrest Park

Tom Lee Park

WAGNER

RIVERSIDE   DR

MAIN   ST

EP DELTA KITCHEN & BAR ▼

WC Handy ★ Park

WC HANDY HOME & MUSEUM ★

THE WESTIN MEMPHIS ●

Church Park

BEALE   ST

QUETZAL ▼

GUS'S WORLD FAMOUS FRIED CHICKEN ▼

PONTOTOC

GIBSON ★ GUITAR FACTORY

MEMPHIS ROCK-N-SOUL MUSEUM ●

THE INN AT ● HUNT PHELAN

BLVD

THE HUNT ● PHELAN

ARKANSAS

TALBOT

VANCE   AVE

51

LINDEN   AVE

HULING   AVE

NETTLETON   AVE

FRONT

NATIONAL CIVIL ■ RIGHTS MUSEUM

HERNANDO   ST

4TH   ST

THOMAS   ST

S. LAUDERDALE   ST

DOWNTOWN

BUTLER   AVE

BUTLER   AVE

S. 3RD   ST

DANNY   ST

WALNUT   ST

SOUTH MAIN

AMTRAK ■ STATION

ARCADE ▼

S. 2ND   ST

0   300 yds

0   300 m

© AVALON TRAVEL

Mississippi River

11 A.M.–4 P.M., adults $3, children $2) is dedicated to telling the story of Handy's life. It was Handy who famously wrote, in his "Beale Street Blues": "If Beale Street could talk, married men would have to take their beds and walk, except one or two who never drink booze, and the blind man on the corner singing 'Beale Street Blues.' I'd rather be there than anyplace I know."

The Handy museum houses photographs of Handy's family, one of his band uniforms, and memorabilia of the recording company that he founded. You can also hear samples of Handy's music.

A. Schwab

During Beale Street's dark days of the 1970s and '80s, when the clubs and restaurants closed and the pawn shops opened, one store remained: A. Schwab (163 Beale St., 901/523-9782, Mon.–Fri. 9 A.M.–5 P.M.). This landmark general store opened in 1876 and has

COURTESY OF MEMPHIS CONVENTION AND VISITORS BUREAU

The Gibson Guitar Factory is one block away from Beale Street.

personal audio guide, which includes recordings of dozens of Memphis-influenced artists from B. B. King to Elvis. Exhibits are dedicated to Memphis radio stations; the influence of the Victrola, Sam Phillips, and Sun Studio; and, of course, all things Elvis, among others. It takes several hours to study all the exhibits in detail and to listen to all (or even most) of the music, so plan accordingly.

There is a free shuttle that runs between the Rock 'n' Soul Museum, Graceland, and Sun Studio. Look for the black van with the Sun label's distinctive yellow sun on the side.

Gibson Guitar Factory

Across the street from the Rock 'n' Soul Museum is the Gibson Guitar Factory (145 Lt. George Lee Ave., 901/544-7998, ext. 4080, www.gibson.com), one of three in the United States. The Memphis plant specializes in the semi-hollow-bodied guitar, and a wide range

been owned and operated by the same family ever since. Originally the source of household necessities for thousands of Delta residents, A. Schwab remains a treasure trove of goods. Here you will find practical things like underwear, hats, cookware, and tools, as well as novelties like old-fashioned candy, incense, and actual cans of Tennessee whoop-ass. Upstairs is the A. Schwab museum, a hodge-podge of old-time tools, clothes, and memorabilia of the store's 130-plus-year history.

Memphis Rock 'n' Soul Museum

Music fans should plan to spend several hours at the Memphis Rock 'n' Soul Museum (191 Beale St., 901/205-2533, www.memphisrocknsoul. org, daily 10 A.M.–7 P.M., adults $10, children 5–17 $7), located right next to FedEx Forum off Beale Street. An affiliate of the Smithsonian Institution, this museum tells the story of Memphis music from the Delta blues to *Shaft*. Your visit starts with a short video documentary and then you can follow the exhibits with your

W. C. HANDY

W. C. Handy was born in a log cabin in Florence, Alabama, in 1873. The son and grandson of African Methodist Episcopal ministers, Handy was exposed to music as a child in his father's church. Handy was also drawn to the music of the black laborers of the area, and when he moved to Memphis in the early 20th century he recognized the wealth of the blues music he heard in bars, on street corners, and in back alleys around Beale Street.

Handy was a trained musician, so he was able to set down on paper the music that had, up until then, been passed from one musician to another.

In 1909 Handy composed Memphis mayor Ed Crump's campaign song "Mr. Crump," which he later published as the "Memphis Blues." But he is most famous for his composition "St. Louis Blues," published in 1914. Handy also created the "Yellow Dog Blues," "Joe Turner Blues," and "Beale Street Blues."

BEALE STREET WALKING TOUR

Beale Street runs from the Mississippi River to Manassas Street in midtown, but it is the three blocks between 2nd and 4th Streets that really matter, at least today. In its heyday, the Beale Street commercial and entertainment district extended farther east and west, but today, it has been condensed into the half dozen blocks from Main Street to 4th Street.

Beale Street is good for walking. Come down during the day to stroll the street and look carefully at what remains of the old architecture. Imagine the street when its cobblestones and sidewalks were jammed with African-American Memphians out doing their Saturday shopping. Then return in the evening for the modern-day experience. This walking tour begins at the intersection of Beale and Main Streets, and heads eastward.

Near the corner of Beale and Main Streets is the **Orpheum Theatre** (203 S. Main St., 901/525-7800, www.orpheum-memphis. com). This site has been used for entertainment since 1890, when the Grand Opera House opened there with a production of *Les Huguenots*. Later, the opera house began vaudeville shows and theater. Fire destroyed the opera house in 1923, but in 1928 it reopened as the Orpheum, a movie theater and performing arts venue for the likes of Duke Ellington, Cab Calloway, Bob Hope, and Mae West. The Orpheum was neglected for many years during the 1960s and '70s, but it reopened in 1984 thanks to the Memphis Development Foundation. It remains one of Memphis's premier venues for the performing arts, with Broadway productions, mainstream musical artists, movies, and much more.

© SUSANNA HENIGHAN POTTER

The First Baptist Beale Street Church was built between 1868 and 1885 and is home to one of the oldest African-American congregations in the city.

A block east of the Orpheum is a statue of Memphis's most famous native son, Elvis Presley. Depicting the King during his early career, the statue sits in **Elvis Presley Plaza.** **A. Schwab** (163 Beale St., 901/523-9782, Mon.-Fri. 9 A.M.-5 P.M.) has served Memphis residents for more than 130 years, although it focuses now on odd, out-of-date, and hard-to-find items rather than general store necessities. Stop in for a souvenir, or to visit the A. Schwab "museum," a collection of old-fashioned household tools and implements.

A few doors down from A. Schwab, at the Irish pub Silky O'Sullivan's, you can see what remains of one of Beale Street's most magnificent old buildings. The facade of what was once the **Gallina Building** is held up by six steel girders. From the 1860s until 1914, this facade kept watch on the business empire of Squire Charles Gallina, who operated a saloon, restaurant, and 20-room hotel, as well as a gambling room. Gallina, who was also a magistrate, held court upstairs above the saloon, and his family lived in an apartment on the top floor. After Gallina's death in 1914, the building was used variously as a pharmacy, clothing store, dry goods shop, and dentist's office.

Beyond 3rd Street, on the northern side of Beale, is **Handy Park,** named for famous blues composer and musician W. C. Handy. Beale Street's markethouse was torn down in 1930 to build the park, which was dedicated during a ceremony attended by blues greats such as Robert Johnson and B. B. King. Since it opened, Handy Park has been a popular place for street musicians, peddlers, concerts, and community events, all of which are presided over by the life-size statue of W. C. Handy.

About midway up the southern side of the next block of Beale Street is the **Daisy Theater** (329 Beale St.). Built in 1917 as a movie house, the theater's domed front speaks of Beale's heyday. Much of the original interior remains today. The theater is closed to the public but may be rented for private events.

Contact the Beale Street Development Corporation (866/406-5986) for information.

Across the street from the Daisy Theater is the **New Daisy Theater,** built in 1941 as another movie house. The New Daisy is one of Memphis's prime live music venues, and it books rock and alternative acts from around the country.

Stately and old, the **First Baptist Beale Street Church** (379 Beale St.) was built between 1868 and 1885 and is home to one of the oldest African-American congregations in Memphis. The church has its roots in praise meetings held in various locations beginning in the 1840s. In the 1860s, the congregation started to meet under brush arbors at the present location, and the first temporary structure was erected in 1865. The cornerstone was laid for the present building in 1871. The First Baptist Beale Street Church was an important force in Memphis's African-American history. It was here that black Memphians published their first newspapers, the *Memphis Watchman* and the *Memphis Free Speech and Headlight.*

Today, **Church Park** is a relatively nondescript city park with benches and some paved walks. But in 1899 when Robert Church built Church Park and Auditorium at the eastern end of the Beale Street commercial district, the park was something truly special. Church, the mixed-race son of a white steamboat captain, is said to have been the first black millionaire in the South. He made his money in real estate, and was troubled that there were no public parks expressly for Memphis's African-American residents. So in 1899 he opened Church Park and Auditorium on six acres of land along Beale Street. The park was beautifully landscaped and manicured, with bright flowers, tropical trees, and peacocks. The auditorium was a venue for black performers and speakers, and became a popular venue for conferences and meetings too. Church Park remains a venue for community events, particularly the annual Africa in April event every spring.

of models are on sale in Gibson's retail shop. For $10, you can get an hour-long tour of the factory floor and see guitars being made, from the shaping of the rim and panels to the painting and buffing of the finished product. Tours leave Monday–Saturday every hour on the hour 11 A.M.–4 P.M., and Sunday noon–4 P.M. Tours can sell out, so it is a good idea to buy your ticket in advance, especially during the busier summer months. Most factory workers leave by 3 P.M. and have the weekends off, so plan ahead if you want to see the factory floor in full swing.

National Civil Rights Museum

If you do nothing else while you are in Memphis, visit the National Civil Rights Museum (450 Mulberry St., 901/521-9699, www.civilrightsmuseum.org, Mon. and Wed.–Sat. 9 A.M.–5 P.M., Sun. 1–5 P.M., adults $12, students and seniors $10, children 4–17 $8.50). Built on the site where Dr. Martin Luther King Jr. was assassinated on April 4, 1968, the museum makes a thorough examination of the American civil rights movement from slavery to the present day. Exhibits display original letters, audio recordings, photos, and newspaper clippings from events including the Montgomery bus boycott, *Brown v. Board of Education,* Freedom Summer, and the march from Selma to Montgomery. Original and re-created artifacts, such as the bus where Rosa Parks made her stand in 1955 and the cell where Dr. King wrote his famous *Letter from a Birmingham Jail,* help to illustrate the story of civil rights.

When Dr. King visited Memphis in March and then again in April 1968, the Lorraine Motel was one of the handful of downtown hotels that welcomed African Americans. The room where he spent his final hours has been carefully re-created, and narration by those who were with him tell the shocking story of his death. Across Mulberry Street, in the building that was once the boardinghouse from where James Earl Ray is believed to have fired his sniper shot, exhibits probe various theories about the assassination, as well as the worldwide legacy of the civil rights movement.

The Lorraine Motel, where Dr. Martin Luther King Jr. was assassinated in 1968, is now the National Civil Rights Museum.

© SUSANNA HENIGHAN POTTER

Visitors to the museum can pay an extra $2 for an audio guide—a worthwhile investment. You must check your still or video camera due to restrictions on taking photographs inside the museum. This is a large museum and it is overflowing with information, so visitors who want to give the displays their due attention should plan on spending between three and four hours here. A good way to visit would be to tour the Lorraine Motel exhibits first, take a break for lunch, and then go across the street for the second half of the museum when you are refreshed.

Admission is free on Monday after 3 P.M. In June, July, and August the museum stays open until 6 P.M.

Belz Museum of Asian and Judaic Art

The Belz Museum of Asian and Judaic Art (119 S. Main St., 901/523-2787, Tues.–Fri. 10 A.M.–5:30 P.M., Sat.–Sun. noon–5 P.M., adults $5, children $4), formerly Peabody Place Museum, houses one of the largest collections of artwork from the Q'ing dynasty. Forged from the private collection of Memphis developers Jack and Marilyn Belz, owners of the Peabody Hotel and Peabody Place mall, the museum features some 1,000 objects, including an array of jade, tapestries, paintings, furniture, carvings, and other artifacts.

UPTOWN

Uptown refers to locations along Union Avenue and points north in the center city district. Here downtown workers are more common than tourists, and tall office buildings rise above the city blocks.

The Cotton Museum

The Cotton Museum at the Memphis Cotton Exchange (65 Union Ave., 901/531-7826, www.memphiscottonmuseum.org, Tues.–Sat. 10 A.M.–5 P.M., Sun. noon–5 P.M., adults $5, seniors $4.50, students $4, children 6–12 $3) is located in the broad rectangular room that once was the nerve center of the Mid-South's cotton trade. The Cotton Exchange was established in 1873, and it was here that buyers and sellers of the South's most important cash crop met, and where fortunes were made and lost. Located just steps away from the Mississippi River, the Exchange was the trading floor of Cotton Row, the area of town that was defined by the cotton industry.

The Cotton Museum features exhibits about cotton's history, its uses, and the culture that its cultivation gave rise to in Memphis and the Mississippi Delta. There are several videos you can watch, as well as a live Internet feed of today's cotton exchange—now conducted entirely electronically. The nicest thing about the museum, however, is seeing the chalkboard where the prices of cotton around the world were written by hand. There is also a replica of the Western Union office where buyers and sellers sent telegrams using an intricate system of abbreviations known only to the cotton trade.

The Peabody Hotel Memphis

The Peabody Hotel Memphis (149 Union Ave., 901/529-4000) is the city's most famous hotel. Founded in 1869, the Peabody was one of the first grand hotels of the South, a place as well known for its elegant balls and big-band concerts as for the colorful characters who sipped cocktails at its famous lounge. Named in memory of the philanthropist George Peabody, the original hotel was located at the corner of Main and Monroe. It closed in 1923 and a new Peabody opened two years later in its present location on Union Avenue. It remained the place to see and be seen for generations of Memphians and Delta residents. It was David Cohn who famously wrote in 1935 that "The Mississippi Delta begins in the lobby of The Peabody Hotel."

The elegant hotel lobby is gathering place for the twice-daily march of the Peabody ducks. They live on the roof of the hotel, and make the journey—by elevator—to the lobby fountain every morning at 11 A.M. At 5 P.M. they march out of the fountain, back onto the elevator, and up to their accommodations on the roof.

The hotel employs a duck master who takes care of the ducks and supervises their daily

The Peabody ducks march daily at 11 A.M. and 5 P.M. at the Peabody Hotel.

trip downstairs. Watching the ducks is free, frenzied, and undeniably fun. It is also one of the most popular activities among visitors to Memphis, so be sure to get there early and secure a good vantage point along the red carpet to watch the duck march.

Mud Island

In Memphis, it is sometimes easy to forget that you are just steps away from the great Mississippi River. A trip to Mud Island will cure this ailment once and for all. A narrow band of land in the river, Mud Island is home to the **Mississippi River Museum** (125 N. Front St., 901/576-7241, www.mudisland.com, adults $8, seniors $6, children $5), which has exhibits about early uses of the river, steam and paddle boats, floods, and much more. The museum and accompanying Mud Island Park are open daily from mid-April to the end of October. Hours in April, May, September, and October are 10 A.M.–5 P.M., and in June, July, and August 10 A.M.–6 P.M.

The museum begins with a refresher course

on European exploration of this region— DeSoto, LaSalle, and Marquette and Joliet— followed by information about early settlement. The highlight is being able to explore a replica of a 1870s steamboat. In the Riverfolk Gallery there are wax depictions of Mark Twain, riverboat gambler George Devol, and steamship entertainers. The museum also remembers the numerous river disasters that have taken place along the Mississippi.

Admission to the Mississippi River Museum includes the **River Walk** at the Mud Island River Park, a five-block scale model of the entire Mississippi River—from Minnesota to the Gulf of Mexico. Walk along the model to see scale representations of cities along the river's path, and read placards about the river's history. On a hot day, wear your bathing suit so you can swim in the pool at the end.

The river park is also home to an outdoor amphitheater, which in summer hosts big-name concerts. You can rent canoes and pedal boats to use in the still waters around the Mud Island harbor.

Admission to the river park is free. You cay pay $4 round-trip to ride the monorail to Mud Island, or you can walk across the monorail bridge for free. The monorail station is on Front Street at Adams Avenue.

Slavehaven Underground Railroad Museum

The legend of the Burkle Estate, a modest white clapboard house on North 2nd Street, has given rise to the Slavehaven Underground Railroad Museum (826 N. 2nd St., 901/527-3427, summer Mon.–Sat. 10 A.M.–4 P.M., winter Wed.–Sat. 10 A.M.–4 P.M., adults $6, youth $4). The museum here tells the story of slavery and the Underground Railroad, which helped thousands of slaves escape to freedom in the North (and, after the 1850 Fugitive Slave Act, to Canada). Jacob Burkle, a German immigrant and owner of the Memphis stockyard, is said to have built the Burkle Estate around 1850. Escaping slaves would have hidden in a root cellar beneath the house before making the 1,500-foot trip to the banks of the Mississippi, where they made a further journey north.

Skeptics say that there is no evidence of this story, and even point to documents that show that Burkle may not have purchased the property until 1871, well after the end of slavery. Advocates for the Underground Railroad story say that it was the nature of the railroad to be secret, so there is nothing unusual about a lack of concrete evidence.

Visitors today need not be too concerned with the details of the debate; the Slavehaven museum does a good job of highlighting the brutality of the slave trade and slavery, and the ingenuity and bravery it took for slaves to escape. Perhaps the most interesting part of the exhibit are the quilts that demonstrate the way that slaves used quilting patterns to send messages to one another. Other displays show advertisements for Memphis slave auctions and images from the early 20th century that depict damaging racial stereotypes.

The museum is operated by Heritage Tours of Memphis and staff are available to conduct guided tours of the property.

Fire Museum of Memphis

The Fire Museum of Memphis (118 Adams Ave., 901/320-5650, www.firemuseum.com, Mon.–Sat. 9 A.M.–5 P.M., adults $6, seniors $4, children $5) is a good place to take children. There is a huge display of fire-engine toys, lots of firefighting paraphernalia, and a "fire room" that presents important lessons on fire safety. You can also see old-fashioned fire engines and youngsters will enjoy playing in the kid-friendly fire truck. The museum is located in the old Fire Station No. 1 in downtown Memphis.

St. Jude Children's Research Hospital

The sprawling complex of St. Jude Children's Research Hospital on uptown's northern fringe has been saving lives and bringing hope to children and their families since 1962. St. Jude was founded by entertainer Danny Thomas in fulfillment of his promise to God to give back to those in need. Over the years and thanks to the success of its fundraising arm—the American Lebanese Syrian Associated Charities—St. Jude has expanded many times over and now leads the world in research and treatment of catastrophic childhood diseases, especially pediatric cancers. The hospital never turns anyone away due to inability to pay, and it never makes families without insurance pay for their treatment.

Visitors can tour a small museum about Danny Thomas and St. Jude in the **Danny Thomas ALSAC Pavilion** (332 N. Lauderdale St., 901/495-4414, daily 8:30 A.M.–4:30 P.M., free), located inside a golden dome on the hospital grounds. Just outside are the graves of Danny Thomas and his wife, Rose Marie.

MUD ISLAND

Mud Island rose from the Mississippi River as a result of two seemingly small events. In 1876, the river shifted slightly about 20 miles south of Memphis, causing the currents that flowed past the city to alter course. And then, in 1910, the U.S. Navy gunboat *Amphitrite* anchored at the mouth of the Wolf River for almost two years, causing a further change in silt patterns. When the ship left in 1912, the sandbar continued to grow, and Mud Island was born.

Residents initially disliked the island, since it was ugly and proved to be a danger to river navigation.

Beginning in the 1930s, poor Memphians – black and white – squatted on Mud Island in ramshackle homes built of scrap metal and wood. Between 200 and 500 people lived on the island during this time.

In 1959, a downtown airport was built on the island, but the airport was closed in 1970 when the DeSoto Bridge was built. In 1974, plans were developed for the present-day Mud Island River Park, which includes a full-scale replica of a river boat, a monorail to the island, and the signature 2,000-foot flowing replica of the Mississippi River.

The Pyramid

The Memphis Pyramid is the most dominating feature of the northern city skyline. Memphis's affiliation with all things Egypt began with its name, and continued in 1897, when a large-scale replica of a pyramid was built to represent Memphis at the Tennessee Centennial Exhibition in Nashville. Pyramids were popular symbols on Memphis paraphernalia for many years.

The first serious proposal for a life-size pyramid to be built in Memphis was written in the 1970s, but the idea did not take off until the 1980s, when the city and county governments agreed to fund it. Denver developer Sidney Shlenker promoted the plan, and promised restaurants, tourist attractions, and lots of revenue for the city. The pyramid was built and opened in 1991, minus the money-making engines that Shlenker promised. Today, the $63 million Great American Pyramid sits empty, but the city is trying to attract a big-box store to turn it into a retail center.

MIDTOWN

You'll need a car to explore the attractions in midtown, which sprawls along Union, Poplar, and Madison Avenues as they head eastward from the city center.

Sun Studio

It is well worth your time to drop by Sun Studio (706 Union Ave., 901/521-0664, www.sunstudio.com, daily 10 A.M.–6 P.M., $10), where Elvis Presley recorded his first hit, "That's All Right," and where dozens of blues, rock, and country musicians were recorded during the 1950s. Founded by radio man and audio engineer Sam Phillips and his wife, Becky, the studio recorded weddings, funerals, events, and, of course, music. Phillips was interested in the blues, and his first recordings were of yet-unknown artists such as Rufus Thomas and Howlin' Wolf. In 1953, Elvis Presley came into the studio on his lunch break to record a $3 record of himself singing "My Happiness" for his mother. Phillips was not impressed with the performance, and it was not for another year—and thanks to the prodding of Phillips's

Sun Studio is where Elvis recorded his first hit in 1954, "That's All Right."

© SUSANNA HENIGHAN POTTER

assistant, Marion Keisker—that Phillips called Presley in to record some more. When Phillips heard Elvis's version of the blues tune "That's All Right," he knew he had a hit. And he did.

But the story of Elvis's discovery is just one of many that took place in the modest home-made Sun Studio, and this attraction is not just for Elvis fans. The one-hour tour of the studio leaves every hour on the half hour, and while you are waiting you can order a real fountain drink from the snack bar or browse the shop's collection of recordings and paraphernalia. The studio is still in business; you can record here for $75 an hour at night, and dozens of top-notch performers have, including U2, Beck, and Matchbox 20.

Lauderdale Courts

The least-known Elvis attraction in Memphis is Lauderdale Courts (252 N. Lauderdale St., 901/523-8662, www.lauderdalecourts.com), the public housing complex where Presley lived with his parents from 1949 to 1953 before his

© AVALON TRAVEL

MEMPHIS

© SUSANNA HENIGHAN POTTER

the Memphis Brooks Museum of Art at Overton Park

rise to fame. The handsome brick building was saved from the wrecking ball in the 1990s, and the apartment where the Presleys lived has been restored to its 1950s glory. Most of the year, the Lauderdale Courts Elvis suite is rented out as a hotel room, but during Elvis's Birthday Week in January and Elvis Week in August it is open for public tours.

Victorian Village

Set on a tree-lined block of Adams Avenue near Orleans Street is Victorian Village, where a half dozen elegant Victorian-era homes escaped the "urban renewal" fate of other historic Memphis homes.

Visitors can tour the **Woodruff-Fontaine House** (680 Adams Ave., 901/526-1469, Wed.–Sun. noon–4 P.M., adults $10, seniors $8, children and students $6), one of the street's most magnificent buildings. Built starting in 1870 for the Woodruff family and sold to the Fontaines in the 1880s, the

house was occupied through 1930, when it became part of the James Lee Art Academy, a precursor to the Memphis Academy of Art. When the academy moved in 1959, the building became city property and stood vacant. Beginning in 1961, city residents raised funds to restore and refurnish the house with period furniture and accessories, and it opened as a museum in 1964. This was during the period of urban renewal that saw to the demolition of many of Memphis's other old homes, and some of the house's furnishings were taken from homes that were later demolished. Visitors to the house are given a guided tour of the 1st floor, and can explore the 2nd and 3rd floors on their own. This is a good stop if you are interested in antiques.

The **Magevney House** (198 Adams Ave., 901/526-4464) and the **Mallory-Neely House** (652 Adams Ave., 901/523-1484) are two other historical homes in the district. The

Magevney House is the oldest middle-class residence still standing in Memphis. It was built in 1836 by an Irish immigrant to the city, Eugene Magevney. The Mallory-Neely House is of the same vintage and is notable for the fact that it was not refurnished in more than 100 years and so remains remarkably true to the era in which it was built.

The Magevney and Mallory-Neely Houses are owned by the City of Memphis, and due to budget cuts have been closed to the public. Call to find out if they have been reopened.

Memphis Brooks Museum of Art

Memphis's foremost art museum is located in Overton Park in midtown, a short drive from downtown. Memphis Brooks Museum of Art (1934 Poplar Ave., 901/544-6200, www.brooksmuseum.org, Tues.–Fri. 10 A.M.–4 P.M., Sat. 10 A.M.–5 P.M., Sun. 11:30 A.M.–5 P.M., adults $7, seniors $6, students $3) is the largest fine art museum in Tennessee, and its permanent collection includes 8,000 works of art. This includes ancient African and Asian art, as well as European, American, and contemporary art. There are 29 galleries at the Brooks, and special exhibitions have focused on the work of Annie Leibovitz, men's fashion in Africa, and the silver work of Paul de Lamerie. There is also a museum shop and restaurant, as well as an auditorium often used to screen films. Admission to the Brooks is free on Wednesday.

The Memphis Zoo

The Memphis Zoo (2000 Prentiss Pl., 901/276-9453, www.memphiszoo.org, Mar.–Oct. daily 9 A.M.–6 P.M., Nov.–Feb. daily 9 A.M.–5 P.M., adults $13, children $8) has been expanding and is now the proud steward of two giant pandas, Le Le and Ya Ya, large cats, penguins, lions, tropical birds, and 3,500 other animal species. Its butterfly exhibit, open from May to October annually, is a popular favorite. The zoo is located on the grounds of Overton Park. Parking is an additional $3.

SOUTH MEMPHIS
◖ Stax Museum of American Soul Music

There is no place in Memphis that better tells the story of the city's legendary soul music than the Stax Museum of American Soul Music (926 E. McLemore Ave., 901/946-2535, www.staxmuseum.com, adults $10, seniors, students, and military $9, children 9–12 $7). Hours are Monday–Saturday 10 A.M.–4 P.M. and Sunday 1–4 P.M., with doors opening on weekdays at 9 A.M. from March to October.

The museum tour starts with a short toe-tapping video that sets the scene for the musical magic that took place here during the 1960s. Exhibits include the sanctuary of an old clapboard Delta church, which illustrates the connection between soul and gospel music. You can also see Booker T. Jones's original organ, Otis Redding's favorite suede leather jacket, and Isaac Hayes's 1972 peacock-blue gold-trimmed Cadillac Eldorado, Superfly.

The museum also takes you through the studio's control room and into the studio itself, slanted floors and all. If you want to try your hand, there is a karaoke machine and a dance floor in case you can't help but move to the music. The Stax museum is a must-see for music enthusiasts, but also an educational journey for those who don't know the story behind some of America's most famous songs. It sits next door to the Stax Music Academy, a present-day music school that reaches out to neighborhood youth.

◖ Graceland

Drive south from downtown on Elvis Presley Boulevard to reach the King's most famous home, Graceland (3717 Elvis Presley Blvd., 901/332-3322 or 800/238-2000, www.elvis.com, $25–70). Graceland's summer (Mar.–Oct.) hours are Mon.–Sat. 9 A.M.–5 P.M. and Sun. 10 A.M.–4 P.M. In November it opens daily 10 A.M.–4 P.M., and from December to February it opens daily 10 A.M.–4 P.M., except Tuesday, when it is closed. Graceland is closed on Christmas and Thanksgiving Days, and sometimes on New Year's Day. There is plenty of parking.

SOULSVILLE

A lucky convergence of people, talents, and social forces led to one of Memphis's – and America's – most unique musical stories. Stax Records was founded in 1960 by Jim Stewart, an aspiring country fiddler, and his sister, Estelle Axton. The first two letters of the brother and sister's surnames came together to form Stax, a name now synonymous with the raw Memphis sound of performers like Rufus and Carla Thomas, Otis Redding, Sam and Dave, Isaac Hayes, Eddie Floyd, the Mar-Keys, the Staple Singers, and Booker T. & the MGs.

Jim Stewart chose a closed movie theater in a working-class South Memphis neighborhood for his recording studio. On a tight budget, he didn't fix the sloped theater floor or angled walls, and the room's reverberating acoustics came to define the Memphis sound.

Motown was known as "Hitsville" for its smooth and palatable sound, so the artists at Stax began to call their neighborhood "Soulsville" – a name that still refers to the area of South Memphis where Stax is located. The soul music that Stax recorded was raw and inventive, influenced by country, blues, gospel, and jazz.

The label's first hit was with WDIA-AM disc jockey Rufus Thomas and his daughter, Carla Thomas, who came in one day and recorded "Cause I Love You." The song became an overnight sensation.

Stax tapped into the talent of the neighborhood, and particularly the African-American Booker T. Washington High School, which graduated such greats as the members of the Soul Children and the Mad Lads. As the Stax reputation developed artists came from out of town to record, including a 21-year-old Otis Redding, who drove up from Georgia in hopes of making a record and made a career instead.

Stax also operated Satellite Records right next door to the studio, and here Estelle Axton was able to quickly test-market new recordings on the neighborhood youngsters who came in for the latest music. Wayne Jackson, a member of the studio's house band, the Memphis Horns, recalls that Estelle and Jim would invite hundreds of young people from the neighborhood into the studio to listen to their newest recording. Based on the group's response, they would choose the single.

Stax was unique for its time as an integrated organization, where the love of music trumped racial differences. As the civil rights movement evolved, Stax artists turned to serious social themes in their music. In 1972 Stax artists organized WattStax, an outdoor black music festival in Los Angeles.

Between 1960 and 1975, when the Stax magic ran out, the studio produced 800 singles and 300 albums, including 243 Top 100 and 14 number-one R&B hits. Isaac Hayes's theme from the movie Shaft was the fastest-selling album in Stax history, and one of three Stax songs went to number one on the pop charts. Other big Stax hits were Otis Reddings' "(Sitting on) the Dock of the Bay"; the Staples Singers' "Respect Yourself"; and Sam and Dave's "Soul Man."

Sadly, Stax was destroyed financially by a bad distribution deal with CBS Records in 1975, and the studio was closed. Its rare master tapes were sold at auction, and the studio where soul was born was demolished.

Thankfully, the story of Stax has not been forgotten. In 2001 ground was broken for a new Stax story, one which grew into the present-day music academy and the Stax Museum of American Soul Music.

Visitors can choose from three tour packages: The mansion-only tour takes about an hour and costs $25; the platinum tour includes the automobile museum, Elvis's two airplanes, and other special perks for $40. Enthusiasts can choose the VIP package for $70, which gives you "front of the line" access, an all-day pass, keepsakes, and access to exclusive exhibits, such as one that features Elvis's first-ever professional photographs, taken in 1955.

The Graceland complex blends into the strip malls and fast-food joints that line the boulevard in this part of Memphis. The ticket counter, shops, and restaurants are located on

PHOTO COURTESY OF TENNESSEE DEPARTMENT OF TOURIST DEVELOPMENT

Elvis Presley's Graceland mansion

the west side of the boulevard, and here you board a shuttle van that drives across the highway and up the curved drive to the Graceland mansion. Graceland managers may have taken full advantage of the commercial opportunities presented by the home that Elvis left behind, but they have not overdone it. The operation is laid-back, leaving the spotlight on Elvis and, of course, his fans, who travel around the world to visit.

The mansion tour is conducted by audio guide. It includes the ground floor of the mansion (the upstairs remains closed to the public) and several outbuildings that now house exhibits about Elvis's life and career. High points include watching the press conference Elvis gave after leaving the army, witnessing firsthand his audacious taste in decor, and visiting the meditation garden where Elvis, his parents, and his grandmother are buried. There is also a plaque in memory of Elvis's lost twin, Jesse Garon. The audio tour plays many of Elvis's songs, family stories remembered by Lisa Marie Presley, and several clips of Elvis speaking. In 2008, Graceland opened two new exhibits: "Private Presley" focuses on the King's service in the army and "Elvis '68" is about the year 1968 in Presley's life and musical career.

The exhibits gloss over some of the challenges Elvis faced in his life—his addiction to prescription drugs, his womanizing and failed marriage, and his unsettling affinity for firearms among them. But they showcase Elvis's generosity, his dedication to family, and his fun-loving character. The portrait that emerges is sympathetic and remarkably human for a man who is so often larger than life.

The automobile museum features 33 vehicles, including his pink Cadillac, motorcycles, and a red MG from *Blue Hawaii,* as well as some of his favorite motorized toys, including a go-kart and dune buggy. His private planes include the *Lisa Marie,* which Elvis customized with gold-plated seat belts, suede chairs, and gold-flecked sinks. Other special Graceland exhibits include "Sincerely Elvis," which chronicles Elvis's life in 1956, and "Elvis After Dark," which describes some of Elvis's late-night passions, like roller skating.

The Graceland mansion was declared a National Historic Site in 2006. It attracts some 600,000 visitors annually.

❰ Elmwood Cemetery

Elmwood Cemetery (824 S. Dudley St., 901/774-3212, www.elmwoodcemetery.org, Mon.–Fri. 8 A.M.–4:30 P.M., Sat. 8 A.M.–noon), an 88-acre cemetery southwest of the city center, is the resting place of 70,000 Memphians—ordinary citizens and some of the city's most prominent leaders. It was founded in 1852 by 50 gentlemen who wanted the cemetery to be a park for the living as well as a resting place for the dead. They invested in tree planting and winding carriage paths so that the cemetery today is a pleasant, peaceful place to spend a few hours.

The cemetery is the resting place of Memphians like Annie Cook, a well-known madame who died during the yellow fever epidemic of 1878; Marion Scudder Griffen, a pioneering female lawyer and suffragette; and musician Sister Thea Bowman. Thousands of anonymous victims of the yellow fever epidemic were buried here, as were both Confederate and Union casualties of the Civil War. Prominent citizens including Robert Church Sr., Edward Hull Crump, and Shelby Foote are also buried at Elmwood.

Visitors to the cemetery may simply drive or walk through on their own. But it is best to rent the one-hour audio guide ($7) of the cemetery, which takes you on a driving tour and highlights 50 people buried in the cemetery. Thanks to a well-written and well-presented narration, the cemetery tour comes closer than any other single Memphis attraction to bringing Memphis's diverse history and people to life.

The cemetery offers occasional lectures and guided tours. Call ahead or check the website to find out if any are scheduled during your visit. To find Elmwood, drive east along E. H. Crump Boulevard, turning south (right) onto Dudley, which dead-ends at the single-lane bridge that marks the entrance to the cemetery.

Church of the Full Gospel Tabernacle

A native of Arkansas and longtime resident of Michigan, Al Green first made his name as one of history's greatest soul singers with hits like "Let's Stay Together," "Take Me to the River," and "Love and Happiness." Following a religious conversion in 1979, he dedicated his considerable talents to God and founded the Church of the Full Gospel Tabernacle (787 Hale Rd., 901/396-9192, www.algreenmusic. com) in Memphis, where his Sunday sermons dripped with soulful gospel.

For almost 16 years, the Reverend Al Green left secular music alone. He dedicated himself to God's music. But in 2005 Green released the first of three new secular albums on Blue Note Records. He's touring again too, in Europe and the United States.

According to his official biography, Rev. Green faced some criticism when he returned to the secular scene. "I've got people in the church saying, 'That's a secular song,' and I'm saying, 'Yeah, but you've got Monday, Tuesday, Wednesday, Thursday, Friday, and Saturday to be anything other than spiritual. You've got to live those days, too!'" Rev. Green says he has not neglected his duty to God. "The music is the message, the message is the music. So that's my little ministry that the Big Man upstairs gave to me—a little ministry called love and happiness."

Despite his rebirth as a secular soul performer, Al Green, now a bishop, still makes time for his church. He preaches regularly, but not every Sunday, and continues to sing the praises of God. The Sunday service at his Memphis church begins at 11:30 A.M. Visitors are welcome, and you can come—within reason—as you are. Please show some respect, though, by being quiet when that's called for and throwing a few bucks in the offering plate when it comes around. And don't forget that the church is a place of worship and not a tourist attraction. If you're not in town on Sunday, you can catch the weekly choir rehearsal on Thursday at 7 P.M.

National Ornamental Metal Museum

An unusual delight, the National Ornamental Metal Museum (374 Metal Museum Dr., 901/774-6380, www.metalmuseum.org, Tues.–Sat. 10 A.M.–5 P.M., adults $5, seniors $4, students and children $3) is dedicated to preserving and displaying fine metalwork. Its permanent collection numbers more than 3,000 objects, and ranges from contemporary American sculpture to works as many as 500 years old. The museum hosts special exhibits several times a year, showcasing various aspects of metalwork. There is also a working metalwork studio, and the museum grounds on the bluff overlooking the Mississippi are an attraction in themselves. This is reputed to be the site where Hernando de Soto and his men camped when they passed through the area in 1542.

Chucalissa

A group of platform and ridge mounds along the Mississippi River are the main attraction at Chucalissa (T. O. Fuller State Park, 901/785-3160, Tues.–Sat. 9 A.M.–4:30 P.M., adults $5, seniors and children $3). The mounds were once part of a Choctaw Indian community that existed between A.D. 1000 and 1550. The village was empty when Europeans arrived, and the name Chucalissa means "abandoned house."

The largest mound would have been where the chief and his family lived. The present-day museum, operated by the University of Memphis, consists of an exhibit about the Native Americans of the area and self-guided tour around the mounds and courtyard area, where games and meetings would have been held. There is also a half-mile nature trail along the bluff overlooking the river. In addition to the opening hours listed above,

Chucalissa is open on Sunday afternoon during the summer months; call ahead for details.

EAST MEMPHIS

East Memphis is home to old suburbs, gracious homes, and some excellent parks and other attractions.

The Dixon

The Dixon (4339 Park Ave., 901/761-5250, www.dixon.org, Tues.–Fri. 10 A.M.–4 P.M., Sat. 10 A.M.–5 P.M., Sun. 1–5 P.M., adults $7, seniors $5, children $3), an art museum housed inside a stately Georgian-style home, has an impressive permanent collection of more than 2,000 paintings, many of them French impressionist and postimpressionist style, including works by Monet, Renoir, Degas, and Cézanne. It also mounts a half dozen special exhibits each year; previous ones have showcased the art of George Rodrigue and David Macaulay.

The Dixon is an easy place to spend several hours, immersed first in art and then in walking the paths that explore the house's 17 acres of beautifully tended gardens. There is a cutting garden, woodland garden, and formal gardens, among others.

Admission to the Dixon is free on Saturday 10 A.M.–noon.

Memphis Botanic Garden

The 100-acre Memphis Botanic Garden (750 Cherry Rd., 901/576-4100, www.memphisbotanicgarden.com, adults $5, seniors $4, children $3) is home to more than 140 different species of trees and more than two dozen specialty gardens, including a Sculpture Garden, Azalea Trail, and Iris Garden. Trails meander through the gardens, but for the greatest fun buy a handful of fish food and feed the fish and ducks that inhabit the pond at the Japanese Garden. The garden puts on a number of events, including blockbuster concerts, plant sales, and programs for children.

The Pink Palace

A good destination for families, the Pink

© SUSANNA HENIGHAN POTTER

The iris garden at the Memphis Botanic Garden blooms in the springtime.

Palace (3050 Central Ave., 901/320-6320, www.memphismuseums.org, Mon.–Sat. 9 A.M.–5 P.M., Sun. noon–5 P.M.) is a group of attractions rolled into one. The Pink Palace Museum (adults $8.25, children $5.75) is a museum about Memphis, with exhibits about the natural history of the Mid-South region and the city's development. There is a full-scale replica of the first Piggly Wiggly market, plus an exhibit about how health care became such a large part of the Memphis economy. The museum is housed within the Pink Palace Mansion, the Memphis home of Piggly Wiggly founder Clarence Saunders.

The Pink Palace is also home to the Sharpe Planetarium (adults $4.50, children $4), which is open on Saturday, and an IMAX movie theater (adults $8, children $6.25), which shows movies daily. Special package tickets are available for all the Pink Palace attractions.

Art Museum of the University of Memphis

The Art Museum of the University of Memphis (3750 Norriswood Ave., 901/678-2224, www.

amum.org, free) houses excellent but small exhibits of ancient Egyptian and African art and artifacts, and a noteworthy print gallery. There are frequent special exhibitions. The museum is closed during University holidays.

Children's Museum of Memphis

You will know the Children's Museum of Memphis (2525 Central Ave., 901/458-2678, www.cmom.com, Mon.–Sat. 9 A.M.–5 P.M., Sun. noon–5 P.M., adults $8, children $7) by the large alphabet blocks outside spelling its acronym, CMOM. Bring children here for constructive and educational play: They can sit in flight simulator and real airplane cockpit, climb through the arteries of a model heart, climb a skyscraper, and more.

Lichterman Nature Center

Lichterman Nature Center (5992 Quince Rd., 901/767-7322, Tues.–Thurs. 9 A.M.–4 P.M., Fri.–Sat. 9 A.M.–5 P.M., adults $6, children $4.50) is dedicated to generating interest and enthusiasm for the Mid-South's nature. The park encompasses some 65 acres, and visitors will enjoy seeing native trees and flowers, including dogwoods, lotus, and pine. There is a museum about the local environment, picnic facilities, and pleasant trails. Environmental education is the center's mission, and this is a popular destination for families and school groups.

TOURS
History Tours
Heritage Tours Memphis (901/527-3427, www.heritagetoursmemphis.com, $25–35) is the city's only tour company dedicated to presenting Memphis's African-American history. Operated by Memphians Elaine Turner and Joan Nelson, Heritage Tours offers black heritage, musical heritage, civil rights, and Beale Street walking tours. They can also arrange out-of-town tours to area attractions, such as the Alex Haley home in Henning, Tennessee. Most local tours cost $25 and last about three hours.

The black heritage tour starts at the W. C. Handy Home and Museum and includes a stop at the Slavehaven Underground Railroad

Museum, plus narration that tells the story of black Memphians such as Ida B. Wells, Robert Church, and Tom Lee, and the events leading up to the assassination of Dr. Martin Luther King Jr. You will drive past the Mason Temple Church of God in Christ at 930 Mason Street, where Dr. King gave his famous "mountain-top" speech the night before his death.

River Tours
The **Memphis Queen Riverboat Tours** (901/527-2628, $18) leave daily at 2:30 P.M. from the Port of Memphis, located at the foot of Monroe Avenue on the riverfront. The afternoon tour lasts 90 minutes and takes you a few miles south of the city before turning around. Commentary tells some of the most famous tales of the river, but the biggest attraction of the tour is simply being on Old Man River. The views of the Memphis skyline from the water are impressive. Concessions are available onboard. The riverboats also offer dinner cruises with live music for about $35 per person.

COURTESY OF MEMPHIS CONVENTION AND VISITORS BUREAU

The *Memphis Queen* riverboat cruises the Mississippi daily.

Music Tours

Memphis just looks better from the passenger window of a 1955 Cadillac. That's as good a reason as any to call Tad Pierson for one of his **American Dream Safari** (901/527-8870, www.americandreamsafari.com) tours of Memphis. Pierson offers tours with a difference—he does not just do sightseeing, he promises experiences and memories for his guests. His tours include juke joints of Memphis, gospel churches, a Mississippi Delta day trip, a special tour for photographers, plus much more. Pierson really gets the unique appeal of Memphis, and he wants to share it with his guests.

Music fans should sign up for one of Sherman Wilmott's **Memphis Rock 'n Roll Tours** (901/359-3102, www.memphisrocktour.com), customized musical tours of Memphis. He will pick you up at any Memphis hotel and then whisk you away to some of the city's best- and least-known musical sites, such as the past and present locations of Memphis recording studios, radio stations, record stores, and even musicians' homes. He is a fountain of music lore. If you have a special interest, speak up: Chances are that Sherman can fix you up. A former curator at the Stax museum and publisher of the *Kreature Comforts Low-Life Guide to Memphis,* Sherman recently started a partnership with Wayne Jackson of the famed Memphis Horns, who will ride along on special tours and tell firsthand stories of Memphis's musical history.

Music-themed tours are also the specialty at **Backbeat Tours** (901/272-2328, www.backbeattours.com, $25–40). You will travel on a reconditioned 1959 transit bus and be serenaded by live musicians. Tours include the Memphis Mojo Tour, which takes you to Memphis music landmarks like Sun Studio and the Stax Museum, and the Hound Dog tour, which follows in Elvis Presley's Memphis footsteps. Backbeat can also take you to Graceland and offers two walking tours of Memphis—a Memphis Ghost Tour and Haunted Pub Crawl—on Wednesday through Sunday evening for $15.

Entertainment

Memphis is a vibrant, diverse city with an entertainment scene that reflects this. Blues, rap, R&B, and gospel are just some of the types of music you can find on any given weekend. Alternative and indie rock finds a receptive audience in Memphis, as does opera, Broadway productions, and the symphony. There's always a good excuse to go out.

LIVE MUSIC AND CLUBS

Memphis may be the birthplace of the blues, but there's a lot more to the music scene than that. It's true that you can catch live blues at a Beale Street nightclub or in a city juke joint. But you can also find hard-edge rock, jazz, and acoustic music most nights of the week. The best resource for up-to-date entertainment listings is the free weekly *Memphis Flyer* (www.memphisflyer.com), which comes out on Wednesday and includes a detailed listing of club dates and concerts.

Keep in mind that big-name artists often perform at casinos in Tunica, just over the state line in Mississippi. Many of these shows are advertised in Memphis media outlets, or check out the upcoming events on the Tunica Convention and Visitors Bureau website, www.tunicamiss.com.

Blues

One of the first things you do when you get to Memphis should be to find out if the **Center for Southern Folklore** (119 S. Main St., 901/525-3655, www.southernfolklore.com, Mon.–Sat. 11 A.M.–5 P.M.) has any concerts or special activities planned during your visit. The center has been documenting and preserving traditional Memphis and Delta blues music for more than 35 years. They put on concerts and lectures, produce documentaries, offer group tours and educational programs, and organize the annual Memphis Music and Heritage Festival over Labor Day weekend. They often have live blues on Friday afternoon, and offer a variety of special shows. This is one of the best places to hear authentic blues. The center has a 250-seat dining room and performance space in Peabody Place, as well as a folklore store that sells folk art, books, CDs, and hot peach cobbler, among other things. A Be Nice or Leave sign sets the tone as soon as you step into this colorful and eclectic shop, one of the best gift shops in the city. The center is a nonprofit organization, and well worth supporting.

Beale Street is ground zero for Memphis's blues music scene. While some people lament that Beale has become a sad tourist trap, it can still be a worthwhile place to spend your evening. Indeed, no other part of Memphis has as much music and entertainment packed into such a small area. On a typical night, Beale Street is full of people of all ages and races strolling from one bar to the next. Beer seems to run a close second to music as the street's prime attraction, with many bars selling directly onto the street through concession windows. "Big Ass Beer" cups used by many establishments say it all.

Nearly all Beale Street bars have live music, but one of the most popular is **B. B. King's Blues Club** (139 Beale St., 901/524-5464, cover $5–7), owned by the legend himself. B. B. King performs here two or three times a year—keep your ear to the ground since the shows are not usually advertised. On other evenings, local acts and some nationally known performers take the stage. B. B. King's draws a mostly tourist crowd, but with the blues on full-throttle, you probably won't care too much.

Also on Beale Street, **Blues City Cafe** (138 Beale St., 901/526-3637, cover $3–5) books blues plus a variety of other acts, including do-wop, Zydeco, R&B, funk, and "high impact rock-a-billy." The café-restaurant is one of the most popular on Beale Street, and the nightclub is right next door. **Rum Boogie Cafe** (182 Beale St.,

901/528-0151, cover $3–5) has an award-winning house band, James Covan and the Boogie Blues Band, that performs most evenings.

Morgan Freeman is part owner of the **Ground Zero Blues Club** (158 Lt. George W. Lee St., 901/522-0130, cover varies), which opened in 2008 next door to the Westin, a few blocks off Beale Street. A satellite of the original Ground Zero in Clarksdale, Mississippi, this club offers real-deal blues seven nights a week.

Jazz

If you want a break from the blues, **King's Palace Cafe** (162 Beale St., 901/521-1851) specializes in jazz. Lots of wood paneling and red paint makes the bar and restaurant warm and welcoming. This is an unpretentious place to have a meal or listen to live music. There is a $1 per person entertainment charge when you sit at a table.

In South Main, **Café Soul** (492 S. Main St., 901/859-0557, cover varies) has live jazz most nights of the week, good for a relaxing evening after browsing the galleries.

Rock

Still on Beale Street, **Alfred's** (197 Beale St., 901/525-3711, cover $5 Fri. and Sat.) has rock acts five nights a week. On Sunday evening, the 17-piece Memphis Jazz Orchestra takes the stage. The dance floor at Alfred's is one of the best on Beale Street.

One of Beale Street's most historic nightclubs, **The New Daisy** (330 Beale St., 901/525-8979, cover $5 and up) books rock 'n' roll, independent, and a few R&B acts. There are shows most nights of the week; call ahead or check the entertainment listings for a schedule. The Daisy is an all-ages club, and many shows attract a young audience.

Off Beale Street, the **Hi-Tone Cafe** (1913 Poplar Ave., 901/278-8663, cover varies) is probably the best place to see live music in town. The Hi-Tone books all kinds of acts, from high-energy rockers to soulful acoustic acts. They are really committed to bringing good live music to Memphis. The cover charge for local shows is a few bucks, but tickets for

MEMPHIS JUKE JOINTS

In Memphis, there are only two reasons to go to a juke joint full of blues: because you feel good or because you feel bad. Beale Street is a reliable source seven nights a week and your visit to Memphis wouldn't be complete without checking out its scene. But if you want to sneak away from the tourist crowd and catch some homegrown talent, check out a Memphis juke joint. Live music is typical on Friday and Saturday nights and sometimes Sunday, but it gets scarce during the week. Generally music starts late (11 P.M.) and finishes early (3 A.M.).

Is it safe? Maybe not, but what is these days? Is it worth it? Most definitely yes! In fact, these clubs are far more safe and friendly than a parking lot at a shopping mall. Just be cool and come for the right reasons and you'll get home to tell the tale.

Some common-sense advice: If you're uncomfortable in a largely black crowd, don't bother. Don't be surprised if the person you've engaged in conversation sitting next to you gets called to the stage sometime during the evening and delivers a beautiful song. If you dress sexy expect results. Don't overdo the dirty dog on the dance floor. If somebody asks your date to dance, relax – it's bound to happen.

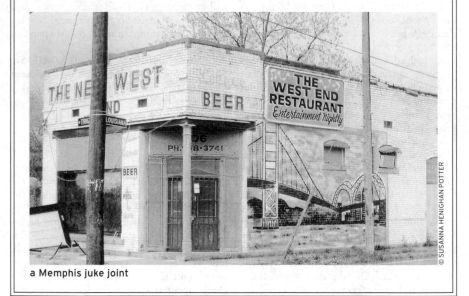

© SUSANNA HENIGHAN POTTER

a Memphis juke joint

Remember that it's in the nature of things for these clubs to come and go. The listings below were current as of this writing, but always subject to change.

- **Wild Bill's** (1580 Vollentine St., 901/726-5473): A legendary club in Memphis. The Patriarch himself passed away in the summer of 2007, but what he established will still carry on. The quintessential juke joint. Small, intimate, an open kitchen serving chicken wings, and ice-cold beer served in 40-ounce bottles. Home to Ms. Nikki and the Memphis Soul Survivors.

- **CC's Blues Club** (1427 Thomas St., 901/526-5566): More upscale. More mirrors. But a great dance floor and don't you dare come under-dressed.

- **One Block North** (645 Marble Ave., 901/525-7505): Friday nights only for live music. Hard to find and that's why you'll be the only tourists there.

- **Executive Inn** (3222 Airways, at the intersection with Brooks Rd., 901/332-3800): Don Valentine is the drummer and bandleader and everybody wants to sit in. This is where Preston Shannon comes to hang out. More soul than blues, but when Preacher Man closes the show you know you'll be satisfied.

- **Handy's Blues Hall** (182 Beale St., 901/528-0150): New Orleans has Preservation Hall. Memphis has Handy's Blues Hall. Everyone bad-raps Beale Street and its jangly tourism scene. But if you catch it on a good night when Dr Feelgood warms up his harmonica and you look around the room at the memorabilia on the walls, you could be in a joint at the end of a country road in Mississippi.

- **The Blue Worm** (1405 Airways Dr., 901/327-7947): When a legendary juke joint band gets old and disintegrates, this is where it ends up. The Fieldstones have been *the* band in Memphis since the early '60s. Now it's down to Wilroy Sanders, the Last Living Bluesman. The house band can get behind anybody and make them a superstar, for one glorious song.

- **Big S Bar and Grill** (1179 Dunnavant Ave., 901/775-9127): They say blues is a feeling. The Big S doesn't have live music, but if you want to sink into the atmosphere of a bar that's dark with mystery and history plus the warmest vibe in town, come on home. Blues DJ on Sunday nights and the jukebox is a veritable encyclopedia of blues.

- **The Boss** (912 Jackson Ave., 901/522-8883): Thursday nights only. Ever heard the overused term "best-kept secret in town"? Jesse Dotson on piano. Leroy Hodges on bass. Roy Cunningham on drums. An array of singers like Preacher Man, Bill Coday, O. T. Sykes. Why wait for the weekend?

Contributed by Tad Pierson, owner and operator of American Dream Safari (www.americandreamsafari.com) and purveyor of true-life expeditions into Memphis and Mississippi bigger-name acts can run $20 and more. The bar serves respectable burgers and finger foods, excellent martinis, and lots of beer.

Also in midtown, **The Buccaneer** (1368 Monroe, 901/278-0909, cover varies) books rock acts most days a week. Cover charge rarely tops $5.

BARS
Downtown
You can head to Beale Street for a night out, even if you're not that into blues. **Coyote Ugly** (326 Beale St., 901/888-8459) attracts a youthful crowd seven days a week. The dance floor here is hot.

The best place to grab a beer downtown is the **Beale Street Tap Room** (168 Beale St., 901/527-4392). With more than 30 beers on tap, this is a great choice for beer lovers. The service is friendly and low-key, and regulars have their own mug.

Off Beale Street, the **Peabody Hotel Memphis** (149 Union Ave., 901/529-4000) may be the best place to enjoy a relaxing drink. The lobby bar offers good service, comfortable seats, and an unrivaled atmosphere.

In Peabody Place about a block from Beale Street, **The Flying Saucer Draught Emporium** (130 Peabody Pl., 901/523-7468) draws a lively happy-hour crowd. The bar offers more than 75 draft beers, plus cocktails and wine. Grab a seat along the windows and watch downtown Memphis come alive as the sun sets.

Also in Peabody Place, **Dan McGuiness** (150 Peabody Pl., 901/527-8500) offers Irish beers and sports on the telly.

In the South Main district, **Ernestine and Hazel's** (531 S. Main St., 901/523-9754) is one of Memphis's most celebrated pit stops for cold drinks and a night out. Once a brothel, Ernestine and Hazel's now has one of the best jukeboxes in town. Take a seat upstairs in one of the old brothel rooms and watch South Main Street below.

For a departure from the usual bar scene, head to the smoke-free **High Point Pinch** (333 N. Main St., 901/619-0061). Also in the Pinch

neighborhood, **Precious Cargo Coffeehouse** (381 N. Main St., 901/578-8446) has a lineup of eclectic music every Friday evening starting about 9 P.M.

Midtown
The **Young Avenue Deli** (2119 Young Ave., 901/278-3123) is a friendly neighborhood bar that books occasional live acts to perform. Located in the Cooper-Young area, Young Avenue Deli has hundreds of different beers on tap or in bottles. The bar attracts a diverse crowd, from young hipsters to older neighborhood denizens.

A favorite place for music, pool, and a night out in midtown is the **Blue Monkey** (2012 Madison Ave., 901/272-2583). Grab a pizza and a beer, shoot some pool, and then rock out to the live band.

Murphy's (1589 Madison Ave., 901/726-4193) is a neighborhood bar with a nice patio, and **Zinnie's Old Place** (1688 Madison Ave., 901/726-5004) is a familiar haunt for many midtowners who are looking for a quiet spot to enjoy a cold one.

Perfect for a business date or after-work pit stop, **The Grove Grill** (4550 Poplar Ave., 901/818-9951) is popular with businesspeople and office-types.

Two of Memphis's best sports bars are found in the eastern reaches of the city. **Brookhaven Pub and Grill** (695 W. Brookhaven Cir., 901/680-8118) has big-screen plasma televisions, great beer on tap, and lots of fans. Tuesday night is quiz night. **Gill's Bar & Grill** (551 S. Highland, 901/458-2787), near the University of Memphis, specializes in cold beers and sports and has a great happy hour.

GAY AND LESBIAN NIGHTLIFE
Many gay and lesbian clubs don't get going until late in the night, after other clubs have closed.

Metro Memphis (1349 Autumn Ave., 901/274-8010, cover varies) is a gay bar and dance club that attracts both gay and straight patrons. The city's largest dance floor may be found at **Backstreet Memphis** (2018 Court

Ave., 901/276-5522, cover varies), a midtown club that has light shows, drag shows, karaoke, and other high-energy entertainment.

A nightclub institution in midtown, **J Wags Bar** (1268 Madison Ave., 901/278-4313, cover varies) doesn't usually get going until the wee hours, after other mainstream clubs have closed.

Attracting mostly women patrons, **Madison Flame** (1588 Madison Ave., 901/278-9839, cover varies) has a popular karaoke night.

THE ARTS

Memphis has a growing arts scene. The **Greater Memphis Arts Council** (901/578-2787, www.memphisartscouncil.com) provides funding for more than 20 local arts groups, and is a good source of information about upcoming events.

Major arts venues include the **Cannon Center for the Performing Arts** (255 N. Main St., 901/576-1201, www.thecannoncenter.com) and the **Orpheum Theatre** (Main and Beale Sts., 901/525-3000, www.orpheummemphis.com). They regularly book major artists and Broadway performances.

Theater

For theater, check out **Playhouse on the Square** (51 S. Cooper St., 901/726-4656, www.playhouseonthesquare.com). This dynamic Memphis institution serves as home to several of the city's acting companies and puts on between 15 and 20 different performances every year. It also offers theater classes, school performances, and pay-what-you-can shows. The playhouse also screens classic movies on the first Sunday of each month.

Theatre Memphis (630 Perkins Ext., 901/682-8323, www.theatrememphis.org) is a community theater company that has been in existence since the 1920s. They stage about 12 shows annually at their theater in midtown. **TheatreWorks** (2085 Monroe Ave., 901/274-7139, www.theatreworks.org) encourages off-beat and new theater with organizations including Our Own Voice Theatre Troupe, the Memphis Black Repertory Theatre, and the Playwright's Forum.

Music

The **Memphis Symphony Orchestra** (3100 Walnut Grove Rd., 901/324-3627, www.memphissymphony.org) puts on a varied calendar of performances year-round in its home at the Cannon Center for the Performing Arts at 2155 North Main Street. The symphony was founded in 1952, and today has more than 850 musicians, staff, and volunteers.

Opera

Opera Memphis (6745 Wolf River Blvd., 901/257-3100, www.operamemphis.org) performs at the historic Orpheum Theatre on Beale Street.

Dance

Ballet Memphis (901/737-7322, www.balletmemphis.org) performs classical dance at the Orpheum and other nontraditional venues throughout the city. The **New Ballet Ensemble** (901/726-9225, www.newballet.org) puts on performances around the city with "dancers in do-rags as well as tights," according to the *Commercial Appeal.*

Project Motion (901/274-7139, www.projectmotiondance.org) is a contemporary dance collective that performs at Theatre Works at 2085 Monroe Avenue.

Cinemas

There are a half dozen multiscreen movie theaters in and around Memphis, including one at Peabody Place downtown. For independent movies, try **Malco's Paradiso** (584 S. Mendenhall Rd., 901/682-1754, www.malco.com) or **Studio on the Square** (2105 Court St., 901/725-71751, www.overtonsquare.com). In the summer, check out the **Orpheum** (203 S. Main St., 901/525-7800) for classic movies, and the **Summer Quartet Drive-In** (5310 Summer Ave., 901/767-4320) for a drive-in experience.

EVENTS
Spring

Memphians celebrate their African heritage over a long April weekend in mid-April. **Africa in April** (901/947-2133, www.africainapril.org)

honors a specific country in Africa each year; activities include cooking, storytelling, music, and a parade. The festival takes place at Church Park on the east end of Beale Street.

In early May, the Memphis-based Blues Foundation hosts the annual **Handy Awards** (www.blues.org), the Grammys of the blues world.

Memphis in May (www.memphisinmay. org), the city's largest annual event, is really three major festivals rolled into one. The **Beale Street Music Festival,** which takes place at Tom Lee Park on the river during the first weekend of May, kicks things off with a celebration of Memphis music. Expect a lot of wow performers, plus many more up-and-coming talents. The festival has grown over the years, and it is now a three-day event with four stages of music going simultaneously. In addition to music, the festival offers excellent people-watching, lots of barbecue, cold beer, and festivity. You can buy daily tickets, or a three-day pass for the whole weekend.

In mid-May, attention turns to the **World Championship Barbeque Cooking Contest,** a celebration of pork, pigs, and barbecue that takes place in Tom Lee Park. In addition to the barbecue judging, there is entertainment, hog-calling contests, and other piggy antics. If you're not part of a competing team (or friends with one) you can buy barbecue from vendors who set up in the park.

Finally, at the end of the month, there is the **Memphis International Festival,** which pays tribute to a different country each year with presentations about its music, food, culture, and history.

Book your hotel rooms early for Memphis in May, since many hotels, especially those downtown, fill up.

Founded by African Americans in 1936 as an alternative to the all-white Cotton Carnival, the **Kemet Jubilee** (www.memphiskemetjubilee.com) was originally known as the Cotton Makers Jubilee. Today, the highlight of the jubilee, which takes place in May, is the parade of marching bands and costumed troupes that runs along 2nd Street in downtown Memphis.

Summer

Carnival Memphis (901/458-2500, www. carnivalmemphis.org), the renamed Cotton Carnival, is now racially integrated and takes place in June. The Carnival features a parade and fireworks.

The annual candlelight vigil at Graceland on August 15, the anniversary of Elvis's death, has grown into a whole week of activities throughout Memphis. More than 30,000 people visit Graceland during **Elvis Week** (www.elvisweek. com), and during the vigil his most adoring fans walk solemnly up the Graceland drive to pay their respects at his grave. Special concerts, tribute shows, and movies are shown during the week, as the city celebrates its most famous export even more than usual.

Fall

Organized by the Center for Southern Folklore, the **Memphis Music and Heritage Festival** (901/525-3655, www.memphis-musicandheritagefestival.com) held over Labor Day weekend sticks close to the roots of Memphis music. Performers include gospel singers, bona fide bluesmen and women, rock-a-billy superstars, and much more. Performances take place in the center's shop and concert hall on Main Street, making them more intimate than other blockbuster music festivals.

End-of-summer fairs are a tradition for southern and rural communities all over the United States. The 10-day **Mid-South Fair** (www.midsouthfair.org) in September is a bonanza of attractions: livestock shows, rodeos, agricultural judging, concerts, beauty pageants, exhibitions, carnival rides, funnel cakes, and cotton candy. In 2008 it moved from the Mid-South Fairgrounds in southeast Memphis to a 150-acre site across the road from the Tunica, Mississippi, Welcome Center, about 30 miles from Memphis.

In mid-September, the Cooper-Young neighborhood throws its annual jamboree at the **Cooper-Young Festival** (www.cooperyoungfestival.com). There is an arts and crafts fair, live music, and food vendors at this street carnival.

Winter

Taking place over the weekend closest to Elvis Presley's January 8 birthday, the **Elvis Birthday Celebration** (www.elvis.com) draws Elvis fans with special performances, dance parties, and a ceremony at Graceland proclaiming Elvis Presley Day.

The two-day **Beale Street Zydeco Music Festival** (901/526-0110) takes place over the last weekend in February and features more than 20 bands paying tribute to Cajun music.

SHOPPING
Gifts and Souvenirs

Any of the half-dozen gift shops along Beale Street sell gifts and souvenirs of the city. **Memphis Music** (149 Beale St., 901/526-5047) has a good selection of CDs and DVDs for music fans. For a unique gift or something practical for yourself, **A. Schwab** (163 Beale St., 901/523-9782) is your best choice, and lots of fun to boot.

Another good place for gift shopping is the **Center for Southern Folklore** (119 S. Main St., 901/525-3655), which has books, art, and music focusing on the region. All of the city's museums have good gift shops, including the **National Civil Rights Museum, Stax Museum of American Soul Music,** and **Sun Studio,** where everything is emblazoned with the distinctive yellow Sun label.

If you have a car, head out to **Shangri-La Records** (1916 Madison Ave., 901/274-1916), the city's best record store, which specializes in Memphis music.

Bookstores

The only downtown bookstore is the aptly named **Downtown Books** (152 Madison Ave., 901/577-6600), which trades in used books from its premises in the basement below the Memphis Coffee Exchange.

You'll need a car to reach the city's major bookstores, however. **Burke's Books** (938 S.

the Cooper-Young Festival, held in September

Cooper, 901/278-7484), in the Cooper-Young district east of midtown, specializes in used and antiquarian books. **Davis-Kidd Booksellers** (387 Perkins Ext., 901/683-9801), a Tennessee-based independent bookseller, is in Laurelwood Shopping Center and is your best choice for new books. Davis-Kidd has weekly book signings and a café.

Bookstar (3402 Poplar Ave., 901/323-9332) in midtown is an outlet store for new books.

Art

For art boutiques and galleries, head south to the South Main arts district, where you will find galleries including **D'Edge Art and Unique Treasures** (550 S. Main St., 901/521-0054), which has contemporary folk art, and **Robinson Gallery/Archives** (44 Huling Ave., 901/683-1132), a photography gallery.

On the last Friday of each month the trolleys are free, the galleries stay open, and hundreds of arts-minded Memphians head to South Main to mingle into the night. For a directory of all South Main galleries, contact the South Main Association (901/578-7262, www.south-mainmemphis.org).

Antiques

Head out Central Avenue, to the area between Cooper and East Parkway, for the greatest concentration of antiques stores. **Flashback** (2304 Central Ave., 901/272-2304) sells both vintage furniture and clothes, including a whole lot of Levi's jeans. **Louedau's** (2174 Young Ave., 901/722-9681) has fabric, lace, and vintage baby clothes. Another good choice is **Toad Hall Antiques** (2129 Central Ave., 901/726-0755), easy to find because of a brightly painted mural on the outside of the building.

Thrift Stores

In a city where vintage never went out of style, you can expect excellent thrift stores. The biggest and best is **AmVets** (2426 Elvis Presley Blvd., 901/775-5018). You can also try the **Junior League of Memphis Thrift Store** (3586 Summer Ave., 901/327-4777).

The most colorful shopping experience in Memphis is found at **The Memphis Flea Market—The Big One** (955 Maxwell Early Blvd., 901/276-3532), which takes place on the third weekend of each month at the Mid-South Fairgrounds. Between 800 and 1,000 vendors turn up each month with housewares, clothing, computers, jewelry, antiques, yard art, and so much more. Between 20,000 and 25,000 people come to shop. Admission is free, but you must pay to park.

Shopping Malls

Memphis proudly welcomed major retail back downtown with the opening of **Peabody Place** (901/261-7529), just a block away from Beale Street, with a Tower Records, Gap, and Victoria's Secret, as well as a movie theater and several restaurants in the food court.

The most upscale shopping mall in the Memphis area is **Wolfchase Galleria** (2760 N. Germantown Pkwy., 901/372-9409). Located in Cordova, an east-lying suburb now consumed by Memphis sprawl, the galleria celebrated its 10th anniversary in 2007. It is aging gracefully, and still boasts some of the most exclusive retailers in the city, including Brooks Brothers, Abercrombie & Fitch, and bebe. Department stores at the mall include Macy's, Dillard's, Sears, and JC Penney. You can take either exit 16 or 18 off I-40 to get to Wolfchase Galleria.

Also in Germantown, **The Shops of Saddle Creek** (West St. at Poplar Ave., 901/761-2571) has Williams Sonoma, Banana Republic, and an Apple computer store, among others.

Closer to the city center, **Oak Court Mall** (4465 Poplar Ave., 901/682-8928) was the location of the very first Starbucks in Tennessee. It is also consistently voted Memphians' favorite mall, no doubt because it offers a good selection of stores in a pleasant atmosphere, and it's relatively close to town. Department stores at Oak Court include Macy's and Dillard's; the mall also has Aveda, Jos A. Bank, Banana Republic, and dozens more stores.

And if that's not enough for you, head across the road to **Laurelwood Shopping Center** (Poplar Ave. at Perkins Ext., 901/794-6022), where you'll find specialty clothing and shoe boutiques, as well as Davis-Kidd Booksellers, Memphis's best large bookstore.

In South Memphis, **Southland Mall** (1215 Southland Mall, 901/346-1210) is Memphis's oldest mall. Built in 1966, Southland soldiers on. There is a Sears, as well as specialty shops including Radio Shack and Bath & Body Works.

Outlet Shopping

You can buy directly from name-brand retailers at rock-bottom prices at the **Lakeland Factory Outlet Mall** (3536 Canada Rd., 901/386-3180). Located at the Canada Road exit off I-40, the mall boasts a number of big-name retailers, including Bass, Van Heusen, Dress Barn, Toy Liquidators, and Old Time Pottery, which sells dinnerware and other pottery.

Sports and Recreation

With a professional basketball team, excellent downtown baseball club, and lots of city parks, Memphis is a great city in which to watch sports or get active yourself.

PARKS
Downtown

Named for the legendary blues composer, **Handy Park,** on Beale Street, between 3rd Street and Rufus Thomas Boulevard, seems a tad out of place among Beale's nightclubs and restaurants. But the park is a site of historic importance, if only because of the statue of its namesake that guards its gates. The park hosts occasional outdoor concerts and festivals, and at other times you will find places to sit and a handful of vendors.

Uptown

Tom Lee Park, a long, narrow grassy park that faces the river, is a popular venue for summertime festivals and events. It is also used year-round for walking and jogging, and by people who simply want to look out at the Mississippi River. The park is named for Tom Lee, an African-American man who saved the lives of 32 people when the steamboat they were on sank in the river in 1925. Lee, who pulled people out of the river and into his boat, "Zev," could not even swim. A dated monument erected at the park in 1954 calls Lee "a very worthy negro."

Located on the northern side of downtown Memphis, **Court Square,** three blocks from

the waterfront along Court Avenue, is a pleasant city park surrounded by historic buildings. Court Square is one of four parks that was included when the city was first planned in 1819. There are benches and trees, and it is a wireless Internet hot spot.

Confederate Park, located on Front Street between Court and Jefferson Streets, commemorates Confederate soldiers who died in the Battle of Memphis, as well as other war dead. There is a statue of Jefferson Davis in the center of the park. This is where many Memphians gathered to watch the Battle of Memphis in 1862, and it remains a good place to view the river below.

Midtown

Located in midtown Memphis, **Overton Park** (1928 Poplar Ave.) is the best all-around park the city has to offer. This 342-acre park has a nine-hole golf course, nature trails through the woods, bike trails, an outdoor amphitheater (called the Overton Park Shell, which is undergoing a major restoration), and lots of green, open spaces. The park shares space with the Memphis Zoo and the Memphis Brooks Museum of Art, making the area a popular destination for city residents and visitors.

The Madison Avenue trolley passes **Forrest Park,** along Madison Avenue, between North Manassas and North Dunlap Streets, an ample city park dedicated to the memory of the controversial Nathan Bedford Forrest. Forrest, a slave-trader, Confederate, and the first grand wizard of the Ku Klux Klan, has an uncomfortable position of prominence in Memphis and the whole of western Tennessee. Both he and his wife are buried in the park.

East Memphis

Located near the University of Memphis and Oak Court Mall, **Audubon Park** (4161 Park Ave.) has a golf course, tennis courts, walking trails, and other sports facilities. The Memphis Botanic Garden is located here.

Memphians celebrate the fact that their largest city park, **Shelby Farms,** is five times the size of New York's Central Park. But the fact is that Shelby Farms is underused, since most of its 4,500 acres are pleasantly undeveloped. There are plans to improve the park by adding more recreational facilities, but for now it is a diamond in the rough. Come here to go mountain biking, horseback riding, inline skating, walking, or running along some of the many trails. You can also fish, raft, canoe, or sail on any of the park's six lakes. There is a wheelchair-accessible trail, areas for picnicking, and a shooting range. Shelby Farms was originally set aside to be the county penal farm, and although it was not used in this way, the county jail is found on the western edge of the park. Shelby Farms is located on the eastern side of the city, just outside the I-40/I-240 loop that circles Memphis. It is easily accessible from Exits 12 and 14 off I-40, and exit 13 off I-240. Or follow Walnut Grove Road from midtown.

South Memphis

Southwest of the city center, about 15 minutes' drive from the airport, is **T. O. Fuller State Park** (1500 Mitchell Rd., 901/543-7581). The visitors center here is open weekdays 8 A.M.–4:40 P.M. Amenities at the 1,138-acre park include sheltered picnic areas, tennis courts, a golf course, swimming pool ($3), basketball courts, softball field, six miles of hiking trails, and camping facilities. T. O. Fuller State Park was the first state park east of the Mississippi River open to African Americans, and the second in the nation.

BIKING

A few brave souls use bicycles to get around Memphis, but most cyclists in the city bike as a form of recreation. The City of Memphis has established five bike routes that circle the city and various neighborhoods. These routes are marked and have designated parking and restroom facilities at the start. They are not bike paths—you share the road with cars—and normal safety measures are necessary.

The **Memphis Hightailers Bicycle Club** (www.memphishightailers.com) organizes frequent rides for various levels, with distances ranging from 20 to 100 miles. In addition, there are rides leaving every Saturday at 8 A.M. and Sunday at 9 A.M. from the Super-Lo parking lot at Southern Avenue and Colonial Street.

For bike rentals, gear, and advice about riding in and around the city, go to **Peddler Bike Shop** (575 S. Highland, 901/327-4833, www.peddlerbikeshop.com), where owner Hal Mabray will happily help you get geared up to ride. A used-bike rental will cost about $25 per day, while a souped-up version can run $50 and up.

There are a number of parks near Memphis that are bike-friendly. **Meeman-Shelby Forest State Park** north of the city has five miles of paved bike paths, and cyclists use the main park roads for more extensive riding. Bicyclists will also find trails at **Shelby Farms.**

It is also noteworthy that the **Mississippi River Trail,** a bicycle route that will eventually run from the headwaters of the Mississippi River in Minnesota to the Gulf of Mexico, runs from Reelfoot Lake in northeastern Tennessee, through Memphis, and on to Mississippi. For maps and details, go to www.mississippirivertrail.org.

GOLF

The City of Memphis operates award-winning 18-hole golf courses at **Audubon Park**

(4160 Park Ave., 901/683-6941) with gently rolling hills; **Fox Meadows** (3064 Clarke Rd., 901/362-0232), which is easy to walk but with several challenging holes; **Galloway Park** (3815 Walnut Grove, 901/685-7805); **Davy Crockett Golf Course** (4380 Rangeline Rd., 901/368-3375); and **Pine Hill Park** (1005 Alice Ave., 901/775-9434), a great course for walkers.

There are two public nine-hole courses: one at **Riverside Park** (465 S. Parkway W., 901/576-4260) and one at **Overton Park** (2080 Poplar Ave., 901/725-9905). Greens fees on the public courses are under $20.

One of the best-kept golf secrets in town is the 18-hole par-71 course at **T. O. Fuller State Park** (1500 W. Mitchell Rd., 901/543-7771) south of downtown.

TENNIS

The City operates public tennis courts at several parks, including **Bert Ferguson Park** (8505 Trinity), **Gaisman Park** (4221 Macon), **Glenview** (1813 Southern), **Martin Luther King Jr. Park** (South Pkwy. at Riverside Dr.), and **University Park** (University at Edward).

There are also four public indoor/outdoor tennis complexes: **Bellevue** (1310 S. Bellevue Blvd., 901/774-7199), **Leftwich** (4145 Southern, 901/685-7907), **Whitehaven** (Finley Rd., 901/332-0546), and **Wolbrecht** (1645 Ridgeway, 901/767-2889). Fees vary per facility; call in advance for information and court reservations.

SWIMMING

The City of Memphis operates a dozen outdoor pools that are open from June to August, and several indoor pools open year-round. Public outdoor pools are open Monday–Saturday noon–6 P.M., and admission is free. The outdoor pools include **L. E. Brown Pool** (617 S. Orleans, 901/527-3620) in southeastern Memphis; **Lester Pool** (317 Tillman Rd., 901/323-2261) in eastern Memphis; **Riverview Pool** (182 Joubert Rd., 901/948-7609) at Kansas Park in south

Memphis; and **Willow Pool** (4777 Willow Rd., 901/763-2917).

Two indoor pools are open to the general public: the **Bickford Aquatic Center** (235 Henry Ave., 901/578-3732, Mon.–Fri. 8 A.M.–6 P.M.) and **Hickory Hill Aquatic Center** (3910 Ridgeway Rd., 901/566-9685, Mon.–Fri. 6 A.M.–9 P.M., Sat. 9 A.M.–2 P.M.). Admission to either pool is $5 per day or $8 for a weekly pass, although there are special free swim periods each day. The pools are closed on Sunday.

GYMS

Out-of-towners can get a day pass to the **Fogelman Downtown** YMCA (245 Madison Ave., 901/527-9622) for $10 and use the indoor pool and track and extensive gym facilities. City residents can buy one of the membership packages.

SPECTATOR SPORTS
Basketball

In 2001, Memphis realized the dream of many in the Mid-South when the Vancouver Grizzlies announced they would be moving south. The NBA team played its first two seasons in Memphis at the Pyramid before the massive $250 million FedEx Forum opened for the 2004–2005 season. The arena is one of the largest in the NBA, and hosts frequent concerts and performances by major artists.

The **Grizzlies** have yet to achieve any major titles, and attendance has been lagging. Ticket prices range from under $20 to several hundred dollars. For ticket information, contact the FedEx Forum box office (191 Beale St., 901/205-2640, Monday–Friday 10 A.M.–5:30 P.M., www.fedex.com). The NBA season runs from October to April.

The **University of Memphis Tigers** surprised many in 2008 by making it all the way to the NCAA Championship. The team's remarkable 38–2 season brought new energy and excitement to the University's basketball program.

You can watch Tigers basketball from November to April at FedEx Forum. Tickets

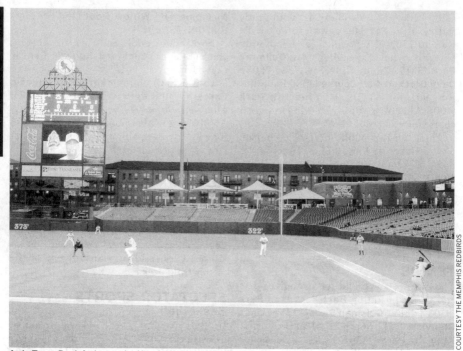

AutoZone Park is home to the AAA Memphis Redbirds, a Cardinals affiliate.

are available from the FedEx Forum box office, or contact University of Memphis Athletics (www.gotigersgo.com) for more information.

Baseball

From April to October, the **Memphis Redbirds** (901/721-6000, www.memphisredbirds.com, $6–20) play AAA ball at beautiful AutoZone Park in downtown Memphis. The stadium is bounded by Union Avenue, Madison Avenue, and 3rd Street, and is convenient to dozens of downtown hotels and restaurants. The Redbirds are an affiliate of the St. Louis Cardinals. Cheap tickets ($6) buy you a seat on the grassy berm, or you can pay a little more for seats in the stadium or boxes.

The Redbirds are owned by a nonprofit organization that also operates a number of community and youth programs in the city.

Racing

The **Memphis Motorsports Park** (550 Victory Ln., 901/358-7223, www.memphismotorsports.com) is located a short drive from downtown Memphis in Millington, northeast of the city center. The park includes a 0.75-mile NASCAR oval, a 0.25-mile drag racing strip, and a 1.77-mile road course. It hosts some 200 race events every year, including a stop in the annual Busch Series races.

Millington is located about 30 minutes' drive north of Memphis.

Ice Hockey

The **Riverkings** (662/342-1735, $10–21) play minor-league ice hockey at the DeSoto Civic Center at 4650 Venture Drive in Southaven, Mississippi, about 20 miles south of Memphis.

Accommodations

There are thousands of cookie-cutter hotel rooms in Memphis, but travelers would be wise to look past major chains. If you can afford it, choose to stay in downtown Memphis. With the city at your doorstep, you'll have a better experience both day and night. Downtown is also where you'll find the most distinctive accommodations, including fine luxury hotels, charming inns, and an antebellum guest home.

Budget travelers have their pick of major chain hotels; the farther from the city center, the cheaper the room. Beware very good deals, however, since you may find yourself in sketchy neighborhoods. There is a campground with tent and RV sites within a 15-minute drive of downtown at T. O. Fuller State Park.

DOWNTOWN
$150-200

The **❰ Talbot Heirs Guesthouse** (99 S. 2nd St., 901/527-9772, www.talborhouse. com, $130–250) in the heart of downtown offers a winning balance of comfort and sophistication. Each of the inn's nine rooms has its own unique decor—from cheerful red walls to black-and-white chic. All rooms are thoughtfully outfitted with a full kitchen and modern bathroom, television, radio and CD player, sitting area, desk and high-speed Internet. Little extras like the refrigerator stocked for breakfast go a long way, as does the cheerful yet efficient welcome provided by proprietors Tom and Sandy Franck. Book early since the Talbot Heirs is often full, especially during peak summer months.

Until the Westin at Beale Street opened in 2007, the **Hampton Inn & Suites** (175 Peabody Pl., 901/260-4000, www.bealestreet-suites.hamptoninn.com, $175) was the only hotel less than a block from Beale Street. The Hampton has 144 standard rooms, with high-speed Internet and standard hotel accommodations. The 30 suites ($250) have kitchens and separate living quarters.

Over $200

For several years, the Hunt-Phelan Home was a museum. Now, it is an inn and restaurant, and it provides the most unique accommodations in Memphis. **❰ The Inn at Hunt Phelan** (533 Beale St., 901/525-8225, www.huntphelan.com, $180–300) has five rooms in the old home, plus six condo-style suites in an adjacent property. Some of the rooms have kitchens and sitting rooms; all have private baths. The Hunt-Phelan Home was built in 1828 and served as Ulysses S. Grant's headquarters while he was in Memphis during the Civil War. After the war, it was a Freedman's Bureau. Although totally modern in amenities, the rooms have been decorated in keeping with the house's history, giving the property a feeling of elegance unmatched by any other Memphis hotel. It is located about three blocks east of Beale Street in a mixed residential and commercial area.

In 2007, Memphis welcomed the **Westin Memphis** (170 Lee Ave., 901/334-5900, $220–300), located across the street from FedEx Forum and one block from Beale Street. The hotel's 203 guest rooms are plush and modern, each with a work desk, high-speed Internet, mp3-player docking station, and super-comfortable beds. The location can be noisy when Beale Street is in full swing.

Plans are afoot for a Hyatt Regency hotel at One Beale (www.onebeale.com), a $175 million mixed-use development that would sit on the riverfront at the head of Beale Street. If condo sales and other financing come through, then this would be Memphis' most luxurious hotel.

UPTOWN
$100-150

The most affordable downtown accommodations are in chain hotels. One of the best choices is the **Sleep Inn at Court Square** (40 N. Front St., 901/522-9700, $100–150), with 124 simple but clean and well-maintained rooms. Guests have access to a small fitness room, free parking, and a free continental breakfast. For those with a bigger appetite, the excellent Blue Plate Café is just across the square. It's a five-block walk to Beale Street from Court Square, but the trolley runs right past the front door of the hotel.

A little closer to the action is the 71-room **Comfort Inn Downtown** (100 N. Front St., 901/520-0583, $100–135). This hotel is within easy walking distance of all the city-center attractions. Rooms are nothing special, but the staff are often quite friendly and guests get free breakfast, Internet access, and indoor parking, and there's an outdoor pool. Ask for a room facing west and you'll have a nice view of the Mississippi River.

$150-200

Near AutoZone Park and lots of restaurants is **Doubletree Downtown Memphis** (185 Union Ave., 901/528-1800, $150–200). A 272-room hotel set in the restored Tennessee Hotel, the Doubletree maintains a touch of the old grandeur of the 1929 hotel from which it was crafted. Rooms are large and there's an outdoor swimming pool and fitness room. Parking is $10 or more per night.

Over $200

If you want to be in the middle of things but can't afford to stay at the Peabody, consider the **Holiday Inn Select** (160 Union Ave., 901/525-5491, www.hisdowntownmemphis.com, $200–250). Located across the street from the Peabody and near AutoZone Park, this Holiday Inn routinely gets good reviews from travelers.

◖ The Peabody Memphis (149 Union Ave., 901/529-4000 or 800/732-2639, www.peabodymemphis.com, $225–350) is the city's signature hotel. Founded in 1869, the Peabody was the grand hotel of the South, and the hotel has preserved some of its traditional Southern charm. Tuxedoed bellhops greet you at the door and all guests receive a complementary shoeshine. Rooms are nicely appointed with plantation-style furniture, free wireless Internet, and in-room safes, as well as all the amenities typical of an upper-tier hotel. Several fine restaurants are located on the ground floor, including the lobby

bar, which is the gathering place for the twice-daily march of the famous Peabody ducks.

One of Memphis's newer hotels is the **River Inn of Harbor Town** (50 Harbor Town Sq., 901/260-3333, www.riverinnmemphis.com, $245–595). A 28-room boutique hotel on Mud Island, the River Inn offers great river views and a unique location that is just minutes from downtown. Set in the mixed residential and commercial New Urban community of Harbor Town, the River Inn provides guests with super amenities like a fitness center, reading rooms, modern decor and furniture, two restaurants, a 1.5-mile walking trail, and spa. Even the most modest rooms have luxurious extras like 32-inch flat-screen televisions, chocolate truffle turn-down service, and full gourmet breakfast at Currents, one of two restaurants on the property. The River Inn offers the best of both worlds—a relaxing and quiet getaway that is uniquely convenient to the center of Memphis.

Seeking to be the finest hotel in Memphis, the **Madison Hotel** (79 Madison Ave., 901/333-1200, www.madisonhotelmemphis.com, $250–450) is appropriately snooty. The decor is modern, with a touch of art deco. Guests enjoy every perk you can imagine, from valet parking to room service from one of the city's finest restaurants, Grill 83. The daily continental breakfast and afternoon happy hour are an opportunity to enjoy the view from the top floor of the old bank building that houses the hotel. The 110 rooms have wet bars, Internet access, and luxurious bathrooms.

MIDTOWN

Midtown hotels are cheaper than those in downtown. If you have a car, they are convenient to city-center attractions as well as those in midtown itself.

Under $100

The refurbished **Artisan Hotel** (1837 Union Ave., 901/278-4100, www.artisanmemphis.com, $80–90) is a smoke-free 160-room boutique hotel in midtown. Each room is decorated with the work of a different classical artist; common areas have lots of heavy-duty wood paneling, lots of stone, and sculpture accents. Amenities include an outdoor swimming pool, Internet access, and an on-site restaurant and lounge.

There are a few budget hotels within trolley distance of downtown. The **Red Roof Inn** (42 S. Camilla St., 901/526-1050, $70–100) is about two blocks from the Madison Avenue trolley and has a dismal, but free, breakfast. The **Motel 6** (210 S. Pauline St., 901/528-0650, $45–70) is about three blocks from the trolley. These choices are certainly not ritzy, but they're acceptable and see a large number of budget travelers.

$100-150

The **Gen X Inn** (1177 Madison Ave., 901/692-9136, www.genxinnhotel.com, $105) straddles downtown and midtown Memphis. Located about two miles from the city center along the Madison Avenue trolley line, Gen Xers can get downtown on the trolley in about 15 minutes with a little luck. The hotel, which has free parking, is also accessible to the city's expansive medical center and the attractions around Overton Park. The Gen X Inn opened in 2006 in a converted medical office building. Its rooms are standard hotel-style, enhanced with bright colors, flat-panel plasma TVs, and a general aura of youthfulness. The whole hotel is non-smoking, and guests enjoy a good continental breakfast and a special partnership with the downtown YMCA for gym use. This is a good choice for travelers who want to be near downtown but are on a budget, especially those with a car.

$150-200

If you want to cook some of your own meals and have comforts like on-site laundry facilities, **Shellcrest** (669 Jefferson Ave., 901/523-0226, www.shellcrest.com, $160) is a good choice. This handsome redbrick town house is about six blocks east of downtown. It is designed to be an extended-stay hotel—most leases are for at least one month. But if they have a vacancy and you are looking to stay for at least three nights, the owners will accommodate short-term guests at a rate of $160 per night. You get a lot for your money; the

accommodations are in spacious one-bedroom apartments with a parlor, sunroom, and study, as well as a gourmet kitchen where you can cook your own meals.

The **Holiday Inn-University of Memphis** (3700 Central Ave., 901/678-8200, $150–160) is part of the university's hospitality school. All rooms are suites, with a wet bar and microwave, sitting room, and spacious bathrooms. The lobby contains an exhibit on Kemmons Wilson, the Memphis-born founder of Holiday Inn who is credited with inventing the modern hotel industry. It is located about six miles from downtown Memphis.

Over $200

You can sleep where Elvis slept at **Lauderdale Courts** (185 Winchester, www.lauderdalecourts.com, $250). The one-time housing project where Elvis and his parents lived after they moved to Memphis from Mississippi is now a neat midtown apartment complex. The rooms where the Presleys lived have been restored to their 1950s greatness, and guests can use the working 1951 Frigidaire. The rooms are decorated with Presley family photographs and other Elvis memorabilia. You can rent Lauderdale Courts No. 328 for up to six nights. It sleeps up to four adults. The rooms are not rented during Elvis Week in August or his birthday week in January when the suite is open for public viewing for $10 per person.

SOUTH MEMPHIS

There are two reasons to stay in south Memphis: the airport and Graceland. But even if you are keenly interested in either of these places, you should think twice about staying in this part of town. With strip malls, seedy neighborhoods, and lots of mediocre chain hotels, there is not much to recommend it.

Under $100

If you need a place to stay near the airport, you can't get any closer than the **Radisson Inn Memphis Airport** (2411 Winchester Rd., 901/332-2370, $90–125), which is right next door. In addition to offering a pool and fitness center, this hotel will shuttle you to the airport terminal for free. Another airport option is the **Holiday Inn Select Memphis Airport** (2240 Democrat Rd., 901/332-1130, $85–130), which caters to business travelers. There is a guest laundry, free airport shuttle, room service, business center, and good fitness room.

You can't sleep much closer to Graceland than the **Days Inn at Graceland** (3839 Elvis Presley Blvd., 901/346-5500, $70–110), one of the most well-worn properties in the venerable Days Inn chain. The hotel has amped up the Elvis kitsch; you can tune into free non-stop Elvis movies or swim in a guitar-shaped pool. There is a free continental breakfast. Book early for Elvis Week.

$100-150

For the most Elvis-y Graceland digs, why not give in and stay at the **Elvis Presley Heartbreak Hotel** (3688 Elvis Presley Blvd., 901/332-1000, www.heartbreakhotel.net, $110–125)? This 128-room hotel has special Elvis-themed suites, and the lobby and common areas have a special Elvis flair. Elvis enthusiasts should check out special package deals with the hotel and Graceland.

CAMPING

You can pitch your tent or park your RV just 15 minutes' drive from downtown Memphis at **T. O. Fuller State Park** (1500 Mitchell Rd., 901/543-7581). The park has 45 tent and RV sites, each with a picnic table, fire ring, grill, lantern hanger, and electrical and water hookups. Sites are allocated on a first-come, first-served basis; reservations are not accepted. Rates are $18.50 a night per site.

On the north side of Memphis, **Meeman-Shelby Forest State Park** (910 Riddick Rd., Millington, 901/876-5215) is a half-hour drive from downtown. Stay in one of six lakeside cabins, which you can reserve up to one year in advance. The two-bedroom cabins can sleep up to six people. Rates are between $50 and $80 per night, depending on the season and day of the week. There are also 49 tent/RV sites, each with electrical and water hookups, picnic tables, grills, and fire rings. The bathhouse has hot showers. Campsite rates are $14.50–17.50 per night.

Food

Eating may be the best thing about visiting Memphis. The city's culinary specialties start—but don't end—with barbecue. Plate-lunch diners around the city offer delectable corn bread, fried chicken, greens, fried green tomatoes, peach cobbler, and dozens of other Southern specialties on a daily basis. And to make it even better, such down-home restaurants are easy on your wallet. For those seeking a departure from home-style fare, Memphis has dozens of fine restaurants, some old established eateries and others newcomers that are as trendy as those in any major American city.

CAFÉS AND DINERS
Downtown

You can order deli sandwiches, breakfast plates, and a limited variety of plate lunches at the **Front Street Deli** (77 S. Front St., 901/522-8943, Mon.–Fri. 7 A.M.–3 P.M., $4–9). The deli serves breakfast and lunch on weekdays only. Its claim to fame is that scenes from *The Firm* were filmed here.

For the best burgers on Beale Street, go to **Dyers** (205 Beale St., 901/527-3937, Mon.–Thurs. 11 A.M.–1 A.M., Fri.–Sat. 11 A.M.–5 A.M., Sun. 11 A.M.–1 P.M., $7–12). The legend is that Dyers' secret is that it has been using the same grease (strained daily) since it opened in 1912. True or not, the burgers here are especially juicy. Dyers also serves wings, hot dogs, milkshakes, and a full array of fried sides.

For coffee, pastries, and fruit smoothies, **Bluff City Coffee** (50 S. Main St., 901/405-

4399, Mon.–Thurs. 6:30 A.M.–8 P.M., Fri.–Sat. 6:30 A.M.–10 P.M., Sun. 8 A.M.–8 P.M., $2–5) is your best bet in this part of the city. Located in the South Main district of galleries and condos, the shop is decorated with large prints of vintage Memphis photographs, and it is also a wireless Internet hot spot.

Located in the "Edge," that no-man's-land between downtown and midtown, **Quetzal** (668 Union Ave., 901/521-8388, Mon.–Thurs. 6:30 A.M.–9 P.M., Fri. 6:30 A.M.–10 P.M., Sat. 7:30 A.M.–10 P.M., Sun. 7:30 A.M.–9 P.M., $4–10) is one of the city's best coffee shops. Fairtrade coffee and cocktails make this a great pit stop, day or night. It is also an Internet café and a popular spot for meetings.

Uptown

The **Bon-Ton Cafe** (150 Monroe, 901/525-0883, Mon.–Fri. 6 A.M.–2:30 P.M., Sat. 7 A.M.–2 P.M., $4–9) serves classic diner fare with a Greek twist. For breakfast get hot cakes, waffles, or biscuits served with your choice of eggs and breakfast meat. If the plate lunch is not your first choice, try pizzas, sandwiches, pasta, or Greek specialties including moussaka or shish-kebob.

Midtown

A block off Cooper Street in a residential neighborhood, **Buns on the Run** (2150 Elzey Ave., 901/278-2867, Tues.–Fri. 7 A.M.–2 P.M., Sat. 7 A.M.–12:30 P.M., $4–8) serves breakfast and lunch. The atmosphere is homey and welcoming, and the food is made from scratch. Breakfast includes omelets, quiches, crepes, and pancakes. For lunch you can get grilled or cold sandwiches, salads with or without meat, or a plate lunch. As the name suggests, Buns on the Run specializes in baked goods, including soft and sweet cinnamon buns, lemon ice-box pie, and a rainbow of cakes.

For a wide selection of vegetarian and organic options, go to **Square Foods** (937 S. Cooper St., 901/274-4222, Mon.–Sat. 9 A.M.–8 P.M., Sun. 10 A.M.–3 P.M., $7–10). The menu here changes regularly, but includes a variety of stir-fries, sandwiches, and wraps,

as well as prepared food like roasted organic free-range chickens.

No restaurant has a larger or more loyal following in midtown than **Young Avenue Deli** (2119 Young Ave., 901/278-0034, Mon.–Sat. 11 A.M.–3 A.M., Sun. noon–3 A.M., $4–8), which serves a dozen different specialty sandwiches, grill fare including burgers and chicken sandwiches, plus salads and sides. The Bren—smoked turkey, mushrooms, onions, and cream cheese in a steamed pita—is a deli favorite. The food is certainly good, but it's the atmosphere at this homey yet hip Cooper-Young institution that really pulls in the crowds. There is live music most weekends, and the bar serves a kaleidoscope of domestic and imported beer, including lots of hard-to-find microbrews. The deli serves lunch and dinner daily.

For a good cup of coffee in the Cooper-Young neighborhood, head to **Java Cabana** (2170 Young Ave., 901/272-7210, Mon.–Thurs. 8:30 A.M.–10 P.M., Fri. 8:30 A.M.–midnight, Sat. 9 A.M.–midnight, Sun. noon–10 P.M., $4–10). Java Cabana serves light breakfast fare, including pancakes and omelets, all day. For lunch or later, you can order simple sandwiches or munchies like apple slices and peanut butter, potato chips, or pop tarts.

For a cold treat during the long, hot Memphis summer, head to **Wiles-Smith Drug Store** (1635 Union Ave., 901/278-6416, Mon.–Fri. 9 A.M.–5 P.M., Sat. 10 A.M.–3 P.M.) for a milkshake. The lunch counter at this old-fashioned drug store also serves sandwiches and snacks, but it is the milkshakes that draw the biggest crowd. They come in chocolate, vanilla, strawberry, and cherry and customers gets to pour the frothy treat into their own glasses.

SOUTHERN
Downtown

Tucked inside an unassuming storefront across from the valet entrance to the Peabody Hotel is **Flying Fish** (104 S. 2nd St., 901/522-8228, daily 11 A.M.–10 P.M., $5–14), your first stop for authentic fried catfish in Memphis. If catfish isn't your thing, try the grilled or boiled shrimp, fish tacos, frog legs, or oysters. The

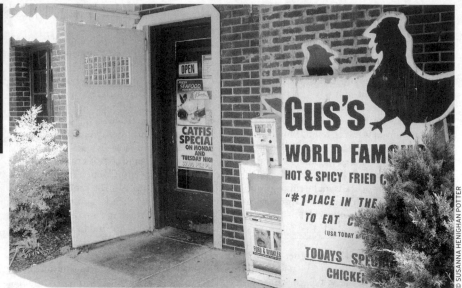

Gus's World Famous Fried Chicken has a well-earned reputation for the best fried chicken in the city.

© SUSANNA HENIGHAN POTTER

baskets of fried seafood come with fries and hush puppies and the grilled plates come with grilled veggies, rice, and beans. The tangy coleslaw is a must. The atmosphere here is laid-back; place your order at the window and come and get it when the coaster they give you starts to vibrate. The checkered tables are well stocked with hot sauce and saltines.

It would be a grave mistake to visit Memphis and not stop at **Gus's World Famous Fried Chicken** (310 Front St., 901/527-4877, $6–12) for some of their delicious fried bird. The downtown location is a franchise of the original Gus's, which is a half-hour drive northeast out of town along U.S. 70, in Mason. It is no exaggeration to say that Gus's cooks up some of the best fried chicken out there: It is spicy, juicy, and hot. It's served casually wrapped in brown paper. Sides include coleslaw, baked beans, and fried pickles. They also serve grilled-cheese sandwiches. Gus's is open daily at 11 A.M., and closes at 9 P.M. on weeknights. Closing time is 10:30 P.M. on Friday and Saturday nights. The service in this hole-in-the-wall establishment is slow, but friendly, so come in with a smile on.

The **Arcade** (540 S. Main St., 901/526-5757, daily 7 A.M.–3 P.M., $5–10) is said to be Memphis's oldest restaurant. Founded in 1919 and still operated by the same family (with lots of the same decor), this restaurant feels like a throwback to an earlier time. The menu is diverse, with pizzas, sandwiches, plate-lunch specials during the week, and breakfast served anytime. The chicken spaghetti is a stick-to-your-ribs favorite.

Uptown

The Little Tea Shop (69 Monroe, 901/525-6000, Mon.–Fri. 11 A.M.–2 P.M., $4.95–7.50) serves traditional plate lunches through the week. Choose from daily specials like fried catfish, chicken pot pie, and meatloaf with your choice of vegetable and side dishes. Every meal (except sandwiches) comes with fresh, hot corn bread that might well be the star of the show. This is stick-to-your-ribs Southern cooking at its best, so come hungry.

If you have room, try the peach cobbler for dessert. The staff's welcoming yet efficient style makes this perfect for a quick lunch. Not to be missed.

The Blue Plate Cafe (113 Court Square S., 901/523-2050, daily 7 A.M.–2 P.M., $4–10) serves hearty breakfasts, plate lunches, and traditional home-style cooking. Its newsprint menu imparts wisdom ("Rule of Life No. 1: Wake up. Show up. Pay attention.") and declares that every day should begin with a great breakfast. It's not hard to comply at the Blue Plate. Eggs come with homemade biscuits and gravy, and your choice of grits, hash browns, or pancakes. For lunch, try a meat-and-three or vegetable plate, slow-cooked white-bean soup, or a grilled peanut butter and banana sandwich. Locals swear by the fried green tomatoes. There are three Blue Plate Cafes in Memphis: the other two are at 2921 Kirby Whitten Road in Bartlett (901/213-1066) and at 5469 Poplar Avenue (901/761-9696) in midtown.

◖ Alcenia's (317 N. Main St., 901/523-0200, Tues.–Fri. 11 A.M.–5 P.M., Sat. 9 A.M.–1 P.M., $4–10), located in the Pinch district, is among Memphis's best Southern-style restaurants. Known for its plate lunches, fried chicken, and pastries, Alcenia's has a style unlike any other Memphis eatery, witnessed in its off-beat decor of '60s-style beads, folk art, and wedding lace. Proprietor B. J. Chester-Tamayo is all love, and she pours her devotion into some of the city's best soul food. Try the spicy cabbage and deep-fried chicken, and save room for Alcenia's famous bread pudding for dessert. Chicken and waffles is the Saturday-morning specialty.

Midtown

Just follow the crowds to the **Cupboard Restaurant** (1400 Union Ave., 901/276-8015, Mon.–Fri. 7 A.M.–8 P.M., Sat.–Sun. 7 A.M.–7 P.M., $6–18), one of Memphians' favorite stops for plate lunches. The Cupboard moved from its downtown location to an old Shoney's about a mile outside of town to accommodate the throngs who stop here for authentic home-style cooking. The Cupboard

gets only the freshest vegetables for its dishes like okra and tomatoes, rutabaga turnips, steamed cabbage, and green beans. The meat specials change daily, but include things like fried chicken, chicken and dumplings, hamburger steak with onions, and beef tips with noodles. The corn bread "coins" are exceptionally buttery, and the bread is baked fresh daily. For dessert, try the lemon icebox pie.

The Women's Exchange (88 Racine St., 901/327-5681, Mon.–Fri. 11:30 A.M.–1:45 P.M., $10) feels like a throwback to an earlier era. Located one block east of the Poplar Street viaduct, the Women's Exchange has been serving lunch since 1936 and the menu has not changed much over the years. The special changes daily and always includes a choice of two entrées, or a four-vegetable plate. Classics like chicken salad, salmon loaf, beef tenderloin, and seafood gumbo are favorites, and all lunches come with a drink and dessert. The dining room looks out onto a green garden, and the atmosphere is homey—not stuffy. The Exchange also sells gifts, housewares, and other knick-knacks.

In the Cooper-Young neighborhood, **Soul Fish** (862 S. Cooper St., 901/725-0722, Mon.–Sat. 11 A.M.–10 P.M., Sun. 11 A.M.–9 P.M., $6–15) offers traditional plate lunches, vegetable plates, and several varieties of catfish. You can get the fish breaded and fried, or blackened with a potent spice mix. Soul Fish is owned in part by Tiger Bryant, owner of the venerable Young Avenue Deli, and it has the hallmarks of a well-conceived eatery. The atmosphere is open and cheerful, with a few touches of subtle sophistication. In this case, the main attraction is good food at a good price—a combination that can be hard to find elsewhere in Cooper-Young.

South Memphis

Gayhawk Restaurant (685 Danny Thomas Blvd., 901/947-1464, Mon.–Fri. 11 A.M.–2:30 P.M., Sat.–Sun. noon–5 P.M., $6–10) serves country-style food that sticks to your ribs and warms your soul. Chef Bobo declares that his specialty is "home-cooked food" and it really is as simple as that. The best thing about Gayhawk is the luncheon buffet, which lets newcomers to Southern cooking survey the choices and try a little bit of everything. The Sunday lunch buffet practically sags with specialties like fried chicken, grilled fish, macaroni and cheese, greens, and much, much more.

(BARBECUE

On the northern fringe of downtown Memphis is one of the city's most famous and well-loved barbecue joints: (**Cozy Corner** (745 N. Parkway, 901/527-9158, Mon.–Sat. 11 A.M.–5 P.M., $4–14). Cozy Corner is tucked into a storefront in an otherwise-abandoned strip mall; you'll smell it before you see it. Step inside to order barbecue pork, sausage, or bologna sandwiches. Or get a 2-bone, 4-bone, or 6-bone rib dinner plate, which comes with your choice of baked beans, coleslaw, or barbecue spaghetti, plus slices of Wonder bread to sop up the juices. One of Cozy Corner's specialties is its barbecued Cornish hens—a preparation that is surprising but delicious. Sweet tea goes perfectly with the tangy and spicy barbecue.

Jim Neely's **Interstate Bar-B-Que** (2265 S. 3rd St., 901/775-1045, Mon.–Thurs. 11 A.M.–11 P.M., Fri.–Sat. 11 A.M.–midnight, $5–20) was once ranked the second best barbecue in the nation, but the proprietors have not let it get to their heads; this is still a down-to-earth, no-frills eatery. Large appetites can order a whole slab of pork or beef ribs, but most people will be satisfied with a chopped pork sandwich, which comes topped with coleslaw and smothered with barbecue sauce. Families can get the fixings for six, eight, or ten sandwiches sent out family-style. For an adventure, try the barbecue spaghetti or barbecue bologna sandwich. If you're in a hurry, the Interstate has a drive-up window too, and if you are really smitten, you can order pork, sauce, and seasoning in bulk to be frozen and shipped to your home.

Although aficionados will remind you that the ribs served at the **Rendezvous** (52 S. 2nd St., 901/523-2746, Tues.–Thurs. 4:30–10:30 P.M., Fri.–Sat. 11:30 A.M.–11 P.M., $8–17) are not technically barbecue, they are one

PIGGLY WIGGLY

Memphian Clarence Saunders opened the first Piggly Wiggly at 79 Jefferson Street in 1916, giving birth to the modern American supermarket. Up until then, shoppers went to small storefront shops, where they would ask the counter clerk for what they needed: a pound of flour, a half-dozen pickles, a block of cheese. The clerk went to the bulk storage area at the rear of the store, and measured out what the customer needed.

Saunders's great idea was self-service. At the Piggly Wiggly, customers entered the store, carried a basket, and were able to pick out pre-packaged and priced containers of food, which they paid for at the payment station on their way out.

The Piggly Wiggly idea took off, and by 1923 there were 1,268 Piggly Wiggly franchises around the country. Saunders used some of his profits to build a massive mansion east of the city out of pink Georgia limestone, but he was never to live in the Pink Palace, which he lost as a result of a complex stock loss.

Today, Saunders's Pink Palace is home to the Pink Palace Museum, which includes, among other things, a replica of the original Piggly Wiggly supermarket.

of the biggest barbecue stories in town. Covered in a dry rub of spices and broiled until the meat falls off the bones, these ribs will knock your socks off. If you prefer, you can choose Charlie Vergos's dry-rub chicken or boneless pork loin. Orders come with baked beans and coleslaw, but beer is really the essential accompaniment to any Vergos meal. The door to Rendezvous is tucked in an alley off Monroe Avenue. The smoky interior, decorated with antiques and yellowing business cards, is low-key, noisy, and lots of fun.

A Memphis chain, **Gridley's** (6842 Stage Rd., 901/377-8055, Sun.–Thurs. 11 A.M.–8 P.M., Fri.–Sat. 11 A.M.–9 P.M.,, $4–20) serves wet-style barbecue ribs, pork shoulder plates and sandwiches, plus spicy grilled shrimp. The shrimp is served with a buttery and delicious dipping sauce. Try the half-pork, half-shrimp plate for a real treat. Meals here come with baked beans, coleslaw, and hot fresh bread.

CONTEMPORARY
Downtown
The Majestic Grill (145 S. Main St., 901/522-8555, Mon.–Thurs. 11 A.M.–11 P.M., Fri.–Sat. 11 A.M.–midnight, Sun. 11 A.M.–9 P.M., $6–29) serves a remarkably affordable yet upscale menu at lunch and dinner. Located in what was once the Majestic Theater, the white tablecloths and apron-clad waiters give the restaurant an aura of refinement. But with main courses starting at just $6, this can be a bargain. Flatbread pizzas feature asparagus, spicy shrimp, and smoked sausage. Sandwiches include burgers and clubs; specialties include pasta, barbecue ribs, grilled salmon, and steaks. Don't pass on dessert, served in individual shot glasses, such as chocolate mousse, key lime pie, and carrot cake, among others.

For a special occasion make reservations at the **Inn at Hunt Phelan** (533 Beale St., 901/525-8225, Wed.–Sat. 5:30 P.M.–1 A.M., Sun. 11 A.M.–3 P.M., $22–36), a stately and sophisticated restaurant in the historic Hunt-Phelan House. The dinner menu is always changing, but expect dishes such as butternut squash ravioli or pepper-crusted tuna with *pommes frites*. If you are feeling really special, treat yourself to the $70 seven-course tasting menu. Diners at the inn can sit inside the elegant dining room, or outside on the charming back patio.

A relative newcomer to the Beale Street dining scene, **E. P. Delta Kitchen and Bar** (126 Beale St., 901/527-1444, Wed.–Sat. 5 P.M.–3 A.M., Sun.–Tues. 5 P.M.–1 A.M., $15–35) is the most upscale eatery on the famed blues drag. Located in what was once the flagship Lansky Brothers clothing store, E. P. (that stands for Elvis Presley) Delta Kitchen has made a name for itself since opening in late 2006. The style here is spicy delta cooking with a refined twist: Imagine upscale jambalaya and bayou duck with pasta. After 11 P.M.,

there is a one-of-a-kind bar menu with offerings like barbecue duck quesadillas and fried green tomatoes. E. P.'s has a stylish and modern atmosphere, with live R&B on weekends. This is a popular place to start an evening out on the town, especially for the professional crowd, and don't miss some of the one-of-a-kind libations like the Memphis BBQ Bloody Mary or the Peanut Butter and Banana Cocktail.

Located on the corner of Madison and Main, **Stella** (39 S. Main St., 901/526-4950, Mon.–Sat. 5:30–10:30 P.M., $27–48) has made a name for itself on Memphis's fine dining scene with dishes like Colorado Lamb Rack, Marinated Filet Mignon, and Oysters Stella. The dining room has expansive high ceilings, and rich wood paneling from the building's previous life as a jewelry store.

It is impossible to pigeonhole **Automatic Slim's Tonga Club** (83 S. 2nd St., 901/525-7948, $12–20), except to say that this Memphis institution consistently offers fresh, spirited, and original fare. They serve lunch Monday–Friday 10 A.M.–2 P.M. and on weekends 11 A.M.–2 P.M.; dinner is served daily 5–9:30 P.M. Named after a character from an old blues tune, Automatic Slim's uses lots of strong flavors to create its eclectic menu; Caribbean and southwestern influences are the most apparent. Take a seat and in two shakes you'll be presented with soft, fresh bread and pesto-seasoned olive oil for dipping. The Caribbean shrimp are a favorite of many diners. A meal at Automatic Slim's would not be complete without a famous Tonga Martini or one of the kitchen's delectable desserts: Pecan tart and chocolate cake are good choices. Automatic Slim's is a welcome departure from barbecue and southern food when you're ready. Its atmosphere is relaxed, and there's often a crowd at the bar, especially on weekends when there's live music on tap.

Long the standard-bearer of fine French cuisine, **Chez Philippe** (149 Union Ave., 901/529-4188, Tues.–Sat. 6–10 P.M., $65–70), located in the Peabody Hotel, now offers French-Asian fusion cuisine. The Asian influences are noticeable in the ingredients, but the preparation of most dishes at Chez Philippe remains traditional French. Entrées include grouper, bass, pork chop, and venison. Chez Philippe offers a prix fixe menu: Three courses is $65 and five courses is $70. Or opt for a seven-course tasting menu for $90; wine pairings are an addition $42 per person.

Midtown

In 2007, Memphis's foremost restaurateur, Karen Blockman Carrier, closed her fine-dining restaurant Cielo in Victorian Village, redecorated, and reopened it as the **Molly Fontaine Lounge** (679 Adams Ave., 901/524-1886, Wed.–Sat. 5 P.M.–2:30 A.M., $12–24). Carrier's vision was an old-fashioned club where guests can order upscale cocktails, relax with live music, and eat tasty Mediterranean and Middle Eastern–inspired tapas. The restaurant has an upmarket but cozy atmosphere, with equal measures of funky and fine. The live piano jazz is the perfect backdrop for the restaurant's artistic small plates.

Surprisingly good for a bookstore café, **Bronte** (387 Perkins Ext., 901/374-0881, Mon.–Sat. 9 A.M.–10 P.M., Sun. 10 A.M.–8 P.M., $8–12), inside Davis-Kidd Booksellers, offers salads, soups, and sandwiches, as well as daily meat and fish specials. The soup-and-sandwich combo is filling and good. Breakfast may well be the best meal on offer, however. The morning menu features specials designed by celebrity chefs, including omelets, baked goods, and crepes.

One of Memphis's most unique restaurant settings is an old beauty shop in the Cooper-Young area. **The Beauty Shop** (966 S. Cooper St., 901/272-7111, $8–32) takes advantage of the vintage beauty parlor decor to create a great talking point for patrons and food writers alike. The domed hairdryers remain, and the restaurant has put the shampooing sinks to work as beer coolers. At lunch, the Beauty Shop offers a casual menu of sandwiches and salads. For dinner, the imaginative cuisine of Memphis restaurateur Karen Blockman Carrier, who also owns Molly Fontaine Lounge and Automatic Slim's Tonga Club, takes over. The Beauty Shop serves lunch Monday–Saturday 11 A.M.–2 P.M. Dinner is served beginning at 5 P.M. nightly, except Sunday. It opens Sunday 10 A.M.–3 P.M.

Right next to the Beauty Shop is **Do** (966 S. Cooper St., 901/272-7111, $6–15), a trendy sushi restaurant that also offers tempura, soups, and salads. It is open for dinner only Tuesday through Saturday.

If you enjoy your beer as much or more than your meal, then head straight for **Boscos Squared** (2120 Madison Ave., 901/432-2222, $12–22). Boscos is a brew pub with fresh seafood, steak, and pizza. Their beer menu is among the best in the city, and many of the brews are made on the premises. Boscos serves lunch daily 11 A.M.–3 P.M., dinner 3 P.M.–midnight, and the late-night munchie menu is available until 2 A.M.

East Memphis

To many minds, Memphis dining gets no better than ◖ **Erling Jensen, The Restaurant** (1044 S. Yates Rd., 901/763-3700, daily 5–10 P.M., $30–50). Danish-born Erling Jensen is the mastermind of this fine-dining restaurant that has consistently earned marks as Memphians' favorite restaurant. Understated decor and friendly service are the backdrop to Jensen's dishes, which are works of art. The menu changes with the seasons and based upon availability, but usually includes about six different seafood dishes and as many meat and game choices. Black Angus beef, elk loin, and buffalo tenderloin are some of the favorites. Meals at Jensen's restaurant should begin with an appetizer, salad, or soup—or all three. The jumbo chunk crab cakes with smoked red-pepper sauce are excellent. Reservations are a good idea at Erling Jensen, and so are jackets for men. Expect to spend upwards of $80 for a four-course meal here; $60 for two courses. Add more for wine.

Memphis's premier steakhouse is **Folk's Folly** (551 S. Mendenhall Rd., 901/762-8200, $30–70), located just east of Audubon Park. Dinner is served nightly beginning at 5:30 P.M., when diners start flocking here for prime aged steaks and seafood favorites. For small appetites, try the 8-ounce filet mignon for $28; large appetites can gorge on the 28-ounce porterhouse for $57. Seafood includes lobster, crab legs, and wild salmon. The atmosphere is classic steakhouse: The lighting is low, and there's a piano bar on the property.

ETHNIC CUISINE
Downtown
For sushi, try **Sekisui** (Union at 2nd Ave., 901/523-0001), where a roll costs between $2.50 and $8, and a filling combo plate will run you about $15. The downtown restaurant is located on the ground floor of the Holiday Inn Select. Sekisui is a Memphis chain, and there are other locations in midtown and the suburbs. The downtown location serves dinner nightly, and lunch Monday–Friday.

For Thai food, try **Sawaddii** (121 Union, 901/529-1818, daily 11:30 A.M.–9:30 P.M., $9–22), which serves a selection of thai curries, noodles, and fried rice, as well as signature dishes like grilled mahimahi. They have an extensive wine list and full bar, too. The waitstaff here is welcoming and down-to-earth, and the atmosphere stylish but not pretentious. It's a good place to come if you tire of barbecue and burgers, but don't want to break the bank.

Midtown
The **Indian Palace** (1720 Poplar Ave., 901/278-1199, daily, $7–17) is a regular winner in reader's choice polls for Indian food in Memphis. The lunch-time buffet is filling and economical, and the dinner menu features vegetarian, chicken, and seafood dishes. The dinner platters are generous and tasty. Lunch is served Monday–Friday 11 A.M.–2:30 P.M. and Saturday–Sunday 11 A.M.–3 P.M., and dinner is available nightly 5–10 P.M.

Pho Hoa Binh (1615 Madison, 901/276-0006, Mon.–Sat. 11 A.M.–9 P.M., $4–9) is one of the most popular Vietnamese restaurants in town. You can't beat the value of the lunch buffet, or you can order from the dizzying array of Chinese and Vietnamese dishes, including spring rolls, vermicelli noodle bowls, rice, and meat dishes. There are a lot of vegetarian options here.

The atmosphere at **Bhan Thai** (1324 Peabody Ave., 901/272-1538, $10–19) in midtown is almost as appealing as the excellent Thai food served there. Set in an elegant 1912 home, Bhan Thai makes the most of the house's space, and seating is spread throughout several colorful rooms and on the back patio. Choose from dishes like red snapper, masaman curry, and roasted duck curry. The Bhan Thai salad is popular, with creamy peanut dressing and crisp vegetables. Dinner here is served Tuesday–Sunday beginning at 5 P.M., and lunch Tuesday–Friday 11 A.M.–2:30 P.M.

It's the regulars who are happy at the **Happy Mexican Restaurant and Cantina** (385 S. 2nd St., 901/529-9991, Sun.–Thurs. 11 A.M.–10 P.M., Fri.–Sat. 11 A.M.–11 P.M., $7–15). Serving generous portions of homemade Mexican food for lunch and dinner, Happy Mexican is destined to become a downtown favorite. The service is efficient and friendly, and the decor is cheerful but not over the top. It's located just a few blocks south of the National Civil Rights Museum.

MARKETS
The only downtown grocery store is the **Easy-Way** (80 N. Main St., 901/523-1323, daily 7 A.M.–6 P.M.) on the corner of Main Street and Jefferson Avenue. For liquor and wine, go to **The Corkscrew** (511 S. Front St., 901/543-9463).

The closest gourmet grocery is located in Harbor Town, the residential community on Mud Island, where **Miss Cordelia's** (737 Harbor Bend, 901/526-4772, daily 7 A.M.–9 P.M.) sells fresh produce, bakery goods, and staples. A deli in the back serves soups, salads, sandwiches, and a wide variety of prepared foods.

For a full-service grocery store in midtown, look for the **Krogers** at the corner of Cleveland and Poplar.

The **Memphis Farmer's Market** (901/575-0580, www.memphisfarmersmarket.com, May–Oct. Sat. 7 A.M.–1 P.M.) takes place in the pavilion opposite Central Station in the South Main part of town.

Information and Services

INFORMATION
Visitors Centers

The city's visitors center is the **Tennessee Welcome Center** (119 Riverside Dr., 901/543-5333) located on the Tennessee side of the I-40 bridge. The center has lots of brochures and free maps and staff who can answer your questions. It is open 24 hours a day, seven days a week. The center assists more than 350,000 travelers annually.

Although it is not designed to be a visitors center, the **Memphis Convention and Visitors Bureau** (47 Union Ave., 901/543-5300, www.memphistravel.com, Mon.–Fri. 9 A.M.–5 P.M.) is a resource for visitors. You can collect maps and ask questions here. The bureau also produces videos highlighting city attractions and restaurants, which are available on many hotel televisions.

Maps

Hand-out maps that highlight key attractions are available from visitors centers in Memphis. If you are only interested in Beale Street, Graceland, and the interstates, these will be fine. The free maps provided at the concierge desk of the Peabody Hotel are especially well marked and useful.

If you want to explore further, or if you plan to drive yourself around the city, it is wise to get a proper city map. Rand McNally publishes a detailed Memphis city map, which you can buy from bookstores or convenience marts in downtown.

Media

The daily *Commercial Appeal* (www.commercialappeal.com) is Memphis's major newspaper, available all over the city. The *Memphis Flyer* (www.memphisflyer.com) is a free alternative weekly, published on Wednesday with the best entertainment listings.

Memphis magazine (www.memphismagazine.com) is published monthly and includes historical anecdotes, restaurant reviews, features on high-profile residents, and lots of advertising aimed at residents and would-be residents.

There are two independent radio stations of note: **WEVL 89.9 FM** is a community radio station that plays blues, country, and other Memphis music. **WDIA 1070 AM,** the historical Memphis station that made the blues famous, still rocks today. Another station of note is **WRBO 103.5 FM,** which plays soul and R&B.

SERVICES
Fax and Internet

Send a fax at **FedEx Kinkos** (50 N. Front St., 901/521-0261), located across from the Peabody's valet entrance.

For Internet access, try **Quetzal Internet Café** (668 Union Ave., 901/521-8388), which is open weekdays 6:30 A.M.–9 P.M. and stays open late on weekends. You can also get online at **Internet Café by Malik** (75 S. Main St., 901/575-9974).

Postal Service

There is a postal retail center, which sells stamps and offers limited postal services, at 100 Peabody Place (901/521-0159). It is open Monday–Friday 8:30 A.M.–5 P.M., and Saturday 9 A.M.–1 P.M.

The full-service downtown post office is located at 1 North Front Street (901/576-2037) and opens weekdays 8 A.M.–5 P.M.

Emergency Services

Dial 911 in an emergency for fire, ambulance, or police. The downtown police department is the South Main Station (545 S. Main St., 901/525-9800). Police patrol downtown by car, on bike, and on foot.

Several agencies operate hotlines for those needing help. They include: Alcoholics Anonymous (901/454-1414), the Better Business Bureau (901/759-1300), Emergency Mental Health Services (901/577-9400), Deaf Interpreting (901/577-3783), Rape Crisis/

Sexual Assault Hotline (901/272-2020), and Poison Emergencies (901/528-6048).

Hospitals

Memphis is chock-a-block with hospitals. Midtown Memphis is also referred to as Medical Center for the number of hospitals and medical facilities there. Here you will find the **Regional Medical Center at Memphis** (877 Jefferson Ave., 901/545-7100), a 620-bed teaching hospital affiliated with the University of Tennessee; and the **Methodist University Hospital** (1265 Union Ave., 901/516-7000), the 669-bed flagship hospital for Methodist Healthcare.

In East Memphis, **Baptist Memorial Hospital** (6019 Walnut Grove Rd., 901/226-5000) is the cornerstone of the huge Baptist Memorial Health Care System, with 771 beds.

Laundry

Try any of these three laundries, which are located near downtown: **Metro Plaza Laundry** (805 S. Danny Thomas Blvd., 901/948-1673), **Crump Laundry Mat and Dry Cleaning** (756 E. Ed Crump Blvd., 901/948-7008), or **Jackson Coin Laundry** (1216 Jackson Ave., 901/274-3536).

Libraries

Memphis has 19 public libraries. The city's main library is **Hooks Public Library** (3030 Poplar Ave., 901/415-2700, Mon.–Thurs. 9 A.M.–9 P.M., Fri.–Sat. 9 A.M.–6 P.M., Sun. 1–5 P.M.), a modern, new public library with 119 public computers, an extensive collection, community programs, meeting rooms, a lecture series, and more. The central library is located on a busy thoroughfare in midtown and would be a challenge to visit without a car.

The downtown branch library, **Cossit Library** (33 S. Front St., 901/526-1712, Mon.–Fri. 10 A.M.–5 P.M.), has a good collection of new releases, and staff there are happy to help visitors looking for information about Memphis. The current building was constructed in 1959, but the Cossit Library was founded in 1888 as the Cossit-Goodwyn Institute.

Getting There and Around

GETTING THERE

By Air

Memphis International Airport (MEM; 901/922-8000, www.mscaa.com) is located 13 miles south of downtown Memphis. There are two popular routes to Memphis from the airport. Take I-240 north to arrive in midtown. To reach downtown, take I-55 north and exit on Riverside Drive. The drive takes between 20 and 30 minutes.

The airport's main international travel insurance and business services center (901/922-8090) is located in ticket lobby B and opens daily. Here you can exchange foreign currency, buy travel insurance, conduct money transfers, send faxes and make photocopies, and buy money orders and travelers checks. A smaller kiosk near the international arrivals and departures area at gate B-36 is open daily and offers foreign currency exchange and travel insurance.

There is wireless Internet service in the airport, but it is not free.

AIRPORT SHUTTLE

TennCo Express (901/345-7962, www.tennco express.com) provides an hourly shuttle service from the airport to many downtown hotels. Tickets are $15 one-way and $25 round-trip. Look for the shuttle parked in the third lane near column number 14 outside the airport terminal. Shuttles depart every half hour 7:30 A.M.–9:30 P.M. For a hotel pick-up, call at least a day in advance.

By Car

Memphis is located at the intersection of two major interstate highways: I-40, which

© SUSANNA HENIGHAN POTTER

Main Street trolleys connect uptown and downtown.

runs east–west across the United States, and I-55, which runs south from St. Louis to New Orleans.

Many people who visit Memphis drive here in their own cars. The city is 300 miles from St. Louis, 380 miles from Atlanta, 410 miles from New Orleans, 450 miles from Dallas, 480 miles from Cincinnati and Oklahoma City, and 560 miles from Chicago.

By Bus

Greyhound (800/231-2222, www.grey-hound.com) runs daily buses to Memphis from around the United States. Direct service is available to Memphis from a number of surrounding cities, including Jackson and Nashville, Tennessee; Tupelo and Jackson, Mississippi; Little Rock and Jonesboro, Arkansas; and St. Louis. The Greyhound station (203 Union Ave., 901/523-9253), in downtown Memphis, is open 24 hours a day.

By Train

Amtrak (800/872-7245, www.amtrak.com) runs the City of New Orleans train daily between Chicago and New Orleans, stopping in Memphis on the way. The southbound train arrives daily at Memphis's Central Station at 6:17 A.M., leaving about half an hour later. The northbound train arrives at 10 P.M. every day. It is an 11-hour ride between Memphis and Chicago and about eight hours between Memphis and New Orleans.

The Amtrak station (901/526-0052) is located in Central Station at 545 South Main Street in the South Main district of downtown. Ticket and baggage service is available at the station daily 5:45 A.M.–11 P.M.

GETTING AROUND
Driving

Driving is the most popular and easiest way to get around Memphis. Downtown parking is plentiful if you are prepared to pay; an all-day pass in one of the many downtown parking garages costs about $10. Traffic congestion peaks, predictably, at rush hours and is worst in the eastern parts of the city and along the interstates.

Public Transportation

BUSES

The **Memphis Area Transit Authority** (901/274-6282, www.matatransit.com) operates dozens of buses that travel through the greater Memphis area. For information on routes, call or stop by the North End Terminal on North Main Street for help planning your trip. The bus system is not used frequently by tourists.

TROLLEYS

Public trolleys run for about two miles along Main Street in Memphis from the Pinch district in the north to Central Station in the south, and circle up on a parallel route along Riverfront Drive. Another trolley line runs about two miles east on Madison Avenue, connecting the city's medical center with downtown. The Main Street trolleys run every 10 minutes at most times, but the Madison Avenue trolleys run less often on weekends and evenings after 6 P.M.

Fares are $1 per ride, or 50 cents between 11 A.M. and 1:30 P.M. You can buy an all-day pass for $3.50, a three-day pass for $8, or a month-long pass for $25. All passes must be purchased at the North End Terminal at the northern end of the Main Street route.

The trolley system is useful, especially if your hotel is on either the northern or southern end of downtown, or along Madison Avenue.

Brochures with details on the routes and fares are available all over town, or you can download one at www.matatransit.com. The trolleys are simple to understand and use; if you have a question, just ask your driver.

SUN STUDIO FREE SHUTTLE BUS

Sun Studio runs a free shuttle between Sun Studio, the Rock 'n' Soul Museum at Beale Street, and Graceland. The first run stops at the Graceland Heartbreak Hotel at 9:55 A.M., Graceland at 10 A.M., Sun Studio at 10:15 A.M., and the Rock 'n' Soul Museum at 10:30 A.M. Runs continue throughout the day on an hourly schedule. The last run picks up at Heartbreak Hotel at 5:55 P.M., Graceland Plaza at 6 P.M., and Sun Studio at 6:15 P.M.

The shuttle is a 12-passenger black van painted with the Sun Studio logo. The ride is free, but it's nice to tip your driver. The published schedule is a loose approximation, so it's a good idea to get to the pick-up point early in case the van is running ahead. You can call 901/521-0664 for more information.

Taxis

Memphis has a number of taxi companies, and you will usually find available cabs along Beale Street and waiting at the airport. Otherwise, you will need to call for a taxi. Some of the largest companies are **Yellow Cab** (901/577-7777), **City Wide Cab** (901/722-8294), and **Arrow Transportation Company** (901/332-7769).

Expect to pay between $25 and $30 for a trip from the airport to downtown; most fares around town are under $10.

WESTERN PLAINS

From the Tennessee River to the Mississippi, Tennessee's western plains are more like the Deep South than any other part of the state. The landscape is spare; in the heart of the delta all you see for mile upon mile are cotton fields—flat with neat rows of the bushy plants. In the south, near the Mississippi state line, piney woods give rise to the state's largest timber industry. Along the Tennessee River, man-made lakes present unmatched opportunities to fish, boat, or simply relax.

Life here was not always peaceful or idyllic. West Tennessee had the largest plantations and the greatest number of slaves before the Civil War. This was confederate territory. The war touched just about every town in Tennessee's western plains, but none more than the quiet, rural community of Shiloh along the Tennessee River. On April 6 and 7, 1862, 24,000 men were killed or wounded on this bloody battlefield. Emancipation brought freedom, but not justice to thousands of African Americans who now struggled as sharecroppers and remained the victims of discrimination and worse. Out of the hardship of life in the Tennessee delta emerged some of the state's most gifted musicians, including "Sleepy" John Estes, Tina Turner, and Carl Perkins.

The knobby knees of Reelfoot Lake and cypress swamps of other natural areas, including Big Hill Pond and the Ghost River, are a landscape unseen in other parts of Tennessee. These habitats give rise to exceptional bird-watching, fishing, and hunting. Come in the spring or fall to avoid the worst heat. Late summer is the

© SUSANNA HENIGHAN POTTER

HIGHLIGHTS

◖ Alex Haley House Museum: One of Tennessee's most celebrated writers grew up in the humble sawmill town of Henning. See the home where Alex Haley first imagined his ancestors (page 82).

◖ Reelfoot Lake State Park Visitor Center: Knob-kneed cypress trees, abundant wildlife, and the fresh air of the country are elixir for those who come to this quiet corner of the delta, and the boardwalk at the state park visitors center is the best place to soak in the setting (page 88).

◖ Tennessee River Folklife Center: Explore the forgotten past of Tennessee river pearls, steamships, and houseboats at this museum located at Nathan Bedford Forrest State Park (page 94).

◖ The Homeplace: Located in beautiful Land Between the Lakes, this living-history museum depicts the farmer's way of life at the midpoint of the 19th century (page 102).

◖ Pinson Mounds State Archaeological Park: The sprawling and mysterious mounds at Pinson are a reminder of those who came before (page 110).

◖ Shiloh National Military Park: The scene of one of the bloodiest Civil War battles is a good place to ponder the meaning of the war and its human cost (page 113).

LOOK FOR **◖** TO FIND RECOMMENDED SIGHTS, ACTIVITIES, DINING, AND LODGING.

season of county fairs and other festivals, and the time when the people of West Tennessee retreat to the nearest lake, river, or stream to cool off.

PLANNING YOUR TIME

A road trip is the best way to experience the western plains; get off the interstate and give small-town restaurants and inns a try. Fresh catfish from the nearby rivers and lakes are served in traditional style—dusted with cornmeal and deep fried. Sample the varieties of hush puppies between Reelfoot Lake

and Shiloh. Campers will find numerous options for shelter in state parks.

The western plains can be toured in about a week, although outdoor enthusiasts may want to budget more time to hike or fish. If you are interested in the cultural and musical attractions of the region, choose Jackson or Brownsville as your home base. If you are interested in Shiloh and the natural attractions along the southern Tennessee River, Savannah is a good choice. For a tour along the Mississippi River, the best accommodations are found around Reelfoot Lake in the

© AVALON TRAVEL

northwest corner of the state. Paris Landing State Park is a good home base for exploring the Kentucky Lakes region.

Driving is the best—only, really—way to get around the western plains. Even in the largest city, Jackson, attractions, restaurants, and accommodations are spread out. A good road map is all you need to find your way around, and residents are friendly and helpful if you get lost.

The Delta

Flat, spare, and rural, the delta region of West Tennessee was, and still is, the state's largest producer of cotton. Cotton fields in cultivation spread out between small towns and farmhouses. County seats of the delta have stately courthouses, enclosed by classic courthouse squares. While the region is home to the cities of Jackson and Brownsville, the delta remains rural, and the way of life is laid-back and traditional.

The delta countryside is fertile soil not only for farming, but for music too. Blues musicians "Sleepy" John Estes, Hammie Nixon, and Yank Rachell are from Brownsville.

BROWNSVILLE

The county seat of the largest cotton-producing county in Tennessee, Brownsville was founded in 1824 and quickly became the home to many of West Tennessee's most affluent settlers. Early leaders carefully mapped out the city lots, and they were sold to doctors, lawyers, and merchants who helped the town develop quickly during its first decades.

Brownsville's first newspaper was founded in 1837, its first bank in 1869, and in its heyday it also boasted an opera house and several hotels and restaurants. It lost hundreds of its residents to the yellow fever epidemic of 1878, and hundreds more fled to avoid becoming ill. A marker in the town's Oakwood Cemetery designates the resting place of the yellow fever victims.

West Tennessee Delta Heritage Center

Half welcome center, half museum, the West Tennessee Delta Heritage Center (121 Sunny Hill Cove, 731/779-9000, Tues.–Sat. 9 A.M.–4 P.M., free) is your best stop for understanding the special music, culture, and history of the delta region. Its exhibits examine the musical heritage of the region, the ecology of the nearby Hatchie River, and cotton, the region's most important crop.

The cotton exhibit illustrates the process from cultivation to baling. A huge basket of picked cotton is there for you to touch, as well as the cotton both before and after being ginned. After driving past miles of cotton fields, visitors will welcome the illustration and explanations.

The heritage center also has displays about each of the counties in the region, with visitor information on each. There is also a gift shop, and you can use their Internet-enabled computer for $5, or for free with a $20 purchase.

Right next to the heritage center is the **"Sleepy" John Estes Home,** a faded clapboard home that was relocated here so tourists could see where the blues legend was living when he died in 1977.

Estes was born in Ripley, Tennessee, in 1904 but lived most of his life in Brownsville. A blues guitarist and vocalist, Estes had a distinctive "crying" vocal style and sounded like an old man, even on his early recordings. Estes made his recording debut in Memphis in 1929 and he recorded regularly until the outbreak of World War II in 1941. Estes spent the end of his life blind and living in poverty.

Sadly, thanks to the risk of liability lawsuits, the old building has been deemed unsafe, so you can't go inside.

WESTERN PLAINS

© SUSANNA HENIGHAN POTTER

"Sleepy" John Estes, a blues legend, was living in this clapboard house in rural Haywood County when he died in 1977.

The heritage center is located at exit 56 off I-40.

Historic Brownsville

It is pleasant to drive or walk around historic Brownsville, a leafy neighborhood of antebellum homes and buildings. Each home is marked with a brown-and-white sign in the yard that is visible from the road and gives the approximate date of construction. For a more detailed guide, visit the Brownsville-Haywood Chamber of Commerce for a copy of their historical guidebook of Haywood County, which includes a walking tour of Brownsville.

Two of the city's most noteworthy old homes are the **Tripp Home** at 420 Main Street, a two-story Greek Revival home built in 1824, and the **Christ Episcopal Church** at the corner of West College and North Washington, organized in 1832. Brownsville is also home to the oldest Jewish temple in continuous service in Tennessee, the **Temple**

of **Adas Israel** at 18 North Court Street, built in 1882.

Historic Brownsville surrounds the College Hill Center, where you will find the **Haywood County Museum** (127 N. Grade Ave., 731/772-4883, Sun. 2–4 P.M., free). This museum is home to a remarkable collection of Abraham Lincoln artifacts and papers, donated by Brownsville native Morton Felsenthal. The museum is open limited hours, so plan accordingly or call ahead to inquire whether someone can open it for you.

The attractive redbrick College Hill Center, which houses the museum, was built in 1851 as the Brownsville Baptist Female College. After 1900 it became the Ogilvie Training School for boys and later it was the Haywood County High School from 1911 to 1970.

Mind Field

Tucked next to a payday-loan storefront and quickmart near downtown Brownsville is the

Mind Field, a steel sculpture created by local artist Billy Tripp. At first glance it looks like an electrical transformer station, but it is truly a work of art. It stands 75 feet tall in places, and includes messages of optimism and open-mindedness from the artist. Find the *Mind Field* off U.S. 70, one block away from the town square.

Hatchie River National Wildlife Area

Just south of Brownsville is the Hatchie River National Wildlife Area (731/772-0501), a 12,000-acre preserve along the Hatchie River. Established to protect the more than 200 species of birds that winter or migrate on the Hatchie, the wildlife area presents excellent opportunities for bird-watching. You can also fish in many areas. Camping is not allowed. For more information, contact the Refuge Office located at the intersection of Highway 76 and I-40.

Events

Brownsville hosts the **Brownsville Blues Fall Festival** in late September or early October, which celebrates blues and the culture of the delta. Come to hear some of the best Delta blues outside Memphis, and enjoy barbecue, regional crafts, and sports activities. The blues festival is followed in October by the **Hatchie Fall Festival** on the courthouse square in Brownsville, which offers more live music and family-oriented fun.

Accommodations

Brownsville has the greatest concentration of hotels in this part of Tennessee. Most of these are located along I-40, a five-minute drive from downtown Brownsville. The **O'Bannon Inn** (120 Sunny Hill Cove Rd., 731/772-4030, $60) at exit 56 is an independent family-run hotel located in an old Holiday Inn. The rooms are comfortable, and guests get free wireless Internet, coffee and snacks all day and night, and a full breakfast with eggs, bacon, sausage, yogurt, fruit, pastries, and biscuits. It is within walking distance of the West Tennessee Delta Heritage Center and fast-food restaurants.

Other chain hotels located here include **Econo Lodge** (2600 Anderson Ave., 731/772-4082, $50–60) and **Days Inn** (2530 Anderson Ave., 731/772-3297, $50–60).

In the historic downtown, try **Lilies' Bed and Breakfast** (508 W. Main St., 731/772-9078, $100). Gail Carver has two rooms in this elegant 1855 home, each with its own private bath.

Food

If you are in town on Friday or Saturday, then don't miss the weekly fish fry at ◖ **City Fish Market** (223 S. Washington Ave., 731/772-9952, Fri. 10 A.M.–5:30 P.M., Sat. 10 A.M.–4:30 P.M., $5–12), on a side street in the old downtown area. Watch the catfish being cleaned and cut up, then deep fried before your eyes. Dinner plates are served with hush puppies and slaw, and you can douse your fish with vinegary hot sauce. Fried catfish does not get much fresher or better than this.

For a home cooked meal during the week, try **The Sugar Palace** (2556 N. Washington Ave., 731/772-3941, Tues.–Fri. 9:30 A.M.–6 P.M., Sat. 10 A.M.–2 P.M., $4–10) on the square, which serves lunch on weekdays and sells candy and sweets all day.

Otherwise, Brownsville has fast-food restaurants, a few barbecue joints, and at least two Mexican restaurants. **Las Palmas** (27 S. Lafayette, 731/772-8004, daily 10 A.M.–9 P.M., $5–11) is on the courthouse square and serves combination plates, fajitas, and grilled seafood.

Information

The **West Tennessee Delta Heritage Center** (121 Sunny Hill Cove, 731/779-9000, Tues.–Sat. 9 A.M.–4 P.M.) near the interstate at Brownsville has comprehensive information about visiting not only Brownsville, but all the counties in West Tennessee. Make this your first stop for information about the area. There is also a gift shop and public Internet access.

The **Brownsville-Haywood Chamber of**

Commerce (121 W. Main St., 731/772-2193, www.haywoodcountybrownsville.com) can also help with information about the city.

NUTBUSH

This rural farming community would be a mere speck on the map were it not for R&B superstar Tina Turner, who was raised in and around Nutbush from her birth in 1936 until she moved to St. Louis at age 16. Turner penned the semi-autobiographical tune "Nutbush City Limits" in 1973, which gave rise to a popular line dance called the Nutbush. Turner re-released the song in 1991.

Reality is that Nutbush is too small to even have city limits; it feels much like a ghost town today. But the lone business, the Nutbush Grocery and Deli on State Highway 19 (renamed in 2001 the Tina Turner Highway), proclaims its association with the R&B superstar with a sign. The home where Tina Turner once lived in Nutbush was torn down long ago, the lumber used to build a barn elsewhere in town.

HENNING

The tiny sawmill town of Henning is a half-hour drive through the cotton fields from Brownsville. It would be unremarkable except for the fact that it nurtured one of Tennessee's greatest writers, Alex Haley.

◖ Alex Haley House Museum

The Alex Haley House Museum (200 S. Church, 731/738-2240, Tues.–Sat. 10 a.m.–5 p.m., Sun. 1–5 p.m., $5) illustrates the early childhood of the Pulitzer Prize–winning author Alex Haley. This is where Haley spent his first 10 years, and he later returned here during the summers to stay with his maternal grandparents, Will and Cynthia Palmer.

Visitors tour the kitchen where Cynthia Palmer told Haley stories of her ancestors, which he later used as inspiration for his masterwork, *Roots*. The museum has artifacts of the period, as well as family pictures and heirlooms. You also hear a recording of Haley describing Sunday dinners served in the family dining room.

This sign is the only evidence of Tina Turner's roots in Nutbush, a rural community west of Brownsville.

© SUSANNA HENIGHAN POTTER

The museum was established with Haley's help, and he was buried here on his death in 1991.

FORT PILLOW STATE HISTORIC PARK

The drive along Highway 87 to Fort Pillow State Historic Park (731/738-5581) takes you through almost 20 miles of rolling cotton fields and past the West Tennessee State Penitentiary. The park, which perches atop a bluff overlooking the Mississippi River, offers group, tent, and RV camping, picnic areas, 15 miles of hiking trails, wildlife viewing, and fishing in Fort Pillow Lake. There is also a museum (daily 8 A.M.–4 P.M., free) that tells the controversial story of the 1864 Battle of Fort Pillow, which many historians say is more aptly referred to as the Fort Pillow Massacre for the brutality displayed by southern troops under the command of Nathan Bedford Forrest.

Visitors to modern-day Fort Pillow can hike to the remains of the fort itself, and see the area where the battle took place. The museum's exhibits and a short video are dated, but an interested visitor will find a great deal of information contained in them. There are reenactments of the battle in April and November. The Mississippi River Bike Trail passes through the park.

HUMBOLDT

Humboldt was chartered in 1866 at the site where the Louisville and Nashville Railroad and the North–South Mobile and Ohio Railroad crossed. It was named for German naturalist and explorer Baron Alexander von Humboldt. Farmers around Humboldt grew cotton and after the 1870s diversified into strawberries, rhubarb, tomatoes, cabbage, lettuce, sweet potatoes, and other crops. Agriculture remains an important industry, but manufacturing is increasingly important. Companies including Wilson Sporting Goods, CON-AGRA, and American Woodmark have plants in Humboldt.

The **West Tennessee Regional Art Center** (1200 Main St., 731/784-1787, www.wtrac.tn.org, Mon.–Fri. 9 A.M.–4:30 P.M., $2) is located in the city's restored city hall building. It houses the Caldwell Collection of oil paintings,

sculpture, watercolor paintings, prints, and lithographs—the only permanent fine-art museum between Nashville and Memphis. The center also showcases memorabilia from the West Tennessee Strawberry Festival, and staff can answer your questions about the area.

Humboldt's Main Street is home to barber shops, real estate agents, banks, and a Mexican grocery. It also has a downtown movie theater, **The Plaza** (1408 Main St., 731/784-7469).

Events

Humboldt is best known for the annual **West Tennessee Strawberry Festival,** which celebrates one of this region's sweetest crops. Established in 1934 to encourage the growing, packing, and consumption of strawberries, the festival takes place in early May at the height of the strawberry harvest. It includes a parade, car show, foot races, beauty pageants, cooking contests, and fireworks. For details, contact the Humboldt Chamber of Commerce (1200 Main St., 731/784-1842, www.humboldttnchamber.org).

Food

For a hearty meal in Humboldt, try the lunchtime buffet at the **Humboldt Grill** (618 N. 22nd Ave., 731/784-4465, Mon.–Fri. 6 A.M.–2 P.M., $5–12). This family restaurant serves breakfast and lunch every day but Monday. Its buffet includes two meats and a variety of side dishes such as green beans, potato salad, mashed potatoes, and creamed corn. They serve eggs, pancakes, and fried potatoes for breakfast, as well as burgers, steaks, and fried chicken.

Accommodations

The pet-friendly **Deerfield Inn** (590 Hwy. 45 Bypass, 731/824-4770, $55) is a standard roadside motel, with single and double rooms, cable TV, and in-room refrigerators.

Information

The **Humboldt Chamber of Commerce** (1200 Main St., 731/784-1842, www.humboldttnchamber.org) can help with information about the town.

WESTERN PLAINS

WESTERN PLAINS

FORT PILLOW

The earthworks at Fort Pillow along the Mississippi River were built by the Confederates in 1861, but the fort was soon abandoned so that the rebels could consolidate their troops farther south. Union forces occupied the fort for several years, owing mainly to its strategic position at a sharp bend in the Mississippi River. On April 12, 1864, there were some 600 Union troops stationed at Fort Pillow – 200 of them were newly freed African Americans who had volunteered to join the Union cause.

By 1864 it was clear to most that the South would lose the war, so when legendary Confederate Gen. Nathan Bedford Forrest attacked Fort Pillow on April 12, it was not a battle of strategic importance but instead a fight for supplies and pride.

Accounts are that the Confederates quickly overcame the fort by land, but that an inexperienced Union commander, Maj. William Bradford, twice declined to surrender. Whether he finally surrendered or not is a matter of debate. Regardless of whether the Union formally surrendered, there was never any question which force would prevail. Forrest had more men and the advantage of surprise. With such a clear-cut victory at hand, it is no wonder that as news of the massive Union casualties emerged, the immediate cry was of massacre.

Forrest reported that a mere 14 Union men were killed in the battle, but Union records say that some 300 men lost their lives, 200 of whom were black. Even Confederate soldiers writing home described the events as "butchery" and told of savagery so great that Forrest himself rode through the ranks and threatened to shoot any Confederate who did not stop the killing.

The U.S. Congress immediately ordered an investigation, and after reviewing a number of accounts and interviewing witnesses, declared the battle a massacre. The Confed-

The cannons are quiet at Fort Pillow, the site of a controversial Civil War battle in 1864.

erates dismissed this as propaganda and blamed the heavy bloodletting on poor command. The precise nature of what happened at Fort Pillow remains a matter of debate.

For Union soldiers, and especially African-American soldiers, there was no ambiguity in their minds over what took place at Fort Pillow. Recognizing that official retribution may never come, black soldiers used Fort Pillow as a rallying cry in battle. "Remember Fort Pillow," they yelled on advance.

Poet Paul Laurence Dunbar immortalized the incident in his poem "The Unsung Heroes," which reads in part: "Pillow knew their blood, That poured on a nation's altar, a sacrificial flood."

DYERSBURG

This town of 20,000 people is the county seat of Dyer County, and was mentioned in the Arrested Development song "Tennessee": "Outta the country and into more country, Past Dyersburg into Ripley, Where the ghost of my childhood haunts me, Walk the roads my forefathers walked; Climbed the trees my forefathers hung from."

The county seat of Dyer County, Dyersburg has a handsome redbrick-and-white courthouse, built in 1912. The courthouse square is home to several antiques shops, professional services, and **Downtown Dyersburg Development Association** (111 W. Market St., 731/285-3433, Mon.–Fri. 8 A.M.–noon), which promotes downtown and can provide visitor information.

You may not need any farming implements, vegetable plants, or fertilizer, but you may still want to check out **Pennington Seed and Supply** (214 S. Main, 731/285-1031) for its pecans and vintage looks. Right next door is **Samkat Books, Records, and More** (216 S. Mill Ave., 731/285-2665), a small shop with used books and music.

Accommodations

Dyersburg has a handful of chain hotels in the delta, outside of Brownsville. They include a **Best Western** (770 Hwy. 51 Bypass, 731/285-8601, $75–85) and **Days Inn** (2600 Lake Rd., 731/287-0888, $80–90).

Food

For a meal in Dyersburg, head to **Cozy Kitchen** (107A W. Market St., 731/285-1054, Mon.–Fri. 5:30 A.M.–1:30 P.M., $5–10), which serves breakfast and lunch on weekdays.

Information

The **Downtown Dyersburg Development Association** (111 W. Market St., 731/285-3433, 8 A.M.–noon Mon.–Fri.) is the best source of information about the town.

ALAMO

The county seat of Crockett County, Alamo was named for the Alamo Mission in Texas where Davy Crockett died. Its population is about 2,500.

You can see exotic animals including zebras, wildebeest, oryx, and water buffalo at the **Tennessee Safari Park at Hillcrest** (Hwy. 412, 731/696-4423, www.tennesseesafaripark.com, open daily early spring–late fall, cars admitted Mon.–Sat. 9:30 A.M.–5 P.M. and Sun. 10:30 A.M.–5 P.M., call for appointment to visit in winter, adults $10, children $6) just outside of town. The park is the creation of the Conley family, who have been collecting and raising exotic animals on their farm since 1963. The farm has more than 250 animals, and visitors can drive a two-mile loop through the farm safari-style. Free-roaming animals come up to your car window to visit. At the barn there is a petting zoo where you can feed and touch more animals. While the Conleys have been raising exotic animals for decades, the park has been open to the public since 2007. The park is 16 miles up Highway 412 from I-40 at exit 78.

Old West Tennessee has been lovingly re-created at **Green Frog Village** (Hwy. 412, 731/663-3319, Tues.–Sat. 10 A.M.–5 P.M., free), located between Alamo and Bells, just north of I-40. The village includes an antique cotton gin, 1830s rural church, antique log cabin, one-room schoolhouse, and country store. It is also an arboretum. The mission of the village is to preserve the rural culture of the Tennessee delta, and it has been the life's work of emergency-room doctor John Freeman and his wife, Nancy.

CHICKASAW NATIONAL WILDLIFE REFUGE

More than 130,000 people visit the 25,000-acre Chickasaw National Wildlife Refuge (731/635-7621) annually. The refuge, located 10 miles north of Ripley along the Mississippi River, is home to dozens of species of birds, including bald eagles. The refuge is a popular area for hunting and fishing—the fall squirrel hunt is one of the largest. You can also bike or hike along the reserve's 20 miles of paved and gravel roads. The refuge was established in 1984 and occupies land once owned by a private timber company.

Find the refuge by driving nine miles north of Ripley on Highway 51. Turn left on Hobe Webb Road for 1.25 miles, and then right onto Sand Bluff Road for half a mile.

BIG CYPRESS TREE STATE NATURAL AREA

You won't find the namesake tree at Big Cypress Tree State Natural Area; the 1,350-year-old tree, which measured 13 feet in diameter, was struck by lightning and died in 1976.

The park, which is near Greenfield, is for day-use only, and has a picnic area, covered pavilion, and a short nature trail.

RIPLEY

Ripley's famous tomatoes take center stage at the annual **Lauderdale County Tomato Festival,** which takes place during the week after July 4 every year. In addition to tomato tasting, cooking contests, and exhibitions, there is live music, a carnival, and a beauty contest. The event is organized by the Lauderdale County Chamber of Commerce (731/635-9541).

HALLS

You can find interesting antiques at a number of stores tucked away in small towns in this part of Tennessee. Perhaps the most interesting is **Murray Hudson's Antiquarian Books and Maps** (109 S. Church St., 731/836-5418, Mon.–Sat. 9 A.M.–5 P.M.). Hudson has been collecting for more than 25 years and has a remarkable collection of old globes, some of them dating back to the early 1700s. He also sells old maps, books, and historic prints.

MASON

Along Highway 70 near Mason, one landmark restaurant attracts Memphians and residents of the delta. 【 **Gus's World Famous Hot and Spicy Chicken** (520 Hwy. 70, 901/294-2028, Mon.–Sat. 11 A.M.–9 P.M., $8–12) has been heralded by the likes of *GQ* magazine and celebrity chef Emeril as *the* place for good fried chicken. Gus's is set in an old frame house, modified over the years to accommodate the thousands of loyal patrons who can't get enough of Gus's hot and spicy fried chicken. Coated in batter and a special seasoning paste, Gus's chicken is fried so that the crust is crispy, the meat juicy, and the taste just spicy enough to be perfect with a cold beer. Just when you think it can't get any better, someone drops a quarter in the old jukebox and the blues fill the air. Wise diners get two orders: one to eat now and one to eat on the way home.

Reelfoot Lake

Tennessee's "earthquake lake" is a landscape of knob-kneed Cyprus trees, gently rippling water, and open spaces. It is a flooded forest, eerie-looking and peaceful. With some 13,000 acres of water, the lake is also a sportsman's dream: 54 species of fish live in Reelfoot, including bream, crappie, catfish, and bass. From January to March—the best fishing season—the lake sees a steady stream of visitors who come to troll its waters.

Reelfoot Lake is home to thousands of wintering and migratory birds. Visitors cannot help but notice the daily symphony of bird calls, not to mention the sight of ducks, herons, wild turkeys, eagles, and geese around the lake. Bird-watchers have identified some 238 species of birds in Reelfoot Lake, and the April turkey hunt in the area is excellent.

Bald eagles are the most iconic of the bird species that winter at the lake, and spotting these majestic creatures is a popular pursuit from January to March. Normally, the winter eagle population on the lake numbers between 100 and 200 birds. Bald eagles had virtually disappeared from the area in the 1960s due to the effects of DDT contamination of their nesting grounds, but thanks to a nesting project started in 1988 they have returned.

REELFOOT LAKE

MISSOURI

KENTUCKY
TENNESSEE

Mississippi River

Reelfoot
National
Wildlife
Refuge

AIRPARK INN
AIRPARK
AIRPARK
TRAIL

To Union City

Clayton

NATIONAL
WILDLIFE REFUGE
VISITOR CENTER

CATES LANDING/
NEW MARKHAM RD

AIRPORT RD

GRASSY ISLAND
HIKING TRAIL

GRASSY ISLAND
AUTO TOUR

Reelfoot Lake
State Park

Reelfoot
National
Wildlife
Refuge

Reelfoot Lake

Spout Springs

BLACK
BAYOU TRAIL

Black
Bayou

CARL PERKINS HWY

Ronaldson Slough

Reelfoot
Lake

Tiptonville

KEYSTONE
TRAIL

REELFOOT LAKE STATE
PARK VISITOR CENTER

Samburg

DRAGONFLY
INN

BOYETTE'S

OLD RIDGLEY RD

BLUE BANK
RESORT

STATE
PARK

CAMPGROUND
TRAIL

BLUE BANK
FISH HOUSE
AND GRILL

0   2 mi

0   2 km

To Troy

Hornbeak   © AVALON TRAVEL

WESTERN PLAINS

Orientation

Reelfoot Lake sits in the extreme northwestern corner of Tennessee. Its northernmost finger nearly touches the Kentucky state line, and the Mississippi River is only a mile to the west. Two-lane state highways circle the lake; the entire loop is about 35 miles. The southern portion of Reelfoot is a state park, and the northern half of the lake is a U.S. National Wildlife Refuge. Several thousand residents live in lakefront communities that dot the area.

The closest town to the lake, Tiptonville is a cluster of homes and businesses at the south-western corner of Reelfoot. The boyhood home of Carl Perkins is found here; look for a sign on Highway 78 south of town to find it.

Most accommodations, restaurants, and provisioning locales are found along the southern shore, just a few minutes drive from Tiptonville. The state park's Air Park Inn, along with one or two private camps and inns, are set on the lake's western shore, about 10 miles from Tiptonville. The trails and visitors center maintained by the U.S. Fish and Wildlife Service are located on the more isolated northern shore of the waters.

SIGHTS
◖ Reelfoot Lake State Park Visitor Center

The State Park Visitor Center (3120 State Road 213, 731/253-7756 or 731/253-8003, Mon.–Fri. 8 A.M.–4:30 P.M., free) provides the best introduction to the lake, with exhibits on its history, wildlife, legends, and ecology. You can see a traditional Reelfoot Lake boat, and read the story of the local vigilantes who took matters into their own hands when the lake was threatened with development. This is also the place to sign up for popular lake cruises and sightseeing tours.

Outside the museum are a couple of mesh cages where you can see bald eagles, owls, and red-tailed hawks. A half-mile boardwalk trail extends out over the lake at the rear of the visitors center and is a must for anyone who wants to experience the special beauty of the lake.

Reelfoot Lake National Wildlife Refuge

On the northern side of Reelfoot, near the intersections of State Highways 22 and 157, is the **National Wildlife Refuge Visitor Center** (4343 Hwy. 157, 731/538-2481, daily 8 A.M.–4 P.M., free). Here you can see exhibits about the lake, with a special focus on the flora and fauna of the area. Take note that the Reelfoot National Wildlife Refuge, which is, essentially, the northern half of the lake, is only open to the public for fishing and wildlife observation March 15–November 15 every year, although the visitors center remains open year-round. Contact the visitors center for specific rules about fishing, hunting, and public access to the refuge.

The wildlife refuge maintains the **Grassy Island Auto Tour,** a three-mile self-guided auto tour, year-round. The tour leads to an observation tower overlooking the Grassy Island part of the lake and is worth the detour required to reach it.

THE SEASONS AT REELFOOT LAKE

There are distinct variations in the type of wildlife you will see in and around Reelfoot Lake throughout the year.

In January and February, the wintering eagle and Canada goose populations peak. Cold water crappie fishing is good. In March, the eagles begin their northward migration, while osprey return from South America. Wild turkeys are often visible in March.

Spring comes to the lake in April and May, with wildflowers in abundance and the best season for bird-watching. It is also the best season to listen for frogs. By June, you may see deer fawns and the floating aquatic plants are in bloom.

July and August are the hottest months at Reelfoot Lake, and also the season of mosquitoes and deerflies. By September, it has cooled off. Fall fishing for crappie and bass begins.

During the fall, migrating and wintering birds begin to return. Short raccoon and archery deer hunting seasons take place in October; the deer gun hunt takes place in November. December is one of the best months to view ducks, geese, and eagles.

SPORTS AND RECREATION
Boating

If you can do only one thing when you visit Reelfoot Lake, get out on the water in a boat. The best cruises are provided by the state park. The three-hour cruises (adults $9, children 5–15 $6, under 5 free) take place from May to September and depart daily at 9 A.M. from the visitors center on the southern side of the lake. Your guide will point out fish, birds, and other distinctive features of the lake. It is a good idea to bring drinks (a cooler with ice is provided) and snacks.

In March and April, the park offers a deep-swamp canoe float that departs on weekends at 8 A.M. and 1 P.M. The cost is $20. From January to March, special bald eagle tours are offered daily at 10 A.M. Call the state park at

731/253-7756 to make a reservation for any of the cruises.

Fishing

Fishing is the most popular recreation activity at Reelfoot Lake. With 13,000 acres of water and an average depth of just over five feet, the lake is a natural fish hatchery. An estimated 54 species of fish live in the lake. The most common fish are bream, crappie, catfish, and bass. The fishing season generally runs from March to July, although some species are plentiful into the fall.

Because Reelfoot Lake is so shallow, and because of the cypress knees which lurk below the surface, most fishermen use a specially-designed Reelfoot Lake boat. If you want to fish on the lake for the first time, sign up with a local guide, who can help make arrangements for a boat rental and will share local fishing knowledge. Experienced guides include Jonathan Moore (731/538-3112), Chuck D's Professional Guide Service (731/885-5696), and Ed Hamilton (731/446-8234). For a complete and current listing of local guides, check with the visitors center or tourist council. Boat rentals usually cost $40 and up per day, and guides charge $100 and up per day.

Several hotels catering to fishermen offer special packages that include room, a boat and motor, bait, ice, and fuel for as little as $120 per night.

Hiking

Campground Trail: A half-mile trail that begins in the spillway area and ends at the state park campground on the southern tip of the lake. The trailhead is located on Highway 21/22.

Keystone Trail: This 1.5-mile path skirts the edge of the lake along part of its southern shore. Hikers should wear shoes or boots that can withstand the sometimes-muddy path. Birds are common. The trailhead is located off Highway 21/22 and is adjacent to a large picnic area.

Black Bayou Trail: This two-mile walk through the cypress swamp follows the Black Bayou Slough. The trailhead is located along Highway 78 on the western shore of the lake.

The Airpark Trail: This 1.5-mile trail winds through cypress and hardwood forest as well as open fields. The trailhead is next to the Airpark Inn off Highway 78.

Grassy Island Hiking Trail: Part of the National Wildlife Refuge at Grassy Island, this half-mile path cuts through lowland forest and over swampy wetlands. A portion follows the paved auto-tour road through Grassy Island.

Biking

The terrain around Reelfoot Lake is flat, and traffic is relatively light. Biking is a good way to get around and explore what the lake has to offer. Bring your own bike, however, since no rentals are available.

ACCOMMODATIONS

The best accommodations on Reelfoot Lake are at the state park–operated ◖ **Airpark Inn** (731/253-7756, $40), on the northwestern side of the lake. Built on a platform over the lake, the inn has 20 comfortable rooms and suites,

The boardwalk trail at the Reelfoot Lake State Park Visitor Center takes you out over Reelfoot Lake.

WESTERN PLAINS

THE NEW MADRID QUAKE

A series of powerful earthquakes struck the central United States between December 1811 and February 1812. Although there was no way of measuring magnitude at that time, modern scientists now say that at least three of these temblors exceeded magnitude 8.0.

The first major quake struck on December 16, 1811, and caused the ground to split open around New Madrid, Missouri. A sulfurous gas filled the air, and witnesses saw thousands of birds flying away from the area. On this day the *New Orleans*, one of the nation's first steamboats, was voyaging down the Mississippi River. The crew was no doubt alarmed to find that as they entered the earthquake-stricken area, riverbanks were shaking and waves were rocking the boat. The steamboat weathered the effects of temblors on December 19, and on December 21 the crew woke to find that the mooring that they had cast the night before was no longer secure because the very island they had anchored to had disappeared under the water.

The final quake struck on February 7, 1812, and gave birth to Reelfoot Lake. The most violent of all the quakes, it caused dishes to shake in Montreal, Canada, and rang bells in Boston. The Mississippi riverbed rose and sank; boats capsized or were sucked into fissures that appeared suddenly in the earth. The quake was so powerful that it caused the Mississippi River to flow northward for a period, and diverted a large amount of water onto once-dry land, creating Reelfoot Lake.

pool, and, for the jet-set, a 3,500-foot landing strip next to the inn. There are also meeting rooms and a boat dock, and a continental breakfast of coffee, orange juice, and pastries.

The **Blue Bank Resort** (3330 State Hwy. 21 E., 731/253-8976, www.bluebankresort.com) has a traditional motel as well as cabins that stand over the lake, with expansive decks and a 12-person hot tub. The cabins can sleep between 3 and 16. All rooms have a lot of exposed wood, giving the resort the feeling of a hunting lodge. The Blue Bank offers fishing packages that cost $200–300 per person for up to four nights and include gear—boat, motor, bait, and ice—for fishing. If you're just interested in a room without the add-ons, call at the last minute to find out if they have a vacancy. Expect to pay $70–100 per night, depending on the season.

For the most intimate accommodations at Reelfoot Lake, try **Dragonfly Inn** (365 Sunkist Beach Rd., 731/442-0750, www.dragonflyinn-reelfootlake.com, $60), formerly Miss Pauline's Bed and Breakfast. Set in an old farmhouse, this friendly bed-and-breakfast is just one mile from Reelfoot Lake but feels removed from the crowds that exist during peak season. The four rooms are homey, and each has a private bath, individual heating and air-conditioning, and a queen-sized bed. Host Marianne serves a full breakfast, and accommodates fishermen with early breakfasts, freezer space, and lots of boat parking in the driveway.

Camping

The state park runs two campgrounds for RVs and tents. A small campground is located next to the Airpark Inn on the northwest coast of the lake. A larger campground is on the southern shore near the visitors center. Rates at both campgrounds are $20 for an RV site and $8 for a tent site. Sites are given on a first-come, first-served basis; no reservations are accepted.

FOOD

Catfish and other lake fish are the food du jour around Reelfoot Lake. **(Boyette's**

each with a private balcony and view of the lake. Guests have reported catching fish right from their porch. Double rooms have refrigerators, microwaves, coffeemakers, and televisions; suites come with all this plus a kitchenette. All guests have access to charcoal grills and freezers as well as a fish-cleaning station. Guests may also take advantage of lighted tennis courts, a swimming

(Hwy. 21, 731/253-7307, daily 11 A.M.–9 P.M., $7–15) is located across the road from the Reelfoot Lake State Park Visitor Center. The catfish platter is the specialty here, and it comes with generous portions of french fries, onion rings, hush puppies, coleslaw, and green beans. If you've worked up an appetite after a day of fishing, go for the all-you-can-eat catfish dinner, a steal at $13. You can also get frog legs, steaks, and burgers.

A little bit farther east along the lakeshore road you will find **Blue Bank Fish House and Grill** (813 Lake Dr., 731/253-8976, daily 11 A.M.–9 P.M., $6–20). The Blue Bank menu is sure to have something that will please anyone. In addition to all-you-can-eat catfish, fried quail, and country ham, you can choose from pasta, shrimp, steak, loaded potatoes, and burgers. The dinner menu is $8–20 and lunchtime entrées are $6–14. They also serve breakfast. The kitchen closes 2–4 P.M. on weekdays.

Around Reelfoot

For a break from the rustic, drive the 20 miles east to Troy, where you'll find **White House**

(106 College St., 731/536-2000, Thurs.–Sat. 11 A.M.–2 P.M. and 5–9 P.M., $14–27), open for lunch and dinner Thursday through Saturday. Set in a gracious old boarding-house, the restaurant serves uncommonly good food in a welcoming environment. The handsome white building on the town square has a lawn and adjoining gift shop, and is a popular venue for weddings and special events. The menu includes a half-dozen different steaks, pork chops, shrimp, salmon, and chicken. At lunch, choose from sandwiches, salads, and pasta.

INFORMATION

Stop at the **State Park Visitor Center** (Hwy. 21, 731/253-7756, daily 8 A.M.–4:30 P.M.) or the **Reelfoot Lake Tourism Council** (4575 Hwy. 21 E., 731/253-6516, www.reelfoot-tourism.com, Mon. 8 A.M.–5 P.M., Thurs. 9 A.M.–5 P.M., Fri.–Sat. 9 A.M.–6 P.M., Sun. 1–6 P.M.) for visitor information. The Reelfoot Lake State Park Auto Tour guide, a single-sheet handout available at any of these offices, is the most useful map of the area.

Kentucky Lake

The part of the Tennessee River which runs from the Land Between the Lakes region near the Kentucky–Tennessee line to Decatur County is commonly referred to as Kentucky Lake. The name reflects the river's breadth ands its lake-like calmness, caused by river dams built in the 1930s and '40s.

The lake provides opportunities for recreation and is home to a one-of-a-kind pearl farm. Off the water, this region includes Fort Donelson National Battlefield, a significant Civil War site, and Hurricane Mills, the town known as the home of country music superstar Loretta Lynn.

HURRICANE MILLS

Loretta Lynn, the country music star, recalls going for a Sunday drive in the countryside

west of Nashville in the early 1960s. That was when she and her late husband, Oliver Lynn, aka Doolittle or Doo, first saw the 1817 plantation home where they would eventually raise their family. "I looked up on this big ole hill and said, 'I want that house right there,'" she said.

Lynn, who moved to Tennessee in 1960 at the beginning of her music career, is one of the most influential female artists in the genre. During the height of her career in the 1970s, she published her autobiography *Coal Miner's Daughter,* later made into a film. In 1979 she was named Artist of the Decade by the Country Music Association.

The mansion that Lynn bought in 1966 is now just one of a half-dozen Lynn-inspired attractions in **Hurricane Mills** (931/296-7700, www.lorettalynn.com), a town that time would have forgotten were it not for Loretta Lynn. First buying just the mansion, Lynn now owns the whole shebang: even the U.S. Postal Service rents the Hurricane Mills Post Office from Lynn.

The town is located seven miles north of I-40, along Highway 13. Waverly and Dickson are the closest large towns.

Sights

Visitors to Hurricane Mills can tour the ante-bellum mansion Lynn bought in 1966, as well as a replica of her childhood home in Butcher Holler, Kentucky, and a simulated coal mine, made to look like the one her father worked in. Guided tours, which cost $12 for adults and $6 for children 6–12, last about an hour and de-part daily at 9:30 A.M., 10:30 A.M., 11:30 A.M., 1 P.M., 2 P.M., 3 P.M., and 4 P.M.

The **Coal Miner's Daughter Museum** (931/296-1840, daily 9 A.M.–5 P.M., adults $10, children 6–12 $5) is an 18,000-square-foot exhibit hall packed with items from Lynn's personal and professional life. Opened in 2001, the museum includes her tour bus, pictures, clothing, portraits, and gifts from celebrity friends. There is also the **Loretta Doll and Fan Museum** (free), located in a beautiful red 1896 gristmill.

The museums and plantation tours are open March through October and are generally closed during the winter. Call ahead to confirm.

Practicalities

The **Loretta Lynn Ranch** (44 Hurricane Mills Rd., 931/296-7700, www.lorettalynn.com) has an RV park, campground, and cabin rentals. There are also canoe rentals, paddle boats, and occasional concerts by Lynn herself. For something a little different, book a night on Lynn's old tour bus. For $125–150 per night, up to four people can sleep tour-bus style, with television, a microwave, refrigerator, and coffeemaker.

The ranch is open from April through the end of September.

For food, entertainment, and shopping, head to **Cissie Lynn's Country Store and Music**

Barn (8000 Hwy. 13 S., 931/296-2275, daily 6 A.M.–6 P.M.). Operated by Loretta Lynn's daughter, Cissie, the restaurant and music hall serves sandwiches and country-style food ($7–15). In the evenings there are writer's nights, live music, and special events.

Closer to the mansion, **Rock-a-Billy Cafe** (Stage Coach Hill, 931/296-1840, daily 9 A.M.–5 P.M.) is a casual restaurant located in the old gristmill.

MOUSETAIL LANDING STATE PARK

Located on land once occupied by an eponymous river town, Mousetail Landing State Park (Linden, 731/847-0841) is one of Tennessee's newest state parks. Dedicated in 1986, this 1,247-acre park lies on the east bank of the Tennessee River in the rural and picturesque Western valley. The town acquired its name from the large number of rodents that took shelter in the town's tanning factories. Tanned hides were shipped northward to markets up the river, including Paducah, Louisville, and St. Louis.

The park contains several ruins from the historic era, including the original pier, a blacksmith shop, and the old community cemetery.

Recreation

There is a three-mile day-use hiking trail through the woods, as well as an eight-mile loop with two overnight shelters along the way. The shelters are well-maintained and provide a lovely escape and relatively easy hiking. You could also complete the entire loop in a day and camp at the park campground.

One half-mile south of the main entrance to the park there is a boat launch and courtesy pier. Fishing is popular and permitted anywhere in the park. Bass, bream, crappie, stripe, and catfish are among the most frequent catches.

Also near the boat dock is a small swimming beach. There is no lifeguard on duty. A small, cold creek near the entrance to the park is ideal for wading and exploration.

There are also playgrounds, an archery range, horseshoes, basketball, and a volleyball court.

Camping

There are two campgrounds at Mousetail Landing. Rates are $16 per site. The main campground, located in a woodland forest, has 24 sites, including 19 with electricity and water. There is a modern bathhouse and laundry facilities, plus picnic tables and grills. There is also a dump station.

The Spring Creek Campground has 21 sites along the banks of the Tennessee River, located at the public boat dock.

NATCHEZ TRACE STATE PARK AND FOREST

Named for the famous old road from Natchez to Nashville, this is one of the largest state parks in Tennessee. The park has four lakes, including Pin Oak Lake, which offers fishing, boating, and swimming. One of the most unique attractions at Natchez Trace is horseback riding. Guided rides of 30 minutes to one hour are available from the **Natchez Trace Equestrian Center** (731/967-5340, Mar.–Memorial Day and Labor Day–late Nov. Fri.–Sat. 9 A.M.–5 P.M., Sun. 1–5 P.M., Memorial Day–Labor Day Tues.–Sat. 9 A.M.–5 P.M., Sun. 1–5 P.M.) for adults and children as young as three years. An hour's guided ride will cost $20.

There are 13.5 miles of hiking trails at the park, as well as a museum about the natural history and wildlife of the area. Tennis courts, baseball fields, basketball course, and an archery and shooting range round out the facilities.

The park also has cabins, a campground, a resort inn, and group lodge.

CAMDEN

The town of Camden is the seat of Benton County, whose eastern edge is bounded by the Tennessee River.

Patsy Cline Memorial

Country music star Patsy Cline, together with Hawkshaw Hawkins, Cowboy Copas, and Randy Hughes, died in an airplane crash about three miles northwest of Camden on March 5, 1963. The Grand Ole Opry stars were heading back to Nashville after playing a benefit concert in Kansas City. The Piper Comanche airplane that they were in stopped in Dyersburg to refuel, and took off shortly after 6 P.M., despite high winds and inclement weather. The plane crashed at 6:20 P.M. in forest west of Camden, just 90 miles from Nashville. Cline was 30 years old.

The site of the plane crash remains a memorial to Patsy Cline, maintained over the years by her loyal fans. There is a memorial stone, bulletin board, and mailbox where fans can leave their personal sentiments about the star. The memorial is located 2.8 miles northwest of town along Mount Carmel Road.

Food

A good choice is the family-friendly **Blackberry Patch Restaurant** (150 S. Forrest Ave., 731/584-9923, Mon.–Thurs. and Sat. 4 A.M.–10 P.M., Fri. 4 A.M.–midnight, Sun. 5 A.M.–10 P.M.).

Near Camden

North America's only freshwater pearl–culturing farm is located a few miles south of Camden on Birdsong Creek, an inlet of the Tennessee River. The **Tennessee River Freshwater Pearl Museum and Farm** (255 Marina Rd., 731/584-7880, www.tennesseeriverpearls.com, Mon.–Sat. 8 A.M.–5 P.M., Sun. 1–4 P.M., free) is the unlikely result of one family's passion for pearls. John and Chessie Latrendressee founded the farm in 1979 and made their first successful harvest in 1984. Wild pearls were harvested from mussels fished from the bottom of the Tennessee River for years, but the Latrendressees were the first to successfully farm the gem.

The small museum explains the culturing process, the history of the Tennessee River pearl farm, and tells the history of pearls. You can also watch a *CBS Sunday Morning* segment produced about the Tennessee River pearl farm. There is a gift shop that sells some of the homegrown pearls; others are exported around the world. For a more detailed look, sign up for one of the farm's tour packages. The full tour ($49) includes lunch and a visit to the farm itself where you can see the phases of pearl culturing. Tours require at least 15 people, but small groups can

often add onto tours that have already been booked. Call ahead to check the schedule.

The pearl farm is located at Birdsong Resort, which is also a favorite place for boaters and fishermen, as well as group getaways. There are dozens of cabins, 50 campsites, a marina, catering facilities, and a pool.

NATHAN BEDFORD FORREST STATE PARK

Dedicated in 1929 to Nathan Bedford Forrest, the controversial confederate Civil War hero, this 2,500-acre state park offers camping, cabins, hiking, swimming, group pavilions, and fishing. There are seven cabins, each of which can sleep up to eight people, plus a group lodge that accommodates up to 64 people. The campground can accommodate tents or RVs.

There are more than 30 miles of hiking trails, ranging from easy to rugged. Swimming is good at Eva Beach, a rough sandy beach on the Kentucky Lake.

The park office is open daily 8 A.M.–4:30 P.M.

(Tennessee River Folklife Center

Located at Pilot Knob overlooking the Tennessee River, the Tennessee River Folklife Center (1825 Pilot Knob Rd., 731/584-2128, daily 8–11 A.M. and noon–4:30 P.M., free) lovingly depicts the traditional ways of river folk. The centerpiece of the museum is Old Betsy, a traditional river boat built from old farm equipment in the 1960s by T. J. Whitfield. Exhibits include photographs of a houseboat family and displays about river mussels, the pearl industry, and traditional foods and music. The museum is comprehensive, but not too large to be overwhelming.

Just steps from the doors to the folklife center is a monument to Nathan Bedford Forrest and his cavalry, which defeated a federal supply depot at Old Johnsonville, near the park, in 1984. There are impressive views of the Tennessee River from the porch outside the museum, including several manufacturing plants that emit not-so-pleasant industrial smells at certain times of the day.

NATHAN BEDFORD FORREST

Nathan Bedford Forrest is one of the most celebrated and reviled historical figures in Tennessee. An accomplished Confederate cavalry commander and the first grand wizard of the Ku Klux Klan, Forrest has come to symbolize the Old South.

Forrest was born in 1821 in Chapel Hill, a small town in Marshall County in Middle Tennessee. At the age of 16, Forrest's blacksmith father died and the young man became the head of his family. He had a mere six months of formal education in his lifetime, yet became a successful businessman, primarily as a plantation owner and slave trader.

Forrest was a staunch believer in the Southern cause, and when Tennessee seceded from the Union in 1861, he enlisted as a private in the Tennessee Mounted Rifles, together with his younger brother and 15-year-old son.

In a peculiar twist, Forrest offered freedom to his 44 slaves at the outbreak of the Civil War, if they would fight for the Confederacy. All agreed, and 43 reportedly served faithfully until the end of the war.

Forrest was daring on the battlefield, often taking great risks to avoid capture and defeat. Historian Brian S. Wills wrote: "His ferocity as a warrior was almost legendary. . . . Forrest understood, perhaps better than most, the basic premise of war: 'War means fighting and fighting means killing.'"

Forrest was involved in dozens of battles – small and large – during the war. In February 1862 he led his men out of Fort Donelson rather than surrender. He was wounded at Shiloh and fought at Chickamauga. In May 1863, he outmaneuvered a stronger Union force in northern Alabama by fooling Col. Abel Streight into believing that Forrest had more men than he did.

Forrest's victory at Fort Pillow in April 1864 was tarnished by the deaths of so many black Union soldiers, allegedly killed after they surrendered.

His victory at Brice's Cross Roads, in Mississippi, where Forrest defeated a much larger force of Union infantry and cavalry in June 1864, is believed by many to be his greatest success.

Forrest ended the Civil War as lieutenant general in command of cavalry in Alabama, Mississippi, and East Louisiana. His last battle at Gainsville, Alabama, in May 1865 ended in surrender.

Following the war, Forrest struggled to adapt to the changes it had brought. He supported the Ku Klux Klan in hopes of restoring the conservative white power structure that existed prior to the war and served as the Klan's first, and only, grand wizard.

His business dealings floundered. Forrest lost a fortune in the railroad industry and he spent his last years running a prison farm and living in a log cabin.

In his last years, Forrest seemed to reconsider many of his views on racial equality. In 1875 he spoke to a local group of freedmen, saying, "I came to meet you as friends, and welcome you to the white people. I want you to come nearer to us. When I can serve you I will do so. We have but one flag, one country; let us stand together. We may differ in color, but not in sentiment." Forrest kissed the cheek of an African-American women who handed him a bouquet of flowers, a gesture of intimacy unknown in that era.

Forrest died in Memphis in October 1877. He was buried at Elmwood Cemetery, but later reinterred at Forrest Park, built in his honor, in midtown Memphis.

In the years since the civil rights movement, many people have questioned Forrest's greatness. In 2005, there was an effort to move the statue over Forrest's grave and rename Forrest Park, and others have tried to get a bust of Forrest removed from the Tennessee House of Representatives chamber; both efforts failed.

WESTERN PLAINS

TENNESSEE NATIONAL WILDLIFE REFUGE

The Tennessee National Wildlife Refuge encompasses more than 51,000 acres along the Kentucky Lake, divided into three units. The Big Sandy Unit is just south of Paris Landing State Park; the Duck River Unit is farther south, near Eagle Creek and where I-40 crosses the river; the Busseltown unit is still farther south, near Perryville and Mousetail Landing State Park.

The refuge was established in 1945 as a safe haven for waterfowl. It consists of several different habitats, including open water, bottomland hardwoods, upland forests, freshwater marshes, and agricultural lands. As a refuge, the first priority here is to protect animal species—not to provide a space for human recreation.

Fishing and hunting are allowed in certain parts of the refuge at certain times of the year. There is an observation deck at the entrance to the Duck River "bottoms" area, where you can see a variety of waterfowl, especially in fall and winter. There is another observation deck at the V. L. Childs Overlook at the Big Sandy Unit off Swamp Creek Road. There is a 2.5-mile hiking trail here too.

The refuge headquarters (3006 Dinkins Ln., 731/642-2091, Mon.–Fri. 7 A.M.–3:30 P.M.) is just east of Paris off Highway 79.

JOHNSONVILLE STATE HISTORIC AREA

This 600-acre park is the site of Johnsonville before the creation of the Kentucky Lake, and this is where the battle of Johnsonville took place during the Civil War. The November 4, 1864, battle is noteworthy because it was the first time that a naval force was engaged and defeated by a cavalry.

The park has picnic pavilions, playgrounds, and six miles of hiking trails.

PARIS

Paris, the largest town in the Kentucky Lake region, was founded in 1823 and named after the French capital in honor of Marquis de Lafayette. Not long after,

© SUSANNA HENIGHAN POTTER

A replica of the Eiffel Tower stands in Paris.

tourists were traveling to Paris to drink and soak in a nearby sulfur well, believed to have health benefits. The well was submerged by Kentucky Lake in 1944 when TVA dammed the Tennessee River.

In keeping with its name, Paris has a model of the Eiffel Tower, donated to the city in 1992 by Christian Brothers University of Memphis. Located in Memorial Park on the outskirts of the city, the model tower is surrounded by a playground, ball field, and walking trails. Don't expect to see it towering over the town, however, since the model is only 60 feet tall.

To learn about the history of Paris and Henry County, visit the **Paris-Henry County Heritage Center** (614 N. Poplar St., 731/642-1030, Tues.–Fri. 10 A.M.–4 P.M., Sat. 10 A.M.–2 P.M.), located in the Cavitt Place, a 1916 Italian Renaissance–style two-story home. The center houses exhibits about the history of Henry County, and can provide an audio walking guide to historic Paris. There is also a gift shop.

Events

More than 12,500 pounds of catfish are served at the **World's Biggest Fish Fry** (www.worldsbiggestfishfry.com), which takes place in Paris in late April every year. The tradition evolved from the annual Mule Day, when farmers traveled to the town to trade their mules and other farm equipment ahead of the summer growing season. In the 1960s, the fish fry was established, and it has grown in popularity every year. Today, the fish fry is a weeklong event with rodeos, races, a parade, and four days of fish dinners, available for $10 a plate at the Bobby Cox Memorial Fish Tent.

Accommodations

In Paris, the **◖ Veranda Bed and Breakfast** (108 N. College St., 731/642-2371, www.verandabandb.com, $80) is in a pleasant historic district near the town square. The 100-year-old home's wide front porch is a perfect place to spend a long summer evening. There are two guest rooms, each with television. The breakfast is hearty and well prepared.

On U.S. Highway 641 one mile outside of Paris, the **Terrace Woods Lodge** (1190 N. Market St., 731/642-2642, www.terracewoodslodge.com, $35) is not as rustic as it sounds. This is a standard motel, but the rooms are clean and the service acceptable.

Food

Knott's Landing (209 N. Poplar St., 731/642-4718, Mon.–Tues. 6 A.M.–2 P.M., Wed.–Sat. 6 A.M.–8:30 P.M., $4–11) specializes in pond-raised catfish served with hot rolls, hush puppies, coleslaw, and more. You can also get a traditional plate lunch, or sandwich, steak, or burger. They also serve breakfast.

Paris distinguishes itself as one of the few small Tennessee towns with a health-food store. **Healthy Thyme** (803 E. Wood St., 731/642-9528, Mon.–Fri. 10 A.M.–5:30 P.M., Sat. 10 A.M.–2 P.M., $3–4) serves fruit smoothies, vegetarian and chicken salads, and sandwiches.

Downtown Paris has a bona fide coffee shop, with espresso, cappuccino, latte, and other specialty coffee drinks. **Jack's Java**

(118 N. Market St., 731/642-5251, Mon.–Fri. 7 A.M.–5 P.M., Sat. 9 A.M.–noon) doubles as a bookstore and florist.

For a sit-down dinner, try **Sepanto Steak House** (1305 E. Wood St., 731/641-1791, Mon.–Sat. 11 A.M.–9 P.M., $10–24), where you can get seafood, pasta, and chicken as well as steaks.

Information

Get visitor information from the **Paris-Henry County Chamber of Commerce** (2508 E. Wood St., 731/642-3431, www.paristnchamber.com) in Paris.

Also in Paris, the **W. G. Rhea Public Library** (400 W. Washington St., 731/642-1220, Mon.–Sat. 9 A.M.–5 P.M.) has 22,000 volumes as well as computers with Internet access. The library is open until 7 P.M. on Tuesday and Thursday evenings.

Near Paris

The most laid-back accommodations in the area are found at **Mammy and Pappy's B&B** (7615 Elkhorn Rd., 731/642-8129, www.mammypappysbb.com, $95), a 1900-era farmhouse in Springville. Located about 13 miles from Paris in rural countryside, this is a real getaway. Dannie and Katie Williams manage this family property, which has been lovingly cared for over the years. Each of the four bedrooms have hardwood floors and private baths. Breakfasts include homemade biscuits, and guests are also provided an evening snack.

PARIS LANDING STATE PARK

One of Tennessee's "resort parks," Paris Landing is an 841-acre park on the banks of Kentucky Lake. The 130-room park inn is located next to a large conference center and dining room, all with views of the lake. There is also an award-winning public golf course and swimming pool.

Day-trippers gravitate to the lake itself. Fishing is the most popular activity; catfish, crappie, bass, sauger, walleye, bluegill, and stripe are some of the most common catches. The park maintains two fishing piers and one launch ramp for public use. There are also more than 200 open and covered slips for rent.

The park has a public swimming beach, hiking trails, tennis, basketball and baseball facilities, and pavilions for picnics and parties.

Accommodations

For accommodations on the lake, you cannot beat **Paris Landing State Resort Park** (16055 Hwy. 79 N., 731/641-4465), which has hotel rooms, cabins, and campground facilities on the water. The 130-room inn ($60–100) looks like a concrete goliath, but the rooms are comfortable and all have beautiful views of the lake. The three-bedroom cabins ($155–175) can sleep up to 10 people, and are set on a secluded point overlooking the lake. The campground ($14.50–17.50) has both RV and tent sites, a laundry, bathhouse, and dump station.

FORT DONELSON NATIONAL BATTLEFIELD

On Valentine's Day in 1862, Union forces attacked the Confederate Fort Donelson on the banks of the Cumberland River. Fort Donelson National Battlefield (Hwy. 79, 931/232-5706, www.nps.gov/fodo) is now a national park. A visitors center with an exhibit, gift shop, and information boards is open daily 8 A.M.–4:30 P.M. The 15-minute video does a good job describing the battle and its importance in the Civil War.

A driving tour takes visitors to Fort Donelson, which overlooks the Cumberland River and may be one of the most picturesque forts in Tennessee. The earthen fort was built by Confederate soldiers and slaves over a period of about seven months.

You are also guided to the **Dover Hotel** (Petty St., 931/232-5706), which was used as the Confederate headquarters during the battle. The hotel, built between 1851 and 1853, is a handsome wood structure and has been restored to look as it did during the battle. It is located a few blocks away from downtown Dover. The hotel is open on weekends noon–4 P.M. from Memorial Day to Labor Day.

The **National Cemetery,** established after the war, was built on grounds where escaped slaves lived in a so-called "contraband camp" during the Civil War. The camp was established by the Union army to accommodate slaves who fled behind Union lines during the war. The freedmen and women worked for the Union army, often without pay. It was not until 1853 that the Union army allowed blacks to join as soldiers.

There are more than five miles of hiking trails at Fort Donelson National Battlefield, including the three-mile River Circle Trail and four-mile Donelson Trail. Both hikes begin at the visitors center. Picnic tables are located next to the river near the old fort.

DOVER

A small town set at the southern shore of the Cumberland River, Dover is a major gateway to the Land Between the Lakes. It is also the place where General Ulysses S. Grant earned the nickname "Unconditional Surrender" during the Civil War.

Accommodations

Located right next to Fort Donelson National Cemetery, **The Riverfront Plantation Inn** (165 Plantation Ln., 931/232-9492, www.riverfrontplantation.com, $85–110) is the best place to stay in Dover. A bed-and-breakfast inn with four rooms and a commanding view of the Cumberland River, this is truly a distinctive retreat. Originally built in 1859, the inn was mostly destroyed by fire in 1865. It served as a Union hospital during the Civil War. After the war, the house was rebuilt and remains much the same today.

The inn is a white brick building, graceful and stately above the river. Guest rooms are neat and cozy, and are named after Confederate generals, including Nathan Bedford Forrest and James Longstreet. All have views of the river, and two rooms may be rented together to form a two-bedroom suite. A hearty breakfast is served on the sunny dining porch overlooking the river.

Just west of the entrance to Land Between the Lakes, the **Dover Inn Motel** (1545 Donelson Pkwy., 931/232-5556, $60–70) has both traditional motel rooms and newly built

UNCONDITIONAL SURRENDER

It was the day after Valentine's Day, 1862, and things were looking bad for the Confederate army at Fort Donelson. The fort, located on the banks of the Cumberland River, was under attack from Federal forces and generals feared a siege.

Southern Generals Floyd and Pillow slipped away overnight, leaving General Buckner, a former friend and schoolmate of General Grant, in command. On the morning of February 16, Buckner wrote to Grant asking for the terms of surrender.

In Grant's famous reply, he said no terms other than "unconditional and immediate" surrender would be accepted. Buckner surrendered, and 13,000 Confederate men were taken prisoner. The path to the heart of the Confederacy was now open, and Grant earned a new nickname: "Unconditional Surrender" Grant.

© SUSANNA HENIGHAM POTTER

Fort Donelson is peaceful now; on Valentine's Day, 1862, it was the site of furious fighting.

WESTERN PLAINS

cabins with full kitchens. All rooms have telephones, cable TV, air-conditioning, and coffeemakers. They cater to hunters and fishermen who are going to Land Between the Lakes but don't want to camp. There is a swimming pool on the property.

Food

The most elegant dining in Dover is at the **Plantation Inn Dining Room** (165 Plantation Ln., 931/232-9492, Thurs.–Sat. 5–9 P.M., Sun. 10 A.M.–2 P.M., $10–25). Located in a bed-and-breakfast overlooking the Cumberland River, the Plantation Inn serves upscale dinners in its old-fashioned dining room or breezy dining porch. Country Cordon Bleu, crab cakes, and cheesy vegetarian pasta are a few of the options on the dinner menu. Entrées are served with your choice of a half-dozen different side dishes, including truffle mashed potatoes and squash casserole. Reservations are recommended, but not essential.

For something entirely different, head to the **B&M Dairy Freeze** (610 Donelson Pkwy., 931/232-5927, daily 10:30 A.M.–7 P.M., $4–8), a casual restaurant with burgers, hot dogs, and ice cream located just west of downtown Dover.

Located downtown, **The Dover Grille** (310 Donelson Pkwy., 931/232-7919, daily 7 A.M.–9 P.M., $5–12) serves burgers, dinner plates, southwestern platters, pasta, and salads.

Several miles east of the town is the **Log Cabin Cafe** (1394 Hwy. 79, 931/232-0220, Mon.–Sat. 6 A.M.–9 P.M., Sun. 6 A.M.–3 P.M., $6–15). The café serves traditional Southern food in a newly built log cabin. It is a popular pit stop for workmen; their breakfast will fuel you all day long.

Information

The **Stewart County Chamber of Commerce** (1008 Moore Rd., 931/232-8290, www.stewartcountyvacation.com) provides visitor information.

CROSS CREEKS NATIONAL WILDLIFE REFUGE

Four miles east of Dover is the 8,862-acre **Cross Creeks National Wildlife Refuge** (643 Wildlife Rd., 931/232-7477). Established in 1962, the refuge includes 12 miles of bottomlands along the Cumberland River, plus nearby rocky bluffs and rolling hills. There is also marsh, brush, and farmland. The refuge is an important habitat for geese, ducks, raptors, shorebirds, wading birds, and neotropical migratory birds. In January, when the bird population is at its peak, as many as 60,000 birds may be in the refuge. Mallard ducks make up the majority. American Bald Eagles also live in the refuge, along with great blue heron, wild turkeys, muskrat, coyote, and bobcat. Farms within the refuge grow corn, soybeans, grain sorghum, and wheat; a portion of each harvest is left in the field for wildlife to consume.

The refuge is open to visitors during daylight hours from March 16 through November 14. The visitors center is open year-round Mon.–Fri. 7 A.M.–3:30 P.M. A network of paved and gravel roads along the southern shore of the Cumberland are the best places to view the refuge. Rattlesnake Trail is a one-mile hiking path through the refuge.

Hunting is allowed in the refuge at certain times of year. Camping and campfires are prohibited.

To find Cross Creeks, drive about four miles east of Dover on Highway 49. Look for Wildlife Drive on your left.

Land Between the Lakes

The narrow finger of land that lies between the Cumberland and Tennessee Rivers is a natural wonderland. Comprising 170,000 acres of land and wrapped by 300 miles of undeveloped river shoreline, the Land Between the Lakes National Recreation Area has become one of the most popular natural areas in this region of the country. Split between Tennessee and Kentucky, the area provides unrivaled opportunities to camp, hike, boat, or just simply drive through quiet wilderness.

The area lies between what is now called Kentucky Lake (the Tennessee River) and Lake Barkley (the Cumberland River). At its narrowest point, the distance between these two bodies of water is only one mile. The drive from north to south is 43 miles. About one-third of the park is in Tennessee; the rest is in Kentucky. It is managed by the U.S. Forest Service, an agency of the U.S. Department of Agriculture.

History

Land Between the Lakes was not always a natural and recreational area. Native

Americans settled here, drawn to the fertile soil, nearness of the rivers, and gentle terrain. European settlers followed, and between about 1800 and the 1960s the area, then called Between the Rivers, saw thriving small settlements. Residents farmed and traded along the rivers, which were served by steamboats.

In many respects, settlers Between the Rivers were even more isolated than settlers in other parts of what was then the western frontier of the United States. They did not necessarily associate with one state or another, instead forming a distinct identity of their own. During the Civil War, it was necessary to finally determine the border between Tennessee and Kentucky, since this line also marked the border between the Union and the Confederacy.

It was during another period of upheaval in the United States that the future of the Between the Lakes region changed forever. In the midst of the Great Depression, Congress created the Tennessee Valley Authority, which would improve soil conditions, ease flooding, bring electricity, and create jobs in Tennessee. One of TVA's projects was the Kentucky Dam, which was built between 1938 and 1944 and impounded the Tennessee River. In 1957, work began on Barkley Dam, which would impound the Cumberland River and put an end to floods that damaged crops and destroyed property along the river.

About 25 years later, president John F. Kennedy announced that the U.S. Government would buy out residents of the land between the Cumberland and Tennessee Rivers to create a new park, which would serve as an example of environmental management and recreational use. The project was to bring much-needed economic development to the area by attracting visitors to the park.

The project was not without opponents, who objected to the government's use of eminent domain to take over lands that were privately owned. Residents lamented the loss of unique communities in the lake region. More than 2,300 people were removed to create Land Between the Lakes. In all, 96,000 of the 170,000 acres that make up LBL were purchased or taken from private hands.

Over time, however, the controversy of the creation of the park have faded, and the Land Between the Lakes has become a well-loved park. It is the third most-visited park in Tennessee, behind only the Smoky Mountains and Cherokee National Forest.

PLANNING YOUR TIME

Several of the best attractions at Land Between the Lakes charge admission. If you are planning to visit all or most of them, consider one of the packages offered by the Forest Service. The discount package allows you to visit each attraction once over a seven-day period. The LBL Fun Card gives you 10 admissions to any of three attractions. It does not expire. You can buy packages at either the north or south welcome station or the Golden Pond Visitor Center.

SIGHTS

Driving south-to-north along the main road, or trace, that runs along the middle of the park, you will find the major attractions within Land Between the Lakes.

Great Western Iron Furnace

About 11 miles inside the park is the Great Western Iron Furnace, built by Brian, Newell, and Company in 1854. If you have traveled around this part of Tennessee much, you would have come to recognize the distinctive shape of the old iron furnaces, which dot the landscape in the counties between Nashville and the Tennessee River. Like the Great Western Furnace, these plants were used to create high-quality iron from iron ore deposits in the earth.

The Great Western Furnace operated for less than two years. By 1856 panic over reported slave uprisings and the coming of the Civil War caused the plant to shut down. It would never make iron again.

◖ The Homeplace

Just beyond the furnace is The Homeplace (Mar.–Nov. daily 10 A.M.–5 P.M., $2–5), a living-history museum that depicts life in Between the Rivers in about 1850. At the middle of the 19th century, Between the Rivers was home to an iron ore industry and hundreds of farmers. These farmers raised crops and livestock for their own use, as well as to sell where they could. In 1850, about 10,000 people lived in Between the Rivers, including 2,500 slaves and 125 free blacks.

The Homeplace re-creates an 1850 farmstead. Staff dress up in period clothes and perform the labors that settlers would have done: They sow seeds in the spring, harvest in the summer and fall, and prepare the fields for the next year in the winter. The farm includes a dogtrot cabin, where you can see how settlers would have lived, cooked, and slept. Out back there is a small garden, a plot of tobacco, pigs, sheep, oxen, and a barn. You may see farmers splitting shingles, working oxen, sewing quilts, making candles, or any other of the dozens of tasks that settlers performed on a regular basis.

The Homeplace publishes a schedule that announces when certain activities will take place, such as canning, sheering of sheep, or harvesting tobacco. Even if you come when there is no special program, you will be able to see staff taking on everyday tasks, and you can ask them about any facet of life on the frontier.

Elk and Bison Prairie

Archaeological evidence shows that elk and bison once grazed in Tennessee and Kentucky, including the area between the rivers. Settlers quickly destroyed these herds, however. Both bison and elk were easy to hunt, and they were desirable for their meat and skins. By 1800, bison had been killed off, and about 50 years later elk were gone too.

When Land Between the Lakes was created, elk and bison were reintroduced to the area. The **South Bison Range** across the road from the Homeplace is one of the places where bison now live. The bison herd that roams on about 160 acres here can sometimes be seen from the main road, or from side roads bordering the range.

You can see both bison and elk at the Elk and Bison Prairie, a 700-acre restoration project located near the mid-point of the Land Between the Lakes. In 1996, 39 bison were relocated from the south prairie here, and 29 elk were transported from Canada. Since then, the population of both animals has grown.

Visitors may drive through the range along a one-mile loop. Admission is $5 per vehicle. You are advised to take your time, roll down your windows, and keep your eyes peeled for a sign of the animals. The best time to view elk and bison is in the early morning or late afternoon. At other times of day, you will enjoy the sights and sounds of the grassland.

Golden Pond Visitor Center and Planetarium

For the best overview of the history, nature, and significance of the Land Between the Lakes, stop at the Golden Pond Visitor Center and Planetarium (daily 9 A.M.–5 P.M., free). The visitors center is home to a small museum about the park, where you can also watch a video about the elk that have been restored on the Elk and Bison Range. There is also a gift shop, restrooms, and picnic area.

The planetarium screens several programs daily about astronomy and nature. On Saturdays and Sundays at 1 P.M. you can get a sneak peak at the night sky above. Planetarium shows cost $3 for ages 13 and up, $2 for ages 5–12, and are free for children four and under.

Golden Pond was the name of Land Between the Lakes' largest town before the park was created. Golden Pond, also called Fungo, was a vibrant town that, at its peak, had a hotel, bank, restaurants, and other retail outlets. During Prohibition, farmers made moonshine in the woods and sold it in Golden Pond. Golden Pond whiskey was sought after in back alley saloons as far away as Chicago. When Land Between the Lakes was created in 1963, Golden Pond had a population of about 200 people. Families moved their homes and relocated to communities outside the park. In 1970, when the historic society unveiled a marker at the site of Golden Pond, the strains of "Taps" rang out over the hills.

You can visit the site of Golden Pond by driving a few miles east of the visitors center on Highway 80. There is a picnic area.

Woodlands Nature Station

The final major attraction in Land Between the Lakes is the Woodlands Nature Station (270/924-2020). Geared to children, the nature station introduces visitors to animals including bald eagles, coyotes, opossum, and deer. There are also opportunities for staff-led hiking trips. Special events and activities take place nearly every weekend, and during the week in summertime.

From April to October the nature station is open Monday through Saturday 9 A.M.–5 P.M. and Sunday 10 A.M.–5 P.M. In March and November it is open Wednesday through Saturday 9 A.M.–P.M. and Sunday 10 A.M.–5 P.M. The nature station is closed December through February.

Center Furnace

You can see the ruins of what was once the largest iron furnace in the Land Between the Lakes along the Center Furnace Trail. Along the short (three-tenths of a mile) walk you will see signs that describe the process of making iron and explain why it was practiced Between the Rivers.

Center Furnace was built between 1844 and 1846. It continued to operate until 1912, much longer than any other furnace in the area.

RECREATION

Promoting outdoor recreation is one of the objectives of Land Between the Lakes. Visitors can enjoy hiking, biking or horseback riding; hunting and fishing; and camping. There is even an area specially designated for all-terrain vehicles.

Trails

There are 200 miles of hiking trails in Land Between the Lakes. Some of these are also open for mountain biking and horseback riding.

The **Fort Henry Trails** are a network of 29.3 miles of trails near the southern entrance to the park, some of which follow the shoreline of the Kentucky Lake. The intricate network of trails allows hikers to choose from a three-mile loop to something much longer.

Access the trails from the south welcome station, or from the Fort Henry Trails parking area, at the end of Fort Henry Road. These trails criss-cross the grounds once occupied by the Confederate Fort Henry. They are for hikers only.

The **North-South Trail** treks the entire length of the Land Between the Lakes. From start to finish, it is 58.6 miles. Three backcountry camping shelters are available along the way for backpackers. The trail crosses the main road in several locations. Portions of the trail are open to horseback riders. The portion from the Golden Pond Visitor Center to the northern end is also open to mountain bikers.

The 2.2-mile **Honker Lake Loop Trail** begins at the Woodlands Nature Station. This trail is open to hikers only. Sightings of fallow deer and giant Canada geese are common along this trail. The banks of nearby Hematite Lake are littered with bits of blue stone, remnants of slag from Center Iron Furnace.

Finally, at the northern end of the park are the **Canal Loop Trails,** a network of hike/bike trails that depart from the north welcome station. These trails meander along the shores of both Kentucky Lake and Lake Barkley. The entire loop is 14.2 miles, but connector trails enable you to fashion a shorter hike or ride if you want.

A detailed map showing all hiking, biking, and horseback trails can be picked up at any of the park visitors centers. You can rent bikes at Hillman Ferry and Piney Campgrounds.

Off-Highway Vehicles

There are more than 100 miles of trail for off-highway vehicles. OHV permits are available for $20 for one to three days, $32 for seven days, and $65 for an annual pass; passes may be purchased at any Land Between the Lakes visitor center. Call 270/924-2000 in advance to find out if any of the trails are closed due to bad weather or poor conditions.

Fishing and Boating

Land Between the Lakes offers excellent fishing. The best season for fishing is spring, from April to June, when fish move to shallow waters to spawn. Crappie, largemouth bass, and a variety of sunfish may be caught at this time.

Summer and fall offer good fishing, while winter is fair. A fishing license from the state in which you will be fishing is required; these may be purchased from businesses outside of the park. Specific size requirements and open dates may be found at any of the visitors centers.

There are 19 different lake access points where you can put in a boat. Canoe rentals are available at the Energy Lake Campground.

Hunting

Controlled hunting is one of the tools that the Forest Service uses to manage populations of wild animals in Land Between the Lakes. Hunting also draws thousands of visitors each year. The annual spring turkey hunt and fall deer hunts are the most popular.

Specific rules govern each hunt, and in many cases hunters must apply in advance for a permit. Hunters must also have a $20 LBL Hunter Use Permit, as well as the applicable state licenses. For details on hunting regulations, call the park at 270/924-2065.

CAMPING

There are nine campgrounds at Land Between the Lakes. All campgrounds have facilities for tent or trailer camping.

Most campgrounds are open from March 1 to November 1. Tent campsites cost $12–13 per night; RV sites range $18–32, depending on whether there is access to electricity, water, and sewer services.

Reservations are accepted for select campsites at Piney, Energy Lake, Hillman's Ferry, and Wrangler Campgrounds up to six months in advance. Call the LBL headquarters in Kentucky at 270/924-2000 or visit the website at www.lbl.org to make a reservation.

Piney Campground

Located on the southern tip of Land Between the Lakes, Piney Campground is convenient to visitors arriving from the Tennessee side of the park. Piney has more than 300 campsites; 281 have electricity, 44 have electricity, water, and sewer, and 59 are primitive tent sites.

There are also nine rustic one-bedroom camping shelters with a ceiling fan, table and chairs, electric outlets, and large porch. Sleeping accommodations are one double bed and a bunk bed. Outside there is a picnic table and fire ring. There are no bathrooms; shelter guests use the same bathhouses as other campers. Camp shelters cost $35–37 per night and sleep up to four people.

Piney's amenities include a camp store, bike rental, archery range, playground, swimming beach, boat ramp, and fishing pier.

Energy Lake Campground

Near the midpoint of Land Between the Lakes, Energy Lake Campground has tent and trailer campsites, electric sites, and group camp facilities.

Hillman Ferry Campground

Located near the northern end of Land Between the Lakes, Hillman Ferry has 380 tent and RV campsites. It is nestled on the shores of Kentucky Lake, between Moss Creek and Pisgah Bay.

Electric and non-electric sites are available. There is a dumping station, bathhouses with showers and flush toilets, drinking water, a camp store, swimming area, coin-operated laundry, and bike rentals.

Boat and Horse Camping

In addition to the campgrounds listed above, Land Between the Lakes operates five lakeside camping areas that are designed for boaters who want to spend the night. Rushing Creek/Jones Creek is the most developed of these camping areas; it has 40 tent or RV sites and a bathhouse with showers and flush toilets. Other campsites, including Birmingham Ferry/Smith Bay, Cravens Bay, Fenton, and Gatlin Point, have chemical toilets, tent camping sites, and grills.

LBL also has Wrangler's Campground, designed for horseback riders. In addition to tent and RV sites, there are camping shelters and horse stalls. Amenities include a camp store, bathhouses, coin laundry, and playground.

Backcountry Camping

Backcountry camping is allowed year-round in Land Between the Lakes. All you need is a backcountry permit and the right gear to enjoy unlimited choices of campsites along the shoreline or in the woodlands.

FOOD

There are no restaurants in Land Between the Lakes. There are vending machines with snacks and sodas at the Homeplace, Golden Pond Visitor Center, and the Nature Station. Picnic facilities abound.

There is a McDonald's at the southern entrance to the park. Dover, five miles east, has a half-dozen eateries. Twenty miles to the west, Paris has dozens of different restaurants.

INFORMATION AND SERVICES

The Forest Service maintains a useful website about Land Between the Lakes at www.lbl.org. You can also call 270/924-2000 to request maps and information sheets. The park headquarters is located at the Golden Pond Visitor Center.

When you arrive, stop at the nearest welcome or visitors center for up-to-date advisories and activity schedules. Each of the welcome centers and the visitors center are open daily 9 A.M.–5 P.M.

The **Land Between the Lakes Association** (800/455-5897, www.friendsof lbl.org) organizes volunteer opportunities and publishes a detailed tour guide to the park, which includes historical and natural anecdotes.

Jackson

Jackson is the largest city between Nashville and Memphis, and the center of commerce and business for rural West Tennessee. Every Pringles potato chip in the world is made in Jackson, which also hosts a number of events including a Division One women's basketball tournament, the Miss Tennessee pageant, and the West Tennessee State Fair.

Jackson owes its existence to the railroads, and the city has preserved this history at a top-notch museum set right next to the railroad tracks. Jackson is also home to a museum dedicated to the life and death of famous railroad engineer Casey Jones, and another that zeroes in on that endearing art form, rock-a-billy.

SIGHTS

Jackson's city center is about five miles south of I-40, and the roadways between the interstate and downtown are cluttered with strip malls, motels, and traffic. Most of the attractions, with the exception of Casey Jones Village, are downtown on the blocks surrounding the stately courthouse square.

Casey Jones Home and Railroad Museum

In 1980, the home of the legendary railroad engineer was moved from the city of Jackson to Casey Jones Village, a plaza of shops and restaurants just off the interstate north of Jackson. The museum includes Jones's white clapboard home and a replica of the engine that he rode to his death in 1900. The home and engine form the centerpiece of the Casey Jones Home and Railroad Museum (56 Casey Jones Ln., 731/668-1222, www.caseyjones.com, Mon.–Sun. 9 A.M.–5 P.M., adults $4, children 6–12 $3, children under 6 free), which tells the story of Casey Jones's life and the legend that surrounds him to this day. Exhibits document every detail

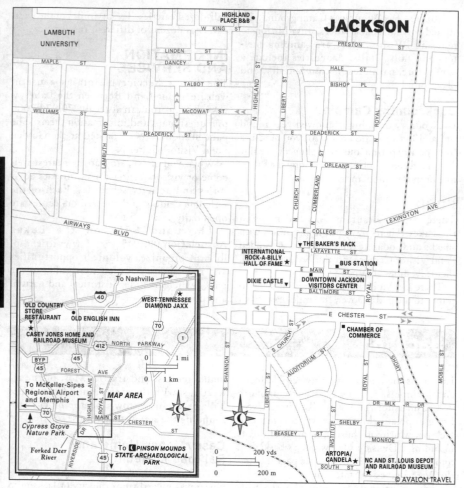

of the deadly 1900 crash that took his life, but some of the most fascinating parts of the museum deal with the legend of Casey Jones that evolved after his death. There are also elaborate model train sets that you can run for a few quarters. The home and museum is open until 8 P.M. from Memorial Day to Labor Day.

N.C. & St. Louis Depot and Railroad Museum

Jackson owes it existence to the railroads that passed through the town, and the N.C. & St. Louis Depot and Railroad Museum (582 S. Royal St., 731/425-8223, Mon.–Sat. 10 A.M.–3 P.M., free) documents much of the city's railroad history. Located inside Jackson's oldest railroad station a few blocks south of downtown, the museum walls are covered with photographs and memorabilia of the railroads. There is a large model train in the rear of the station, and outside visitors can explore a dining car and engine.

Over the railroad tracks from the museum is a covered fountain whose waters once drew thousands of people to Jackson. The **Electro Chalybeate Well** (604 S. Royal St.) was discovered in the late 1800s and its waters were reputed to cure a host of ailments. In recent years the city of Jackson built the fountain, gazebo, and benches around the well. You can drink the water from a circle of water fountains if you like.

International Rock-a-Billy Hall of Fame

As the city that lays claim to Carl Perkins, Jackson is home to the International Rock-a-Billy Hall of Fame (105 N. Church St., 731/423-5440, www.rockabilly.org, Mon.–Fri. 10 A.M.–4 P.M., adults $10). This storefront museum features exhibits about a number of the genre's famous performers. There is also a room of Elvis memorabilia, and a performance space for concerts and dancing. A tour with enthusiastic guide Linda McGee costs $10 and is best-suited for hard-core rock-a-billy fans. There are line-dancing lessons Monday beginning at 6 P.M., and live music on Friday night starting at 6:30 P.M.

Bemis Mill Village Museum

The history of Bemis, a cotton mill town established in 1900, is recorded at the Bemis Mill Village Museum (2 N. Missouri St., 731/424-0739, www.bemishistory.org). The museum is housed in the Bemis Auditorium, a large, imposing building constructed in 1922 to be the focal point of community life for the townspeople. The building is an elegant, sophisticated example of Beaux Arts design. It houses exhibits about the Bemis Brothers Bag Company, as well as life in an early-20th-century company town.

ENTERTAINMENT
Shopping

Across Royal Sreet from the N.C. & St. Louis Depot and Railroad Museum is **Artopia** (575 S. Royal St., 731/554-2929), a gallery housed in an old hotel. Each old guest room is filled with the work of different artists, and items include paintings, sculpture, fabric, and much more.

There is also a salon, coffee shop, and restaurant. Artopia is open every day, and stays open until 9 P.M. on Thursday, Friday, and Saturday.

The **Old Medina Winery** (2894 Old Medina Rd., 731/256-1400, Mon.–Sat. 9 A.M.–6 P.M., Sun. noon–5 P.M.) has two rooms and a pleasant outdoor patio where you can taste Tennessee-made wine and other food products. Old Medina Winery is the new home of Lauderdale Cellars, a winery once located in Ripley.

Events

Jackson puts on three major annual events. The **Shannon Street Blues and Heritage Festival** (731/427-7573, www.jacksondowntown.com) takes place in June at the West Tennessee Farmer's Market and is the work of the Downtown Development Corporation. The Rock-a-Billy Hall of Fame organizes an **International Rock-a-Billy Festival** (731/427-6262, www.rockabillyhall.org) every August, and the Casey Jones Village puts on an **Old Time Music Fest** (731/668-1223, www.caseyjonesvillage.com) in September.

Every September sees the **West Tennessee State Fair** (731/424-0151), a week of competitions, amusements, performances, and rides at the Jackson Fairgrounds Park.

SPORTS AND RECREATION
Parks

A few miles southwest of downtown Jackson is **Cypress Grove Nature Park** (Hwy. 70 W., 731/425-8316), a pleasant park with boardwalks, picnic facilities, walking paths, and an observation tower.

Spectator Sports

The **West Tennessee Diamond Jaxx** (4 Fun Pl., 731/988-5299, www.diamondjaxx.com) play in Pringles Field just off I-40 in Jackson. A farm team of the Chicago Cubs, the Jaxx put on a good show for fans during their season from April to October. Admission is $4.50–9.50.

ACCOMMODATIONS

For the most luxurious accommodations in Jackson, choose (**Highland Place Bed &**

THE LEGEND OF CASEY JONES

Casey Jones was born John Luther Jones, but was better known as Casey after his hometown, Cayce, in Kentucky. He started as a telegrapher for the Mobile and Ohio Railroad in Kentucky, and worked his way up to be brakeman, fireman, and eventually engineer. Casey had a reputation for running the trains on time, whatever it took.

In the early-morning hours of April 30, 1900, Jones was running a passenger train from Memphis to Canton, Mississippi, when he crashed into the tail end of a freight train that was blocking a portion of the track near Vaughn, Mississippi. Jones died when his engine No. 382 collided with the freight train and veered off the tracks. Jones was the only person killed in the accident.

The story of Casey Jones did not end with his death, however. An African-American engine wiper, Wallace Saunders, started to sing a song that he composed about the dead engineer, and soon "The Ballad of Casey Jones" was a well-known folk song. The professional songwriting team Sibert and Newton copyrighted the song in 1909 and it became one of the most famous songs in America. Neither the Jones family or Wallace Saunders ever received a penny from its success.

The story of Casey Jones's life and death was immortalized on television, film, and stage. His widow, Janie Jones, and accident survivor, Simeon Webb, remained minor celebrities for the rest of their lives.

The story of Casey Jones is told at the Casey Jones Home and Railroad Museum in Jackson.

the Casey Jones Home and Railroad Museum

© SUSANNA HENIGHAN POTTER

Breakfast (519 N. Highland Ave., 731/427-1472, www.highlandplace.com, $145–175). Set in a stately redbrick historic home along central Highland Avenue, a five-minute drive from downtown, the inn has four rooms ranging from a three-room suite to single rooms. Each room has a private bath, cable television, and wireless Internet access. The rooms are decorated with antique and modern handmade furniture. All guests have the run of the numerous public rooms, including a living room, library, and breakfast room. It sure beats a standard hotel room.

The Old English Inn (2267 N. Highland Ave., 731/668-1571, www.oldenglishinn.com, $60–75) is set a mile or so south of the interstate. Its 103 rooms include suites and wheelchair-accessible rooms. The lobby and common areas enjoy distinctive flair, included stained glass and a fireplace, and all the rooms are nicely furnished with dark wood. The Old English Inn calls itself a Christian hotel, although guests of all religious affiliations are welcome.

FOOD

C Dixie Castle (215 E. Baltimore, 731/423-3359, Mon.–Fri. 10:30 A.M.–2 P.M., Mon.–Sat. 5–9 P.M., $5–12) attracts a large local crowd for lunch and dinner. This diner-style restaurant serves plate lunch specials, burgers, and sandwiches. The food is home-style, with large portions. You'll be hard-pressed to find a table at the peak of the lunch rush. At dinner, they offer steaks, pork chops, and chicken dinners. They do a brisk take-out trade as well, and the servers are some of the friendliest in town.

Also downtown, **The Baker's Rack** (203 E. Lafayette, 731/424-6163, Mon.–Thurs. 7 A.M.–5 P.M., Fri. 7 A.M.–3 P.M., $2.50–9) serves a diverse menu of hot and cold sandwiches, baked potatoes, plate lunches, and salads. They also make decadent desserts: Try the red velvet cake or "better than sex" cake. For breakfast, choose from biscuits, eggs on toast, oatmeal, French toast, or a generous breakfast platter with all the fixings.

In Casey Jones Village off I-40, the **Old Country Store Restaurant** (56 Casey Jones Ln., 731/668-1223, www.caseyjones.com,

daily 6:30 A.M.–9 P.M., $5–9) serves specials like country ham, smothered chicken, and fried catfish, plus burgers and barbecue. The breakfast bar is a popular choice for those with a big appetite. They also have a fruit bar and the usual breakfast choices of eggs, biscuits, pancakes, and omelets.

One of the best of the newer restaurants in town is **Candela** (575 S. Royal St., 731/554-3663, Tues.–Sat. 11 A.M.–2 P.M., Thurs.–Sat. 5–9 P.M., $7–17). Located in Artopia, Candela takes a creative approach to dining, and the results are usually excellent. Lunch features tortellini pasta, seared salmon, shrimp salad, and a variety of sandwiches. For dinner try the stuffed mushrooms, lobster ravioli, or fish of the day.

The **West Tennessee Farmer's Market** (91 New Market St., 731/425-8310) takes place under shelters in downtown Jackson daily 7 A.M.–4 P.M. in the summer.

INFORMATION AND SERVICES

Maps and general information on Jackson can be found at the **Jackson Downtown Development Corporation** (314 E. Main St., 731/427-7573) or the **Jackson Area Chamber of Commerce** (197 Auditorium St., 731/423-2200).

The **Jackson-Madison County Library** (433 E. Lafayette St., 731/425-8600) is one of the nicest public libraries in West Tennessee.

GETTING THERE AND AROUND

Jackson is located about midway between Nashville and Memphis along I-40, and most people drive here. The regional McKellar-Sipes Airport (MKL, www.mklairport.com) has on-and-off commercial air service, subject to the ups and downs of the airline industry. Check with airport officials to find out if commercial service is available.

Photographers have been known to make a detour to photograph the iconic Jackson Main Street Greyhound bus terminal, with its retro art deco style. The station is convenient to several attractions and restaurants, but not close to any hotels. There is daily service to

WESTERN PLAINS

Memphis and Nashville; Paducah, Kentucky; and Jackson, Mississippi.

While trains still travel on Jackson's famous tracks, there is no passenger service to or from the city.

◖ PINSON MOUNDS STATE ARCHAEOLOGICAL PARK

One of the largest complexes of mounds ever built by Woodland Indians is found 10 miles south of Jackson. Pinson Mounds (460 Ozier Rd., 731/988-5614, free), now a state park, is a group of at least 17 mounds believed to have been built beginning around 50 B.C. The mounds were discovered in 1820 by Joel Pinson, part of a surveying team that was mapping new territory bought from the Chickasaw Indians in 1818. Early archaeological digs were carried out in the late 1800s, but it was not until 1961 that the first major investigation of the site was completed by scientists from the University of Tennessee.

Despite continuing archaeology on the site, many mysteries remain: Among them is the significance of the design and arrangement of the mounds and why the mound-builders abandoned the site around A.D. 500. Some scientists have argued that the mounds were arranged as markers for the summer and winter solstices.

Visitors to Pinson Mounds begin within a mound replica, which houses a museum and bookstore. The museum is dedicated to telling the story of what is known about the mysterious mounds and the people who built them. The mounds themselves are spread out along six miles of hiking trails that meander through the archaeological park. Many of the trails are across open fields, and walking can be hot during the summer months. A bike is an ideal way to get around, but you need to bring your own since there is no rental facility.

The park museum is open Monday–Saturday 8 A.M.–4:30 P.M. and Sunday 1–5 P.M. The rest of the park, including its hiking trails and picnic area, are open until dusk.

Events

Archaeofest is a festival celebrating Native American culture. It takes place every September and includes artistic demonstrations, food and craft vendors, storytelling, flintknapping, and more. Contact the park office for more information.

Camping

Pinson Mounds has a group camp facility that can accommodate up to 32 people. There is also a day-use picnic area.

BETHEL SPRINGS

About 30 miles south of Jackson on Highway 45, near the community of Bethel Springs, is **Ada's Unusual Country Store** (9653 Hwy. 45, 731/934-9310, Mon.–Sat. 8 A.M.–5 P.M.), which is unusual indeed. The shelves are packed with organic and natural food items, including grains, flour, pastas, and snacks. You can buy fresh local eggs, honey, and milk; Amish cheese and cookbooks; and homemade breads and sweets. For a meal on the go, you can get cold drinks, fresh-made sandwiches, and ice cream.

© SUSANNA HENIGHAN POTTER

The tallest of the mounds at Pinson Mounds, shown here, is 33 feet.

South Along the Tennessee

The Tennessee River flows by Clifton and southward to the state line. It passes Tennessee's most lovely river town, Savannah, and the site of the state's bloodiest Civil War battle, Shiloh.

CLIFTON

Pulitzer Prize–winning author T. S. Stribling was born in the river town of Clifton in 1881. His works include the 1,479-page trilogy *The Forge, The Store,* and *Unfinished Cathedral,* which portray the history of a Florence, Alabama, family from the Civil War to the 1920s. He won the Pulitzer Prize for fiction in 1933 for *The Store.* Stribling was one of the first Southern writers to speak out about issues of social conscience. He also wrote formulaic adventure novels and detective stories. His autobiography, *Laughing Stock,* was published posthumously in 1969.

A museum dedicated to Stribling and his life's work is located in the Clifton Public Library. This 1924 Craftsman bungalow is where Stribling and his wife, Lou Ella, lived in their retirement. The museum includes Stribling's typewriter, Bible, papers, and other personal articles. The **T. S. Stribling Museum** (300 E. Water St., 931/676-3678, Tues.–Fri. 11:30 A.M.–6:30 P.M., free) is operated by the City of Clifton.

SAVANNAH

A picturesque town on the eastern bank of the Tennessee River, Savannah has historic homes, a good museum, and the greatest selection of restaurants and accommodation in this part of the state.

In its early life, the town was Rudd's Ferry, named for James Rudd, who operated a ferry across the river. The ferry was taken over by David Robinson, whose wife is said to have renamed the town Savannah after her hometown in Georgia. In 1830, Savannah became the seat of Hardin County and soon developed a reputation as a wealthy, cultured town.

Tennessee River Museum

Savannah is a river town, and the river is one of its main attractions. The Tennessee River Museum (507 Main St., 731/925-2364, Mon.–Sat. 9 A.M.–5 P.M., Sun. 1–5 P.M., $2) documents the history of the region and the river. Exhibits detail the prehistoric peoples of the region, and include an original red stone effigy pipe found inside one of the Shiloh Indian Mounds a few miles south. There are also exhibits on Shiloh and the river during the Civil War, riverboats, and the economic uses of the river, including pearl farming and mussels. One of the most interesting exhibits features receipts issued by Savannah merchants to the U.S. Army party that was escorting 2,500 Cherokee Indians down the river on the Trail of Tears in 1838.

The museum is a good first stop for visitors to the area, and staff can provide information about other attractions in the area. Through a partnership with Shiloh National Military Park, guests who show their Shiloh parking pass receive free entry to the museum.

Historic Homes

David Robinson built the **Cherry Mansion** (265 W. Main St.) on the riverbank, on top of what historians believe was an Indian mound. Robinson gave the mansion to his daughter when she married William H. Cherry, for whom it was named. The house, which is closed to the public, is where U.S. General Ulysses S. Grant stayed during the days leading up to the battle of Shiloh. Cherry was a noted Union sympathizer, and the mansion remained a Union headquarters and field hospital during the war. Although the house is privately owned, visitors are welcome to stop and look. There is a river overlook next door.

Savannah was settled between 1830 and 1850, but many of the old houses were damaged or destroyed during the Civil War. However, beautiful homes were rebuilt and many of these remain in the leafy residential

WESTERN PLAINS

GENERAL JOHNSTON

Gen. Albert Sidney Johnston, the Confederate commander of the western department of the army, was concentrating all available forces at Corinth, Mississippi, in early April 1862. His objective was to launch an offensive against the Union army under the command of Gen. Ulysses S. Grant at Pittsburg Landing, Tennessee, before Union reinforcements arrived.

On April 3, Johnston ordered his troops to march north, towards the engagement. Heavy rains and bad roads slowed their forward progress, and the Southern troops lost a day on their journey, a delay that would prove significant in the coming days.

The Confederates arrived at their camp south of Pittsburg Landing on the late afternoon of April 5, and Johnston decided to delay the attack until morning. During the evening, he and his second-in-command, P. G. T. Beauregard, disagreed about the coming fight; Beauregard argued against attack, saying that the Union army would not be surprised. But Johnston would not be deterred. He wanted to attack the Union forces before reinforcements from Nashville arrived.

As it turned out, the Union army was surprised by the Confederate attack in the early-morning hours of April 6. Soldiers described the disorder and chaos of the Union camps as word was quickly spread about the advancing fighters. Gen. Grant, who was breakfasting at the Cherry Mansion in Savannah, a few miles north of Shiloh, was surprised by the sound of gunfire and rushed to the scene.

Gen. Johnston would not live to see the outcome of the battle that he orchestrated. In the middle of the afternoon on the first day of fighting, just before the Confederates reached the high-water mark of their efforts, Johnston was struck by a mini-ball in the leg. His companions did not realize at first the seriousness of his injury, and neither did Johnston. But at 2:45 P.M. on April 6, the Confederate general died, passing command to Beauregard.

Johnston was the highest-ranking officer on either side of the Civil War to be killed in active duty.

area just north of Savannah's Main Street. The homes are elegant examples of fine homes of the late 19th century.

Pick up a guide to the **Savannah Walking Tour** at the Tennessee River Museum (507 Main St., 731/925-2364).

Haley Memorial

Savannah is where the paternal grandparents of Pulitzer Prize–winning author Alex Haley are buried. Alex Haley Sr. operated Rudd's Ferry, and his wife, Queen Haley, worked in the Cherry mansion for the Cherry family. Haley's novel *Queen* was inspired by his grandmother's life. The couple's shared tombstone is located in the Savannah Cemetery. To find the Haley Memorial, take Cherry Street from downtown Savannah and over a small bridge and enter the cemetery. Take the first gravel road to your right, and then walk over the hill, taking a right at the Y. The Haleys,

as well as Alex Haley Sr.'s first wife, Tennie, share a gravestone.

Accommodations

You can get a comfortable bed at the **Savannah Lodge** (585 Pickwick St., 731/925-8586, $35–55), a motel that boasts the basics for its guests. Several national chains also have locations in Savannah.

Food

Worleybird Cafe (990 Pickwick St., 731/926-4882, Mon.–Sat. 5 A.M.–9 P.M., Sun. 5 A.M.–2 P.M., $5–12) is a popular choice for Savannah's locals. Named for beloved son of the soil, country musician Daron Worley, the café serves sandwiches, Cajun catfish, steaks, chicken cordon bleu, and salads, plus eggs, biscuits, and pancakes in the morning.

Another good choice for home-style cooking in Savannah is **Toll House Restaurant**

(610 Wayne Rd., 731/925-5128, Mon.–Sat. 5 A.M.–9 P.M., Sun. 6 A.M.–2 P.M., $4–9), whose home fries and eggs draw a crowd in the morning. At lunch and dinner, there is an ample buffet with traditional favorites like macaroni and cheese, fried catfish, and beef tips.

For a more refined dining experience, go to the **Uptown** (390 Main St., 731/926-1911, Mon.–Sat. 11 A.M.–8 P.M., $12–19), a wine bar and bistro with seafood, pasta, and steak, as well as superb desserts.

Information

Stop at the **Tennessee River Museum** (507 Main St., 731/925-2364, Mon.–Sat. 9 A.M.–5 P.M., Sun. 1–5 P.M.) to pick up maps and other information about Savannah.

You can also contact the **Hardin County Convention and Visitors Bureau** (731/925-8181, www.tourhardincounty.org) for information.

(SHILOH NATIONAL MILITARY PARK

The Shiloh National Military Park (1055 Pittsburg Landing Rd., 731/689-5696, www.nps.gov/shil, daily 8 A.M.–5 P.M., $3) is set along the western shore of the Tennessee River about eight miles south of Crump. The Battle of Shiloh is one of the most remembered of the Civil War; it was the battle which demonstrated to both North and South that the war would be a longer and harder fight than either side had imagined. Shiloh today is a landscape of alternating open fields and wooded forest, populated by hundreds of monuments to soldiers who fought and died at Shiloh on April 6–7, 1862. The peacefulness of the present brings into even greater focus the violence of the battle that took place here almost 150 years ago and claimed nearly 24,000 casualties.

You can drive around the battlefield, but some of the most important sites are a short walk from the road. At the visitors center there is a small

WESTERN PLAINS

© SUSANNA HENIGHAN POTTER

Some two-thirds of the 3,695 people buried at the Shiloh National Cemetery are unidentified.

museum and you can watch a 25-minute video about the battle. The film, made in 1956, was one of the first park service films to use live actors. A new movie is in the works.

Sights within the park include the peach orchard, now being regrown, where soldiers described the peach blossoms falling like snow on the dead and injured; the "bloody pond," where injured men crawled for water, and in some cases, to die; and the Hornet's Nest, the site of some of the most furious fighting.

The 10-acre **Shiloh National Cemetery** is located next to the visitors center. Two-thirds of the 3,695 bodies interred here are unidentified. Most are Union soldiers killed at Shiloh, but there are others from nearby battles, the Spanish-American War, both World Wars, and the Revolutionary War. The Confederate dead were buried in five trenches around the battlefield, and remain there today.

Nearly 800 years before the Civil War, the riverbank near present-day Shiloh was home to a mound-building Mississippian Indian community. The **Shiloh Indian Mounds** that they left behind sit along the west bluff of the riverbank, and are one of the largest mound groups in the country. A remarkable effigy pipe was discovered here in the 1890s and is on display at the Tennessee River Museum in Savannah. The mounds are accessible on foot from two points in the park.

Practicalities

A printed guide and map to the battlefield is available at the visitors center, and it takes about an hour to follow it. For a more detailed examination, you can buy an audio tour from the park bookstore for $12. This tour takes about two hours to complete and includes narratives by soldiers, historians, and civilians.

Shiloh National Military Park is closed on Christmas Day. The bookstore is one of the best in the area, and has an extensive collection of books on the Civil War, Tennessee, Native Americans, and African-American history.

There are snack and drink vending machines at the visitors center, and a picnic area in the park. The closest restaurants are in Shiloh,

Savannah, and Counce. For accommodations, look in Savannah.

With its miles of flat roads and restrained traffic, Shiloh is a good place to bicycle. There are no rental facilities nearby, however, so plan on bringing your own wheels.

SHILOH

There is not much to the modern town of Shiloh, except a few souvenir shops and one excellent catfish restaurant. **◖ World Famous Hagy's Catfish Restaurant** (off Hwy. 22, 731/689-3327, Tues.–Sat. 11 A.M.–10 P.M., Sun. noon–9 P.M., $9–15) is set off by itself in a beautiful clearing overlooking the Tennessee River. You can stretch your legs with a walk down to the water's edge. Hagy's menu has fried and grilled catfish, plus other favorites like chicken and steak. But choose the catfish, which is nicely seasoned and expertly fried. It comes with hush puppies and coleslaw. This will be a meal to remember.

Find Hagy's by looking for the large sign for the turn-off along Highway 22 on the northern side of Shiloh National Military Park.

PICKWICK LANDING STATE PARK

Pickwick Landing was a riverboat stop from the 1840s until the 1930s when Pickwick Dam was built and the lake formed. Pickwick Lake was created in December 1937 when the Tennessee Valley Authority dammed the Tennessee and flooded farmland in the valley. The lake was dedicated in 1940, and a crowd of 30,000 people attended the services on the southern earth dam. Today it attracts vacationers from around the region who enjoy the laid-back atmosphere and top-flight bass fishing.

The lake lies in Tennessee, Alabama, and Mississippi and is one of the premier spots for recreation in the area. Boating, fishing, and swimming are especially popular. There are several nearby golf courses, and opportunities to camp, hunt, and hike.

Pickwick Landing State Park (Rte. 57, 731/689-3129) is one of Tennessee's resort parks, with a new hotel, conference center, golf course, and marina.

Hiking

There is an easy three-mile hiking trail that meanders along the lakeshore.

Golf

The Pickwick Landing State Park golf course is a par-72 champion's 18-hole course. The pro shop rents clubs and carts and sells golf accessories. Call 731/689-3149 to reserve a tee time. Greens fees range $13–22, depending on the season and day of the week.

Boating

Pleasure riding, sailing, waterskiing, and fishing are all popular activities on Pickwick Lake. There are three public boat-launch ramps at Pickwick Landing State Park, and marine fuel and other boating items are available from the park marina.

You can rent a pontoon boat from **Pickwick Boat Rentals** (731/689-5359) for $175 and up per day.

Fishing

Fishing on Pickwick Lake is best in the spring and fall. Conditions here include shallow stump flats, well-defined channels, active feeder creeks, steeply falling bluffs, rocky ledges, and long grass beds.

Pickwick Outdoors, Inc. (877/214-4924) organizes fishing vacations for groups. For a fishing guide, contact **Big Orange Guide Service** (731/689-3074) or **Rick Matlock's Guide Service** (731/689-5382).

Swimming

Pickwick Landing State Park has three swimming beaches. Circle Beach and Sandy Beach are in the day-use area; Bruton Beach is in the primitive area, which is located across the lake from the main park.

Accommodations

Pickwick Landing State Resort Park (Hwy. 57, 731/689-3135, $70–80) is the home of one of Tennessee's newest state park inns and conference centers. The modern hotel has 75 rooms, each with a balcony looking out over the lake and the dam. Cabins are available for between $100 and $125 per night, and campsites are available for under $20. There is a pool and a 135-seat restaurant at the inn, which serves three meals a day.

COUNCE

This humble town is the western gateway to Pickwick Lake. It is also a hub in the region's hardwood timber industry, and you will smell the fumes of the local paper plant at certain times of the day.

Accommodations

If you're planning to stay more than a few days at Pickwick Lake, consider renting a cabin. **Pickwick Lake Cabin Rentals** (11268 Hwy. 57, 731/689-0400, www.pickwicklakecabins.com) represents the owners of two dozen one-, two-, and three-bedroom cabins on and around the lake. Lakefront cabins will cost from $300 to $400 per night; water-view cabins will cost $200 to $300, and cabins off the water cost between $100 and $200. Many lakefront cabins come with a private dock and can accommodate large groups.

Food

Don't be mistaken by the rustic appearance of the **Broken Spoke** (7405 Hwy. 57, 731/689-3800, Wed.–Sat. 11 A.M.–10 P.M., $12–27). This is the most upscale and creative dining around Pickwick Lake. The decor is comfortably eclectic, but not trashy, and there is tasteful live music several nights a week. The menu is remarkably diverse: You can choose from catfish, po-boys, and burgers, or steaks, pork chops, and chicken cooked expertly on the grill. There are also salads, pasta, and daily specials. Come with an appetite—there are no small portions. The adjacent bar is a popular hangout spot any night of the week, and **Mombie's Pizza** (731/689-8646, Tues.–Sat. 11 A.M.–10 P.M., $9–15), right next door, serves the best pizza, burgers, and wings in Pickwick. You will find the Broken Spoke and Mombie's one mile west of the dam on Highway 57.

WESTERN PLAINS

Southwestern Tennessee

The southernmost stretch of West Tennessee spans Adamsville in the east to La Grange in the west. Here you'll find a museum dedicated to sheriff Buford Pusser, another dedicated to bird dogs, and one of the loveliest small towns in all of Tennessee.

Information

Seven Tennessee counties have come together to form the **Tourism Association of Southwest Tennessee** (866/261-7534, www.tasttn.org), which produces brochures and stocks information stands at interstate rest stops and other crossroads. Their guide to the region has helpful listings and a map.

ADAMSVILLE

Famed McNairy County sheriff Buford Pusser worked in Selmer, the McNairy County seat, but he lived in Adamsville, a small town a few miles down Highway 45. Fans of Pusser and the movies that his legacy inspired, starting with the 1973 film *Walking Tall,* can learn more about his life at the **Sheriff Buford Pusser Home and Museum** (342 Pusser St., 731/632-4080, Mon.–Fri. 11 A.M.–5 P.M., Sat. 9 A.M.–5 P.M., Sun. 1–5 P.M., $5). Pusser earned a reputation as a no-nonsense lawman during his eight-year career as sheriff. He was famous for raiding moonshine stills, and for fighting criminals with little regard for his own personal safety. In 1967 his wife, Pauline, was killed in an ambush when she was riding along with him in his patrol car. Seven years later, Pusser was killed in a single-car accident while he was driving home from the McNairy County Fair in Selmer. When Pusser died, hundreds of people came to his funeral. Elvis Presley visited the family privately to offer his condolences.

The home and museum features a video about Pusser's life, family memorabilia, and two cars that Pusser used.

Shiloh Golf Course and Restaurant

(2915 Caney Branch Rd., 731/632-0678) in Adamsville is a par-71 course and driving range.

SELMER

In Selmer, the McNairy County seat, you can see the courthouse where Buford Pusser worked, and where Mary Winkler was put on trial in 2007 for the murder of her preacher husband, Matthew Winkler.

This quiet town is also home to the **McNairy County Historical Museum** (114 N. Third St., 731/646-0018, Sat. 10 A.M.–4 P.M., Sun. 1–4 P.M., free), located in the old Ritz theater. Exhibits are dedicated to schools, the Civil War, churches, the healing arts, business, and agriculture.

Selmer is most famous for its so-called slugburgers, deep-fried grain burgers that are sold at lunch counters around town.

LA GRANGE

La Grange, a mere speck of civilization 50 miles east of Memphis, feels like the town that time forgot. Old homes—some elegant, some ramshackle—line narrow drives. The post office, town office, and an old-fashioned country store constitute the business district. Unfortunately, since the closure in 2007 of Cogbill's Store and Museum, there is not much to do here except look. If you are here on Saturday morning, stop at the La Grange General Store for a cup of coffee and conversation. The town office is open weekday mornings.

Despite the dearth of outright attractions, La Grange, also called "La Belle Village," delivers an experience unlike any other town in this part of Tennessee. Its lovingly preserved antebellum homes, rural landscape, and charming people are truly unique.

History

La Grange, named in honor of the Marquis de Lafayette's ancestral home in France, seemed destined for great things when it was chartered in 1829. Its population quickly swelled to more than 3,000. The first Episcopal church in West Tennessee was founded here, and in 1835 stockholders chartered the La Grange & Memphis Railway. The plans for a railroad faltered, however, and La Grange suffered from Union occupation during most of the Civil War. A tornado destroyed part of the town in 1900, and La Grange lost its telegraph station and express mail delivery to nearby Grand Junction. Hopes for La Grange to grow into a city dwindled.

Despite its size, La Grange was and is known for a special refinement and pursuit of the arts and education. In 1855, the La Grange Female College and the La Grange Synodical College for Men were chartered. The town's local newspapers, *The Monitor* and, later, the *Spirit of the Age,* were respected in the region. During the Civil War, La Grange native Lucy Pickens was depicted on the face of the Confederate $1 note, and three different $100 notes. Pickens, whose childhood home at 290 Pine Street is still standing, was known as the "Queen of the Confederacy."

In 1998, La Grange dedicated a 2.5-ton bronze and limestone monument to the nearby Wolf River. The **Wolf River Monument,** located near the post office and fire department, was rendered in the shape of a wolf's head and was created by Memphis sculptor Roy Tamboli.

Information

La Grange City Hall (20 Main St., 901/878-1246, Mon.–Fri. 8 A.M.–noon) is the best source of information about the town. They can provide you with a large fold-out map of the town's historic homes.

Ghost River State Natural Area

The Ghost River is a 14-mile section of the

© SUSANNA HENIGHAN POTTER

the Ghost River

WESTERN PLAINS

Wolf River that meanders through bottom-land forest, cypress-tupelo swamps, and open marshes. The river got its name from the loss of river current as the water flows through marshes and swamps.

About a three-mile drive south of La Grange you can hike or canoe in the Ghost River State Natural Area. To find the 600-foot boardwalk and hiking trail, drive south from La Grange on Yager Road, and then turn west on Beasley Road. The parking area is about 1.5 miles down the road. There is another parking area and a place to put in a canoe along Yager Road, and a marked canoe path so you don't get lost in the swamp. There is another parking area at the canoe take-out on Bateman Road. You can get a map from the La Grange town office, or from the State of Tennessee website (www.state.tn.us).

GRAND JUNCTION

A few miles east of La Grange on Highway 57 is the **National Bird Dog Museum** (5050 Hwy. 57 W., 731/764-2058, Tues.–Fri. 10 A.M.–2 P.M., Sat. 10 A.M.–4 P.M., Sun. 1–4 P.M., free). The collection includes paintings and photographs of champion sporting dogs, plus lots of taxidermy. The National Field Trials take place just down the road at the Ames Plantation.

CHICKASAW STATE PARK

Named for the Indians who once lived and hunted in this part of Tennessee, Chickasaw State Park encompasses Lake Placid and a golf course. The 14,400-acre park lies midway between Jackson and Bolivar. There are roads for hiking or biking, tennis courts, an archery range, horseback riding, campsites, and a 40-room inn.

Bear Trace at Chickasaw (9555 State Route 100, 731/989-4700, www.beartrace.com) is a Jack Nicklaus golf course with natural beauty and challenging holes.

BIG HILL POND STATE PARK

Big Hill Pond was created in 1853 when dirt was removed from a borrow pit to build a levee across the Tuscumbia and Cypress Creek bottoms for the Memphis to Charleston Railroad. Over the years, a stand of cypress tress has grown in and around the 35-acre pond.

The highlight of the state park (11701 Hwy. 57, 731/645-7967) is the boardwalk through the scenic swamp and the observation tower, which provides views of the swamp and lake. There are 30 miles of hiking trails, 14 miles of horseback riding and mountain bike trails, a campground with 30 sites, a picnic area, and opportunities to fish and hunt.

NASHVILLE

Nashville is the home of country music. This city of 600,000 on the banks of the Cumberland River is where tomorrow's hits are made and where you can hear them performed on the stage of the longest-running live radio variety show, the Grand Ole Opry.

There is a twang in the air all around the city—in the honky-tonks along lower Broadway, on the streets of downtown Nashville, and in Music Valley, modern home of the Opry. During the annual Country Music Association Festival in June, the whole city is alive with the foot-tapping rhythm of country music.

Nashville is also the city where performers and songwriters come to make it in the music business. Listening rooms and nightclubs all over the city are the beneficiaries of this abundance of hopeful talent. There is no excuse to stay home after night falls.

It is wrong to think that country music is all there is to Nashville. After the Civil War and Reconstruction, Nashville became known as the Athens of the South because it was a center for education and the arts. Still today, Nashville offers visitors much more than a night at the Opry. Excellent art museums include the Frist Center for Visual Arts and the Cheekwood. The Nashville Symphony Orchestra plays in the elegant and acclaimed Schermerhorn Center downtown.

Come to watch the Tennessee Titans play football, or to play golf at one of the award-winning courses nearby. Admire the Parthenon in Centennial Park, or drive to the southern outskirts of the city for a hike at Radnor Lake State Natural Area.

PHOTO COURTESY OF TENNESSEE DEPARTMENT OF TOURIST DEVELOPMENT

HIGHLIGHTS

(Country Music Hall of Fame: Pay homage to the kings and queens of country music while you trace its evolution from old-time Appalachian mountain music to today's mega-hits (page 124).

(Civil Rights Room at the Nashville Public Library: The public library houses the best exhibit about the historic Nashville sit-ins of 1960 (page 130).

(The Parthenon: First built in 1897 to mark the 100th anniversary of the state of Tennessee, this life-sized replica of the Greek Parthenon is as beautiful as it is unusual (page 132).

(Cheekwood: Art and nature are perfectly balanced in this exceptional museum and botanic garden built on an estate financed by Maxwell House coffee (page 138).

(The Grand Ole Opry: The live radio variety show that's been on the air for more than 80 years is still the best place to be entertained in Music City (page 147).

(The Bluebird Cafe: The quintessential Nashville listening room, the Bluebird hosts intimate music sessions every night of the week (page 150).

LOOK FOR **(** TO FIND RECOMMENDED SIGHTS, ACTIVITIES, DINING, AND LODGING.

Downtown is dominated by tall office towers and imposing government buildings, including the state Capitol. Meat-and-three restaurants serve irresistible Southern-style meals, while eateries along Nolensville Pike reflect the ethnic diversity of the city.

Nashville is a city that strikes many notes, but sings in perfect harmony.

PLANNING YOUR TIME

Nashville is a popular destination for weekend getaways. Over two days you can see a few of the city's attractions and catch a show at the Grand Ole Opry. Musical pilgrims and history enthusiasts should plan to spend more time in Music City. Even the most disciplined explorers will find themselves happily occupied if they choose to stay a full week.

Downtown is a good home base for many visitors. Hotels here are within walking distance of many attractions, restaurants, and nightclubs. They are also the most expensive accommodations in the city. Visitors who are primarily interested in seeing a show at the

© AVALON TRAVEL

Grand Ole Opry or shopping at Opry Mills should shack up in Music Valley, where you will find a smorgasbord of affordable hotel rooms.

Visitors with a car can also look for accommodation outside of the city center. There are affordable hotels in midtown, and charming bed-and-breakfasts in Hillsboro and East Nashville. All these neighborhoods are nicely off the tourist track. The city's lone hostel is in midtown and is a good choice for budget travelers.

When to Go

Summer is the most popular time to visit Nashville. The CMA Music Festival in June draws thousands to the city. Temperatures in August top out around 90 degrees, although it can feel much hotter.

Spring and fall enjoy mild temperatures, and are the best time to visit Nashville. You will avoid the largest crowds but still sample all that the city has to offer. In spring you will enjoy sights of tulips, dogwoods, and magnolias in bloom. Beginning in mid-October, foliage around the city starts to turn blazing red, brown, and yellow.

In winter, temperatures range from 30 to 50 degrees. During November and December, holiday concerts and decorations liven up the city. Many attractions cut back hours during winter, and some outdoor attractions are closed altogether.

ORIENTATION

For a city of its size, Nashville takes up a lot of space. In fact, Nashville has the second-largest footprint of any major American city. But don't picture a scene of concrete: Nashville is a leafy, suburban city. Outside downtown is a patchwork of traffic lights, strip malls, and tree-lined residential neighborhoods, several of which are incorporated towns with their own elected officials, city halls, and police.

Nashville's attractions are spread out among the city's various neighborhoods. Learn the locations and identities of a few parts of town, and you are well on your way to understanding Music City.

City Center

Nashville straddles the Cumberland River, a waterway that meanders a particularly uneven course in this part of Tennessee. Downtown Nashville sits on the west bank of the river, climbing a gradual incline from Broadway to the Tennessee State Capitol. It is defined by landmarks including the BellSouth tower, the tallest building in Tennessee, better known by many as the Batman building for the two tall antennae that spring from the top.

Downtown is divided into two general areas: **Broadway and the District** is the entertainment area, and where you will find major attractions like the Country Music Hall of Fame, the Ryman Auditorium, and Printer's Alley, a hotbed of clubs and bars. **Downtown** refers to the more traditional city zone, where you'll find office buildings, the Tennessee State Museum, and city parks.

It is a good plan to walk around central Nashville since traffic and parking are about as difficult here as in any city of this size. But do remember that Nashville is built on a hill. Walking between Broadway and the state Capitol is perfectly doable, but on a hot summer day, or with small children in tow, you may think otherwise.

East Nashville

Shelby Street Pedestrian Bridge spans the Cumberland at McGavock Street and takes you straight to the heart of East Nashville. Now dominated by humongous LP Field, home of the Tennessee Titans, the eastern reaches of Nashville are also home to some of the most charming residential neighborhoods. **Edgefield,** Nashville's oldest suburb, was a separate city when it first sprang up in the 19th century. Many of its most elegant homes were destroyed in the great East Nashville fire of 1916, but it still boasts a lovely mix of Victorian, Princess Anne, and Colonial Revival homes. Farther east is **Lockeland Springs.**

While there are no blockbuster attractions in East Nashville, visitors should consider the growing number of bed-and-breakfast accommodations here. The neighborhoods are close

Downtown Nashville sits on the west bank of the Cumberland River.

to downtown, but also boast their own unique nightlife, restaurants, and character.

North Nashville

North of the state Capitol and Bicentennial Mall is **Germantown,** a quaint, compact neighborhood now awash with galleries, restaurants, and studios, once the home of European immigrants. Heading west from Germantown, **Jefferson Street** takes you past several of Nashville's African-American landmarks, including Fisk University and Meharry Medical College.

A neighborhood created entirely for the tourist trade, **Music Valley** is the zone of hotels, restaurants, and retail that has popped up around the Opryland Hotel and the Grand Ole Opry House. Located inside a narrow loop of the Cumberland River, Music Valley lies northeast of downtown Nashville. It is convenient to the airport along the Briley Parkway.

If Music Valley is actually a valley, you wouldn't know it. The strip of hotels, restaurants, souvenir shops, and malls is just about as far removed from the natural environment as you can get. The Grand Ole Opry is the

best thing that Music Valley has going for it. Opryland Hotel is an attraction in its own right, however, and Opry Mills is a discount shopper's paradise. Music Valley is also home to a wide variety of hotel accommodations, including some budget-friendly choices.

West Nashville

Perhaps the most famous neighborhood in all of Nashville, **Music Row** is where country music deals are done. The tree-lined streets of 16th and 17th Avenues, a few blocks southwest of downtown, shade dozens of different recording studios, record labels, and producers.

Lying just west of downtown, **Elliston Place** is a block of nightclubs, restaurants, and two famous Nashville eateries: Elliston Place Soda Shop and Rotier's.

The neighborhood is surrounded by medical complexes, and is a few blocks from the city's only downtown hostel. Centennial Park, Nashville's best urban park, is a few blocks farther west.

The youthful energy of nearby Vanderbilt University and Belmont College keep **Hillsboro Village** one of the most consistently hip neighborhoods in Nashville. Located on both sides of 21st Avenue, Hillsboro and the related neighborhood of Belmont are about as far away from the Grand Ole Opry as you can get in Nashville.

Hillsboro is home to one of Nashville's finest used book stores, stylish and pricey boutiques, and notable restaurants, including the upscale Sunset Grill, the down-home Pancake Pantry, and Fido, a coffeehouse for all seasons. Hillsboro is also where you will find the alternative movie house the Belcourt, which screens independent and arts movies every day of the week.

South of Hillsboro is **Green Hills,** whose primary attraction is a shopping mall. Together, Hillsboro, Elliston Place, and Green Hills are Nashville's **Midtown.**

Sylvan Park is an old suburb of the city, located between Charlotte Avenue and Murphy Road, just west of the city center. Noted for neat homes and state-named roads, the neighborhood is quiet and residential.

Along Charlotte Avenue, facing Sylvan Park, you will find antiques and thrift stores, the Darkhorse Theater, and Rhino Books, specializing in used and rare books. Farther out along Charlotte is the Goodwill Superstore, a dream come true for thrift store aficionados, and a burgeoning number of ethnic eateries.

West End refers to the neighborhoods along West End Avenue. It includes Belle Meade, an incorporated city and one of the wealthiest in the whole state. Head in this direction to find good restaurants, the Belle Meade Plantation, and Cheekwood.

South Nashville

South of the city center are several distinct neighborhoods. **8th Avenue South,** close to downtown, is the antiques district. Restaurants like Arnold's Country Kitchen and clubs including the Douglas Corner Cafe draw people to this neighborhood.

Follow 12th Avenue as it heads south from downtown to find **the Gulch.** Rising from what was once a railroad wasteland, the Gulch is now the city's hot spot for high-rise housing and urban condos.

A few miles farther south along 12th Avenue is **12 South,** another of Nashville's most newly gentrified neighborhoods. An influx of young professional property owners has given rise to new restaurants, boutiques, and coffee shops.

There is not much greenery left in **Green Hills,** a retail hot spot south of Hillsboro Village. If you can stand the traffic jam, follow 21st Avenue south to find upscale Green Hills Mall and the venerable Bluebird Cafe, tucked away in a strip mall a few blocks farther south.

Sights

BROADWAY AND THE DISTRICT

This is the entertainment and retail hub of Nashville. Walk along lower Broadway, as the blocks from 5th Avenue to the river are called, and you will pass a dozen different bars, restaurants, and shops catering to visitors. The District, located along 2nd Avenue near where it crosses Broadway, is a neighborhood where old warehouses have been converted to nightclubs, shops, office space, and loft condominiums.

◖ Country Music Hall of Fame

The distinctive design of the Country Music Hall of Fame and Museum (222 5th Ave. S., 615/416-2001, www.countrymusichalloffame.com, daily 9 A.M.–5 P.M., $15.95–19.95) is the first thing you will notice about this monument to country music. Vertical windows at the front and back of the building resemble piano keys; the sweeping arch on the right side of the building portrays a 1950s Cadillac fin; and from above, the building resembles a bass clef. The Hall of Fame was first established

The Country Music Walk of Fame leads to the Hall of Fame in downtown Nashville.

in 1967, and its first inductees were Jimmie Rodgers, Hank Williams, and Fred Rose. The original Hall was located on Music Row, but in 2002 it moved to this brand-new signature building two blocks off Broadway in downtown Nashville.

Country music fans are drawn by the carload to the Hall of Fame, where they can pay homage to country's greatest stars, as well as the lesser-known men and women who influenced the music. The hall's slogan is "Honor Thy Music."

The museum is arranged chronologically, beginning with country's roots in the Scotch-Irish ballads sung by the southern mountains' first settlers, and ending with displays on some of the genre's hottest stars of today. In between, exhibits detail themes including the rise of bluegrass, honky tonk, and the world-famous Nashville Sound, which introduced country music to the world.

There are a half-dozen private listening booths where you can hear studio-quality recordings of seminal performances, as well as a special display of a few of the genre's most famous instruments. Here you can see Bill Monroe's mandolin, Maybelle Carter's Gibson, and Johnny Cash's Martin D-355.

If you are truly interested in learning something about country music while you're here, splurge on the $5 audio guide, which adds depth to the exhibits and helps to drown out distractions caused by your fellow museumgoers.

The Hall of Fame itself is set in a rotunda. Brass plaques honor the 100 inductees, and around the room are the words "Will the Circle Be Unbroken," from the hymn made famous by the Carter Family.

The Ryman Auditorium

Thanks to an $8.5 million renovation in the 1990s, the historic Ryman Auditorium (116 5th Ave. N., 615/889-3060, www.ryman.com, daily 9 A.M.–4 P.M., $12.50–16.25) remains one of the best places in the United States—let alone Nashville—to hear live music. Built in 1892 by Captain Thomas Ryman, the Union Gospel Tabernacle, as the Ryman was then called, was designed as a venue for the charismatic preaching of Rev. Samuel P. Jones, to whom Ryman owed his own conversion to Christianity.

Managed by keen businesswoman Lula C. Naff during the first half of the 20th century, the Ryman began to showcase music and performances. In 1943, Naff agreed for the Ryman to host a popular barn dance called the Grand Ole Opry. The legacy of this partnership gave the Ryman its place in history as the so-called Mother Church of Country Music.

The Opry remained at the Ryman for the next 31 years. After the Opry left in 1974, the Ryman fell into disrepair and was virtually condemned when Gaylord Entertainment, the same company that owns the Opry, decided to invest in the grand old tabernacle. Today, it is a popular concert venue, booking rock, country, and classical acts, and performers still marvel at the fabulous acoustics of the hall.

Seeing a show at the Ryman is by far the best way to experience this historic venue, but if you can't do that, pay the $12.50 admission

© SUSANNA HENIGHAN POTTER

The Ryman Auditorium is also called the Mother Church of Country Music.

to see a short video and explore the auditorium on your own. You can sit a few minutes on the old wooden pews and even climb on stage to be photographed in front of the classic Opry backdrop. A guided tour that takes you backstage costs $16.25.

Shelby Street Pedestrian Bridge

Built in 1909, the Sparkman Street Bridge was slated for demolition in the 1998 after inspectors called its condition "poor." But citing the success of the Walnut Street Bridge in revitalizing downtown Chattanooga, Tennessee, advocates succeeded in saving the bridge. The Shelby Street Bridge reotpened in 2003 as a pedestrian and bike bridge.

The Shelby Street Bridge connects East Nashville neighborhoods with downtown. It is also convenient on Titan game days since the eastern terminus is a few hundred yards from LP Field. Perhaps most significant for visitors, however, is the fact that the views of the downtown cityscape are excellent from here.

Fort Nashborough

Fort Nashborough (170 1st Ave., 615/862-8400, Mon.–Sat. 10 A.M.–5:30 P.M., Sun. 1–5 P.M., free) is a one-quarter-sized replica of the fort erected by James Robertson and John Donelson when they first settled what was then called French Lick on Christmas Day 1779. Visitors here will get the feeling that this site has seen better days. While the replica fort is open, it is mostly left unattended and there is little to see or learn here. The interiors of the five cabins have been gated with iron bars, seemingly to prevent neighborhood vagrants from settling in. The site is mostly fascinating simply because it looks so out of place among Nashville's skyscrapers and the Tennessee Titans' stadium nearby. It has a nice view of the river too.

Tennessee Sports Hall of Fame

Sports fans will enjoy the Tennessee Sports Hall of Fame (Nashville Arena, 615/242-4750, www.tshf.net, Mon.–Sat. 10 A.M.–5 P.M., $3). Located in a state-of-the-art 7,500-square-foot exhibit space, the hall chronicles the history of sports in Tennessee from the 1800s to today's heroes.

Customs House

Located at 701 Broadway, the old Nashville Customs House is a historic landmark and architectural beauty. Construction on the Customs House began in 1875 and President Rutherford B. Hayes visited Nashville to lay the cornerstone in 1877. The building is an impressive example of the Victorian Gothic style. It was designed by Treasury architect William Appleton Potter and was completed in 1916. Although it is called a customs house, the building served as the center of federal government operations in the city: Federal government offices, courts, and treasury offices were housed in the building. For many years it held the city's U.S. Post Office.

Ownership transferred from the federal to the city government in 1979 and the building was later leased for redevelopment. It currently houses federal bankruptcy court and other offices.

NASHVILLE

Hume Fogg

Located across Broadway from the Customs House is Hume Fogg Magnet School. It sits on land formerly occupied by Hume School, Nashville's first public school. The four-story stone-clad 1912 building was designed by William Ittner of St. Louis in the Norman Gothic style with Tudor Gothic details. Today, it is a public magnet school with a reputation for high academic standards.

The Frist Center for the Visual Arts

Nashville's foremost visual art space is the Frist Center for the Visual Arts (919 Broadway, 615/744-3247, www.fristcenter.org, Mon.– Sat. 10 A.M.–5:30 P.M., Thurs. and Fri. until 9 P.M., Sun. 1–5 P.M., adults $8.50, seniors and military $7.50, students $6.50). The Frist is located in a stately building that once housed the 1930s downtown post office. High ceilings, art deco finishes, and unique hardwood tiles distinguish the museum.

With no permanent collection of its own, the Frist puts on about 12 different major visiting exhibitions annually. At any given time, you will see between three and four different exhibits. ArtQuest, a permanent part of the Frist, is an excellent hands-on arts activity room for children and their parents.

DOWNTOWN

The greater part of downtown is dominated by large office buildings and federal, state, and city government structures. From Commerce Street northward to the state Capitol, you will find historic churches, museums, and hordes of office workers.

Tennessee State Capitol

Set on the top of a hill and built with the formality and grace of classic Greek architecture, the capitol building of Tennessee strikes a commanding pose overlooking downtown Nashville. Construction of the Capitol began in 1845, two years after the state legislature finally agreed that Nashville would be the permanent capital city. Even with the unpaid labor

of convicts and slaves, it took 14 years to finish the building.

The Capitol is built of limestone, much of it from a quarry located near present-day Charlotte and 13th Avenues. In the 1950s, extensive renovations were carried out and some of the original limestone was replaced. The interior marble came from Rogersville and Knoxville, and the gasoliers were ordered from Philadelphia. The Capitol was designed by architect William Strickland, who considered it his crowning achievement and is buried in a courtyard on the north end of the Capitol.

Visitors are welcome at the Capitol. Ask at the information desk for a printed guide that identifies each of the rooms and many of the portraits and sculptures both inside and outside of the building. If the legislature is not in session, you can go inside both the House and Senate chambers, which look much as they did back in the 19th century. In the 2nd-floor lobby, you can see two bronze reliefs depicting the 19th and 14th amendments to the United States Constitution, both of which were ratified by the State of Tennessee in votes held at the Capitol.

Guided tours of the Capitol depart hourly Monday–Friday 9 A.M.–3 P.M. Ask at the information desk inside for more information.

Other important State buildings surround the Capitol. The **Library and Archives** sits directly west of the Capitol, and next to the **Tennessee Supreme Court**. The **Tennessee War Memorial** is a stone plaza on the south side of the Capitol, and a nice place to people-watch. A number of State office buildings are nearby, and State employees can be seen walking to and fro, especially at lunchtime.

Tennessee State Museum

If you are used to the flashy multimedia exhibits found in many of today's top museums, the Tennessee State Museum (5th Ave., 615/741-2692, www.tnmuseum.org, Tues.–Sat. 10 A.M.–5 P.M., Sun. 1–5 P.M., free) will seem like a musty throwback to the past. The displays are largely straightforward combinations of text and images, and they require visitors to read and examine on their own. There are but

NASHVILLE

NASHVILLE

© AVALON TRAVEL

a few video presentations. But for patrons with enough patience to give the displays their due, the museum offers an excellent overview of Tennessee history from the Native Americans to the New South era of the 1880s.

Exhibits detail the state's political development, the Revolutionary and Civil Wars, and profile famous Tennesseans including Andrew Jackson and Davy Crocket. They also cast a spotlight on the lifestyles and diversions of Tennesseans of various eras, from the early frontiersmen and -women to a free African-American family before emancipation. Special artifacts include the top hat worn by Andrew Jackson at his presidential inauguration, a musket that belonged to Daniel Boone, and the jaw bone of a mastodon.

The **Tennessee Military Museum** (Legislative Plaza, 615/741-2692, Tues.–Sat. 10 A.M.–5 P.M., free) is associated with the Tennessee State Museum and highlights America's overseas conflicts, beginning with the Spanish-American War in 1989 and ending with World War II. The exhibits examine the beginnings of the wars, major battles, and the outcomes. There is a special exhibit about Alvin C. York, the Tennessee native and World War I hero. The military museum is located in the War Memorial Building on the south side of the Capitol.

◖ Civil Rights Room at the Nashville Public Library

The Nashville Public Library (615 Church St., 615/862-5800, Mon.–Thurs. 9 A.M.–8 P.M., Fri.

NASHVILLE SIT-INS

Greensboro, North Carolina, is often named as the site of the first sit-ins of the American civil rights movement. In truth, activists in Nashville carried out the first "test" sit-ins in late 1959. In these test cases, protesters left the facilities after being refused service and talking to management about the injustice of segregation. In between these test sit-ins and the moment when Nashville activists would launch a full-scale sit-in campaign, students in Greensboro took that famous first step.

The Nashville sit-ins began on February 13, 1960, when a group of African-American students from local colleges and universities sat at a downtown lunch counter and refused to move until they were served. The protesting students endured verbal and physical abuse, and were arrested.

Community members raised money for the students' bail, and black residents of the city began an economic boycott of downtown stores that practiced segregation. On April 19, the home of Z. Alexander Looby, a black lawyer who was representing the students, was bombed. Later the same day, students led a spontaneous, peaceful, and silent march through the streets of downtown Nashville to the courthouse. Diane Nash, a student leader,

asked Nashville mayor Ben West if he thought it was morally right for a restaurant to refuse to serve someone based on the color of his or her skin. Mayor West said no.

The march was an important turning point for the city. The combined effect of the sit-ins, the boycott, and the march caused, in 1960, Nashville to be the first major Southern city to experience widespread desegregation of its public facilities. The events also demonstrated to activists in other parts of the South that non-violence was an effective tool of protest.

The story of the young people who led the Nashville sit-ins is told in the book *The Children* by David Halberstam. In 2001, Nashville resident Bill King was so moved by the story of the protests that he established an endowment to fundraise for a permanent civil rights collection at the Nashville Public Library. In 2003, the Civil Rights Room at the Nashville Public Library was opened. It houses books, oral histories, audio-visual records, microfilm, dissertations, and stunning photographs of the events of 1960. The words of one student organizer, John Lewis, who went on to become a congressman from Georgia, are displayed over the entryway: "If not us, then who; if not now, then when?"

9 A.M.–6 P.M., Sat. 9 A.M.–5 P.M., Sun. 2–5 P.M., free) houses the city's best exhibit on the movement for civil rights that took place in Nashville in the 1950s and '60s. Nashville was the first Southern city to desegregate public services, and it did so relatively peacefully, setting an example for activists throughout the south.

The story of the courageous men and women who made this change happen is told through photographs, videos, and displays in the Civil Rights Room at the public library. The library is a fitting location for the exhibit, since the block below on Church Street was the epicenter of the Nashville sit-ins during 1960.

Inside the room, large-format photographs show school desegregation, sit-ins, and a silent march to the courthouse. A circular table at the center of the room is symbolic of the lunch counters where young students from Fisk, Meharry, American Baptist, and Tennessee A&I sat silently and peacefully at sit-ins. The table is engraved with the ten rules of conduct set out for sit-in participants, including rules to be polite and courteous at all times, regardless of how you are treated. A timeline of the national and Nashville civil rights movements is presented above the table.

Inside a glass-enclosed viewing room you can choose from six different documentary videos, including an hour-long 1960 NBC news documentary about the Nashville sit-ins. Many of the videos are 30 minutes or longer, so plan on spending several hours here if you are keenly interested in the topics.

The centerpiece of the Civil Rights Room is a glass inscription by Martin Luther King, who visited the city in 1960 and said, during a speech at Fisk University: "I came to Nashville not to bring inspiration, but to gain inspiration from the great movement that has taken place in this community."

Nashville is planning a new and much-needed museum dedicated to its African-American history and culture, which will be located at the corner of Jefferson and 8th Avenues, near the farmer's market. Until this museum is built, the Nashville Public Library is the best place to learn about the city's racially segregated past and the movement that changed that.

The Civil Rights Room is located on the 2nd floor of the library, adjacent to the room that houses its Nashville collection.

The Arcade

One of Nashville's most unique urban features is the covered arcade that runs between 4th and 5th Avenues and parallel to Union Street. The two-story arcade with a gabled glass roof was built in 1903 by developer Daniel Buntin, who was inspired by similar arcades he saw in Italy.

From the moment it opened, the Arcade was a bustling center for commerce. Famous for its peanut shop, the Arcade has also been the location of photo studios, jewelers, and a post office for many years. Today, restaurants crowd the lower level, while professional offices line the 2nd floor.

Downtown Presbyterian Church

William Strickland, the architect who designed the Tennessee State Capitol, also designed the Downtown Presbyterian Church (154 5th Ave. N., 615/254-7584, www.dpchurch.com), a place of worship now on the National Register of Historic Places. Built in 1848 to replace an earlier church destroyed by fire, the church is in the Egyptian revival style that was popular at the time. It is, however, one of only three surviving churches in the country to be built in this style.

Downtown Presbyterian, which added the word "Downtown" to its name in 1955, was used as a Union hospital during the Civil War, and it is where James K. Polk was inaugurated as Tennessee governor in 1839. Visitors are welcome to come for a self-guided tour during regular business hours. Groups of five or more can call in advance for a guided tour of the building.

MUSIC ROW

Home to the business end of the country music industry, Music Row can be found along 16th and 17th Avenues south of where they cross Broadway. While there are few bona fide attractions here, it is worth a jaunt to see the

NASHVILLE

headquarters of both major and independent music labels all in one place.

Music Row's most famous, or infamous, landmark is **Musica,** the sculpture at the Music Row traffic circle. The Alan LeQuire sculpture caused a stir when it was unveiled in 2003 for the larger-than-life anatomically correct men and women it depicts. Regardless of your views on art and obscenity, it is fair to say that *Musica* speaks more to Nashville's identity as the Athens of the South than as Music City USA.

RCA Studio B

As a rule, the music labels in Music Row are open for business, not tours. The lone exception is Historic RCA Studio B (Music Square W., 615/416-2001, www.countrymusichalloffame.com, $12.95). The RCA studio was the second recording studio in Nashville and the place where artists including the Everly Brothers, Roy Orbison, Dolly Parton, Elvis Presley, and Hank Snow recorded hits. Also called the RCA Victor Studio, this nondescript studio operated from 1957 to 1977. Visitors on the one-hour tour, which departs from the Country Music Hall of Fame downtown, hear anecdotes about recording sessions at the studio and see rare footage of a 1960s Dottie West recording session. The studio no longer operates, but it is used in courses at nearby Belmont College.

Tours can only be purchased in conjunction with admission to the Country Music Hall of Fame. Tours depart hourly Sunday–Thursday 10:30 A.M.–2:30 P.M. On Friday and Saturday, tours leave every half-hour 10:30 A.M.–2:30 P.M.

The Upper Room

Three million Christians around the world know the *Upper Room Daily Devotional Guide,* a page-a-day pocket devotional available in 106 countries and 40 languages. Headquartered in Nashville, the Upper Room Ministry has established a bookstore, museum, and chapel to welcome visitors. **The Upper Room Chapel and Museum** (1908 Grand Ave., 615/340-7207, www.upperroom.org/chapel, Mon.–Fri.

8 A.M.–4:30 P.M., free) features a small museum of Christian-inspired art, including a wonderful collection of nativity scenes from around the world made from materials ranging from needlepoint to camel bone. Visitors may also tour the chapel, with its 8-foot-by-20-foot stained-glass window and 8-foot-by-17-foot wood carving of Leonardo DaVinci's *The Last Supper.* A 15-minute audio presentation discusses features of the carving and tells the history and mission of the Upper Room.

Admission to the Upper Room is free; donations are accepted.

MIDTOWN

Encompassing the neighborhoods of Elliston Place, Hillsboro Village, and Green Hills, midtown refers to the parts of Nashville between downtown and the West End.

◖ The Parthenon

In 1893, efforts began to raise funds for a mighty exposition that would celebrate the 1896 centennial of the state of Tennessee. Though the exposition would start a year late—in 1897—it would exceed all expectations. The old West Side Race Track was converted to a little city, with exhibit halls dedicated to transportation, agriculture, machinery, minerals, forestry, and African Americans, among other themes. There were Chinese, Cuban, and Egyptian villages, a midway, and an auditorium. The exposition attracted 1.7 million people between May 1 and October 31. While the event turned only a modest profit for its organizers, it no doubt contributed in other ways to the local economy and to the stature of the state.

When the exposition closed in the fall of 1897, all the exhibit halls were torn down, except for a life-sized replica of the Greek Parthenon, which had housed an art exhibit during the centennial. The exposition grounds were made into a public park, aptly named Centennial Park, and Nashvillians continued to admire their Parthenon.

The Parthenon replica had been built out of wood and plaster, and it was designed only to last through the centennial. Remarkably, it survived well beyond that. But by the 1920s, the Parthenon was crumbling. City officials, responding to public outcry to save the Parthenon, agreed to restore it, and they hired a contractor to rebuild the replica. The contractor did so using tinted concrete.

Today, the Parthenon remains one of Nashville's most iconic landmarks. It is a monument to the creativity and energy of the New South, and also to Nashville's distinction as the Athens of the South.

You can see and walk around the Parthenon simply by visiting Centennial Park. It is, in many respects, most beautiful from the outside. You can also pay to go inside.

The Parthenon (Centennial Park, 2600 West End Ave., 615/862-8431, Tues.–Sat. 9 A.M.–4:30 P.M., Sun. June–Aug. only 12:30–4:30 P.M., adults $5, seniors and children $2.50) has three gallery spaces; the largest is used to display works from its permanent collection of 63 pieces of American art. The other two galleries host changing exhibits. Visitors to the museum are also able to go inside the Parthenon to view the 42-foot statue of Athena Parthenos.

Belmont Mansion

The elaborate "summer home" of Adelicia Acklen was constructed in 1853 and was named Belle Monte. Belmont Mansion (1900 Belmont Blvd., 615/460-5459, www.belmont-mansion.com, Mon.–Sat. 10 A.M.–4 P.M., Sun. 1–4 P.M., adults $10, seniors $9, children 6–12 $3), as it is known today, is a monument to the excesses of the Victorian age.

Adelicia was born to a wealthy Nashville family in 1817. When she was 22, Adelicia married Isaac Franklin, a wealthy bachelor 28 years her senior. When Franklin died seven years later, Adelicia inherited his substantial wealth. Adelicia remarried to Joseph Acklen, a young lawyer, and together they planned and built Belmont Mansion. The home was built in the Italian style, with touches of Egyptian revival style.

The home boasted 36 rooms and 16,000 square feet of space including a grand gallery

© SUSANNA HENIGHAN POTTER

The Parthenon in Centennial Park is one of Nashville's most extraordinary structures.

NASHVILLE

MIDTOWN NASHVILLE AND THE WEST END

To Downtown

MUSIC ROW

UPPER ROOM CHAPEL

OUTLAND CAFÉ

CITY HOSTEL

GREENHOUSE

ELLISTON PLACE SODA SHOP

LOEWS VANDERBILT PLAZA

INNS AND SUITES

EXIT/IN

VANDERBILT FINE ARTS GALLERY

JIMMY KELLY'S

ROTIER'S

MARRIOTT NASHVILLE VANDERBILT

VANDERBILT UNIVERSITY

AARON DOUGLAS GALLERY

CARL VAN VECHTEN GALLERY

FISK UNIVERSITY

MEHARRY MEDICAL COLLEGE

SWETT'S

THE PARTHENON

Centennial Park

TENNESSEE STATE UNIVERSITY

Hadley Park

NASHVILLE

13TH AVE

EDGEHILL RD

18TH AVE S

17TH AVE S

WEDGEWOOD AVE

BELMONT MANSION ★

BELMONT UNIVERSITY

12 SOUTH

12TH AVE S

HILLSBORO HOUSE •

BELMONT BLVD

PORTLAND AVE

PANCAKE PANTRY ▼

FIDO ▼

LINDEN HOUSE B&B •

BONGO JAVA ▼

0.25 mi

0.25 km

0

0

SARRATT GALLERY ■

VANDERBILT UNIVERSITY

BLAKEMORE AVE

BELCOURT THEATER ★

HILLSBORO VILLAGE

BOSCOS ▼

21ST AVE S

440

WOODLAWN DR

HOG HEAVEN ▼

RESTAURANT ZOLA ▼

31ST ST

WEST END AVE

NATCHEZ TRACE

GOLF CLUB LN

440

MURPHY RD

BOWLING AVE

CENTENNIAL BLVD

41

40

65

MAP AREA

WOODMONT BLVD

SHALIMAR ▼

SCOTT'S ▼

BRONTE ▼

THE MALL AT GREEN HILLS ■

GREEN HILLS

THE BLUEBIRD CAFE ◄

0.5 mi

0.5 km

0

0

WHITE PIKE

BATTERY LN

HARDING PL

To Radnor Lake State Natural Area

HILLSBORO PIKE

440

SYLVAN PARK

40TH AVE N

DARKHORSE THEATER ★

46TH AVE N

McCABE PUB ▼

CAFÉ NONNA ▼

Richland Park

McCABE GOLF COURSE ★

51ST AVE N

CHEROKEE RD

HARDING RD

155

BELLE MEADE BLVD

BELLE MEADE PLANTATION ★

BELLE MEADE

CHEEKWOOD ◄

PAGE RD

Percy Warner Park

To Chaffin's Barn Dinner Theater & the Loveless Café

WHITE BRIDGE PIKE

40

BRILEY PKWY

© AVALON TRAVEL

where the Acklens hosted elaborate balls and dinner parties. The property included a private art gallery, aviary, zoo, and conservatory, as well as a lake and acres of manicured gardens. After the Civil War, Adelicia traveled to Europe, where she purchased a number of paintings and sculptures that are now on display in her restored mansion.

Shortly before her death, Adelicia sold Belmont to two female educators who ran a girls school from the property for 61 years. Later, it was purchased by the founders of Belmont College, a private college known for its music and music business programs.

Visitors to the mansion are given a 45-minute guided tour of the property, which includes the downstairs sitting and entertaining rooms and three of the upstairs bedrooms.

Vanderbilt University

Named for philanthropist Commodore Cornelius Vanderbilt, who donated $1 million in 1873 to found a university that would "contribute to strengthening the ties which should exist between all sections of our common country," Vanderbilt University (www.vanderbilt.edu) is now one of the region's most respected institutions of higher education.

A private research university, Vanderbilt has an enrollment of 6,300 undergraduates and 5,200 graduates. The university comprises 10 schools, a medical center, public policy center, and The Freedom Forum First Amendment Center. Originally just 75 acres, the university had grown to 250 acres by 1960. When the George Peabody School for Teachers merged with Vanderbilt in 1979, another 53 acres were added.

Vanderbilt's campus life is vibrant, and there is a daily roll call of lectures, recitals, exhibits, and other special events. Check http://calendar.vanderbilt.edu for an up-to-date listing of all campus events.

Prospective students and their parents can sign up for a campus tour. Vanderbilt also offers a self-guided tour of the campus's trees, which form the Vanderbilt Arboretum. Most trees on the tour are native trees common to Nashville and Middle Tennessee. This is a nice activity for people who want to hone tree identification skills. Download a podcast or print a

McKISSACK AND McKISSACK ARCHITECTS

The oldest African-American architectural firm in Tennessee can trace its roots to Moses McKissack (1790-1865), a member of the West African Ashanti tribe, who was sold into slavery to William McKissack of North Carolina. Later, McKissack moved to Middle Tennessee. Moses became a master builder, and he passed his knowledge on to his son, Gabriel Moses McKissack, born in 1840. Gabriel Moses passed his knowledge of the building trade to his own son, Moses McKissack III, born in 1879.

Moses McKissack III was born in Pulaski, where he received a basic education in the town's segregated schools. In 1890 he was hired by a local white architect. From then until 1905, McKissack designed and built homes throughout the area, including many in Mount Pleasant in Maury County. He developed a reputation as an excellent architect and tradesman.

In 1905 McKissack moved to Nashville, where he started his own construction company. Within a few years, he was working on major projects. He built a home for the dean of architecture and engineering at Vanderbilt University and the Carnegie Library at Fisk University. In 1922, Moses's brother, Calvin, joined him and they opened McKissack and McKissack, Tennessee's first black architectural firm.

The McKissacks have continued to distinguish themselves in the building industry, and they have also kept the business in the family. Since 1991 the company has been led by Cheryl McKissack, a fifth-generation McKissack. The firm employs more than 100 people and has corporate offices in Philadelphia and New York City.

paper copy of the tour from the website or contact the university for more information.

Vanderbilt University also has two excellent art galleries: The **Sarratt Gallery** (Sarratt Student Center, Vanderbilt Place near 24th Ave., 615/322-2471, Mon.–Fri. 9 A.M.–9 P.M., Sat.–Sun. 11 A.M.–10 P.M.) has a more contemporary bent than the **Vanderbilt Fine Arts Gallery** (Fine Arts Bldg., Mon.–Fri. noon–4 P.M., Sat.–Sun. 1–5 P.M., free), which includes works that demonstrate the development of both Eastern and Western art, plus six different traveling exhibits annually. The Fine Arts Gallery is located near the intersection of West End and 23rd Avenues. Both galleries are closed or limit their hours during university holidays and semester breaks, so it's a good idea to call ahead.

There is designated visitor parking in several lots on the Vanderbilt campus. Look on the eastern edge of the sports facilities parking lot off Natchez Trace, in the Wesley Place parking lot off Scarritt Place, or in the Terrace Place parking lot between 20th and 21st Avenues north of Broadway.

Belmont University

The school for girls founded in the Belmont Mansion in 1890 evolved in 1913 to the Ward-Belmont School for Women and in 1951 to coed Belmont College. Since 1991, it has been Belmont University, a higher-education institution with links to the Tennessee Baptist Convention. Belmont is a fast-growing university with highly respected music and music business programs. It has a student enrollment of 4,800.

WEST END

Nashville's most posh neighborhood, Belle Meade, is actually a city with its own government. Named after an antebellum plantation, Belle Meade the city is home to Nashville's elite, and famously possesses one of the most wealthy zip codes in America. Drive through to spy on mansions that look more like museums and lawns that look like botanical gardens.

Around Belle Meade are other nice neighborhoods where Nashville's professionals and upper class live. West End Avenue, the area's thoroughfare, is home to lots of nice restaurants. As you head westward, you pass Cheekwood, the Warner Parks, and eventually run into the Natchez Trace Parkway.

Belle Meade Plantation

The mansion at the former Belle Meade Plantation is the centerpiece of present-day Belle Meade Plantation and one of the finest old homes in the city. Its name means "beautiful pasture," and indeed it was Belle Meade's pastures that gave rise to the plantation's fame as the home of a superb stock of horses. Purchased as 250 acres in 1807 by Virginia farmer John Harding and his wife, Susannah, the estate grew to 5,400 acres at its peak in the 1880s and 1890s.

Belle Meade was never a cotton plantation, although small amounts of the cash crop were grown here, along with fruits, vegetables, and tobacco. Instead it was the horses, including the racehorse Iroquois, that made Belle Meade famous. The mansion was built in 1820 and expanded in 1853. Its grand rooms are furnished with period antiques, more than 60 percent of which are original to the house. The estate also includes outbuildings, including a smokehouse, dairy, and the original log cabin that Harding built for his family when they moved to Belle Meade in 1807.

The plantation also includes a slave cabin, which houses an exhibit on Belle Meade's enslaved population, which numbered more than 160 at its peak. Two of these slaves are described in detail. Susanna Carter was the mansion's housekeeper for more than 30 years, and remained with the family even after the end of slavery. On her deathbed, Selena Jackson, the mistress of Belle Meade for many years, called Susanna "one of the most faithful and trusted of my friends." The other African American who features prominently at the museum is Bob Green, whose skill and experience as a hostler earned him one of the highest salaries ever paid to a horse hand of the day.

Visitors to Belle Meade are given a one-hour guided tour of the mansion and then visit the outbuildings and grounds on their own.

◖ Cheekwood

Plan to spend a full morning or afternoon at Cheekwood (1200 Forrest Park Dr., 615/356-8000, www.cheekwood.org, Tues.–Sat. 9:30 A.M.–4:30 P.M., Sun. 11 A.M.–4:30 P.M., adults $10, seniors $8, students and children $5) so you can experience the full scope of this magnificent art museum and botanical garden. Galleries in the Cheekwood mansion house the museum's American and European collections, including an excellent contemporary art collection. Cheekwood has the largest public collection of works by Nashville artist William Edmondson, the sculptor and stoneworker. Cheekwood usually displays items from its permanent collection as well as traveling exhibitions from other museums. Many exhibits have special ties with Nashville.

But the Cheekwood is far more than just an art museum. The mansion overlooks hundreds of acres of gardens and woods, and it is easy to forget that you are near a major American city when you're at the Cheekwood. Walk the mile-long Carell Woodland Sculpture Trail past works by 15 internationally acclaimed artists, or stroll past the water garden to the Japanese garden. There are dogwood gardens, an herb garden, a delightful boxwood garden, and much more. Wear comfortable shoes and pack a bottle of water so you can enjoy the grounds in comfort.

The Cheekwood owes its existence to the success of the coffee brand Maxwell House. During the 1920s, Leslie Cheek and his wife, Mabel Wood, invested in the new coffee brand being developed by their cousin, Joel Cheek. Maxwell House proved to be a success and earned the Cheeks a fortune, which they used to buy 100 acres of land in West Nashville. The family hired New York residential and landscape architect Bryant Fleming to create a 30,000-square-foot mansion and neighboring gardens. Cheekwood was completed in 1933.

Leslie Cheek lived in the mansion just two years before he died, and Mabel lived there for another decade before deeding it to her daughter and son-in-law, who later offered it as a site

THE SCULPTURE OF WILLIAM EDMONDSON

The first African-American artist to have a one-man show at the Museum of Modern Art in New York was Nashville-born sculptor William Edmondson.

Edmondson was born around 1870 in the Hillsboro area of Nashville. He worked for decades as a laborer on the railroads, a janitor at Women's Hospital, and in other similar jobs before discovering his talent for sculpture in 1929. Edmondson told the Nashville *Tennessean* that his talent and passion were God-given: "God appeared at the head of my bed and talked to me, like a natural man, concerning the talent of cutting stone He was about to bestow. He talked so loud He woke me up. He told me He had something for me."

Edmondson was a prolific sculptor. He worked exclusively with limestone, and he created angels, women, doves, turtles, rabbits, and other "varmints." He also made tombstones. Edmondson never learned to read or write, and he called many of his works "mirkels" because they were inspired by God.

In the 1930s, Louise Dahl-Wolfe, a photographer for *Harper's Bazaar* magazine, brought Edmondson and his work to the attention of Alfred Barr, the director of the Museum of Modern Art. Barr and other trustees of the museum admired what they termed as Edmondson's "modern primitive" work, and they invited him to display a one-man show at the museum in 1938. In 1941, the Nashville Art Museum put on an exhibit of Edmondson's work.

Edmondson continued to work until the late 1940s, when he became ill with cancer. He died in 1951 and is buried in an unmarked grave at Mt. Ararat Cemetery in Nashville. The city park at 17th Avenue North and Charlotte Avenue is named in honor of William Edmondson.

You can see an exhibit of Edmondson's work at the Cheekwood Museum.

for a museum and garden. Cheekwood opened to the public in 1960.

Visitors pay admission at a guard gate at the entrance; there is a total family cap of $30 per car. Once inside, drive to parking lot B so you can explore the art museum and grounds. Parking lot A is for the museum shop and restaurant.

SOUTH NASHVILLE

Head south on 4th Avenue, which becomes Nolensville Pike, towards a diverse array of attractions.

Fort Negley

Early in the Civil War, the Union army determined that taking and holding Nashville was a critical strategic link in their victory. So after Nashville fell in 1862, the Federals wasted no time fortifying the city against attacks. One of the city's forts was Fort Negley, built between August and December 1862 on St. Cloud Hill south of the city center.

Fort Negley owes its existence to the 2,768 men who were enrolled to build it. Most were blacks, some free and some slave, who were pressed into service by the Union army. These men felled trees, hauled earth, and cut and laid limestone for the fort. They slept in the open and enjoyed few, if any, comforts while they labored. Between 600 and 800 men died while building the fort, and only 310 received payment.

When it was completed, Fort Negley was the largest inland masonry fortification in North America. It was never challenged. Fort Negley was abandoned by the military after the war, but it remained the cornerstone of one of Nashville's oldest African-American communities, now known as Cameron-Trimble. During the New Deal, the Works Progress Administration rebuilt large sections of the crumbling fort, and it became a public park.

In 2007, the city opened a visitors center to tell the story of the fort. **Fort Negley Park** (Fort Negley Dr., 615/862-8470, Tues.–Sat. 9 A.M.–4:30 P.M., free) includes a museum about the fort and Nashville's role in the Civil War. There is a short paved loop trail around the base of the fort, plus raised boardwalks

© AVALON TRAVEL

through the fortifications themselves. Historic markers tell the story of the fort's construction and detail its military features.

City Cemetery

Right next to Fort Negley Park, off Chestnut Street, is the old City Cemetery. Opened in 1822, City Cemetery (1001 4th Ave. S., www.thenashvillecitycemetery.org) was the final resting place of many of Nashville's most prominent early citizens, including founder James Robertson;

NASHVILLE

William Driver, the U.S. Navy captain who named the flag "Old Glory"; Mabel Lewis Imes and Ella Sheppard, members of the original Fisk Jubilee Singers; and 14 Nashville mayors.

During the Civil War, the cemetery was contracted to bury more than 15,000 Union and Confederate dead, although they were later reinterred in different cemeteries.

Visitors are welcome 8 A.M.–5 P.M. daily. Consult the information board in the Keeble Building for help with your self-guided tour. Guided tours and special events, such as living history tours, garden tours, and historical lectures, take place on the second Saturday of each month. The events are aimed at telling the history of Nashvillians who are buried at this historical cemetery.

Adventure Science Center

Children will enjoy learning about science at the Adventure Science Center (800 Fort Negley Blvd., 615/862-5160, Mon.–Sat. 10 A.M.–5 P.M., Sun. 12:30–5:30 P.M., adults $9, children $7). Interactive exhibits explore how the body works, the solar system, and other scientific areas. The center's new Sudekum Planetarium opened in June 2008. With 164 seats, it is the largest planetarium in Tennessee.

Tennessee Central Railway Museum

Railroad enthusiasts should make a detour to the Tennessee Central Railway Museum (220 Willow St., 615/244-9001, www.tcry.org, Tues., Thurs., and Sat. 9 A.M.–3 P.M., free). This institution is best known for its special railroad excursions (see *Tours* later in this chapter), but they also collect railroad equipment and paraphernalia, which are on display at the museum. The museum is located in an otherwise industrial area between the interstate and the railroad tracks, one block north of Hermitage Avenue and east of Fairfield Avenue.

Nashville Zoo at Grassmere

See familiar and exotic animals at the Nashville Zoo at Grassmere (3777 Nolensville Pike,

615/833-1534, www.nashvillezoo.org, adults $13, seniors $11, children 3–12 $8, children under 3 free). From April 1 to October 15, the zoo is open daily 9 A.M.–6 P.M. The rest of the year, opening hours are daily 9 A.M.–4 P.M. The zoo is closed Thanksgiving, Christmas, and New Year's Days. Parking is free.

Many of the zoo's animals live in beautiful habitats like Lorikeet Landing, Gibbon Islands, and Bamboo Trail. The zoo's meerkat exhibit, featuring the famously quizzical and erect animals, is one of its most popular. The Wild Animal Carousel is an old-time carousel with 39 different brightly painted wooden animals. Two of the newest exhibits feature African wild dogs and Eurasian Lynx.

The zoo is located at Grassmere, the one-time home and farm of the Croft family. The historic Croft farmhouse has been preserved and is open for guided tours in October and December every year.

Travellers Rest Plantation and Museum

Travellers Rest (636 Farrell Pkwy., 615/832-8197, www.travellersrestplantation.org, Tues.–Sat. 10 A.M.–4 P.M., Sun. 1–4 P.M., $2–10) was the home of John Overton, a Nashville lawyer who helped found Memphis, served on the first Tennessee Supreme Court, and was a trusted advisor to Andrew Jackson, the seventh U.S. president and the first from Tennessee.

Overton was born in Virginia and studied law in Kentucky before he decided to move to Middle Tennessee, what was then the western frontier of the United States. When workmen were digging the cellar for the original home in 1799, they uncovered Native American skeletons and artifacts—Overton had chosen a Mississipian-era Indian mound for the site of his home. But the archaeological finds did not stop Overton, who initially named his home Golgotha, or hill of skulls. The name did not stick, however; tradition has it that Overton later named the home Travellers Rest because it was his place of rest between long trips as a circuit judge in Middle and East Tennessee.

Travellers Rest underwent two major

expansions in its lifetime: one in 1808 and another 20 years later. The additions allowed Overton first to accommodate a growing number of young law students who wished to study law with him, later his wife, Mary, and their children, and, finally, the elaborate parties that Overton hosted to further the political career of Andrew Jackson.

John Overton was many different things in his lifetime. Among them was slave owner. Records show that between 30 and 80 slaves lived at Travellers Rest before emancipation. While Overton's plantation was not the primary source of his wealth, it no doubt contributed to his status and prominence. Sadly, when the L&N Railroad purchased the Overton property in the 1940s, the company destroyed not only the Overton family burial ground and peach orchard, but also the slave cabins that remained at the rear of the house.

Visitors to Travellers Rest may choose to skip the mansion tour; admission to the grounds alone is just $3. But to get the full story and flavor of the property, choose the 45-minute guided tour.

Tennessee Agricultural Museum

The Tennessee Agricultural Museum (Ellington Agricultural Center, 615/837-5197, www.tnagmuseum.com, Mon.–Fri. 9 A.M.–4 P.M., free) celebrates the ingenuity and dedicated labors of farm life from the 17th to the 20th century. Operated by the Tennessee Department of Agriculture and set on the department's pleasant south Nashville campus, the museum depicts various facets of Tennessee farm life. There are exhibits about clothes-washing, blacksmithing, coopers, plows, and weaving, just to name a few. Outside, there is a small kitchen garden with heirloom vegetables, and replicas of a log cabin, one-room schoolhouse, and outdoor

THE BATTLE OF NASHVILLE

During most of the Civil War, Nashville was occupied by Federal forces. After Fort Donelson, 90 miles northeast of Nashville, fell in mid-February 1862, Nashville was in Union hands. The Federals turned Nashville into an important goods depot for the Northern cause, and set strict rules for city residents during occupation.

As the war drew to a close in late 1864, Nashville was the site of what war historians now say was the last major battle of the Western Theater.

The Battle of Nashville came after a string of defeats for the Confederate army of Tennessee, commanded by John Bell Hood. After his bloody and humiliating losses at Spring Hill and Franklin a few miles south, Hood moved north and set up headquarters at Travellers Rest, the home of John Overton. His plan was to set up his troops in an arc around the southern side of the city. Union Maj. Gen. George H. Thomas did not plan to wait for Hood's attack, however. He devised to attack first and drive the Confederates away from Nashville.

A winter storm and frigid temperatures delayed the battle. For two weeks, from December 2 to 14, 1864, the two armies peered at one another across the no-man's-land between two lines. Then, at dawn on December 15, 1864, the Union attack began. Union troops on foot and horse, including at least four U.S. Colored Infantry brigades, attacked various Confederate posts around the city. By the close of the first day of fighting, Hood withdrew his troops two miles farther south from the city.

The dawn of the second day of battle augured more losses for the Confederates. Unable to hold their line against the Union assault, they fell back again. As darkness fell, Union Maj. Gen. Thomas wired Washington to announce his victory. Pursued by a Union cavalry commanded by Maj. Gen. James Wilson, what remained of the Confederate army of Tennessee marched south and on the day after Christmas crossed the Tennessee River into Alabama. Four months later, the war was over.

kitchen. There is also a short self-guided nature trail illustrating the ways that settlers used various types of native Tennessee trees.

Admission to the museum is free, but you can pre-arrange demonstrations for a fee. Staff are also available to answer any questions. This is a good choice for families.

JEFFERSON STREET

Jefferson Street runs from downtown through northwestern Nashville, past several of the city's African-American landmarks.

Bicentennial Mall

Just as Tennessee celebrated its 100th anniversary in 1896 with the construction of Centennial Park, Tennessee celebrated its 200th anniversary in much the same way. The **Bicentennial Capitol Mall State Park** occupies 19 acres on the north side of the capitol building. It offers excellent views of the Capitol, which towers over the mall. The mall and the Capitol are separated by a steep hill

and more than 200 steps, which prove daunting to all but the fittest among us.

The mall has dozens of features that celebrate Tennessee and Tennesseans, including a 200-foot granite map of Tennessee embedded in concrete; a River Wall with 31 fountains, each representing one of Tennessee's rivers; and a timeline with Tennessee events, inscriptions, and notable quotes from 1796 to 1996. There is also a monument to Tennessee's WWII veterans and casualties, and a walk of counties that depicts each of the state's 95 counties. A one-mile path that circles the mall's perimeter is popular with walkers and joggers, and a 2,000-seat amphitheater is used for special events. The park may be a civics lesson incarnate, but it is also a pleasant place to pass the time.

To the west of the mall is the **Nashville Farmer's Market,** where you can buy fresh produce, hot food, and arts and crafts.

Fisk University

Founded in 1866 to educate newly freed slaves,

The Tennessee State Capitol overlooks the Bicentennial Mall, built in 1996 to commemorate Tennessee's 200th anniversary.

FISK'S STIEGLITZ COLLECTION

When photographer Alfred Stieglitz died in 1946, his wife, Georgia O'Keeffe, herself one of the most important artists of her generation, was left with the responsibility of giving away his massive art collection. Stieglitz had collected more than 1,000 works by artists including Arthur Dove, Marsden Hartley, O'Keeffe, Charles Demuth, and John Marin. He also owned several African sculptures.

Stieglitz's instructions regarding this art collection were vague. In his will he asked O'Keeffe to select the recipients "under such arrangements as will assure to the public, under reasonable regulations, access thereto to promote the study of art."

O'Keeffe selected several obvious recipients for parts of the collection: the Library of Congress, the National Gallery of Art in Washington, the Metropolitan Museum of Art, the Art Institute of Chicago, and the Philadelphia Museum of Art. Fisk University in Nashville was a surprise, and Carl Van Vechten, a writer, photographer, and friend of Stieglitz and O'Keeffe, is credited with making the suggestion. Van Vechten was keenly interested in African-American art and was close friends with Fisk president Charles Johnson.

O'Keeffe and Fisk were not an easy partnership. According to an account by C. Michael Norton, when she first visited the university a few days before the Carl Van Vechten Gallery would open on campus, O'Keeffe ordered major changes to the gallery space, eventually flying in a lighting designer from New York on the day before the opening. At the opening ceremony on November 4, 1949, held at the Memorial Chapel at Fisk, O'Keeffe declined President Johnson's invitation to the lectern and spoke from her chair, saying curtly: "Dr. Johnson wrote and asked me to speak and I did not answer. I had and have no intention of speaking. These paintings and sculptures are a gift from Stieglitz. They are for the students. I hope you go back and look at them more than once."

The Stieglitz Collection at Fisk consists of 101 works of art, including two by O'Keeffe, 19 Stieglitz photographs, prints by Cezanne and Renoir, and five pieces of African tribal art.

Cash-strapped Fisk has sought to sell parts of the collection to raise funds. A proposal to sell a 50 percent share in the collection for $30 million to Wal-Mart heiress Alice Walton's Crystal Bridges Museum in Bentonville, Arkansas, has been rejected by a court, but Fisk continues to press its case. In 2008, an alternative proposal was made to house the collection in the planned museum of African-American culture, art, and history, to be located near the Bicentennial Mall. But that idea offered no immediate financial relief for Fisk and raised many unanswered questions. Meanwhile, Fisk reopened the Van Vechten Gallery in October 2008 so that the legendary collection is once again accessible to the public.

Fisk University (www.fisk.edu) has a long and proud history as one of the United States' foremost black colleges. W. E. B. Du Bois attended Fisk, graduating in 1888, and Booker T. Washington married a Fisk alumna and sent his own children to Fisk. In more modern times, Knoxville native and poet Nikki Giovanni attended Fisk.

Fisk sits at the corner of Jefferson Street and Dr. D. B. Todd Jr. Boulevard, about 10 blocks west of downtown Nashville. The campus is a smattering of elegant redbrick buildings set on open green lawns, although a few more modern buildings, including the library, detract from the classical feel. One of the oldest Fisk buildings is **Jubilee Hall,** on the north end of the campus, which is said to be the first permanent building constructed for the education of African Americans in the country. It was built with money raised by the Fisk Jubilee Singers, who popularized black spirituals during a world tour from 1871 to 1874. Another notable building is the **Fisk Little Theatre,** a white clapboard building that once served as Union hospital during the Civil War.

At the corner of Jackson Street and Todd Boulevard is the **Carl Van Vechten Gallery** (615/329-8720, Tues.–Sat. 10 A.M.–5 P.M., free),

THE JUBILEE SINGERS

In 1871, Fisk University needed money. Buildings at the school established in old Union army barracks in 1866 were decaying while more and more African Americans came to seek education.

So, the school choir withdrew all the money from the University's treasury and left on a world tour. The nine singers were Isaac Dickerson, Maggie Porter, Minnie Tate, Jennie Jackson, Benjamin Holmes, Thomas Rutling, Eliza Walker, Green Evans, and Ella Sheppard. Remembering a biblical reference to the Hebrew "year of the jubilee," Fisk treasurer and choir manager George White gave them their name, the Fisk Jubilee Singers.

The singers struggled at first, but before long audiences were praising them. They toured first the American South, then the North, and in 1873 sailed to England for a successful British tour. Their audiences included William Lloyd Garrison, Wendell Phillips, Ulysses S. Grant, William Gladstone, Mark Twain, Johann Strauss, and Queen Victoria. Songs like "Swing Low, Sweet Chariot" and "Nobody Knows the Trouble I've Seen" moved audiences to tears. The singers introduced the spiritual to mainstream white audiences and erased negative misconceptions about African Americans and African-American education.

In 1874 the singers returned to Nashville. They had raised enough money to pay off Fisk's debts and build the University's first permanent structure, an imposing Victorian Gothic six-story building now called Jubilee Hall. It was the first permanent structure built solely for the education of African Americans in the United States.

Every October 6, the day in 1871 that the singers departed Fisk, the University recalls their struggle and their triumph with a convocation featuring the modern-day Jubilee Singers.

© SUSANNA HENIGHAN POTTER

Jubilee Hall on the Fisk University campus was paid for by the proceeds of the Fisk Jubilee Singers.

named for the art collector who convinced artist Georgia O'Keeffe to donate to Fisk a large portion of the work and personal collection of her late husband, Alfred Stieglitz. The college still retains much of this collection, although they have sought to sell parts of it to raise funds for the cash-strapped private school. The legal and financial uncertainty over this art collection has forced the college to put it in storage for many years, but the gallery reopened to the public in 2008. The collection includes works by Stieglitz and O'Keeffe, as well as acclaimed European and American artists including Pablo Picasso, Paul Cezanne, Pierre-Auguste Renoir, Diego Rivera, Arthur Dove, Gino Severini, and Charles Demuth. It is truly a remarkable collection.

The **Aaron Douglas Gallery** (Jackson St. and 17th Ave. N., Tues.–Fri. 11 A.M.–4 P.M., Sat. 1–4 P.M., Sun. 2–4 P.M., free) houses Fisk's collection of African, African-American, and folk art works. It also hosts visiting exhibits, and others by Fisk students and faculty. It is named after painter and illustrator Aaron Douglas, who also established Fisk's first formal art department. The gallery is located on the top floor of the Fisk library.

Fisk welcomes visitors, but there is no central information desk or printed guide. A map is posted just inside the library, and this is the best place to go to start your visit. Historical markers provide details of each of the main campus buildings. To see the famous painting of the Jubilee Singers, enter Jubilee Hall and bear right to the Appleton Room, where it hangs at the rear.

Meharry Medical College

Just across Dr. D. B. Todd Jr. Boulevard from Fisk is Meharry Medical College, the largest private, comprehensive, historically black institution educating medical professionals. It was founded in 1876 as the Medical Department of the Central Tennessee College of Nashville, under the auspices of the Freeman's Aid Society of the Methodist Episcopal Church.

Meharry was at one time responsible for graduating more than half of all African-American doctors and nurses in the United States. Today it has an enrollment of more than 700 students.

Hadley Park

Founded in 1912, Hadley Park is believed to be the oldest public park developed for African Americans in the South and, most likely, the United States. The park got its start when Fisk University president George Gates requested that the city buy land and create a park for its black citizens. This was in the era of segregation, so other city parks were not open to blacks. The request was granted, and the park opened in July 1912. An old farmhouse was converted into a community center, and benches and a playground were installed. It is now home to a state-of-the-art gym and fitness center, computer labs, meeting rooms, and tennis courts.

Tennessee State University

Founded in 1912 as a normal school for blacks, Tennessee State University (www.tnstate.edu) is now a comprehensive university with more than 9,000 students. In 1979, as a result of a court order to desegregate the state's universities, TSU merged with the Nashville campus of the University of Tennessee. Today, TSU's student body is 75 percent African American.

MUSIC VALLEY

A knot of tourist attractions separated from the rest of Nashville by the Cumberland River, Music Valley has little to recommend it other than the Grand Ole Opry. A strip of motels, restaurants, and dubious country music "museums," this is one tourist zone that you will be just as happy to skip. Unless, of course, you just want to soak up the trashy side of Music City tourism.

If you're game, however, head straight for **Cooter's** (2613 McGavock Pk., 615/872-8358, Mon.–Thurs. 9 A.M.–7 P.M., Fri.–Sat. 9 A.M.–8 P.M., Sun. 9 A.M.–6 P.M., free), a gift shop and museum dedicated to the *Dukes of Hazzard* television show. The museum features a mind-boggling array of toys, ornaments, and model cars manufactured in the 1970s and '80s

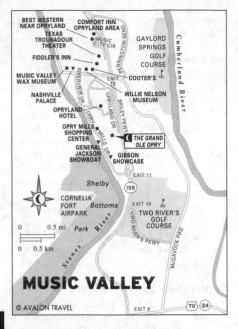

BEST WESTERN NEAR OPRYLAND
COMFORT INN OPRYLAND AREA
TEXAS TROUBADOUR THEATER
MUSIC CITY CIR
GAYLORD SPRINGS GOLF COURSE
FIDDLER'S INN
MUSIC VALLEY WAX MUSEUM
COOTER'S
NASHVILLE PALACE
WILLIE NELSON MUSEUM
OPRYLAND HOTEL
OPRY MILLS SHOPPING CENTER
THE GRAND OLE OPRY
GENERAL JACKSON SHOWBOAT
GIBSON SHOWCASE
EXIT 12
FRANKLIN LIMESTONE RD
RIVERVIEW DR
OPRYLAND DR
OPRY MILLS DR
BRILEY PKWY
Cumberland River
EXIT 11
Shelby
155
CORNELIA FORT AIRPARK
Bottoms
EXIT 10
TWO RIVER'S GOLF COURSE
Park
Stones River
TWO RIVER'S PKWY
McGAVOCK PIKE
0   0.5 mi
0   0.5 km

MUSIC VALLEY

© AVALON TRAVEL
EXIT 8
70 24

to profit off the Dukes' wild popularity. You can also see one of the bright-orange Dodge Chargers that became the Dukes' icon. In the gift shop, buy a pair of "official" Daisy Dukes, or any number of General Lee souvenirs. Cooters is operated by Ben Jones who played Cooter, the affable sidekick mechanic, in the original television series. In recent years, Jones has been one of the forces behind DukeFest, a wildly popular annual celebration of fast cars and the General Lee held at the Nashville Motor Speedway.

A few doors down from Cooters, you will find **Willie Nelson and Friends Museum** (2613 McGavock Pike, 615/885-1515, summer daily 9 A.M.–8 P.M., winter daily 9 A.M.–7 P.M., $10), which showcases a number of things that once belonged to Willie Nelson, including his golf bag, a replica of his tour bus, and the guitar he played during his first performance on the Grand Ole Opry. Many of the Willie Nelson items were purchased by museum operators Jeannie and Frank Oakley at an IRS auction.

Another choice is the **Music Valley Wax Museum of the Stars** (2515 McGavock Pike, 615/884-7876, daily 9 A.M.–5 P.M., $12), which advertises itself thus: "As close as you can get to Nashville's biggest stars without being slapped with a restraining order." Enough said.

The Grand Ole Opry

Since 1974, the Grand Ole Opry (2802 Opryland Dr., 615/871-6779, www.opry.com) has been performed at the specially built Grand Ole Opry House in Music Valley.

The Opry performs at least two times a week, Friday and Saturday, with additional shows on Tuesday night most weeks. If you don't come to see a show, you can stop at the **Grande Ole Opry Museum** (2802 Opryland Dr., 615/889-6611, Mon., Wed., and Thurs. 10 A.M.–6 P.M., Tues. 10 A.M.–7:30 P.M., Fri. 10 A.M.–8:30 P.M., Sat. 10 A.M.–10 P.M., Sun. noon–5 P.M., free). The museum has exhibits about many early Opry members and performers, including Minnie Pearl and Roy Acuff. It also emphasizes the important link between the Opry and WSM radio, which still broadcasts the Opry live in Nashville and on the Internet. The museum is closed in January and February.

If the Opry isn't occupied with a performance or special event, you can take a backstage tour for $11.

TOURS
Nash Trash Tours

Nashville's most notorious tour guides are Sheri Lynn and Brenda Kay Jugg, sisters who ferry thrill-seekers around Nashville in a big pink school bus. The Nash Trash Tour (615/226-7300 or 800/342-2123, www.nash-trash.com, $30) is a raunchy, rollicking, rib-tickling tour of city attractions, some of which you won't even find in this guidebook. Be prepared to be the butt of some of the jokes yourself; their "I Got Trashed" T-shirts have a double meaning. You'll snack on canned cheese and there's a pit stop to buy beer. Not appropriate for children or adults who aren't comfortable laughing at themselves and others. As Sheri Lynn says: "If we haven't offended you, just give us some time."

Gray Line Tours

Nashville's largest tour company, Gray Line (2416 Music Valley Dr., 615/883-5555 or 800/251-1864), offers no fewer than 12 different sightseeing tours of the city. The three-hour Discover Nashville tour costs $40 per adult and includes entrance to the Ryman Auditorium, the Country Music Hall of Fame, and stops at other city landmarks.

The three-hour Homes of the Stars tour takes you past the homes of stars including Alan Jackson, Vince Gill, Dolly Parton, and the late Tammy Wynette for $35. There is also a one-hour downtown trolley tour for $12 and a 90-minute downtown walking tour for $20.

General Jackson Showboat

Enjoy lunch or dinner, live entertainment, and a cruise along the Cumberland on the General Jackson Showboat (2812 Opryland Dr., 615/458-3900, www.generaljackson.com). Midday tickets range $30–50 and include

lunch. Evening tickets are $35–90 and include a three-course dinner. You can cruise and skip the meal at midday or in the evening for $17.

Tennessee Central Railway

The Tennessee Central Railway Museum (220 Willow St., 615/244-9001, www.tcry.org) offers an annual calendar of sightseeing and themed railway rides in central Tennessee. Excursions include fall foliage tours, Christmas shopping expeditions, and trips to scenic small towns. All trips run on the Nashville and Eastern Railroad, which runs east, stopping in Lebanon, Watertown, and Cookville, and terminates in Monterrey.

Trips sell out early, so book your tickets well in advance.

Nashville Black Heritage Tours

Call ahead to book a tour for your family or group with Bill Daniel of Nashville Black Heritage Tours (5188 Almaville Rd., Smyrna, 615/890-8153), who will craft a tour of the city's most important African-American heritage sites

Entertainment

From shopping to live music, Nashville offers visitors plenty of diversions. Even if you are not a fan of country music, you will find plenty to do in Music City.

LIVE MUSIC AND CLUBS

No trip to Nashville is complete without listening to some live music. Music City overflows with musicians and opportunities to hear them. So whether you catch a show at the Opry, stake out a seat at the Bluebird Cafe, or enjoy a night at the symphony, be sure to make time for music during your visit.

Even before you arrive in the city, you can plan out your nights thanks to the Nashville Convention and Visitors Bureau (www.nashvillecvb.com). Through a handy feature on the bureau's website you can check out upcoming

concerts a month or more in advance. Many venues will let you buy tickets in advance over the phone or online.

Published on Wednesday, the *Nashville Scene* always includes detailed entertainment listings and recommendations. The *Tennessean*, the city's daily paper, publishes its entertainment insert on Friday.

◖ The Grand Ole Opry

If there's anything you really must do while in Nashville, it's go to see the Grand Ole Opry (2802 Opryland Dr., 615/871-6779 or 800/733-6779, www.opry.com, $35–50). For more than 80 years this weekly radio showcase of country music has drawn crowds to Nashville. Every show at the Opry is still broadcast live on WSM, a Nashville AM radio

NASHVILLE

THE GRAND OLE OPRY

Nashville's most famous broadcast can trace its roots to October 1925, when Nashville-based National Life and Accident Insurance Company opened a radio station in town. Its call letters, WSM, stood for "We Shield Millions," the company's motto.

WSM hired George D. Hay, a radio announcer who had worked in Memphis and Chicago, to manage the station. Hay – who, while in Chicago, had announced one of the nation's first live country radio shows – planned to create a similar such program in Nashville.

On November 25, 1925, Hay invited a 78-year-old fiddler, Uncle Jimmy Thompson, to perform live on Saturday night over the radio waves. The response was electric, and WSM continued to broadcast live old-time music every Saturday night. In May 1927, the program developed the name the Grand Ole Opry, practically by chance. An announcer named Judge Hay was segueing from the previous program of classical opera to the barn dance. "For the past hour, we have been listening to music taken largely from Grand Opera. From now on, we will present the Grand Ole Opry," he said. The name stuck.

During the first few years, most Opry performers were unknowns who worked day jobs in and around Nashville. But as the show gained popularity, some acts were able to make it professionally, including Uncle Dave Macon, the Vagabonds, and the Delmore Brothers. By 1939, the Opry gained a slot on the nationwide NBC radio network, allowing it to reach a national audience every week.

Always a live audience show, the Opry was performed in several different venues over the years. It started in the WSM studio, then moved to the Hillsboro Theater (now the Belcourt), the Dixie Tabernacle on Fatherland Street, and the War Memorial Auditorium downtown. In 1943 it moved to the Ryman Auditorium, where it remained until 1974, when National Life built a new 5,000-seat auditorium in a rural area north of Nashville. The first show from the new Opry House in Music Valley was broadcast on March 16, 1974. President Richard Nixon attended. In 1983, the Opry was acquired by Oklahoma-based Gaylord Broadcasting Company. The Opry is still owned by Gaylord Entertainment.

The music that flows from the Opry's stage on a Saturday night (and now, Tuesday and Friday too) has changed since the first fiddler took the airwaves. Just as country music broadened its appeal by softening its hard edges, the Opry has evolved with its audience. Today it is a showcase for all types of country and country-inspired music, including bluegrass, gospel, honky-tonk, and zydeco. It remains, however, one of the most esteemed and celebrated institutions in country music.

The Opry is the most famous stage in country music.

station. Shows are also streamed online and some are televised on cable. But nothing quite beats being there.

The Opry runs on Friday and Saturday night, with two two-and-a-half-hour shows each night. The early show starts at 6:30 P.M. and the late show starts at 9:30 P.M. Sometimes there is a bonus show on Tuesday evening. Since this is a radio broadcast, shows start and end right on time.

Every Opry show is divided into 30-minute segments, each of which is hosted by a different member of the Opry. This elite country music fraternity includes dozens of stars that you've heard of and others you haven't. The host performs two songs; one at the beginning of their half-hour segment and one at the end. In between they will introduce two or three other performers, each of whom will sing about two songs. In between segments, the announcers read radio commercials and stagehands change around the stage set.

All in all, it is a fast-paced show that keeps your toes tapping. Even if there's an act that you don't like, they won't be on the stage for too long. Of course, the flip side is that if it's an act you love, well, they're only on the stage for two songs too. Even when the biggest stars appear on the Opry stage, they rarely sing more than a few numbers.

The Opry usually releases the full line-up for each show about a week in advance. Some fans wait until then to buy their tickets so they're sure to catch a big-name artist. My advice is to forget about bragging to your friends back home about who you saw at the Opry and buy tickets to any show at all. Each show is carefully balanced to include bluegrass, classic country, popular country, and, sometimes, gospel. It is a true showcase that every fan of country music will enjoy.

Most Opry shows take place in the Grand Ole Opry House, a 4,400-seat auditorium in Music Valley. The interior of the hall was designed to look like the Ryman Auditorium, although the seats are much more comfortable. A circle of the original stage from the Ryman was cut out and placed in the center of the Opry House stage, and it is here that artists stand when they perform. Several months out of the year the Opry returns to the Ryman for its Opry at the Ryman season.

Ernest Tubb Midnite Jamboree

Texas Troubadour Ernest Tubb started a tradition when he set up a live radio show at the back of his Broadway record shop. The show was broadcast after the Opry shut down across the street, and it lived up to its name, the Midnite Jamboree. The Jamboree continues, now broadcast from the **Texas Troubadour Theatre** (Music Valley Village, 2416 Music Valley Dr., 615/889-2472, www.ernesttubb.com, no cover). Located across the street from the Opryland Hotel, the Jamboree gets started early in the evening, while the Opry is still on, but things really get swinging after midnight.

The Texas Troubadour Theatre is also home to the **Cowboy Church** (2416 Music Valley Dr., 615/859-1001, www.nashvillecowboychurch.org). Every Sunday morning at 10 A.M., locals and tourists dressed in anything from shorts to Stetsons gather here for a lively praise-and-worship country gospel church service led by Dr. Harry Yates and Dr. Joanne Cash Yates. The church was founded in 1990 with just six souls; today it attracts hundreds to its weekly services. Country and gospel music legends make cameo performances now and again, but the real star is Jesus.

The Gibson Showcase

Guitar manufacturer Gibson has a concert venue next to its Nashville retail store. The Gibson Showcase (161 Opry Mills Dr., 615/514-2200, ext. 231, cover varies) puts on weekday bluegrass concerts, evening dinner events, and special shows. Bluegrass jams start at 8 P.M. on Monday nights; there's no cover charge and reservations are not accepted. Just Country and More is a showcase of country music classics, pop tunes, and family entertainment performed while guests chow on a Southern dinner menu. Special events include performances by jazz, blues, bluegrass, and country greats.

The Ryman Auditorium

The most famous music venue in Nashville, the Ryman Auditorium (116 5th Ave. N., www.ryman.com, cover varies) continues to book some of the best acts in town, of just about every genre you can imagine. On the good side, the hall still boasts some of the best acoustics around. On the bad, the bench seats are just as uncomfortable as ever. But if the show is good, you probably won't even notice.

Country Music Hall of Fame

The Country Music Hall of Fame (222 5th Ave. S., 615/416-2100, www.countrymusichalloffame.com) hosts concerts, readings, and musical discussions regularly in an auditorium located inside the hall. These daytime events are often aimed at highlighting one type of country music or another, but sometimes you'll find big names playing. Admission is free with your paid admission to the hall, so it is a good idea to plan your trip to the hall on a day when there's a concert scheduled (separate admission to concerts is not available). Check the website for a listing of upcoming events.

(The Bluebird Cafe

For a certain type of music fan, the Bluebird Cafe (4104 Hillsboro Pike, 615/383-1461, www.bluebirdcafe.com, cover varies) has a whole lot going for it. It is intimate and homey. It books some of the best up-and-coming country and acoustic acts in the business. Its shows start as early as 6:30 P.M. There's no smoking, no talking during the acts, and virtually none of the usual bar pick-up scene. In short, the Bluebird is a place where music comes first, and everything else is a far second.

Opened in 1982 by Amy Kurland, the Bluebird started out as a casual restaurant with live music. It's located next to a dry cleaners in a nondescript shopping mall a few miles south of Hillsboro Village. Over the years, it has evolved into a destination for music lovers who appreciate its no-nonsense take on live music, and who hope that they just might stumble in on the next big thing. The Bluebird is famous as an early venue for the then-unknown

Garth Brooks, but its stage has also hosted the likes of Emmylou Harris, Kathy Mattea, Gillian Welch, Trisha Yearwood, and Steve Earl, among many more.

The Bluebird opens every night of the week, and most evenings the entertainment starts at 6:30 P.M. Cover is usually under $10. There is no cover charge and no reservations accepted for the shows on Sunday, songwriters' night, or Monday, open-mic night, but guests should arrive by 5:30 P.M. to get one of the first-come, first-served seats. There are only 21 tables and a few additional seats at the bar, so you have to be on your toes to get a spot in the house. For shows on Friday and Saturday nights, the Bluebird takes reservations the Monday of that week noon–5 P.M. Be advised that many weeks the shows sell out in a mere half hour, so keep hitting that redial button! Reservations for Tuesday–Thursday shows are available a week ahead 11 A.M.–5 P.M. You can also make reservations online. There is a $7 minimum per seat at all shows, so come hungry or thirsty. The food is standard bar fare, nothing more and nothing less. No outside drinks are allowed.

Once you've successfully navigated the rules of getting a seat at the Bluebird, sit back and enjoy some fine live music. Nashville is the city where anybody can become a somebody, and it's places like the Bluebird that make that happen. Be a part of it.

Clubs

If there is one false assumption that many people have about Nashville, it is that this is a strictly country town. In fact, Nashville has a vibrant rock 'n' roll music scene, plus good blues and jazz. So in a city where country music rubs shoulders with great rock, blues, and Americana, most live music venues refuse to be pigeonholed.

Venues here are categorized by their predominant music type, but keep in mind that variety is the name of the game. Most bars and clubs charge a cover when there is a band or performer, while songwriter nights and open mics are usually free.

COUNTRY

Nashville's most colorful country music establishments are the honky-tonks that line Broadway. Once places where country boys and girls would come to shake a leg or meet a beau, these all-day, all-night bars and music clubs now cater to visitors. **Tootsie's Orchid Lounge** (422 Broadway, 615/726-0463, no cover) is painted purple and exudes classic country every day of the week beginning as early as 10 A.M. Three doors down from Tootsie's is **Robert's Western World** (416 Broadway, 615/244-9552, no cover), voted the city's best honky-tonk. Originally a store selling boots, cowboy hats, and other country music regalia, Roberts morphed into a bar and nightclub with a good gift shop. Another choice is **The Stage** (412 Broadway, 615/726-0504, no cover), with a large dance floor and music seven nights a week.

After the Opry moved to Music Valley in the late 1970s, taking with it the customers who kept Broadway businesses afloat, the street's honky-tonks subsisted first on local bar flies and later on the tourist trade. Whether you're looking for a place to drown your sorrows or kick off a night on the town, Broadway's honky-tonks are a good place to go.

Probably the most popular country music nightclub downtown, the **Wildhorse Saloon** (120 2nd Ave. N., 615/902-8200, www.wildhorsesaloon.com, cover varies) is a boot-scootin' and beer-drinking place to see and be seen. When the Wildhorse opened in 1994, promoters drove a herd of cattle through the streets of downtown Nashville. Today, the Wildhorse is still a place where a good show and a good time are the top priorities. The huge dance floor is often packed with cowboys and cowgirls line dancing to the greatest hits of the country music genre. Dance lessons are offered every day (Mon.–Thurs. 6:30–8:30 P.M., Fri. 6–9:30 P.M., Sat. noon–9:30 P.M., Sun. 2–7:30 P.M.). The Wildhorse books big-name acts many nights of the week, including country music, roots rock, and classic rock stars. The Wildhorse opens Thursday through Sunday at 11 A.M., and on Monday at 5 P.M. When there is a show on, doors normally close at 6 P.M. and re-open at 7 P.M. for people with tickets. On other nights the cover charge ranges $4–6. From 10 P.M. on, the Wildhorse is a 21-and-up club.

The city's most popular venue for bluegrass and roots music, **The Station Inn** (402 12th Ave. S., 615/255-3307, cover varies) showcases fine artists every night of the week. This homey and casual club opens nightly at 7 P.M., with music starting about 9 P.M. This is a 21-and-over club, unless you come with a parent or guardian. There is no cover for the Sunday-night bluegrass jam.

The **Douglas Corner Cafe** (2106-A 8th Ave. S., 615/298-1688, cover varies) offers a Tuesday-night open mic, and country acts the rest of the week. It is known as a place where singer-songwriters are discovered, and it is not unlike the Bluebird Cafe in attitude and ambience. An intimate setting, full menu, and good acoustics make this a popular choice for music listening. Several live albums have been recorded here.

The **Nashville Palace** (2400 Music Valley Dr., 615/889-1540, no cover) is a restaurant, nightclub, and dance floor across from the Opryland Hotel. Live music is on tap daily starting at 5 P.M., and talent nights on Tuesday and Wednesday always draw a crowd.

JAZZ AND BLUES

If you need to get that country twang out of your head, a good dose of the blues will do it. **B. B. King Blues Club** (152 2nd Ave. N., 615/256-2727, cover varies) is a good place to start for a night of the blues. The club is a satellite of King's original Beale Street club, and it books live blues every night. The cover charge is usually under $10, unless B. B. King himself is making one of his rare appearances.

In Printer's Alley, the **Bourbon Street Blues and Boogie Bar** (220 Printer's Alley, 615/242-5867, cover varies) is a hole-in-the-wall nightclub that specializes in New Orleans–style jazz and blues.

A fine dining restaurant next door to Green Hills Mall, **F. Scott's** (2210 Crestmore Rd.,

NASHVILLE

615/269-5861, no cover) is also the city's premier venue for live jazz. The music goes well with the restaurant's art deco appeal. Come for dinner or for a few drinks at the bar while you listen in. Although there's no cover at the door, there is a two-drink minimum if you're not dining.

ECLECTIC

Clubs listed here may book a rock band one night and folk the next. Always check the free weekly *Nashville Scene* for the latest entertainment listings.

12th and Porter (114 12th Ave. S., 615/254-7250, cover varies) is a favorite venue for live music in the city. Second only to the Ryman in popularity, 12th and Porter books all kinds of acts. They are a popular choice for music-label showcases, and legendary performers have been known to stage impromptu shows here. Spacious and offering a full menu, including good Mexican food, 12th and Porter is a great hangout and place to hear live music.

The **Exit/In** (2208 Elliston Pl., 615/321-3340, cover varies) has been a favorite rock music venue for years, although it also books alternative country, blues, and reggae. Located on Elliston Place, the club is convenient to Vanderbilt and downtown.

Coffee shop by day, bar and live music venue by night, **Café Coco** (210 Louise Ave., 615/321-2626, cover varies) in Elliston Place is the best of both worlds. Monday is songwriter's night, Tuesday is open-mic poetry, and Thursday is open-mic music. Jazz and rock bands play other nights, when the cover ranges $2–5.

The Basement (1604 8th Ave. S., 615/254-8006, www.thebasementnashville.com, cover varies) calls itself a cellar full of noise, but it's a good kind of noise. Indie rock is the most common art form here, but they book other types of acts too. The Basement's New Faces Night on Tuesday is a popular place to hear singer-songwriters. Admission is 21 and over, unless accompanied by a parent or guardian. There is a full bar and light menu. Note that inside the

club is totally smoke-free; there is an outdoor smoking porch. The brick walls and subterranean feel give the Basement its cool atmosphere. Park behind the club and on side streets.

Located in an old warehouse that has housed a flour mill, jam factory, and country music concert hall, **Cannery Row** (One Cannery Row, 615/251-3020, www.mercylounge.com, cover varies) and its derivative **Mercy Lounge** are two cool venues for live music. Cannery Row is a large, somewhat cavernous space with lots of nice cherry-red touches, hardwood floors, and a shiny red bar. It can hold up to 1,000 people. The Mercy Lounge upstairs is a bit more intimate, with a capacity of up to 500 people. The Mercy Lounge hosts 8 off 8th on Monday nights, an open mic where eight different bands get to perform three songs. Both venues book rock, country, soul, and all sorts of other acts. It is located off 8th Avenue South.

A music venue designed by performers, **The Rutledge** (410 4th Ave. S., 615/782-6858, www.therutledgelmv.com, cover varies) has some of the most ear-pleasing acoustics in the city. An intimate venue—it seats only 250—the Rutledge books a wide variety of acts, hosts industry events, and even puts on tribute shows now and then. It is a smoke-free club and serves a limited food menu.

3rd and Lindsley (818 3rd Ave. S., 615/259-9891, www.3rdandlindsley.com, cover varies) is a neighborhood bar and grill that showcases rock, alternative, progressive, Americana, soul, and R&B music. Over the years they have developed a reputation for booking good blues acts. They serve a full lunch and dinner menu, the bar is well-stocked, and the club offers a great atmosphere and sound quality. Smoking is allowed.

Over in East Nashville, the **French Quarter Cafe** (823 Woodland St., 615/227-3100, cover varies) offers a Thursday night in-the-round songwriter's night. Weekends will find blues, rock, and soul musicians on the stage at this New Orleans–style nightclub. Dine on spicy po-boys, muffaletta, or other Cajun specialties while you enjoy a night out.

CONCERT SERIES

Dyer Observatory (1000 Oman Dr., 615/373-4897, www.dyer.vanderbilt.edu), a working space observatory operated by Vanderbilt University, has emerged as a popular venue for music, thanks to two ongoing concert series. **Music on the Mountain,** with Blair School of Music, and **Bluebird on the Mountain,** with the Bluebird Cafe, bring live music to this dramatic and one-of-a-kind spot. Imagine a night of fine music enjoyed under the stars, with the fresh air and the atmosphere of the forest all around you.

Every October the Grand Ole Opry celebrates its birthday with **Opry Month,** four weeks of star-studded performances, including several at the Opry's original home, the Ryman Auditorium. Get your tickets early, since these shows are always popular.

Also taking place on Thursday nights in the summer, **Bluegrass Nights at the Ryman** is a concert series that features some of the best pickers in the country. Starting in June and ending in July, this Ryman Auditorium series is always popular.

For a laid-back evening in a one-of-a-kind setting, check out the Tennessee Jazz and Blues Society's concert series **Jazz on the Lawn** (www.jazzblues.org). On Sunday evenings from May to October, jazz and blues artists take the stage on the lawns of some of Nashville's most historic homes, including Belle Meade and Cheekwood. Bring your own picnic and blanket.

BARS

Bar-hopping is best enjoyed downtown, where there is the greatest concentration of nightclubs, restaurants, and bars. Even on weeknights, the District, which lies along lower Broadway and its side streets, is crowded with people dressed in designer cowboy boots and fringed shirts. This is the official entertainment district of Nashville, and it is well-patrolled by police and cruisers alike.

Outside of the District, there are several other enclaves of nightlife that cater more to residents than visitors.

Nashville won't issue a liquor license unless the establishment also serves food, so all of the bars listed below double as restaurants.

The District

The honky-tonks along Broadway, Wildhorse Saloon, and B. B. King Blues Clubs are several of the most popular nightclubs in the District. Right next to the Wildhorse Saloon in the heart of the District, **Coyote Ugly** (154 2nd Ave. N., 615/254-8459, www.coyoteugly.com) draws a youthful, raucous crowd. Drinking beer and making friends are the two primary pursuits here, and for many people, there's no better place to do either.

Memorabilia of Nashville's past adorns the walls at **Legends Corner** (428 Broadway, 615/248-6334), a popular club for live music and rollicking crowds. There is never a cover, but be sure to put in a few bucks when they pass the hat for the performer.

Farther afield, but still downtown, you'll find one of the city's best beer bars. Behind the Union Station Hotel on the west side of downtown, the **Flying Saucer** (1001 Broadway, 615/259-7468) has one of the best selections of beer in town. Monday is pint night, when you can get $2.50 pints of just about any of the beers on the wall.

Duck into **The Beer Sellar** (107 Church St., 615/254-9464) to experience its "50 draughts, 150 bottles and 1 bitching jukebox." Located within walking distance of downtown, this is a cozy bar for conversation and fun.

Another popular brewpub is **Big River Grille and Brewing Works** (111 Broadway, 615/251-4677), an imposing bar and restaurant in the heart of the District. They serve food as well as boutique beers from around the world.

Printer's Alley

This narrow patch of downtown, located in between 3rd and 4th Avenues off Church Street, is home to a half-dozen nightclubs and bars, many that cultivate a seedy reputation. While reality may be a bit more tame, it is still a popular place to let loose. Elaborate wrought-iron balconies and the cobblestone underfoot evoke

Bourbon Street, a parallel that seems to suit the place. Bars here include **Bourbon Street Blues and Boogie Bar** (220 Printer's Alley, 615/242-5867) and **Fiddle and Steel** (201 Printer's Alley, 615/251-9002). Printer's Alley also has a karaoke bar and one of the city's most storied adult-entertainment bars.

Midtown

Elliston Place is home to several live music clubs plus a few neighborhood bars. The Exit/In and The End have live bands most nights of the week. You can play a game of pool at **Elliston's Pool Place Hall** (2200 Elliston Pl., 615/320-9441). This is a back-to-the-basics hangout where good drinks, good pool, and good people make for a good night out. **The Gold Rush** (2205 Elliston Pl., 615/321-1160) is a popular late-night mellow hangout. Finally, **Sherlock Holmes' Pub** (2206 Elliston Pl., 615/327-1047), which models itself as an old-fashioned English pub, has fish-and-chips and pints of beer.

Also an upscale restaurant, **Virago** (1811 Division St., 615/320-5149) in Music Row is a trendy bar and late-night pit stop. The S-shaped bar is the perfect place to order a martini and imagine you're in a big city.

Boscos (1805 21st Ave. S., 615/385-0050) calls itself a beer-lover's restaurant. While food is important here, it is Boscos' reputation for good beer that keeps patrons coming back. Stake out a front window seat to people-watch in trendy Hillsboro Village while you drink your beer.

Also in Hillsboro Village, **Cabana** (1910 Belcourt Ave., 615/577-2262) is a popular place to people-watch and unwind. It is a bar/restaurant/late-night hangout that attracts a youthful and well-dressed crowd. Lounge at the bar or in the expansive backyard. Choose from dozens of beers, wines, and some excellent martinis.

In the Green Hills area, **The Greenhouse** (2211 Bandywood Dr., 615/385-3357) offers specialty drinks, beers, and lots of hanging plants. To find it, look for the Green Hills Kroger and take a left. A few doors down, **The Box Seat** (2221 Bandywood Dr., 615/383-

8018) is a bona fide sports bar with televisions in every direction.

South Street Original Crab Shack and Authentic Dive Bar (907 20th Ave. S., 615/320-5555) is an institution, serving Cajun specialties and a relaxed atmosphere. Head upstairs to the open-air Treehouse, perfect for a warm Nashville night.

Broadway Brewhouse (1900 Broadway, 615/340-0089) has more than 70 different beers on tap and 100 more in coolers.

East Nashville

Edgefield Sports Bar and Grille (921 Woodland St., 615/228-6422) is a no-frills watering hole that caters to East Nashville residents.

The Family Wash (2038 Greenwood Ave., 615/226-6070) is a live music listening room where people come for a pint of beer and food too. It's also a neighborhood joint for the up-and-coming East Nashville community.

For a fun, retro vibe and a dance floor that gets hopping most nights of the week, grab a table at the **Alleycat Lounge** (1008-B Woodland St., 615/262-5888).

You might think you're in Austin at the **Rosepepper Cantina** (1907 Eastland Ave., 615/227-4777), a Mexican restaurant and bar. Choose from 30 different variations on the margarita, and enjoy the house band on weekend nights.

12 South

The up-and-coming neighborhood on 12th Avenue South is attracting new residents and businesses. Here you can enjoy a martini at **Mirror** (2317 12th Ave. S., 615/383-8330), a Miami Beach–inspired restaurant and bar. Enjoy the tapas menu while you sip your drink and people-watch.

Snag a seat on the crowded patio outside **Mafiaoza's Pizzeria and Neighborhood Pub** (2400 12th Ave. S., 615/269-4646, www.mafiaozas.com), a popular neighborhood hangout known for its top-notch pizza.

For something a little different, head to **Rumors Wine and Art Bar** (2304 12th Ave. S., 615/292-9400), a homey wine bar and art gallery. Good for wine lovers and aspiring wine lovers alike, this is a popular place for residents of the trendy 12 South district to get together. Rumors has a satellite location in East Nashville, at 112 Woodland Street (615/262-5346).

GAY AND LESBIAN NIGHTLIFE

You don't have to be gay to enjoy **Tribe** (1517-A Church St., 615/329-2912), but it helps to be beautiful, or at least well-dressed. The dance floor here is one of the best in the city, and the atmosphere is hip. Martinis and other specialty drinks are the poison of choice at this standard-setting club, which stays open until the wee hours.

Right next door to Tribe is **Play** (1519 Church St., 615/322-9627), the city's newest gay club, with drag shows and performances by adult-film stars.

The Chute Complex (2535 Franklin Rd., 615/297-4571) has karaoke, drag shows, and a dance floor. It caters to gay men.

Women outnumber men at the **Lipstick Lounge** (1400 Woodland St., 615/226-6343), a cool yet homey club in East Nashville. Live music, pool, and great food attract a crowd nearly every night.

For a low-key evening of pool or a happy hour stop before dinner, **TRAX** (1501 2nd Ave. S., 615/742-8856) is the place to go. The patio is a nice place to sit in warm weather. There is wireless Internet and big-screen televisions.

Outloud Cafe (1707 Church St., 615/329-8006) is a casual restaurant, coffee shop, and low-key venue for entertainment, catering to the gay and lesbian crowd. Thursday is movie night, there are monthly art exhibits, and game night is Monday beginning at 7 P.M.

COMEDY

Nashville's only comedy club is **Zanies** (2025 8th Ave. S., 615/269-0221), where you can hear stand-up comics every weekend and some weeknights.

FAMOUS NASHVILLIANS

Nashville is used to celebrity, what with all the country music stars around. But it's not just musicians who call, or called, Nashville home:

- **"Jefferson Street Joe" Gilliam,** one of the first African-American quarterbacks in the National Football League, played his college ball at Tennessee State University. The former quarterback for the Pittsburgh Steelers died in 2000 in his hometown of Nashville, five days before his 50th birthday.

- **Madison Smartt Bell** was born and raised in Nashville. The novelist's works include *All Souls Rising, Ten Indians*, and *The Year of Silence.*

- **Oprah Winfrey** was raised in Nashville by her father, Vernon. In her second year at Tennessee State University she was hired as Nashville's first female and first African-American TV news anchor on WTVF-TV.

- **Julian Bond,** civil rights activist, political activist, and the chairman of the NAACP, was born in Nashville and lived here until he was five years old.

- **Bobby Jones,** host of BET's Bobby Jones Gospel, was once a professor at Tennessee State University. The program is the longest-running show on cable television and is taped in Nashville.

- **Red Grooms** was born and raised in Nashville. Grooms is a prominent modern American artist, whose pop art depicts frenetic scenes of urban life.

- **Al Gore Jr.,** though born in Washington, D.C., and raised in Carthage, Tennessee, is closely associated with Nashville. After the Vietnam War he attended Vanderbilt University for one year and then spent five years as a reporter for the *Tennessean.* The former U.S. vice president and his wife, Tipper, have had a home in Nashville for many decades.

THE ARTS

Before Nashville was Music City, it was the Athens of the South, a city renowned for its cultural, academic, and artistic life. Universities, museums, and public arts facilities created an environment for artistic expression unparalleled by any other Southern city.

These days, most people think that country music is Nashville's only art form. But the truth is that Nashville offers far more than honkytonks and the Opry. It has an opera company of its own, not to mention an award-winning symphony, buoyant arts scene, and ample opportunities to sample contemporary and classic music, film, and theater.

Theater

The **Tennessee Repertory Theatre** (505 Deaderick St., 615/782-4000, www.tennesseerep.org) is Tennessee's largest professional theater company. It stages five big-name shows and three off-Broadway productions annually. The Rep performs in the Tennessee Performing Arts Center, located in the James K. Polk Cultural Center in downtown Nashville. This is the same building that houses the Tennessee State Museum, plus the Nashville Opera Association and the Nashville Ballet. Some of their productions have included *The Crucible, I Hate Hamlet,* and *Doubt.* The season runs from October to May.

Artists' Cooperative Theatre (615/726-2281, www.act1online.com) is an organization dedicated to bringing theatrical gems, both classic and modern, to Nashville audiences. Founded in 1989, ACT 1, as it is called, has presented productions of more than 90 of the world's greatest plays. Each year the theater puts on four or five productions. ACT 1 performs at the Darkhorse Theater at 4610 Charlotte Avenue.

New theatrical works are given the spotlight by the **Actors Bridge Ensemble** (1312 Adams St., 615/341-0300, www.actorsbridge.org), a theater company for new and seasoned actors. The Ensemble brings provocative and new plays to Nashville, often performing at the Belmont Black Box Theater in midtown.

Circle Players (www.circleplayers.net) is the oldest nonprofit, all-volunteer arts association in Nashville. As a community theater, all actors, stagehands, directors, and other helpers are volunteers. The company stages four or five performances every year at a variety of theater locations around the city. Performances include classic theater, plus stage adaptations of popular cinema and literature.

Nashville's leading experimental theater group is the **People's Branch Theatre** (615/254-0008, www.peoplesbranch.org). Founded in 2000, the group brings together local actors to produce bold and innovative professional theater. They perform at the Belcourt Theatre in Hillsboro Village.

Children's Theater

Nashville Children's Theatre (724 2nd Ave. S., 615/254-9103, www.nashvillechildrenstheatre.org) is the oldest children's theater company in the United States. During the school year, the theater puts on plays for children from preschool to elementary-school age in its colorful theater. In the summer there are drama classes for youngsters.

Teenagers own and operate the **Real Life Players,** a stalwart theater company that produces original plays written by Nashville teens. Profits are donated to teen-related community organizations. Plays are performed at the Darkhorse Theater at 4610 Charlotte Avenue. Call the theater at 615/297-7113 to find out when the next Real Life performance will be held.

Don't miss the **Marionette Shows at the Nashville Public Library** (615 Church St., 615/862-5800). Using marionettes from the collection of former library puppeteer Tom Tichenor, plus others acquired from Chicago's Peekabo Puppet Productions, the library's children's room staff put on excellent one-of-a-kind family entertainment.

Music

The **Nashville Symphony Orchestra** (One Symphony Place, 615/687-6400, www.nashvillesymphony.org) is now housed in the Schermerhorn Symphony Center next to the

Country Music Hall of Fame. Nominated for four Grammies and selling more recordings than any other American orchestra, the symphony is a source of pride for Music City. Costa Rican conductor Giancarlo Guerrero will begin his tenure as music director in 2009.

The symphony puts on more than 200 performances each year, including classical, pops, and children's concerts. Its season spans September to May. Buying tickets online is a breeze, especially since you can easily choose where you want to sit. There is free parking for symphony-goers in the Sun Trust parking garage on the corner of 4th Avenue and Commerce Street.

During the summer, the symphony plays its **Centennial Park Concert Series.** Come to the Centennial Park band shell to hear free big-band, ballroom, and classical concerts.

The **Blair School of Music** (2400 Blakemore Ave., 615/322-7651) presents student, faculty, and visiting artist recitals frequently during the school year. Vanderbilt University's music school, Blair addresses music through academic, pedagogical, and performing activities.

Listen to new works by American composers performed by the **Nashville Chamber Orchestra** (615/322-1226, www.nco.org). The orchestra's concerts include masterpieces and new works commissioned by the chamber orchestra, many of which fuse tradition with new genres, including jazz, Celtic, Latin, and world music.

Opera

Middle Tennessee's only opera association, the **Nashville Opera Association** (www.nashvilleopera.org) puts on an average of four mainstage performances per season (October–April) and does a six-week tour to area schools. They perform at the Tennessee Performing Arts Center at 505 Deaderick Street.

Ballet

Founded in 1981 as a civic dance company, the **Nashville Ballet** (www.nashvilleballet.com) became a professional dance company in 1986. Entertaining more than 40,000 patrons each year, the ballet performs both classical and contemporary pieces at the

Tennessee Performing Arts Center at 505 Deaderick Street.

Dinner Theater

Chaffin's Barn Dinner Theatre (8204 Hwy. 100, 615/646-9977, www.dinnertheatre.com, $33–50) was Nashville's first professional theater and continues to put on popular Broadway-style plays for dinner patrons. If mystery is more your style, have dinner at **Miss Marple's Mystery Dinner Theatre** (135 2nd Ave. N., 615/242-8000, www.missmarples.com, $50), where you and your friends try to guess who done it.

Cinemas

Once the home of the Grand Ole Opry, the **Belcourt Theatre** (2102 Belcourt Ave., 615/383-9140, www.belcourt.org) is Nashville's best venue for independent films. Built in 1925 as a silent movie house, the Belcourt now screens a refreshing variety of independent and unusual films.

More mainstream arty flicks are shown at the **Regal Cinemas Green Hills** (3815 Green Hills Village, 615/269-5910). Mainstream multiplex cinemas can be found on the outskirts of town in nearly every direction.

EVENTS
February

The second week of February is **Antiques Week** in Nashville. During this period, four separate antiques events top the bill. At the Tailgate Antique Show at the Fiddler's Inn Hotel in Music Valley, antiques dealers set up their shops in hotel rooms and parking spaces. A similar set-up exists at the Radisson Hotel Opryland for the Music Valley Antiques Market. The biggest sale is at the Gaylord Opryland Hotel and Convention Center. The final event for Antiques Week is the upscale Antiques and Garden Show of Nashville, which features antique dealers, exhibition gardens, and lectures at the Nashville Convention Center.

April

Nashville celebrates the coming of spring in a big way. **Awesome April** (www.visitmusiccity.com)

FAN FAIR

Like country music itself, the annual event known as Fan Fair has evolved from a down-home meet-and-greet to large-scale musical theater.

Fan Fair began in 1972 as a convention for music fans. Each year, the event grew as more and more people wanted to meet their country idols in person. Fans bought tickets months in advance, camped out at the state fairgrounds, and yearned to see, touch, and speak with the stars. Fan Fair delivered. Stars endured marathon autograph sessions – Garth Brooks famously spent 23 hours signing autographs without a bathroom break – and they performed to crowds of their most dedicated fans.

But country music's remarkable boom of the 1990s was the end of that kind of Fan Fair – the music simply outgrew the event. Country music was no longer the step-child of the recording industry; it was corporate, and it was big business. Fans, politicians, and industry representatives tangled over the future of Fan Fair. One plan to move Fan Fair to the Nashville Superspeedway in Lebanon was nixed because it would take the event out of Nashville.

In the end, the CMA (Country Music Association) Music Festival replaced Fan Fair in 2000. With venues at Riverfront Park and LP Field, there is still plenty of music. Stars perform day and night. The autograph sessions continue in the Nashville Convention Center, but the artists you'll find here are the unknowns and up-and-comings. You need an invitation to meet and greet the stars.

The rebirth of Fan Fair as the CMA Music Festival still attracts criticism, especially from those who remember the glory days of the old Fan Fair. But today's fans delight in the modern event, and even some of the critics are coming around.

is the name that encompasses the half dozen or more big events that take place during this month, one of the most pleasant on the city's weather calendar.

The **Country Music Television Music Awards** (www.cmt.com) was country music's first fan-voted awards show. Founded in 2002, the show lets fans participate in both the first and final rounds of voting. The show is broadcast live on television from Nashville, usually from the Curb Event Center at Belmont University.

Gospel music hosts its annual awards night in April too. The **Gospel Music Association Dove Awards** (www.gospelmusic.org) is billed as gospel music's biggest night. The celebration takes place at the Grand Ole Opry House in Music Valley, and is preceded by Gospel Music Week at the Nashville Convention Center, part trade show and part fan fair.

Film lovers throughout Tennessee look forward to the **Nashville Film Festival** (www.nashvillefilmfestival.org) held every April at the Green Hills Cinema 16. The film festival was founded in 1969 as the Sinking Creek Film Celebration. These days, upwards of 20,000 people attend the weeklong event, which includes film screenings, industry panels, and lots of parties.

Tin Pan South (www.tinpansouth.com) is an annual celebration of songs and songwriting organized by the Nashville Songwriters Association International. The event features five nights of performances by some of the best singers and songwriters around. Shows are held in 10 different intimate venues around the city, presenting music fans with the tough choice of where to go each night.

The **Country Music Marathon** (www.cmmarathon.com) takes place every April. More than 15,000 professional and amateur runners take part, and tens of thousands more come out for the live music and cheer squads that line the racecourse. The post-race concert usually boasts nationally known country music artists.

May

Held in Centennial Park, the **Tennessee Crafts Fair** (www.tennesseecrafts.org) showcases the work of more than 180 different fine craftsmen and women. More than 45,000 people come to the three-day event every year, which also includes craft demonstrations, a food fair, and entertainment. The fair repeats in September.

For something a little different, plan to attend the **Running of the Iroquois Steeplechase** (www.iroquoissteeplechase.org) at Percy Warner Park. Taking place on the second Saturday of May, the race is the nation's oldest continuously run weight-for-age steeplechase in the country. Fans in sundresses or suspenders and hats enjoy watching some of the top horses in the country navigate the race course. You can pay $15 general admission to sit on the hillside overlooking the stadium. Pack a blanket, food, and drinks, and you'll have an excellent day. Various tailgating tickets are available and are priced according to how good the view is from the parking spot. If you want to tailgate, you need to buy tickets well in advance.

Taking place every weekend in May, the **Tennessee Renaissance Festival** (www.tnrenfest.com) celebrates all things medieval. Come to watch jousting matches, hear 16th-century comedy, or buy capes and swords. The festival takes place off Highway 96 between Franklin and Murfreesboro, about 25 minutes' drive south from Nashville.

June

What was once called Fan Fair, and is now called the **Country Music Association Music Festival** (www.cmafest.com), is a four-day music mega-show in downtown Nashville. The stage at Waterfront Park along the Cumberland River is occupied by day with some of the top names in country music. At night the hordes move to LP Field across the river to hear a different show every night. Four-day passes, which cost between $80 and $300 per person, also give you access to the exhibit hall, where you can get autographs and meet up-and-coming country music artists. This is Nashville's biggest event of the year, and you are wise to buy your tickets and book your hotel early. Get a room downtown

so you don't need a car; parking and traffic is a nightmare during the festival.

Early June sees Nashville's gay, lesbian, bisexual, and transgender community show its colors at the **Nashville Pride Festival** (www.nashvillepride.org), a one-day event at Centennial Park.

July

Independence Day (www.visitmusiccity.com) is celebrated in a big way with fireworks and a riverfront concert that's broadcast live on television. The event is free and attracts upwards of 100,000 people every year.

The **Music City Brewer's Festival** (www.musiccitybrewersfest.com) is a one-day event on the lawn behind the Hilton Hotel downtown. Come to taste local brews, learn about making your own beer, and enjoy good food and live music. Tickets are required, and the event often sells out.

August

The **East Nashville Tomato Art Festival** (www.tomatoartfest.com) is a tongue-in-cheek celebration of tomatoes and the hip, artsy vibe of East Nashville. Events include a parade of tomatoes, the "Most Beautiful Tomato Pageant," biggest and smallest tomato contests, tomato toss, and Bloody Mary taste-off. The festival usually takes place on the second Saturday of August.

September

The Belle Meade Plantation (www.bellemeadeplantation.org) hosts its biggest fundraising event of the year, **Fall Fest,** every September. The two-day festival features antiques, arts and crafts, live music, and children's activities.

Nashville's annual **Greek Festival** (615/333-1047) is hosted by the Holy Trinity Greek Orthodox Church. Nashville residents flock here for homemade Greek food and entertainment, which includes dancing and tours of the historic cathedral.

The **John Merritt Classic** (www.johnmerrrittclassic.com) held over Labor Day starts with fashion shows and concerts and culminates with a football contest between the Tennessee State University Tigers and another historically black collegiate football team. The annual showdown is named for legendary former TSU football coach John Ayers Merritt.

The **Music City Jazz and Blues Festival (JAMS)** (www.nbl4u.com) over Labor Day is a two-day festival featuring jazz, blues, soul, R&B, and reggae performers. It is held at Riverfront Park along the Cumberland.

October

The **Southern Festival of Books** is held during the second full weekend of October on Legislative Plaza in downtown Nashville. Featuring book readings, autograph sessions, and discussions, the festival is a must for book lovers. It has activities for children, too. The festival is organized by Humanities Tennessee (www.tn-humanities.org).

Oktoberfest (www.nashvilleoktoberfest.com) is a Nashville tradition. Held in historic Germantown north of the Bicentennial Mall, this weekend festival is enhanced by its setting in what was once Nashville's German enclave. The events include a walk-run, church services, and a street fair with German music, food, and other entertainment. Oktoberfest usually takes place in mid-October.

Vanderbilt's Scarritt-Bennett Center hosts the **Celebration of Cultures** (www.celebrationofcultures.org) every October in Centennial Park. This international festival features food and music from around the world.

November

Beginning in November and continuing through the new year, several Nashville institutions put up special holiday decorations. Belmont University, Travellers Rest Plantation and Belle Meade all celebrate the holiday season with special decorative flair.

December

The **Music City Bowl** (www.musiccitybowl.com) pits a Southeastern Conference team against a Big Ten rival. This nationally televised football game is held at LP Field.

SHOPPING

You'll find many good reasons to shop in Nashville. Who can pass up Western wear in Music City? Fine boutiques cater to the well-heeled in tony West End. Malls in the suburbs offer upscale department stores or outlet bargains. And downtown you'll find unique art and gifts.

One of the best all-around shopping districts is **Hillsboro Village,** the commercial district that borders Vanderbilt University in midtown. Upscale clothing stores, used books, and trendy housewares are just a few of the things you'll find in this neighborhood, best explored on foot.

Music

The Texas Troubadour, Ernest Tubb, founded his famous record store on Broadway in 1947. **Ernest Tubb's Record Shop** (417 Broadway, 615/255-7503) remains an excellent source of classic and modern country music recordings, as well as DVDs, books, clothing, and souvenirs. At the back of the shop you can see the stage where Ernest Tubb's Midnite Jamboree was recorded and aired after the Grand Ole Opry on Saturday nights. The Jamboree still airs, but it's recorded at the Texas Troubadour Theatre in Music Valley.

For new and used CDs, DVDs, and vinyl, go to **Grimey's** (1604 8th Ave. S., 615/254-4801). Here you'll find a wide selection of not just country, but rock, folk, blues, R&B, and other genres. The staff are knowledgeable and friendly.

If you want to make your own music, head to **Gruhn Guitars** (400 Broadway, 615/256-2033), a guitar shop with one of the best reputations in the music world. Founded by guitar expert George Gruhn, the shop is considered by some the best vintage guitar shop in the world. Shiny guitars, banjos, mandolins, and fiddles looks like candy hung up on the walls of the Broadway storefront that serves both up-and-coming and established Nashville musicians.

Nashville's other guitar shop is the **Gibson Bluegrass Showcase** (Opry Mills, 615/514-2233). Part retail outlet, part live music venue, the Gibson store celebrates both the instruments and the sound of bluegrass music. You can buy fiddles, mandolins, Dobros, or guitars, and they will ship all over the world.

If country music is just one of many musical interests, head to **The Great Escape** (1925 Broadway, 615/327-0646). This record and comic book shop was founded in 1977, and continues to offer a pleasing array of used CDs, records, and cassettes for music fans. The location near Vanderbilt attracts a youthful clientele.

Western Wear

No city is better endowed with places to buy Western-style wear. The best selection is found in shops along Broadway in downtown Nashville, where you'll find hats, boots, shirts, belts, jeans, and everything else you'll need to look the part. Opry Mills, the mall next to the Grand Ole Opry, also has a good selection of Western wear.

Trail West (312 Broadway, 615/251-1711) is a one-stop shop for country clothes. **Boot Country** (304 Broadway, 615/259-1691) specializes in all styles and sizes of cowboy boots.

Music-industry men and women get dressed at **flavour** (1522-B Demonbreun, 615/254-2064), a hip clothing store on Music Row. Come here for stylish denim, cowboy boots, plus casual and dressy wear for ladies and gents. This is not your daddy's boot store; this is country music chic.

The name says it all at **Manuel Exclusive Clothier** (1922 Broadway, 615/321-5444), a clothing shop where the cowboy shirts start at $750 and jackets at over $2,000.

Even without a ton of cash you can outfit yourself in some of the best Western designs at **Katy K Designs Ranch Dressing** (2407 12th Ave. S., 615/297-4242). This is the showplace of designer Katy K's unique clothing line, which has been worn by the likes of Loretta Lynn and BR549. Ranch Dressing has a well-curated selection of vintage goods, plus clothing from other designers' lines. To find the shop, look for the giant cowgirl on the facade of an otherwise nondescript office building.

Clothing

Ginette's Boutique (2420 Elliston Pl., 615/327-1440) offers the latest fashions in women's clothes, handbags, and accessories at non-runway prices.

With two locations, one in Hillsboro Village and one downtown at 305 Church Street, **Fire Finch** (615/942-5271) is known for trendy jewelry and accessories. Its downtown location also has a few home decor items as well.

A relative newcomer on the Nashville clothing scene, **Nashville Clothing Company** (2922 West End Blvd., 615/577-5346) sells stylish men's and women's clothes and shoes. This includes a wide selection of funny T-shirts, purses, and bags.

Men can get outfitted from toe to top hat at **J. Michael's Clothiers** (2525 West End Ave., 615/321-0686). An old-fashioned clothing store that specializes in one-on-one advice, J. Michael's is famous for its personal touch; in addition to selling off-the-rack name brand they tailor to suit. Whether you're just starting a new career or looking for a special-occasion outfit, you'll find what you need at J. Michael's.

Art

While not exactly a gallery, **Hatch Show Print** (316 Broadway, 615/256-2805) is one of Nashville's best-known places to buy art. Hatch has been making colorful posters for decades, and their letterpress style is now one of the trendiest looks in modern design. They continue to design and print handouts, posters, and T-shirts for local and national customers. Visitors to the shop can gaze at the cavernous warehouse operation, and buy small or large samples of their work, including reproductions of classic country music concert posters. This is a great place to find a special souvenir of your trip to Nashville.

At **All Fired Up** (21st Ave. S., 615/463-8887), choose a piece of unfinished pottery for between $5 and $50, then pay an additional $6 "painting fee," and choose from hundreds of different paints and glazes to finish your piece. This is a great way to spend a rainy afternoon or have fun with a date.

Transplanted New Yorkers Theo Antoniadis and Veta Cicolello opened **Ovvio Arte** (42 S. Chestnut St., 615/256-8756, www.ovvioarte.com) in 2008. This art gallery and performance space is a venue for the unexpected. It offers regular theater, dramatic readings, and art shows.

The Tennessee Artists Guild operates **TAG Gallery** (83 Arcade, 615/429-7708, www.tagartgallery.com), one of the best galleries in Nashville. Founded in 2000, the TAG specialized in selling affordable art to up-and-coming collectors. They offer a regular diet of unique shows.

Garage Mahal (1106 Woodland St., 615/226-2070), also known as the Art and Invention Gallery, is an East Nashville institution. Proprietors Meg and Bret MacFayden put on between five and six shows each year, including their signature Tomato Art Show, part of the annual Tomato Art Festival.

Also in East Nashville, **Plowhaus** (211 S. 17th St., 615/349-3777) is an artists' co-op with a gallery and lots of community outreach activities.

Home Decor

Find fine crystal, tableware, jewelry, and other upscale housewares at **AshBlue** (4231 Harding Rd., 615/383-4882). This sophisticated shop is perfect for bridal registries, housewarming gifts, or that special touch for your home or office.

Natural soaps, hand-crafted fragrances, and soy candles are just a few of the things you will find at **Green Pergola Aromatherapy and Soap Company** (223 Donelson Pk., 615/889-0044). One of the best things about the store, however, is its unique partnership with two other businesses. **Teas for Two** sells loose tea and **One 2 Yoga Studio** offers one-on-one and group yoga instruction. You can also buy a hot or cold cup of tea to drink while you enjoy the relaxing atmosphere of the store.

Modern home furnishings, large and small, are what draws shoppers to **Mad Mod** (162 8th Ave. N., 615/244-6807). A complete line of bamboo textiles, local art, and trendy furniture make this a popular stop for the downtown condo set.

Books

Nashville has several good bookstores, and at least one is bound to suit your taste. **Bookman Bookwoman Used Books** (1713 21st Ave. S., 615/383-6555), in the trendy Hillsboro neighborhood, is chock-a-block with used books, including cheap paperbacks and rare must-haves. **Elder's Books** (2115 Elliston Pl., 615/327-1867), close to Vanderbilt and Centennial Park, is a book-lover's bookstore. The store is packed with books, but not just any books. The collection is carefully chosen and includes many signed and first editions. Elder's has an excellent collection of books about Nashville, Tennessee, the Civil War, and the South, as well as lots of other topics. Be warned that this is a store for book-loving adults, not their children. Noisy or misbehaving children are not tolerated.

For new books, head to **Davis-Kidd Booksellers** (Green Hills Mall, 615/385-2645), a Nashville-based independent bookseller with locations throughout Tennessee. Davis-Kidd puts on a number of literary events, such as book signings, discussions, and readings.

Outloud! Books and Gifts (1701 Church St., 615/329-8006) specializes in books, videos, music, and gifts with a gay or lesbian theme. There is an adjoining café, special events, and comfortable couches for relaxing.

The newest addition to the Nashville book scene is **McKays** (5708 Charlotte Pike, 615/353-2595), which sells used books, CDs, and DVDs. A Knoxville institution for years, McKays moved to Music City in 2007. Calling itself a "free enterprise library," McKays encourages readers to return books for store credit after they've read them.

Antiques

Near 100 Oaks Mall in South Nashville you'll find Nashville's largest and most popular antiques mall. **Gaslamp Antique and Decorating Mall** (100 Powell Ave., 615/297-2224, www.gaslampantiques.com) is squeezed between a Staples and Home Depot. It has more than 150 vendors and a great selection of all types of antiques.

For something closer to town, head to

Eighth Avenue Antiques Mall (2015 8th Ave. S., 615/279-9922) or **Wonders on Woodland** (1110 Woodland St., 615/226-5300) in East Nashville.

Malls
The finest shopping mall in Nashville is the **Mall at Green Hills,** an indoor mall located about 15 minutes' drive south from downtown Nashville along Hillsboro Road. Stores include Macy's, Dillard's, Tiffany & Co., and Davis-Kidd Booksellers. The mall has spawned additional shopping opportunities nearby, so this is a good place to head if you're in need of just about anything. Call the mall concierge (615/298-5478, ext. 22) to find out if your favorite store is there.

Farther south of Nashville, at the Moore's Lane exit off I-65, is **Cool Springs Galleria** (1800 Galleria Blvd., 615/731-6255, www.cool-springsgalleria.com), the newest mall in the area. Four major department stores anchor the mall, which includes 100 specialty shops. The mall is surrounded by acres more of drive-up shopping centers and restaurants.

Heading west from town on Highway 70, you'll run into **Bellevue Center** (7620 U.S. 70, 615/646-8690, www.bellevuecenter.com), where you'll find Dillard's, Sears, Hecht's, and more than 115 specialty shops. Many Nashvillians consider this the city's best mall.

Outlet Malls
Some Nashville residents look down their nose

at **Opry Mills** (433 Opry Mills Dr., 615/514-1000), the discount mall in Music Valley that sits across the street from the Grand Ole Opry. Indeed, if upscale shopping is your thing, don't come here. But if good deals on name-brand merchandise appeal to you, Opry Mills is the mall for you. Brands include Corning, Levi's, Banana Republic, American Eagle Outfitters, Barnes & Noble, Gap, and Off Fifth. There is also a 20-screen movie theater, IMAX, and Bass Pro Shop with all sorts of outdoor equipment.

A bit farther down the highway in Lebanon, about 30 miles east of Nashville on I-40, **Prime Outlets** (800/617-2588) features name-brand outlet stores. Brands include Polo Ralph Lauren, Coach, Tommy Hilfiger, and Ann Taylor. To get to Prime Outlets, take I-40 east from Nashville and get off at exit 238.

Flea Markets
Nashville's largest flea market takes place on the fourth weekend of every month at the Tennessee State Fairgrounds. The **Tennessee State Fairgrounds Flea Market** (615/862-5016, www.tennesseestatefair.org) is a bargain-lover's dream, with thousands of sellers peddling clothes, crafts, and all sorts of vintage and used housewares. The fairgrounds are located on 4th Avenue, south of downtown.

The **Nashville Farmer's Market** next to the Bicentennial Mall downtown has a flea market on weekends.

Sports and Recreation

Nashville has good parks, numerous sports teams, and nice weather to enjoy both.

PARKS
Centennial Park
Nashville's best city park, Centennial is best-known as home of the Parthenon. It is also a pleasant place to relax. A small lake provides a habitat for ducks and other water creatures; paved walking trails are popular for walking

during nice weather. The park hosts numerous events during the year, including Shakespeare in the Park.

Radnor Lake State Natural Area
Just seven miles southwest of downtown Nashville, Radnor Lake State Natural Area (Otter Creek Rd., 615/373-3467) provides a natural escape for visitors and residents of the city. Eighty-five acre Radnor Lake was

created in 1914 by the Louisville and Nashville Railroad Company, which impounded Otter Creek to do so. The lake was to provide water for the railroad's steam engines. By the 1940s, the railroad's use of the lake ended and 20 years later the area was threatened by development. Local residents, including the Tennessee Ornithological Society, successfully rallied against development and Radnor Lake State Natural Area was established in 1973.

There are six miles of hiking trails around the lake, and Otter Creek Road, which is closed to vehicular traffic, is open to bicycles and walkers. A nature museum at the visitors center describes some of the 240 species of birds and hundreds of species of plants and animals that live at Radnor. The visitors center is open Sunday–Thursday 9 A.M.–4 P.M. and Friday–Saturday 8 A.M.–4 P.M.

Radnor is well-used and well-loved by Nashvillians, and for good reason. Very few American cities have such a large and pristine natural area so close to the urban center.

Edwin and Percy Warner Parks

The largest city parks in Tennessee, Edwin and Percy Warner Parks (Hwy. 100) are a 2,600-acre oasis of forest, fields, and quiet pathways located just nine miles southwest from downtown Nashville. Nashvillians come here to walk, jog, ride bikes and horses, and much more. The parks have scenic drives, picnic facilities, playgrounds, cross-country running trails, an equestrian center, bridle trails, a model-airplane field, and athletic fields. Percy Warner Park is also home to the Harpeth Hills Golf Course, and Edwin Percy Park has a nature center that provides year-round environmental education. The nature center also hands out maps and other information about the park.

Warner Parks hosts the annual Iroquois Steeplechase Horse Race in May. A 10-mile bridle path is open to horseback riding year-round. Visit the park's Equestrian Center (2500 Old Hickory Blvd.) for more information.

J. Percy Priest Lake

J. Percy Priest Lake was created in the mid-

1960s when the Army Corps of Engineers dammed Stones River east of Nashville. The lake is a favorite destination for fishing, boating, swimming, and picnicking.

J. Percy Priest Lake sprawls over 14,200 acres. Access is provided through more than a dozen different parks and access areas on all sides of the lake. Many of these areas bear the names of communities that were inundated when the lake was created.

The lake's main visitors center, operated by the Army Corps of Engineers, is located at the site of the dam that created the lake. The visitors center is located on Bell Road at exit 219 off I-40 heading east from downtown Nashville. There you will find a lake overlook and one of four marinas on the lake.

In addition to access areas managed by the Corps of Engineers, Nashville operates **Hamilton Creek Park** on the western shore of the lake. The State of Tennessee operates **Long Hunter State Park** on the eastern shore.

There are several hiking trails around the lake. The **Three Hickories Nature Trail** is an easy 1.6-mile trail found in the Cook Recreational Area. **Anderson Road Fitness Trail** is a paved one-mile trail that travels through woodlands and along the lake.

For a long hike, or for horseback riding, go to the **Twin Forks Horse Trail,** an 18-mile trail located in the East Fork Recreation Area on the southwestern shore of the lake. Within Long Hunter State Park there are three hiking trails, including a nature loop trail and the mile-long Deer Trail leaving from the visitors center.

Boating, fishing, and watersports are among the most popular activities on J. Percy Priest Lake. Launch ramps are found in Long Hunter State Park and at several marinas around the lake. Elm Hill Marina (3361 Bell Rd., 615/889-5363, www.elmhillmarina.com) is the marina closest to downtown Nashville.

The Corps of Engineers operates three day-use swim areas that have sand beaches, bathrooms, and other amenities for a day in the water. These swim areas are located at Anderson Road, Cook Campground, and Seven Points Campground. There is a $4 per-vehicle fee at Anderson and Cook. There is swimming at Long Hunter State Park's Bryant Grove as well.

GOLF

Nashville operates seven public golf courses in the city. Many of these are in parks and offer excellent golf in beautiful settings. You can find details about all city courses at www.nashville.gov/parks/golf/golf.htm. Most courses are open year-round; call ahead for operating hours and to reserve a tee time.

Harpeth Hills Golf Course (2424 Old Hickory Blvd., 615/862-8493) is a par-72 course built in 1965 and renovated in 1991. It is located in Percy Warner Park, and is considered one of Tennessee's best public golf courses. Green fees are $23 on weekdays and $25 on weekends.

Percy Warner Park is home of **Percy Warner Golf Course,** a nine-hole course good for beginner golfers, available on a walk-in basis only.

Probably the most-used public golf course in Nashville, **McCabe Golf Course** (615/862-8491) is located in West Nashville near Sylvan Park. McCabe consists of a par-70 18-hole course and 9-hole course. Upgrades have introduced new green complexes and tee complexes. Green fees are $20 on weekdays and $22 on weekends.

The oldest city golf course in Nashville is **Shelby Golf Course** (615/862-8474), located in Shelby Park in East Nashville. Shelby is a short course with small mounded greens that places a premium on accuracy. Green fees are $16.

Situated on the Cumberland River in North Nashville, **Ted Rhodes Golf Course** (615/862-8463) is scenic, and pleasant to walk. Built in 1953 as a nine-hole course, Ted Rhodes was expanded to 18 holes in 1992. It is par 72. Green fees are $20 on weekdays and $22 on weekends.

Located near Music Valley in Donelson, **Two Rivers Golf Course** (615/889-2675) offers a challenging course for golfers of all skill levels. A bonus is the view of the Nashville skyline at the eighth hole. Greens fees are $20 on weekdays and $22 on weekends.

There are many privately owned golf courses in Nashville, some of which are open to the public. **Gaylord Springs** (18 Springhouse Ln., 615/458-1730), located next to the Gaylord Opryland Hotel in Music Valley, is a par-72 18-hole course built in 1990. Greens fees are $50–90. **Nashboro Golf Club** (1101 Nashboro Blvd., 615/367-2311) offers a par-72 18-hole course with fees between $27 and $41. **Hillwood Country Club** (6201 Hickory Valley Rd., 615/352-5600) is a par-72 6,903-yard course built in 1955. Greens fees are around $85.

BIKING

The first destination for bikers around Nashville is the **Natchez Trace Parkway** (www.nps.gov/natr), a two-lane 444-mile blacktop scenic drive that originates in Nashville and journeys south through Tennessee and Mississippi countryside, eventually terminating in Natchez, Mississippi. The parkway is closed to commercial traffic and the speed limit is strictly enforced, making it popular for biking.

Biking the Trace can be an afternoon outing or a weeklong adventure. The National Park Service maintains three campgrounds along the Trace, plus five bicyclist-only campsites with more modest amenities. The northernmost bike campsite is located at the intersection of the Trace and Highway 50, about 36 miles south of Nashville.

When biking on the Trace, ride in a single-file line and always wear reflective clothing and a helmet. Pack food and water, and carry a cell phone, ID, and emergency information.

Short paved trails good for biking can be found at Radnor Lake State Natural Area, Warner Parks, and in any of Nashville's greenways, including those at Shelby Bottoms along the Cumberland River.

Nashville's only dedicated mountain bike trail is at **Hamilton Creek Park** (www.hamcreek.com) on J. Percy Priest Lake, on the east side of the Nashville airport. This 10-mile bike trail consists of an eastern trail better for beginning bikers and a western trail for advanced bikers. The two trails meet at a tunnel that crosses Bell Road.

NASHVILLE

Bike Shops

There are several good bike shops in Nashville. If you need bike gear, repairs, or advice, check out **Cumberland Transport** (2807 West End Ave., 615/321-4069), **Nashville Bicycle Company** (2817 West End Ave., 615/321-5510), or **Trace Bikes** (8400 Hwy. 100, 615/646-2485), located next to the Loveless Cafe near the Natchez Trace Parkway.

Resources

If you're looking for the inside scoop on biking around Nashville and recommended routes in the surrounding countryside, check out www.nashvillecyclist.com, an online community of bikers.

The **Harpeth Bike Club** (www.harpethbikeclub.com) is Nashville's largest bike club. It organizes weekend and weekday group rides from April to October, plus races and social events where you can meet other bike enthusiasts.

TENNIS

The **Centennial Sportsplex** (222 25th Ave. N., 615/862-8480, www.sportsplextennis.com) has 15 lighted outdoor tennis courts and four indoor courts, as well as a ball machine, pro shop, and concession stand. The center is open seven days a week; specific hours vary by season. Indoor court rental fees are $18 per hour; courts may be booked up to three days in advance. Outdoor courts are available for $3 per hour per person and they can be reserved up to six days in advance.

The Sportsplex organizes numerous tennis tournaments, leagues, and classes during the year. Call or stop by for details.

SWIMMING

The city's biggest pool is found at the **Centennial Sportsplex Aquatic Center** (222 25th Ave. N., 615/862-8480, www.centennialsportsplex.com, Mon.–Thurs. 5:30 A.M.–7:50 P.M., Fri. 5:30 A.M.–5:50 P.M., Sat. 9 A.M.–4:50 P.M., adults $6, children under 13, military, disabled, seniors, and students $5, children 4 and under free). The center, located near Centennial Park in midtown, has both a large lap pool and a small play pool. Various swim classes are offered; call for a schedule.

Take the kids to **Wave Country** (2320 Two Rivers Pkwy., 615/885-1052, daily 10 A.M.–6 P.M., adults $8, children under 12 $7, children under 4 free), a waterpark with exciting slides, wave pool, and sand volleyball courts. Wave Country is managed by the city parks commission, and is open from Memorial Day to Labor Day.

A great destination for swimming and watersports is **Nashville Shores** (4001 Bell Rd., Hermitage, 615/889-7050, www.nashvilleshores.com, Mon.–Sat. 10 A.M.–6 P.M., Sun. 11 A.M.–6 P.M.). Here you'll find miles of sandy beaches along the shore of J. Percy Priest Lake, pools, waterslides, and watersports. Admission includes the opportunity to take a 45-minute lake cruise. Admission rates are based on height; 48 inches and taller pay $22, shorter than that $17. Children two years and under are free. General admission is half-price after 3 P.M. Nashville Shores is open from Memorial Day to Labor Day.

GYMS

The City of Nashville operates a fitness center in the **Centennial Sportsplex** (222 25th Ave. N., 615/862-8480, www.centennialsportsplex.com, Mon.–Thurs. 5:30 A.M.–8 P.M., Fri. 5:30 A.M.–6 P.M., Sat. 9 A.M.–5 P.M., adults $6, children under 13, military, disabled, seniors, and students $5, children 4 and under free). The fitness center has modern cardiovascular and weight-lifting machines. Fitness classes are also offered.

The Sportsplex also has two pools, tennis courts, and an ice rink. The ice rink offers public skate periods every week, with more during the winter months and holiday season.

SPECTATOR SPORTS
Football

You simply cannot miss 68,000-seat LP Field, home of the **Tennessee Titans** (460 Great Circle Rd., 615/565-4000, www.titansonline.com). The stadium, which was finished in 1999, towers on the east bank of the

The Tennessee Titans play at LP Field, on the east bank of the Cumberland River.

Cumberland River, directly opposite downtown. Since their move to the stadium in 1999, the Titans have sold out each and every home game. They play from September to December.

Tickets sell out early—often months in advance. If you want to see a game on short notice, your best bet is a program where season ticket–holders can sell their seats to games they don't want to attend.

For an altogether different football experience, catch a home game of the **Nashville Dream** (615/907-6617, www.nashville-dream.com) at Glencliff High School. The Nashville Dream is a women's football team and a member of the National Women's Football Association. The season runs from April to July.

Finally, the most unique brand of football played in Nashville is Australian rules. The **Nashville Kangaroos** (www.nashvillekanga-roos.org) were founded in 1997 and were one of the first Australian football teams in the United States. The "Roos" play at Elmington Park (3500 West End Ave.), and sometimes practice with Vanderbilt's own Aussie rules squad. One of the missions of the club is to promote cultural understanding and exchange, so the social calendar can be just as grueling as the sports one. The Roos also sponsor a women's netball team.

Racing

The **Nashville Superspeedway** (4847-F McGreary Rd., Lebanon, 615/547-7223, www. nashvillesuperspeedway.com) is a 1.33-mile course that hosts Indy Racing League, NASCAR Craftsman Trucks, and two NASCAR Busch Series races. Seating up to 150,000 fans, Nashville Superspeedway has been drawing capacity crowds since it opened in 2001. The Superspeedway is located in Lebanon, Tennessee, about 30 minutes' drive east of town.

Baseball

What a fine name for a minor-league baseball team! The **Nashville Sounds** (534 Chestnut St., 615/242-4371, www.nashvillesounds.com) are a AAA affiliate of the Milwaukee Brewers, and they play about 30 home games a year from June to October. Before the 2008 season opener, the team invested $1 million in stop-gap improvements to the aging Greer Stadium, their home in south Nashville. In 2008, the team sold to new owners, who promised to do more to improve the Sounds' home in the coming years, part of a plan to draw larger crowds to the games.

Tickets are $10 for reserved seats or $6 general admission.

Soccer

Nashville's professional soccer team, the **Metros** (Ezell Park, 5135 Harding Pl., 615/832-5678, www.nashvillemetrosoccer.com), play just south of Nashville International Airport. Founded in 1989, the Metros have endured a half-dozen name, field, and league changes. They have survived thanks to the dogged support of soccer fans in the city.

The Metros are a member of the United Soccer League's Premier Development League, and the season runs from May to July. They play other teams from the southeastern United States. Single-game tickets are $7 for adults and $4 for youths.

Ice Hockey

Nashville celebrated the 10th anniversary of its National Hockey League franchise, the **Predators** (501 Broadway, http://predators. nhl.com), in 2008. It was a sweet victory for fans, who fought to keep the team in the city in the face of lackluster support from the community. The Predators play in the 20,000-seat Sommet Center, also called the Nashville Arena, located on Broadway in the heart of downtown. The regular season begins in October and ends in early April. Single-game tickets start at $17 and can cost as much as $150.

College Sports

In addition to Nashville's smorgasbord of professional and semi-professional sports teams, the city's colleges provide lots of good spectator sports. Vanderbilt plays football, men's and women's basketball, and baseball in the Southeastern Conference. Tennessee State University and Belmont University play Division 1-A basketball, and Lipscomb University is a member of the Atlantic Sun Division.

Accommodations

Nashville has more than 32,000 hotel rooms. Accommodations range from historic downtown hotels to standard motels. Some of the city's most distinctive accommodations are in bed-and-breakfast inns in Hillsboro and East Nashville.

Downtown has the most appealing and convenient hotels. More budget-friendly options are found in midtown and Music Valley.

BROADWAY AND THE DISTRICT

Hotels in this neighborhood are as close as you can get to attractions including the Country Music Hall of Fame and Broadway honky-tonks.

$150-200

Located across Broadway from the Frist Center for the Visual Arts, **Holiday Inn Express Nashville-Downtown** (902 Broadway, 615/244-0150, $150) offers a comfortable compromise between value and location. There is an on-site fitness room, free wireless Internet, a business center, and a guest laundry. Guest rooms have desks, coffeemakers, and two telephones. Suites ($250) have refrigerators and microwave ovens. All guests enjoy free continental breakfast. On-site parking is available for $14 a day. The Holiday Inn is located about five blocks away from lower Broadway.

Over $200

Nashville's most notable downtown hotel is **Union Station** (1001 Broadway, 615/726-1001, $160–270), a 125-room Wyndham Hotel located in what was once the city's main train station. Distinctions include magnificent iron work and molding, and an impressive marble-floored great hall that greets guests. High ceilings and lofty interior balconies make this one of Nashville's great old buildings, and hotel guests get to make it their home away from home. Union Station is a fine hotel, with amenities like free turn-down service, a fitness center, wireless Internet, plasma televisions, complimentary morning newspapers, and room service. Rooms have cathedral ceilings, stylish furnishings, and a subtle art deco touch. The bathrooms have soaking tubs, walk-in showers, and expansive marble vanities. You can choose from a standard room with one double bed or a premium room with a king-sized bed or two double beds. Four suites are also available.

The all-suite **(Hilton Nashville Downtown** (121 4th Ave. S., 615/620-1000, www.nash-villehilton.com, $170–240) is next door to the Country Music Hall of Fame, Broadway's honky-tonks, and the home of the Nashville Symphony. It's also across the street from the Nashville Convention Center. All of the hotel's 330 suites have two distinct rooms—a living room with sofa, cable television, microwave oven, refrigerator, and coffeemaker, and a bedroom with one or two beds. The rooms are appointed with modern, stylish furniture and amenities. An indoor pool, workout room, valet parking, and two award-winning restaurants round out the hotel's amenities. The Hilton's combination of luxury and location make it one of the best choices for travelers to Nashville.

The **Renaissance Hotel** (611 Commerce St., 615/255-8400, $290–310) is connected to the Nashville Convention Center by a raised and covered walkway. Located one block north of Broadway, it stands 25 stories, providing impressive views of the city below. The Renaissance's 646 rooms offer web TV, hairdryers and ironing boards, crisp linens, coffeemakers, and business services. For an additional $12 daily, guests can enjoy high-speed wired Internet access and unlimited local and U.S. long-distance calls. The fitness center is next door to an indoor heated swimming pool, whirlpool, and sauna.

DOWNTOWN

Downtown hotels are convenient to downtown businesses and government offices, and a short walk from tourist attractions along Broadway.

Over $200

The last of a dying breed of downtown hotels, the **(Hermitage Hotel** (231 6th Ave., 615/244-3121, www.thehermitagehotel.com, $300–800) has been the first choice for travelers to downtown Nashville for almost 100 years. The 123-room hotel was commissioned by prominent Nashville citizens and opened for business in 1910, quickly becoming the favorite gathering place for the city's elite. Prominent figures including Al Capone, Gene Autry, and seven U.S. presidents have stayed at the Hermitage. In modern times, its roll call includes some of country music's biggest names. You don't have to be famous to stay at the Hermitage, but having plenty of cash will help your cause. Rooms start at $300 a night, but check for last-minute specials on its website when rates will dip to $200. Guests enjoy top-of-the-line amenities, including 24-hour room service, pet walking, valet parking, and laundry services. Rooms are furnished in an opulent style befitting a luxury urban hotel, and have CD/DVD players, refreshment centers, marble baths, and high-speed wireless Internet access. Many rooms have lovely views of the Capitol and city.

Courtyard by Marriot (179 4th Ave. N., 615/256-0900, $200–250) is a 181-room renovated hotel set in a century-old downtown high-rise. It is located right next to Printer's Alley, and is set midway between the downtown business district and Broadway's entertainment attractions. Guest rooms are tastefully decorated, with web TV, wired Internet access, coffeemakers, ironing boards, cable TV, voice mail, and super-comfortable beds. There are two restaurants on-site, and guests can take advantage of valet parking for $20 a day.

Located just steps from the Tennessee State Capitol and near dozens of downtown office buildings, the **Doubletree Hotel Nashville** (315 4th Ave. N., 615/244-8200, $190–250) is a popular choice for business travelers. Rooms are spacious and bright, and even basic rooms have a comfortable desk and chair, coffeemaker, free Internet access, voice mail, and ironing boards. The hotel boasts a beautiful indoor swimming pool, business center, above-average fitness center, and on-site restaurant and coffee shop. Parking at the Doubletree is valet only and costs $20 per day.

The **Sheraton Downtown Nashville** (623 Union St., 615/259-2000, $200–270) is a city landmark. The 476-room hotel stands tall above neighboring buildings, providing most guest rooms with views of the city below. Located in the middle of Nashville's bustling downtown business district, it is another good option for business travelers. The hotel is 100 percent smoke-free, and has a fitness room, business center, indoor pool, and laundry and concierge services. Internet access and on-site parking is available for an additional fee.

MIDTOWN

Midtown hotels are near Music Row, Vanderbilt and Belmont Universities, and the entertainment, dining, and shopping attractions of Hillsboro Village.

Under $100

One of two hostels in Nashville, **Music City Hostel** (1809 Patterson St., 615/692-1277, www.musiccityhostel.com, $25) is located among doctor's offices and commercial buildings in between downtown Nashville and Elliston Place. The low-slung '70s-style building looks like nothing much on the outside, but inside it is cheerful, welcoming, and a comfortable home base for budget travelers. Music City Hostel offers the usual dorm-style bunk-bed accommodations, as well as a handful of private apartments, which rent for $75–85 a night. You can also have a private bedroom with private bath plus shared kitchen and common room for $60 a night. Common areas include a large kitchen, dining room, reading room, cable TV room, computer with Internet access, and a coin laundry. The entire facility is smoke-free.

Parking is free, and the hostel is within walking distance of restaurants, a bus stop, car rental agency, post office, and hospitals. It would be a hike to get downtown on foot from here.

$100-150

Best Western Music Row (1407 Division St., 615/242-1631, $90–110) is a no-nonsense motel with an outdoor pool, free continental breakfast, Internet access, and indoor corridors. Rooms have cable TV, AM/FM alarm clocks, and coffeemakers. Pets are allowed for $10 a day, and parking is free. The 75-room hotel is located a few steps away from the Music Row traffic circle and nearby restaurants.

Located near Elliston Place and Vanderbilt University, **Guesthouse Inn and Suites** (1909 Hayes St., 615/329-1000, $109) offers a free shuttle to nearby hospitals, including Baptist Hospital, Vanderbilt Medical Center, and the Veterans Administration Hospital. All rooms have microwave ovens, refrigerators, and coffeemakers, and guests enjoy free breakfast including made-to-order waffles. Suites ($140) include a sleeper couch. Rooms are typical motel-style, with two double beds or a single king-sized bed. The property is convenient to Hillsboro Village, Music Row, and Centennial Park.

Come home to **Hillsboro House** (1933 20th Ave. S., 615/292-5501, www.visitnashville.net, $130–175), a restored Victorian buttercup cottage in a quiet residential neighborhood near Vanderbilt, Hillsboro Village, and Belmont University. The bed-and-breakfast offers three mini-suites, each with a private bathroom and telephone. Rooms have comfortable feather beds, antique furniture, and touches of home. Guests are invited to lounge in an upstairs library. There is free wireless Internet access for guests, and the full breakfast includes homemade breads.

Another bed-and-breakfast choice in this part of the city is **1501 Linden House Bed and Breakfast** (1501 Linden Ave., 615/298-2701, www.nashville-bed-breakfast.com, $110–165). This cheerful yellow-brick home on a corner lot has three guest rooms, each with stylish furniture and hardwood floors; one room has a private whirlpool and another has a fireplace.

Over $200

For luxurious accommodations near Vanderbilt, choose **(C Loews Vanderbilt Plaza** (2100 West End Ave., 615/320-1700, $260–310), a 340-room hotel on West End Avenue close to Centennial Park and Hillsboro Village. Loews boasts 24-hour room service, luxurious sheets, towels, and robes, natural soaps, and spacious bathrooms. Guests enjoy top-of-the-line coffee and tea kettles, evening turn down service, and free high-speed Internet access. Many rooms have views of the Nashville skyline; premium rooms provide guests with access to the concierge lounge, with continental breakfast and evening hors d'oeuvres and a cash bar. All guests can enjoy a fine fitness room, spa, art gallery, and gift shop.

You can't get closer to Vanderbilt University than the **Marriott Nashville Vanderbilt** (2555 West End Ave., 615/321-1300, $180–300). Set on the northern end of the university campus, the Marriott has 301 guest rooms, six suites, and meeting space. It is located across West End Avenue from Centennial Park, home of the Parthenon, and a few steps from Vanderbilt's football stadium. There is an indoor pool, full-service restaurant, deli, concierge lounge, ATM, and business center.

EAST NASHVILLE

While it does not have many attractions, there are a few good reasons to stay in East Nashville. For football fans, this part of the city is close to the Tennessee Titans' stadium. Others will enjoy bed-and-breakfasts in Edgefield, a cool, laid-back, and diverse residential neighborhood. Good dining abounds, and downtown is a short drive or walk across the Cumberland River.

Under $100

Located on the east bank of the Cumberland River, **Days Inn at the Stadium** (211 N. 1st St., 615/254-1551, $75–100) is near LP Field, where the Tennessee Titans play. The hotel's 180 rooms have clock-radios, cable TV, and

wireless Internet. Some have nice views of the Nashville skyline. Guests enjoy access to a fitness room, indoor pool, and laundry facilities, plus free breakfast. There is a bar and restaurant inside the hotel. While not within easy walking distance of downtown Nashville, the Days Inn is just across the river from the city's premier attractions. Free parking is a plus.

$100-150

Carole's Yellow Cottage (801 Fatherland St., 615/226-2952, $100–125) is a bed-and-breakfast offering two comfortable guest rooms. The decor is not as fussy as many bed-and-breakfasts, and the atmosphere is homey and low-key. Rooms have a private bathroom, and guests can relax in a library with a TV/VCR. Breakfasts are homemade and feature organic foods when available.

The Big Bungalow (618 Fatherland St., 615/256-8375, www.thebigbungalow.com, $110–160) a Craftsman-style early-1900s townhouse, offers three guest rooms, each with its own private bath and television. Guests have shared access to a computer, microwave, and refrigerator. Common areas are comfortable and stylish, with tasteful decor and hardwood floors. Hostess Ellen Warshaw prepares breakfast for her guests and sometimes hosts in-the-round concerts in her living room. She is also a licensed masseuse. This is a pet-free, non-smoking facility; children over 10 years are welcome. The bed-and-breakfast is located about seven blocks from the Shelby Street Pedestrian Bridge that takes you to the heart of the District.

$150-200

The East Park Inn (822 Boscoble St., 615/226-8691, $155) is a brightly painted Queen Anne–style bed-and-breakfast in Edgefield, on the east bank of the Cumberland River. Two guest suites offer private bathrooms and elegant furnishings. Guests also enjoy a relaxing terrace and garden, comfortable common rooms, and delicious breakfasts of fresh fruit, breads, quiche, waffles, and fresh-squeezed orange juice, served by host Brooks Parker. Afternoon

NASHVILLE

tea or wine is served on the front porch, which enjoys a pleasant view of the Nashville skyline. The inn is located 10 blocks from downtown Nashville, and three blocks from coffee shops and restaurants.

You'll be happy to call **Top O'Woodland** (1603 Woodland St., 888/288-368, www.topofwoodland.com, $160) home during your stay in Nashville. This redbrick home on a corner lot is distinctive and beautiful. Features include a spacious wraparound front porch, original stained-glass windows, a turret, a baby grand Steinway piano, and lots of period and original antiques. The bed-and-breakfast is within five blocks of restaurants and pubs, and a short drive over the Cumberland to downtown Nashville. Guests can choose to stay in the master suite, with a king-sized four-poster bed, working fireplace, private bath, and private entrance, or in Mr. Green's Cottage, a detached cottage with kitchenette that can sleep up to six people. The home has wireless high-speed Internet access, and a generous continental breakfast is served at your convenience. Hostess Belinda Leslie is a chaplain and a certified wedding and event planner, and Top O'Woodland is a beautiful place for an old-fashioned wedding or quiet elopement.

MUSIC VALLEY

There are a dozen or more chain hotels in Music Valley, all close to restaurants and a short drive from the Grand Ole Opry and Opry Mills mall. Nashville's most famous hotel, Opryland, is luxurious and within walking distance of the Opry.

These hotels tend to provide more for your money than downtown digs, but they are a 10-to-15-minute drive to the city center.

Under $100

If you're looking for a clean, comfortable room and friendly welcome, look no farther than the 〔 **Fiddler's Inn** (2410 Music Valley Dr., 615/885-1440, www.fiddlers-inn.com, $60–75). This 204-room no-frills hotel offers a solid Tennessee welcome to its guests, who come in droves to see the Opry and enjoy other Music

Valley attractions. It's right next to a Cracker Barrel restaurant and there's plenty of parking for cars and tour buses. Guests enjoy cable TV, free coffee and pastries in the morning, an outdoor pool, and a gift shop stocked with Nashville souvenirs.

The all-suite **Best Western Suites near Opryland** (201 Music City Cir., 615/902-9940, $70–80) is a comfortable compromise between the luxury of the Opryland Hotel and the affordability of a motel. Each of the hotel's 100 suites has a couch, desk, high-speed Internet access, coffee- and tea-maker, microwave, ironing board, and refrigerator. Rooms with whirlpools tubs are available for about $80 more per night. Guests enjoy an on-site fitness room, 24-hour business center, outdoor pool, free continental breakfast, and weekday newspaper. The Best Western is located along a strip of motels and restaurants about one mile from the Grand Ole Opry and other Opryland attractions.

Located about two miles from the Opryland, **Comfort Inn Opryland Area** (2516 Music Valley Dr., 615/889-0086, $70–75) offers 121 clean, comfortable guest rooms with cable TV, wireless Internet, ironing board, hair dryer, and free daily newspaper. There is free outdoor parking, and interior corridors.

$100-150

Guests at the **Courtyard by Marriott Opryland** (125 Music City Cir., 615/882-9133, $140–150) enjoy refurbished rooms with soft beds, wireless Internet, coffeemakers, ironing boards, and refrigerators. The on-site restaurant serves breakfast, and business rooms come with a desk, dataport, voice mail, and speakerphone.

Over $200

The **Gaylord Opryland Hotel** (2800 Opryland Dr., 615/889-1000, $240–310) feels like a cruise ship on land. This 2,881-room luxury hotel and convention center is built around a nine-acre indoor garden. Glass atriums invite sunlight, and miles of footpaths invite you to explore the climate-controlled gardens.

Highlights include a 40-foot waterfall and flat-boats that float along a river.

Set among the gardens are dozens of different restaurants and cafés, ranging from casual buffets to elegant steakhouses. A few shops are sprinkled in, but it has not yet totally morphed into a mall. Hundreds of room balconies overlook the gardens, providing some guests with views of the well-kept greenery, even in winter. If you stay, choose between a "traditional view" looking outside the hotel, or an "atrium view" for about $60 more per night.

The property has a full-service salon and fitness center, on-site child care and "kid's resort," and a car rental agency. You can walk to Opry Mills mall and the Grand Ole Opry from the hotel or take the free shuttle. Guest rooms are luxurious and feature coffee- and tea-makers; two telephones; wireless Internet access; pay-per-view movies, games, and music; daily national newspapers; and other usual amenities. You can add a refrigerator for a one-time $20 fee, and you get up to 20 minutes of local calls free per day. Guests can buy one-time or daily passes on the downtown shuttle for about $15 a day, and the airport shuttle costs $35 round-trip.

While room rates at the Opryland are steep, the hotel offers attractive packages that add on other Gaylord-owned attractions and properties. These often include tickets to the Grand Ole Opry, a ride on the General Jackson Showboat, trips into Nashville to visit the Ryman Auditorium or the Wildhorse Saloon, and extras like spa visits and golf games at the hotel. Many of these packages are a good deal for travelers who want to pay one price for their whole vacation.

AIRPORT
Under $100
The **Alexis Inn and Suites Nashville Airport** (600 Ermac Dr., 615/889-4466, www.nashvillealexishotel.com, $60–70) is a comfortable and convenient place to stay near the airport. Rooms have all the usual amenities, plus guests get free popcorn in the lobby, a free airport shuttle daily between 7 A.M. and 9 P.M., and a business center. All rooms have refrigerators, and most have microwaves. There is a free continental breakfast. Suites cost $80–100 per night.

$100-150
Drury Inns and Suites (555 Donelson Pike, 615/902-0400, $100–130) offers guests an appealing array of extras, including a free hot breakfast, free evening beverages and snacks, a free airport shuttle, 60 minutes of free long-distance calls, and $7 daily park-and-fly parking. There is both an indoor and outdoor pool and a fitness center. Drury Inn is about two miles north of the airport and five miles south of Music Valley.

Hotel Preston (733 Briley Pkwy., 615/361-5900, www.hotelpreston.com, $110–140) is a boutique hotel near the airport. Youthful energy, modern decor, and up-to-date rooms set this property apart from the crowd. Rooms are stocked with Tazo tea and Starbucks coffee and there's and a 24-hour fitness center. The "You-Want-It-You-Got-It" button in each room beckons the 24-hour room service, and whimsical extras including a lava lamp, pet fish, and art kit are available by request when you check in. High-speed Internet is an add-on extra. Naughty packages—like the "Ooey Gooey Night Out" couple's getaway with late check-out, wine, and whipped cream on request—prove that this isn't your parents' motel, though the hotel caters equally to business travelers with meeting rooms and a business center. Two restaurants, including a bar and nightclub, provide food and entertainment.

SOUTH OF NASHVILLE
Under $100
Nashville's second hostel is located a half-hour drive south of the city in Brentwood. **Country Hostel Nashville** (9900 Maxwell Ln., 615/578-7207, www.countryhostelnashville.com, $22) is indeed semi-rural, and guests can enjoy bike riding (the hostel rents bikes) or sitting out on the comfortable deck. The hostel

has free wireless Internet, a barbecue, and a spacious kitchen. It is non-smoking inside and air-conditioned in summer. Accommodations are divided into male and female dorm-style rooms with bunk beds and clean sheets. Towels and linens are provided, and the hostel will pick you up from the airport or bus station for an additional fee.

This hostel is also convenient to attractions in Franklin, Tennessee, and close to malls, shopping, and dining. You need a car to explore any of these areas, however.

Food

You can eat in a different restaurant each day in Nashville and never get bored. Southern cooking stars at meat-and-three diners and barbecue joints, fine dining restaurants cater to the well-heeled, and ethnic eateries reflect the city's diversity.

The Arcade
One of two downtown food destinations, the Arcade is an old outdoor shopping mall that lies between 4th and 5th Avenues. The ground floor of the Arcade is full of hole-in-the-wall restaurants that cater to the downtown lunchtime crowd with quick, cheap eats. Upstairs are professional offices and a few galleries.

Katie's Meat & Three (10 Arcade, 615/256-1055) has four different meat specials daily, which you can get with sides like turnip greens, mashed potatoes, and white beans. A meat-and-three plate costs $7; order your choice of four sides for $5. The Greek Touch (13 Arcade, 615/259-9493) has gyro, sausage, veggie, and chicken divine sandwiches, platters, and salads, all for under $6. There are also several sandwich shops, a pizza parlor, and a Chinese restaurant.

Most restaurants at the Arcade have some seating inside, or you can sit outside and watch the world go by around you. The outdoor experience is made slightly less enjoyable by the presence of smokers who have been forbidden to enter many eateries.

Nashville Farmer's Market
Organizers of the Nashville Farmer's Market have hit upon a good thing. The outdoor components of the market include a farm shed with fresh produce year-round and a flea market with arts and crafts on weekends. The interior of the market is a food court with choices ranging from Southern specialties to Caribbean cuisine. **Swett's** (900 8th Ave. N., 615/742-9699), a popular soul food restaurant, has an outpost here. **Jamaicaway** (900 8th Ave. N., 615/255-5920) serves oxtail, steamed fish, and Jamaican patties. There are also Mexican, Chinese, and Greek choices, as well as a super salad bar. The food court is open daily 9 A.M.–5 P.M.

DINERS AND COFFEE SHOPS
Downtown
Provence (601 Church St., 615/664-1150, Mon.–Fri. 7 A.M.–6 P.M., Sat. 8 A.M.–5 P.M., $5–12), located inside the Nashville Public Library, serves excellent European-style pastries, breads, and salads, as well as coffee. Provence's signature sandwiches include creamy chicken salad and turkey-and-brie. Or you can try a sampler of the café's salads, including roasted-vegetable salad, parmesan potato salad, or creamy penne pasta. Save room for a decadent pastry, or at least a cookie, which come in varieties like raspberry hazelnut, chocolate espresso, and ginger molasses. For breakfast, nothing beats a buttery croissant spread with jam. Provence also has locations at 1600 Division Street at Roundabout Plaza; at 315 Deaderick Street in the AmSouth Building downtown; and in Hillsboro at 1705 21st Avenue South.

For homemade salads, wraps, and sandwiches, follow the crowds of downtown office workers to the **Frist Center Cafe** (919 Broadway, 616/244-3340, Mon.–Wed. and Sat. 10 A.M.–5:30 P.M., Thurs.–Fri. 10 A.M.–9 P.M.,

Sun. noon–5 P.M., $5–8), located at the rear of the Frist Center for the Arts. Sandwiches are available whole or half, and you can add a soup, salad, or fries for a well-rounded lunch. The café has daily hot lunch entrées, plus a case of tempting desserts.

Midtown

When Nashvillians are in the mood for a hearty deli sandwich, they head to **Noshville** (1918 Broadway, 615/329-6674, Mon. 6:30 A.M.– 2:30 P.M., Tues.–Thurs. 6:30 A.M.–9 P.M., Fri. 6:30 A.M.–10:30 P.M., Sat. 7:30 A.M.–10:30 P.M., Sun. 7:30 A.M.–9 P.M., $7–12), which is as close to a genuine New York delicatessen as you'll find in this town. Lox and bagels, oatmeal, and a variety of egg dishes are popular at breakfast. At lunch and supper choose from a variety of sandwiches, all served double-stacked, which means it's really more than any one person should eat. To find Noshville, look for the miniature statue of Lady Liberty on the roof. There is a second location in Green Hills at 4014 Hillsboro Circle, 615/269-3535.

The hype surrounding Nashville's favorite breakfast restaurant, the **Pancake Pantry** (1796 21st Ave. S., 615/383-9333, Mon.–Fri. 6 A.M.–3 P.M., Sat.–Sun. 6 A.M.–4 P.M., $6–14) is deserved. Founded in 1961 and still family-owned, the Pantry serves the best pancakes in the city, and probably the state. Owner David Baldwin says that the secret is in the ingredients, which are fresh and homemade. Many of the flours come from Tennessee, and the syrup is made right at the restaurant. The Pantry proves that a pancake can be much more than plain. The menu offers no less than 21 varieties, and that doesn't include the waffles. Try the fluffy buckwheat cakes, savory cornmeal cakes, sweet blintzes, or the old standby buttermilk pancakes. And if you decide to order eggs instead, the good news is that most of the other breakfast platters on offer come with a short stack of pancakes too. To its credit, the Pantry offers no-yolk omelets for the health-conscious, and it's very kid-friendly as well.

The Pantry also serves lunch, which is limited to sandwiches, salads, and soups. Beware that on many weekend mornings, and some weekdays, the line for a seat at the Pantry goes out the door.

In today's retro-happy world, it isn't too hard to find an old-fashioned soda shop. But how many of them are the real thing? **Elliston Place Soda Shop** (2111 Elliston Pl., 615/327-1090, Mon.–Fri. 7 A.M.–7 P.M., Sat. 7 A.M.–5 P.M., $5–9), near Centennial Park and Vanderbilt, is one of these rare holdovers from the past, and it's proud of it. The black-and-white tile floors, lunch counter, and Purity Milk advertisements may have been here for decades, but the food is consistently fresh and good. Choose between a sandwich or a plate lunch, but be sure to save room for a classic milkshake or slice of hot pie with ice cream on top. Yum!

Nashville's original coffee shop, **Bongo Java** (2007 Belmont Blvd., 615/385-5282, Mon.– Fri. 7 A.M.–11 P.M., Sat.–Sun. 8 A.M.–11 P.M.) is just as popular as ever. Located near Belmont University, Bongo, as its frequent patrons call it, is regularly full of students chatting, texting, and surfing the Internet thanks to free wireless Internet. Set in an old house with a huge front porch, Bongo feels homey and welcoming, and a bit more on the hippie side than other Nashville coffee shops. Nonetheless, expect the latest in coffee drinks, premium salads, and sandwiches. Breakfast, including Bongo French toast, is served all day. There is a bulletin board, a good place to find and seek roommates or apartments.

Voted Nashville's favorite coffee shop, **Fido** (1812 21st Ave. S., 615/777-3436, Mon.–Fri. 7 A.M.–11 P.M., Sat. 8 A.M.–midnight, Sun. 8 A.M.–11 P.M.) near Vanderbilt is a place to see and be seen. Take a seat along the front plate-glass windows to watch the pretty people as they stroll between the Sunset Grill and Posh, one of Nashville's most upscale clothing boutiques. Fido's is a tad dark, with sleek furnishings and rock music playing. It is not unfriendly, but has a harder edge than Bongo Java. In addition to coffee, sandwiches, salads, and baked goods are also on the menu.

Said to have the best burger in Nashville, **Rotier's** (2413 Elliston Pl., 615/327-9892,

Mon.–Fri. 10:30 A.M.–10 P.M., Sat. 9 A.M.–10 P.M., $5–12) is also a respected meat-and-three diner. Choose from classic sandwiches or comfort-food dinners. The Saturday breakfast will fuel you all day long. Ask about the milkshake, a city favorite that appears nowhere on the menu.

Dessert takes center stage at **Bobbie's Dairy Dip** (5301 Charlotte Ave., 615/292-2112, Mon.–Thurs. 11 A.M.–9 P.M., Fri.–Sat. 11 A.M.–10 P.M., Sun. noon–9 P.M., $4–7). The cheeseburgers and chili dogs are the comfort food you've dreamed of, and you can finish off with soft-serve ice cream, dipped cones, sundaes, and banana splits. Bobbie's closes during the winter months; call ahead to confirm they're open.

South Nashville

Aurora Bakery and Cafe (3725 Nolensville Pike, 615/837-1993, Mon.–Sat. 7 A.M.–8 P.M., $5–6) offers one of the most cheerful welcomes among Nashville eateries. The café is clean, bright, and full of the smell of fresh baked goods. Come here to buy loaves of fresh white bread, or to sample one of the dozens of types of pastries, cookies, and cakes, many of them traditional Hispanic recipes. Specialties include empanadas and *tres leche* cake.

East Nashville

The most creative deli in Nashville is **Mitchell's Delicatessen** (1402 McGavock Pk., 615/262-9862, Tues.–Sat. 7 A.M.–7 P.M., Sun. 7 A.M.–4 P.M., $5–9). Order the roasted lamb and raita; a Vietnamese-style creation with pork, liver pate, and veggies; or a BLT fit for a king. Breakfast is served until 11 A.M., and there is also a daily menu of soups and hot plate specials. Stop here for top-notch bread, cheese, and meats for your own sandwiches, too.

SOUTHERN SPECIALTIES
Downtown

Run, don't walk, to 【 **Arnold's Country Kitchen** (605 8th Ave. S., 615/256-4455, Mon.–Fri. 10:30 A.M.–2:45 P.M., $7–10) for some of the best Southern cooking in town. Set in a red cinder-block building on the southern outskirts of downtown, Arnold's is a food-lover's dream. No haute or fusion cuisine here—this is real food! It's set up cafeteria style, so start out by grabbing a tray while you peer at the wonders before you: chocolate pie, congealed salad (that's Jell-O to those who don't know), juicy sliced tomatoes, turnip greens, mashed potatoes, squash casserole, macaroni and cheese—and that's just the "vegetables." Choose a vegetable plate, with either three or four vegetables, or a meat-and-three for just about a buck more. Common meat dishes include ham, baked chicken, fried fish, and beef tips. All meals come with your choice of pillowy yeast rolls or corn bread. The full lunch, plus a drink, will run you under $10. As you leave, full and happy, the only question on your mind will be, When can I come back?

Midtown

One of Nashville's most beloved meat-and-threes is **Swett's** (2725 Clifton Ave., 615/329-4418, daily 11 A.M.–8 P.M., $7–10), family owned and operated since 1954. People come from all over the city to eat at this North Nashville institution, which combines soul food and Southern cooking with great results. The food here is homemade and authentic, down to the real mashed potatoes, the vinegary greens, and the yeast rolls. Swett's is set up cafeteria style. Start by grabbing dessert—the pies are excellent—and then you move on to the good stuff: Country-fried steak, pork chops, meatloaf, fried catfish, and ham are a few of the usual suspects. A standard plate comes with one meat, two sides, and a serving of either yeast roll or corn bread, but you can add more sides if you like. Draw your own iced tea—sweet or unsweet—at the end and then find a seat, if you can.

North Nashville

Nashville's most sublime food experience is not to be found in a fine restaurant or even at a standard meat-and-three cafeteria. The food that you'll still be dreaming about when you get home is found at 【 **Prince's Hot**

© SUSANNA HENIGHAN POTTER

a typical meat-and-three plate lunch, as served at Swett's

Chicken Shack (123 Ewing Dr., 615/226-9442, Tues.–Thurs. noon–10 P.M., Fri.–Sat. 2 P.M.–1 A.M., $4–6) in North Nashville. Hot chicken is skillet-fried chicken that is also spicy, and you can find hot chicken outlets in Nashville, Memphis, and a few other Southern cities. But no hot chicken shop does it quite as well as Prince's, where the hot chicken comes in three varieties: mild, hot, and extra-hot. Most uninitiated will find the mild variety pretty darn spicy, so beware. It is served with slices of white bread—perfect for soaking up that spicy chicken juice—and pickles. You can add a cup of creamy potato salad, coleslaw, or baked beans if you like. When you walk into Prince's, head to the back where you'll place your order at the window, pay, and be given a number. Then take a seat—if you can find one—while you wait for your food. You can order to go or eat in. Your food is made to order, and Prince's is very popular, so the wait often exceeds 30 minutes. Have heart though—Prince's chicken is worth the wait.

West End

For a refined Southern food experience there's **Martha's at the Plantation** (5025 Harding Rd., 615/353-2828, daily 11 A.M.–2 P.M., $9–15), a sunny family-friendly café located above the gift shop at Belle Meade Plantation. Proprietor Martha Stamps offers favorites like chicken croquettes, fried chicken, and fried catfish sandwiches. Salads include cornmeal-crusted oysters on a bed of romaine, and popular side dishes are squash casserole, baked cheese grits, and spicy kale. For your main dish, try the boneless pork chop with cranberry glaze or a patty melt on sourdough toast. Her chicken and tuna salad sandwiches are also consistently good. Kids can choose from favorites including macaroni and cheese and peanut butter and jelly sandwiches.

© SUSANNA HENIGHAN POTTER

The Loveless Cafe is a culinary landmark.

West of Nashville

The **Loveless Cafe** (8400 Hwy. 100, 615/646-9700, daily 7 A.M.–9 P.M., $7–13) is an institution, and some may argue it's a state of mind. But this little café-that-could is increasingly a destination too, for visitors not just to Nashville but the entire heartland of Tennessee. The Loveless got its start in 1951 when Lon and Annie Loveless started to serve good country cooking to travelers on Highway 100. Over the years the restaurant changed hands, but Annie's biscuit recipe remained the same, and it was the biscuits that kept Nashvillians, including many famous ones, coming back for more. In 1982 then owner George McCabe started the Hams & Jams mail-order business, and in 2003 the Loveless underwent a major renovation that expanded the kitchen and dining rooms and added additional shops in the rear. The food at the Loveless is good, no doubt about it. The biscuits are fluffy and buttery, the ham salty, and the eggs, bacon, and sausage will hit the spot. The supper and lunch menu has expanded to include Southern standards like fried catfish and chicken, pit-cooked pork barbecue, pork chops, and meatloaf, as well as a few salads. The prices are a bit on the high side—a basic plate of bacon and eggs will run you at least $9—but a destination restaurant can do that. Parties of four or more can choose the family-style breakfast, which offers all the fruit, bacon, sausage, fries, gravy, eggs, biscuits, and preserves you can eat for $11 per adult and $6 per child. The Loveless is located about 20 miles from downtown Nashville; plan on a 30-minute drive out Highway 100. Once you get out of the clutter of West End, it's a pretty trip.

BARBECUE
Downtown

Thousands of tourists can't be wrong; **Jack's Bar-b-que** (416 Broadway, 615/254-5715, Mon.–Thurs. 10:30 A.M.–9 P.M., Fri.–Sat. 10:30 A.M.–10 P.M., Sun. noon–6 P.M., $4–13) is a great place to grab a bite on Broadway. Choose from barbecue pork shoulder, brisket, turkey, ribs, or sausage, and pair it with classic Southern sides like green beans, macaroni and cheese, and fried apples. Jack's serves five types of barbecue sauce, including classic Tennessee, Texas, and Kansas City. Most diners opt for a plate of one meat, two vegetables, and bread for $8–9, but if you're really hungry go for the three-meat platter for $13. Adding to the appeal of the good, affordable food is the fact that Jack's service is fast and friendly.

Midtown
Near Centennial Park and Vanderbilt, **Hog Heaven** (115 27th Ave. N., 615/329-1234, Mon.–Sat. 10 A.M.–7 P.M., $5–10) is a small yet well-known landmark for barbecue. Pulled-pork sandwiches and beef brisket are among the most popular at this mostly take-out eatery.

East Nashville
Family-operated **Dee's Q** (1000 Riverside Dr., 615/227-0024, Mon.–Thurs. 11 A.M.–9 P.M., Fri. Sat. 11 A.M. 10 P.M., Sun. 11 A.M.–7 P.M., $2.50–10) serves up Memphis-style barbecue dry ribs, brisket, turkey, and chicken. He smokes his meats over hickory fire right next door to the open-air seating area. Call for winter hours.

South Nashville
Tucked on Nolensville Pike, the land of ethnic eateries, is one of Nashville's best barbecue houses. **Martin's Bar-B-Que Joint** (7215 Nolensville Pike, 615/776-1856, Tues.–Sat. 11 A.M.–8 P.M., $3.50–20.50) has pulled pork, barbecue spareribs, smoked wings, and beef brisket, plus all the side dishes you could want: coleslaw, green beans, potato salad, and the best corncakes this side of town. You can also order burgers and a mean catfish po-boy. Martin's is located inside the Nolensville city limits, about 30 minutes' drive south from downtown Nashville.

STEAKHOUSES
Downtown
Most everything about **Demos' Steak and Spaghetti House** (300 Commerce St.,

615/256-4655, daily 11 A.M.–11 P.M., $6–15) is upscale except the price. Just as the name suggests, Demos' specializes in steaks and spaghetti, and it has earned a reputation among Nashville residents for quality food and good value. Choose from hamburger steak, rib eye, or sirloin, or try one of the 12 different spaghetti dinners, including seafood sauce and browned butter with garlic. The portions are more than generous, pleasing to the biggest appetites. The original Demos' is in Murfreesboro, and there are other locations in Lebanon and Hendersonville.

Midtown
C Jimmy Kelly's (217 Louise Ave., 615/329-4349, Mon.–Sat. 5 P.M.–midnight, $12–36) is a family-run old-school steakhouse. Set in an old Victorian mansion a few blocks from Centennial Park and Vanderbilt, Jimmy Kelly's has been operated by the Kelly family since 1934. During its lifetime, food fads have come and gone, but Jimmy Kelly's has continued to serve excellent steaks and other grill foods. Dinner begins with irresistible corn cakes, and continues with classic appetizers like crab cakes or fried calamari. Entrée choices include a half-dozen different steaks, lamb, grilled chicken, and seafood, including the best blackened catfish in the city. Jimmy Kelly's offers low lighting, wood paneling, and attentive, but not fussy, service. Tables are set throughout what were once parlors, bedrooms, and porches in the old home, giving diners a feeling of homey intimacy.

CONTEMPORARY
Downtown
The thoughtful menu, careful preparations, and intimate atmosphere at the **C Mad Platter** (1239 6th Ave. N., 615/242-2563, Mon.–Fri. 10 A.M.–2 P.M., Wed.–Sat. 5:30–11 P.M., Sun. 5–11 P.M., $18–29) have made it one of Nashville's favorite "nice" restaurants for years. Located among restored townhouses in the tiny Germantown neighborhood just north of the Bicentennial Mall, the Mad Platter is the work of Craig and Marcia

Jervis, two chefs who met while catering the mid-1980s Michael Jackson's Victory tour. The Jervises married and opened the Mad Hatter, where they demonstrate their love for food, and each other, every day. Signature entrées include the Mad Platter rack of lamb, which is tender and juicy, and the porcini-dusted shrimp. For a special occasion, or just to enjoy one of the city's best dining deals, choose the five-course special. Add $20 to your favorite entrée and you'll get soup, appetizer, salad, and dessert, too. Talk about a meal to remember! Lunch features sandwiches, pasta, and salads for $7–13. The chicken salad is sweet and tangy, and comes with fresh banana bread. Reservations are advisable at dinner; for lunch, come early to head off the business crowd.

Rub elbows with legislators, lobbyists, and other members of the jet set at the **Capitol Grill** (23 6th Ave. N., 615/345-7116, daily 6:30 A.M.–2 P.M. and 5:30–10 P.M., $16–47). Located in the ground floor of the elegant Hermitage Hotel and set a stone's throw from the Tennessee State Capitol, this is the sort of restaurant where marriages are proposed and deals are done. The menu is fine dining at its best: choice cuts of meat prepared with exacting care. Dinner features rack of elk, sea bass, and pork chops; the provenience of each is noted on the menu. The lunch menu is more modest, including the Capitol Grill burger, a grilled pimento cheese sandwich, and meat entrées for $11–18. The business lunch offers a lunch entrée and your choice of soup or salad for $20. Breakfast ($4–16) may be the most decadent of all, with cinnamon-swirl French toast, eggs Benedict, lobster and shirred eggs, and an array of fresh pastries and fruit. The Sunday Brunch features the best of the grill's lunch and breakfast menus, and is consistently popular.

Adjacent to the Capitol Grill is the Oak Bar, a wood-paneled and intimate bar for pre- or post-dinner drinks and conversation.

Midtown

Restaurant Zola (3001 West End Ave., 615/320-7778, Mon.–Thurs. 5:30–10 P.M., Fri.–Sat. 5:30–11 P.M., $16–30) is consistently among Nashville's favorite restaurants for romance, special occasions, and its menu. Located in a strip mall in the city's upscale West End, Restaurant Zola wows with its intriguing fusion of Mediterranean and Southern cuisine and superb wine list. Fresh seafood, top-grade meats, and vegetarian entrées that are much more than an afterthought define the menu. Zola's paella and the lobster omelet headline the seafood menu; pork tenderloin and grilled venison highlight the meats, and the signature vegetable tower will make even meat-eaters smile. Be sure to save room for some of the best desserts in town.

◖ F. Scott's (2210 Crestmore Rd., 615/269-5861, Mon.–Thurs. 5:30–10 P.M., Fri.–Sat. 5:30–11 P.M., Sun. 5:30–9 P.M., $26–38) is an upscale restaurant and jazz bar with one of the best wine lists in Nashville. Diners are ushered into a black-and-white-tiled dining room, where the sounds of live jazz from the adjacent listening room follow them. Enjoy a relaxed meal with wine pairings and great conversation. Food at F. Scott's is meant to be savored. Appetizers include rabbit tart, or pancetta and scallops with caviar, and entrées might be pan-seared seafood, dressed-up shepherd's pie, and grilled beef tenderloin. Save room for dessert: homemade ice cream, coconut cake, or a cheese plate paired with the perfect dessert wine.

A favorite for Music Row power lunches, special occasions, and late-night bar food, **Sunset Grill** (2001 Belcourt Ave., 615/386-3663, $11–30) serves lunch Tuesday–Friday 11 A.M.–3 P.M., dinner nightly 5–11 P.M., and late-night Monday–Saturday until 1:30 A.M. Dinner favorites include Voodoo Pasta, a spicy pasta dish with shrimp and andouille sausage, and the grilled beef tenderloin. At lunch, when most choices clock in at under $12, you can order salads, sandwiches, and pasta. The Cobb salad and chicken-salad sandwiches are always popular. Food here is prepared with care, often using organic and locally produced ingredients. The outdoor patio is popular during warm weather, and it is a great place to people-watch.

East Nashville

The Family Wash (2038 Greenwood Ave., 615/226-6070, Tues.–Sat. 6 P.M.–midnight, $9–15) is a live music listening room that serves good food at surprisingly low cost. Where else can you get a well-cooked steak for just $14? Choose from baked mac and cheese, the killer meat or vegetarian shepherd's pie, or roasted salmon and jasmine rice. Pizzas and the flank steak sandwich are always good. Reservations are accepted, and a good idea, especially when a popular musician is on the stage. The Wash, located in an old laundry, books up-and-coming singer-songwriters, and when the music is on, the conversation stops. This is a restaurant with a lot of energy and a little attitude.

ETHNIC CUISINE
Downtown

There are several Greek restaurants amid Nashville's office towers and State buildings. One of the best is **Santorini** (210 4th Ave., 615/254-4524, Mon.–Fri. 10:30 A.M.–3 P.M., $3.50–5.75). Choose from falafel, gyro, chicken, or spinach pie, served as a plate (with rice, salad, and pita), salad (with pita, tabouli, and salad), or meal (with fries). The food is fresh and well prepared, and the premises are neat and clean.

Located in the downtown Arcade, **House of Pizza** (15 Arcade, 615/242-7144, Mon.–Fri. 10 A.M.–6 P.M., Sat. 11 A.M.–4:30 P.M.) serves up thick- and thin-crust varieties, massive stromboli, mighty lasagna, and huge meatball subs. The restaurant is small; eating in can be a challenge, especially since Nashvillians flock here for the best pizza in town.

Midtown

The venerable **International Market and Restaurant** (2010 Belmont Blvd., 615/297-4453, daily 10:30 A.M.–9 P.M., $4–10) near Belmont University and Hillsboro Village may well be the best choice for a cheap lunch in Nashville. The cafeteria serves lots of vegetable, noodle, and rice dishes, many of them Thai in origin, at prices that seem not to have risen much since the restaurant was established in 1975. If you want to splurge, order a "from the kitchen" special of pad thai or another dish, which will be made from scratch just for you.

For the best Italian food in Nashville, head west to the neighborhood of Sylvan Park, where you'll find **Caffe Nonna** (4427 Murphy Rd., 615/463 0133, Tues.–Fri. 11 A.M.–2 P.M., Mon.–Thurs. 5–9 P.M., Fri.–Sat. 5–10 P.M., $12–21). Inspired by chef Daniel Maggipinto's own Nonna (grandmother), the café serves rustic Italian fare. Appetizers include salads and bruschetta and entrées include the divine Lasagne Nonna, made with butternut squash, ricotta cheese, spinach, and sage. One of the best deals is the mix-and-match pasta; choose your own pasta and sauce for $10 at lunch and $12 at dinner. The lunch menu offers a dozen different sandwiches, including basil chicken salad and Italian-fried tilapia, for under $10. The service at Caffe Nonna is friendly and attentive, and the atmosphere is cozy.

Located just west of the Kroger food store and on the opposite side of the street, K&S World Market on Charlotte Avenue, the second in a chain whose original location is on Nolensville Pike, will keep any foodie happy for hours with its obscure and unusual food items. In the same shopping center you'll find Nashvillians' favorite Vietnamese restaurant, **Kien Giang** (5825 Charlotte Ave., 615/353-1250, Tues.–Fri. 11 A.M.–9 P.M., Sat.–Sun. 10 A.M.–9 P.M., $4–12).

Drive a bit farther out to find **La Hispana Panaderia** (6208 Charlotte Pike, 615/352-3798, daily 6 A.M.–9 P.M.), whose bread and pastries are as good as the finest European bakery but at a fraction of the cost.

One of Nashville's oldest Indian restaurants, **Shalimar** (3711 Hillsboro Rd., 615/269-8577, Mon.–Sat. 11 A.M.–10 P.M., $11–17) offers fine food and efficient service. The $11 lunch combo of entrée, rice,

Fresh vegetables are on sale at the Nashville Farmer's Market on 8th Avenue.

© SUSANNA HENIGHAN POTTER

naan, salad, and a drink is popular, along with the Saturday lunch buffet. At dinner, Shalimar takes on a slightly more elegant cast with vegetarian, chicken, lamb, and seafood entrées in popular preparations including masala, biryani, tikka, saag, or korma. Shalimar is a few blocks away from the Green Hills Mall.

South Nashville

Chosen by Nashvillians as the best Mexican restaurant in a very crowded field, **La Hacienda Taqueria** (2615 Nolensville Pike, 615/256-6142, Mon.–Thurs. 10 A.M.–9 P.M., Fri. 10 A.M.–10 P.M., Sat. 9 A.M.–10 A.M., Sun. 9 A.M.–9 P.M., $2–14) is located within a colorful storefront on Nolensville Pike, Nashville's most ethnically diverse thoroughfare. The menu offers a dizzying array of choices—tacos, enchiladas, tamales,

burritos, quesadillas, and *tortas,* just to name a few. Most come with your choice of chicken, chorizo, tripe, pork, or steak filling, and many have an authenticity often missing from Mexican restaurant fare. Combination platters, which offer three items plus rice and beans, are a good way to sample the options if you aren't sure what to order.

If you aren't in the mood for Mexican, just drive a bit farther along Nolensville Pike for other choices. Among them is **Dunya Kebob** (2521 Nolensville Pike, 615/242-6664, Mon.–Thurs. 11 A.M.–9:30 P.M., Fri.–Sat. 11 A.M.–10:30 P.M., Sun. noon–9:30 P.M., $5–10), which offers chicken, lamb, beef, and seafood kebobs and gyro sandwiches.

Not far from Nolensville, you'll find two more international favorites in the same shopping center on Trousdale Drive. **Back to Cuba** (4683 Trousdale Dr., 615/837-6711, Tues.–Sat. 11 A.M.–9 P.M., $8–12) serves traditional Cuban favorites: Grilled sandwiches of pork, ham, cheese, and pickle are a popular choice at lunchtime. For dinner, try the roast pork or grilled shrimp and don't skip the lacy fried plantains and spicy black beans.

For homemade Italian fare, go to **Mama Mia's** (4501 Trousdale Dr., 615/331-7207, Mon.–Fri. 11 A.M.–2 P.M., Mon.–Sat. 5–10 P.M., $7–16), which offers lasagna, ravioli, chicken, veal, and seafood dishes. Bring your own wine.

MARKETS

For fresh fruits, vegetables, preserves, and honey, go to the **Nashville Farmer's Market** held daily in the large covered building between 8th Avenue and the Bicentennial Mall. Many of the goods for sale here are homegrown at farms near Nashville; to be sure, ask whether you're getting Tennessee products.

There is an abundance of traditional grocery stores around Nashville. Common chains are Kroger, Publix, and H. G. Hill. Drive out any of the main corridors into the city and you will quickly find a grocery store. There is a Trader Joe's, which specializes in organic and specialty items, in Green Hills, just south of the Green Hills Mall.

Information and Services

INFORMATION
Visitors Centers
The main visitors center (615/259-4747, Mon.–Sat. 8 A.M.–5 P.M., Sun. 10 A.M.–5 P.M.) is located at the corner of 5th Avenue and Broadway, inside the Nashville Arena. Here you can pick up brochures, get a free map, and find answers to just about any question. It is open late when there is an event at the Nashville Arena.

There is another visitors center a few blocks uptown at 1 Nashville Place (615/259-4730, Mon.–Fri. 8 A.M.–5 P.M.).

Maps
Visitors centers offer a free hand-out map of downtown and an area map that shows major thoroughfares. This will be sufficient for many travelers. However, if you plan to do a lot of driving or off-the-beaten-track exploring, pick up a city map such as those published by Rand McNally or AAA. Detailed maps may be purchased from local drugstores and bookstores. Save time by buying a map before you arrive.

Media
NEWSPAPERS
Nashville's daily morning broadsheet is the *Tennessean* (www.tennessean.com). Published under various names since 1812, the *Tennessean* offers what every big-city newspaper does: local, regional, and national news, plus lots more. The paper's entertainment insert is published with the Friday newspaper. The newspaper is available all over town for 50 cents on weekdays and Saturdays, $1.75 on Sundays.

The *City Paper* (www.nashvillecitypaper.com) is a free twice-weekly tabloid with a strong website that specializes in local news, sports, and events. It offers an alternative viewpoint to that of the *Tennessean* and makes a good, compact read for locals and visitors. You can pick up *City Paper* in dozens of downtown locations.

The *Nashville Scene* is a fat tabloid-sized alternative weekly that balances its coverage of the local arts, music, and social scene with some political and local news coverage. This is a good go-to choice to understand what's going on in the city. *All the Rage,* owned by the *Tennessean,* is also published on Thursdays and focuses solely on entertainment and events.

Nashville Music Guide (www.nashvillemusicguide.com) is a free tabloid published twice a month. It covers the local music scene and music-industry news.

In addition, the *Nashville Business Journal* (615/248-2222, $1) is a weekly business publication covering industry, commerce, and finance. It is distributed on Mondays. *Nashville Pride* (615/292-9150, 50 cents) covers African-American news and is distributed on Fridays.

Also published by the *Tennessean, Nashville Lifestyles* is a monthly magazine with local celebrity profiles, home and garden tips, event information, and advertising. You can pick it up at newsstands throughout the city.

American Songwriter Magazine (1303 16th Ave. S., 615/321-6069, www.americansongwriter.com) is a bimonthly magazine devoted to the art of songwriting. It has been published in Nashville since 1984.

RADIO
The Nashville dial is chock-a-block with the usual commercial radio prospects. There are a few radio stations worth mentioning, however. **WSM 650 AM** is the legendary radio station that started it all when it put a fiddler on the air in 1925. Still airing the Grand Ole Opry after all these years, WSM plays country music at other times.

Nashville Public Radio is **WPLN 90.3 FM.** Tune in here for classical music and National Public Radio news. **WPLN 1430 AM** is a companion station with all-day news and talk, including BBC broadcasts. Nashville's only community radio station is **Radio Free Nashville** (98.9 FM, www.radiofreenashville.org). While its signal only reaches a small part of the city now, Radio

Free Nashville is looking to expand its reach as soon as it raises the necessary funds.

WKDA 900 AM is Nashville's Spanish-language radio station. **WAMB 1160 AM** plays big-band music, and **WNAH 1360 AM** plays old-fashioned Southern gospel.

Several Nashville universities liven up the radio dial. Fisk's **WFSK 88.1 FM** plays jazz. Middle Tennessee State University has **WMTS 88.3 FM,** the student-run station, and **WMOT 89.5 FM,** a jazz station. Vanderbilt University's student radio station is **WRVU 91.1 FM.**

TELEVISION
Nashville's network affiliates offer local news morning and night. These include **WKRN** (Channel 2 ABC), **WSMV** (Channel 4 NBC), **WTVF** (Channel 5 CBS), and **WZTV** (Channel 17 FOX).

The local public-television station is **WNPT** (Channel 8 PBS).

Remember that since Nashville is in the Central time zone, most nationally televised programs air one hour earlier than they do on the East Coast.

SERVICES
Internet
You can go online free at the **Nashville Public Library** (615 Church St., 615/862-5800). There is free wireless access at the visitors center located at 5th and Broadway.

Postal Service
Mail a letter or buy stamps from the downtown post offices at 901 Broadway and 1718 Church Street. Both are open Monday–Friday 8:30 A.M.–5 P.M. There is also a post office in the downtown Arcade.

Emergency Services
Dial 911 for police, fire, or ambulance in an emergency. For help with a traffic accident, call the Tennessee Highway Patrol at 615/741-2060. The Davidson County Rescue Squad can be summoned by calling 615/226-0462.

Libraries
Nashville's downtown library is the crown jewel of its library system. The **Nashville Public Library** (615 Church St., 615/862-5800, www.library.nashville.org, Mon.–Fri. 9 A.M.–8 P.M., Fri. 9 A.M.–6 P.M., Sat. 9 A.M.–5 P.M., Sun. 2–5 P.M.) opened in 2001, replacing an older library that had served the city since 1965. The new library is dynamic and busy serving its community. There are story hours, children's programs, art exhibits, a local history collection, and meeting rooms. Visitors to the city will find the public Internet access and wireless Internet network most useful. There is a nice courtyard inside the library where people eat lunch, relax, and enjoy occasional concerts.

If you are visiting the library, you can park in the Nashville Public Library Parking Garage. Enter on 6th or 7th Avenues between Church and Commerce Streets. The first hour of library parking is free, and the daily maximum is $6. Be sure to validate your ticket at the security desk as you enter the library.

Getting There and Around

GETTING THERE
By Air
Nashville International Airport (BNA; 615/275-1675, www.nashintl.com) is located eight miles east of the city center. To get downtown from the airport, head west on I-40; it's a short 15-minute drive. One-way taxi fare from the airport to most hotels is $22.

AIRPORT SHUTTLE
ShuttleMax (615/361-6184 or 888/500-7629, www.shuttlemax.net) provides regular shuttle service from the airport to hotels in Brentwood, Franklin, and the Opryland area. One-way fare is between $11 and $30, depending on the location of your hotel. Round-trip is between $20 and $50. Reservations are highly recommended.

Gray Line Transportation (615/883-5555, www.graylinenashville.com) offers regular shuttle service from the airport to downtown, West End, and Music Valley hotels. The shuttle departs from the airport every 15–20 minutes between 5 A.M. and 11 P.M.; reservations are not required. Call ahead to book your hotel pick-up. Fare is $11 one-way and $18 round-trip.

By Car
Driving is the most popular way to get to Nashville. The city is 250 miles from Atlanta, 330 miles from St. Louis, 400 miles from Charlotte, 550 miles from New Orleans, and 670 miles from Washington, D.C.

No less than three major interstate highways converge in Nashville. I-40 runs east–west, connecting Nashville with Knoxville and Memphis. I-65 runs north–south, and connects the city with Louisville, Kentucky, and Birmingham, Alabama. I-24 travels at a southeastern angle down to the city, connecting it with the cities of Clarkesville and St. Louis in the north, and Chattanooga and Atlanta in the south.

By Bus
Greyhound (800/231-2222, www.greyhound.com) serves Nashville with bus service to the city from Memphis, Jackson, Chattanooga, and Knoxville, Tennessee, as well as Paducah and Bowling Green, Kentucky. The Greyhound station (200 8th Ave. S., 615/255-3556) is on the southern end of downtown Nashville.

Expect to pay about $40 for a one-way ticket from Memphis to Nashville.

GETTING AROUND
Driving
The best way to get around Nashville is by car. Although visitors staying downtown will be able to find plenty to do and places to eat all within walking distance, many of the best attractions are located outside of the city center. So unless your stay is but a few days, it is best to bring or rent a car to get around.

If you don't bring your own, a dozen different major rental agencies have a fleet of cars, trucks, and SUVs at the airport. Agencies include **Alamo** (615/361-7467, www.alamo.com), **Avis** (615/361-1212, www.avis.com), and **Hertz** (615/361-3131, www.hertz.com). For the best rates, use an online travel search tool, such as Expedia (www.expedia.com) or Travelocity (www.travelocity.com), and book the car early, along with your airline tickets.

NAVIGATING NASHVILLE
Nashville is quite easy to navigate. I-65 and I-24 create a tight inner beltway that encircles the heart of the city. I-440 is an outer beltway that circles the southern half of the city. Briley Parkway, shown on maps as Highway 155, is a limited-access highway that circles the northern outskirts of the city.

City residents use the interstates not just for long journeys but for short cross-town jaunts as well. Most businesses give directions according to the closest interstate exit.

Non-interstate thoroughfares emanate out from Nashville like spokes in a wheel. Many are

NASHVILLE

named for the communities that they eventually run into. Murfreesboro Pike runs southeast from the city; Hillsboro Pike (Rte. 431) starts out as 21st Avenue South and takes you to Hillsboro Village and Green Hills. Broadway becomes West End Avenue and takes you directly to Belle Meade and, eventually, the Loveless Cafe. It does not take long to realize that roads in Nashville have a bad habit of changing names all of a sudden, so be prepared and check the map to avoid getting too confused.

For real-time traffic advisories and road construction closures, dial 511 from any touchtone phone, or go to www.tn511.com.

PARKING

There is metered parking on most downtown streets, but some have prohibited-parking signs effective during morning and afternoon rush hours. Always read the fine print carefully.

There is plenty of off-street parking in lots and garages. Expect to pay about $10 a day for garage parking. Meters are free after noon on Saturday, and on Sunday and holidays.

Public Transportation

Nashville's **Metropolitan Transit Authority** operates city buses. Pick up a map and schedule from either of the two downtown visitors centers, or online at www.nashvillemta.org.

Few tourists ride the buses because they can be difficult to understand if you're new to the city, and because they are not the most efficient use of your time. One route that is helpful, however, is the Opry Mills Express that travels from downtown Nashville to Music Valley, home of the Grand Ole Opry, Opryland Hotel, and Opry Mills, a shopping mall. The Opry Mills Express departs the Nashville Arena 13 times a day on weekdays. Fare is $1.75 one way; $0.60 for senior citizens. You can pick up a detailed route

timetable from either of the two downtown visitors centers.

On Tennessee Titans' game days, the MTA offers its End Zone Express. Park at either Greer Stadium (where the Nashville Sounds play) or the State employee lot at 4th Avenue North and Harrison, and for just $6 you get shuttled straight to LP Field.

COMMUTER RAIL

In 2006 Nashville debuted the **Music City Star Rail** (501 Union St., 615/862-8833, www.musiccitystar.org), a commuter rail system designed to ease congestion around the city. With service Monday through Friday, three morning trains and three afternoon trains connect Donelson, Hermitage, Mount Juliet, and Lebanon to downtown Nashville. More routes are planned for the future.

One-way tickets can be purchased for $5 each from vending machines at any of the stations. You can pre-purchase single-trip tickets, 10-trip packs, and monthly passes at the Regional Transportation Authority Office at 501 Union Street Monday–Friday 10 A.M.–2 P.M. For a complete list of ticket outlets, contact the railway.

Taxis

Licensed taxicabs will have an orange driver permit, usually displayed on the visor or dashboard.

Several good cab companies are **Allied Cab Company** (615/244-7433 or 625/320-9083), **Checker Cab** (615/256-7000), **Music City Taxi Inc.** (615/262-0451, www.musiccitytaxi.com), and **United Cab** (615/228-6969).

If cruising around in a stretch limo is more your style, call **Basic Black Limo** (615/430-8157, www.basicblacklimo.net). The rate is $125 per hour on Saturday nights; the limo seats up to 14 passengers.

THE HEARTLAND

No region of Tennessee is as diverse as the Heartland. From Clarksville on the Cumberland River to Cowan at the foot of the Cumberland Plateau, the Heartland manages to surprise and satisfy its visitors.

The Heartland is familiar. Its scenes are winding country roads cutting through horse pasture; perfectly fried chicken; and charming old railroad towns where the trains still run.

But there are other attractions that just might surprise you: Amish buggies traveling the back roads, a celebration dedicated to the lowly mule, and some of the best shopping in the whole state of Tennessee. The Heartland is a landscape of quiet beauty and some outstanding stories that will captivate its visitors.

There's the tale of Sam Davis, boy hero of the Confederacy, who went to his grave without divulging the name of his Union informant. There's the story of the sanctuary for retired circus and zoo elephants, tucked in the lush Tennessee countryside near Hohenwald. And there's the legend of the Natchez Trace, the old Indian road that cuts from Nashville through the countryside bound for the Mississippi port town of Natchez.

In the end, there are dozens of good reasons to travel Tennessee's Heartland. But the best one is a wish to slow things down a bit and enjoy the simple pleasure of natural beauty, notable history, and the company of friendly people.

PLANNING YOUR TIME

The rural byways of Tennessee's Heartland are best explored at a slow pace. The beauty of the

HIGHLIGHTS

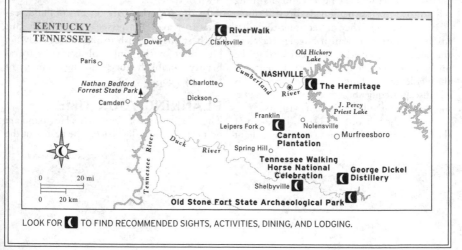

◖ **RiverWalk:** Clarksville's city park is a celebration of the Cumberland River (page 191).

◖ **The Hermitage:** The home of America's seventh president is also one of Tennessee's finest historic homes, which preserves not only the story of Andrew Jackson, but also that of his family, paid staff, and slaves (page 197).

◖ **Carnton Plantation:** Let your imagination run free at this mansion, which served as a Confederate field hospital during the Battle of Franklin. It is the setting of the novel *The Widow of the South* (page 209).

◖ **Tennessee Walking Horse National Celebration:** Watch the world's greatest show horses compete in the heart of Tennessee horse country (page 233).

◖ **George Dickel Distillery:** Tennessee whiskey is world-famous, but you can beat the crowds at this lesser-known distillery in beautiful Cascade Hollow (page 248).

◖ **Old Stone Fort State Archaeological Park:** An ancient earthen structure, the Old Stone Fort has confounded scientists for decades. Come here to ponder the lives of the earliest Tennesseans (page 251).

LOOK FOR ◖ TO FIND RECOMMENDED SIGHTS, ACTIVITIES, DINING, AND LODGING.

region is best enjoyed on small back roads; the friendliness of its people appreciated over a leisurely conversation.

Explore the Heartland gradually if you can. The region can be dipped into over a series of weekend drives or week-long expeditions. If you have only a few days, choose one of the subregions to explore. If shopping and dining are your preferences, Franklin is a natural choice. For quaint small-town feel, go to Bell Buckle and Wartrace, crown jewels in Tennessee Walking Horse Country. For a natural escape, drive down the Natchez Trace Parkway.

Tours

The Tennessee Department of Tourism promotes several self-guided tours through the Heartland. The **Tennessee Antebellum Trail** (www.antebellumtrail.com) is a 90-mile loop beginning at the Hermitage in Nashville. It stops at several of the best-known antebellum homes in the region, including Belle Meade and the Carnton Plantation.

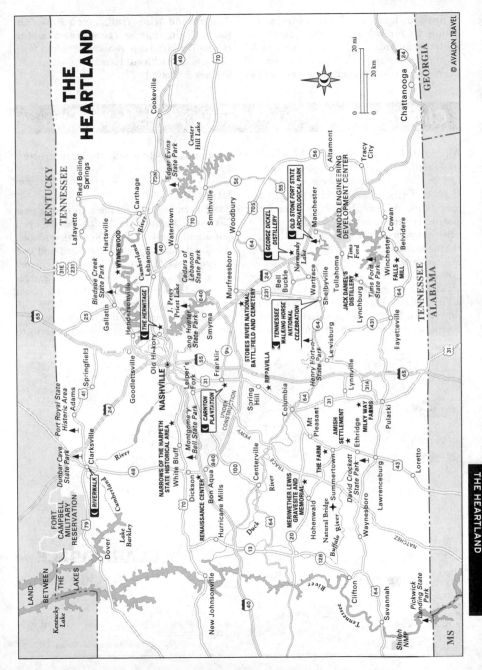

THE HEARTLAND

THE **HEARTLAND**

© AVALON TRAVEL

KENTUCKY
TENNESSEE

GEORGIA

Chattanooga

20 mi
20 km

Cookeville

Red Boiling Springs

Lafayette

Carthage

Center Hill Lake

Edgar Evins State Park

Altamont

Tracy City

Arnold Engineering Development Center

Manchester

OLD STONE FORT STATE ARCHAEOLOGICAL PARK

Smithville

Woodbury

WYNNEWOOD

Hartsville

Cumberland River

Watertown

Cedars of Lebanon State Park

GEORGE DICKEL DISTILLERY

Cowan

Belvidere

Winchester

TENNESSEE
ALABAMA

Hendersonville

THE HERMITAGE

J. Percy Priest Lake

Long Hunter State Park

Murfreesboro

STONES RIVER NATIONAL BATTLEFIELD AND CEMETERY

Bell Buckle

Wartrace

Normandy Lake

Shelbyville

Tullahoma

Tims Ford

Tims Ford State Park

FALLS MILL

JACK DANIEL'S DISTILLERY

Lynchburg

Fayetteville

Gallatin

Bledsoe Creek State Park

Springfield

Goodlettsville

Old Hickory

NASHVILLE

Smyrna

Leiper's Fork

Franklin

TENNESSEE WALKING HORSE NATIONAL CELEBRATION

RIPPAVILLA

Henry Horton State Park

Lewisburg

Adams

Port Royal State Historic Area

Clarksville

Dunbar Cave State Park

FORT CAMPBELL MILITARY RESERVATION

Dover

Lake Barkley

Cumberland River

RIVERWALK

Montgomery Bell State Park

White Bluff

NARROWS OF THE HARPETH STATE HISTORICAL AREA

RENAISSANCE CENTER

Bon Aqua

Dickson

Hurricane Mills

Spring Hill

CARNTON PLANTATION

UNDER CONSTRUCTION

Columbia

Centerville

Mt Pleasant

Summertown

AMISH SETTLEMENT

THE FARM

MERIWETHER LEWIS GRAVESITE AND MEMORIAL

Hohenwald

Natural Bridge

David Crockett State Park

MILKY WAY FARMS

Ethridge

Pulaski

Lynnville

Lawrenceburg

Loretto

Waynesboro

New Johnsonville

Buffalo River

Duck River

Hurricane Mills

Clifton

Savannah

Pickwick Landing State Park

Shiloh NMP

Tennessee River

MS

BETWEEN THE LAKES

LAND

Kentucky Lake

NATCHEZ

TRACE PKWY

Bedford, Franklin, Coffee, Lincoln, and Moore Counties have joined forces to promote back-roads tourism in south-central Tennessee. They publish guides to several themed "trails," including a **Tennessee Spirits and Wine Trail,** a **You Pick 'Em Farm Trail,** and the **Tennessee Walking Horse Trail.** You can request free guides from Tennessee's Backroads Heritage (www.tennesseebackroads.org).

Clarksville

Alternately known as the town of spires—for its beautiful historic church spires—and the Queen City—for the Cumberland River that flows by, Clarksville is an old city with a new lease on life. By some accounts the oldest incorporated city in Tennessee, Clarksville owed its early prosperity to the Cumberland River and the tobacco industry. Today, the Fort Campbell military base is the city's biggest economic engine and Clarksville is Tennessee's fourth-largest city. In recent years, Clarksville has done a lot to preserve its waterfront and historic downtown. Its centerpiece waterfront park is a major draw, and so is its historic downtown, which was largely rebuilt after a destructive 1999 tornado.

History

Early attempts to settle the area that is now Clarksville began in the 1760s, and the town was founded in 1785. In 1806 the first school, the Rural Academy, was established and two years later the *Clarksville Chronicle* newspaper began publication. By 1819 there were 22 stores in town, and one year later the first steamboat began to navigate the Cumberland River.

During the second half of the 19th century, no crop or industry was more important to

© SUSANNA HENIGHAN POTTER

RiverWalk lines the Cumberland River as it passes through Clarksville.

Clarksville than tobacco. In 1855, a special variety of tobacco grown in the fields and valleys of north-central Tennessee was known as the strongest in the world. This "Clarksville dark" tobacco was used primarily to make cigar wrappers and snuff—not cigarettes. During these years, Clarksville grew to be the second-largest tobacco market in the United States, and in 1880 sales moved to a brand-new Tobacco Exchange built near the public square.

The tobacco industry declined by the 1930s, due to changing agricultural practices and the Great Depression, although you can still see small farms of tobacco in the valleys and pastures around Clarksville.

The most disruptive event of recent Clarksville history was a F3 tornado that struck downtown at 4:15 A.M. on January 22, 1999. The twister left a 4.3-mile-long 880-yard-wide path. It destroyed 124 buildings and damaged 562 more, many of them in the historic downtown district.

Clarksville has seen its share of celebrities. It is the home of Miss USA 2007, Rachel Smith, and was the birthplace of U.S. Olympic track-and-field gold medalist Wilma Rudolph. Poet Allen Tate, a member of the Fugitive poets at Vanderbilt in the 1920s, was from nearby Benfolly, and Robert Penn Warren attended Clarksville High School. Jimi Hendrix lived in Clarksville while he was stationed with the 101st Airborne Division at Fort Campbell in 1962.

SIGHTS
RiverWalk

Opened in 1987, RiverWalk is Clarksville's crown jewel. The 15-acre park stretches along the Cumberland River, and paved walkways make it easy to enjoy a stroll along the banks of the river. There are also playgrounds, a boat ramp, picnic tables, and an amphitheater where the city hosts events like summer's RiverFest and Christmas on the Cumberland. The Rotary Clubs of Clarksville have also built an avenue of flags designed to reflect the diversity of the city.

If you want to learn more about the river, visit the **Cumberland River Center** (931/645-7476) near the center of the park, where a permanent

THE HEARTLAND

exhibit chronicles the history of the river and of Clarksville. Among other things, the exhibit describes the river's significances in the Civil War and also its role in the city's lucrative tobacco industry. The center is located near the main parking lot for RiverWalk and is open daily.

At the southern end of RiverWalk you will find a bronze statue of Clarksville native and U.S. Olympic gold medalist **Wilma Rudolph.** The statue sits at the base of the pedestrian overpass at College Street and Riverside Drive.

Historic Clarksville

Pick up a copy of "Walk Clarksville" from the visitors center, RiverWalk, or at the Customs House. This 2.2-mile walking tour allows you to slow down and appreciate the city's fine architecture and its interesting history. The tour begins at the Customs House Museum on South 2nd Street, and includes the downtown historic district, the public square, the Smith-Trahern Mansion, and Austin Peay State University. Along Franklin Street you will see a large outdoor mural, "Bursting with Pride," which depicts several

PHOTO COURTESY OF TENNESSEE DEPARTMENT OF TOURIST DEVELOPMENT

Clarksville's Customs House Museum and Cultural Center is a good place to start your exploration of the city.

WILMA RUDOLPH: A TRUE OLYMPIAN

Wilma Glodean Rudolph was born on June 20, 1940, the 20th of 22 children born to her parents, Ed and Blanche Rudolph, in Clarksville. Wilma was diagnosed with polio as a young child, and she used leg braces to walk. Blanche Rudolph took her daughter to Meharry Medical College in Nashville, a hospital for African Americans, as often as she could. When they could not travel, Blanche treated her daughter with homemade remedies, and she spent many evenings massaging her daughter's stricken legs.

When Wilma was 12 she overcame her polio, and quickly became a stand-out athlete. She was a high school basketball star and earned a spot on the U.S. Olympic track-and-field team when she was just 16 years old. At the 1956 Summer Olympics Wilma brought home a bronze medal in the 4-x-100-meter relay.

Four years later, Wilma Rudolph made Olympic history when she became the first American woman to win three gold medals in a single Olympic games. Her medals came in the 100 meters, 200 meters, and the 4-x-100-meter relay. Rudolph was heralded as the "fastest woman in history."

Wilma returned home to Tennessee and retired from athletics in 1962. A year later she enrolled at Tennessee State University, where she earned a degree in education. She later married and had four children. Rudolph wrote her autobiography, *Wilma: The Story of Wilma Rudolph,* in 1977. She died at her home in Brentwood in 1994 of brain and throat cancer; she was just 54 years old.

A bronze statue depicting the young Wilma Rudolph stands on the waterfront in her hometown of Clarksville.

THE HEARTLAND

of the city's most historic buildings. The walking tour includes a number of historic downtown churches, including Mount Olive Baptist Church, where Wilma Rudolph worshipped as a child, and the First Presbyterian Church, founded in 1822. Don't skip the walk through the Dog Hill Historic District, a clutch of 1890s wood-frame cottages, named Dog Hill because neighborhood dogs would howl at the whistles of passing trains and steamboats. Plan on 2–2.5 hours for the walking tour.

Customs House Museum and Cultural Center

Clarksville's old post office houses its largest museum, which has a wide-ranging collection including regional art and historical artifacts. The Customs House Museum and Cultural Center (200 S. 2nd St., 931/648-5780, www.customshousemuseum.org, Tues.–Sat. 10 A.M.–5 P.M., Sun. 1–5 P.M., adults $5, seniors $4, students $1–2) gets points for variety, if nothing else. Its permanent exhibits include Dunwody Boehm porcelains and a "memory lane" exhibit with clothes, forms of transportation, and firearms from the 18th and 19th centuries. The "explorers' floor" has exhibits and activities for children, including bubbles and a grocery store and optical illusions. A wonderfully intricate model train set is on display, and volunteer engineers run trains on Sunday afternoons.

There is also a small exhibit about the remarkable building itself, which was built in 1898 as a post office and customs house for the collection of tobacco taxes. The unique architecture consists of Italianate ornamentation, a Far East–inspired slate roof, Romanesque arches, and Gothic copper eagles perched at four corners. In addition to the permanent exhibit, the Customs House hosts traveling exhibits year-round.

The Customs House Museum has free admission on Sundays.

Smith-Trahern Mansion

Built around 1858 by tobacconist Christopher Smith, this Greek Revival and Italianate

mansion sits high above the bank of the Cumberland River. The Smith-Trahern Mansion (311 N. Spring St., 931/648-9998, Mon.–Fri. 9:30 A.M.–2:30 P.M., $2) contains a unique curved staircase and a widow's walk looking out at the river. It is now the setting for an education outreach program provided by the University of Tennessee's extension office. Tours are also available to visitors, and the home is used frequently for weddings and other private functions.

Dunbar Cave

The Dunbar Cave has been a site of importance to successive waves of people living around present-day Clarksville. Prehistoric Native Americans took shelter inside the cave as early as 10,000 years ago. Mississippian Indians also used the cave, leaving as evidence cave art on the cavern's walls.

In the 1930s it became a mineral bath resort, and people traveled for miles to take the baths and enjoy big band and swing music

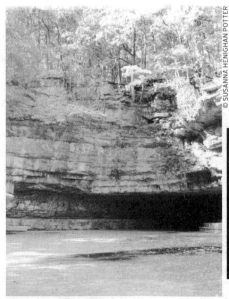

© SUSANNA HENIGHAN POTTER

THE HEARTLAND

The mouth of Dunbar Cave was once the site of concerts and summertime parties.

played on the stage at the mouth of the cave. Artie Shaw and Benny Goodman were among the artists who performed at Dunbar Cave. In 1948, country music star Roy Acuff bought the property and broadcast a live country music show from the location.

Dunbar Cave was purchased by the state in 1973. It is located just four miles from downtown Clarksville, making it a popular retreat for the city's residents. There are three miles of hiking trails, including one-mile and two-mile loops and a short 0.7-mile paved walk to the mouth of the cave. Guided hikes inside the cave are offered on weekends year-round and on certain weekdays in summer. Reservations are essential, and the tours cost $5 per person. You can also visit the nature museum at the park office (401 Old Dunbar Cave Rd., 931/648-5526) daily 8 A.M.–4:30 P.M., staff permitting.

There are plans for an interpretive center to be added to the park, which would describe how the cave was used by Native Americans, early European settlers, and the early-20th-century vacationers who came to Dunbar to get well.

Beachaven Vineyards and Winery

You can get a vineyard tour and sample wines at Beachaven Vineyards and Winery (1100 Dunlop Ln., 931/645-8867, www.beachavenwinery.com, Mon.–Sat. 9 A.M.–5 P.M., Sun. noon–5 P.M.).

ENTERTAINMENT
Theater

You can see professional company shows and black-box theater at the **Roxy Regional Theatre** (100 Franklin St., 931/645-7699, www.roxyregionaltheatre.org) in downtown Clarksville. First opened as a movie house in 1912, the Roxy (then called the Lillian Theater) was a first-run movie house until 1980. In 1983 it reopened as a regional theater. The Roxy puts on 10 shows per year, including musicals and classic American and European drama. The Other Space is a black-box theater also located at the Roxy that puts on innovative and cutting-edge productions.

Events

Clarksville's biggest party is **Riverfest,** an end-of-summer extravaganza held at the Cumberland RiverWalk. It includes live music, food vendors, children's activities, and fireworks.

Other annual events include **Oktoberfest,** held at the Fairgrounds Park in October, and **Jazz on the Lawn,** monthly free concerts held during the summer at Beachaven Vineyards and Winery.

Sports and Recreation

There are three golf courses around Clarksville: **Mason Rudolph Golf Course** (1514 Golf Club Ln., 931/645-7479), which offers inexpensive rates for 9- and 18-hole play; **Swan Lake** (581 Dunbar Cave Rd., 931/648-0479), right next to Dunbar Lake State Natural Area; and **Eastland Green** (550 Clubhouse Ln., 931/358-9051).

There are eight outdoor lighted tennis courts at Swan Lake Tennis Complex, which you can use for $4 per hour. Call the city's parks department at 931/647-6511 for details.

ACCOMMODATIONS

The best hotel in Clarksville has the best location. The **Riverview Inn** (50 College St., 931/552-3331, www.theriverviewinn.com, $84–120) is located just steps from the Cumberland River and Clarksville's historic downtown. Probably even more in its favor, it is located miles from the noisy, congested, and unappealing strip of highway that is home to a seemingly endless array of chain hotel choices. The Riverview offers suites, king-sized rooms with a desk and couch, and traditional double rooms. All guests can enjoy breakfast, a fitness room, business center, free wireless Internet, free daily newspaper, and laundry. You can even get your hair done at the on-site salon. And while the exterior of the hotel is about as charming as a concrete box, the inside is cheery and the staff pleasant. A real winner for road warriors.

If you prefer more homey accommodations, call Margaret Welker at **Magnolia House** (1231 Madison St., 931/552-4545, www.magnoliabb.com, $110), a well-run and welcoming bed-and-breakfast in Clarksville's historic district. Margaret has two guest suites, each with a private bathroom, desk, wireless Internet access, fine linens, and a refrigerator. One of the rooms also has a kitchenette, and can sleep up to three people.

FOOD

Every town deserves a restaurant like ◖ **Silke's Old World Breads** (1214A College St., 931/552-4422, Mon.–Sat. 7:30 A.M.–6 P.M., $5–7). Silke's is a bakery that makes European pastries and breads in a stone hearth oven. There is sourdough, whole wheat, rye, and lots more. On the sweet side, they offer traditional coffeeshop favorites like cheesecake and tiramisu, plus European-style fruit cobblers, turnovers, and genuine pretzels. If you're dining in, you can get sandwiches, salads, or pizzas. The salmon burger is a delicious alternative to another beef burger, and the pizzas are crisp and chewy. Or try one of the German sausage sandwiches, which feature long skinny sausages served on a little round bun. The menu offers a variety of choices for vegetarians, and decidedly different breakfast specialties: Try the cheese plate of fresh-baked bread, sliced cheese, herb/cheese spread and fruit. And don't forget your coffee; you can choose from varieties that include Silke's Old World Blend, designed to taste German! To ease the conscience while you eat, know that Silke goes out of her way to use organic and local ingredients and that she donates leftovers to charity. Silke's is located just north of town inside an old tobacco warehouse.

Keeping with the German theme, Clarksville is home to an old-school German restaurant, **Brunie's** (101 Legion St., 931/645-8414, Mon.–Sat. 8:30 A.M.–11 P.M., $6–14), a block off the public square. Brunie's is dark and smoky, with a pool table in the back and live music on the weekends. There are at least eight beers on tap. The menu features such German favorites as schnitzel, bratwurst, and sauerkraut, plus American stand-bys like burgers and steak. Most of the German dishes are available for dinner only, but there

is usually one German lunch special, served with a hot toasted roll, potato salad, and cucumber salad.

Clarksville's most upscale restaurant is the **Gas Lantern** (512 Madison Ave., 931/906-1000, Wed.–Sat. 4:30–10:30 P.M., $18–24). The Gas Lantern is located in the ground floor of the Rose Garden, an 1886 Victorian with a hand-carved staircase and wrought-iron mantles. The atmosphere is refined and luxurious, aided by the namesake garden and old-fashioned elegance of the home. The menu is traditional Italian, and is set out in four courses, with antipasto, salads, pastas, and meats. Shrimp Sambuco, fettucine Bolognese, and roasted rack of lamb are just a few of the specialties. For dessert try bread pudding or crème brûlée. A multicourse meal, excluding wine, could easily exceed $60 per person.

INFORMATION AND SERVICES

Clarksville and Montgomery County operate a tourist information center near exit 4 north of Clarksville. The center is open daily 8 A.M.–5 P.M. during the summer and 8 A.M.–4 P.M. in winter. Call them at 931/553-8467. You can also pick up brochures and maps of Clarksville at the Customs House Museum and at RiverWalk.

The **Clarksville-Montgomery County Public Library** (Montgomery County Veterans Plaza, 350 Pageant Ln., 931/648-8826) has free public Internet access.

Clarksville's *Leaf-Chronicle,* one of the oldest newspapers in Tennessee, is published daily. Its name reflects the prominence of tobacco during Clarksville's earlier years.

AROUND CLARKSVILLE
Port Royal State Historic Area

One of the earliest settlements in West Tennessee was at Port Royal, along the Red River, about 15 miles west of Clarksville. The town was settled in 1782 and incorporated in 1797. Set along an old Native American trail that later became a major stagecoach route, Port Royal was a waypoint for travelers of all kinds.

In the 1830s, hundreds of Cherokee Indians who were forcibly removed from their lands in Tennessee, North Carolina, and Georgia traveled through Port Royal on their way to Oklahoma. Diaries of soldiers who traveled with the displaced Cherokee say that some groups remained camped at Port Royal for a day or two to grind corn and rest before they left Tennessee.

Port Royal became a state historic area in 1977 and was later designated one of five sites in Tennessee along the National Trail of Tears Historic Trail.

Sadly, visitors to the park will see little evidence of Port Royal's interesting past, except what they can conjure up in their imaginations while strolling along the bank of the Red River. There are a few picnic tables and a parking area.

Adams

A picturesque rural town, Adams is located about 30 miles west of Clarksville along the Red River. The town isn't famous for much, but it is known as the home of the Bell Witch, a spooky specter that captivated the imaginations of Tennesseans in this neck of the woods around the turn of the 19th century. According to lore, the witch haunted the Bell family after they moved to Adams from North Carolina. The Bell Witch was never visible, but it threw objects, spoke, pulled hairs, yelled, and generally behaved very badly. Hearing stories of the witch, Andrew Jackson and some friends came up from Nashville to combat the terror, only to give up after suffering a night of the witch's inhospitable treatment.

You can revel in tales of the Bell Witch at the **Bell Witch Cave** (430 Keysburg Rd., 615/696-3055, $10). Here you can tour a cave that was on the Bell property, as well as tour a replica of the Bell log home. The cave and cabin are open Wednesday–Monday 10 A.M.–5 P.M. during June, July, and August, and on weekends only during May, September, and October. The cave is closed from November to April.

Historic Collinsville

Proprietors JoAnn and Glen Weakley have re-created the old settlement of Collinsville, about 15 miles south of Clarksville in lovely rural countryside. Historic Collinsville (4711 Weakley Rd., 931/648-9141, www.historiccollinsville.com, March 15–Nov. 15 Thurs.–Sun. 1–5 P.M., $5, children under 5 free) includes a restored schoolhouse, log cabin, dogtrot house, and other buildings that would have been seen in the period from 1830 to 1870. There is also a "wildlife center" with a number of stuffed wild animals, including wildcats, owls, and deer.

Fort Campbell

In February 1942, during World War II, construction began on Camp Campbell, which came to be a training ground for the 12th, 14th, and 20th Armored Divisions, and headquarters of the IV Armored Corps and the 26th Infantry Division. In 1950, the camp was redesignated Fort Campbell and became a permanent base.

Over the years, Fort Campbell soldiers have been deployed to many parts of the world and in every war since World War II. The fort is home to more than 30,000 soldiers and 10,500 military family members; 4,300 civilian employees work there. An additional 46,000 military family members live off the base in the Clarksville area. The presence of the military base has a major economic and social impact on Clarksville and the surrounding area. For example, the median age of Clarksville is 32 to the statewide average of 36.

Visitors to Fort Campbell should stop at the **Pratt Museum** (Bldg. 5702, Tennessee Ave., 270/798-3215, Mon.–Sat. 9:30 A.M.–4:30 P.M., free), which traces the history of the Screaming Eagles from World War II to the Iraq War. The museum also includes the history of Fort Campbell, from its initial survey as Camp Campbell in 1941 to the present day. The museum displays more than 50 uniformed figures and nine historical aircrafts, plus military vehicles and artillery pieces.

Along the Cumberland

Northeast of Nashville, the Cumberland River winds emphatically like holiday wrapping ribbon. It is a calm river, though, and in places impoundment has created "lakes": Old Hickory Lake close to Nashville, Cordell Hull Lake in Jackson County, and Dale Hollow Lake along the Kentucky border.

The Nashville suburbs absorb a little more of this quiet countryside every year. Towns like Hendersonville and Gallatin are within the city commuters' range. Out in the countryside, historic homes and the charm of an almost-forgotten resort town are the main attractions.

This part of Tennessee was hit by powerful tornadoes in February 2008. Macon and Sumner Counties were the most badly affected, with more than two dozen fatalities and widespread damage.

OLD HICKORY

Old Hickory was once a village distinct from Nashville, but now this enclave east of the city is part of the city. Old Hickory is named for Andrew Jackson, whose home, the Hermitage, is located nearby. The town has an interesting history, however. It was founded in 1918 by DuPont as a company town for a new smokeless gunpowder plant being built nearby. Hundreds of "temporary homes" were built for workers using materials made with asbestos. The "permanent village" consisted of more substantial buildings for managers.

The gunpowder plant was short-lived. By 1919 it had closed, and workers moved away. In 1923, however, DuPont returned and retooled the factory into one that would make rayon. The asbestos-riddled houses were torn down, but the permanent village was restored and once again became homes for people employed at the factory. In 1946 DuPont sold the village and Old Hickory ceased operating as a company town. Many of the old-style company homes are still standing, however.

(The Hermitage

Andrew Jackson's plantation and home 16 miles east of Nashville is the area's best historical tourist attraction. The Hermitage (4580 Rachel's Ln., 615/889-2941, www.thehermitage.com, daily 9 A.M.–5 P.M., $7–15, family pass $40) is where Jackson retired following his two terms as president of the United States, and it is where he and his beloved wife, Rachel, are buried.

Jackson bought the property in 1809; he and Rachel initially lived in a rustic log cabin, which has since been restored. Jackson first named the home and property Rural Retreat, and later he chose the more poetic name the Hermitage. Jackson ran a successful cotton plantation on the property, owning as many as 150 slaves. In 1819 he and Rachel started construction of what is now the mansion. They moved in in 1821.

In 1831, two years after he became the nation's seventh president, Jackson expanded the mansion so it was more suitable for presidential entertaining. While Jackson was in Washington, his adopted son, Andrew Jackson Jr., managed the property, and when a chimney fire damaged the house in 1834, Jackson Jr. and his wife, Sarah, saw to its restoration. At the end of Jackson's second term in office in 1837, he retired to the Hermitage and lived here happily until his death in 1845.

Following President Jackson's death, the Hermitage remained in family hands until 1853, when it was sold to the State of Tennessee to pay off the family's debts. It opened as a museum in 1889 and was restored largely due to the persistence of the Ladies Hermitage Association. Because the property never left family hands before it was sold to the State, many of the furnishings are original and even the wallpaper in several rooms dates back to the years when Andrew Jackson called it home.

One major strength of the present-day Hermitage tour and museum is that it focuses not only on Jackson and the construction

OLD HICKORY

Andrew Jackson, the seventh president of the United States, was one of the most important American political figures of the first half of the 19th century. His impact was so great that we now refer to his era as the Age of Jackson and his ideology as Jacksonian Democracy.

Jackson was born in 1767 on the American frontier in South Carolina. His father, an immigrant from Northern Ireland, died before Jackson was born. At age 12, Jackson volunteered for the American army in the Revolutionary War. Jackson's two brothers, Hugh and Robert, died during the war. His mother, Elizabeth, died of smallpox in 1781. Jackson was 14 years old, and alone in the world.

Remarkably, Jackson not only survived; he flourished. In 1784 he moved to Salisbury, North Carolina, where he studied law. In 1787 he became a licensed lawyer and moved west, to Washington County, now part of Tennessee. In 1788 he was appointed the district attorney for the Mero District, now Middle Tennessee.

In Nashville, a city that was founded less than 10 years earlier, Jackson met Rachel Donelson, the daughter of John Donelson. Jackson fell in love with Rachel and in 1781 they were married. Later, when they learned that Rachel's earlier, unhappy marriage to Lewis Robards of Kentucky was not legally dissolved, they remarried in 1794 before a Davidson County justice of the peace.

The Jacksons set about to establish a home and livelihood. Jackson practiced law, speculated in land, and dabbled in politics. They bought farmland in Davidson County where they built the Hermitage, which would be the Jacksons' home for the rest of their lives. The couple never had children of their own, but they adopted a nephew, who was known as Andrew Jackson Jr., and reared several Indian orphans.

By 1798 Jackson was a circuit-riding judge on the Tennessee Superior Court, but he also developed a reputation for resolving his own conflicts through violence. He brawled with a set of brothers, killed a man in a duel, caned another, and ran a sword through a third. In 1803 he quarreled publicly with governor John Sevier and nearly dueled him as well.

Jackson's violent temper was better suited for the battlefield. In 1802 he was elected Major General of the Tennessee militia and with the outbreak of war in 1812, his leadership was required. Jackson earned the nickname "Old Hickory" in 1812 when he disobeyed orders and refused to dismiss his Tennessee soldiers in Natchez, Mississippi, marching them back to Tennessee under great hardship instead. He earned national fame three years later when he marched his men from Florida

---

and decoration of the mansion, but also the African-American slaves who worked at the Hermitage plantation. Curators and archaeologists have studied the Hermitage to learn about the hundreds of men and women who made the Hermitage profitable and successful for so many years. The tour of the grounds takes visitors to Alfred's Cabin, a slave cabin occupied until 1901 by former Hermitage slave Alfred Jackson. You also learn about the agriculture that took place on the Hermitage, and can see cotton being cultivated during the summer months. To learn even more about the Hermitage's slaves, take an add-on wagon tour, offered from April to October.

Visitors to the Hermitage begin with a video about Andrew Jackson and the Hermitage, and can continue on to a museum. You take an audio tour of the grounds, and guided tours are offered of the mansion. You wind up in the gift shop and café. Plan on spending at least three hours here to make the most of your visit. Try to come when the weather is good.

Old Hickory Lake

The Old Hickory Dam was built in 1952 and became operational in 1957. At normal water levels, the lake is 22,500 acres.

Old Hickory is well within Nashville's sprawl-zone, and private development along to New Orleans, where he resoundingly defeated the British. The American public was so pleased with their new war hero that they did not mind when they learned the British had actually surrendered two weeks earlier. Neither did they mind some of his tactics: military executions, imposition of martial law, suspension of habeas corpus, and defiance of a federal court order.

In the succeeding years, Jackson fought battles with Native American tribes, and negotiated land treaties with them. By 1821, he quit his post as Major General and came home to the Hermitage for a short retirement.

In 1822 the Tennessee state legislature nominated Jackson for U.S. president and his nomination was seconded by other states. In the 1824 contest, Jackson received more votes than any other contender in the crowded field. But when the U.S. House of Representatives gave the presidency to John Quincy Adams, Jackson called the decision a "corrupt bargain" that violated the will of the voters. His 1828 presidential campaign had begun.

The 1828 campaign was spirited and dirty. Opponents found seemingly countless stories of Jackson's indiscretions, and they accused him and Rachel of committing adultery by marrying before Rachel's divorce was final. When Rachel Jackson died on December 22, 1828, Jackson accused his opponents of hastening her death by slander.

Jackson was raised as a Presbyterian and held strong religious beliefs throughout his life. He resisted Rachel Jackson's encouragements to formally join a church, however, saying that he feared the charge of hypocrisy that could be leveled against him as a public churchgoer. Jackson promised Rachel that when he left public life he would join the church, and he was true to his word. In July 1838, Jackson, then in his 70s, joined the church.

During his two terms as president, Jackson enraged his opponents and delighted supporters. He took unprecedented actions in the name of reform, including several controversial banking decisions. He believed in a strong federal government and stood in the way of state nullification of federal laws. By the end of his eight years in the White House, Jackson was known by his opponents as "King Andrew," while his supporters still saw him as a spokesman of the common man.

Jackson, who never remarried, spent the remaining eight years of his life at the Hermitage, where he entertained guests, helped to manage the farm, and dispensed advice to politicians. His health declined, though, and in 1845, at age 78, he died and was buried in the Hermitage garden, next to his beloved Rachel.

---

the lakeshore is extensive. The Army Corps of Engineers manages the lake, including its public recreation areas.

There are nearly a dozen different day-use facilities along Old Hickory Lake. The following have covered picnic facilities, swimming beaches, and restrooms: Rockland and Lock 3 in Hendersonville; Cedar Creek in Mount Juliet; Old Hickory Beach in Old Hickory; and Laguardo in Laguardo.

Located on the shore of Old Hickory Lake, **Bledsoe Creek State Park** has six miles of hiking trails, a 26-site campground, boat ramp, and day-use facilities. Bledsoe Creek is located just east of the city of Gallatin.

HENDERSONVILLE

A speck of a town that has become an upscale suburb of Nashville, Hendersonville has a few things going for it: It is home to some of country music's most famous names; it is near Old Hickory Lake; and it is the locale of Trinity Music City U.S.A., a major religious broadcasting attraction.

Trinity Music City U.S.A. (1 Music Village Blvd., 615/822-0093, www.tbn.org, Tues.–Sat. 11 A.M.–6 P.M., Sun. 1–5 P.M., free) owes its existence to Conway Twitty, a rock and country musician who opened his house in Hendersonville to fans and called it Twitty City. After Twitty died in 1993, the property

THE HEARTLAND

sold to Trinity Broadcasting Network (TBN), which retooled the idea and came out with its own "City" destination.

Nationally televised programs are produced at the Hendersonville TBN campus, and visitors can sit in on weekly church services on Friday nights and Sunday afternoons, or a live taping on Tuesday evenings from 7 to 9 P.M. Special religious films are screened throughout the day, and there are exhibits about TBN and Trinity City. Special events are held year-round, and visitors are welcome at other times to tour the grounds and browse the gift shop.

Another star long associated with Hendersonville is Johnny Cash, and his second wife, June Carter Cash. The couple's home on Old Hickory Lake in Hendersonville was where they lived for 35 years. The Cashes died in 2003, and in 2006, former Bee Gee Barry Gibb bought the property for $2.3 million. The home was destroyed by fire in 2007. A small cabin used by June and Johnny, and later restored by their son John Carter Cash, survived, but is not open to the public.

CASTALIAN SPRINGS

This small town a few miles east of Gallatin was one of the towns devastated by tornadoes in 2008. Twisters destroyed whole houses and tossed mobile homes around like they were toys. The town made headlines when rescuers found alive an 11-month-old boy who had been tossed some 150 yards.

Previously, what put Castalian Springs on the map were its mineral springs and two nearby historic homes.

Wynneworld

The largest existing log structure in Tennessee, this imposing home was built in 1828 by A. R. Wynne, William Cage, and Stephen Roberts as a stagecoach inn on the Nashville–Knoxville Road. Six years after it was built, Wynne purchased his partners' shares and moved his family to the inn, where he lived until his death in 1893. Over the years, the inn saw many guests who came to drink and soak in the

mineral springs. In the 1940s the present name, Wynneworld, was given to the property, and in 1971 the Tennessee Historical Commission acquired the building as a historic site.

Today, Wynneworld (210 Old Hwy. 25, 615/452-5463, Mon.–Sat. 10 A.M.–4 P.M., Sun. 1–5 P.M., free) is open to the public from April through December.

Cragfont

General James Winchester was one of those men who seems to have been just about everywhere. He fought in the American Revolution and the War of 1812, was a Middle Tennessee pioneer, and one of the founders of Memphis. Winchester's home, Cragfont (200 Cragfont Rd., 615/542-7070, www.cragfont.org, Apr. 15–Nov. 1 Tues.–Sat. 10 A.M.–5 P.M., Sun. 1–5 P.M., adults $5, seniors $4, children 6–12 $3) is now a Tennessee Historic Site.

Construction on Cragfont started in 1798 and finished four years later. It was the finest mansion of the Tennessee frontier—appropriate for a man of Winchester's stature. Cragfont was named because it stood on a rocky bluff with a spring at its base. The home was built in the late Georgian style. Today it is furnished with Federal-period antiques.

Following his involvement in the War of 1812, Winchester moved to Cragfont full time, where he farmed and speculated in land. Winchester died in 1826, but his wife, Susan Black Winchester, lived here until 1862. The property was purchased by the Tennessee Historical Commission in 1958.

CARTHAGE

Carthage, the seat of Smith County, is a river town. The first steamship traveled here from Nashville in 1829, and the trade persisted even into the 20th century, when the first good paved roads were constructed through the rugged countryside.

Landmarks in this quiet town include the **Cordell Hull Bridge,** built in 1936 and noteworthy for its intricate steel grid work, and the **Smith County Courthouse,** a Second Empire–style structure built in 1875. About five miles outside of town is the **Cordell Hull Lock and Dam.**

The **Smith County Heritage Museum** (3rd Ave. N., Wed., Fri., Sat. 10 A.M.–2 P.M., free) houses historical exhibits, including Civil War, steamboat, and farm memorabilia.

Carthage is best known in some circles as the hometown of former U.S. vice president Al Gore. **Markham's Department Store** (222 Main St. N., 615/735-0184) has a special "Gore-Lieberman Store" where campaign memorabilia from the historic 2000 presidential election is on sale. You can even buy a coffee cup that celebrates a Gore victory in 2000. The Gore farm is located a few miles outside Carthage along U.S. 70. It's closed to the public.

Accommodations

There is a lovely river getaway located just outside Carthage. **Dreaming by the River** (136 Gibbs Landing, 615/823-1566, www.dreamingbytheriver.com, $115–155) is a bed-and-breakfast inn located overlooking the Cumberland River. Guest rooms are modern and tasteful, with hardwood floors, elegant beds, and private, modern baths. There is wireless Internet throughout the building. The home is set on five acres, and there are walking paths to the waterfront.

CORDELL HULL LAKE

The 72 miles of the Cumberland River impounded by the Cordell Hull Dam are popular areas for recreation. Operated by the U.S. Army Corps of Engineers, Cordell Hull Lake's recreation areas consist of two large campgrounds and numerous day-use areas with swimming beaches, picnic facilities, and boat ramps.

Cordell Hull Lock and Dam

The lock and dam that impounds the river was built between 1963 to 1973. You can see the dam from the Tater Knob overlook, located about four miles outside of Carthage off State Route 263. It is an impressive vista.

You can learn more about the science of hydroelectric power and the natural history of the Cumberland River at the **Cordell Hull Lake Visitor Center** (71 Corps Ln., 615/735-1034,

www.lrn.usace.army.mil/op/COR/rec, Mon.–Fri. 9 A.M.–3 P.M., free), located adjacent to the dam off State Route 263 east of Carthage.

The half-mile **Turkey Creek Nature Trail** departs from the visitors center.

There is a lovely six-mile hiking trail from the Tater Knob overlook to the Defeated Creek Campground and recreation area. The **Bearwaller Gap Trail** follows the lakeshore, and is named after bear "wallers," cool depressions where black bears once came to wallow. Today, there are no black bears in these hills. There is a backcountry campsite for hikers about half-way at the Two Prong camping area.

A campground, marina, and day-use facility, **Defeated Creek** was named by early settler John Peyton after his party defeated an Indian attack where they had camped along the creek. (The nearby town, Difficult, was named by the same party after they made the difficult trek back home after the attack.)

Day-trippers will enjoy the sandy beach and marina facilities. The **Bear Wheels Mountain Bike Trail** trailhead is also located at Defeated Creek. The 155-site campground can accommodate tents and RVs; it has showers, bathhouses, a playground, and laundry.

The marina at Defeated Creek offers power-boat rentals for between $175 and $225 per day. Paddle boats are also available for $15 for two hours.

Cordell Hull's second campground, **Salt Lick,** is a 150-site campground. It also has a swim beach, playground, water and electric hook-ups, dump stations, laundry, and a shower house.

Two more day-use areas have picnic facilities and public swimming beaches. **Wartrace Creek** is located near the town of Gladdice and Roaring River is located near Gainesboro.

RED BOILING SPRINGS

This one-time resort town is still welcoming visitors. Red Boiling Springs had as many as eight different hotels during its heyday from 1890 to 1930, when thousands of people traveled by train and horse-drawn wagon to "take the waters" at the town's mineral springs.

According to accounts, the atmosphere in

the holiday town was relaxed, but also a tad refined. Tourists spent their days enjoying the cool air, playing croquet on the lawn, taking walks, and soaking in mineral baths. There was live music, good conversation, and meal-times were a celebration.

Times have changed in Red Boiling Springs, but not as much as in some Tennessee towns. The Salt Lick Creek flows through the city park and is a lovely place to stroll or even wade. Three hotels keep up the town's tradition, and each offers a bona fide welcome to its guests.

If old-time atmosphere is not your thing, perhaps **Cyclemo's Motorcycle Museum** (319 E. Main St., 615/699-5049, Thurs.–Sat. 10 A.M.–5 P.M., Sun. 1–5 P.M., adults $8, seniors $6, children $4) is. Here you can see restored antique motorcycles and bike memorabilia, and buy biker clothing and other goods. There are plans in the works for a full restoration center that would specialize in fixing up old bikes. The business hopes to attract bikers who come to the area for the winding country roads so good for motorcycles. The museum has extended hours in the summertime.

About two miles west of Red Boiling Springs along Highway 52 is the turn-off for **Long Hungry Creek Farm** (Long Hungry Rd., 615/699-2493, www.barefootfarmer.com), one of Tennessee's largest and most established organic and biodynamic farms. Farmer Jeff Poppen has also written and taught extensively on the subject of farming. Visitors are welcome, but should always call in advance. The farm hosts special events and workshops during the year.

Shopping

You can order custom-made wooden chairs from **Newberry and Sons Chairs** (1593 Jennings Creek Rd., 615/699-3755, www.newberryandsonschairs.com). Located in the countryside along State Route 56 south of Red Boiling Springs, the Newberry workshop is a testament to doing things the old-fashioned way. Foot stools, rocking chairs, corner chairs, and traditional ladder-back dining chairs are

Armour's Hotel in Red Boiling Springs dates from the days when the town was a rural wellness retreat.

among the styles available. Call in advance if you would like to visit the workshop.

Accommodations

The **Donoho Hotel** (500 Main St., 615/699-3141, www.thedonohohotel.com, $62) first opened in 1914 and was renovated in 2001. Guest rooms open onto a generous wraparound porch, where rocking chairs invite you to sit a spell and relax. Rooms have an antique feel but modern amenities, including central air and heating and new bathrooms. Guests can relax in the parlor or lobby, where there are board games and memorabilia from the hotel's early days. Or walk to the nearby Salt Lick Creek. As part of the 2001 renovations, the owners built an entertainment hall that can be used for meetings, performances, or conferences. Family-style meals are served in the 128-seat dining room, and feature home-style Southern cooking. Meal plans, including breakfast and supper, are available for about $18 extra per person per night.

Located on the outskirts of town atop a quiet hill, **The Thomas House** (520 E. Main St., 615/699-3006, www.thomashousehotel.com, $60) is a brick-and-lumber structure dating to the 1890s. Its guest rooms are furnished with antiques and each is decorated with its own individual flair. There is also a swimming pool. The Thomas House stages frequent dinner theater. Meal plans are available for about $20 per person per night, and include breakfast and dinner.

Armour's Red Boiling Springs Hotel (321 E. Main St., 615/699-2180, www.armourshotel.com, $85) is the only hotel with a working mineral bath on the property. Guests (and non-guests) can enjoy a massage, a stint in the steam room, and a soak in the town's long-revered mineral waters. Built in 1924, Armour's has 16 rooms, including two suites. It was the first brick hotel in Red Boiling Springs, and so was known for several years as Smith's Brick Hotel, after John Smith, the first owner. Later the hotel was called the Counts Hotel. All rooms have private baths and each is decorated just a little bit differently. Breakfast is included in the room rate; dinner is available family-style for $14 per person, with advanced reservations. Perhaps the greatest attraction is the wide, open porch that looks out on the hotel's lush green lawn. It is a scene that asks you to stop and relax.

Food

Red Boiling Springs' three hotels serve breakfast and dinner daily; reservations are recommended. You can also drive about seven miles east along Highway 52 to the **Hermitage Hill Restaurant** (16150 Hwy. 52, 615/699-3919, daily 6 A.M.–8 P.M., $4–15). This is a

---

THE LONGEST YARD SALE

In a place where "yard saleing" is a bona fide activity, you can expect good things. The best of the good things takes place on the third Friday and Saturday in May and it is considered in some circles to be the longest yard sale in the whole state.

It works like this: Between the towns of Orlinda and Celina, along Tennessee Highway 52, hundreds of people set up booths and tents to sell their unwanted goods. When it started, mostly locals were the sellers, but now people travel sometimes great distances to set up along the route. Neighbors often team up together with a booth, and nonprofits like schools, civic organizations, and even political parties use the yard sale as a fundraiser.

The sale passes through four counties and covers some 95 miles. In 2008, some 550 vendors took part, and it is growing bigger every year. There is no limit to what you'll find for sale, but expect things like quilts, antiques, household items, books, clothing, crafts, and toys. Vendors normally set up early on Friday morning for the early birds. By Saturday afternoon, many have sold out and may pack up by mid-afternoon.

For details on the Longest Yard Sale, contact Escape Nashville (www.escapenashville.com), a group of towns and counties located along Highway 52 north of Nashville.

traditional country-cooking restaurant with full breakfast offerings, steak, burgers, grilled sandwiches, and country ham. The lunch buffet is served daily, and there is a dinner buffet on Friday and Saturday nights.

Big Ed's BBQ (111 Whitley Hollow Rd., 615/699-3288, Wed.–Sat. 8 A.M.–8 P.M., $3–6) serves plates of pork and beef barbecue as well as sandwiches, burgers, and sides like coleslaw and baked beans.

Information

You can get information about Red Boiling Springs and other towns in Macon County from the **Macon County Chamber of Commerce** (208 Church St., Lafayette, 615/666-5885).

West of Nashville

The countryside that lies south of Clarksville, west of Nashville and north of Columbia, is the most rural and sparsely populated in the Heartland. It is ideal for back-roads driving. There are excellent state parks and a few notable pit-stops, such as Montgomery Bell State Park and an old-fashioned tea room at Bon Aqua.

The Duck River, the longest river totally contained in Tennessee, flows from the east towards Hickman and Perry Counties, eventually emptying into the Tennessee River near Johnsonville. The Buffalo River, a tributary of the Duck and the largest unimpounded river in Middle Tennessee, flows westward through Wayne and Lawrence Counties before turning northward through Perry County. Both rivers contribute natural beauty and recreational opportunities to the area.

HARPETH RIVER STATE PARK

Harpeth River State Park (615/952-2009) follows the Harpeth River as it winds through parts of Dickson County near the towns of Bell Town, Kingston Springs, and Pegram. This is a do-it-yourself state park. Bring a map (available at www.tennessee.gov) with you, since there are few signs and even fewer people about to assist you.

The **Narrows of the Harpeth,** located north of Highway 70, is where the river nearly bends back onto itself. Here iron magnate Montgomery Bell built the Pattison Forge, which harnessed the power of the river to manufacture a wide range of iron implements.

Slaves built the forge between 1818 and 1820, and it remains a marvel of engineering and labor. The tunnel that brought water power to the forge was 300 feet long, 15 feet wide, and six feet high. When the river is low, visitors can wade into the tunnel and look at it.

Recreation

Canoeing and fishing are popular along the river. Canoe accesses are found at the U.S. Highway 100 bridge southwest of Nashville, the 1862 Newsom's Mill ruins, and at the McCrory Lane Bridge at Hidden Lake. Downstream, the Narrows of the Harpeth provides an upstream and downstream access, the Bell's Bend five-mile float, and a unique 0.25-mile portage. Swimming is also permitted, but there are no lifeguards.

Three different trails originate at a common trailhead at the Narrows. The trails include a two-mile bluff overlook trail, a half-mile trail leading to the site of Pattison Forge, and a half-mile spur that connects the canoe launch to the canoe take-out.

At Gossett Tract, a few miles downriver from the narrows, there are two hiking trails. A one-mile trail circles a meadow and another one-mile trail winds along the river providing a glimpse of Mound Bottom Archaeological Site. There are also picnic tables and grills here.

At Hidden Lake, near the town of Pegram, a one-mile trail meanders around and through a wildflower meadow. Another trail offers a half-mile hike through the forest and along majestic bluffs to a small lake with a one-mile spur trail

MINNIE PEARL'S HOMETOWN

Centerville, in Hickman County, is best known as the hometown of Minnie Pearl. What's less well-known is that the first lady of country comedy was not a real person, but rather a character created and portrayed by actress and comedian Sarah Ophelia Colley (1912-1996).

Colley, born in 1912 and raised in Centerville, attended Nashville's prestigious Ward-Belmont College, a finishing school for women, where she majored in expression. In 1934, Colley joined a theater group for women that traveled throughout the South to organize local dramatic productions. It was in the course of these journeys that Colley experienced the Southern culture that she would later portray through her alter ego, Minnie Pearl. The real Minnie Pearl, to the extent that she was real at all, was a kind country woman from Sand Mountain, Alabama, who housed Colley when she was stuck in town with no lodging. This lady's comic stories, impeccable timing, and outlook on life left an impression on young Colley, who began performing as Minnie Pearl soon after.

Colley's big break came in 1939 when a Centerville banker invited Colley to perform at a Lions Club event. WSM radio program director Harry Stone spotted her, and the rest is history. "Minnie Pearl" performed on the Grand Ole Opry for more than 50 years. Generations of Americans have heard her greeting: "Howdee! I'm just so proud to be here," and witnessed her frilly dresses and outlandish hats (with the price tag hanging over the brim).

Off-stage, Colley married Air Army Corps pilot Capt. Henry Cannon and worked for a number of charities. Colley had a foot in both of Nashville's worlds: its hillbilly opry and the Athens of the South. She was uniquely able to shuttle between these two very different universes.

Minnie Pearl's legacy is on display at the **Grinder's Switch Center** (405 W. Public Sq., Centerville, 931/729-5774). Operated by the local Chamber of Commerce, the center houses Minnie Pearl memorabilia and recordings of the famous lady of country comedy.

---

ascending to the top of a ridge where the remains of an old marble dance floor are all that remain of a 1940s resort.

MONTGOMERY BELL STATE PARK

One of Tennessee's resort parks, Montgomery Bell State Park (615/797-9052) offers a great deal to its visitors. Named for iron magnate Montgomery Bell, who established the iron ore industry in this part of Tennessee, the 3,842-acre park is set amid rolling hills. It was one of three parks built in Tennessee by the federal government in the 1930s. Young men in the Civilian Conservation Corps built the original structures at Montgomery Bell, including the stone dams that impound Lakes Woodhaven and Acorn. In more recent years, the park inn and golf course were built as Montgomery Bell became one of the state's resort parks.

The hardwood forest that was cut to clear farmland and to produce charcoal for the iron furnaces has given way to second-growth forest and a habitat for fox, squirrel, raccoon, opossum, deer, and a wide variety of birds and wildflowers.

The park's proximity to Nashville makes it quite popular for weekend retreats, conferences, and family getaways.

Golf

Montgomery Bell has a par-72 18-hole golf course. Built in 1973 and redesigned by Gary Roger Baird in 1988, the course is considered one of the top public courses in the state. The entire course is heavily wooded and you will often see wildlife, including deer and wild turkey.

Tee times are required; greens fees are $14–24. There is a pro shop with club and cart rentals. Call 615/797-2578 for reservations or more information.

THE HEARTLAND

Other Recreation

There are some 20 miles of dirt **mountain bike trails,** ranging from easy to difficult. No motorized vehicles are allowed, and bikers must not use hiking trails (and vice versa).

There are 19 miles of **hiking trails** in the park. The longest is 12 miles and the shortest is less than a mile. There are three overnight shelters for backpackers. You can pick up detailed maps from the park office or at the inn. A short nature trail that departs from the park office is ideal for those with less grand ambitions.

You can rent paddle and johnboats Monday–Saturday from Memorial Day through Labor Day at **Lake Acorn,** a 17-acre lake in the park. Private boats are allowed on Lake Acorn from September through April, or on Lake Woodhaven year-round. Outboard attached motors are not allowed; trolling motors are permitted. There is no boating permitted on Creech Hollow Lake, the third lake at Montgomery Bell.

Fishing is allowed in all three lakes. Bluegill, catfish, bass, and creel are some of the species that you will find. A valid Tennessee fishing permit is required; you must also adhere to seasonal limits.

There is a **swimming** beach on Lake Acorn, open from Memorial Day to Labor Day annually. No lifeguards are on duty. There is also a swimming pool for inn and cabin guests.

Other recreation facilities include horseshoes, softball fields, basketball, playgrounds, and tennis courts.

Accommodations

Montgomery Bell has a 120-room, five-suite park inn (120 Jackson Hill Rd., Burns, 615/797-3101 or 800/250-8613). Rooms are equipped with two beds, telephones, television, and views of Acorn Lake. Rates are $68–80 for regular rooms, $145–195 for suites. There are also conference and meeting facilities.

Camping

There are eight two-bedroom vacation cabins,

with kitchens, bathrooms, and modern amenities. They rent for $75 per night.

There are 40 tent sites ($11) and 75 RV campsites ($17.50) at the Montgomery Bell campground, which is set in a woodland along a creek.

One of the most unique features of Montgomery Bell State Park are the 47 1930s-era stone rustic cabins built by the Civilian Conservation Corps during the Depression. These cabins are available for group rental only. The beautiful buildings overlook Lake Woodhaven and are considered a historic site. Central bathroom and cooking facilities are provided.

Food

The restaurant at the park inn and conference center serves breakfast (7–10 A.M.), lunch (11 A.M.–2 P.M.), and dinner (5–8 P.M.) seven days a week. Friday night there is a seafood buffet, Saturday night a steak buffet.

DICKSON

Tennessee governor Frank Clemet was born in the old Halbrook Hotel in Dickson, the largest city, but not the county seat, of Dickson County. This old railroad town has a pleasant downtown district.

The **Renaissance Center** (855 Hwy. 46 S., 615/740-5600, www.rcenter.org, Mon.–Fri. 8 A.M.–9 P.M., Sat. 9 A.M.–9 P.M.) is a unique multimedia, technological, and arts center. Designed to encourage interest in all types of artistic expression, the center has visual art exhibits, theater, a planetarium, computer courses, and dance classes. The center is located a few miles south of downtown Dickson, heading towards the interstate.

House Blend (124 N. Main St., 615/446-3311, Mon.–Thurs. 6 A.M.–9 P.M., Fri. 6 A.M.–10 P.M., Sat. 9 A.M.–6 P.M., $4–6) has above-average sandwiches, salads, and a whole array of coffee drinks and fruit smoothies. The grown-up grilled cheese is perked up with some parmesan and feta cheeses, and the Mighty Mississippi is a delicate barbecue delight. You get to choose between tortilla chips and orange mini-muffins to accompany your sandwich. The chefs will gladly prepare a half-salad, half-sandwich plate; just ask.

WHITE BLUFF

This small hamlet along Highway 70 is home to one of the region's most celebrated barbecue joints. **Carl's Perfect Pig** (4991 Hwy. 70 E., 615/797-4020) lives up to its name with tender and tangy pulled-pork shoulder and ribs. Chef Carl Teitloff also serves popular lunch specials and grill foods, including fried catfish and burgers. Open at 10:30 A.M. Wednesday–Sunday, Carl closes up at 6 P.M. on weeknights, 7 P.M. on Friday and Saturday nights, and at 2:30 P.M. on Sunday.

BON AQUA

Named for the healing waters that once drew people to this area, Bon Aqua is now little more than a huddle of homes and a small business district. Today, its chief attraction is the **Beacon Light Tea Room** (6343 Hwy. 100, 931/670-3880, Tues.–Fri. 4–10 P.M., Sat.–Sun. 9 A.M.–10 P.M., $7–12), a glorious stop for country ham, skillet-fried chicken, and Biblical wisdom reproduced on the walls, tables, and decor of this unique country eatery. The menu encourages you to "please give your order by number" and you'll be good enough to comply. The No. 4, half a skillet fried chicken, two vegetables, biscuits, preserves, and gravy, will have you whistling all day long. Breakfast is available on weekends.

Franklin

For most of its life, Franklin was just another small town in Tennessee. The bloody Battle of Franklin that took place in the fields surrounding the town on November 30, 1864, was probably the single most important event to take place in the town. Like other towns in the region, it took many years for Franklin to fully recover from the impact of the Civil War.

Franklin underwent a metamorphosis starting in the 1960s. Construction of I-65 near the town spurred economic development. Today, Franklin is a well-heeled bedroom community for Nashville professionals. The city, whose population runs around 50,000, is the tenth-largest in Tennessee, and one of the wealthiest in the state. What sets Franklin apart from other small towns in the state is the efforts it has made to preserve and protect the historic downtown. Its location only 20 miles from Nashville is also a major plus.

Franklin's attractions are all within a few miles of the city center, except for Cool Springs Galleria, a mega-mall located several miles out of town along the interstate.

SIGHTS
Historic Downtown

Franklin is one of the most picturesque small towns in Tennessee. Contained within four square blocks, downtown Franklin consists of leafy residential streets with old and carefully restored homes. The center of town is a traffic circle, crowned by a simple white Confederate monument. The circle is fronted by banks, more offices, and the 1859 Williamson County courthouse.

The best way to explore downtown Franklin is on foot. Free parking is available along the streets or in two public lots, one on 2nd Avenue and one on 4th Avenue. Pick up a printed walking-tour guide from the visitors center on East Main Street.

The walking tour takes you past 39 different buildings, including the **Hiram Masonic Lodge,** the oldest Masonic Lodge in Tennessee and also the building where Andrew Jackson in 1830 signed the treaty that led to the forced removal of thousands of Native Americans from Tennessee, Georgia, and other Southern states. You will also see the old city cemetery and the old **Franklin Post Office,** as well as lots of beautiful old houses and churches, all of which remain in use today. The walking tour is a good way to become familiar with the town and to appreciate the different types of architecture. It takes between one and two hours to complete.

Guided walking tours of Franklin are offered by **Franklin on Foot** (www.franklinonfoot.com, 615/400-3808). The Classic Franklin tour provides an overview of the history of the town and its buildings. The *Widow of the South* tour is combined with admission to the Carnton Plantation and is a must for lovers of that popular novel. Other tours include a children's tour and Haunted Franklin tour. Tours cost between $5 and $18 per person.

McLemore House

Five generations of the McLemore family lived in the white clapboard home at the corner of Glass Street and 11th Avenue in downtown Franklin. McLemore House was built in 1880 by Harvey McLemore, a former slave and farmer. Inside, a small museum has been created that documents the story of African Americans in Williamson County.

McLemore House is open by appointment only. Contact Mary Mills at 615/794-2270 or the Convention and Visitors Bureau to arrange a tour.

(Carnton Plantation

When Robert Hicks's novel *The Widow of the South* became a bestseller in 2005, the staff at the Carnton Plantation (1345 Carnton Ln., 615/794-0903, www.carnton.org, Mon.–Sat. 9 A.M.–5 P.M., Sun. 1–5 P.M., $3–8) noticed an uptick in the number of visitors. The novel is a fictionalized account of Carrie McGavock and how her home, the Carnton Plantation, became a Confederate hospital during the Battle of Franklin in the Civil War.

The Carnton mansion was built in 1826 by Randal McGavock, a former Nashville mayor and prominent lawyer and businessman.

The Carnton Plantation in Franklin was made famous by the novel *The Widow of the South*.

Randal had died by the time of the Civil War, and it was his son, John, and John's wife, Carrie, who witnessed the bloody Battle of Franklin on November 30, 1864. Located behind the Confederate line, the Carnton Plantation became a hospital for hundreds of injured and dying Confederate soldiers. As late as six months after the battle, the McGavock home remained a refuge for recovering veterans.

In the years that followed the battle, the McGavocks raised money, donating much of it themselves, to construct a cemetery for the Confederate dead, and donated two acres of land to the cause.

A new visitors center opened at Carnton in 2008, providing much-needed space for the museum and gift shop. Visitors to the Carnton Plantation can pay full price for a guided tour of the mansion and self-guided tour of the grounds, which include a smokehouse, slave house, and garden. You can also pay $3 for the self-guided tour of the grounds. There is no admission charged to visit the cemetery.

Fort Granger

An unsung attraction, Fort Granger is a lovely and interesting place to spend an hour or so. Built between 1862 and 1863 by Union forces, the earthen fort is set on a bluff overlooking the Harpeth River just south of downtown Franklin. The fort was the largest fortification in the area built by Captain W. E. Merrill during the Federal occupation of Franklin. It saw action twice in 1863 and also in 1864 during the Battle of Franklin.

Many features of the fort remain intact for today's visitors. You can walk around portions of the breastworks. The interior of the fort is now a grassy field, perfect for a summer picnic or game of catch. An overlook at one end of the fort provides an unmatched view of the surrounding countryside.

You can reach Fort Granger two ways. One is along a short but steep trail departing Pinkerton Park on Murfreesboro Road

THE HEARTLAND

east of town. Or you can drive straight to the fort by heading out of town on East Main Street. Turn right onto Liberty Pike, right onto Eddy Lane, and, finally, right again onto Fort Granger Drive.

The fort, which is maintained by the City of Franklin, is open during daylight hours only. While there is no office or visitors center at the fort, you may contact Franklin's parks department (615/794-2103) for more information.

The Carter House

Some of the fiercest fighting in the Battle of Franklin took place around the farm and house belonging to the Carter family on the outskirts of town. The family took refuge in the basement while Union and Confederate soldiers fought hand to hand right above them. Today, the Carter House (1140 Columbia Ave., 615/791-1861, www.carter-house.org, Mon.–Sat. 9 A.M.–5 P.M., Sun. 1–5 P.M., adults $8, seniors $7, children 7–13 $4) is the best place to come for a detailed examination of the battle and the profound human toll that it exacted on both sides.

You will see hundreds of bullet holes, which help to illustrate the ferocity of the fight. Guides describe some of the worst moments of the battle, and bring to life a few of the people who fought it. The house also holds a museum of Civil War uniforms and memorabilia, including photographs and short biographies of many of the men who were killed in Franklin. There is also a video about the battle, which shows scenes from a reenactment.

PARKS AND RECREATION

Pinkerton Park (405 Murfreesboro Rd.), just southeast of town off Murfreesboro Road, is a pleasant city park. Walking trails, playgrounds, and picnic tables draw dozens of town residents, who come to exercise or simply relax. A short hiking trail takes you to Fort Granger overlooking the city. You can also take the Sue Douglas Berry Memorial pedestrian bridge over the Harpeth River and walk the six blocks to the town square.

Jim Warren Park (705 Boyd Mill Ave., 615/794-2103) is a large public park with baseball and softball fields, tennis courts, covered picnic areas, and 2.5 miles of walking trails.

Harlinsdale Farm

One of the most famous Tennessee Walking Horse breeding farms became a public park in 2007. Harlinsdale Farm (239 Franklin Rd., 615/794-2103) was a famed Franklin landmark for many years, thanks to a very famous horse. Midnight Sun, a stallion, was world champion walking horse in 1945 and 1946, and all subsequent champions can trace their ancestry to him.

In 2004, Franklin bought the 200-acre farm for $8 million and three years later the first 60 acres opened as a public park. It is a pleasant place to walk or picnic. There are plans for a visitors center, overlook, and extensive walking trails.

Golf

Located a few miles southeast of Franklin, **Forrest Crossing Golf Course** (750 Riverview Dr., 615/794-9400) is an 18-hole par-72 golf course designed by Gary Roger Baird. Just shy of 7,000 yards, the course rating is 77.8 and the slope is 135.

There are more golf courses in Cool Springs, a few miles north of Franklin. **Vanderbilt Legends Club** (1500 Legends Club Ln., 615/791-8100) is a top-of-the-line golf club. There are two 18-hole courses at the club, as well as a complete array of club services, including a putting green and chipping green. Green fees are $75–85 and include a cart. Lower rates are available after 3 P.M. No blue jeans, T-shirts, or athletic shorts are allowed.

The **Fairways on Spencer Creek** (285 Spencer Creek Rd., 615/794-8223) is a nine-hole alternative. The course rating is 64.6 and slope is 105.

ENTERTAINMENT
Theater

The **Boiler Room Theatre** (The Factory, 615/794-7744, www.boilerroomtheatre.com)

is a professional theater company that performs seven or eight productions each year. Shows take place in a 120-seat theater in building six at the Factory (see *Shopping*), and range from light-hearted musical theater to dramas. The theater's season runs year-round.

Franklin's community theater is **Pull-Tight Players** (112 2nd Ave. S., 615/791-5007 or 615/790-6782, www.pull-tight.com). Performing in an intimate theater in downtown Franklin, Pull-Tight Players put on about six productions each season, which runs from September to June. Productions include many classic stage favorites.

Cinema

The 70-year old Franklin Cinema at 419 Main Street closed in 2007 because of rising rents in the downtown area. A few months later, the Heritage Foundation of Williamson County purchased the theater for $1.75 million with plans to renovate and reopen the classic theater.

For now, head to Cool Springs to find **Thoroughbred 20** (633 Frazier Dr., 615/778-0775), a 20-screen multiplex showing first-run movies.

Live Music

The **Listening Room Cafe** (500 W. Main St., 615/591-5725) hosts in-the-round and other intimate concerts several nights a week. Songwriters and musicians from Nashville frequently head down here for a night's show, which typically begins around 7 P.M.

Other venues that sometimes offer live music include restaurants **Saffire** (The Factory, 615/599-4995) and **The Bunganut Pig** (1143 Columbia Ave., 615/794-4777).

EVENTS

Franklin hosts a number of events throughout the year.

Spring

On the Saturday before St. Patrick's Day, in March, the **Feile Franklin Festival** on Main Street includes Irish dance, music, and vendors.

The city's biggest festival of the year is the **Main Street Festival** during the last full weekend of April. Local arts and crafts are the major draw of this showcase, which also includes food, music, theater, and children's activities.

The town's Rotary Club organizes the annual **Franklin Rodeo** (www.franklin-rodeo.com), a weeklong event in May that includes a Rodeo Parade, Miss Tennessee Rodeo pageant, and a PRCA-sanctioned rodeo with steer wrestling and bronco and bull riding. It takes place at the Williamson County Ag Expo Park, and proceeds go to local service projects.

Summer

During the first full weekend of June you can join the Heritage Foundation on a **Town and Country Tour of Homes** (www.historic-franklin.com). Tours go to private and historic homes that are closed to the public during the rest of the year.

Franklin celebrates Independence Day with **Franklin on the Fourth,** a patriotic family concert on the public square. The fireworks finale takes place near Mack Hatcher/Hillsboro Road.

During the last weekend in July the city celebrates **Bluegrass Along the Harpeth,** a music festival featuring bluegrass, old-time string bands, and buck dancing.

The **Williamson County Fair** (www.williamsoncountyfair.org) starts on the first Friday in August and features agricultural exhibits, a Midway, live entertainment, and competitions.

Fall

The **Franklin Jazz Festival** is a two-day music festival that features jazz, Dixieland, and big-band acts in downtown Franklin. Admission is free; the festival takes place on the Sunday and Monday of Labor Day weekend.

Winter

The Carter House organizes a holiday tour of homes during the first full weekend of December. During the second full weekend of the month, the city of Franklin is transformed into a bustling English Victorian town at **Dickens of a Christmas.** There are costumed characters, carolers, artisans, strolling minstrels, and unique foods.

SHOPPING

In many respects, shopping is Franklin's greatest attraction. Trendy downtown shops, the unique environment of the Factory, and proximity to a major mall make this a destination for shoppers. It is also one of Tennessee's most popular antiques shopping destinations.

Antiques

Franklin declares itself "the new antiques capital of Tennessee." Indeed, antiquing is one of the most popular pursuits of Franklin's visitors, and at least two dozen antiques shops serve to quench the thirst for something old. The town's antiques district is huddled around the corner of Margin Street and 2nd Avenue. Here you'll find no less than six major antiques stores. Other shops are found along Main Street in the downtown shopping district.

The best place to start antiquing is the **Franklin Antique Mall** (251 2nd Ave. S., 615/790-8593), located in the town's old ice house. The mall is a maze of rooms, each with different goods on offer. Possibilities include books, dishware, quilts, furniture, knick-knacks, and housewares. You can also follow 5th Avenue about two blocks south of downtown to find **Country Charm Antique Mall** (301 Lewisburg Ave., 615/790-8998), whose three buildings house a vast array of furniture, quilts, glassware, china, and home decor.

Just outside the Franklin Antique Mall are at least five other antiques shops to roam through, including **J. J. Ashley's** (125 S. Margin St., 615/791-0011), which specializes in French and English Country accessories, as well as European furniture. **Scarlett Scales Antiques** (212 S. Margin St., 615/791-4097), located in a 1900s shotgun house, has American country furnishings,

accessories, and architectural elements arriving daily.

Downtown

Retail is alive and well in Franklin's downtown. West Main Street is the epicenter of the shopping district, although you will find stores scattered around other parts of downtown as well. Home decor, classy antiques, trendy clothes, and specialty items like candles, tea, and gardening supplies are just a few of the things you'll find in downtown Franklin.

Most shops in downtown Franklin are open by 10 A.M. and many stay open until the evening to catch late-afternoon visitors. You can easily navigate the downtown shopping district on foot, although you may need to stow your parcels in the car now and then.

Bink's Outfitters (421 Main St., 615/599-8777) sells outdoor clothing and equipment. Stylish ladies' apparel and accessories are sold at **Chico's** (348 Main St., 615/599-8471). Go to **ENJOUE** (400 Main St., 615/599-8177) for funky fashions and trendy styles.

The city's best bookstore is **Landmark Booksellers** (114 E. Main St., 615/791-6400), found on the other side of the town square. They have a wide selection of used and new books, including many regional titles. It is friendly and welcoming, with fresh coffee for sale in the mornings.

Franklin Tea Merchant (430 Main St., 615/794-6311) has a wide selection of loose tea and various tea accessories. Toys old and new are on sale at **Main Street Toy Co.** (412 Main St., 615/790-4869). For the best in paper, wrappings, and stationery, go to **Rock Paper Scissors** (317 Main St., 615/791-0150). **Heart and Hands** (418 Main St., 615/794-2537) is one of several shops specializing in crafts and home decor.

The Factory

Franklin's most unique retail center is the Factory (230 Franklin Rd., 615/791-1777, www.factoryatfranklin.com). A 250,000-square-foot complex of 11 different old industrial buildings, the Factory once housed stove factories and a textile mill. In the mid-1990s, Calvin Lehew bought the dilapidated eyesore and began the lengthy process of restoring the buildings and converting them to a space for galleries, retail shops, restaurants, and other businesses.

Today, the Factory is a vibrant commercial center for the city of Franklin. It houses a refreshing array of local independent retailers, including galleries, salons, candy shops, and a pet boutique. **The Little Cottage** (615/794-1405) sells children's fashions. Quilting supplies and fabric are the mainstays at **The Smocking Loft** (615/794-6226).

There are also 11 different studios and learning centers, including the **Viking Store** (615/599-9617), which offers cooking demonstrations and classes; **Creation Station** (615/791-9192), where you can practice scrapbooking; and **Arts for Life** (615/995-2778), which offers art classes and music lessons. There are also talent agencies and a tae kwon do academy.

In addition to retail and learning centers, the Factory has four restaurants and a fish market.

Cool Springs Galleria

Cool Springs Galleria (1800 Galleria Blvd., Cool Springs, 615/771-2128, www.coolspringsgalleria.com) is a mall with 165 specialty stores, 5 major department stores, 20 restaurants, and a 500-seat food court. It is located a few miles north of Franklin, convenient to I-65. Shops include Zales, Wild Oats, Talbots, Pier 1, Pottery Barn, Macy's, JC Penney, and Eddie Bauer. The mall is found at exits 68B and 69 on I-65.

ACCOMMODATIONS

Franklin has two types of accommodation: cozy bed-and-breakfast inns and chain motels. The bed-and-breakfasts are located in downtown Franklin and the surrounding countryside. The chain motels are located around exit 65 off I-65, about two miles from the city center. The bed-and-breakfast accommodations are far more congruous with Franklin's charm than the interstate motels.

Under $100

Several chain motels surround the interstate near Franklin. Closest to town are the 89-room **Quality Inns and Suites** (1307 Murfreesboro Rd., 615/794-7591, $65–110) and the 142-room **Best Western** (1308 Murfreesboro Rd., 615/790-0570, $55–70). Both offer wireless Internet, free continental breakfast, and an outdoor pool.

$100-150

The **Magnolia House Bed and Breakfast** (1317 Columbia Ave., 615/794-8178, www.bbonline.com/tn/magnolia, $100–120) is less than a mile from downtown Franklin, near the Carter House. A large magnolia tree shades the early 20th-century Craftsman home. There are four carpeted guest rooms, each with a private bath. Three house queen-sized beds; the fourth has two twin beds. Common areas include a polished sitting room, cozy den, and sunroom that looks out on the quiet residential neighborhood. Hosts Jimmy and Robbie Smithson welcome guests and prepare homemade breakfast according to your preferences.

Also less than a mile from downtown, **Franklin House Bed and Breakfast** (304 Stewart St., 615/791-9895, www.bbonline.com/tn/franklinhouse, $125) has two queen-sized guest accommodations located upstairs in the 100-year-old farmhouse. Common areas include a gracious wraparound porch. Breakfast of homemade bread, breakfast casseroles, and other favorites is served in the spacious dining room.

⟨ **Old Marshall House Bed and Breakfast** (1030 John Williams Rd., 615/791-1455, www.oldmarshallhouse.com, $120–170) is the best bed-and-breakfast in the Franklin area. The 19th-century farmhouse located about five miles east of the city has three bedrooms plus a unique log cabin on the grounds. King-sized guest rooms feature handmade quilts, large bathrooms, fireplaces, and private sitting areas. The queen-sized guest room, the most modestly priced, also has a private bathroom and its own cable TV and DVD player. Outside is a restored 1850s log cabin that has been carefully converted into a perfect overnight retreat. Guests enjoy a living room made cozy by a cast-iron gas stove, modern bathroom with a claw-foot tub, and king-sized sleeping loft. The cabin has a microwave, coffeemaker, and refrigerator and rents for $170 a night. Weather permitting, breakfast is served on a terrace overlooking the five-acre yard. Dishes include French toast, fruit compote, and hashbrown quiche. The property is equipped with wireless Internet, and owners Glen and Ursula Houghton are friendly, knowledgeable, and seasoned hosts.

Over $200

Designed especially for couples, **Blue Moon Farm Bed and Breakfast** (4441 N. Chapel Rd., 800/493-4518, www.bluemoonfarmbb.com, $350–475) is a three-room cottage complete with kitchen, spa-style bathroom, and master bedroom. The art deco decor is unique among country bed-and-breakfasts, as is the sophistication of the welcome. Touches like spa robes, an ultra tub, and a decadently dressed king-sized bed make this a real getaway. The kitchen is stocked with drinks, snacks, and the ingredients for light meals. A "Grocery Bag Breakfast" is left in the refrigerator for you and your companion to enjoy when you want, and in privacy. During waking hours, you can stroll the grounds or take advantage of wireless Internet access. Hosts Susan and Bob Eidam will also be happy to recommend and arrange activities for your stay in the Franklin area. Children over one year are welcome at a cost of $20 extra per night.

FOOD
Downtown

Think country buffet, and then think ten times better. (**Monell's** (108 Bridge St., 615/790-6993, Mon.–Fri. 10:30 A.M.–2 P.M., Tues.–Sat. 5–8:30 P.M., Sat. 8:30 A.M.–1 P.M., Sun. 8:30 A.M.–4 P.M., $13–20) does fine Southern cooking, served all-you-can-eat family style. Come in and you'll be seated at a long table with other diners. If you feel weird about that, well, get over it and just remember to pass the dishes to the left. Chances are you'll wind up enjoying the unexpected company. The tables at Monell's sag with good food. When you're seated you'll find cold cucumber salad, coleslaw, and iced tea already on the table. Soon after, the server will bring out plate after plate of more temptations: savory greens, fluffy biscuits, cheesy potato casserole, golden skillet-fried chicken, and much more. Each lunch or dinner they offer three different main-course meats, including things like chicken and dumplings, skillet-fried chicken, pot roast, pork chops, and meatloaf. The main dishes are accompanied by traditional country sides. Dessert may be banana pudding, fruit cobbler, or some other sweet specialty. For breakfast, expect smoked sausage, bacon, country ham, pancakes, hash browns, grits, and—if you can imagine it—more. Monell's is a great choice for those who love country cooking, for the uninitiated who want to try it out, and for all those in between.

The best choice for baked goods, coffee, and light fare, including soups, salads, and sandwiches, is **Merridee's Breadbasket** (110 4th Ave., 615/790-3755, Mon.–Sat. 7 A.M.–5 P.M., $3–7). Merridee grew up in Minnesota and learned baking from her mother, a Swede. When Merridee married Tom McCray and moved to Middle Tennessee in 1973, she kept up the baking traditions she had learned as a child. In 1984, she opened Merridee's Breadbasket in Franklin. Merridee McCray died in 1994, but her restaurant remains one of Franklin's most popular. Come in for omelets, scrambled eggs, or sweet bread and fruit in the morning. At lunch choose from the daily soup, casserole, or quiche, or order a cold or grilled sandwich. Merridee's also bakes fresh bread daily; take home a loaf of the always-popular Viking bread. Merridee's attracts a variety of people—students, businesspeople, and families out on the town. The creaky wood floors and comfortable seating make it a pleasant and relaxing place to refuel.

Puckett's Grocery and Restaurant (120 4th Ave. S., 625/794-5527), the Leiper's Fork institution, has expanded with a second location in Franklin. The Franklin shop offers traditional breakfasts with eggs, bacon, country ham, and biscuits and plate lunches in the day. In the evening, order up a handmade burger (the locals swear that they're the best in town), a Southern dinner of fried catfish, or a traditional steak, chicken, or fish entrée. For vegetarians, they offer a veggie burger or a vegetable plate, as well as salads. The food is well prepared and the service friendly, and there's almost always a crowd.

Award-winning and always popular, (**Saffire** (The Factory, 615/599-4995, Tues.–Sun., $14–35) serves lunch 11 A.M.–3 P.M. and dinner beginning at 5 P.M. Using primarily organic and biodynamic ingredients, Saffire's menu sparkles with unique dishes. Try the tender and flavorful Cuban roasted-pork appetizer plate, or a simple salad of heirloom tomatoes. Entrées include upscale dishes like prime rib and ahi tuna. Their fried chicken is dusted with Panko flakes, topped with country ham gravy, and served with luscious macaroni and cheese. Saffire has an extensive wine and cocktail list, including organic choices. Take $4 off signature cocktails during happy hour (5–6 P.M.) and on Tuesday night most bottles of wine go for half-price. The lunch menu is casual, featuring sandwiches, salads, and lunch-sized entrées. Or choose the "green plate" daily special, featuring local and organic ingredients. There is also a midday kid's menu with favorites like grilled cheese and chicken bites. Set within an old warehouse, Saffire's dining room is spacious with exposed brick and beams. The kitchen opens out onto the dining room, so you can watch the cooks work. With live music many nights, Saffire is a fine choice for excellent food in a pleasant and exciting environment.

Farmer's Market

The Franklin Farmer's Market takes place at the rear of the Factory on Saturday mornings during spring, summer, and fall 8 A.M.–noon. This is one of the finest small-town farmer's markets in the state, featuring a wide variety of fruit and vegetable growers, and cheese, milk, and meat sellers, as well as craftspersons and live music.

INFORMATION AND SERVICES

The **Williamson County Convention and Visitors Bureau** (615/791-7554 or 866/253-9207, www.visitwilliamson.com) publishes guides and maintains a website about Franklin and the surrounding area. They also operate the **Williamson County Visitor Center** (209 E. Main St., 615/591-8514, Mon.–Fri. 9 A.M.–4 P.M., Sat. 10 A.M.–3 P.M., Sun. noon–3 P.M.).

The **Williamson Medical Center** (Hwy. 96 E., 615/435-5000) is a 185-bed full-service medical facility with a 24-hour emergency room.

King Neptune (1533 Columbia Ave., 615/790-7682) is a clean and comfortable laundry, open 24 hours a day. A single wash costs $1.50.

GETTING AROUND

Traffic can be heavy in and around Franklin. As a bedroom community for commuters working in Nashville, the morning and afternoon rush hours are to be avoided. The City of Franklin offers a trolley bus service around the town and to outlying areas, including Cool Springs Galleria, Williamson Medical Center, Watson Glen Shopping Center, and Independence Square. The trolleys run four different routes; the route most useful for visitors is the yellow route, which runs from the Factory at Franklin to Cool Springs Galleria hourly on the hour 7 A.M.–5 P.M.

You can pick up a full schedule and route map from the visitors center. Trolley stops are well marked with a brown-and-white sign, plus a schedule. The fare is $1 for adults and 50 cents for seniors and children. Exact change is required.

If you need a taxi, call Brentwood Taxi at 615/373-4950.

The Natchez Trace

The Natchez Trace Parkway cuts a diagonal path through the Heartland south of Nashville. The two-lane limited-access highway passes through mostly undeveloped countryside.

Towns and sites in this region are a short drive off the trace, and bring you to villages and county seats that embody small-town Tennessee.

LEIPER'S FORK

Part small town, part yuppified enclave, Leiper's Fork is a pleasant place to spend a few hours. It is located about 15 minutes' drive from Franklin and near milepost 420 on the Natchez Trace Parkway. The town runs for several miles along Leiper's Fork, a tributary of the West Harpeth River. Beautiful old farmhouses line Old Hillsboro Road, which serves as the main thoroughfare through town.

One of the earliest settlers of the area was the Benton family, including Thomas Hart Benton, who would go on to become a U.S.

senator from Missouri. For many years, Leiper's Fork was called Hillsboro after Hillsborough, North Carolina, where many of its early settlers came from. There is another Hillsboro in Coffee County, Tennessee, however, so when this Hillsboro petitioned for a post office in 1818, the U.S Postal Service insisted that it change its name. Leiper's Fork was born.

Acclaimed furniture-maker Dick Poyner was from the Leiper's Fork area. Poyner, a former slave, was famous for his sturdy ladder-back wooden chairs, one of which is on display at the Tennessee State Museum in Nashville.

Leiper's Fork is a pleasant community. Art galleries and antiques shops line the short main drag. Unusually good food can be found at local restaurants and a laid-back let's-laugh-at-ourselves attitude prevails.

Bed-and-breakfast inns in the area make it a viable destination, or a pleasant pit-stop during a tour of the region.

driving along the Natchez Trace Parkway

PHOTO COURTESY OF TENNESSEE DEPARTMENT OF TOURIST DEVELOPMENT

THE HEARTLAND

Shopping

Leiper's Fork retailers are open Wednesday–Saturday 10 A.M.–5 P.M. and Sunday 1–5 P.M.

Opening its doors in 2007, **R Place** (4154 Old Hillsboro Rd., 615/794-8592) sells the artwork of Anne Goetz, the handmade furniture of Reed Birnie, and used books curated by Renee Armand. You can also get homemade pie and coffee if you need sustenance while you browse the shop, housed in an old home.

The **Leiper's Creek Gallery** (4144 Old Hillsboro Rd., 615/599-5102) is the finest gallery in town. It shows a wide selection of paintings by local and regional artists and hosts a variety of arts events year-round.

Neena's Primitive Antiques (4158 Old Hillsboro Rd., 615/790-0345) specializes in primitive antiques, linens, home decor items, and leather goods.

Entertainment

Friday night is songwriter night at **Puckett's Grocery** (4142 Old Hillsboro Rd., 615/794-1308, www.puckettsgrocery.com). For $30 you enjoy dressed-up dinner—fresh seafood, poultry, and steak are usually among the options—at 7 P.M. and an in-the-round performance from Nashville singer-songwriters starting at 8:30 P.M. If you prefer, pay $15 for the concert only. Reservations are essential for either, so call ahead. Check the website to find out who is performing.

Jailhouse Industries operates the Leiper's Fork **Lawn Chair Theatre** from May to September. Bring your lawn chair or blanket and enjoy classic movies and kids' favorites on Friday and Saturday nights. Call 615/477-6799 for more information, or just ask around.

Hiking

The Leiper's Fork District of the Natchez Trace National Scenic Trail runs for 24 miles, starting near milepost 427 and ending at milepost 408, where State Highway 50 crosses the parkway. The trail follows the old Natchez Trace through rural countryside.

The best access point is from Garrison Creek Road, where there is parking, restrooms, and picnic facilities. You can also access the trail from Davis Hollow Road.

Accommodations

Namaste Acres (5436 Leiper's Creek Rd., 615/791-0333, www.bbonline.com/tn/namaste, $120–175) is a unique bed-and-breakfast. Located on a working horse farm, Namaste Acres guests are treated to beautiful farm views and hearty country breakfasts. Three guest suites are decorated with a Western flair: lots of exposed wood, rocking chairs, and woven Indian rugs. Horse owners can board their horses here too. Each suite has a private bathroom, deck, and fireplace, as well as a TV/VCR, telephone, refrigerator, and coffeemaker.

Food

(**Puckett's Grocery** (4142 Old Hillsboro Rd., 615/794-1308, www.puckettsgrocery.com, $6–25) is home to the heartbeat of Leiper's Fork. An old-time grocery with a small dining room attached, Puckett's serves breakfast, lunch, and dinner to the town faithful and visitors alike. The original country store opened about 1950. In 1998, Andy Marshall bought the store and expanded the restaurant offerings. Solid country breakfasts are the order of the day in the mornings, followed by plate lunches. The pulled pork is a favorite, as is the Puckett Burger. Dinner specials include catfish nights, family nights, and a Saturday-night seafood buffet. Friday night the grocery turns upscale with a supper club and live music. Reservations are essential for Friday night. Puckett's hours vary by the season, so it is best to call ahead, especially for dinner arrangements. Summer hours are Monday–Thursday 6 A.M.–7 P.M., Friday–Saturday 6 A.M.–10:30 P.M., Sunday 6 A.M.–6 P.M. From December through February, the grocery cuts back its hours, often closing about an hour early. A second Puckett's Grocery location in Franklin offers a more varied menu.

For a casual sandwich, decadent pastry, or cup of coffee, head to the **Backyard Cafe** (4150 Old Hillsboro Rd., 615/790-4003, Mon.–Sat. 11 A.M.–3 P.M., Sun. noon–3 P.M.).

THE HEARTLAND

THE NATCHEZ TRACE PARKWAY

The first people to travel what is now regarded as the Natchez Trace were probably Choctow and Chickasaw Indians, who made the first footpaths through the region. French and Spanish traders used the 500 miles of intertwining Indian trails that linked the Mississippi port of Natchez to the Cumberland River.

Early white settlers quickly identified the importance of a land route from Natchez to Nashville. In 1801, the Natchez Trace opened as an official post road between the two cities. Boatmen who piloted flatboats from Nashville and other northern cities to Natchez and New Orleans returned along the Trace by foot or horse, often carrying large sums of money. One historian characterized the diverse array of people who used the Trace: "robbers, rugged pioneers, fashionable ladies, shysters, politicians, soldiers, scientists, and men of destiny, such as Aaron Burr, Andrew Jackson and Meriwether Lewis."

The Trace developed a reputation for robberies, and few people traveled its miles alone. Many thieves disguised themselves as Indians, fanning the flames of racial distrust that existed during this period of history. By 1820, more than 20 inns, referred to as "stands," were open. Many were modest – providing food and shelter only.

In 1812, the first steamship arrived at Natchez, Mississippi, marking the beginning of the end of the Trace's prominence. As steamboat travel became more widespread and affordable, more and more people turned away from the long, laborious, and dangerous overland route along the Trace.

The road's historical importance is evident in the fact that it was not easily forgotten. While it faded from use, the Natchez Trace was remembered. In 1909, the Daughters of the American Revolution in Mississippi started a project to mark the route of the Trace in each county through which it passed. The marker project continued for the next 24 years and eventually caught the attention of Mississippi Rep. Thomas J. Busby, who introduced the first bills in Congress to survey and construct a paved road along the route of the old Natchez Trace.

During the Great Depression, work on the Natchez Trace Parkway began under the Public Works Administration, the Works Project Administration, and the Civilian Conservation Corps. Following the New Deal, construction slowed dramatically and it was not until 1996 that the final leg of the parkway was completed.

The 445-mile parkway follows the general path of the old Natchez Trace; in a few places, they fall in step with each other. Just over 100 miles of the parkway lie within Tennessee. It runs along the Western Highland Rim through Davidson, Williamson, Hickman, Maury, Lewis, and Wayne Counties.

The parkway passes scenic overlooks, historic sites, and quiet pastures. In many places along the route you have the opportunity to walk along the original Trace.

ACCOMMODATIONS AND FOOD

There are no hotels on the parkway. Look for accommodations in nearby cities, including Franklin, Columbia, and Lawrenceburg. The Hampshire-based **Natchez Trace Reservation**

Information

The **Leiper's Fork Merchant's Association** (615/972-2708, www.leipersforkvillage.com) promotes the town, maintains a listing of local businesses, and publishes an annual calendar of events.

SPRING HILL

A small town midway between Franklin and Columbia, Spring Hill is best known by many as the site of a large General Motors automobile factory. To students of the Civil War, the town is the site of one of the South's greatest missed opportunities of the war. While it is doubtful that a different outcome at Spring Hill would have changed the course of war, it would very likely have saved the many thousands of lives lost at the Battle of Franklin.

Spring Hill is located along U.S. Highway 31. Downtown consists of a few blocks between Beechcroft and Kendron Roads. The town's main street was destroyed by fire and

Service (800/377-2770, www.bbonline.com/natcheztrace) books bed-and-breakfast inns along the parkway, from Nashville all the way to Natchez. This service is worth considering, especially since many of these inns are located closer to the parkway than motels are.

The closest accommodations to the parkway are three **campgrounds,** one of which lies in Tennessee. The Meriwether Lewis Campground at milepost 385 has 32 sites and a bathhouse. The next campground is Jeff Busby at milepost 193, in Mississippi.

There are no restaurants or food concessions along the parkway. Picnic facilities abound, however, so wise travelers will pack a few sandwiches and avoid traveling off the parkway to eat.

INFORMATION AND SERVICES

The **National Park Service** (800/305-7417, www.nps.gov/natr) publishes a fold-out map and guide to the parkway. The official visitors center for the parkway is in Tupelo, Mississippi. For detailed hiking information, visit the website about the Natchez Trace National Scenic Trail at www.nps.gov/natt.

The only gas station along the parkway is at Jeff Busby, milepost 193, in Mississippi. Fill up your tank before you take off to explore.

PHOTO COURTESY OF TENNESSEE DEPARTMENT OF TOURIST DEVELOPMENT

Cattle graze along the Natchez Trace Parkway.

THE HEARTLAND

tornado in 1963, leaving only a few remnants of Spring Hill's former charm. To see them, drive up and down the town's side streets, including Murray Hill, Depot, and McLemore Streets. Spring Hill's main attractions are along Highway 31 less than a mile outside of town.

The **Spring Hill Battlefield** (931/486-9037) is a 118-acre park with a one-mile trail that climbs to the top of a hill overlooking the battlefield. Interpretive markers tell the story of Spring Hill. The park is open during daylight hours. To find it, turn east onto Kendron Road and look for the park on the right-hand side of the road, just before the road passes I-65.

Rippavilla

You can tour an 1850s-era mansion at Rippavilla Plantation (5700 Main St., aka Hwy. 31, 931/486-9037, www.rippavilla.org, Tues.–Sat. 9 a.m.–5 p.m., adults $8, seniors $6, children 6–12 $5, children under

THE SOUTH'S LAST STAND

In the waning days of the Confederacy, its president, Jefferson Davis, met with his commanders to plan strategy. It was September 1864, and the Federals were pushing southward in Virginia and Georgia.

The plan that Davis and his commanders, including Gen. John Bell Hood, agreed was a daring march northward through Middle Tennessee. It was hoped that Gen. Hood's Army of the Tennessee would draw Federal forces away from the battles elsewhere and that they would eventually be repelled from the South entirely.

The last-ditch plan failed, and cost the Confederacy some 13,500 lives. The battles of Spring Hill, Franklin, and Nashville were major blows to the Southern cause and its last losing stratagem.

SPRING HILL

On November 29, 1864, Gen. John M. Schofield and his federal troops were stationed in Columbia. Moving northward, Hood went around Columbia and headed towards Spring Hill. From here, Hood could either have marched to Nashville ahead of the Federals or returned to Columbia and attacked them from the rear. It was a promising position.

But the opportunity was squandered when the Confederates camped just short of a critical road northward. Schofield, who suspected Hood's strategy and realized his grave error, moved his men in the dead of night and marched them safely northward, passing within "talking distance" of the encamped Southern army.

Explanations for Hood's mistake suggest that he was not himself on that day. He was probably in tremendous physical pain from earlier war injuries (Hood had already lost the use of his left arm and had his right leg amputated below the hip), and was probably taking opium. He may also have been drunk. If walls could talk, the ones at Oaklawn on Denning Lane in Spring Hill, an 1835 mansion that served as the Confederate headquarters, would have a tale to tell.

Whatever the cause, on the morning of November 30, when Hood realized what had happened, he resolved to battle the Federals in Franklin. Fueled by shame and desperation, Hood ordered the charge at the Battle of Franklin, one of the South's bloodiest defeats of the war.

FRANKLIN

By the time Hood and his army reached Franklin on November 30, 1864, the general was frustrated and the men exhausted. The missed opportunity at Spring Hill stung, but worse was yet to come.

Ignoring the advice of his commanders, including Nathan Bedford Forrest and Benjamin Franklin Cheatham, Hood ordered a full frontal attack on the federal line around Franklin. Unlike many other battles of the Civil War, the troops at Franklin had a full view at each other. There were some 23,000 Federal soldiers on one side, and 20,000 Confederates on the

6 free), just south of downtown Spring Hill on Highway 31. Rippavilla, originally called Rip-o-villa, was built in 1851 by wealthy plantation owner Nathaniel Cheairs and his wife, Susan. The story is told that there was a tradition in the Cheairs family for the men to marry women named Sarah, so when Nathaniel told his father that he intended to ask Susan McKissak to marry him, his father offered to pay the young man $5,000 in gold not to. Susan McKissak's father, one of the richest men in the area, heard of this and in reply he offered Cheairs all the bricks and slave labor he needed to build his home.

In the end, Cheairs married Susan and received both the gifts from his father-in-law and the $5,000 from his father—not a bad way to start out in life.

Rippavilla was sold out of the family in the 1920s, and the new owner modernized many of the finishes and also connected what was once a detached smokehouse and kitchen to the main building. Guided tours of the mansion last about 45 minutes and guests may also other. At about 4 P.M. on the last day of November, 1864, 18 brigades of Confederate soldiers, many of them from Tennessee, marched towards the Federal line. With the rebel yell that made them famous, the attack had begun. It was like sending soldiers to the slaughter.

It was a bloody and fierce battle. Even those commanders and soldiers on the Confederate side who had doubts about the battle strategy fought bravely and often to the death. The hand to hand combat around the Carter House near downtown Franklin was some of the fiercest of the battle. One Federal soldier said that the fighting was in such close quarters that "even the poorest marksman could not fail to hit a human target."

The Confederate assault failed. The fighting ended around 9 P.M. and overnight Federal Gen. John M. Schofield and all his soldiers who could walk marched to Nashville. They left their dead on the battlefield. Two weeks later, they defeated Hood's army again during the Battle of Nashville.

The death toll at Franklin was staggering. Some 7,000 Confederate were killed, wounded, or captured in just five hours of battle. The Federals lost 2,500 men. Many injured warriors died on the battlefield overnight, when temperatures dropped below freezing.

The townspeople of Franklin were left to tend to the wounded on both sides of the battle. Nearly every home in the city became a makeshift hospital. The most famous of these was the Carnton Plantation, where visitors today can still see blood stains on the floor, left by injured and dying soldiers.

In 1866, John and Carrie McGavock established a Confederate cemetery on the grounds of Carnton. It holds 1,500 graves, making it the largest private military cemetery in the nation. Carrie kept a careful record of the men who were buried there, and her cemetery book was used by thousands of people who came to Franklin to mourn loved ones who died there.

COURTESY CF LIBRARY OF CONGRESS

an unidentified Confederate soldier

walk around the property, which includes an 1870s Freedman's School that was moved from another part of the county when it was threatened to be destroyed.

Tennessee Museum of Early Farm Life

For an educational trip back in time, stop at the Tennessee Museum of Early Farm Life (5700 Main St., aka Hwy. 31, 931/381-3686, Fri.–Sat. 9 A.M.–3:30 P.M., adults $3, children and seniors $2), which displays farm, kitchen, and other useful implements used at Tennessee farms and homes in days gone by. Operated by a group of enthusiastic and knowledgeable retired farmers, the museum lovingly preserves plows, cultivators, seeders, wagons, and many other pieces of machinery that helped make a hard life just a bit easier for farmers and their families. You can see machinery and equipment used to make brooms, to make molasses, to sow seeds, to bale hay, and to cure pork. Through the descriptions provided by your tour guide, you begin to understand the ingenuity and inventiveness

THE HEARTLAND

of these pioneers, as well as the hard work that went into fulfilling their basic needs.

The museum is open on Friday and Saturday only, but call ahead for an appointment if you'd like to visit on a different day. It is located a few hundred yards behind the Rippavilla Plantation and was once called the Mule Museum, the name that is still reflected on the road sign at Rippavilla.

General Motors Plant

Spring Hill's one-time Saturn automobile plant now produces the Chevy Traverse cross-over vehicle; in 2009, production was cut back due to the nationwide economic slowdown. The plant's Welcome Center (Hwy. 31, 931/486-5000, Mon.–Fri. 6 A.M.–3 P.M., free) provides information about the plant and schedules tours.

Accommodations

There is a **Best Western** (102 Kedron Pkwy., 931/486-1234, $90–130) in town with an outdoor pool, laundry facility, free full breakfast, fitness room, and business services.

COLUMBIA

Columbia is the seat of Maury County. Founded in 1809 and named for Christopher Columbus, Columbia was the commercial hub for Middle Tennessee's rich plantations. In 1850 it became the third-largest city in Tennessee, behind Nashville and Memphis. A decade later Maury County was the wealthiest county in the whole state. The city's prominence did not survive, however. The economic trauma of the Civil War was largely to blame.

No city in all of Tennessee is more closely associated with mules than Columbia. During the 19th and early 20th centuries, Columbia's mule market opened on the first Monday of April and people flocked here to buy and sell mules. Other towns, including Lynchburg and Paris, were known for large "First Monday" sales, but Columbia's was the largest.

Ancestral Home of James Knox Polk

The United States' 11th president, James Knox

President James K. Polk's family home in Columbia is now a museum.

Polk, was born in North Carolina but moved to Middle Tennessee with his family when he was 11 years old. Before moving to town, Polk's family lived for several years on a farm north of Columbia, from where Polk's father ran successful plantations, speculated in land, and was involved in local politics.

The home where James Polk lived as a teenager and young man in Columbia is the only house remaining, besides the White House, where Polk ever lived. It is now the Ancestral Home of James Knox Polk (301–305 W. 7th St., 931/388-2354, www.jameskpolk.com, Apr.–Oct. Mon.–Sat. 9 A.M.–5 P.M., Sun. 1–5 P.M., Nov.–Mar. Mon.–Sat. 9 A.M.–4 P.M., Sun. 1–5 P.M., adults $7, seniors $6, youths 6–18 $5, children under 6 free), and home to a museum about Polk's life and presidency.

The home has a number of furnishings that belonged to President Polk and his wife, Sarah, while they lived at the White House. Other pieces come from Polk Place, the home that the couple planned and built in Nashville following the end of Polk's presidency in 1849. Sadly, Polk died of cholera just five months after leaving office and so had little opportunity to enjoy the home; Sarah Polk lived for another 42 years following her husband's death and she spent them all at Polk Place.

The Polk home in Columbia was comfortable, but not luxurious, for its time. It was while living here that Polk began his career as a Tennessee lawyer, and eventually won his first seat in the U.S. House of Representatives. He would go on to serve 14 years in the House, four of them as Speaker. He was governor of Tennessee from 1839 to 1841 and defeated Henry Clay, a Whig, to become president in 1845. Polk's presidency was defined by his drive to expand the Union westward, and it was during his term in office that the United States added California, Texas, and Oregon to the territory of the United States.

The Polk home provides a good introduction to this little-known, but nonetheless important, U.S. president.

The Athenaeum Rectory

Once part of a famous finishing school for girls, The Athenaeum Rectory (808 Anthenaeum St., 931/381-4822, Tues.–Sat. 10 A.M.–4 P.M., adults $6, seniors $5, children $1–4) is also an unusual architectural gem. Designed and built by Maury County master builder Nathan Vaught, the Rectory was the home of Rev. Franklin Gillette Smith and his family. Smith came to Columbia from Vermont in 1837 to run the Columbia Female Institute, an Episcopal girls' finishing school.

In 1851, Smith decided to open his own school for girls. He built the Columbia Athenaeum School next to the Rectory, which remained his family home. Its name refers to Athena, the goddess of wisdom, and has come to mean "seat of learning."

For 52 years the Athenaeum educated young women in art, music, history, science and business. The library houses more than 16,000 volumes and the school sat on 22 wooded acres of land. Ladies took part in gymnastics, bowling, croquet, and tennis. At its peak, the Athenaeum housed 125 boarding students, plus day students from the surrounding area.

The Athenaeum remained open until 1904; after the deaths of Rev. Smith and his wife, it was operated by their son. From 1904 to 1914, the Athenaeum served as the community's high school, and in 1915 the school was torn down and the Columbia High School built in its place. The Athenaeum Rectory was preserved, however, and visitors can tour the Moorish-Gothic structure that housed the parlor and reception area for the school.

The rectory is operated by the Association for the Preservation of Tennessee Antiquities. For a week every summer they offer the 1861 Athenaeum Girls' School, when girls 14–18 years dress up in period clothing and study topics like etiquette, penmanship, and archery. Every May, they offer a weekend course for women 19 years and older.

Mule Day

Columbia's Mule Day (931/381-9557, www.muleday.com) takes place over four days in mid-April. The festival's roots are in the First Monday mule market that took place in Columbia during the period when work animals were indispensable to Tennessee farmers. In many cases, mules were a farmer's most valuable asset—a good pair of mules could make a poor farmer rich.

Mules were more expensive than horses or oxen, and more highly prized. They were said to be stronger, smarter, and more surefooted than other work animals. Their temperament can be stubborn, but some mules are easy and willing to work. For this reason, mule breeders were important, influential, and, often, quite wealthy.

Today's Mule Day is more festival than mule market, although the event does includes mule sales, mule and donkey seminars, and mule shows and competitions. The highlight is the Mule Day Parade on Saturday morning, when thousands of people crowd to see school bands, mules, and colorful troops parade down the

THE HEARTLAND

PHOTO COURTESY OF TENNESSEE DEPARTMENT OF TOURIST DEVELOPMENT

Mule Day in Columbia

road. There is also live music, storytelling, dancing, gospel singing, and the crowning of the Mule Day Queen. Activities take place at various locations in Columbia, but the heart of Mule Day is the Maury County Park on Lion Parkway.

Accommodations

Columbia has more choices of chain hotels than any other city in Maury County. **Jameson Inn** (715 S. James M. Campbell Blvd., 931/388-3326, $85–90) is a 55-room hotel with all the amenities: complimentary breakfast, fitness center, free wireless Internet, pool, big televisions, movie channels, and ironing boards. Premium rooms add microwaves, refrigerators, and coffeemakers. The inn is located across the street from the Columbia Mall and downtown.

Locally owned, the **Richland Inn** (2405 Hwy. 31, 931/381-4500, www.columbia-richlandinn.com, $70–100) is a 147-room inn with singles, doubles, and suites. There is a continental breakfast and a family restaurant next door.

A host of motels are found around exit 46 on I-65, about 10 miles east of Columbia. They include **Comfort Inn** (1544 Bear Creek Pike, 931/388-2500, $75–100) and **Holiday Inn Express** (1558 Bear Creek Pike, 931/380-1227, $75–120).

Food

Located on the courthouse square, **Square Market and Cafe** (35 Public Sq., 931/840-3636, Mon.–Thurs. 9 A.M.–2:30 P.M., Fri. 9 A.M.–9 P.M., Sat. 10:30 A.M.–9 P.M., $6–19) serves breakfast and lunch throughout the week, and dinner on Friday and Saturday nights. The weekday menu features salads, sandwiches, and soups. The signature Polk's Roasted Pear Salad of greens, blue cheese, walnuts, and roasted-pear vinaigrette is a favorite for lunch. Heartier appetites can choose hot steamed sandwiches, or the Tennessee Hot Brown, a hot open-faced turkey sandwich topped with white sauce, cheddar cheese, and bacon. The café brews good coffee and the desserts are homemade. Weekend dinner includes entrées like baked salmon with dill caper sauce, spinach-and-garlic ravioli, and Eastern Shore crab cakes. There is live music, too.

For country cooking, hearty breakfasts, and plate-lunch specials, head to **Bucky's Family Restaurant** (1102 Carmack Blvd., 931/381-2834, daily 5 A.M.–2 P.M., $4–12).

The best steakhouse in the area, **The Ole Lamplighter Inn** (1000 Riverside Dr., 931/381-3837, Mon.–Sat. 4:30–9 P.M., $10–26) will satisfy the biggest appetite with charbroiled steak, all-you-can-eat soup and salad buffet, bottomless soft drinks, plus seafood and shrimp options. The Lamplighter looks a bit like a log cabin from the outside, and inside it has a low-light tavern feel that hastens relaxation. Come here to enjoy good food at good prices.

Information

The **Middle Tennessee Visitors Bureau** (302 W. 7th St., 931/381-7176 or 888/852-1860, www.antebellum.com) operates a visitors center across the street from the James K. Polk house. The visitors center (931/840-8324) is open Monday–Saturday 9 A.M.–4 P.M.

MOUNT PLEASANT

A few miles down Highway 43 from Columbia is the small town of Mount Pleasant. Once known as the Phosphate Capital of the World, Mount Pleasant is now a quiet town with an unusually large number of beautiful old homes. Many of them were built with money earned from the phosphate industry. During the early boom years of the 1890s, the promise of quick money attracted hundreds of men to work in the mines. Law and order was haphazard until a Texas Ranger named Captain Russell arrived.

Sights

You can learn about the phosphate industry at the **Mount Pleasant/Maury County Phosphate Museum** (Public Sq., 931/379-9511, Mon.–Sat. 9:30 A.M.–4:30 P.M., $1). In addition to information about phosphate, the museum houses artifacts of local history, Civil War memorabilia, and local crafts.

Mount Pleasant has a nice variety of historic homes, but most are closed to the public. The **Breckenridge Hatter's Shop** (205 N. Main St.), believed to be the oldest building still standing in town, is an original log cabin covered with weatherboarding in the 1920s. The **Price-Jackson House** (209 N. Main St.) was built in 1849 and served as an insurance office for many years.

A few blocks away from the town square, Pleasant Street is home to at least three elegant old homes. **Manor Hall** (300 Pleasant St.) once sat on a property of more than 1,200 acres. Martin Luther Stockard had it built in 1859 for his second wife, using money he inherited from his first wife and her brother. The **John Ruhm-Graham Home** (106 Pleasant St.) was built in 1910 for Mr. John Rhum, one of the "captains of the phosphate industry." It has the only elevator in Mount Pleasant. The **Jenkins-Bradburn House** (104 Pleasant St.) is a three-story log house built in 1917.

Drive northward on Main Street (Hwy. 243) to find more stately homes. **Walnut Grove** (510 N. Main St.) was built in 1858 and includes a detached kitchen believed to be the oldest brick building in Mount Pleasant. Inside, ash floors are laid at random widths.

Rattle and Snap

Considered by some to be the finest antebellum home in Tennessee, Rattle and Snap (1522 N. Main St., aka Hwy. 243, 931/379-1700, www.rattleandsnapplantation.com) was built by George Washington Polk in 1845. Its extravagance was unmatched by any other home of the period: the 10 Corinthian columns that stand at the front of the mansion were made in Cincinnati, shipped by steamboat to Nashville, and brought over land by oxcart to Maury County. The marble mantels came from Italy; the gardens were designed by a German landscape architect; and a glorious Waterford chandelier hangs over the dining room table. The fine craftsmanship throughout the home is attributed to slaves who labored on the construction.

The story goes that Rattle and Snap was named after an eponymous popular game of the period involving dried beans that were rattled and rolled with a snap of the fingers. Polk claimed that he won the land on which the mansion sits in a rattle and snap game with the governor of North Carolina.

The house was spared during the Civil War, reportedly after the Union commander and field captain noticed that Polk was wearing a Masonic ring in his portrait. Polk's wealth did not survive the war, however, and in 1867 he sold the property to J. J. Granberry, who occupied the home for 50 years and renamed it Oakwood Hall. In 1919 it changed hands again and for many years tenant farmers lived in the deteriorating mansion. Rattle and Snap owes its restoration to Amon Carter Evans, former publisher of the *Tennessean*.

Today, Rattle and Snap is open for group tours of 15 people or more. Overnight guests are also welcome at its Carriage House, and special events are hosted here. Tours, offered year-round, are $13 for adults and $8 for children, and must be booked and paid for in

THE HEARTLAND

advance. Casual visitors will enjoy admiring the property from the highway.

Accommodations

Sleep in the Carriage House at **Rattle and Snap Plantation** (1522 N. Main St., aka Hwy. 243, 931/379-1700, www.rattleandsnapplantation.com, $250), and you will enjoy your own private tour of one of the state's most famous antebellum homes. The Carriage House is a three-bedroom guesthouse located at the rear of the mansion. It includes two queen-sized bedrooms and a sleeping loft with two twin beds. There is also a kitchen, sitting room, and patio where guests can relax and prepare meals. No children are allowed, and smoking is not permitted. There is a two-night minimum stay.

Located about 15 minutes from Mount Pleasant in Hampshire, **Ridgetop Bed and Breakfast** (Hwy. 412, 931/285-2777, www.bbonline.com/tn/ridgetop, $85–100) is a rural getaway with a standard guest room and two private cottages. The cottages are unique: the Swiss Cottage is a postage stamp–sized Swiss chalet, with a queen-sized bed downstairs and upstairs sleeping loft with two additional beds. The log cabin evokes frontier life, but with modern amenities including air-conditioning and a private bathroom. All meals are served in the main dining room. Proprietors Bill and Kay Jones run a reservation agency for bed-and-breakfasts along the Natchez Trace Parkway, and will be happy to book onward accommodation for you.

HOHENWALD

The unassuming county seat of Lewis County, Hohenwald developed in the 1890s, when a railroad was built through rural Lewis County. Starting in 1895, immigrants from Switzerland moved to the area as part of a settlement scheme advanced by a Swiss-American developer, J. G. Probst. The immigrants laid out and built New Switzerland immediately adjacent to the older town of Hohenwald. The two communities are now united.

THE ELEPHANT SANCTUARY

Tucked into the rural landscape of central Tennessee, near the small town of Hohenwald, more than 20 African and Asian elephants retired from circuses and zoos have found refuge.

The Elephant Sanctuary at Hohenwald is a licensed and enlightened nonprofit program that provides a place where retired elephants can live peacefully and as naturally as possible.

The sanctuary was established in 1995 and has grown with support from donors and grants. Today it is a 2,700-acre park, with a heated barn (it can get cold in January) and a spring-fed lake. There are presently 23 elephants living at the sanctuary. They spend their days walking around, interacting with each other, eating, and being bathed or cared for in other ways.

In 2006, elephant caregiver Joanna Burke was killed in a tragic accident when Winkie, one of the sanctuary elephants, knocked her over and stepped on her. The elephant was apparently afraid that Joanna would touch her right eye, which had been stung and was swollen and painful. Elephant experts say that Winkie's behavior was consistent with post-traumatic stress disorder, which has been diagnosed in other retired zoo and circus elephants.

Burke's death was a sad event for the sanctuary, but in keeping with the wishes of Burke and her family, Winkie was not put to sleep, although new protocols were established for animals with a history of aggression. Burke is buried at the elephant sanctuary.

Visitors are not allowed at the elephant sanctuary (unless you are a major donor), but you can watch live elephant cams on their website at www.elephants.com. The sanctuary is planning to build a visitors center once they raise the necessary funds.

For many years, the Alpine character of Hohenwald was evident. A Swiss Singing Society was formed, and Swiss and German Reformed Churches held services in German. The European heritage survived until World War II, when anti-German sentiment caused many to abandon their cultural heritage. Today, traces of Hohenwald's Alpine heritage are faint, having been supplanted by those of Middle Tennessee.

Meriwether Lewis Gravesite and Memorial

Lewis County is named for Meriwether Lewis, the U.S. army captain and private secretary to president Thomas Jefferson, who is best known as the leader, along with William Clark, of the Lewis and Clark expedition to the Pacific Ocean from 1805 to 1806. His gravesite and a memorial sit along the Natchez Trace Parkway about seven miles east of Hohenwald. This is where Lewis died, under mysterious circumstances, while traveling the trace bound for Washington, D.C., in 1809.

According to accounts, Lewis, who was appointed governor of the Louisiana Territory following his successful expedition, was upset by accusation of financial mismanagement. He was traveling to Washington to clear his name, and on the night of October 11, 1809, he stayed at Grinder's Stand, a homestead whose owners boarded travelers along the trace. In the morning, Lewis was found shot to death in his bed. His death was called a suicide, although a few months later a friend came to investigate the circumstances and pronounced that Lewis was murdered. Lewis was just 35 years old when he died.

While the circumstances of Lewis's death remain a mystery, his legacy remains alive. Several monuments to him have been erected at and around his gravesite, and a modest museum tells the story of his life.

The Meriwether Lewis site is located at the intersection of the Natchez Trace Parkway and U.S. Highway 20. There is a campground, picnic area, and restroom nearby.

Natural Bridge

Hidden away at the privately owned and operated Tennessee Fitness Spa and Retreat (299 Natural Bridge Rd., 931/722-5589) is one of this area's most remarkable natural attractions, a double-span natural bridge.

Here a tributary of the Buffalo River has etched away at the bedrock for thousands of years, eventually creating a natural bridge formation that is marvelous to look at.

The bridge invites exploration. You can walk along the side of the trickling stream, and climb up to view the bridge from above. The sight of layer upon layer of rock, which has been carved out over many thousands of years, is remarkable.

A few hundred yards from the natural bridge is a small cave, also open to visitors. Lights have been placed inside to make it easy to explore.

Natural Bridge is located along State Route 99, between Hohenwald and Waynesboro. Tennessee Fitness allows the public to visit natural bridge and the cave on Sundays only. Come between 9 A.M. and 5 P.M. and check in at the office first. Admission is free.

Buffalo River

The Buffalo River, a tributary of the Duck River, flows through northern Wayne County. It is a picturesque and placid river, ideal for canoeing.

Located on Highway 13 where it crosses the Buffalo, **Clearwater Canoe Rental** (931/722-3081, www.clearwatercanoes.com) offers canoe rentals, an RV park, and rustic cabins. A five-hour float costs $30 per canoe; discounts are available for large groups.

Accommodations

Look for accommodations in Lawrenceburg, Columbia, and Mount Pleasant.

Food

The **General Cafe** (101 Park Ave. N., 931/796-3990, Mon.–Thurs. 5 A.M.–8 P.M., Fri.–Sat. 5 A.M.–9 P.M., Sun. 5 A.M.–2 P.M., $3–7) is the best place to eat in Hohenwald, and a good place to meet lots of people. The menu has burgers and sandwiches, catfish, and daily plate-lunch specials, like meatloaf, chicken and dressing, and baked chicken. For breakfast, have the ham and eggs with biscuits.

THE FARM

In 1970, hippie spiritual leader Stephen Gaskin and 320 others established a commune in the rural Tennessee countryside near Summertown, Tennessee. Initially governed by beliefs that forbade alcohol and birth control and promoted nonviolence and respect for the environment, the Farm has evolved over the years. While it has loosened some rules, it remains committed to peace, justice, and environmental sustainability.

The Farm (Summertown, 931/964-3574, www.thefarmcommunity.com) has established a number of successful businesses, and it has contributed to its mission for a more peaceful and healthy world. Its businesses include a book publishing company, a soy dairy that manufactures tofu and soy milk, and a yoga studio. Farm books include *The Farm Vegetarian Cookbook* and Ina May Gaskin's works on natural childbirth. Nonprofits on the Farm include Plenty International, an international aid organization, and the Farm School, which provides alternative education for primary through secondary grades.

The Farm is glad to receive visitors. The Ecovillage Training Center puts on workshops and conferences throughout the year, many of them dealing with organic gardening, permaculture, construction, and other sustainable technologies. The Farm also operates a midwifery training center and birthing houses, where women can come to give birth.

About 200 people live at the Farm today. A few have been there since the beginning, but there are also recent transplants. Some work at Farm enterprises, but others have jobs "off the Farm." Farm members become shareholders in the company that owns the Farm land and other assets.

Visiting the Farm

The Farm is a welcoming and friendly place, where people wave at each other and you can strike up a conversation with just about anybody. The **Welcome Center** (100 Farm Rd.) has a museum about the community and sells Farm books, T-shirts, and other products. It is usually open Monday–Friday 1–5 P.M., but it is a good idea to call ahead to confirm; hours are normally cut back from November to March. You can arrange for a tour with a member of the Farm by calling ahead to the welcome center. There are also twice-yearly Farm Experience weekends for people who want to see what Farm living is about.

The **Farm Store** (931/964-4356) is open daily 9 A.M.–7 P.M. and sells organic and natural groceries, household items, vegetarian sandwiches, and drinks.

Accommodations

You can sleep the night at the Farm. The Inn at the Farm is part of the Ecovillage Training Center, and it offers dormitory-style accommodations. Reservations are required, and the inn is sometimes full when there are workshops or conferences underway.

A half-dozen Farm residents rent out rooms to visitors, usually for about $35 a night per person. Meals may be available for an additional fee. There is also a campground, where you can pitch your own tent. For more information about staying at the Farm, call the welcome center or go online.

Getting There

The Farm is located off Drake's Lane Road, a few miles west of Summertown along Route 20. Detailed directions and a map are available on the Farm website.

ETHRIDGE

In 1944, three Amish families moved to the countryside near Ethridge, in rural Lawrence County. According to some accounts, they came seeking a place where they would not be required to send their children to large, consolidated secondary schools. They also were in search of land where they could farm and make a home.

Over the years the Amish population in Lawrence County has waxed and waned, and estimates put it between 100 and 200 families now. The Amish are known for their conservative dress, rejection of modern technology, including electricity, and their preference to keep to themselves. They are also excellent farmers, craftsmen, and cooks, devout Christians, and peace-lovers. Most of the Amish in this part of Tennessee speak English and Pennsylvania Dutch, and some also know German.

As you drive through the back roads that criss-cross the Amish area, you will be able to identify the Amish homes because they are old-fashioned farmhouses, without electricity wires, cars, or mechanized farm equipment. You will also notice their fields of corn, peanuts, wheat, oats, tobacco, hay, and oats, and you may see a black horse-drawn buggy—their primary form of transportation.

Many Amish sell goods, ranging from handmade furniture to molasses. As you drive, you will see signs advertising various products for sale. You are welcome to stop by and buy something. Remember that due to their religious beliefs, the Amish do not allow their pictures to be taken. Please respect this fact when you visit them.

If you prefer, you can explore Amish country with a guide on a wagon tour. Such tours are offered by local Lawrence County residents, who are not Amish. Each tour lasts about 90 minutes and will take you to several farms where you can meet the Amish and buy products from them. Tours are provided twice daily Monday–Saturday at 10 A.M. and 3:30 P.M. by the **Amish Country Store** (4011 Hwy. 43 N., 931/829-1621). The rate is $10 for adults. You can also call **Jerry's Amish Buggy and Wagon Tours** (931/629-5055).

If you want to drive through on your own, start in Ethridge and explore the narrow back roads bounded by Highway 43 on the east, State Route 242 on the west, Highway 20 on the north, and U.S. Route 64 on the south. You can pick up a free detailed map of Amish country, with specific farms identified, from the **Lawrence Chamber of Commerce** (1609 Locust Ave., aka Hwy. 43, 931/762-4911, www.chamberofcommerce.lawrence.tn.us). You can also buy a map from the **Amish**

Country Mall (4011 Hwy 43 N., 931/829-1621) for $3.

A half-dozen stores along Highway 43 just north of Ethridge sell Amish-made goods for those who don't have time to venture into Amish territory themselves. One of the best is **Dutch Country Bakery** (3939 Hwy. 43 N., 931/829-2147, Mon.–Sat. 7 A.M.–5 P.M.), which sells Amish baked goods, cheeses, and bulk goods. It also serves breakfast and lunch daily.

The Amish work Monday through Saturday. Sunday is their Sabbath, the day that they worship and spend time with family. You won't find any Amish farm stands or homes open for business on Sunday.

LAWRENCEBURG

Lawrenceburg is the seat of Lawrence County, named for a U.S. naval hero of the War of 1812. Built along the Jackson Military Road, Lawrenceburg has long been a center of trade and commerce for the surrounding countryside. It is the hometown of former Tennessee Senator, actor, and unsuccessful presidential aspirant Fred Thompson.

Sights

Founded in 2003 by local Cherokee, the **Cherokee and Davy Crockett Museum** (1 Public Sq., 931/762-3733, Mon.–Sat. 9:30 A.M.–4 P.M.) seeks to preserve the heritage of Lawrence County's Native Americans. It also pays tribute to Davy Crockett, who lived in Lawrence County for about four years and won his first elective office, as justice of the peace, while there.

You can see a replica of Davy Crockett's office at the **Davy Crockett Museum,** located one block south of the public square. It is free and open daily during daylight hours.

The man who popularized Southern Gospel music called Lawrenceburg home, and the town has remembered him with a museum. The **James D. Vaughan Museum** (SunTrust Bank Bldg., Public Sq., 931/762-8991, www.members.tripod.com/vaughanmuseum, Mon.–Fri. 9:30–11:30 A.M. and 1–2:30 P.M., weekends by appointment, free) tells the story of its namesake, who sponsored and recorded the first professional gospel quartets and established the first Southern gospel magazine and radio station. He also established the Vaughn School of Music, where he taught students to sing, and published millions of shape-note songbooks. Vaughn has been called the father of Southern gospel music, and Lawrenceburg has been declared its birthplace.

Events

Taking place in early June and again over Labor Day weekend, the **Summertown Bluegrass Reunion** (64 Monument Rd., Summertown, 931/964-2100, www.webpages.charter.net/terrypierce) is an authentic showcase of homegrown bluegrass music. Bring your lawn chair and take a seat under the canopy of trees to enjoy a seemingly limitless smorgasbord of bluegrass music. During the late afternoons, the main stage closes for an hour for a shade-tree band contest, a real case of dueling banjos. The audience picks the winner. Dance for fun, or in one of the afternoon buck dancing contests.

The bluegrass reunions take place at a private campground in Summertown, located about 13 miles north of Lawrenceburg. Admission is under $10 each day. Most festival attendees camp in RVs on the grounds; tents are also allowed.

Accommodations

Choose from a handful of standard-issue motels in Lawrenceburg. The **Best Western/Villa Inn** (2126 N. Locust Ave., aka Hwy. 43, 931/762-4448, $66–75) has been refurbished. The **Richland Inn** (2125 N. Locust Ave., aka Hwy. 43, 931/762-0061, $63–73) has double and king-sized rooms, plus executive suites. Rooms have cable TV, in-room data jacks, and irons. There is a free continental breakfast, business center, and plenty of RV and truck parking.

Food

The **Paradise Cafe** (12 Public Sq., 931/762-0067, Mon.–Thurs. 10 A.M.–3 P.M., Fri.–Sat. 10 A.M.–8 P.M., $3–9) is a homey establishment that serves spaghetti dinners as well as traditional dishes like chuck steak, chicken and dressing, and pork chops. They also serve breakfast.

Square Forty Restaurant (40 Public Sq., 931/762-2868, Mon.–Sat. 7:30 A.M.–2 P.M., $5–15) also serves traditional Southern food and a popular Sunday-morning buffet.

Information

Visitor information for Lawrenceburg and Lawrence County is available from the **Cherokee and Davy Crockett Museum** (1 Public Sq., 931/762-3733). The **Lawrence County Chamber of Commerce** (1609 Locust Ave., aka Hwy 43, 931/762-4911, www.chamberofcommerce.lawrence.tn.us) publishes brochures and has information about local businesses and attractions.

DAVID CROCKETT STATE PARK

One of Lawrenceburg's most famous residents was also one of its earliest. David Crockett, the larger-than-life frontiersman who seems to have been everywhere in Tennessee, was one of Lawrenceburg's first commissioners and justices of the peace. He and his family operated a gristmill, powder mill, and distillery on the Shoal River a few miles west of town starting in 1817. In 1821, after a flood swept away their home and businesses, the Crocketts moved to northwest Tennessee, where Crockett was elected to Congress. Crockett died in 1836 at the Alamo Mission. The place where he lived in Lawrence County is now the David Crockett State Park.

Recreation

David Crockett is a pleasant park with a lot of amenities, including picnic tables, tennis courts, a restaurant, and an Olympic-sized swimming pool. Crockett Falls is a pleasant place for a picnic.

You can rent paddle boats or fishing boats to explore 40-acre Lindsey Lake (no private boats are allowed). Fishing is permitted from the lake banks or from a boat; people over 13 years old need a valid Tennessee fishing license and everyone must follow state regulations. There is a paved 2.3-mile bike trail and three different hiking trails.

Camping

There are 107 campsites, each with a picnic table, fire pit, and electrical and water hookups for RVs. Bathhouses have hot showers and commodes. Sites are allocated on a first-come, first-served basis only.

Events

Davy Crockett and the pioneer spirit that he symbolizes is celebrated during **Davy Crockett Days** (931/762-9408), a two-day festival that takes place in early August at David Crockett State Park. Festival enthusiasts spend the weekend dressed in period costumes and do thing things that Crockett and his contemporaries would have. Activities include shooting, games, music, food, and old-time traders.

Walking Horse Country

The countryside surrounding Shelbyville is the capital of the Tennessee Walking Horse. The beloved high-stepping creatures known for their smooth gait are bred and shown at farms that dot the rolling hills of south-central Tennessee. The annual Walking Horse National Celebration is one of the largest horse shows in the world. Small towns Wartrace and Bell Buckle are two of the most charming in the whole of Middle Tennessee.

The Tennessee Walking Horse Parkway

Highway 31A from Pulaski to Lewisburg, and Highway 64 from Lewisburg to Wartrace, via Shelbyville, has been designated the Tennessee Walking Horse Parkway and it is the best scenic route through this beautiful terrain. You will pass dozens of horse farms—some large and some small—and you will see some of the handsome horses out grazing in the field.

LEWISBURG

Lewisburg is best known for two very different animals: the Tennessee Walking Horse and the fainting goats of Marshall County. Lewisburg is the home of the business end of the famous horse breed: It is here that the Tennessee Walking Horse Breeders' and Exhibitors' Association is located. As for the goats, the story goes that in the 1880s, a mysterious man named Tinsley moved to Marshall County with four goats and a cow. He stayed for only

one growing season, and when he left, he sold his "bulgy-eyed" goats to a local doctor. The goats displayed a strange habit of becoming rigid to the point of losing their balance when startled. Over the years, the fainting goats reproduced. It is now known that their condition is a neurological abnormality called mytonia, which doesn't harm the animals.

Downtown Lewisburg is set around the 1920s-era courthouse. On the north side of the square you'll find one of the most unusual buildings in all of Tennessee. The **Ladies' Rest Room** on 3rd Avenue was built in 1924 to accommodate rural women who traveled to town to shop or sell goods. The building included a reception room, toilets, a bedroom, and a kitchen. In his excellent guide to the area, Judge Robert Brant quotes an unsigned letter received at the county court not long after the restroom was built: "In behalf of the ladies of the county, I desire to thank the gentlemen of the County Court for the beautiful restroom they have given us. . . . We praise this beautiful gift, not merely for its beauty and many conveniences but because it shows that the women of the county are held in love and honored by our men."

Today, the restroom is no longer open to the public, and is in disrepair, although efforts are being made to preserve it.

Entertainment

The **Marshall County Community Theater** operates in the historic Dixie Theater on the

THE HEARTLAND

east side of the town square. Check local listings or contact the chamber of commerce to find out about upcoming performances.

There is an authentic 1940s-era drive-in movie theater less than two miles out of town. The **Hi-way 50 Drive In** (1584 Fayetteville Hwy., 931/270-1591) screens first-run movies Friday, Saturday, and Sunday evenings. For just $5 for adults and $2 for children, guests get to see back-to-back movies at this vintage drive-in theater. The sound system is modern, however (it's tuned to your car radio). There is a concession stand that sells burgers, fries, pizza, and popcorn, but patrons are also welcome to bring their own food. This is a popular weekend treat for local residents.

Events

To celebrate Marshall County's fainting goats, the city of Lewisburg hosts the **Goats, Music, and More Festival** (931/359-1544, www.goatsmusicandmore.com) in October. The free two-day fair features goat shows, arts and crafts displays, and a barbecue cook-off. In the evening major country music and rock acts perform at the town's Rock Creek Park.

Practicalities

For accommodations and food, see *Shelbyville.* For information about Lewisburg, contact the **Marshall County Chamber of Commerce** (227 2nd Ave. N., 931/359-3863, www.marshall chamber.org).

HENRY HORTON STATE PARK

A few miles north of Lewisburg, near the small town of Chapel Hill, is Henry Horton State Park (4358 Nashville Hwy., 931/364-2222). The park is known for its 18-hole championship golf course, skeet range, and inn and conference facilities.

Park amenities include an on-site restaurant that serves country-style meals and buffets, an Olympic-sized swimming pool (inn and cabin guests swim free), hiking trails, and a gift shop.

The park's 18-hole Buford Ellington golf course is a popular destination for golfers in the region. It has a pro shop, dressing rooms, rental clubs, gasoline and pull carts, a driving range, and a practice green. Greens fees are $14–24, depending on the season and day of the week. Call 931/364-2319 to reserve a tee time.

Day-trippers can also enjoy the skeet range, fishing on the Duck River, picnics, horseshoes, tennis courts, volleyball, basketball, andtable tennis.

Accommodations

Accommodations include the park inn, with motel-style rooms, a campground with both tent and RV sites, and seven cabins ideal for families or small groups. Rooms at the park inn rent for between $65 and $80, depending on the season and day of the week. Rooms are air-conditioned and come with a television and telephone. Cabins, which are fully equipped for cooking and housekeeping, rent for $110 a night. Campsites are available for $14.50 or $17.50, depending on the season.

SHELBYVILLE

If any one Tennessee city is home to the Tennessee Walking Horse, it is Shelbyville. Considered the world's greatest pleasure, trail, and show horse, the Tennessee Walking Horse is the first breed of horse to bear the name of a state. Tennessee Walkers existed for many years before the breed was identified and named; early settlers needed horses that could travel easily and comfortably over rocky and uneven terrain. These early walkers were not trained to show—they were purely utilitarian.

Tennessee Walkers are known for their docile temperament and kind manner. They are also known for their unique running walk—in which each of the horse's hooves hit the ground separately at regular intervals. In this gait, the animal's front legs rise in an exaggerated step and the horse's head nods in time with the rhythm of its legs.

Sights

A few miles east of Shelbyville on Highway 64 is **Waterfall Farms** (2395 Hwy. 64 E.,

931/684-7894, www.waterfallfarm.org), one of the few horse farms in this area with an open-door policy on visitors. Just drive on in and check in at the office, where you can ask questions and see photographs of some of the farm's award-winning stallions. You are welcome to walk around the farm and see the magnificent horses, who may be out in the field, in their stables, or otherwise occupied.

For information on other farms that welcome visitors, or opportunities to ride a Tennessee Walking Horse, contact the **Walking Horse Owners' Association** in Murfreesboro at 615/494-8822.

One of only two wineries in the region, **Tri-Star Vineyards and Winery** (168 Scales Rd., 931/294-3062, www.tristarwinery.com) is located about seven miles north of Shelbyville, off Highway 41A. In operation for more than 40 years, Tri-Star makes wines from grapes, muscadines, berries, and fruit. Visitors are welcome Friday and Saturday 10 A.M.–5 P.M. and Sunday noon–5 P.M. The winery is closed during the month of January and on all major holidays.

◖ Tennessee Walking Horse National Celebration

The premier event in Shelbyville is the annual Tennessee Walking Horse National Celebration (931/684-5915, www.twhnc.com), which takes place in late summer for 11 days, ending on the Saturday before Labor Day. This is the event that determines the best of the high-stepping Walking Horses, and it is an exciting time to be a horse fan.

The national celebration routinely attracts 30,000 people per night and more than 5,000 entries. The event takes place at the Celebration Grounds, a few blocks from the courthouse square in Shelbyville.

The Celebration was founded in 1939 as a way to promote Tennessee Walkers. It is an economic experiment that worked. Prize money now tops the half-million-dollar mark, and organizers boast that more than a quarter-million tickets are sold over the 10-day event.

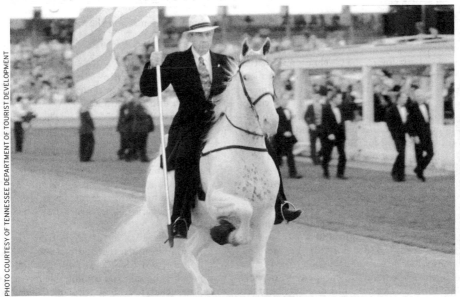

PHOTO COURTESY OF TENNESSEE DEPARTMENT OF TOURIST DEVELOPMENT

THE HEARTLAND

The Tennessee Walking Horse is a champion show horse.

VANNOY STREETER'S WIRE HORSES

Self-taught folk artist Vannoy Streeter drew inspiration for his life's work from the elegant stride and unique step of the Tennessee Walking Horse. Born in Wartrace in 1919 and raised on a horse farm, Streeter first displayed his remarkable talent as a child. His family could not afford to buy toy airplanes and cars, so he made them – bending them out of bailing wire.

Streeter was in Wartrace for the first Walking Horse Celebration, and in later years he returned to the event after it moved to Shelbyville. Streeter was proud of the fact that African Americans trained Strolling Jim and many other world-champion walking horses. He created hundreds, if not thousands, of sculpted horses, each with the distinctive high-stepping front leg and each with an African-American rider on the back. Other favorite subjects were performers – he sculpted Tina Turner and Elvis Presley in particular – and vehicles, including big-rig trucks, locomotives, and airplanes.

Streeter made most of his sculptures out of coat-hanger wire; he bought hangers by the hundreds. He did detail work with fine-gauge wire and large-scale work with bracing wire. He worked with regular pliers, wire cutters, and needle-nosed pliers.

Streeter worked on the railroads, and as a lumberyard hand, janitor, and hospital orderly. In 1960 he met and married his wife, Marie, and became father to her six children. He continued to make his wire sculptures, eventually gaining national attention. In 1990 he was a demonstrating artist at the National Black Arts Festival in Atlanta and in 1992 Shelbyville proclaimed Vannoy Streeter Day. His work has been displayed in the White House and at the Tennessee State Museum in Nashville.

Streeter continued to work until his death in 1998, although his productivity declined after his wife's death. His work is sold in folk art galleries in Nashville and other cities, and has been included in African-American and folk art exhibits in Tennessee and elsewhere.

Winning a show at the Celebration makes a horse more valuable and cements its reputation in the industry.

For horse lovers, the Celebration is exciting and beautiful. For breeders and horse farmers, it is their chance to make it in this competitive and high-stakes business. For the city of Shelbyville and the whole region, it is an economic powerhouse, pumping more than $20 million into the local economy every year.

The Celebration Grounds are used for other horse shows, plus sporting and musical events, year-round. The Nashville Symphony has played here, and shows featuring alpaca, miniature horses, and ponies take place.

Tickets for reserved seats at the Celebration range $7–20 per night and a pass for the whole event is $105. Box seats are more expensive, while general admission tickets to the South Grandstand are cheaper. While tickets for the best seats must be reserved in advance, you can almost always get a seat at the Celebration, even if you show up on the day of the event.

Accommodations

Located within walking distance to the Celebration Grounds in Shelbyville, **Cinnamon Ridge Bed and Breakfast** (799 Whithorne St., 931/685-9200, $65–75) is a five-bedroom guesthouse. Each room has a private bath and television; provisions may be made for a private telephone, daily newspaper, and other services that appeal to business travelers. Full breakfast is served in your choice of the formal dining room or the sunny garden room. There is also a family room, patio, and backyard deck where you can unwind.

Also within walking distance from the Celebration Grounds, the **Bedford Inn** (727 Madison St., 931/684-7858, $40) is a stalwart motel with clean and comfortable rooms. Amenities include televisions, telephones, microwaves and refrigerators, and plenty of parking.

Located in the countryside between Shelbyville and Lynchburg, the **Bottle Hollow Lodge Bed and Breakfast** (Bottle Hollow Rd., 931/695-5253, www.bbonline.com/tn/bottlehollow, $105–150) is a ranch-style single-story building with a commanding view of the surrounding countryside. The lodge has five bedrooms, including a 600-square-foot master suite with a full-sized bathroom, fireplace, and sitting area. Other bedrooms have private bathrooms, TV, and telephones.

You will enjoy privacy in a rural setting at the **Tennessee Horse Country Bed and Breakfast** (311 Robinson Rd., 931/684-1863, www.tennesseehorsecountry.com, $55–145), located on a horse farm about eight miles south of Shelbyville along Highway 231. The property has a guesthouse that sleeps up to four people with a whirlpool tub, full kitchen, living room, and porch, as well as a smaller cottage with a queen-sized bed, full bath, and kitchenette. Both accommodations are entirely private. Your kitchen will be stocked with breakfast foods if you request.

Immerse yourself in the world of the Tennessee Walking Horse at the C **Clearview Horse Farm** (2291 Hwy. 231 S., 931/684-8822, www.clearviewhorsefarm.com, $75). This working horse farm has an indoor area for horse shows, a comfortable and modern barn, and horse trainers. There are three guest rooms at the farm, each with a private bath. The rooms are modern and neat, with ranch-like touches. The Tennessee Walking Horse Room can sleep up to four and would be ideal for families. Guests can enjoy a pool on the property, as well as a fishing lake. There is a continental breakfast. Many guests here are horse owners themselves, although "non-horseys" are welcome too.

Located in the countryside between Lewisburg and Shelbyville, **Haha Farm** (482 Cortner Hollow Rd., Petersburg, 931/680-0423, www.hahafarm.com, $80–90) is a working alpaca and llama farm. The guest room is modest, but the experience here is one-of-a-kind. Breakfast is served family style, and you are invited to explore the farm and meet its unusual residents. The farm-hand special offers accommodation at a reduced rate ($60 per night) in exchange for three hours of work on the farm. On the other side of the spectrum is the farm spa pampering special, which includes a daily massage, for about $145 a night. Owners Steve and Kathy Haber warn that alpacas and llamas are addictive, and that your first llama kiss might well change your life.

Food

For coffee and other pick-me-ups, try **The Coffee Break** (121 South Side Sq., 931/680-2552, Mon.–Fri. 7 A.M.–3 P.M., Sat. 8 A.M.–3 P.M., $4–7).

WARTRACE

This tiny railroad town about 10 miles east of Shelbyville is the birthplace of the Tennessee Walking Horse. It was on the grounds of the town's Walking Horse Hotel, across the railroad tracks from the town square, that Albert Dement trained a $350 plow horse into **Strolling Jim,** the first world grand champion walking horse. Strolling Jim died in 1957, and is buried in the pasture behind the hotel.

The annual walking horse celebration that now draws a quarter million people to Shelbyville every year started in Wartrace, but got too big for the small town and moved to Shelbyville in 1935.

Today, Wartrace is a sleepy yet surprisingly pleasing town. The old residential district lies along a few quiet side streets that climb gently along a hillside. The howl of frequent freight trains—between 20 and 25 pass through daily—harkens to an earlier era.

Shopping

In certain circles, the name J. W. Gallagher is well known. Gallagher was born near Wartrace in 1915 and opened a woodworking shop in 1939. Skilled at furniture and cabinet-making, it was Gallagher's guitars that made him famous. From 1969 onwards Gallagher only made guitars. In 1976, Gallagher's son, Don, took over the business. There are not many Gallagher guitars out there—between 1965 and 1990 just over 2,000 were made—because each instrument is handcrafted from beginning to end.

Gallagher's Guitar Shop (5 Main St., 931/389-6455, www.gallagherguitar.com) is a non-descript storefront with the word "Gallagher's" on the front.

Accommodations

The ☾ **Walking Horse Hotel** (101 Spring St., 931/389-7030, www.walkinghorsehotel.com, $100) is the best place to stay not only in Wartrace, but for a good distance in any direction. When Joe Peters bought the hotel in 2007 he was intent on paying tribute to his late wife, Chais, who loved the old 1917 hotel. Peters and his family have brought new life to the old hotel by refurbishing the rooms, recruiting beloved chef Bill Hall to run the Strolling Jim Restaurant, and opening the Chais Music Hall, a state-of-the-art venue for all types of music. Rooms are a fusion of old and new. Classic touches from the hotel's early days have been preserved, but guests can expect the best modern amenities, including flat-screen televisions, wireless Internet, super-comfortable beds, and good linens.

Another choice in Wartrace is the **Historic Main Street Inn** (207 Main St. E., 931/389-0389, www.historicmainstreetinn.com, $95–115), a bed-and-breakfast located half a block from main street. Each of the five guest rooms are lavishly decorated in a romantic style fitting for the 1906 Queen Anne home. All rooms have a private bath—some have antique claw-footed tubs. Breakfast here is nothing simple or quick; expect choices like homemade fruit crepes, baked apple pancake, or stuffed French toast. Built by a local banker, the home has been operated as a bed-and-breakfast since 1996.

Food

The **Iron Gait** (106 Fairfield Rd., 931/389-6001, Mon.–Fri. 7 A.M.–2 P.M., Sat. 7 A.M.–7 P.M., Sun. 1–4 P.M., $3–8) serves breakfast, burgers, and meat-and-three dinners. The monster burger is a favorite, as are the plate lunches. Find the Iron Gait just

around the corner from Main Street, on the road to Bell Buckle.

For other dining choices, look in Bell Buckle, Normandy, and Shelbyville.

Information

The **Wartrace Chamber of Commerce** (931/389-9999, www.wartracechamber.com) promotes the town.

BELL BUCKLE

A tiny town nestled in the northern reaches of the Walking Horse region, Bell Buckle is a charming place to visit. Once a railroad town, Bell Buckle has successfully become a destination for antiques shopping, arts and crafts, small-town hospitality, and country cooking. The town's single commercial street faces the old railroad tracks; handsome old homes—some of them bed-and-breakfast inns—spread out along quiet residential streets.

What makes Bell Buckle so appealing is the sense of humor that permeates just about everything that happens here. T-shirts for sale on the main street proclaim "Tokyo, Paris, New York, Bell Buckle," and the town's quirky residents feel free to be themselves. Tennessee's poet laureate, Margaret "Maggi" Britton Vaughn, who operates the Bell Buckle Press and had an office on Main Street for many years, once told an interviewer that William Faulkner "would have killed" for a community with the ambience, and characters, of Bell Buckle.

Bell Buckle's name is derived from the Bell Buckle Creek, named thus because a cow's bell was found hanging in a tree by the creek, attached by a buckle.

The town's annual RC and Moon Pie Festival in June attracts thousands to the small town, and the Webb School Arts and Crafts Festival in October is one of the finest regional arts shows in the state.

Sights

Bell Buckle is noted as the home of the elite and well-regarded **Webb School.** Founded in 1870 and led by William Robert Webb until his death in 1926, Webb School has graduated

10 Rhodes scholars, several governors, attorneys general, and numerous successful academics. The school now has about 300 students in grades 8 through 12 from around the country and the world. While it was all-male for many years of its life, Webb School now admits both male and female students. Its athletic mascot is the "Webb Feet."

The Webb campus is about three blocks north of downtown Bell Buckle. You can visit the main administrative office during regular business hours, where there are photographs and school memorabilia on display.

Events

Bell Buckle's biggest annual event is the **RC and Moon Pie Festival** in mid-June. This weekend event includes country and bluegrass music, Moon Pie games, arts and crafts booths, the crowning of a Moon Pie King and Queen, and a 10-mile run. You can also witness the cutting of the world's largest Moon Pie. In case you're wondering why Bell Buckle has rights to the Moon Pie festival, it's because they asked for it.

The **Webb School Arts and Crafts Festival** in October brings hundreds of artisans to town. It is one of the finest arts and crafts shows in the region, attracting fine and folk artists from Tennessee and beyond.

Shopping

The single most popular pursuit in Bell Buckle is shopping. Antiques are the main attraction, but arts and crafts are a close second.

The **Bell Buckle Art Gallery** (26 Railroad Sq., 931/389-0004) sells a wide selection of artwork, from pottery and sculpture to paintings. Most pieces here have a fresh, modern appeal.

The **Cat's Meow** (25 Railroad Sq., 931/389-0064) has purses, totes, linens, throws, and jewelry, plus lots of gifts for babies and new parents. The **Doodle Bug** and **Doodle Bug Too** (Railroad Sq., 931/389-9009) are sister shops that sell jewelry, housewares, gifts, and folk art.

For antiques try the **Bell Buckle Antique Mall** (112 Main St., 931/389-6174) or **Blue Ribbon Antiques** (Railroad Sq., 931/684-2588).

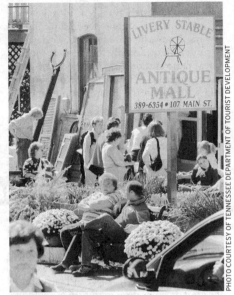

antique shopping in Bell Buckle

PHOTO COURTESY OF TENNESSEE DEPARTMENT OF TOURIST DEVELOPMENT

Accommodations

Hostess Ina Mingle runs the **Mingle House Bed and Breakfast** (116 Main St., 931/389-9453, $80–85) in a restored 1898 Victorian home. Rooms are furnished with antiques, and guests can fuel up with a country-style breakfast of eggs, sausage, bacon, and more in the morning.

Food

There's no debate about where to eat in Bell Buckle. The **Bell Buckle Cafe** (Railroad Sq., 931/389-9693, Mon. 10:30 A.M.–2 P.M., Tues.–Thurs. 10:30 A.M.–8 P.M., Fri.–Sat. 10:30 A.M.–9 P.M., Sun. 11 A.M.–5 P.M., $5–15) is not only a Bell Buckle institution, it's the only game in town. The menu is Southern, with a few refined touches (like ostrich burgers and spinach-strawberry salad) you won't find at most small-town cafés. The menu is also mighty diverse, with seafood, pasta, and sandwiches in addition to the usual plate lunches and dinner entrées. The large dining room fills up quick, especially for lunch, so there's no shame in coming a

THE HEARTLAND

bit early. The Bell Buckle Cafe takes care of your entertainment needs too. There's always live music on Thursday, Friday, and Saturday night, usually bluegrass or country. Local radio station WLIJ broadcasts a musical variety show from the café on Saturday 1–3 P.M., which is a great reason to come to the café for lunch.

If you managed to pass up homemade dessert at the Bell Buckle Cafe, then head to **Bluebird Antiques and Ice Cream Parlor** (15 Webb Rd., 931/389-6549). Here you'll find a turn-of-the-20th-century soda fountain with hand-dipped ice cream and homemade waffle cones. Come in the morning to see (and smell) them making the cones. Not to be missed.

Information

The **Bell Buckle Chamber of Commerce** (931/389-9663, www.bellbucklechamber.com) publishes brochures, promotes the town, and operates as a clearinghouse for information.

The Southern Heartland

The region of Tennessee south of Walking Horse Country and east of the Natchez Trace is a fertile area known for farming, the railroad, and a very famous brand of sipping whiskey. The Jack Daniel's Distillery in Lynchburg is the greatest single draw in this region, but there are other reasons to come.

Tims Ford Lake near Winchester and Tullahoma is ideal for boating and fishing. The Elk River that runs near Fayetteville is perfect for canoeing, and the tiny railroad town of Cowan is a down-home gem waiting to be discovered. The biggest music festival in all of Tennessee, Bonnaroo, takes place every summer near Manchester. Perhaps the best-kept secret in the whole area is the George Dickel Distillery in lovely Normandy.

PULASKI

The city of Pulaski has two significant claims to fame. The first is that it was here that a 21-year-old Confederate soldier, Sam Davis, was executed by the Union army for spying. Davis was captured in Giles County on November 20, 1863, carrying sensitive Union papers. When he refused to say where he got them, Davis was sentenced to death. The young soldier's final words, written in a letter to his mother, immortalized his sacrifice: "If I had a thousand lives, I would give them all before I would betray a friend or the confidence of my informer."

Pulaski's second, and better-known, claim to fame is that it was here that the Ku Klux Klan was established. The Klan that came to life in Pulaski in the spring of 1866 was a different organization than the one which is now associated with that name.

Sights

If you see only one county courthouse in this part of Tennessee, let it be the **Giles County Courthouse,** an elegant neoclassical courthouse that has been called the most beautiful in Tennessee. Built of brick and marble, the finest feature is a three-story rotunda capped by a dome and skylight. In the cupola, the 1858 bell strikes the hours. A ladies' restroom in the basement was a place where women and children who had come to town to shop could rest a spell before making the long journey back into the countryside. The restroom was furnished with several beds and a cradle.

The courthouse is the county's fifth. The first was a rough log cabin, and it was abandoned as the county grew. The second and third courthouses were destroyed by fire, and the fourth courthouse, completed in 1859, survived the Civil War only because Thomas Martin, a prominent citizen and the founder of Martin College, paid a $3,000 bribe to the Federals. The fourth courthouse did not survive to the present, however; it too was destroyed by fire, this time in 1907. The current

© SUSANNA HENIGHAN POTTER

A statue of Confederate hero Sam Davis stands sentry outside the Giles County Courthouse in Pulaski.

courthouse was completed in 1909 at a cost of $132,000 and was made fireproof.

The courthouse is surrounded by a bustling courthouse square, fronted by businesses including antiques shops and restaurants.

Pulaski has two monuments to the boy hero of the Confederacy. A statue of Sam Davis stands at the south side of the courthouse. The statue was erected in 1909 by the United Daughters of the Confederacy.

The second monument is on Sam Davis Avenue, where Davis was executed. A small museum is located here, but it does not have regular hours. Call the Giles County Tourism Foundation at 931/363-3789 to arrange for someone to open it for you.

Pulaski is a lovely town, with a number of beautiful old homes. Two of the most noteworthy are the **Brown-Daly-Horne Home** (307 West Madison St.), which was the home of one-time Tennessee Governor John C. Brown. Brown served as the chairman of the convention that rewrote the Tennessee constitution in 1870. He did so well that Tennesseans elected him their 19th governor in 1870. The home is an excellent example of the Queen Anne style. It now houses a bank.

The second prominent home is the **Thomas Martin House** (302 S. 2nd St.), built in 1842 by Thomas Martin, who founded Martin College. It was a hotel in the early 20th century, and is now a bank.

Two different groups of Cherokee Indians passed through Pulaski during the 1838–1839 removal, now called the Trail of Tears. The city is developing a park and interpretive center about the Trail of Tears on Stadium Street. The center is projected to open in 2009, pending funds. Until then, you can see the site of its future home.

Entertainment

The **Martin Movie Theater** (S. 5th St., 931/424-7373, www.moviesatmartin.com) shows movies on Friday and Saturday nights and Saturday and Sunday afternoons.

THE HEARTLAND

Accommodations

Located on a quiet residential street in town, **Miss Butler's Bed and Breakfast** (429 W. Jefferson St., 931/424-0014, www.missbutlers.com, $80–110) is an 1888 Georgian-style townhouse that has five separate guest rooms. Each room is named for a historical figure with ties to Giles County: among them are Sam Davis, Frank Mars, and Tennessee governor John C. Brown. The house is named after Miss Margaret Butler, an educator and historian of the area. Each room has a private bath and telephone. Guests have access to a fax machine and there is wireless Internet throughout the home. Guests also enjoy privileges at a local country club, where you can play golf or tennis or swim.

For hotel accommodations, choose from the **Richland Inn** (1020 W. College St., 931/363-0006, $80–85) and the **Comfort Inn of Pulaski** (1140 W. College St., 931/424-1600, $130).

Food

There are several casual restaurants downtown, perfect for lunch. **Reeves Drugs** (125 N. 1st

THE ORIGINS OF THE KU KLUX KLAN

The Ku Klux Klan was established in the spring of 1866 in Pulaski by six ex-Confederate soldiers, who saw it as a secret society for fun and entertainment. They adopted some of the trappings of a college fraternity, and performed initiation rituals and pranks. During the second half of 1866, new "dens" of the Ku Klux Klan were formed in nearby counties, but there was no evidence of the vigilantism and violence that has come to be associated with the KKK.

Between 1867 and 1868, the political nature of the KKK emerged. Ex-Confederate soldiers home from the war were unhappy with Reconstruction policies that promoted voting rights for African Americans and gave preferences to former Union soldiers and sympathizers. The KKK was seen as a way to resist these policies. Members met for a convention in Nashville in 1867 and a year later Nathan Bedford Forrest was elected to be the first and only Grand Wizard of the Klan.

During this period, the Klan was strongest in Giles, Humphreys, Lincoln, Marshall, and Maury Counties in Middle Tennessee and Dyer, Fayette, Gibson, Hademan, and Obion Counties in West Tennessee. Klansmen intimidated African Americans with attacks, whippings, and murder. They were particularly active during the 1868 election, when many African Americans voted for the first time.

Tennessee governor William Brownlow was a staunch Unionist and was resolved to put an end to the Klan's activities. In 1868 he announced new, harsh penalties for being associated with the Klan. He hired a private detective from Cincinnati to infiltrate the Klan and give names of people who were involved. After the detective turned up dead in February 1869, Brownlow declared martial law in six Middle Tennessee counties.

Brownlow's tenure as governor was just about up, however. A week later he resigned to take a seat in the U.S. Senate. His successor, Dewitt Senter, was less strident in his views and less controversial in his actions. Later that year, Forrest called for the end of the Klan, saying that it had served its purpose.

For about 50 years, the KKK was dormant. But in Georgia in 1915 it was resurrected, and remained active in the Deep South, including Tennessee, for the next 30 years. Members intimidated and terrorized blacks, Jews, and other minorities; they murdered and maimed men and women; they attacked whites who were seen to sympathize with minorities. The Klan's political influence helped to elect Tennessee governor Austin Peay in 1923 and U.S. senator Lawrence D. Tyson in 1924, among others.

Since the Klan was disbanded in 1944, its name has been adopted by various right-wing, extremist, and racist organizations, some of whom have tried to stage events in Pulaski, the birthplace of the KKK. Town residents have fought these events, wishing to leave behind their historic association with the Ku Klux Klan.

St., 931/363-2561, Mon.–Sat. 8 A.M.–5:45 P.M., $3–5) is an old-fashioned drugstore lunch counter, serving sandwiches and ice cream. **The Coffee Corner** (102 S. 2nd St., 931/363-1911, Mon.–Fri. 7 A.M.–6 A.M., Sat. 10 A.M.–4 P.M., $2–5) serves sandwiches, wraps, salads, pastries, and coffee.

The Pulaski farmer's market takes place on Saturday mornings during the growing season on the south side of the courthouse.

Information
The **Giles County Tourism Foundation** (110 N. 2nd St., 931/363-3789, ext. 22, www.gilescountytourism.com) publishes brochures and keeps information about attractions, events, and accommodations. Stop in at their office in Pulaski to ask questions or pick up brochures.

CORNERSVILLE
If you've ever fantasized about staying in a log cabin, here's your chance. (**Lairdland Farm Bed and Breakfast** (3174 Blackburn Hollow Rd., 931/363-9090, www.bbonline.com/tn/lairdland, $115–125) consists of two genuine log cabins, set on a large 19th-century horse farm. Both the Clock Creek Cabin and the Springhouse Cabin can sleep up to six people. And while they are log cabins, modern amenities abound. Each has a kitchen, bathroom, television, and heating and air-conditioning. The downstairs living rooms are centered on a working fireplace.

The kitchens come stocked with the makings for a country breakfast—ham, coffee, biscuits, pastries and more—and you can prepare other meals in the kitchen or on the grill. Since Lairdland is a working horse farm, there are also opportunities for recreation. Horse owners can bring their own animals and board them for $15 per night. Miles of wooded trails on the farm are ideal for horseback riding, hiking, or mountain biking.

Lairdland Farm is located about 15 minutes' drive northeast of Pulaski, off Highway 31A.

LYNNVILLE
About 15 miles north of Pulaski is the quaint town of Lynnville. Almost 60 different buildings in this small town of just about 400 people are listed on the National Register of Historic Places.

Sights
The **Lynnville Depot Museum and Train Station** (162 Mill St., 931/527-3158, Tues.–Sat. 10 A.M.–4 P.M., Sun. noon–4 P.M., free) is the town's main attraction. Built around a 1928 locomotive, the museum invites you to climb aboard an old passenger train.

The museum also includes an exhibit about the nearby Milky Way farm, where candy bar giant Frank Mars lived. The farm was built between 1930 and 1934 with money Mars earned from the sale of Milky Way candy bars. He had invented the Milky Way in 1923 and by 1930 it was the number-one-selling candy bar in the world. The Milky Way farm included several dozen buildings, cottages, and miles of fences. The crown jewel was a 25,000-square foot 21-bedroom English Tudor–style Manor House. Frank Mars died in 1934 and the farm operated as a horse farm for many years. More recently, it fell into disrepair and parts of the more-than-2,000-acre estate were sold. In 2005, the property was purchased by a real estate development company which plans to preserve the Manor House and turn it into a clubhouse and inn. On the surrounding farm land, they will build an upscale gated community with amenities including a polo field, golf course, equestrian center, spa, and shopping complex.

Accommodations
The **Historic Lynnville Bed and Breakfast** (1565 Main St., 931/527-0270, www.bbonline.com/tn/lynnwood, $85) has two suites in an 1860 Victorian townhouse. Guests enjoy a private bath and in-room television, as well as wireless Internet.

Food
In Lynnville, you must stop at **Soda Pop Junction** (111 Mill St., 931/527-0001, Mon.–Thurs. 7 A.M.–7 P.M., Fri.–Sat. 7 A.M.–10 P.M., Sun. 11 A.M.–3 P.M., $3–13), a classic old soda

fountain. Besides the fountain drinks, malts, and other treats, Soda Pop Junction serves breakfast, grilled sandwiches, and dinner plates. The ⅓-pound burger is juicy and costs less than $3. The grilled bologna sandwich is a favorite, and dinners include steak, pork chops, and fried catfish. Friday night is the fish fry and on Sunday a country buffet is on offer for just $7 per person. The Soda Pop Junction is a great place to fuel up.

Information

The **Giles County Tourism Foundation** (110 N. 2nd St., 931/363-3789, ext. 22, www.giles-countytourism.com) publishes brochures and keeps information about attractions, events, and accommodations. Stop in at their office in Pulaski to ask questions or pick up brochures.

FAYETTEVILLE

The county seat of Lincoln County, Fayetteville is a bustling little city. Its proximity to Huntsville, Alabama, helps keep it lively, and its old homes and classic courtyard square make it attractive.

Sights

From 1861 until 1969, Fayetteville's most famous structure was a stone bridge that spanned the Elk River. It included six elliptical arches spanning 450 feet, and was very rare. Legend has it that after marching his troops over it in 1863, Union General William Tecumseh Sherman ordered it destroyed, but the man chosen to carry out the mission could not bear to destroy such a beautiful bridge.

In 1969 the bridge collapsed into the Elk River, but the town has built a replica at **Stone Bridge Memorial Park,** located at the corner of Highway 431/231 and Thornton Taylor Parkway.

The history and heritage of Fayetteville and Lincoln County is preserved at the **Fayetteville Lincoln County Museum** (521 Main Ave. S., 931/438-0339, www.flcmuseum.com, free). The museum, located in the old Borden Milk factory, is open from May to November on Thursday and Saturday 12:30–4:30 P.M. To visit outside these hours, call the chamber of

commerce at 931/433-1234 in advance to make arrangements.

The museum houses military, medical, and agricultural exhibits, including an outstanding arrowhead collection. The building also houses a community center.

Fayetteville's town square and the adjoining residential streets are dotted with beautiful and historic buildings. Ask at the Chamber of Commerce Welcome Center for a printed guide to historic structures, and spend an hour or so strolling the streets of this lovely town.

Shopping

Fayetteville may be the only city in Tennessee whose most celebrated retail establishment is a fabric store. **Sir's Fabric Store** (110 N. Elk Ave., 931/433-2487) has been in business since the 1940s and is still operated by the Sir family. It receives new fabric shipments every week and sells them at outlet prices.

Events

The second week of September is the **Lincoln County Fair** (931/433-6387), considered by some as the best county fair in the whole state. Come for demolition derbies, harness races, farming exhibits, carnival rides, pageants, and other entertainment.

The **Lincoln County Bluegrass and Crafts Festival** (931/433-1234) in September attracts regional musicians who compete in bluegrass, band, and dance contests. It takes place at the Lincoln County Fairgrounds.

Fayetteville gets a head-start on the holiday season with **Host of Christmas Past** (931/433-1234) over the second weekend of November. The festival includes high tea, trolley rides, strolling musicians, and a candlelight walking tour of the city.

Accommodations

Little Young House Bed and Breakfast (210 Bright Ave., 931/433-5873, www.tennesseebb.com, $80) is an 1869 townhouse that is listed on the National Register of Historic Places. Located four blocks from the town square, Little Young has three guest rooms, each furnished with elegant antiques and wall-to-wall carpeting. Afternoon tea is served in the parlor and breakfast in the dining room. A modern entertainment room is decorated to resemble an old-fashioned gentleman's smoking room; it houses a television, DVD player, and DVD library.

The **Fayetteville Bed and Breakfast** (1111 W. Washington St., 931/433-9696, $55–65) is a 1915 bungalow located one mile from the town square. Each room has a private bath, and breakfast is served.

Two miles outside of town in an 1880s colonial mansion, the **Old Cowan Plantation** (126 Old Boonshill Rd., 931/433-0225, $65) is a peaceful country getaway. Two guest rooms with private baths are comfortable and well appointed. A continental breakfast is served downstairs; sip your morning coffee out on the verandah overlooking the rural landscape.

Food

The old Fayetteville jail is now **Cahoots Restaurant** (114 W. Market St., 931/433-1173, Mon.–Thurs. 10:30 A.M.–8 P.M., Fri.–Sat. 10:30 A.M.–9:30 P.M., $13–20). This is a popular choice for just about any meal; the menu is diverse, with burgers, chicken, and Mexican cuisine on offer.

For steak and barbecue, choose the top-rated **Cattleman's Steakhouse** (520 Main Ave. S., 931/433-8834, Sun.–Thurs. 5–9 P.M., Fri.–Sat. 5–10 P.M., $13–40), which scores a 10 for its hand-carved steaks and satisfying sides. Also choose from seafood and chicken.

Information

The **Fayetteville-Lincoln County Chamber of Commerce** (208 S. Elk Ave., 931/433-1234, www.fayettelincolncountychamber.com) operates a welcome center and publishes visitor information, including a guide to historic homes and buildings in the city.

KELSO

Located about 10 miles east of Fayetteville along the Elk River is Kelso. Here you will find **Prichard's Distillery** (11 Kelso Smithland Rd., 931/433-5454, www.prichardsdistillery.com), which uses water and premium molasses to create rum, which they then age in handmade charred white-oak barrels. Visitors can see the copper pot stills and the barrel warehouse. The distillery is open Monday through Saturday 9 A.M. to 4:30 P.M., but they ask that you call before visiting.

Recreation

The Elk River winds up from Alabama and empties into Tims Ford Lake. The river, tamed by damming, is an ideal river to float in a canoe. Its current is strong yet calm, and it winds through beautiful countryside. **Elk River Canoe Rental** (190 Smithland Rd., 931/937-6886, www.elkrivercanoes.com) is a rental outfit located nine miles east of Fayetteville along Highway 64. They rent top-quality canoes ($14–25 per person), along with lifejackets and paddles. They also provide transportation to and from put-in and take-out points, and will arrange for multiple-day journeys if you like. They are open April through October. Call ahead to reserve your canoe.

Just a few miles east of town is **Elk River Adventures and Outfitters** (2167 Winchester Hwy., aka Hwy. 64, 931/433-9946, www.kelsostore.com) also rents canoes by the day. The store sells gear and goodies, and the restaurant is open daily for lunch and dinner.

LYNCHBURG

Lynchburg, no longer population 361, has been transformed by the popularity of Jack Daniel's Tennessee Whiskey, which is made a few blocks from the town square. No other small town in Tennessee sees as many visitors, from as many different places, as this one.

Critics may object to the tour buses and crowds, but for now, the town has managed to survive its success with relative grace. It has maintained its small-town feel, and it offers its guests a hospitable and heartfelt welcome.

Lynchburg is centered around the Moore County courthouse, a modest redbrick building. Souvenir shops, restaurants, and a few

© SUSANNA HENIGHAN POTTER

the Lynchburg town square

local businesses line the square. Outside of this, Lynchburg is quiet and residential. The Jack Daniel's Distillery is about three blocks away from the town square; a pleasant footpath connects the two.

Jack Daniel's Distillery

As you drive into Lynchburg, or walk around the town, you might notice some odd-looking grey warehouses peeking out above the treetops. These are barrel houses, where Jack Daniel's Distillery ages its whiskey. Around Moore County there are 74 of these warehouses, and each one holds about one million barrels of whiskey.

Thousands of whiskey drinkers make the pilgrimage every year to Jack Daniel's Distillery (280 Lynchburg Hwy., aka Hwy. 55, 931/759-4221, www.jackdaniels.com, daily 9 A.M.–4:30 P.M., free) to see how Jack Daniel's is made. And what they find is that, aside from the use of electricity, computers, and the sheer scale of the operation, things have not changed too much since 1866 when

Jack Daniel registered his whiskey still at the mouth of Cave Spring near Lynchburg.

Jack Daniel was an interesting man. He stood just five feet, two inches tall and liked to wear three-piece suits. He was introduced to the whiskey business by a Lutheran lay preacher named Dan Call, who sold the distillery to Daniel shortly after the Civil War. In 1866, Daniel had the foresight to register his distillery with the federal government, making his the oldest registered distillery in the United States. He never married and had no known children.

Daniel died of gangrene in 1911. He got it from kicking a metal safe in frustration after he couldn't get it open, and breaking his toe. After Daniel died, the distillery passed to his nephew, Lem Motlow. The distillery remained in the Motlow family until it was sold in 1957 to the Brown-Forman Corporation of Louisville, Kentucky.

The one-hour tour of the distillery begins with a video about the master distillers—Jack Daniel's has had seven in its lifetime—who are the final authority on all facets of the product. You then board a bus that takes you up to the far side of the distillery, and from here you'll walk back to the visitors center, stopping frequently to be told about the key steps in the process. The highlight of the tour for some is seeing Cave Spring, where the distillery gets its iron-free spring water. Others enjoy taking a potent whiff of the sour mash and the mellowing whiskey.

The tour ends back at the visitors center where you are served free lemonade and coffee. Moore County, where Lynchburg is located, is a dry county and for 86 years the irony was that Jack Daniel's could not sell any of its whiskey at the distillery. In 1995, however, the county approved a special exemption that allows the distillery to sell souvenir bottles of whiskey at its visitors center. That is all they sell, however; you have to buy other Jack Daniel's merchandise at one of the gift shops in town.

Other Sights

A stately two-story brick building on the southwest corner of the square is the **Moore County**

THE HEARTLAND

Jail (231 Main St., mid-Mar.–Dec. Tues.–Sat. 11 A.M.–3 P.M., free), which served as the sheriff's residence and the county jail until 1990. The building is now a museum and is operated by the local historical society. You can see law-enforcement memorabilia, old newspaper clippings, and vintage clothes. Go upstairs to see the prisoners' cells.

Just down Main Street is the **Tennessee Walking Horse Museum** (Public Sq., 931/759-5747, Tues.–Sat. 9 A.M.–5 P.M., free). The museum was originally located in Shelbyville, but moved to Lynchburg in the early 2000s to take advantage of the bustling tourist trade here.

The Walking Horse Museum displays photographs, trophies, and other memorabilia from walking horse champions. You can admire both show and posed photographs of top horses, and watch a video that explains what makes the walking horse so special. The films include show footage of the breed's distinctive flat walk, fast walk, and canter.

Events

Spring in the Hollow is an arts, crafts, and music festival that takes place in early May. At the end of May, the **Spotted Saddle Horse Show**, an annual horse show, takes place.

Frontier Days in mid- to late June is a weekend celebration of early settlers. Costumed performers and traders evoke bygone days. July sees the **Tennessee Walking Horse Show** and August the second Spotted Saddle Horse Show.

The biggest event of the year in Lynchburg is the **Jack Daniel's World Champion Invitational Barbeque,** which takes place over the last weekend of October. Teams must qualify to take part—they must have won another large barbecue tournament—and even then teams must be invited. Despite serious competition, the event is a whole lot of fun. Spectators compete in bung tossing and butt bowling. There is clogging and bluegrass music, and lots of county fair-type food is sold. The barbecue competition takes place at Wiseman Park on the outskirts of the town square. An arts and crafts festival takes place at the town square.

Christmas in Lynchburg livens up an otherwise quiet time in town with seasonal performances and decorations.

For information about any events, contact the Lynchburg–Moore County Chamber of Commerce at 931/759-4111.

Accommodations

The **Lynchburg Bed and Breakfast** (Mechanic St., 931/759-7158, www.bbonline.com/tn/lynchburg, $70) has been welcoming guests to Lynchburg since 1985. There are two guest rooms; one has a queen-sized bed and one has two twin beds. Each room has a private bathroom and cable TV; a shared telephone and refrigerator are in the hallway between the two rooms. Guests are served a continental breakfast. Accommodations are homey, but not luxurious.

The **Tolley House** (1253 Main St., 931/759-7263, www.tolleyhouse.com, $135–150) is located about a mile from the town square, and is a pleasant country retreat. A handsome antebellum farmhouse once owned by Jack Daniel's master distiller Lem Motlow, the Tolley House provides touches of luxury. Rooms have private baths, television, and wireless Internet access, and are furnished tastefully with antiques. Hosts Frank and Karen Fletcher provide your choice of a full country or light continental breakfast. Discounts are available for stays of two or more nights.

The closest thing to a motel in Lynchburg is the **Lynchburg Country Inn** (423 Majors Blvd., 931/759-5995, www.lynchburgcountryinn.com, $55–65). Its 25 rooms are each furnished with a microwave, refrigerator, and cable TV. There's a pool out back and rocking chairs on the front and back porches. The building is modern, built in 2003, but the decor is pure country.

NEAR LYNCHBURG

Dream Fields Country Bed and Breakfast (9 Back St., Mulberry, 931/632-0336, www.bbonline.com/tn/dreamfields, $100–120) is located in the tiny town of Mulberry, about seven miles south of Lynchburg. It is about halfway between Lynchburg and Fayetteville. The handsome old farmhouse, once owned by Jack Daniel's older brother, Willy, has two guest rooms inside and a private cottage on the grounds. The guest rooms ($100–105) have queen-sized beds, private baths, and satellite television. The cottage ($120) has a bathroom, refrigerator and microwave, television, air-conditioning, and fire place. The property is rural, and you just might see deer grazing out your window. Sit a spell in the front porch, or take a dip in the spring-fed creek on the grounds.

For other accommodations near Lynchburg, look in Tullahoma and Fayetteville.

Food

The most popular place to eat in Lynchburg is **Miss Mary Bobo's Boarding House** (295 Main St., 931/759-7394, Mon.–Sat. lunch only, $19). Miss Mary's started life as the home of Thomas Roundtree, the founder of Lynchburg. It later became the home of Dr. E. Y. Salmon, a Confederate captain, who maintained an office there and rented out rooms to boarders. In 1908, Lacy Jackson Bobo and his wife, Mary Evans Bobo, bought the house and continued to operate it as a boardinghouse until the 1980s. Over the years, word of Mary Bobo's legendary home-cooked meals spread and this boardinghouse became one of the region's best-known eating houses. Today, Miss Mary's is no longer a boardinghouse, and the restaurant is operated by Miss Lynne Tolley, who has worked hard to keep up the traditions established by Miss Mary. The restaurant is owned by the Jack Daniel's Distillery, and servers are hired from the local community college. A meal at Miss Mary's will easily be the most unique of your trip. On most days there are two seatings—11 A.M. and 1 P.M. Guests should arrive at least 15 minutes early so you can check in, pay, and be assigned to a dining room. When the dinner bell rings, you will be taken to your dining room by a hostess, who stays with you throughout the meal. Everyone sits family-style around a big table. The meal served at Miss Mary's is a traditional Southern dinner. You'll find no less than six side dishes

and two meats, plus iced tea (unsweetened), dessert, coffee, and bread. Almost every meal features fried chicken. Side dishes may include green beans, mashed potatoes, fried okra, carrot slaw, and corn bread. Your hostess will make sure that everyone has enough to eat, answer questions about the food, and tell you some stories about the restaurant—if you ask. Be sure to call well ahead to make your reservations. Meals are fully booked weeks and even months in advance, especially during the busy summer months and on Saturdays.

For a more low-key meal, go to the **Bar-B-Que Caboose Cafe** (217 Main St., 931/759-5180, daily 11 A.M.–5 P.M., $7–12). The menu offers pulled-pork barbecue sandwiches, jambalaya, red beans and rice, and hot dogs. You can also get pizzas. On Friday night (Apr.–Oct.) the restaurant opens for dinner 6:30–8 P.M. and you can get a barbecue plate dinner for $9 while you listen to live music. On Saturday morning from 10 to 11 A.M. a live country music radio show is broadcast from the Caboose Cafe.

There are a handful of other restaurants in Lynchburg, all on the town square. **Elk Coffee** (12 Short St., 931/759-5552, Mon.–Sat. 8 A.M.–5:30 P.M., Sun. noon–5 P.M., $6–12) sells lighter fare, including wraps and salads.

Be forewarned that it is next to impossible to get an evening meal in Lynchburg. By 6 P.M. the place is a ghost town.

Information

The Lynchburg Welcome Center (182 Lynchburg Hwy., aka Hwy. 55, 931/759-6357, www.lynchburgtenn.com) is open daily at the intersection of Majors Boulevard and Mechanic Street. The welcome center has public restrooms and information about local businesses and attractions.

TULLAHOMA

A quintessential railroad town, Tullahoma straddles what was once the Nashville and Chattanooga Railroad. Atlantic Street, actually two streets, runs on both sides of the tracks. The Depot Historic District on the east side of the railroad has a fine collection of old Victorian-era homes.

Sights

Arnold Engineering Development Center

(Arnold Air Force Base, 931/454-5655, www.arnoldaf.mil) is the nation's premier aerospace ground flight testing facility. Founded in 1951 by President Truman and named for Gen. Henry H. Arnold, a World War II commander, the center is also a major economic engine for the Tullahoma and Manchester area. The base has more than 50 different test facilities, ranging from large wind tunnels to space chambers. It has played a key role in developing all of the military's high-performance jet aircraft, missiles, and space systems.

Free tours for groups of 12 or more are available by prior reservation only. They last about three hours and require a good deal of walking; wear comfortable shoes. While individual tours are not provided, you can ask to be scheduled with a larger group, usually on Fridays.

Immediately adjacent to the Tullahoma Regional Airport is the **Beechcraft Heritage Museum** (570 Old Shelbyville Hwy., 931/455-1974, www.beechcraftheritagemuseum.org, Mon.–Fri. 8:30 A.M.–4:30 P.M., Sat.–Sun. 1–4 P.M., adults $10, students $5, children under 12 free). The museum tells the story of Beech Aircraft Company, founded by aviation pioneer and Pulaski native Walter H. Beech. The museum features dozens of antique airplanes, including the very first Beechcraft ever made. Built out of love of aviation and Beechcraft planes, the museum is a must if you share either of those passions. Children will also enjoy seeing old-fashioned planes that look like modern-day cartoon characters.

The Arts

The **Tullahoma Fine Arts Center** (401 S. Jackson St., 931/455-1231, www.tullahoma-finearts.org) offers art classes, hosts the annual Tullahoma Fine Arts and Crafts Festival every May, and operates a Regional Art Museum. The museum exhibits local and regional art on a changing basis. The center is usually open

Mon.–Fri. 10 A.M.–4:30 P.M., but it is a good idea to call ahead. Look for the bronze sculpture of a female dancer, called *Summer Song,* in the front yard of the center.

The arts center is located in a historic Italianate home built by the Baillet family after they migrated from New York to rural Tennessee in 1868. The three Baillet sisters, Jane, Emma, and Affa, were noted milliners, poets, and artists, and it was their memory and legacy which inspired local residents to restore the home and open the arts center in the 1960s and '70s.

Located in the South Jackson Civic Center at 404 South Jackson Street, the **Mitchell Museum** (931/455-5321, www.southjackson.org, free) displays items collected over a lifetime by former Tullahoma postmaster Floyd Mitchell and his wife, Margaret Noland Mitchell. Other citizens have donated artifacts to the collection over the years. The museum is open on the first Sunday of each month from 1 to 4 P.M., and at other times by appointment.

Accommodations

Designed for business travelers, small-scale conferences, and those seeking upscale accommodations, **℃ The Grand Lux Inn** (212 E. Lincoln St., 931/461-9995, www.thegrandluxinn.com, $115–125) is a stunning old Victorian home now converted into a thoroughly modern inn. Six guest rooms are available, each with a private entrance, bath, and amenities including cable television, writing desks, hair dryers, and wireless Internet. The styling is modern. A continental breakfast of hot and cold cereals, fruit, pastries, coffee, and juice is served in the Breakfast Room, but this is not a traditional bed-and-breakfast. An added bonus is that Tullahoma's best restaurant, Emil's, is right next door.

Jameson Inn (2113 N. Jackson St., 931/455-7891, $75–85) is a 60-room motel with the usual amenities: continental breakfast, fitness room, outdoor pool, cable TV, wireless Internet, and free weekday newspapers.

About three miles north of Tullahoma, off Highway 41A, you'll find one of this region's best and most beautiful bed-and-breakfasts.

Ledford Mill (1195 Shipman Creek Rd., 931/455-2546, $95–125) is set at a historic gristmill, founded in 1884 and restored in 1996 to become a country inn. The grounds are beautiful—so beautiful, in fact, that people come here just to look at them. The highlights are the two waterfalls, which invite a relaxing stroll and quiet reflection.

The grounds of the inn are open to the public daily 9 A.M.–4 P.M. After that, registered guests have the run of this most beautiful place. Rooms at the inn have carefully incorporated distinctive features of the old mill. The Falls Room has a wall of Chattanooga shale, and you can still see the main wheel of the old mill in the bathroom.

Breakfast can be served in the dining room, or you can ask for a picnic to be enjoyed in your room or the gardens.

The **Lodge at Gunter Hollow** (149 Gunter Hollow Rd., 931/433-5214 or 931/438-1665, www.lodgeatgunterhollow.com, $95) is a Christian conference center and bed-and-breakfast inn. Its seven guest rooms are new, neat, and comfortable. Each has its own private entrance, a spacious private bath, and a covered deck outside. Breakfast is served in the conference center dining room. There is also a parlor where you can watch television or relax with a book.

Food

The best place to eat in Tullahoma is **Emil's** (210 E. Lincoln St., 931/461-7070, www.emilsfinedining.com, Tues.–Fri. 11 A.M.–2 P.M., Thurs.–Sat. 5:30–8:30 P.M., lunch $7.50–14, dinner $16–30). Chef Georges Martin is the brain behind the menu, which combines genteel Southern fare and fine French cuisine. Lunch is casual, with an array of salads (the crab cake salad is a favorite), as well as sandwiches and entrées like penne pasta with ham and peas. Many diners opt for the daily lunch special ($7.50), or the platter of soup, chicken salad, crackers, dessert, and a drink ($9). Three nights a week Emil's serves dinner. Entrées include roast duck, braised lamb shank, and barbecue salmon. In deference to the region, you'll also find fried chicken.

Emil's is located in a restored 1905 home, and it is almost always full. It is a good idea to reserve your table in advance.

For something a bit more casual, head to **Fast Jack's** (122 W. Lincoln St., 931/455-2194, Mon.–Thurs. 10:30 A.M.–11 P.M., Fri.–Sat. 10:30 A.M.–midnight, Sun. 3 P.M.–midnight, $5–8). At this popular lunch spot you can choose from the daily plate-lunch special, burgers, or a nine-inch lunch pizza. The plate lunches are the real draw: hamburger steak, fried shrimp, meatloaf, chicken and dressing, and a host of tempting side dishes are usually on offer. There's extra parking at the rear of the restaurant.

On the outskirts of town, as you drive towards Lynchburg, you'll find **Sweet Aroma Cafe** (401 Wilson Ave., 931/461-5535, Mon.–Fri. 7 A.M.–4 P.M., Sat. 7 A.M.–2 P.M., $6–9). Stop here for breakfast or lunch; breakfast runs the gamut from hearty omelets and biscuits and gravy to pastries and peanut butter and banana sandwiches. At lunch they serve wraps, salads, and specialty sandwiches, including an appetizing chicken peach salad adorned with tomato slices and crackers. They serve hot and cold coffee all day long.

Information

The **Tullahoma Chamber of Commerce** (135 W. Lincoln St., 931/455-5497, www.tullahoma.org) publishes a directory of local businesses and hands out brochures and other information to stoppers-by.

NORMANDY

Normandy is a tiny one-street town, notable for its position on the railroad and its location amid some of the most beautiful countryside in this part of Tennessee. The rural routes surrounding Normandy are well worth exploring.

◖ George Dickel Distillery

About seven miles south of Wartrace, just outside of the old railroad town of Normandy, is one of the best-kept secrets in this part of Tennessee. The George Dickel Distillery (931/857-3124, Tues.–Sat. 9 A.M.–4 P.M., free) makes thousands of gallons of Tennessee sipping whisky every year, and all of it comes from the Dickel distillery up Cascade Hollow on the Highland Rim of the Cumberland Plateau. (In deference to its connection to scotch, Dickel uses the Scottish spelling for whisky, without the "e.")

It's no secret that the best-known name in whiskey is distilled a few miles down the road in Lynchburg, but the folks at George Dickel don't seem to mind. The Dickel distillery is a smaller operation, and visitors are given a more personalized and detailed look at the operations of the plant. And the setting in the Cascade Hollow is one of the most charming in this part of the state.

George Dickel, a German immigrant, distilled his first bottle of whisky at Cascade Hollow in 1870. Dickel created a unique cold mellowing process, which made his product smoother than others. The distillery still uses Dickel's cold mellowing process, as well as his signature proportions of corn, malt, and rye. The Dickel distillery closed down during Prohibition, only to reopen in the 1950s. The distillery has changed hands several times over the past 50 years, and it is now owned by Diageo, one of the largest beer, wine, and spirits manufacturers in the world.

Visitors can get a free one-hour tour of the distillery, which takes you through every step in the process. The last tour departs at 3:30 P.M.

To find George Dickel, take Route 269 to Normandy, where you will see signs pointing you to Cascade Hollow Road.

Accommodations

For a high-class country escape, head to the **Parish Patch Farm and Inn** (1100 Cortner Rd., 931/857-3017, www.parishpatch.com, $80–220), an inn, conference center, and restaurant set in the rural countryside near Normandy. The more than 30 guest rooms are scattered in various buildings on this working farm. They include spacious suites, private cottages, standard-sized bedrooms, and rustic rooms in an old gristmill. The two least expensive rooms share a bath; all other rooms have private bathrooms, televisions, and telephones.

Rollaway beds are available. All guests can enjoy the full country breakfast served daily in the inn dining room. Other amenities include a swimming pool, walking trails, a book and video library, hammocks, and lots of countryside to explore. Parish Patch is a working farm, so you can also watch (or join in) on farm chores, pick your own blackberries (in season, of course) or just watch the animals. The Duck River flows through the property, providing opportunities for fishing or canoeing.

Food

The **Cortner Mill Restaurant** (1100 Cortner Rd., 931/857-3018, www.parishpatch.com, Tues.–Sat. 5:30–9 P.M., $16–42) is an upscale country restaurant that serves dinner five nights a week and is often booked for special events. Specialties include Memphis-style dry-rub barbecue ribs, grilled rack of lamb, baked rainbow trout, and frog legs. There is an extensive wine list, and desserts include a flaming bananas foster made tableside. The restaurant hosts special buffets on Easter, Thanksgiving, Christmas, and New Year's Day, and the Champagne Sunday Brunch (Sun. 11:30 A.M.–1:30 P.M.) is a popular treat for locals and visitors.

The restaurant is located in a restored 1825 gristmill and the dining room overlooks the river. It is an elegant choice for a special dinner.

NORMANDY LAKE

The largest non-power-generating lake created by the Tennessee Valley Authority, Normandy Lake is a 3,200-acre reservoir located between Tullahoma, Shelbyville, and Manchester. It is named for the tiny railroad town of Normandy nearby.

The lake was created in 1976 by a 2,800-foot long dam across the Duck River. The river was dammed to control flooding and create recreational opportunities.

On the southern shore of the lake is the **Barton Creek Recreational Area** (158 Barton Springs Rd., 931/857-9222). Here you will find a campground with 67 sites, including 40 with electricity and water, a swimming beach, boat dock, picnic tables, and

BONNAROO MUSIC AND ARTS FESTIVAL

Bonnaroo Music and Arts Festival (www. bonnaroo.com) started out in 2002 as a jam band music festival, but diversification has made this summertime mega event a destination for all types of music fans. The 'Roo takes place over four days in June on a rural farm in Manchester. Between 75,000 and 90,000 people come each year.

Bonnaroo has a hippie heart with a slightly hard edge. Place names are Suessian – the music tents are called, from largest to smallest, What Stage, Which Stage, This Tent, That Tent, and The Other Tent. Activities run the gamut from a Mardi Gras parade to kid's art activities. Of course, it's the music that really draws the crowds: reggae, rock, Americana, jam bands, world, hip-hop, jazz, electronic, folk, gospel, and country. The event is truly a feast for the ears.

In 2007, the Police were reunited at Bonnaroo. In 2008, headliners included Kanye West, Willie Nelson, and Pearl Jam. But quality permeates every echelon of the stage. Unknowns and barely-knowns routinely wow audiences. There is a big emphasis on world artists and folk music. A jazz tent provides nightclub ambience, and there's even a comedy tent.

A few things to know about Bonnaroo: First, it's huge. The event takes place on a 700-acre farm, and the list of offerings is seemingly endless: four stages of music, whole villages dedicated to the arts, a 24-hour movie tent, yoga studio, salon, children's activity tents, music-industry showcase, food vendors, and a whole lot more.

Second, Bonnaroo has above-average logistics. Organizers seem to consider everything, including the basics: drinking water, medical care, parking, traffic control, and a general store where you can buy necessities. Food vendors sell Tennessee barbecue, veggie burgers, and just about everything in between. A shuttle service between the Nashville airport and the 'Roo helps minimize traffic. Rules about camping, RVs, re-entry, and security are common-sense and easy to follow.

All that said, you can't turn up with the clothes on your back and expect to have much fun. It's important to pack well: A good camping tent, folding chairs, and water bottles are important. Even if you plan to buy most of your food, at least pack some snacks. There are ATMs at the 'Roo, but lines can be very long, so bringing plenty of

---

playground. Campsites cost $16–20 per night. The facility is managed by the Tennessee Valley Authority.

A 420-acre protected area near Normandy Lake north of Tullahoma, **Short Springs Natural Area** is a delightful corner of the world. Gorges and slopes carved by water, waterfalls, and abundant wildflowers characterize the area. It also captures two of Tennessee's defining geologic regions, the Highland Rim and the Central Basin. Because of the difficult terrain, parts of the natural area were never farmed and remain undisturbed to this day.

Access to the area is provided across from a parking area and water tower on Short Springs Road. To find the access point from Tullahoma, drive northward on Jackson Street (Hwy. 41A). Turn right onto Hogan Street

after four blocks, and then left onto Country Club Drive after five blocks. Country Club Drive becomes Short Springs Road.

From the parking area, hiking trails head to Upper and Lower Busby Falls as well as the 60-foot Machine Falls. The Machine Falls loop is 1.4 miles and the Busby Falls Loop is just under one mile. The 1.4 mile Laurel Bluff Loop circles the top of Laurel Bluff, providing lovely views of the area.

Short Springs is managed by the Tennessee State Natural Area Program and the City of Tullahoma. Camping, biking, horseback riding, rock climbing, motorized vehicles, and collecting plants are all prohibited.

You can download a color map from the State of Tennessee website (www.state.tn.us/environment), or call 615/532-0431 for more information.

cash is also a good idea (but not too much, since you don't want to attract trouble). Also bring garbage bags, sunscreen, and hot-weather, comfortable clothes. Rain renders the farm to mud, so if the weather is iffy – or even if it's not – pack sturdy shoes and a rain coat.

Plenty of Bonnaroo fans take the opportunity to do a lot of drinking and drugs. There are police at the festival, but they don't seem to crack down on every recreational drug user. Beer – including good microbrews – are sold, and consumed generously. That said, getting wasted is not everyone's idea of a good time and if you decide to stay sober, you'll be in good company.

Most people buy a four-day pass to the festival, but day-pass tickets are available too. Four-day passes cost $200 and up; a limited number of reduced-price early-bird tickets go on sale in January each year. Regular tickets go on sale in the spring, after the line-up has been announced.

In 2007, Bonnaroo producers bought most of the farm where the festival is held, saying that they want to improve water lines and roads. They may also start hosting smaller events there during the year.

PHOTO COURTESY OF TENNESSEE DEPARTMENT OF TOURIST DEVELOPMENT

Bonnaroo is the biggest music festival in all of Tennessee.

Long a favorite destination for area residents, **Rutledge Falls** is a natural beauty. Located near Short Springs Natural Area, and sharing many of its characteristics, Rutledge Falls is on private property. Look for the Rutledge Falls Baptist Church on Short Spring Road. There is a parking lot just beyond the church, in front of an old brick farmhouse. Follow the short path to the falls.

MANCHESTER

Opened in 2003, **Beans Creek Winery** (426 Ragsdale Rd., 931/723-2294, www.beanscreek.com, Mon.–Sat. 10 A.M.–6 P.M., Sun. 1–5 P.M.) is a pleasant diversion. Using grapes and fruits grown themselves or on farms in the region, Beans Creek makes a wide variety of wines, ranging from dry to sweet to sparkling. Their tasting bar and store is welcoming and spacious, and they sell other Tennessee wines as well. "Walk throughs" around the property and plant are also offered.

People come from around the world to visit **Northside Clocks** (2032 McArthur Dr., 931/728-4307) in Manchester. This family-owned clock shop sells and repairs clocks. Its inventory includes new and antique pieces, including beautiful grandfather clocks, mantel clocks, and cuckoo clocks. They also sell exquisite Lefton Lighthouses and Fenton Glass porcelain.

◖ OLD STONE FORT STATE ARCHAEOLOGICAL PARK

Located a few miles' drive north of Manchester, on Highway 41, is one of the most mysterious

THE HEARTLAND

historic sites in Tennessee. The Old Stone Fort State Archaeological Park (732 Stone Fort Dr., 931/723-5073) is home to a Native American construction some 2,000 years old.

History

Sometime around the birth of Christ, early Woodland Indians started to build a massive stone and dirt embankment encompassing 52 acres of woodland between two branches of the Duck River. The embankment was not constructed for military purposes, and there is no evidence that it was the site of a settlement. Archaeologists don't know why the Native Americans undertook such a mammoth job—without pack animals or wheels—but they suspect that the site was of spiritual, political, or community significance for a great number of Woodland Indians. Studies have shown that the site was built and used for 13 generations.

After Indians left the area, white settlers used the site for industry. They built mills on the river, and called the enclosure a "stone fort" since that is what it looked like to them.

Sights

Since the 1970s, the site has been owned by the State of Tennessee, and it is now a state park. The **museum** (8:30 A.M.–4 P.M., free) explains what is known about the so-called fort, including the people who built it. You can watch a 15-minute video about the site, and learn about the paper and gristmills that 19th-century settlers built on the site.

The museum gift shop has a wide selection of works about Native Americans.

Recreation

About two miles of trails circle the fort and are a delightful and easy hike. The paths take you along the Duck River, past three waterfalls, and along the interior of the site, now a serene and beautiful prairie. The sound of rushing water mingles with the symphony of prairie insects and birds.

Parts of the trail take you along and over the embankments constructed so painstakingly by Native Americans more than 2,000 years ago.

The Old Stone Fort park also has a picnic area with grills, a restroom, and picnic shelters.

About two miles down the highway from the park is the **Old Stone Fort Golf Course** (931/5075) a nine-hole golf course built along the Duck River. It is open year-round; carts and clubs are available for rent from the pro shop.

Events

Flintknapping is the art of creating spear and arrowheads from stone, and twice a year the Old Stone Fort plays host to an eponymous event celebrating the ancient art form. Held over the first weekend of May and the last weekend of September, Flintknapping includes demonstrations, competitions, and material sales.

Camping

There are 51 campsites with water and electrical hook-ups, grills, picnic tables, and hard-surface pads. A dump station is available during the summer. One of two restroom facilities includes showers. Campsites are available on a first-come basis; the maximum stay is two weeks.

WINCHESTER

The seat of Franklin County is named for Gen. James Winchester, whose influence during the first 50 years of Tennessee state history went far beyond the military. Among other things, Winchester was Tennessee's first Speaker of the Senate and voted in the North Carolina convention that ratified the U.S. Constitution in 1788. He fought in both the Revolutionary War and the War of 1812. When Franklin County was created in 1807, it was decided to name its main city in honor of Winchester.

The town's most famous daughter is Dinah Shore, born Francis "Fannie" Rose Shore. Although she moved away at age seven, Dinah Shore is remembered fondly in her hometown. So fondly, in fact, that the main drag is name Dinah Shore Drive. Shore became famous singing for World War II troops and is best known for her television shows, including *The Dinah Shore Chevy Show*. She wrote cookbooks, was an avid golfer, and won nine Emmy awards. Shore died of cancer in 1994. There is a Dinah Shore exhibit at Winchester's Jail House Museum.

Sights

Franklin County's old jail was retired from use as a detention center in 1972, but instead of tearing it down, city officials decided to turn it into a museum. **The Jail House Museum** (400 Dinah Shore Dr., 931/967-0524, 10 A.M.–4 P.M., $1) now houses exhibits on local history, the Civil War, and Dinah Shore, among other things. The highlight for many is seeing an old jail cell, leg irons, and handcuffs. The museum is open from mid-March to mid-November.

One of Winchester's most notable structures is the **Hundred Oaks Castle** (Hundred Oaks Dr., 931/967-8583). Originally built as a two-story plantation home in the 1830s, the property was purchased in the 1860s by Albert Marks, the 21st governor of Tennessee. Marks's son, Arthur Handley Marks, was inspired by the castles and estate homes of Europe. Starting around 1880, Arthur Marks and his wife, Mary Hunt, a wealthy native of Nashville, turned Hundred Oaks into a castle. When the work was completed, Hundred Oaks was a 12-bedroom building with a 40-foot-high Great Hall, a wine cellar, and many features of medieval architecture. The stones were quarried at Sewanee and the bricks baked locally. Unfortunately for Arthur Marks, he did not get to enjoy the fruits of his investment. Marks died in 1882 at age 28 of typhoid fever. Mary Hunt remarried, and the estate was the subject of a long-running legal battle. From 1900 until 1990, the property went through a number of different incarnations, from a Roman Catholic church and school to a dairy creamery and a private restaurant and club. In 1981 it was leased to the Franklin County Adult Activity Center, which used it as an adult training center for many years. The castle was badly damaged by fire in 1990. In 1997 it was purchased by the Kent Bramlett Foundation, a charitable organization. The home is open by appointment only; call for a guided tour. Special events also take place here.

Entertainment

Winchester's downtown movie theater is **The Oldham** (115 1st Ave. NE, 931/967-2516).

AROUND WINCHESTER
Estill Springs

Found north of Winchester on the road to Tullahoma, Estill Springs is home to the **Montana Drive-In** (10251 Tullahoma Hwy., 931/694-3454, www.montanadrivein.com), one of only a few drive-in movie theaters left in the state. The double feature begins at 7 P.M. nightly.

Franklin State Forest

A 7,291-acre forest managed by Tennessee's Forestry Division, Franklin State Forest was acquired in 1936 from the Cross Creek Coal Company. Trails were built by the Civilian Conservation Corps during the Great Depression. Many of these trails remain today. Hunting and hiking are the two most popular activities here.

Belvidere

Named for Belvidere, Illinois, this community set amid beautiful and productive countryside west of Winchester was settled by Midwesterners after the Civil War.

A few miles west of Belvidere on Highway 64 there is a historical marker for Polly Finlay, Davy Crockett's first wife. The Crocketts settled on the banks of Beans Creek in Franklin County in 1812. The couple had two sons, and they named their Franklin County home "Kentuck." In 1815 Polly died. A year later, Davy Crockett married Elizabeth Patton, a widow with several small children of her own. The new family moved to Lawrence County in 1817.

The pretty **Falls Mill** (134 Falls Mill Rd., 931/469-7161, www.fallsmill.com, Mon.–Tues. and Thurs.–Sat. 9 A.M.–4 P.M., Sun.

12:30–4 P.M., adults $4, seniors $3, children $2), makes a perfect pit stop. The large three-story mill is a lovingly restored 1873 cotton factory. The water-powered mill now grinds flour and corn meal, and the Falls Mill country store sells whole wheat flour, grits, cornmeal, and pancake mix. Visitors can also pay the modest admission fee to hear a presentation about the old mill and take a self-guided tour of the picturesque grounds.

In addition to a grain mill and country store, Falls Mill also has a two-story log cabin **bed-and-breakfast cottage** (134 Falls Mill Rd., 931/469-7161, www.fallsmill.com, $100). The cozy cabin includes a full kitchen, sitting room, and queen-sized bedroom. There is a television, heat and air-conditioning, and a working fireplace. The kitchen is stocked with the makings for breakfast, and guests can sample the home-milled pancake mix and grits. The cabin can sleep up to five people.

To find Falls Mills, travel to the Old Salem community along Highway 64. Turn north off the highway onto Salem-Lexie Road. Drive 1.3 miles, and turn left onto Falls Mill Road.

TIMS FORD STATE PARK

Tims Ford State Park (931/962-1183) is a 431-acre park built on the shores of Tims Ford Lake, between Winchester and Tullahoma. Tims Ford Lake was created in 1970 when the Tennessee Valley Authority dammed the Elk River; eight years later the park opened. The park is named for an early river crossing.

Recreation

Fishing and boating on the lake are the two most popular activities at the park. There are seven public boat ramps in the park, and two marinas: **Lakeview Marina** (931/967-6711) has pontoon and johnboat rentals, fishing bait, camp supplies, and marine gas; **Holiday Landing Resort and Marina** (931/455-3151) is a full-service marina with slip rentals, gas, and pontoon boat rentals.

The lake is known for smallmouth and striped bass, but you may also catch large-mouth bass, crappie, catfish, and bluegill.

Bait and cleaning stations are available at the Lakeview Marina.

There are eight miles of trails. They include the **Marble Plains Trail,** a 1.1-mile handicapped-accessible paved path that winds through trees and fields past the Old Marble Plains Church and ends at an overlook of the Tims Ford Lake. From the overlook you can press on along the **Shoreline Trail,** a 3.1-mile path that follows the shoreline of the lake. The **Bicycle Trail** is a 4.4-mile paved path that winds through wooded coves on the Weaver's Point peninsula. Walking is also allowed.

There is an Olympic-sized swimming pool, open from Memorial Day until mid-August.

Bear Chase at Tims Ford is an award-winning 18-hole Jack Nicklaus signature golf course. It is located on a peninsula and offers beautiful views of the lake. Call 931/968-0995 for tee times. Greens fees are $40–50, but there are reduced rates for senior citizens and juniors.

Camping

There are two campgrounds associated with the park. The Tims Ford Campground has 52 RV and tent sites set in a wooded area in the main park. It is open year-round and has bathhouses with hot and cold showers. The Fairview Campground is located eight miles away on Highway 50, towards Winchester. Its 88 RV and tent sites are located on the lake. Fairview Campground is open from April to October. Campsites are $17.50 per night, or $20.50 with a sewer connection. No reservations are accepted for campsites.

Cabins

The park has 20 large cabins overlooking the lake. Each cabin can sleep up to eight people in two bedrooms. There is a full kitchen with modern appliances, a full bath with shower, a living area with a gas log fireplace, and a deck off each room overlooking the lake. Cabins rent for $90–125 a night, depending on the season and day of the week. There is a two-night minimum stay and the cabins are open year-round. For reservations, call 800/471-5295.

Food

There is a full-service restaurant at the Holiday Landing Resort and Marina inside the park. Call 931/455-3151 for more information.

COWAN

The town of Cowan, a few miles east of Winchester, is proving itself to be the little engine that could. A town of and for the railroad, Cowan is reinventing itself as a lovely tourist destination. Located just off the Cumberland Plateau, its attractions include historical railroad-inspired landmarks and the lovely scenery of the surrounding countryside.

The railroad was important in Cowan's history and development. The Nashville & Chattanooga line, chartered in 1848, made its first complete journey between the two cities in 1854. Engines based in Cowan helped trains make it up the steep, winding track to Tracy City. This portion of the rail rose 1,200 feet in seven miles and was referred to as the "Mountain Goat" because of the steepness of the climb. The Cowan station that still exists was built in 1904.

The last passenger train stopped in Cowan in 1965. Eleven years later a group of citizens with foresight purchased the old railroad depot with the hopes of turning it into a museum. They succeeded, and it is now the most charming railroad museum in the state. And while passenger trains no longer pass through Cowan, it remains a stop on the CSX freight train system.

Sights

Cowan's old railroad station is now the **Cowan Railroad Museum** (108 Front St., 931/967-7365, www.cowanrailroadmuseum.org, May–Oct. Thurs.–Sat. 10 A.M.–4 P.M., Sun. 1–4 P.M., free). The museum displays an antique locomotive and train memorabilia and equipment. Photographs, period costumes, old railroad timetables, and machinery combine to evoke the heyday of railroad travel and transportation. There are also model trains and a pleasant

park with picnic tables and other facilities outside. Call in advance if you would like to see the museum outside its usual summer season.

Accommodations

Cowan's heyday as a railroad depot is remembered at the **Franklin Pearson House Bed and Breakfast** (108 E. Cumberland St., 931/962-3223, www.franklinpearson.com, $75–110). Once a railroad hotel, this historic downtown property is now a nine-room bed-and-breakfast. Originally a modest railroad boardinghouse, the hotel enjoyed a period of success from 1906 until World War II as the elegant and sophisticated Franklin House, and, later, the Parker House.

The end of passenger rail service and a major fire in 1965 threatened to destroy Cowan's downtown hotel. After almost 40 years of various uses, the property was restored and reopened in 2003 as a bed-and-breakfast. The handsome white brick facade and elegant reception era evoke a bygone era, but one which is alive in spirit.

Each of the nine rooms has its own look and feel. Antique furniture, some of it original to the property, adds to the ambience. Rooms include several king- and queen-sized beds, one room with twin-bed accommodations, and two suites. All rooms have a private bathroom, cable television, and a telephone. Breakfast is served in the lobby each morning, and includes cereal, fruit, and hot specialties including eggs. In addition to the lobby, guests can relax in an upstairs library and sitting room.

Food

For a town of its size, Cowan offers a pleasant variety of dining. The **Corner House** (401 E. Cumberland St., 931/967-3910, Mon.–Sat. 11 A.M.–2 P.M., $7–9) is a traditional Southern teahouse located in a Victorian-style home. Dine in homey sophistication on seasonal sandwiches, salads, and casserole entrées. The luncheon plate includes a muffin, entrée, and salad. Be sure to save room for dessert.

If Italian cooking is more your style, then head to **Sernicola's** (108 S. Tennessee Ave.,

931/962-3380, Tues.–Sat. 11 A.M.–2 P.M. and 5–8 P.M., $9–15). Sernicola's has taken the unusual path of combining Italian specialties with good Southern cooking. The result is bound to please just about anyone. The weekday lunch buffet ($6–8) is always popular, as are the pizzas and the "Pusher Burger," named for Cowan's pusher railroad engines.

Cumberland Street Bakery (209 E. Cumberland, 931/962-1788) is a wholesale bakery. They open for retail sales on Friday and Saturday mornings.

Information
Cowan welcomes its visitors at the **Monterey Café and Welcome Center** (101 E. Cumberland, 931/968-9877, www.visit-cowan.com, daily 9:30 A.M.–5 P.M.), in the Texaco Station. Stop here for a refreshment and to pick up brochures and maps.

Murfreesboro

A city of more than 80,000 people, Murfreesboro is, quite literally, the heart of Tennessee. The geographic middle of the state lies just northeast of the city's courthouse square and is commemorated with a stone marker.

The presence of **Middle Tennessee State University** enlivens Murfreesboro. The public university with more than 22,000 students was founded in 1911 as a teacher's college and became a university in 1965. Student life revolves around the campus, located just east of downtown.

SIGHTS
Murfreesboro's downtown is centered on its 1857 **courthouse,** the oldest in the state. It is one of only six pre–Civil War courthouses remaining in Tennessee.

Stones River National Battlefield
The second most deadly Civil War battle in Tennessee is remembered at the Stones River National Battlefield (3501 Old Nashville Hwy., 615/893-9501, www.nps.gov/stri). Only a fraction of the actual battlefield is included in the national park, but enough remains to give you a sense of the battle that took place here from December 31, 1862, to January 2, 1863.

Start your visit to Stones River at the **Visitor Center** (daily 8 A.M.–5 P.M., free). Here is one of the best interpretive Civil War museums in all of Tennessee. It is modern and dynamic, and portrays much more than the tactical events of the battle. It depicts the lives and privations experienced by Civil War soldiers, the effect of the battle on Murfreesboro, and the propaganda war that took place after the battle to determine which side was considered "winner." Plan on spending at least one hour at the museum; the visitors center also houses a gift shop and bookstore, restrooms, and staff who can answer your questions.

There are self-guided walking and driving tours to other Stones River landmarks. These include the **Stones River National Cemetery,** where some 6,100 Union dead were buried. Confederates killed at Stones River were taken to their hometowns or buried in a mass grave south of town. Later, these soldiers were reinterred in a mass grave at Evergreen Cemetery in Murfreesboro.

Following the Battle of Stones River, Gen. Rosecrans ordered the construction of the depot and fortification at Murfreesboro. He wanted to press on along the railroad to Chattanooga, but he needed a place from which to launch the attack. From January to June 1863, soldiers and African-American laborers built **Fortress Rosecrans,** the largest enclosed earthen fortification built during the Civil War. Part of the fort remains standing today.

Historic Sites
The elegant Italianate mansion at **Oaklands** (900 N. Maney Ave., 615/893-0022, www.oaklandsmuseum.org, Tues.–Sat. 10 A.M.–4 P.M.,

THE BATTLE OF STONES RIVER

After Union forces took Nashville in early 1862, the Federals looked southward towards Chattanooga and Atlanta. It was their objective to drive a wedge through the southland, using the railroad as their path.

Following the Battle of Perryville in October 1862, two large armies were gathering for a battle. Maj. Gen. William S. Rosencrans's 43,000-strong Army of the Cumberland was camped in Nashville, and Gen. Braxton Bragg's 38,000 Confederates were camped 33 miles southeast in Murfreesboro. On the day after Christmas, 1862, Rosencrans marched his men to Murfreesboro to prepare for the fight that was to come.

In a strange prelude to battle, on the still night of December 30, 1862, military bands from both sides played long into the night. It began as a musical duel between armies, with songs like "The Bonnie Blue Flag" and "Hail Columbia." But after one army began playing "Home Sweet Home," the other joined in. It was a poignant and unusual moment before one of the war's bloodiest battles.

The Battle of Stones River took place on December 31, 1862, and January 2, 1863. The first day's fighting was fierce and deadly. When dawn broke on New Year's Day, both sides tended to wounded men and gathered the dead from the battlefield. Fighting resumed on January 2, in a cold and driving rain. In what would eventually become the definitive moment of the battle, a brutal Confederate drive to push the Federals back failed in the late afternoon on January 2. Overnight, after he heard that Rosencrans was getting reinforcements, Bragg ordered retreat. The low-spirited Southerners, who up until the retreat felt they had won the battle, marched 30 miles south towards Tullahoma in cold, wet weather. They were forced to leave their fallen brothers on the battlefield.

Tactically speaking, the battle was a draw, but Bragg's withdrawal allowed Rosencrans to declare it a Union victory. His claim was quickly accepted by the North, which was in bad need of a win. President Abraham Lincoln wrote to Gen. Rosencrans these words: "I can never forget, whilst I remember anything, that about the end of last year and at the beginning of this, you gave us a hard-earned victory, which, had there been defeat instead, the nation could scarcely have lived over."

Stones River was the second-bloodiest Civil War battle in Tennessee, behind Shiloh. Some 24,645 men were killed or injured at the battle – 13,249 Federal and 10,266 Confederate.

Sun 1–4 P.M., adults $7, students and children $5) was one of Murfreesboro's finest. It started as a modest two-room brick house in 1818 on the property of Dr. James Maney and his wife, Sallie Hardy Murfree. Additions in 1820, 1830, and 1857 left an elaborate and elegant mansion, now restored to its former glory. The tour of the home lasts about 45 minutes. You will see evidence of the various additions and hear stories about some of the notable people who visited at Oaklands, including Confederate president Jefferson Davis. Oaklands was badly deteriorated, vandalized, and quite nearly razed during the 1950s. Local residents fought for its preservation, and in 1958 it was purchased by the City of Murfreesboro. It was later deeded to Oaklands Association, which restored the home and opened it as a museum in the early 1960s. Today, Oaklands offers a range of special events and educational programs for local schools.

The **Bradley Academy Museum and Cultural Center** (415 S. Academy St., 615/867-2633, www.bradleymuseum.org, Tues.–Sat. 10 A.M.–4 P.M., adults $5, students and seniors $3, children under 13 $1) is located in an old schoolhouse. Bradley Academy was established in 1806 as the only school for Rutherford County. Students paid $24 a session and were required to bring firewood. Courses included Latin, Greek, mathematics, logic, writing, and literature. James K. Polk, who would go on to become president of the United States, was one of the school's early students.

THE HEARTLAND

Bradley Academy closed in the 1850s after it was absorbed into the newer Union University. During the Civil War the building served as a hospital for the wounded. In 1884, it was repaired and opened as a school for African Americans. In 1918, the old building was torn down and a new one built in its place.

Bradley Academy remained a school, cultural center, and gathering place for the African-American community until it closed in 1955. Today, it houses a museum about Rutherford County, a restored 1917 classroom, and changing local art exhibits. It also serves as a community center.

The museum is sometimes closed, even during its published opening hours. It is a good idea to call ahead.

Murfreesboro pays tribute to its pioneer past at **Cannonsburgh Village** (312 S. Front St., 615/890-0355, Tues.–Sat. 10 A.M.–5 P.M., Sun. 1–5 P.M., adults $2.50, children $1.50) Reconstructed log cabins, a one-room schoolhouse, general store and working blacksmith's shop evoke the town's early settlement. Cannonsburgh was the original name for Murfreesboro. The village grounds are open year-round and admission is free if you simply want to look around. Fees are charged for a guided tour.

ARTS AND ENTERTAINMENT
The Arts
Local and regional artists are shown at the **Murfreesboro/Rutherford County Center for the Arts** (110 W. College St., 615/904-2787, www.boroarts.org, Tues.–Sat. 10 A.M.–4 P.M., free). The center is located in a restored 1909 Italian Renaissance building that served as the Customs House and later a post office. Since 1995 it has been an arts center with gallery space. Theater performances take place on weekends in a charming 168-seat theater. Tickets are usually $12 for adults with discounts for students and seniors.

Nightlife
Liquid Smoke (Public Sq., 615/217-7822) sells cigars and specialty and imported beer. It opens at 2 P.M. and closes late. Not open on Sundays.

For live music, head to **Wall Street Restaurant and Bar** (121 N. Maple St., 615/867-9090). In addition to serving breakfast and lunch daily, they have happy hour 5–10 P.M. and live music on the weekends.

Other Entertainment
Check the calendar at the **Tennessee Miller Coliseum** (340-B W. Thompson Ln., 615/494-8961, www.mtsu.edu/~tmc), a 220,000-square-foot air-conditioned coliseum specially designed for horse and other livestock shows.

Events
In May, the Main Street Association and MTSU's McLean School of Music present the two-day **Main Street JazzFest** (www.mainstreet-jazzfest.com) in downtown Murfreesboro.

Oaklands presents **Oaklands Victorian Fair** (www.oaklandsmusuem.org) in early June. This daylong event features tours, craft and game demonstrations, storytelling, Victorian music, and an old-fashioned cake walk.

In mid-July, Murfreesboro celebrates **Uncle Dave Macon Days Festival** (615/890-0355) in Cannonsburgh Village. Old-time music is the main draw at this free festival, which features banjo music, buck dancing, and clogging. There is also a gospel showcase.

Parks and Recreation
Murfreesboro has 4.5 miles of paved greenways for walking, biking, and in-line skating. There are two canoe access points and four fishing piers. Trailheads are located at Thompson Lane, Broad Street, Redoubt Brannan, Manson Pike, and Cannonsburgh Village.

ACCOMMODATIONS
The **Carriage Lane Inn** (337 E. Burton St., 615/890-3630, www.carriagelaneinn.com, $100–150) is unique among bed-and-breakfasts, quite simply for its size. The property comprises three individual buildings, located next to each other in a quiet residential neighborhood. All three are historic homes, and each has been carefully restored to preserve the antique feel of the homes but to also provide guests with modern comforts

and amenities. The Main Inn, the Cottage, and the Yellow House can each be rented as a whole or by the room. Individual rooms are rented for between $125 and $150 a night, including a hearty breakfast. The property hosts frequent family reunions, weddings, and special events.

Byrn-Roberts Inn (346 E. Main St., 615/867-0308, www.byrn-roberts-inn.com, $140–225) is an upscale bed-and-breakfast. Each of the five guest rooms have hardwood floors, comfortable beds, and private bathrooms. Guests share a business center, fitness room, and several sitting areas for relaxation. The three-course breakfast is sure to get you going right. The inn is perfectly suited for business travelers as well as couples on a romantic getaway.

The interstate exits surrounding Murfreesboro are host to dozens of different chain motels, including **Fairfield Inn and Suites** (175 Chaffin Pl., 615/849-1150, $90–120), **Wingate Inn** (165 Chaffin Pl., 615/849-9000, $80–100), and **Super 8** (127 Chaffin Pl., 615/867-5000, $60–90).

FOOD

Soup is the specialty at **All Souped Up** (115 E. Vine St., 615/494-0092, Mon.–Fri. 10:30 A.M.–7 P.M., $5–9). The chef's 100-plus different varieties of soup are the star of the show, but you can also order sandwiches and salads. The half-sandwich, bowl of soup combo is the most popular choice. The restaurant closes at 5 P.M. on Friday.

For something a bit more elegant, go to **B. McNeel's** (215 N. Church St., 615/896-1002, www.bmcneels.com, lunch Mon.–Fri. 11 A.M.–2 P.M., dinner Tues.–Thurs. 5–10 P.M., Fri.–Sat. 5–11 P.M., brunch Sun. 10:30 A.M.–2 P.M., $10–30). Exposed brick walls, high ceilings, and a charming outdoor patio put this downtown restaurant high on the ambience list. At lunch you can choose from designer salads and sandwiches or midday versions of the restaurant's excellent entrées, including steak, chicken, and seafood. The fried oysters are a favorite. At dinner, you can choose from any of McNeel's salads or sandwiches or its upscale entrées, including herb-encrusted rack of

lamb or baked grouper. The popular Sunday brunch buffet is $13 per adult and $7 for children between 4 and 10 years.

Another favorite downtown eatery is **Marina's Italian Restaurant** (125 N. Maple St., 615/849-8881, Tues.–Sat. 11 A.M.–9 P.M., $5–14). Choices include pizzas, calzones, pasta, and the gargantuan stuffed pizza, a real crowd-pleaser. The lunchtime menu features full- and half-sized plates, all under $8. For dinner you can choose from the standards, as well as upscale dishes like shrimp pasta and baked salmon.

One of Murfreesboro's most popular restaurants is located in the sprawl-zone, a few miles away from the city center. **Demo's** (1115 Northwest Broad St., 615/895-3701, 11 A.M.–10 P.M., $6–15) was established in Murfreesboro and now has several locations in the area. Steak and spaghetti are their signature dishes. You can order spaghetti plates with up to three different sauces—brown butter and the classic meat sauce are among the favorites. Steaks are served with your choice of a baked potato or spaghetti. Service is attentive, and the prices are reasonable, making this a popular restaurant. Arrive early if you don't want to wait for a table.

INFORMATION

The **Rutherford County Chamber of Commerce and Visitors Center** (501 Memorial Blvd., 615/893-6565, www.rutherfordchamber.org, Mon.–Fri. 8 A.M.–4:30 P.M.) publishes visitor information and operates a visitors center. If you arrive on the weekend or after hours, there is an outdoor information kiosk available.

AROUND MURFREESBORO
Smyrna

Boy hero of the Confederacy Sam Davis grew up in Smyrna, once a hamlet, now a stop on the interstate highway. Davis's legacy brings travelers here today to see his boyhood home. The city of more than 33,000 people is also home to Nissan's North American headquarters, which attracts workers and a few visitors interested in seeing how cars are made.

Sam Davis Home and Museum (1399 Sam Davis Rd., 615/495-2341, www.samdavishome.org, Mon.–Sat. 10 A.M.–4 P.M., Sun. 1–4 P.M., adults $8.50, seniors $6.50, children $3) is the childhood home of Confederate hero Sam Davis. Born in Smyrna and raised in an upper-middle-class family, Davis was enrolled at the Western Military Academy in Nashville when the Civil War broke out.

Davis volunteered for the Confederate cause, and in 1863 he was a member of "Coleman's Scouts," soldiers who worked behind enemy lines to disrupt communications. He was detained by Union troops in November 1863 on his way to Chattanooga. Davis had in his possession papers that could only have been given to him by a high-level Union official.

Thinking that Davis would betray the name of his informant, Gen. Grenville Dodge arrested Davis and charged him with spying. Sentenced to hang, Davis still refused to say the name of his source, and he went to the gallows with the secret. His sacrifice made him a legend and a hero among Confederates.

His childhood home and museum keep this legend alive. Visitors see a short video about Davis and his sacrifice, and are then taken on a guided tour of the boyhood home. The house, which has been a museum since the 1930s, includes hundreds of original Davis family items.

Nissan North America (983 Nissan Dr., 615/459-1444) is Rutherford County's largest single employer with some 6,700 workers. The plant sprawls over 884 acres and cost $2.1 billion to build. Some half-a-million vehicles roll off the assembly line yearly, including Maxima and Altima sedans, Frontier pick-ups, and Xterra and Pathfinder SUVs. Tours of the plant are offered on Tuesday and Thursday at 10 A.M. and 1 P.M. Advance reservations are required; no children under 10 are allowed and cameras, including camera phones, are not permitted.

LONG HUNTER STATE PARK

Long hunters were traders and hunters who ventured into the yet-unsettled western frontier to trap wild animals and trade with Native Americans. They existed in Middle Tennessee during the 18th century, sometimes establishing rough farmsteads, called stations. One such long hunter was Uriah Stone, and the river that runs southeast of Nashville still bears his name.

Stones River was impounded in the mid-1960s to form J. Percy Priest Lake. Located on the lake's eastern shore is **Long Hunter State Park** (2910 Hobson Pk., 615/885-2422). Consisting of some 2,600 acres, the park comprises four units: Couchville, Baker's Grove, Sellar's Farm, and Bryant Grove, each named for farming communities that were inundated when the lake was made. Notably, Bryant Grove was named for Sherrod Bryant, who in the 1850s was one of the state's wealthiest African-American landowners. In addition to the park's natural attractions, hikers may see stone remnants of early homesteads, standing witness to the area's past.

Recreation

J. Percy Priest Lake is the main attraction at Long Hunter State Park. There are two boat ramps that provide access to the 14,000-acre lake. Pleasure boating, fishing, and water-skiing are popular pursuits. Catches include large- and small-mouth bass, rockfish, stripe, crappie, bream, and catfish. Rental boats are available at the Couchville unit.

For hiking, choose from the short Lake Trail, Nature Loop Trail, or Inland Trail. Deer Trail is a mile-long path through woodland beginning at the park office. The Bryant Grove Trail connects Bryant Grove and Couchville.

Longer hikes include the Day Loop and Volunteer Trail. Overnight camping shelters are available on these longer hikes.

In addition, there is a small swimming beach, volleyball courts, playground, and picnic facilities.

Camping

There is no campground at Long Hunter State Park. A group camp facility can be reserved by youth groups and other organized groups with advance reservations.

CUMBERLAND PLATEAU

The Cumberland Plateau stretches from north to south across the entire state of Tennessee. A flat-topped ridge that stands some 1,000 feet higher than its surroundings, the plateau covers 4,300 acres, or about 10 percent of the state.

In the northeastern corner of the plateau are the Cumberland Mountains, a rugged and rural region with Tennessee's greatest deposits of coal. At the southern end of the plateau is the Sequatchie Valley, a pleasant, agriculturally rich valley that lies in the middle of the plateau.

The Cumberland Plateau takes in swaths of wilderness including Fall Creek Falls, one of the state's best parks and home of the eponymous Fall Creek Falls, the highest waterfall east of the Rockies. In the northern plateau is the Big South Fork National River and Recreation Area, where the Big South Fork River cuts a dramatic gorge into the plateau. Hiking, horseback riding, and rafting are popular here. In the southern plateau, Savage Gulf is a natural area with dramatic rock formations and steep gorges.

Cookville and Crossville are the largest cities of the plateau—mostly it is a rural, sparsely populated area. The New Deal–era project at Cumberland Homesteads is a remarkable story of idealism and perseverance. Historic Rugby, an English-style village founded by British author Thomas Hughes, is enchanting even today. The story of the Children's Holocaust Memorial at Whitwell Middle School on the lower plateau is a modern-day miracle, which inspired a major studio film in 2004.

PHOTO COURTESY OF TENNESSEE DEPARTMENT OF TOURIST DEVELOPMENT

HIGHLIGHTS

◖ Historic Rugby: In the 1880s English settlers founded a utopian colony on the Cumberland Plateau; the site remains a beautiful and spellbinding place (page 266).

◖ The Big South Fork: The river gorge carved by the Big South Fork over millions of years is untamed wilderness. This is a playground for hikers, bikers, riders, and paddlers (page 268).

◖ Cumberland Homesteads: Remnants of a New Deal project to bring homesteaders to the plateau are still apparent in this town near Crossville (page 279).

◖ Fall Creek Falls: The tallest falls east of the Rocky Mountains are dramatic, but they are not the only waterfalls at Fall Creek Falls State Park; four others dot this expansive and popular outdoor destination (page 287).

◖ Children's Holocaust Memorial: What started as a project to teach middle school students about tolerance is now a public monument to peace and activism (page 296).

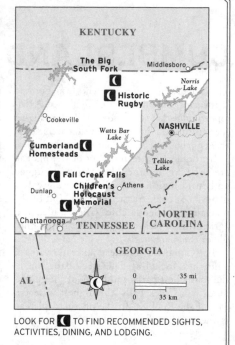

LOOK FOR ◖ TO FIND RECOMMENDED SIGHTS, ACTIVITIES, DINING, AND LODGING.

PLANNING YOUR TIME

The Cumberland Plateau is a region best explored leisurely. You should get off the interstate and take secondary routes to small towns like Jamestown, Oneida, Grassy Cove, Dayton, and Sewanee. Many of the parks and recreation areas are relatively rugged and undeveloped, so you will need to get out of the car and hike a little.

Remember that it is usually a few degrees cooler on the plateau than it is in the surrounding countryside, a plus during the hot, humid Tennessee summer. Also remember that the boundary between **Eastern Time** and **Central Time** cuts right through the plateau, so you need to be extra careful when making plans in this part of Tennessee.

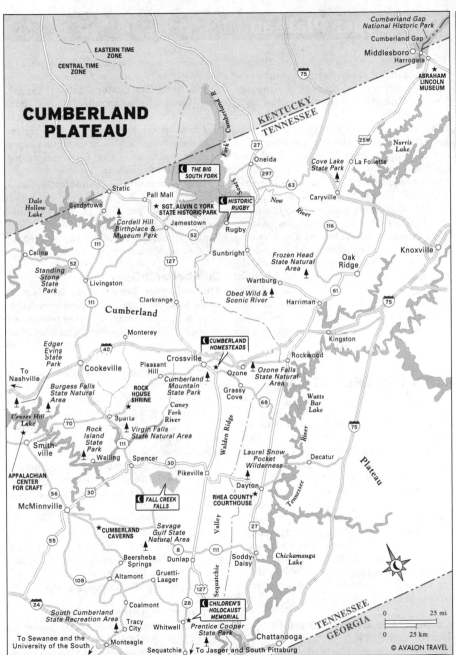

CUMBERLAND PLATEAU

Cumberland Gap
National Historic Park

Cumberland Gap

Middlesboro
Harrogate

ABRAHAM
LINCOLN
MUSEUM

EASTERN TIME
ZONE

CENTRAL TIME
ZONE

75

CUMBERLAND
PLATEAU

KENTUCKY
TENNESSEE

25W
Norris
Lake

Oneida
297

Cove Lake
State Park
La Follette

THE BIG
SOUTH FORK

63

Caryville

Static

Pall Mall
SGT. ALVIN C YORK
STATE HISTORIC PARK

HISTORIC
RUGBY
New

River

Dale
Hollow
Lake
Byrdstown

Cordell Hill
Birthplace &
Museum Park
Jamestown

Rugby

116

52

Celina
111

127
Sunbright
Frozen Head
State Natural
Area
Oak
Ridge
Knoxville

52

Standing
Stone
State
Park
Livingston

Wartburg
61

75

Clarkrange
Obed Wild &
Scenic River
Harriman

Cumberland

Monterey

Kingston

Edger
Evins
State
Park
40

CUMBERLAND
HOMESTEADS

Rockwood

To
Nashville
Cookeville
Pleasant
Hill
Crossville
Ozone
Ozone Falls
State Natural
Area

Burgess Falls
State Natural
Area
ROCK
HOUSE
SHRINE
Cumberland
Mountain
State Park
Grassy
Cove
68
Watts
Bar
Lake

Center Hill
Lake
70
Sparta
Caney
Fork
River

75

Smith-
ville
Rock
Island
State
Park
111
Virgin Falls
State Natural Area

Laurel Snow
Pocket
Wilderness
Decatur
Plateau

APPALACHIAN
CENTER
FOR CRAFT
Walling
Spencer
30

56
30
Pikeville
Dayton

McMinnville
FALL CREEK
FALLS
RHEA COUNTY
COURTHOUSE

55
CUMBERLAND
CAVERNS
Savage
Gulf State
Natural
Area
8
111
27

Beersheba
Springs
Dunlap
Soddy-
Daisy
Chickamauga
Lake

108
Altamont
Gruetti-
Laager

24
Coalmont
28
CHILDREN'S
HOLOCAUST
MEMORIAL

South Cumberland
State Recreation Area
Tracy
City
Whitwell
Prentice Cooper
State Park
Chattanooga
TENNESSEE
GEORGIA

To Sewanee and the
University of the South
Monteagle
Sequatchie
To Jasper and South Pittsburg

0   25 mi

0   25 km

© AVALON TRAVEL

The Upper Plateau

The northern reaches of the Cumberland Plateau contain some of the most rural and isolated countryside in the state of Tennessee. Here the flat expanse of the plateau gives way to the rugged terrain of the ancient Cumberland Mountains, creating a landscape that is as beautiful as it is difficult to penetrate.

Case in point: When Tennessee officials were looking for a remote and desolate place to put a state prison back on 1893, they chose Brushy Mountain in Morgan County, where the prisoners could conveniently work in nearby coal mines too. The isolation of this region makes it a lovely place to visit, as long as you are happy slowing down to the pace of winding two-lane roads.

Today, visitors who make the journey to the northern plateau are rewarded with beautiful landscape—mostly rural with small towns here and there. Prosperity is only modest in these parts; these counties are among the poorest in the state of Tennessee. Coal mining has been and continues to be a mainstay of the economy here, along with logging and manufacturing.

THE CUMBERLAND GAP

Once the gateway to the western frontier, Cumberland Gap is now a national park with great natural beauty and historical significance. An estimated 30,000 people walked, rode, or were carried through the Cumberland Gap over the Appalachian Mountains between 1760 and 1850.

Located where Tennessee, Virginia, and Kentucky come together, the Cumberland Gap has remained an important transportation link. The first tunnel through the gap was constructed in 1888, and soon after a macadamized road was built. In 1996, new twin tunnels were built through the mountain and the aboveground highway removed in an effort to return the gap to its 1750 appearance.

Cumberland Gap National Historical Park

Most of Cumberland Gap National Historical Park lies in Kentucky and Virginia; only the southernmost reaches are in Tennessee. The **Cumberland Gap Visitor Center** (U.S. 25E, Middlesboro, Kentucky, 606/248-2817, daily 8 A.M.–5 P.M., free) is located just over the state line and has exhibits about the Cumberland Gap and information about recreation opportunities, and tours of Gap Cave and the historic Hensley Settlement.

Take a drive to the **Pinnacle Overlook.** The overlook is located at the end of a windy four-mile road that climbs more than 1,000 feet. From the pinnacle you can see the Great Smoky Mountains 80 miles away, and the gap itself, some 900 feet below.

Cumberland Gap

The small, quiet town of Cumberland Gap sits on the southern side of the gap, surrounded on all sides by hills. Set as it is in the bottom of a geological bowl, the town of Cumberland Gap has been protected from the ravage of development. Historic homes line the streets, and there is a circa-1899 railroad depot and a railroad tunnel that was carved by hand in the late 1890s. Modern-day improvements include a network of greenways and hike-bike trails, which connect the town with the Wilderness Road Trail, which in turn makes its way to the saddle of the Cumberland Gap.

One of the most unusual attractions in town is **Little Congress Bicycle Museum** (Llewellyn St., 423/869-9993, www.bicyclemuseum.net, Sat.–Sun. 8 A.M.–dusk, free). Here you can see antique bicycles from the 19th and 20th centuries, including a 1934 quadrocycle and an 1895 Penny Farthing. Curator and owner Ralph McClanaham II, a district judge in Kentucky, is a bicycle enthusiast who grew up in Cumberland Gap.

Accommodations and Food

The **Cumberland Gap Inn** (630 Brooklyn St., 423/869-3996, www.cumberlandgap.net, $75–80) is a folksy 31-room motor inn, located within walking distance of Cumberland Gap restaurants and attractions. Rooms are comfortable motel-style, with microwaves, coffee makers, refrigerators, and broadband Internet.

Located in a charming historic mill, the **Olde Mill Bed and Breakfast Inn** (603 Pennlyn Ave., 423/869-9839, www.oldemillbbinn.com, $75–130) offers unique accommodations in a lovely setting. The six rooms and one suite range from rustic comfort to modern luxury. There is a private log cabin, cozy upstairs "pinnacle" room, and a honeymoon suite with whirlpool tub and a beautiful four-poster bed. All rooms have private bathrooms and comforts like air-conditioning, microwave, refrigerator, and Internet access. A hearty home-style breakfast is served buffet-style in the morning.

For a bite to eat, look no further than **Webb's Country Kitchen** (602 Colwyn Ave., 423/869-5877, Tues.–Thurs. 8 A.M.–8 P.M., Fri.–Sat. 8 A.M.–9 P.M., Sun. 8 A.M.–4 P.M., $5–15), where biscuits and gravy, country ham, and delicacies like chicken-fried steak are the specialties. At lunch you can order a bowl of pinto beans or a four-vegetable plate, or any number of sandwiches. On Friday nights there is an open mic with bluegrass, country, and gospel music; on Saturday nights there is live bluegrass.

HARROGATE

This small town a few miles south of the Cumberland Gap is home to Lincoln Memorial University, an independent four-year university with more than 3,200 students. The LMU mascot is the Railsplitters. To the visitor, LMU offers the **Abraham Lincoln Museum** (U.S. 25E, 423/869-6235, Mon.–Fri. 9 A.M.–4 P.M., Sat. 11 A.M.–4 P.M., Sun. 1–4 P.M., adults $5, seniors $3.50, children 6–12 $2.50, under six free), dedicated to the life of this most celebrated president. This somewhat musty museum follows Lincoln from his boyhood in Kentucky to his leadership during the Civil War. A highlight is a wall that contains more than 100 different photographs of Lincoln, from the iconic to lesser-known images, which gives the viewer a greater sense of what Lincoln actually looked like. Among the museum's collection are the bed in which Lincoln slept on the night of his 52nd birthday and a rare photograph of his father, Thomas Lincoln.

ONEIDA

Oneida is the largest town in Scott County, and one of the principal gateways to the Big South Fork National River and Recreation Area. Incorporated in 1913, it was a way station for the Cincinnati Southern Railroad. After Highway 27 opened in the late 1920s, Oneida continued to serve as a transportation hub for the logging and mining industries of this remote and largely rural county.

Today, Oneida is a workingman's town. The railroad still passes through town, and local industries include manufacturing, health care, and education.

Accommodations and Food

For accommodations, check into the **Grand Vista Hotel** (11597 Scott Hwy., 423/663-4100, www.grandvistahuntsville.com, $80), located at the intersection of Highways 27 and 63, near Huntsville. This full-service hotel offers free hot breakfast, refrigerators and microwaves, a heated pool, a business center, and a fitness room.

Phillip's Drive In (18499 Alberta St., 423/569-4002, Mon.–Thurs. 8 A.M.–10 P.M., Fri.–Sat. 8 A.M.–10:30 P.M., $5–14) is home to the juicy "jerryburger," plus milkshakes, hot dogs, chicken tenders, taco salad, BLTs, and just about anything else you may desire.

RUGBY

North of Wartburg, the terrain of the plateau becomes more rugged, and the towns less frequent. Settlements like Deer Lodge, Sunbright, and Burrville appear to have seen better days. If the countryside seems remote now, imagine how it must have felt to hundreds of young English gentry and American settlers, who came to the Tennessee wilderness in the 1880s to develop a new type of colony.

21ST-CENTURY COLONISTS

Historic Rugby is expanding. Since 1992, the organization has been selling lots at Beacon Hill and Boyle Woods for private residential development. The lots range from 0.7 to 2.5 acres, and development must be compatible with the Victorian architecture and atmosphere of Rugby. Both areas were intended as areas for residential development under the original Rugby plan, but the colony never grew large enough to warrant it.

At this writing, all but a few lots were sold. Perhaps Rugby's time has finally come.

◖ Historic Rugby

The story of these unlikely settlers, and what remains of their community, is preserved at Historic Rugby (5517 Rugby Hwy., aka Hwy. 52, 888/214-3400, www.historicrugby.com, adults $7, children $3), located in the northernmost corner of Morgan County (and, incidentally, the westernmost edge of Eastern Standard Time).

Rugby was the creation of British author and social reformer Thomas Hughes, who imagined a place where the second sons of English gentlemen, who would not inherit their fathers' wealth, could come to make their way in the world. Rugby was founded on principles of community, hard work, education, and the arts. Rugby opened in 1880, and "colonists" from America and Europe settled here. The experiment attracted considerable attention from the media, which both praised and ridiculed Rugby's unusual ambitions.

There were triumphs and tragedies: Typhoid outbreaks felled dozens of settlers and economic pursuits failed due to harsh weather, poor soil, and the seeming lack of interest in hard manual labor among many colonists. For a time, tourism was a mainstay of the enterprise, since people were attracted to this odd English village in the Cumberland Mountains, where residents stopped to drink tea in the afternoon. One of the oldest libraries in the state of Tennessee was founded in Rugby in 1882, and other pursuits such as a letterpress and restaurant were successful.

But Rugby could not overcome its challenges. A bad drought in 1887 was the final blow. When Thomas Hughes died in 1896, after investing a considerable portion of his own personal fortune in the colony, Rugby was considered to be a failure and an embarrassment. While most settlers moved away by the turn of the 20th century, a handful stayed on and passed the old Victorian-era homes built by colonists down to their children and grandchildren.

In the 1960s, a young man from Deer Lodge name Brian Stagg became fascinated by the enchanting ghost town of Rugby, and he organized Historic Rugby, the private nonprofit corporation that now runs the town.

Begin your visit to Historic Rugby at the **visitors center** (5517 Hwy. 52, 10 A.M.–5 P.M.),

© SUSANNA HENIGHAN POTTER

Christ Church Episcopal at Historic Rugby

where, after paying admission, you will watch a video about Rugby and view a small museum. A guided tour of the grounds includes **Christ Church Episcopal,** a one-room wooden chapel with original hanging lamps, stained glass, and an 1849 rosewood organ. The church was built in 1887, and remains in use today. The **Hughes Public Library** looks almost exactly as it did when it opened in 1882. Its simple unadorned walls are covered floor to ceiling with one of the best collections of Victorian literature in the country. The tour also stops at Kingstone Lisle, the modest home that Hughes built for his mother, who lived out the end of her years, happily by all accounts, at Rugby.

Rugby's old commissary has been restored and converted into a gift shop, which stocks an above-average selection of handicrafts, plus English- and Victorian-inspired specialty items. You can also pick up a copy of *Tom Brown's School Days,* the novel that made Thomas Hughes famous and rich enough to bankroll Rugby in the first place.

Rugby today is a marriage of old and new. The new visitors center was opened in 2006, and house lots are being sold according to the original Rugby development plan. But the presence of original Rugby buildings like the Hughes Public Library anchors the newness to its past.

In Rugby you cannot help but be enchanted by the atmosphere of natural beauty, unhurried life, and Victorian-era buildings. Coming here is a journey, not necessarily back in time, but certainly away from it.

Events

Rugby puts on dozens of workshops and special events year-round. Naturalists, artists, craftspeople, and historians lead these courses, which take place many weekends during the year. Download a calendar from the Historic Rugby website.

Rugby's premier event is the **Festival of British and Appalachian Culture** in mid-May. Entertainers usually include well-known bluegrass and folk musicians, and there are traditional arts-and-crafts demonstrations. The British bit comes in with a maypole, bagpipe players, and food of the British Isles.

Accommodations

Fall completely under Rugby's spell by staying the night at (**Historic Rugby Lodging** (423/628-2441, $74–105). Historic Rugby offers overnight accommodation in the Newbury House, Pioneer Cottage, Percy Cottage, and Linden Carriage House. In Newbury House, restored in 1985, there are five guest rooms and one suite. Two of the guest rooms share a bath; others have private facilities. All guests can relax in the downstairs parlor or on the sun porch, and there are coffee, tea, and cookies in the kitchen. Rates at Newbury range $74–103 for double accommodation, and include breakfast. The three- and five-bedroom cottages rent for $80–90 per room, and guests have the use of a kitchen.

All Rugby accommodations are comfortable and unique among Tennessee lodging. Not quite your typical bed-and-breakfast, and certainly not your average hotel, these accommodations are rustic, yet entirely comfortable. They are a favorite escape for many travelers in the region.

Grey Gables (Hwy. 52, 423/628-5252, www.rugbytn.com, $125) is a bed-and-breakfast unaffiliated with Historic Rugby, but influenced by it nonetheless. The farmhouse-style inn has eight bedrooms, each furnished with antique furniture and colorful draperies and linens. Your overnight rate includes breakfast and dinner prepared by hostess Linda Brooks Jones, a celebrated local chef.

Food

The (**Harrow Road Cafe** (5517 Hwy. 52, Sun.–Thurs. 8 A.M.–6 P.M., Fri.–Sat. 8 A.M.–9:30 P.M., $5–12) rounds out Rugby's attractions. Serving breakfast, lunch, and dinner daily (they close at 6 P.M. on weekdays, but offer a special dinner menu on the weekends), the café is the heartbeat of Rugby. Tourists, residents, and the legions who drive Highway 52 daily meet here in the name of good eats. The menu reflects the hybrid nature of Rugby's appeal: there is Welsh rarebit and shepherd's pie next to fried catfish and turnip greens. All the food is good, though, and there is an effort to stay true to some of the English traditions. You can order hot tea without fear of being laughed out of the room. They may even offer milk.

The Harrow Road Cafe closes at 4 P.M. on weeknights in January and February.

◖ THE BIG SOUTH FORK

Big South Fork National River and Recreation Area (4564 Leatherwood Rd., Oneida, 423/286-7275, www.nps.gov/biso) was established in 1974 to preserve this northern-flowing large tributary of the Cumberland River and approximately 119,000 surrounding acres. Threatened with coal-mine damage and what would have been the highest dam in the eastern United States, local conservationists with the help of then U.S. senator Howard Baker from nearby Huntsville, Tennessee, succeeded in saving this outstanding gorge and rim terrain in one of the most remote areas of Tennessee and Kentucky. About three-fourths of the park is in Tennessee. It is a land bejeweled with a wild river surrounded by natural forms such as steep sandstone bluffs and high arches, including famous side-by-side arches, arguably the largest in the eastern United States.

Orientation

State Highway 297 cuts through the Tennessee portion of the Big South Fork. It is a pleasant, scenic drive that takes you down to the bottom of the river gorge and back up again. The closest towns are Oneida to the east and Jamestown to the west.

Sights

Soon after you enter the park from the east, you pass the park headquarters and a turn-off to the East Rim Overlook, a picturesque spot where you can peer out over the gorge. From the overlook it is a quick, steep descent to the bottom of the gorge at Leatherwood Ford, where you'll find picnic tables, an information kiosk, and trailheads.

Past the gorge is Bandy Creek, a focus of activity and recreation on the Tennessee side of the park. The complex, which sits on the site of an abandoned homestead of earlier days, includes a campground, horse stables, visitors center, and trails. The visitors center (423/286-7275, daily 8 A.M.–4 P.M.) offers free information and detailed maps, guidebooks, and ice for sale. For those preferring a pool to the many swimming holes along the river, there is Bandy Creek Pool.

A favorite destination for hikers in the Big South Fork is the Twin Arches, a remarkable double natural bridge formation.

In the Kentucky portion of the park there are attractions that commemorate the historic coal-mining communities and railroads

---

NEW RIVER SCENIC RAILWAY

In 2008 a new scenic railroad excursion opened for business. The New River Scenic Railway (443 Jeffers Rd., Huntsville, 423/663-8899, www.newriverscenicrailway.com) follows the New River through surprisingly wild country on the northeast corner of the Cumberland Plateau.

The railway is a labor of love for co-owners Jimmy Byrge and Scotty Phillips, who see it as a way to bring tourists to this sparsely populated part of East Tennessee. The railroad, which extends some 62 miles, served the coal fields and logging camps of the plateau for years. It cuts through remote parts of Scott, Campbell, and Anderson Counties, past sandstone bluffs, green fields, and along the clear, sparkling New River. Towns along the way have winsome names: Winona, Devonia, Norma, Rosedale. It is a seldom-seen corner of Appalachia.

Excursions depart from Huntsville on the southeastern edge of the Big South Fork. Choose between the 62-mile, 4.5-hour full journey ($44 adults, $22 children) or a 24-mile, 2.5-hour trip ($28 adults, $14 children). Some cars are air-conditioned, but in mild weather you may prefer to sit in a window-cooled car. There are snacks on sale, or you can pack a bag lunch.

Excursions run on Friday, Saturday, and Sunday. Call to confirm departure times.

of the region. From 1937 to 1962, people lived in Blue Heron, a remote coal mining town operated by the Stearns Coal and Lumber Company. Today, **Blue Heron Mining Community** (Kentucky Hwy. 742, 606/376-3787) is an outdoor museum where visitors can hear the stories of one-time residents, told through audio recordings and displays about daily life in this remote and beautiful place. Blue Heron Mining Community is open year-round during daylight hours. From April to October, rangers are on hand to answer questions. At other times, you may explore on your own. From mid-April through November you can ride the **Big South Fork Scenic Railroad** (800/462-5664, www.bsfsry.com, adults $18, seniors $16.50, children 3–12 $3) from Stearns, Kentucky, to Blue Heron.

In addition, the park hosts two festivals each year, usually in late April and late September, which celebrate the cultural heritage of the area. While Blue Heron is the largest cultural heritage site in the park, the Big South Fork is sprinkled with the remains of many more old settlers' cabins and farmsteads. Hikers, bikers, and horseback riders are asked not to disturb or dig around ruins that you may encounter.

River Recreation

The Big South Fork is a center for white-water sports, including canoeing, kayaking, and rafting. Floating through the Big South Fork gives you entry to a remote and beautiful countryside, where you can still see evidence of previous agricultural, mining, and logging use. The rivers and streams in the park offer placid floats and dangerous white water. The character of the rivers can change with heavy rains; check conditions before setting out.

For those without their own craft, there is only one permitted outfitter. **Sheltowee Trace Outfitter** (Whitley City, KY, 800/541-7238, www.ky-rafting.com) leads beginner and intermediate white-water rafting trips down the Big South Fork from mid-March to mid-May each year. Participants in these trips meet near Oneida. Sheltowee also rents canoes, kayaks, and tubes. They offer shuttle service to put-in

points, and provide maps and itineraries to help plan your river outing.

For those needing only a guide, **Against the Flow** (Byrdstown, 931/510-6939) offers professional guide services for the park's waters and others in the area. The river can be hazardous and floaters need to be sure of their skills and equipment and know the area they are floating.

Horseback Riding

On land, there are 300-plus miles of trails, marked by self-evident icons for specific uses. The remoteness of this park calls for horseback travel, and there are 130 miles of backcountry horse trails. The *Trails Illustrated* map of the Big South Fork is the best resource for trail navigation in the park.

Southeast Pack Trips (276 Dewey Burke Rd., Jamestown, 931/879-2260, www.southeastpacktrips.com) and **Saddle Valley Campground** (350 Dewey Burke Rd., Jamestown, 931/879-6262, www.saddlevalleycampground.com) are permitted horse outfitters for the Big South Fork. They offer overnight horseback excursions or half-day journeys. Expect to pay about $20 per hour to rent a horse, or $100 per day for a guide if you have your own horses. Short as well as longer rides may be arranged directly at the **Bandy Creek Stable** (1845 Old Sunbright Rd., 423/286-7433) in the park, which is also a place to board horses while you camp in the nearby Bandy Creek Campground.

Other Recreation

Big South Fork allocates trails for all manner of uses. Hikers may use any trail in the park. Mountain bikers may use specified bike trails or any horse trail. Wagon trails are open for all non-motorized traffic and multi-use trails include motor vehicles, such as ATVs. Users should check for specific ATV regulations before setting out.

Fishing and hunting in season and with appropriate State licenses are allowed and popular. Big South Fork also has many locations open for rock climbing and rappelling, though arches and other fragile land forms are closed to these activities. There are no outfitters for these activities.

Camping

Bandy Creek Campground ($19–22) is the only campground in the Tennessee section of the Big South Fork, and it is easily accessible from Leatherwood Road (Hwy. 297), the only paved road through the heart of the park. There are 180 sites, 100 with water and electricity hook-ups, and 49 for tents only. The facility is open year-round with reservations (877/444-6777, www.recreation.gov) accepted from April through October. Campgrounds located in Kentucky include Blue Heron ($17) and Alum Ford ($5).

Backcountry camping is allowed in some areas with a permit, available at the park and from many area businesses.

Accommodations

For an experience unique in the Big South Fork, reserve a bed at the 【 **Charit Creek Lodge** (865/429-5704, www.charitcreek.com). This is a privately operated concession offering rustic overnight stays at an old farmstead, plus supper and breakfast. It is especially good for groups, since each cabin or lodge room can sleep up to 12 people.

The complex consists of three cabins (two for visitors), a barn, and a communal dining/gathering hall. There is no electricity or telephones, and the lodge is accessible only on horseback, foot, or bike. Full accommodations cost $65 per night per adult ($53 for children under 10), and includes dinner and breakfast. Hostel accommodations cost $20 per night and include access to showers, restrooms, and modest kitchen privileges. All guests enjoy wood-burning fireplaces, heated (in season) showers, and access to outdoor games, including volleyball and horseshoes. Meals are hearty, and served family-style.

Charit Creek Lodge is situated about a mile down the trail from the Fork Ridge Road, at the confluence of the Charit Creek and the Stations Camp Creek. You can also reach it via the Twin Arches Trail.

Charit Creek is operated by the same company that operates LeConte Lodge in the Great Smoky Mountains National Park, and the reservation office is at 250 Apple Valley Road, in Sevierville.

© RICHARD HENIGHAN

Charit Creek Lodge in the Big South Fork provides rustic accommodations in the wilderness.

PICKETT STATE PARK

Pickett CCC Memorial State Park and the surrounding Pickett State Forest comprise 11,000 acres of land obtained by the State from the Sterns Coal & Lumber Company in the midst of the Great Depression of the 1930s. The park is named after the small and isolated county in which it is located, which in turn was named after Howell L. Pickett, an otherwise unnoted Tennessee state representative involved in the county's formation in 1879. The Civilian Conservation Corps, a New Deal program to assist the unemployed, built the basic infrastructure of the park in its early days. The original administrative buildings, various roadside and trailside improvements, several rustic stone cabins (still comfortably in use), and the Thompson Creek Dam that creates the park's 15-acre recreation lake, were constructed by the local workers who joined the CCC.

Recreation

Seasonal uses of the lake include a free swimming area with a fine sand beach, changing facilities, and rental canoes and fishing boats. No private boats are allowed. Limited recreation equipment such as horseshoes and tennis rackets can be borrowed.

The jewels of Pickett, however, are the natural features and forms that the slow forces of deep geological time have wrought. The soft sandstone under harder cap rock and above less permeable layers eroded to form numerous rock overhangs, called variously caves or rock houses, or more spectacularly, the famous natural bridges of the park. In the case of natural bridges, the forces of erosion have worked on both sides of a narrow ridge to form a passage all the way through the sandstone. Several of these forms such as **Hazard Cave, Indian Rock House,** and a natural bridge can be reached by short and clearly marked walks from State Highway 154, the road to and through the park.

There are 58 miles of hiking trails in Pickett. A network of one- to two-mile loops highlights the park's features. Those seeking backcountry hiking can set out on either the **Hidden Passage Trail** or the **Rock Creek Trail.** The former follows Thompson Creek into the adjacent Big South Fork National River and Recreation Area, where it becomes the Shiltowee Trace Trail and can take the hiker some 40 miles into the Daniel Boone National Forest in Kentucky. The Rock Creek Trail follows this creek into the Big South Fork where it becomes the John Muir Trail and extends a further 40 miles. The two Pickett trails intersect and form a pair of double loops each about 8 to 10 miles long, just right for a pleasant day of hiking.

Backcountry camping in Pickett can be arranged at the park office, and Big South Fork allows it with a permit as well. Pets are allowed on a leash on trails, but only one cabin is pet-friendly. Hunting is allowed in backcountry areas during specific fall and winter hunting seasons.

Camping and Accommodations

Pickett's overnight facilities include 34 tent and trailer camping sites available on a year-round first-come, first-served basis ($13 per night); a large group facility with dorm space for 144 people and an indoor dining and cooking facility ($3 per person per night, minimum charge $200 per night); and four types of cabins: rustic (sleeps four), chalet (sleeps two), deluxe (sleeps six), and villa (sleeps eight). Cabins cost between $80 and $120 per night, with a $20-per-night discount during the off-season, from November to March. There is no restaurant, but there is a large picnic area with a few rentable covered sites.

For more information contact the park office (4605 Pickett Park Hwy., 931/879-5821). Cabin reservations are made by calling 877/260-0010.

JAMESTOWN

Jamestown is the second gateway city to the Big South Fork. Located on the western side of the wilderness, Jamestown is the seat of Fentress County and features a lovely stone courthouse. The town's claim to fame is that Samuel Clemens, better known as Mark Twain, was conceived here. Twain was born in Missouri seven months after his family left Jamestown. It is said that Obedstown in Twain's book *The*

Gilded Age approximates Jamestown. The folk of Jamestown created **Mark Twain Spring Park,** across from the post office, to celebrate their connection with this literary genius. (For those who want to take the story even further, note that you may see the Tennessee home where the Clemenses lived on display at the Museum of Appalachia, in Norris.)

Jamestown's main attraction is the **Ye Olde Jail Museum** (114 Central Ave. W., 931/879-9948, Mon.–Fri. 8 A.M.–4:30 P.M., free). Located in the same building as the Fentress County Chamber of Commerce, the old jail housed prisoners from 1900 to 1979. You may tour the old cells, which now house exhibits about local history.

Tennessee's oldest licensed winery is the **Highland Manor Winery** (2965 S. York Hwy., 931/879-9519, Mon.–Sat. 9 A.M.–5 P.M., Sun. 11 A.M.–5 P.M., free), located about four miles south of Jamestown. This Tudor-style winery makes grape, muscadine, and other fruit wines for sale and tasting.

Practicalities

Visitors to Jamestown will find plenty of grocery stores, gas stations, and camp supplies with which to stock a trip to the Big South Fork or Pickett State Park. Highways 154 and 297 leading out of town towards the parks are littered with enterprises geared to outfitting hunters and hostlers.

For a casual meal near Jamestown, try **Cherokee Trails Market and Cafe** (2880 Pickett Park Hwy., 931/879-0895, Mon.–Fri. 6:30 A.M.–9 P.M., Sat. 7 A.M.–9 P.M., Sun. 7 A.M.–4 P.M., $2–5) for burgers, sandwiches, and hearty breakfasts.

ALVIN C. YORK STATE HISTORIC AREA

Alvin C. York State Historic Area, established in 1968, is located approximately 8.5 miles north of Jamestown on U.S. Highway 127. Situated on the edge of the beautiful valley of the Wolf River, not far from Kentucky, it is a remembrance of the most decorated American military hero of World War I. The small town

of Pall Mall includes the York home and farm, which he received as a gift from grateful Tennesseans when he returned here. There is also his store and gristmill. Nearby are York's grave and the church where he served as Sunday school teacher, elder, and occasional preacher.

Alvin York was a poor, ill-educated farm boy when he left America to fight in World War I. He returned an international hero, after his courage and marksmanship led him and seven surviving members of his squad to kill 25 German soldiers and capture 132 prisoners in a single engagement on October 18, 1918. York was feted by the Allied countries and their leaders and offered wealth and fame when he returned to the United States. He chose instead to return to rural Tennessee, marry his childhood sweetheart, and live his life there, while seeking to improve the future for his remote community. York used his celebrity to obtain better roads and educational improvements for the upper Cumberland Plateau. The Alvin York Institute was founded in 1929 and provided generations of mountain children with education and vocational opportunities. When York died in 1964, 7,000 people attended his funeral.

The bucolic Alvin York State Historic Area (Pall Mall, 931/879-6456, free) is a fitting tribute to this most remarkable American war hero. The park includes the old York home, which is full of photographs and memorabilia reflecting on the famous soldier and his community. The old York gristmill is picturesque, and a picnic ground provides an excuse to linger. As of this writing, York's son, Andy, remains the park ranger, and on most days he is there to tour you through the home.

DALE HOLLOW LAKE

Dale Hollow Lake is a 27,700-acre manmade lake located in parts of Pickett, Clay, Fentress, and Overton Counties, plus Clinton and Cumberland Counties in Kentucky. Created in 1943, the Dale Hollow Dam impounds the Obey River, about seven miles above its junction with the Cumberland. Byrdstown on the east and Celina on the

PHOTO COURTESY OF TENNESSEE DEPARTMENT OF TOURIST DEVELOPMENT

Fishing is a popular pursuit at Dale Hollow Lake near Byrdstown.

west are the main gateways to the lake and its recreational opportunities.

The **Dale Hollow National Fish Hatchery** (50 Fish Hatchery Rd., Celina, 931/243-2443, www.fws.gov/dalehollow, daily 7 A.M.–3:30 P.M., free) produces rainbow, brown, and lake trout for restocking rivers and lakes in Tennessee and neighboring states. The hatchery produces more than 300,000 pounds of trout each year for stocking programs. There is a visitors center where you can learn about trout and the hatchery process. You can also tour the facility.

Recreation

Fishing and boating are popular pastimes on Dale Hollow Lake. There are 14 commercial marinas on the lake, including **East Port** (5652 East Port Rd., 931/879-7511) near Alpine, and **Star Point** (4490 Star Point Rd., 931/864-3335) and **Sunset Marina** (Hwy. 111, 931/864-3115), both near Byrdstown. Because of its above-average water quality,

the lake is sometimes used by scuba divers. The only commercial dive shop is located at **Willow Grove Marina** (9990 Willow Grove Hwy., 931/823-6616, www.willowgrove.com) near Allons.

Camping

The U.S. Army Corps of Engineers provide six campgrounds around the lake. They include the **Obey River Campground** (931/864-6388, $12–24), which has 132 RV and tent sites, dump stations, electrical hook-ups, bath houses, and a developed swimming area on the lake. Obey River Campground is located near Byrdstown, and sits picturesquely on the lakeshore. You may reserve campsites by calling 877/444-6777, or by visiting www.reservation.gov.

CORDELL HULL BIRTHPLACE STATE HISTORIC AREA

Congressman, U.S. secretary of state, and Nobel Laureate, Cordell Hull was born in 1871 and raised in upper Pickett County. Hull's family was poor; he was educated in part at home and then in free schools until his parents were able to afford a private education.

Education was not wasted on Cordell Hull, who possessed a quick and astute mind. In 1891 he received a law degree after just one year of course work at Cumberland University in Lebanon. Hull went on to work as a lawyer and judge before entering into a political career that would eventually take him to the highest reaches of the U.S. government.

Hull was a member of the U.S. House of Representatives from 1906 to 1931, when he was elected to the U.S. Senate. In 1933, Hull was chosen as secretary of state under president Franklin D. Roosevelt, a position which he would hold for 11 years. Hull received the Nobel Peace Prize in 1945 for his role in helping to establish the United Nations. He was also an ardent supporter of free trade, believing that world peace and progress depended on nations having free access to the raw materials and markets of the world.

Hull left public service in 1944 and lived out the remainder of his years in Washington,

D.C. He did not return to the rural Tennessee countryside from whence he came.

The Cordell Hull Birthplace State Historic Area (Hwy. 325, Byrdstown, 931/864-3247) consists of a visitors center, replica of Hull's childhood home, and a natural trail. A museum contains artifacts belonging to Hull, including his Nobel Peace Prize, plus original papers and photographs. The cabin portrays the lifestyle that Hull would have experienced while he lived here from 1871 to 1874.

There is a one-mile hiking trail, as well as a picnic area for day use.

STANDING STONE STATE PARK

Covering nearly 11,000 acres of hills and valleys on the Upper Cumberland Plateau, Standing Stone State Park (1674 Standing Stone Hwy., Hilham, 931/823-6347) is a place for relaxing recreation. The 12-foot-tall "standing stone" for which it was named once stood along the Avery Trace, an early road which is now Highway 70. The stone is no longer in its original site; a portion of it is on display in Monterey.

Recreation

The 70-acre Standing Stone Lake offers fishing and boating. Paddle boats may be rented from the park office year-round, and you can bring your own electric trolling motor and battery if you wish. No private boats are allowed. Fishers often catch large-mouth bass, blue gill, crappie, lake trout, and catfish.

There are eight miles of day-use hiking trails, including several that climb to points where you can enjoy views of the surrounding area.

The park swimming pool is open from Memorial Day to Labor Day.

Camping

A pleasant campground has 36 trailer and tent sites ($20), each equipped with a table, charcoal grill, and water and electrical hookups. The campground is open year-round, but the bathhouses close from December to March. Sites are available on a first-come, first-served basis.

Cabins

Standing Stone has 14 rustic cabins ($60–65), which can accommodate between two and eight people and are open from April through October. Eight timber lodges ($90–120) have central heat and air-conditioning and are open year-round. They sleep up to 10 people. Four modern cabins ($70–90) are also open year-round and can accommodate up to eight people. There is also a group lodge, and a meeting room.

All cabins are equipped for housekeeping. However there are no televisions, microwaves, or telephones in the cabins.

CLARKRANGE

Located on Highway 127 south of Jamestown is Clarkrange and the **Cumberland Mountain General Store** (Hwy. 127, 931/863-3880, May–Nov. Tues.–Sat. 10 A.M.–5 P.M., Sun. noon–5 P.M.), an old-time general store that dates back to 1923. Inside, it is stocked with old-fashioned household items, antiques, and local crafts. A '50s-style diner serves burgers, fries, and milkshakes.

COOKEVILLE

Cookeville is the seat of Putnam County and the largest city on the Upper Cumberland Plateau. Cookeville is closely associated with I-40, which passes just south of town. For road-weary travelers, Cookeville is a pit stop or a mile mark to show one's progress.

Off the interstate, Cookeville's greatest source of energy and vitality is **Tennessee Tech University** (1000 N. Dixie Ave., 931/432-5312, www.tntech.edu), a public university with an enrollment of more than 10,000. Tennessee Tech was founded in 1909 as Dixie College, and was affiliated with the Church of Christ. Since 1965 it has been part of the state's higher-education system. The campus is located on the northwest side of town, near 12th Street and Peachtree Avenue, and includes historic Henderson and Derryberry Halls.

Sights

Visitors to Cookeville should find their way to the **West Side District,** located along West

Broad Street, North Cedar and Church Avenues, and 1st Street. This is the best area for shopping and dining. It is also where you will find the **Cookeville Depot Museum** (116 W. Broad St., 931/528-8570, Tues.–Sat. 10 A.M.–4 P.M., free). Located in the town's old train depot, the museum houses railway artifacts, memorabilia, and photographs of the railroad in Putnam County over the years. The depot was built in 1909.

The **Cookeville History Museum** (40 E. Broad St., 931/520-5455, Wed.–Sat. 10 A.M.–4 P.M., free) houses an extensive collection of artifacts, photographs, and other items of interest from Cookeville's history.

Cookeville's newest attraction is the **Cookeville Children's Museum** (36 W. 2nd St., 931/979-7529, Wed.–Fri. 10 A.M.–2 P.M., Sat. 10 A.M.–4 P.M., adults $4, children 2 years and up $3). Opened in 2007, the children's museum houses interactive and educational exhibits for children aged 2–12 years. They include music-making, arts exploration, and outdoor games.

The Arts

Tennessee Tech University lends sophistication to Cookeville's arts scene. The university's Bryon Fine Arts Building is home of the Bryon Symphony Orchestra, which performs six times per year. The **Jean Derryberry Gallery** (Roaden University Center, 931/372-3123, Mon.–Fri. 10 A.M.–4:30 P.M., free) exhibits student and faculty work, plus special exhibits from the university's collection.

The **Cookeville Drama Center** (10 E. Broad St., 931/528-1313, www.cookville-tn.org/dramacenter) is a performing-arts venue where local and touring productions are staged. The Cookeville Mastersingers also perform here. The Drama Center also organizes summer shows at the **Dogwood Park and Performance Pavilion,** including Shakespeare in the Park and Symphony in the Park.

For visual arts, visit the **Upper Cumberland Arts Alliance Gallery** (Cookeville Mall, 931/265-0338), which displays and sells works from artists in 14 Upper Cumberland counties. The **Cumberland Art Society Backdoor Gallery** (186 S. Walnut St., 931/526-2424) showcases fine art and photography, plus an annual juried membership show. Visitors may see an artist at work in the open studio space. The gallery offers special workshops and demonstrations throughout the year.

Accommodations

There is a host of chain hotels and motels in Cookeville, with most found around exit 287 off I-40. The town's most distinctive accommodations are found at **Cookeville Manor Bed and Breakfast** (7241 Hilham Hwy., 931/372-8236, $80–110), a redbrick colonial house near downtown. Guest accommodations include one suite and two rooms. A full breakfast is served, and guests may use several downstairs sitting rooms, plus a conference room facility.

Food

For a fine Italian meal, make reservations at **Mauricio's Ristorante Italiano** (232 N. Peachtree Ave., 931/528-2456, Thurs.–Fri. 11 A.M.–2 P.M., Tues.–Sat. 4–9 P.M., $15–32), a perfect place for a special night out or a business meal. The richly painted walls and rustic decor is easy yet elegant, and the service is careful but not fussy. The menu offers authentic and well-executed Italian dishes.

For a casual lunch in the West Side district, head to **The Soup Kitchen** (20 W. Broad St., 931/528-7687, Mon.–Fri. 8 A.M.–8 P.M., $5–12) for deli-style sandwiches, fresh soups, and salads.

Dipsy Doodle Drive Inn (2331 W. Broad St., 931/372-2663, Mon.–Thurs. 5:30 A.M.–8 P.M., Fri.–Sat. 5:30 A.M.–8:30 P.M., $5–12) offers Southern-style cooking, and **Bobby Q's BBQ** (1070 N. Washington Ave., 931/526-1024 or 931/526-1024, Tues.–Thurs. 11 A.M.–8:45 P.M., Fri.–Sat. 11 A.M.–9:45 P.M., $5–12) is one of Cookeville's oldest, and most favorite, barbecue restaurants.

MONTEREY

The city park in downtown Monterey is home to part of the stone that once stood in Standing Stone State Park, north of town.

The countryside north of Monterey is home to the Muddy Pond Mennonite Community. This is good countryside to explore if you are looking for handicrafts or home-baked bread and other specialty items. It is also a beautiful area to drive through.

To find Muddy Pond, drive north from Monterey on Highway 164, until you reach Muddy Pond Road. Turn right onto Muddy Pond, and travel a couple miles. You have arrived. The **Muddy Pond General Store** (3608 Muddy Pond Rd., 931/445-7829) sells handcrafts, quilts, pottery, bulk foods, and clothing. The **Country Porch** (3130 Muddy Pond Rd., 931/445-7370) also has gift items,

as well as light lunch fare, including soups and sandwiches.

One of the community's best attractions is the **Guenther's Sorghum Mill** (4064 Muddy Pond Rd., 931/445-3357). On Tuesday, Thursday, and Saturday in September and October you can watch as the sorghum mill makes its molasses. If you come at this time, you may see a horse-powered mill squeezing cane juice from the sorghum stalks. The juice is boiled in the evaporator pan until it turns into the thick, golden-hued syrup.

At other times of the year, come by the mill to purchase sorghum and other specialty items in their variety store.

CUMBERLAND TRAIL STATE PARK

In 1998, Tennessee established its 53rd state park, the **Justin P. Wilson Cumberland Trail State Park** (423/566-2229). When it is completed, the park will be a 300-mile linear trail that runs from Cumberland Gap National Park on Tennessee's northern border, all the way to Chickamauga and Chattanooga National Military Park and Prentice Cooper Wildlife Management Area in the south.

Some 150 miles of the Cumberland Trail are open, and others are being developed. The nonprofit **Cumberland Trail Conference** (www.cumberlandtrail.org) is spearheading trail projects and is the best source of information on current conditions, campsites, and other useful hiking information.

The trail traverses the ancient Cumberland Mountains. Passing through 11 counties, the trail and associated parklands encompass gorges, valleys, mountain peaks, waterfalls, and geological formations.

Portions of the trail include:

· **Cumberland Mountain,** which begins in Cumberland Gap National Park and travels to Cove Lake State Park;

· **Smoky Mountain,** a 25-mile segment beginning at Cove Lake and crossing through the heart of the Cumberland Mountains to Frozen Head State Park;

· **Frozen Head,** which begins at Frozen Head State Park and ends at the Obed Wild and Scenic River, traversing from the ridgeline to a watershed gorge;

· **Obed River,** a 17-mile pass through the Obed Wild and Scenic River and the Catoosa Wildlife Management Area;

· **Grassy Cove,** which traverses Brady and Black Mountains surrounding Grassy Cove;

· **Stinging Fork,** a 15-mile segment using an already-established trail system through the Bowater Pocket Wilderness;

· **Piney River,** a 22-mile segment that includes 10 miles of the Piney River Pocket Wilderness Trailhead, and then leaving the escarpment above Spring City;

· **Laurel-Snow,** a 32-mile segment passing through the existing Laurel-Snow Bowater Pocket Wilderness Trail;

· **North Chickamauga,** a 20-mile segment located almost exclusively within the North Chickamauga Creek Gorge; and

· **Tennessee River Gorge,** the final leg of the trail located in Prentice Cooper State Forest.

The trail terminates at Signal Mountain.

Accommodations

For lodging, check out the chain hotels along the interstate, or call for a room at **The Garden Inn Bed and Breakfast** (1400 Bee Rock Rd., 931/823-1400, $135–145). This 11-room inn offers private bathrooms, full breakfast, and a lovely, rural location on the plateau. The grounds include the Bee Rock overlook, from which you can see Calfkiller Valley and Stamps Hollow below.

OBED WILD AND SCENIC RIVER

The Obed Wild and Scenic River, added to the National Park system in 1976, is—like its nearby and better-known neighbor, the Big South Fork National River and Recreation Area—based around a prized white-water recreation stream. The Obed park, managed jointed by the U.S. Deptartment of Interior and the Tennessee State Wildlife Management Agency, encompasses 56 miles of the rugged Obed and Emory River system, with adjacent riparian areas. The park offers Class II–IV white water, and excellent rock-climbing opportunities. For hikers there is a 14.2-mile section of the Cumberland Trail State Park along the Obed and its Daddy's Creek tributary, though portions of this trail are closed during certain hunting seasons.

Camping

The Rock Creek Campground, a no-reservation, 12-site facility with pit toilets and no water or electric hook-ups, provides a place to sleep. Backcountry camping is also allowed.

Information

The park's **visitor center** (208 N. Maiden St., Wartburg, 423/346-6294, www.nps.gov/obed, daily 8 A.M.–4:30 P.M., free) has a small museum and information about recreation in the park.

FROZEN HEAD STATE NATURAL AREA

Frozen Head State Natural Area (964 Flat Fork Rd., Wartburg, 423/346-3318) is famous for its beautiful spring wildflowers. The park takes its name from Frozen Head Mountain, a 3,324-foot peak often covered by ice and snow in winter.

On a clear day, the views from the top of Frozen Head extend to the Smoky Mountains in the east, the Cumberland Mountains to the north, and the Cumberland Plateau to the west. Cross Mountain (3,534 feet), the tallest peak in the Tennessee portion of the plateau, is within view.

You can reach the summit of Frozen Head Mountain on the South Old Mac Trail (2.4 miles), or the North Old Mac Trail (3.3 miles).

The land here was not always a park. Much of Frozen Head State Natural Area was part of Brushy Mountain State Prison, and convict labor was used to mine coal from the hills. During the early 20th century, the forest was heavily logged and in 1952 it was burnt by forest fire. Over the past decades, a new forest has grown up, including an exceptional array of spring wildflowers.

To see the blooms, hike along any of the lower

falls along the Flat Fork Creek in Frozen Head State Natural Area

PHOTO COURTESY OF TENNESSEE DEPARTMENT OF TOURIST DEVELOPMENT

trails, especially those that hug the Flat Fork Creek that flows through the park. Panthers Branch Trail (2.1 miles) is a favorite walk for flowers. It also passes the DeBord Falls.

There are 20 primitive campsites for backpackers in Frozen Head. As many as 75 people can be accommodated at the group camp.

There are picnic tables, pavilions, an amphitheater, and a visitors center, plus a 6.9-mile bike-horse trail. All the rest of the 50 miles of trail are for hiking only.

The Flat Fork Creek is stocked with rainbow trout in the spring, and it is a favorite place for fishing.

The Middle Plateau

The center swath of the plateau is the most populated—it is close to I-40 and the population centers of Crossville and Cookeville. Universities in the area lend greater sophistication and wealth to some parts of the middle plateau. Highway 70, once called the Broadway of America, runs east–west through this part of the plateau, providing a much more pleasant experience than the nearby interstate.

KINGSTON

This town, the seat of Roane County, sits on the banks of Watts Bar Lake. The lake was formed in 1942 when the Clinch, Emory, and Tennessee Rivers were dammed by the Tennessee Valley Authority's Watts Bar Dam.

Kingston is an old city. It was founded in 1799 around an army garrison on the Clinch River. You can see a replica of this installation at **Fort Southwest Point** (1226 Hwy. 58, 865/376-3641, www.southwestpoint.com, Apr.–mid-Dec. Mon.–Sat. 10 A.M.–4 P.M., $1). The fort was built in 1797 as settlers moved westward and came into conflict with Native Americans whose lands were being encroached upon. The fort and its soldiers were supposed to protect the Cherokee land from white settlement. At its peak, Fort Southwest Point housed 600 soldiers.

Fort Southwest Point was abandoned by the army in 1811. Beginning in 1974, archaeologists began to study the ruins. Today, parts of the original fort have been re-created, including a barracks, blockhouse, and more than 250 feet of palisade walls. The museum also has artifacts found on the site.

In the heart of downtown Kingston is the **Roane County Courthouse,** one of only seven remaining pre–Civil War courthouses in Tennessee. Inside is the **Roane County Museum of History** (119 Court St., 865/376-4201, www.roanetnheritage.com, Mon. 8:30 A.M.–6:30 P.M., Tues.–Fri. 8:30 A.M.–4:30 P.M., free), which is part of the Roane County Archives.

Recreation

Watts Bar Lake is located just a few blocks from downtown Kingston. There is a walking trail along the riverbank. Popular activities include fishing and boating.

The *Watts Bar Belle* (695 S. Kentucky St., aka Hwy. 58, 865/376-5995, www.wattsbar-belle.com) is a small riverboat that cruises the lake and offers lunch and dinner cruises ($9–25), sightseeing tours ($17), and private events. It operates year-round.

Accommodations

Woodland Cove Bed and Breakfast (Rockwood Ferry Rd., 865/717-3719, www.woodlandcov-ebb.com, $120–175) is located on Watts Bar Lake, about 15 minutes' drive south of Kingston. This lovely waterfront retreat offers a dock, water activities including canoeing, swimming, and paddle-boating, and lovely views of the lake. Rooms have private bathrooms and guests get a full breakfast, evening dessert, and drinks.

HARRIMAN

Harriman, a town of less than 10,000, has an interesting history. It was founded in 1890 by a Methodist minister who wanted to form a town on the foundation of social temperance and industry, where no alcohol would be permitted. His idea struck a chord with people from all over the country, and when he held a one-day land sale in 1890 more than 570 lots were sold and more than $600,000 made.

The town's **Cornstalk Heights** historic district between Roane and Cumberland Streets comprises 135 historic Victorian houses, many built by these early investors. The **Harriman Heritage Museum** (330 Roane St., 865/882-3122) is open by appointment and tells the story of the city's founding. A guide to the town's historic homes has been published by the Cornstalk Heights Community Organization and is available from the **Roan County Visitors Bureau** (119 Court St., 423/376-4201), located in the courthouse.

The **Midtown Drive-In Theatre** (2734 Roane Hwy., aka Hwy. 70, 865/882-6119), located just south of town, shows movies during the summer.

OZONE FALLS STATE NATURAL AREA

This dramatic waterfall is located a few steps from Highway 70, near the town of Ozone, located between Harriman and Crossville. Ozone Falls is also a short drive from I-40 (you can get there from either exit 329 or 338), and so a poplar stop for road-weary travelers who want to breath some fresh air and stretch their legs. Be wary, however, because the path that goes to the top of the falls dead-ends at a 110-foot drop. There is no guard rail or fence to keep you from falling, so exercise caution. Families with small children may want to skip this trail altogether.

For a safer and better look at the falls, take the half-mile path to the bottom of the falls. It passes through a lovely gorge with interesting rock formations and old-growth forest.

Ozone Falls is a unit of the Cumberland Mountain State Park. There is an information board at the parking area, but no rangers on duty.

GRASSY COVE

On Highway 68, just a few miles outside the town of Homestead, is the lovely rural community of Grassy Cove. Surrounded by Brady and Black Mountains, the cove is more than 10,000 acres. In 1974 it was declared a National Natural Landmark because it is one of the largest limestone sinkholes in North America. Remarkably, the cove is drained by a cave and after the water flows into the cave it emerges some six to seven days later at the mouth of the Sequatchie River, on the other side of the mountain.

For casual visitors, however, Grassy Cove's appeal is not geologic: It is the countryside. Drive along any of the secondary roads and soak in the landscape of lightly rolling hills, largely used for livestock farming, surrounded by steep wooded hillsides. Take Kemmer Road off Highway 70 to find the **Grassy Cove Methodist Church and Cemetery,** built in 1803, and the picturesque **Grassy Cove Community House,** built in 1894 and used as part of the Presbyterian Grassy Cove Academy from 1880 to 1906.

On Highway 68 there are two general stores, distinguishable by a single letter. The **J. C. Kemmer & Sons General Store** at the south side of the cove offers old-fashioned cookware, overalls and other workingman's attire, and an array of other odds and ends, some of which you may need. The **J. A. Kemmer & Son General Store,** on the north end of the cove, doesn't have as much inventory (but what it does have is similar), but it does have an old-fashioned wood-burning stove where you can sit and visit with the proprietor, if he is around.

◖ CUMBERLAND HOMESTEADS

The town of Homestead southeast of Crossville is named for Cumberland Homesteads, the New Deal project that saw the construction of more than 250 homesteads for poor families during the Great Depression. Organized by the government's Division of Subsistence Housing (later called the Resettlement Administration),

CUMBERLAND HOMESTEADS

During president Franklin Roosevelt's New Deal anything was possible. On several thousand remote acres of land atop the Cumberland Plateau, that thing was Cumberland Homesteads, a radical project to give hundreds of out-of-work laborers a second chance.

Under the scheme, poor families would agree to work and contribute to collective projects, including the construction of their own homes. In return, workers were paid for a portion of their labor. The rest was turned into credits in order to pay off their own homestead, which consisted of a family home, chicken pen, smokehouse, privy, two-story barn, and lands where families were expected to raise their own food.

Between 1934 and 1938, some 262 homesteads were built and thousands of people, many of them from other parts of Tennessee, moved to the Cumberland Plateau to make a new life. It was, by all accounts, a hard life, but also a happier and more promising one than many people left behind. In addition to the homesteads themselves, the community built a school where children could be educated. There were also opportunities to learn new skills – from canning to masonry – which would help families after the Depression, and the New Deal, ended.

There were a handful of similar homestead projects around the country, including one for African Americans in Virginia. To reformers and planners, the project meant an opportunity to demonstrate that a planned, cooperative community could work.

Cumberland Homesteads did work for several years. A labor dispute in which homesteaders complained they were being shortchanged on work credits created animosity between the project architects and those who actually lived there. But despite the difficulties, most homestead families remained, even after the formal project wrapped up around 1940.

The legacy of Cumberland Homesteads is strong. A handful of homestead family members are still alive, and their descendents live all over the plateau. Some still live in the homestead houses, distinctive for their common Tudor-style cottage design and the Crab Orchard stone with which they were built. An association of Homestead descendents and other supporters runs the Cumberland Homesteads Museum in the old administration building and water tower, at the intersection of Highway 68 and U.S. Highway 70 southeast of Crossville.

the project was designed to give poor Tennessee families an opportunity to work for the basics of life, plus learn new skills and acquire a permanent home.

The countryside around Homestead—U.S. Highways 127 and 70, and Highway 68—is dotted with old homestead houses, distinctive for their cottage features and the use of golden-hued Crab Orchard stone.

To learn more about the Homestead experiment, visit the **Homesteads House Museum** (2611 Pigeon Ridge Rd., aka U.S. 127, 931/456-9663, www.cumberlandhomesteads.org, Mon.–Sat. 10 A.M.–5 P.M., Sun. 1–5 P.M., adults $2, youths $1, children under 6 free), which is open from March through mid-December. Located in the distinctive

Homestead tower and administration building, the museum tells the story of the project, depicts what life was like for homesteaders, and includes a gallery about the original homestead families. The building itself is remarkable; the ground floor consists of four "wings," each of which now houses exhibits. The tower, which housed a water tank for the homesteaders, reaches up above the trees and offers views of the surrounding countryside. No one can really explain why the planners chose to build such an unusual building, but one theory is that it was to expose the workmen to advanced building techniques.

The folks at the Homesteads museum are remarkably friendly, and the gift shop has local-made crafts, books and pamphlets about the project, and a hefty cookbook of recipes collected from homesteaders.

CUMBERLAND MOUNTAIN STATE PARK

Cumberland Mountain State Park (U.S. 127 S., 931/484-6138) was developed as a recreation area for the Cumberland homesteaders and built between 1938 and 1940 by the Civilian Conservation Corps (CCC). Its focal point is a seven-arch dam and bridge made from Crab Orchard stone, which impounds Byrd Creek to make pleasant 50-acre Byrd Lake. The 70-year-old dam, which got a facelift in 2008, is a monument to the labors of the young men of the CCC. WWI hero Sgt. Alvin York briefly served as a foreman on the project until he was called away in 1940 for the filming of his life story.

Recreation

There are six **hiking** trails, ranging from easy paths around the lake to an overnight loop. During the summer months, you can rent boats for use on Byrd Lake and fishing is popular. There is a swimming pool and tennis courts.

Accommodations

There are 37 cabins, which range from modern to rustic, and a group lodge. The campground has 147 sites with electric and water hook-ups.

Food

The park restaurant (931/484-6138, summer daily 11 A.M.–2:30 P.M. and 4–8 P.M., Jan.–Apr. Tues.–Sat. 11 A.M.–2:30 P.M., Fri.–Sat. 4–8 P.M., $6–16) overlooks the lake and serves three meals daily. Friday evening is catfish night.

CROSSVILLE

Named because it was here that the old Nashville–Knoxville road crossed the Chattanooga–Kentucky road, Crossville is now a pleasant town and the unofficial capital of the Cumberland Plateau. Smaller than nearby

© SUSANNA HENIGHAN POTTER

The Palace Theatre in Crossville is one of many buildings on the plateau constructed out of distinctive Crab Orchard stone.

Cookeville, and more appealing, Crossville is a pleasant place to spend a few hours.

One of the first things you should look for in Crossville is Crab Orchard stone, a distinctive tan-colored sandstone that is quarried in the area and derived its name from the community of Crab Orchard just down the road. Crab Orchard stone was used by local builders for years, but in 1925 it grew in popularity after a Nashville architect used it at Scarrit College. It has been used all over the country.

Crab Orchard stone was used to build Crossville's first courthouse and the Palace Theatre on Main Street, among many other buildings around town.

Sights

The **Cumberland County Courthouse,** designed by W. Chamberlin and Company and built in 1905, sits in the center of town. Its yard has been used over the years for public art displays and memorials, the most recent being a memorial to U.S. soldiers killed in Iraq and Afghanistan. Across Main Street from the present-day courthouse is the older one, built in 1886. It houses the homegrown **Upper Cumberland Military Museum** (20 S. Main St., 931/456-5520, Mon.–Fri. 10 A.M.–3 P.M., free) with memorabilia from the Civil War through to the war in Iraq. There is an interesting display about the Prisoner of War camp built in Crossville during World War II.

About a block away from the courthouse is the **Palace Theatre** (72 S. Main St., 931/484-6133, www.palacetheatre-crossville.com). Built in 1938 out of Crab Orchard stone with art deco flourishes, the Palace was a first-run movie theater for 40 years. In 1993 it was listed on the National Register of Historic Places, and after being abandoned and derelict for many years, the community decided to preserve the Palace. A restored and expanded Palace Theatre opened in 2001.

The 302-seat facility hosts events ranging from high school band concerts to regional musical events. They also show movies. Pop in while you're in town and someone is bound

to offer to show you around, as long as it is not in use.

At the corner of North and Main Streets is the old **Crossville Depot** (931/456-2586). The depot was built in 1900 and served as the town's train station until 1968, when the trains stopped running through Crossville. In the 1980s the old tracks were removed. In 1996 three local Rotary Clubs spearheaded a project to restore the old depot. Today, it houses a gift shop. Inside there are a few photographs and displays about the old railroad.

Golf

Crossville calls itself the Golf Capital of Tennessee because there are 10 different golf courses in the area. **The Bear Chase at Cumberland Mountain** (407 Wild Plum Ln., 931/707-1640, www.tngolftrail.net) is one of the public golf courses operated in partnership with the state park system. It was designed by Jack Nicklaus. The 6,900-yard, par-72 layout features a design that capitalizes on elevation changes as well as nature features, such as flowing brooks and clustered, mature pines. The club also offers a driving range, practice green, pro shop, rental clubs, and golf lessons.

Lake Tanasi Village (2479 Dunbar Rd., 931/788-3301, www.laketansipoa.com) is a top-rated golf course that places a premium on accuracy off the tee. The fairways of this 6,701-yard course are gently rolling, with tiered greens, water hazards, bunkers, and thick rough. There is also a driving range, practice green, pro shop, rental clubs, golf lessons, and on-site lodging.

For a detailed rundown of each golf course in the Crossville area, contact the Crossville Chamber of Commerce's special golf desk (877/465-3861, www.golfcapitaltenn.com).

Entertainment

The Cumberland Plateau's foremost arts facility is the **Cumberland County Playhouse** (221 Tennessee Ave., 931/484-5000, www.ccplayhouse.com), located a few miles west of downtown Crossville, near the Crossville airport. Founded in 1965 and nurtured by successive generations of committed Cumberland residents, the playhouse presents mainstream theatrical works like *Hello Dolly* and *Oklahoma*, plus regional and local works. They also organize acting, dance, and music classes for all ages.

Accommodations

A number of chain hotels are located near Crossville's three interstate exits. The **Best Western Leisure Inn** (exit 317, 4035 Hwy. 127 N., 931/484-1551, $75–100) is a sprawling hotel with indoor corridors, queen- and king-sized rooms, and a hot breakfast. There is also an indoor heated pool, fitness room, and business center. Children 12 and under stay free. Discounts are available for 7-, 14-, and 30-day nonrefundable advance reservations.

The **Cumberland Mountain Lodge** (1130 Clint Lowe Rd., 931/788-5833, www.cumberlandmountainlodge.com, $250) is a rural bed-and-breakfast located on a working livestock farm. The farmhouse was fully restored in 2005, however, and the three guest rooms are comfortably and elegantly furnished in Mission style. Hardwood paneling and Crab Orchard stone feature prominently in the construction. Amenities include continental breakfast, high-speed Internet, wood-burning fireplaces, stocked fishing pond, and miles of hiking trails. Guests may also relax in the common areas, including the great room and a large, homey dining area.

Rates at Cumberland Mountain Lodge are $250 per night per couple, and $50 for each additional adult in your party. The lodge can sleep up to six adults.

The farm is located on a permanent conservation easement, and it is a relaxing and quiet place. It is located about 15 miles from Crossville, south of Cumberland Mountain State Park.

Food

Folks in Crossville like to eat lunch at **Boston's** (42 North St., 931/456-1925, Mon.–Fri. 10:30 A.M.–3 P.M., Sun. 11 A.M.–2 P.M., $4–12). They offer daily hot lunch specials plus sandwiches, salads, and soups.

For something a bit more upscale, try **Rembrandt's Cafe** (52 N. Main St., 931/456-

3636, $5), which serves pasta dishes, salads, paninis, and delectable desserts. You won't find food like this in many small Tennessee towns. There is also a full coffee bar. This friendly shop also has an Internet café and tables for playing cards.

Information

The **Cumberland County Chamber of Commerce** (34 S. Main St., 931/484-8444, www.crossville-chamber.com, Mon.–Fri. 9 A.M.–5 P.M.) has an information center, or you can order a package of brochures before you arrive. The Palace Theatre (72 S. Main St.) also has an information center with brochures, and the staff there are friendly and helpful.

PLEASANT HILL

About 10 miles west of Crossville on Highway 70 is the small town of Pleasant Hill. The **Pioneer Hall Museum** (Main St., 931/277-3872, Wed. 10 A.M.–4 P.M., Sun. 2–5 P.M., free), open from May through October, is a local history museum. Pioneer Hall was a dormitory for the Pleasant Hill Academy, established in 1884 and closed in 1947.

SPARTA

There is just something special about downtown Sparta, but it's hard to put your finger on the one thing that makes it so. Taken individually, each component seems insignificant, but together they make a pleasant whole, and a nice place to stop to stretch your legs or grab a meal.

Storefronts along Liberty Square and Bookman Way are colorful with art deco touches. The old movie theater facade was rebuilt, and there are plans to fix up the inside and make it into a functioning performing-arts center. The town amphitheater is used frequently for concerts and civic events, plus a monthly bluegrass concert. Down by the Calfkiller River, the river park has covered picnic tables, a playground and walking paths.

Lester Flatt was raised in Sparta, and he maintained a home here throughout this life. There is a historical marker on the east side of town and a monument to the bluegrass star in front of the courthouse.

Sparta, the seat of White County, was founded in 1809. Over the years the town grew along with coal, lumber, and other industries on the plateau. Sparta's newspaper is the *Expositor,* and it has been in print for more than 125 years.

Shopping

Sparta has several antiques stores. **Brasel's Antiques and Collectibles** (222 W. Bockman Way, 931/837-2805) has furniture, glass, quilts, porcelain, and Barbies, just for starters. **Anderson Antiques** (9 Maple St., 931/837-9044) on Liberty Square specializes in imported Scottish period antiques. The shop is usually open Friday and Saturday from 10 A.M. to 3 P.M. and at other times by appointment. A few blocks from the town square is **J&J Antiques** (133 S. Young St., 931/836-8123), three buildings of antiques, primitives, and collectibles.

Wheel-thrown pottery, soaps, and candles are the specialties at **The Fragrant Mushroom Pottery Gallery & Studio** (15 Rhea St., 931/836-8190).

Perhaps Sparta's most distinctive store is **Simply Southern Quilts & Gifts** (12 Liberty Sq., 931/836-3271). Opened in 2007, Cheryl Hackett's shop sells all the equipment you need to make a quilt. But what makes her store special are the sewing and quilting classes that she offers upstairs, and her open-door policy for area quilters. Anyone who wants is welcome to come in and sew in her spacious third-floor classroom (provided there's not a class in session, of course). There is a "men's lounge" on the mezzanine with a television, comfortable couch, and snacks. Crafters of all kinds will feel as if they have come home when they reach Simply Southern.

Food

Brenda Pope serves homemade soups, fresh salads, and light sandwiches at **Miss Marenda's Tea Room** (5 E. Maple, 931/836-2542, Tues.–Fri. 11 A.M.–2 P.M., $5–8). The

Sparta Cafe (104 E. Bockman Way, 931/837-2233, $2–8) is the place to come for a hearty breakfast, lunch, or dinner. The breakfast menu offers variations on a theme: "Hungry Man's Breakfast," "Big Breakfast," and "Steak Breakfast." Lighter appetites can order a bowl of oatmeal for 80 cents. At lunch and dinnertime, choose from entrées like country ham, popcorn shrimp, and catfish. Sandwiches are also on offer.

For pizzas and Italian food, the **Brick Oven** (125 Church Hill Dr., 931/836-3444, www.brick-oven.net) sells calzones, strombolis, sandwiches, subs, salads, pasta, and all sorts of pizzas.

Information

Stop at the **Sparta-White County Chamber of Commerce** (16 W. Bockman Way, 931/836-3552, www.sparta-chamber.net) for information, maps, and brochures.

AROUND SPARTA
Rock House Shrine

About four miles east of Sparta off Highway 70 is Rock House Shrine (931/761-2885, Wed., Fri., Sat. 10 A.M.–3 P.M., adults $5, children $3), a 175-year-old sandstone house that once served as a stagecoach stop on the Wilderness Road. The likes of Andrew Jackson and Sam Houston slept here, along with hundreds of less-famous men and women. The Daughters of the American Revolution has maintained and protected the building over the years, and it is usually open for tours from April to October. Call to confirm.

You can get to the Rock House from Sparta two ways. Follow the new Highway 70 if you like, but a more pleasant drive departs Gains Street downtown and becomes Country Club Lane. This is the old Highway 70, and takes you directly to the Shrine.

Virgin Falls State Natural Area

One of the best all-day hikes in the Sparta area is the **Virgin Falls,** a mysterious 110-foot waterfall. No surface water leads to the falls or away from it; the falls appear from an underground stream and disappear at the bottom into another cave. It is quite a sight.

The eight-mile round-trip hike to Virgin Falls is through the state-owned 1,157-acre Virgin Falls State Natural Area. The natural area has at least three additional waterfalls and several caves and sinkholes. From the Caney Fork Overlook you enjoy a dramatic view of Scott's Gulf and the Caney Fork River 900 feet below.

The parking lot for the natural area is located on Scotts Gulf Road southeast of Sparta. To find it, drive 11 miles east of Sparta along Highway 70. Turn onto Eastland Road (also called Mourberry Road), and drive six miles until you reach Scotts Gulf Road. The parking lot and trailheads are two miles up the road, on the right side.

For information contact the State's Division of Natural Areas in Nashville at 615/532-0431.

Mennonite Community

There is a Mennonite community just outside of Sparta. Follow Young Street south out of town about three miles and look for Pleasant Hill Road. Take a right and in less than 100 yards is the **Country Store and Bakery**, operated by Mennonites. The store carries salvage groceries, a handful of Amish and Mennonite-made goods, and some practical goods specific to Mennonite people, such as dark-blue cloth. You can also buy bulk cheese and Amish and Mennonite cookbooks. The store is next door to a Mennonite school and church. It is open Monday through Saturday, and does not allow patrons wearing shorts, sleeveless shirts, or tank tops.

Walling

Real Cajun food is on the menu at the **Foglight Foodhouse** (275 Powerhouse Rd., 931/657-2364, Tues.–Sat. 5–9 P.M., $15–38). The first thing you will notice here is the view of the Caney Fork River. In nice weather, you can eat in the fresh air on a deck overlooking the river. Cajun specialties include

pecan fried catfish, smoked rib-eye steak, and grilled entrées.

CENTER HILL LAKE

Formed when the Army Corps of Engineers dammed the Caney Fork River, Center Hill Lake sprawls out between Smithville and Sparta. There are seven recreation areas around the lake, where you can picnic, swim, and enjoy being near the water. Eight commercial marinas cater to boaters. **Edgar Evins State Park** (Silver Point, 931/858-2446) sits on the northern banks of the lake, near I-40. Boating and other forms of water recreation are the focus at this 6,000-acre park. The Edgar Evins Marina (931/858-5695) is the center of activity for boating and fishing.

There are also 11 miles of hiking trails, including the nine-mile Jack Clayborn Millennium Trail and a short nature walk departing from the park visitors center.

Rock Island State Park (931/686-2471) at the south end of the lake is located near the town of Walling, southwest of Sparta. The Tennessee Electric Power Company built a dam and hydroelectric plan here in 1917, creating the Great Falls Reservoir. Later, the Tennessee Valley Authority took over the facility, and in 1971 the state leased the first 350 acres from TVA to form the park.

Rock Island has a sandy beach for swimming, public boat ramps, picnic tables, playgrounds, and facilities for basketball, volleyball, tennis, and more. Fishing is popular on the lake, especially during spring.

You can stay in one of 10 cabins ($100–135), or at the 60-site campground ($20).

BURGESS FALLS STATE NATURAL AREA

The Falling Water River is the focal point of Burgess Falls State Natural Area (931/432-5312), located northwest of Sparta near the town of Bakers Crossroads. A three-quarter-mile hike brings you to the 130-foot Burgess Falls, named for the 18th-century Revolutionary War veteran who received this land as payment for his service to the young country. There is also a picnic area and fishing piers.

This stretch of river has long been acknowledged as a source of energy. The Burgess family operated a gristmill here for many years, which used the power of the water to grind flour and cornmeal. During the early 1920s, the City of Cookeville built a dam and power plant along the river to provide electricity for the city. The dam broke during a 1928 flood, but a new one was built in its place. The new dam operated until 1944 when it became obsolete due to the Tennessee Valley Authority's hydroelectric projects.

Get to Burgess Falls along Tennessee Highways 135 or 136. The park is located between Sparta and Smithville, north of Highway 70.

SMITHVILLE

Smithville, the seat of DeKalb County, is known as the venue for the **Smithville Fiddler's Jamboree** (615/587-8500, www.smithvilletn.com), held over Fourth of July weekend. Arts-and-crafts sellers line the street and a stage is built in front of the courthouse for two days of Appalachian music and dance.

Smithville is also associated with the Evins family, prominent businesspeople and politicians. Joe L. Evins was a U.S. congressman representing Smithville and its neighbors from 1947 to 1977. Joe's father, Edgar, was one of the chief developers of Smithville. The nearby state park is named in his honor.

Quilters, sewers, and other craftspeople might like to stop at **Becky's Fabrics and More** (105 W. Main St., 615/597-8521, Mon.–Tues. and Thurs.–Fri. 9 A.M.–5 P.M., Sat. 9 A.M.–2 P.M.), which has more than 2,000 bolts of fabric in stock plus fat quarters by the thousands. It also stocks specialty equipment for hand- and machine-quilting.

Food

Smithville is a good place to stop for lunch. **Ashburn's Alley Cafe** (109 W. Walnut St., 615/597-2559, Tues.–Sat. 10 A.M.–2 P.M., $4–8) serves a daily plate-lunch special, plus salads, soups, and sandwiches. Across the street is **Fiddler's** (108 W. Walnut St., 615/597-8646, Mon., Tues., Thurs. 7 A.M.–2 P.M., Fri.–Sat. 7 A.M.–9 P.M., Sun. 8 A.M.–2 P.M., $8–18), with home-style luncheon fare. Try the shepherd's pie or roasted rib eye. Fiddler's presents live music after 6 P.M. on Friday and Saturday evening.

On the other side of the courthouse you'll find (**Sundance** (107 E. Main St., 615/597-1910, Tues.–Fri. 10 A.M.–2 P.M., Fri.–Sat. 5–8:30 P.M., $7–20), a popular choice for its daily home-cooked lunch specials, specialty salads, fresh-brewed fruit teas, and hot-from-the-oven desserts. The menu is not extensive, but it changes daily and you can be assured that everything is made from scratch. Sundance serves dinner on weekends, when diners will also enjoy live acoustic guitar music while they eat.

AROUND SMITHVILLE
Appalachian Center for Craft

A fine-arts education center affiliated with Tennessee Tech University in Cookeville, the Appalachian Center for Craft (615/597-6801, www.tntech.edu/craftcenter, daily 9 A.M.–5 P.M., free) is located on the banks of Center Hill Lake about six miles north of Smithville.

The name is a bit misleading: The center is not located in the Appalachian Mountains (it's on the Cumberland Plateau), and it is not focused on traditional crafts. Instead, the center teaches students the latest techniques in clay, fibers, glass, metal, and woods. The results are pieces which are more a reflection of trends in modern art-making than of the mountain heritage of the area.

Visitors can tour three exhibit areas, which feature the works of Artists in Residence, students, and others. The gallery has a variety of artwork for sale, ranging from jewelry to candles and sculptures. The pieces are serious works of art.

The center has a few walking trails, and the **Walkway Cafe** (615/597-3287) serves meals seven days a week, with a focus on what is healthy, wholesome, and fresh. You will find no chicken fingers here.

The Lower Plateau

As you head south, the Cumberland Plateau narrows, eventually reaching a width of about 38 miles near Chattanooga. The Sequatchie River flows down the southern half of the plateau, creating the Sequatchie Valley, a wide, fertile valley that extends all the way to Chattanooga. West of the Sequatchie Valley is the Cumberland Plateau, and to the east the ridge is called Walden's, or Walling, Ridge.

FALL CREEK FALLS STATE PARK

Tennessee's largest state park, Fall Creek Falls State Park (2009 Village Camp Rd., Pikeville, 800/250-8611) is a prime area for outdoor recreation on the Cumberland Plateau. The 25,000-acre park derives its name from its largest waterfall and chief attraction, but there are four other falls within the bounds of the park. In addition, Fall Creek Lake offers fishing and boating, and the Cane Creek Gorge offers dramatic vistas and bluffs. An oak and hickory forest that covers most of the park gives way to tulip poplar and hemlock in the gorges.

Fall Creek Falls got its start as a public park in the 1930s when the National Park Service established a Recreation Demonstration Area here, around the falls. During the New Deal, some park infrastructure was built. In 1944, the park was deeded to the State of Tennessee. Construction of the dam began in 1966, and in 1970 other major park facilities, including the inn, were built. In the 1990s, an 18-hole golf course was added.

Planning Your Time

If you have only a few minutes, go to the Fall Creek Falls overlook and then drive to the Nature Center, where you can see two more waterfalls and walk across a swinging bridge. If you have a few hours, travel to the Nature Center, view the Cane Creek Falls, and then hike the two-mile loop that takes you along the Cane Creek Gorge and Fall Creek Falls.

Over a few days you could hike to all the falls and add the recreational activity of your choice: swimming, boating, bicycling, fishing, or even shuffleboard.

Fall Creek Falls is located within a few hours' drive of three of Tennessee's biggest cities, but it is far from any real towns. The park is about a 45-minute drive along two-lane blacktop roads to the nearest towns of McMinnville, Sparta, Crossville, and Dayton. On the outside bounds of the park are convenience stores that sell canned goods and a few basic necessities. Pikeville, a small town with a few restaurants and a grocery, is located about 20 minutes' drive away.

Fall Creek Falls is beautiful year-round—there are those who think the falls are especially lovely in winter—but the summer and fall are the most popular times to visit. The fall foliage show here is spectacular; book your cabin or other accommodations early to avoid being disappointed.

(Fall Creek Falls

At 256 feet, Fall Creek Falls is the tallest waterfall east of the Rocky Mountains. Here water plunges past millennia of rock layers and into a pool of water that is deep and mysterious. Talking is difficult at the overlook, because you have to shout to speak over the sound of falling water.

Visitors to Fall Creek Falls can take an easy stroll from the parking lot to the overlook. For a more strenuous half-mile trip, hike down to the bottom of the falls. You can also hike a two-mile loop from the Nature Center to Fall Creek Falls.

There are other waterfalls at the state park. **Cane Creek Falls** and **Cane Creek Cascade** are immediately behind the park's Nature Center. Though not as tall as Fall Creek Falls, these are just as splendid. **Piney Falls,** accessible from an overlook on the western side of the park, is considered by some to be the park's most beautiful falls.

For impressive views of the Cane Creek Gorge,

Fall Creek Falls is the tallest waterfall east of the Rocky Mountains.

go to **Millikan's Overlook** and **Buzzard's Roost.** At Millikan's you are looking out at the point where the Cane Creek Gorge joins the Piney Creek Gorge. A five-minute walk from the parking lot brings you to Buzzard's Roost, where you are eye-level with the hawks and turkey vultures that soar along the bluffs.

For information about the flora, fauna, and geologic history of the Cumberland Plateau, visit the **Nature Center** (423/881-5708, daily 9 A.M.–4 P.M., free). Here you can see a three-dimensional map of the park and learn about the plants and animals that make it home. There is also a movie about the park.

Recreation

Fall Creek Lake is fun to explore by **boat.** Paddle boats, canoes, and fishing boats without motors are available for rent for between $6 and $9 a day; hourly rates are available. A fishing permit costs an extra $2, and you'll need to make sure you have a Tennessee fishing license too. You can also fish from the lakeshore.

There is an 18-hole **golf** course at the park.

Greens fees are $22–25 depending on the day. You can rent carts and clubs, and there is a driving range and practice green. Call the Pro Shop for details at 423/881-5706.

There is a **swimming** pool at the inn, which non-guests can use for $3. Swimming is not permitted in the lake.

There are three paved **bicycle** paths, for a total distance of just over three miles. Bikes are also permitted on the park roads. Chinquapin Ridge and Piney Creek are mountain bike trails. Both are about seven miles long and are appropriate for intermediate or advanced mountain bikers. For details on the trails, including current conditions, call the nature center.

During the summer, the Fall Creek Falls Stables, a private concession, offers guided **horseback riding** tours of the park for $20 per person. Contact them directly at 423/881-5952 for reservations.

There are a half-dozen **hiking** trails in the park, many of which leave from the nature center. The **Woodland Trail** is a 0.8-mile path that passes through forest to Fall Creek Falls. The **Gorge Overlook Trail** is 1.1 miles and passes three overlooks on its way to Fall Creek Falls. The three-mile **Paw Paw Trail** is the longest hike at the park and crosses Rockhouse Creek. Experienced hikers may want to try the **Cable Trail,** a steep path which runs from the Paw Paw Trail to the base of the Cane Creek Falls. It's so steep that the park has erected a cable to help you, and you should consult with park staff about the trail's condition before setting out.

Leaving from the rear of the inn parking lot is a paved 1.35-mile trail that follows the lakeshore.

Several of the trails can be combined to make for longer hikes, and there is one overnight campsite for backpackers.

Accommodations

Fall Creek Falls has an inn, campground, and cabins for its visitors. The lovely blue **fisherman's cabins** sit picturesquely on the lakefront. The landside cabins are tucked into the woods with partial views of the water. All cabins sleep up to eight people and rent for

$135 per night; between Memorial Day and Labor Day you must rent them by the week.

The inn is a concrete fortress on the lake, with about as much charm as a worn-out college dormitory. The view of the lake out your window is not enough consolation for the spiritless decor and institutional feel. Nonetheless, the beds are comfortable and it does beat an interstate motel—but just barely. Rooms rent for $80 from November to March and $93 the rest of the year.

Campsites are set in a pleasant forest near the Nature Center. Rates are $20, but you'll pay $5 extra for a site with sewer hook-up.

For inn and cabin reservations, call 423/881-5241 or 800/250-8610. For camping information, call 800/250-8611.

Food

The **Fall Creek Falls Restaurant** (daily 7 A.M.–8 P.M., $4–12) is located at the inn and serves breakfast, lunch, and dinner seven days a week. Billing itself as country cooking at affordable rates, the menu features burgers, sandwiches, fried fish, and a buffet. The buffet ($10 at supper, less at other times) includes a salad bar, about five side dishes, and three main-dish meats, plus dessert and soup. The quality of food is mediocre, however, and the health-conscious will struggle to cobble together a satisfying meal.

Around the Park

A few commercial enterprises have popped up around Fall Creek Falls. Four miles from the south gate of the park is **The Way Inn Grill** (Hwy. 284, 931/946-2800, Mon.–Sat. 7 A.M.–5 P.M., Sun. 10 A.M.–5 P.M., $2–4), which serves food off the grill daily. Their lunch special is popular and home-cooked. They also stock groceries and selected camping supplies.

On the north side of the park, **The Fire House Grill** (12959 Park Rd., 423/881-5118, Fri. 4–8 P.M., Sat. noon–8 P.M., Sun. noon–6 P.M.) sells pizza, barbecue, and groceries.

For more luxurious accommodations near the park, go to the **Fall Creek Falls Bed and Breakfast** (184 Deweese Rd., 423/881-5494, www.fallcreekfalls.com, $86–150). Located

near the north entrance of the park, the bed-and-breakfast has six guest rooms, a two-room suite, and a private cabin that overlooks the rural countryside. Rates include breakfast and tax.

Also near the north entrance to the park, **Dogwood Manor** (34 Rozzell Rd., 423/881-5898, www.dogwoodmanorbb.com, $125–130) is a four-suite inn. Built in 2006, the inn features suites with living rooms and kitchenettes. Breakfast is served on the upstairs balcony.

DAYTON

This town of 7,000 is the seat of Rhea County and the site of one of Tennessee's most famous legal events: the trial in July 1925 of teacher John Scopes on the charge that he taught evolution at the local high school.

Sights

Visitors should head directly to the **Rhea County Courthouse,** where the trial took place. In the basement there is a **museum** (Mon.–Fri. 8 A.M.–4:30 P.M., free) that gives an overview of the trial, including panels about its two principal characters: defense attorney Clarence Darrow and lawyer for the prosecution Williams Jennings Bryan. Thanks to the widespread media coverage of the trial, there are photographs and contemporary accounts of the events themselves.

If court is not in session, you can head upstairs and see the courtroom, a broad, high-ceilinged, and elegant room. The original hard-backed chairs fill the gallery and it is easy to imagine the heat and emotions that were stirred up here in 1925. It was so hot, in fact, that on at least one occasion court adjourned to a stage set up on the lawn outside the courtroom.

Bryan, who won the case for the prosecution, died during an afternoon nap five days after the trial, while he was still in Dayton. A college was founded in his honor five years later, and today **Bryan College,** on the outskirts of town, is a Christian college with an extensive collection relating to Bryan and the Scopes trial. The college celebrates Bryan's position that the Bible is the literal truth.

THE SCOPES MONKEY TRIAL

For a few weeks in the heat of July 1925, Dayton was the site of much national attention. High school football coach and biology teacher John Scopes was on trial for violating a new and controversial Tennessee law, passed just four months earlier, which made it illegal to teach "any theory that denies the story of Divine Creation of man as taught in the Bible, and to teach instead that man has descended from a lower order of animal."

F. E. Robinson, owner of a local drug store, is often credited with proposing and championing the cause that Dayton be the first city to test Tennessee's new anti-evolution law. He recruited Scopes, who agreed to be the test case. Scopes' alleged "crime" took place the previous April when he taught biology out of a state-sanctioned text book.

Dayton's interest in testing the law had little to do with the issue of evolution (although most town residents took the fundamentalist view of Divine Creation). Instead, it was an economic decision, since many in town knew that a trial like this would fill up all the hotels and put Dayton on the map in a way it had never been before. But Robinson and other organizers probably never imagined that more than 80 years after the fact, people would still be coming to Dayton on account of the trial.

One reason for the continued interest in the Scopes trial is the arresting cast of characters who took part. Clarence Darrow was one of three volunteer lawyers who took up for Scopes's defense. "Great Commoner" William Jennings Bryan was a special prosecutor. The climax of the trial took place on July 20, when Darrow called Bryan to the stand as an expert witness on the Bible.

The courtroom dual between these two lawyers was captured in the 1955 play *Inherit the Wind*, which was performed on Broadway and was made into a Hollywood film in 1960 starring Gene Kelly, Spencer Tracy, and Fredric March. The story has been the subject of at least three subsequent television remakes.

The narrow legal question of whether Scopes taught evolution to Dayton high school students was not at issue during the trial, and on July 21 the jury took 10 minutes to return a guilty verdict. The judge fined Scopes $100. Later, the Tennessee Supreme Court overturned the conviction on a technicality. Dayton prosecutors decided not to retry John Scopes, who by now was at the University of Chicago studying geology.

The legacy of the Scopes trial, and the publicity it stirred, was a wave of similar state laws banning the teaching of evolution. Tennessee's own anti-evolution statute remained on the books until 1967, although there were no other prosecutions.

© SUSANNA HENIGHAN POTTER

The Rhea County Courthouse in Dayton was the scene of the Scopes Monkey Trial in 1925.

Events

Every July since 1988, the Dayton Chamber of Commerce and Bryan College have organized a four-day performance of *The Scopes Trial,* a documentary drama of the court case, based closely on the actual transcripts. Tickets are about $15 per person, and onlookers are expected to dress as their counterparts in the mid-1920s would have: no blue jeans or T-shirts, and no pants for the ladies.

During the Scopes festival, there are arts-and-crafts booths open on the courthouse lawn, while the reenactment takes place upstairs in the courthouse. For information and tickets, call the chamber of commerce at 423/775-0361.

Accommodations

Rooms at the **Holiday Inn Express** (2650 Rhea County Hwy., 423/570-0080, $80–105) come with cable TV, microwaves, refrigerators, and coffeemakers, hair dryers, and speakerphones, among other things. There is a free hot breakfast in the morning, a business center, and a fitness room.

The Historic Magnolia House (656 Market St., 423/570-1200, www.bbonline.com/tn/magnoliahouse, $125–150) is an elegant Greek Revival home built in 1890 by a railroad doctor. There are four plush guest rooms with private baths and antique furniture. There is an air of antiquity in the home; guests are encouraged to wear 19th-century hats when they take afternoon tea in the parlor.

Food

Dayton's most distinctive restaurant is the **Fehn's 1891 House** (449 Delaware Ave., 423/775-1892, www.fehns1891house.com, Thurs. 5–8:30 P.M., Fri. 5–9 P.M., Sat. 4–8:30 P.M., 2nd and 4th Sun. 11:30 A.M.–2:30 P.M., $12–20), located in an old boarding school. The setting is elegant, yet relaxing, and the menu features stand-by favorites, such as prime rib, fried chicken, salmon, and filet mignon. Try the homemade fruit tea and the daily special dessert.

For the best deli sandwiches in Dayton, go to **Jacob Meyer's Deli** (1368 Market St.,

423/570-0023, Mon.–Sat. 9 A.M.–11 P.M.). Meyer's serves sandwiches and lunch specials 11 A.M.–5 P.M. Otherwise, come here for coffee, pastries, and desserts. Coffee and pastries are also available at **Harmony House Coffee** (447 Haywood Ln., 423/570-7656, Mon.–Fri. 7 A.M.–6 P.M., Sat. 8 A.M.–8 P.M.).

McMINNVILLE

The roads leading to McMinnville are scattered with dozens of tree nurseries. A few are retail operations, but most are wholesale, selling only to garden and home stores around Tennessee and the southeast. As a result, McMinnville and Warren County are known as the Nursery Capital. The nurseries are attracted by the good soil, temperate climate, and availability of supplies and specialist services.

The greatest tourist attraction in this part of the plateau is **Cumberland Caverns** (1437 Cumberland Caverns Rd., 931/668-4396, www.cumberlandcaverns.com, May–Aug. daily 9 A.M.–5 P.M., Sept.–Apr. daily 10 A.M.–4 P.M., adults $15, children $10). Best known for its underground ballroom, equipped with seating and a 0.75-ton crystal chandelier, Cumberland Caverns also has cave formations, underground waterfalls and pools, and a historic 1812 saltpeter mine. The underground tour is 1.5 miles long and includes the sound and light show "God of the Mountain." Kids will also enjoy the Cumberland Caverns gem mine, where they can search for semiprecious stones. It is a constant 56 degrees down in the cave.

Cumberland Caverns is located six miles southeast of McMinnville, off Highway 8.

SAVAGE GULF STATE NATURAL AREA

Carved over millions of years by Big Creek, Collins River, and Savage Creek, Savage Gulf is a network of gorges resembling a giant chicken's foot. It is also one of the Cumberland's most lovely natural areas, but you have to get out of your car to enjoy it. Fast-moving streams, steep bluffs, and the divergent habitats of the gorge and the plateau make it a fascinating place to explore.

Savage Gulf comprises 14,500 acres, 500 of which is virgin forest. There are 55 miles of trails. We owe its existence to several local residents who raised money and support for the area to be preserved. Several of the most prominent champions of the park were descended from the Swiss immigrants who settled this area in the 19th century.

Orientation

There are two ways to access Savage Gulf. The Stone Door Ranger Station (931/692-3887) is located off Highway 56 near Beersheba Springs. The Savage Ranger Station (931/779-3532) is located off Route 399 between Palmer and Cagle. It is a half-hour drive from one ranger station to the other.

The park offers programs and guided hikes year-round. Contact South Cumberland State Park (931/924-2956) for an upcoming calendar.

Recreation

There are 16 hiking trails through the natural area. Some are easy and flat, others are strenuous, taking you up, down, and around the deep gorges. Some 10 primitive campsites scattered throughout the park make it easy to plan an overnight hiking trip. A camping permit is required; contact the ranger stations for details.

The single greatest sight at Savage Gulf is the **Stone Door,** a rock formation that looks like a giant door that has been left ajar. Native Americans used it to travel from the plateau to the gorges. It is a 0.8-mile hike from the Stone Door Ranger Station along the plateau to the Stone Door. Also leaving from the Stone Door Ranger Station is the **Laurel Falls Loop,** a short 0.3-mile walk to a waterfall.

The **Savage Day Loop** is a 4.2-mile hike that begins and ends at the Savage Ranger Station. Along the way you walk across a suspension bridge, stop at Rattlesnake Point Overlook, and follow an old logging road.

For a detailed map of the hiking trails and

campsites at Savage Gulf, stop by or call one of the ranger stations and ask for the trails map.

DUNLAP

Dunlap, Tracy City, Coalmont, and other small towns in this part of the plateau owe their existence to coal. From the 1860s until the 1920s, coal was mined in this area. During the 20th century, much of the coal was turned to coke—a refined coal product used in iron and steel foundries. Coke ovens were built all over the countryside.

Dunlap has preserved the history of these coke ovens at the **Dunlap Coke Oven Park** (423/949-3493, www.cokeovens.com, free), a 62-acre park where some 268 old coke ovens have been preserved. The Coke Oven Museum at the park is open by appointment. To find the park, drive south on Highway 127 through Dunlap and turn right on Cherry Street at the stoplight. Cross the railroad tracks and follow the signs to the park.

For more information about the park and the coke ovens, contact the Sequatchie Valley Historical Association at 423/949-2156.

TRACY CITY

Tracy City is a quiet town today. From 1858 until the 1920s, it was a busy coal mining town, and the site of bitter labor disputes between miners and the owners of the mines.

Sights

Several historic buildings have links to the city's mining history. **Miner's Hall** on Jasper Road was the headquarters of the local United Mine Workers Union. You can see homes built by coal capitalists next door to each other along Depot Street.

Grundy Lakes State Park (Hwy. 41, 931/924-2980) is a lovely little park, and the best place in the area to see old coke ovens. A one-way road skirts a small lake, built by the Civilian Conservation Corps during the New Deal of the 1930s. You can see old ovens across the lake from the swimming beach, and also along the road just past the beach entrance. As you become better at spotting the

PHOTO COURTESY OF TENNESSEE DEPARTMENT OF TOURIST DEVELOPMENT

Thousands of coke ovens, like these in Dunlap, were built to process raw coal into clean-burning coke.

ovens, you will notice that they are scattered all over the forest through the park.

In addition to the coke ovens, Grundy Lakes has a playground, picnic tables, and walking trails. The 1.3-mile **Lone Rock Trail** skirts the lake. The 12.5-mile **Fiery Gizzard Trail** starts at Grundy Lakes and traces the Fiery Gizzard gorge. It is a beautiful and challenging walk through a diverse and rugged landscape. There are two backcountry campsites along the way, and the trail ends up at the parking area for **Foster Falls,** a 60-foot waterfall. You can also drive to Foster Falls by heading east along Highway 41 from Tracy City. The access point is located shortly after you pass into Marion County.

Shopping

Stop at **The Marugg Company** (88 Depot, 931/592-5042), manufacturers of hand-hewn rakes and other implements. They also operate an antiques shop next door. Hours are limited in the winter.

Food

The Swiss heritage of this part of Tennessee is evident at **Dutch Maid Bakery** (931/592-3171, Mon.–Sat. 7 A.M.–5 P.M., Sun. 10 A.M.–2 P.M.). The bakery was founded in 1902 by six brothers of the Baggenstoss family, and it remained in the Baggenstoss family until 1992. In 2005, it was purchased by Cynthia Day, who continues to use the old Baggenstoss recipes, plus some of her own. You will find loaves of breakfast bread and whole wheat, potato, and salt-rising bread, along with pastries and fruitcakes.

A café ($4–8) next door serves breakfast and lunch Monday through Saturday, and a buffet lunch on Sundays. There are traditional breakfast options, all served with toasted bread made at the bakery. At lunch you can get sandwiches or choose the daily lunch special, such as pork chops, chicken and dumplings, or meatloaf. The café closes at 2:30 P.M. throughout the week.

SOUTH CUMBERLAND STATE PARK

To newcomers, South Cumberland State Park (Hwy. 41, 931/924-2980) is confusing because it seems to be in so many places at the same time. The reality is that South Cumberland is an umbrella park for 10 different "units" that are scattered around the southern plateau. Units will be presented in this book where they fit in geographically.

The headquarters of the park is located along Highway 41 about halfway between Monteagle and Tracy City. There is a visitors center, museum, and recreation facilities including a ball field, picnic tables, and gift shop. The museum eloquently describes the natural and human history of the area through hand-stitched narrative panels. It is a good starting place for an overview of the area.

MONTEAGLE

Few communities in Tennessee are as surprising as Monteagle. A speck on the map, and a rest stop on the interstate, Monteagle is also home to a 125-plus-year-old summer retreat that continues to this day. The **Monteagle Assembly** (931/924-2286, www.monteagle-sundayschoolassembly.org) was founded in 1882 as the Chautauqua of the South. Created out of enthusiasm for Christian living, temperance, and intellectual and artistic development, the Monteagle Sunday School Assembly was initially meant as an ecumenical training center for Sunday School teachers. Over the years, the assembly became more secular in its focus; the annual summer program taught literature, physics, drawing, music, and education. For a time, Nashville's Peabody College held its summer school here.

What is most remarkable about the Monteagle Assembly is that it persists. Of the hundreds of similar assemblies patterned after the Chautauqua Institution in New York, fewer than 10 remain active. Monteagle is one of them. After a period of decline in the mid-20th century, Monteagle came back and the 100th-anniversary celebrations in 1982 were a major success.

Every summer, from early June until August, families return to Monteagle to live and take part in workshops, church activities, lectures, and community events. If you are having a hard time understanding what happens, imagine it as a wholesome summer camp for the whole family.

Even if you're not a member of the Assembly, you can attend workshops and other events by buying a daily gate ticket ($16). Temporary passes are also available if the workshop lasts only a few hours. Workshops range from art classes to bridge instruction. Lecture topics are equally diverse. Many have a religious perspective, but others focus on local history, health and fitness, or nature and the environment. There are also musical performances.

Part of Monteagle's appeal comes from its physical setting. The assembly is located in a wooded, hilly area, and the 161 cottages are charming examples of 19th and early-20th-century architecture, including Carpenter Gothic, Queen Anne, and Craftsman. All are well maintained, and walking or driving through the community makes you feel as if you have stepped back in time.

If you visit during the summer, you will have to pay the gate fee, which is $16 for adults per day. Outside of the summer season, visitors may drive or walk through the assembly on their own. Stop in at the office, located to the right of the gate, for a map and other information. If you come during the summer, please respect the quiet hours, which are 1–2:30 P.M. daily.

Accommodations

The (**Edgeworth Inn** (No. 23 Monteagle Assembly, 931/924-4000, www.edgeworthinn.com, $110–225) is an 11-room bed-and-breakfast located inside Monteagle Assembly. Built in 1896, this handsome Victorian offers atmosphere unmatched by other area bed-and-breakfasts. Each room has a private bath, and several suites are available. The generously proportioned porch is a focal point for visitors, as is the lovely garden.

Just outside the gates of the Assembly is the (**Monteagle Inn** (204 W. Main St., 931/924-

3869, www.monteagleinn.com, $175–205), a 13-suite boutique bed-and-breakfast. Guest rooms are neatly appointed with plush linens, four-poster beds, newly refurnished bathrooms, and color schemes reminiscent of Italy. Common rooms include a comfortable sitting room, gardens, and a front porch.

You can also rent a room inside the Assembly from one of the more than 150 assembly members. Ask at the office for a listing of properties and contact information. Rates, policies, availability, and amenities vary considerably among properties, and many book up well in advance for the season.

Food

Thanks to the presence of the Assembly, Monteagle supports more than the average number of upscale restaurants. **The High Point** (931/924-4600, daily 5–10 P.M., $24–46) is Monteagle's original fine-dining restaurant. Built in 1929 by Al Capone, the High Point is famous for its hidden escape hatches and secret storage areas, where Capone hid liquor and other contraband. Today, the High Point is hardly criminal. Its upscale ambience emanates from a sturdy stone facade, hardwood floors, and beautiful dark-wood window casings. During the summer, you may dine on the stone terrace. The menu features an array of fresh seafood—grouper, mahi-mahi, lobster, and shrimp—plus prime steaks, pork chops, and lamb. The wine and spirits bar is superb.

Located on the road to Sewanee, ◖ **Pearl's Foggy Mountain Cafe** (15344 Sewanee Hwy., 615/598-9568, dinner daily at 5 P.M., Sun. brunch 11 A.M.–2 P.M., $18–32) is your best choice for an innovative yet comforting meal in these parts. Proprietors Jim and Susan Wofford escaped the rat race of Atlanta to open a high-quality restaurant in the wilds of the Cumberland Plateau. A favorite among Sewanee and Monteagle residents and visitors, the Foggy Mountain serves a modern version of Southern-style cuisine. Home-smoked trout, stuffed pork chops, and lots of fresh salads are just some of the dishes you can expect.

For something more everyday, go to **Papa**

Ron's Pizza and Pasta Grill (402 W. Main St., 931/924-3355, daily 11 A.M.–9 P.M., $6–18), which serves lunch and dinner daily. The menu offers a variety of creamy and tomato-based pasta dishes, personal and large pizzas, soup, and sandwiches. The service is efficient.

The **Monteagle Diner** (740 W. Main St., 931/924-4177, Sun.–Mon. 6:30 A.M.–3 P.M., Wed.–Sat. 6:30 A.M.–9 P.M., $4–12) serves comfort food for breakfast, lunch, and dinner. The breakfast buffet and lunch specials are popular.

SEWANEE

The town of Sewanee is synonymous with the **University of the South** (735 University Ave., 931/598-1000, www.sewanee.edu), the private liberal arts college that has educated 24 Rhodes scholars and earned a reputation as one of the South's finest universities.

It was 1857 when the Episcopal Church announced it was planning to establish an educational center in the region. The plans were grand: the center would include 30 schools and colleges offering classical education as well as practical subjects like agriculture and forestry. The citizens of Franklin County and the Sewanee Mining Company offered 10,000 acres of land on the Cumberland Plateau for the school, and in 1860 the cornerstone was laid.

The Civil War nearly dashed all hopes for this educational paradise. By the end of the war all the original leaders were dead, and the cornerstone had been blown apart. Promised funds for the school had evaporated.

Despite the challenges, Bishops Charles T. Quintard and William M. Green persisted with the dream. They raised 2,500 British pounds, built a clapboard chapel, donned ecclesiastical robes, and led a procession to establish the University of the South on September 18, 1868. During its first year, nine students were enrolled.

Over the years, Sewanee's fortunes have improved. Today, its endowment is one of the largest per-student endowments in the country. Its academic reputation is strong, and the *Sewanee Review* is the oldest literary quarterly in the United States. The university is still owned by the Episcopal Church, and in addition to its undergraduate liberal arts college, it is home to the Episcopal School of Theology.

Sewanee enrolls about 1,500 students. The original "domain" of 10,000 acres that was donated to establish the school remains, making it the largest college campus in America. The campus, with its Gothic-style architecture and classical feel, is a pleasant place for a walk. Stop at the admissions office for a campus map.

Sewanee's architecture is grand. Even the newer buildings are carefully constructed to fit in on the campus, which feels like it would be just as at home in old England as on the Cumberland Plateau of Tennessee.

For a dramatic view over the western edge of the plateau, drive to an overlook located at the end of Tennessee Street, past the School of Theology.

Of note is the University Bookstore (735 University Ave., 931/598-1153), which is the best bookstore between Chattanooga and Nashville. The shelves include an extensive selection of religious works, Sewanee merchandise, and a wide selection of modern and classic works. The *Sewanee Review* is on sale for $8 a copy.

Accommodations

Accommodations in Sewanee itself are limited. **Cabin 111** (289 University Ave., 931/598-5311, www.cabin111.com, $95) is a cozy one-bedroom cottage located half a mile from the university campus. The simple yet comfortable accommodations include a queen-sized bed and kitchenette.

If you are in some way affiliated with the university, you may reserve a room at **The Sewanee Inn** (University Ave., 931/598-1686). For other choices, look in Monteagle.

Food

On campus, the **Global Cafe** (735 University Ave., 931/598-1120, Mon.–Sat. 8 A.M.–10 P.M., $5–13) serves breakfast, lunch, and dinner six days a week. The menu is sandwiches, salads,

and homemade potato chips. You can also get coffee and snacks. The café is next-door to the campus bookstore.

Sewanee's commercial district is located along Highway 41, a few blocks south of the university. **The Blue Chair** (41 University Ave., 931/598-5434, $7–14) should be your first stop for coffee, sandwiches, breakfast, and takeaway dinners and boxed lunches. The Blue Chair opens at 7 A.M. Monday–Friday, and 7:30 A.M. on Saturday. Closing time varies with the season and the university's schedule.

Around Sewanee

The **Sewanee Natural Bridge** is about four miles outside of town. Part of South Cumberland State Park, the rock formation is 25 feet tall with a 50-foot span. Visitors reach it at the end of a short footpath from a parking area. Take care as you walk over and around the natural wonder.

To find the natural bridge, drive west out of town along Highway 41. Turn left onto Highway 56 and follow the signs.

WHITWELL

A small town on the southern end of the Sequatchie Valley, Whitwell is the type of place you might just pass right through. Don't. This rural community that huddles along Highway 28 northeast of Chattanooga is home to one of the most moving sights in this part of Tennessee, the Children's Holocaust Memorial.

◖ Children's Holocaust Memorial

The story started in 1998, when the principal of Whitwell Middle School wanted to start a project about tolerance. She sent an eighth-grade teacher, David Smith, to a workshop on the subject. Mr. Smith returned with an idea to offer an after-school class about the Holocaust. Another teacher, Sandra Roberts, led the first session in the fall of 1998. As Roberts told the students about the six million Jews killed by the Nazis, she realized that six million was a number that her students just could not grasp.

It was a student who first suggested the paper clips. The idea was for students to collect 6 million paper clips as a way of demonstrating the horrific scale of the Holocaust. The idea caught on. Over the years that followed, Whitwell Middle School received paper clips from all 50 states, and more than 50 countries. Along with them have come letters and documents, over 30,000 of them. The school still receives paper clips.

The tale of the Children's Holocaust Memorial goes even farther. After the paper clips began to pour in, and interest in the project grew, the school recognized the need for a memorial. Things came together when two correspondents for a German newspaper bought a 1917 German rail car, which had been used to transport Jews during the Holocaust, and donated it to the school. Local businesses pitched in to build the memorial, where visitors can come to see the millions of paper clips that the students collected. The message of the memorial is one of rebirth and call to action: The students ask you as you leave to reflect on what you can do to eliminate hatred and bigotry from the world.

Visitors can see the Children's Holocaust Memorial (1130 Main St., 423/658-5631, www.marionschools.org/holocaust) at any time. During school hours, stop at the front door of the school where you can pick up an audio tour. On Fridays when school is in session there are student-led tours at 10:40 A.M.

(CST). Reservations are required. After-hours you can pick up an audio tour from the police station, or simply look at the memorial on your own.

In 2004, Miramax Pictures released a documentary by Joe Fab about the project, titled *Paper Clips*.

SOUTH PITTSBURG

Established in the 1870s and named in the hope it would become an industrial center of the New South, South Pittsburg is a small town that has seen better days. It is located just a few miles north of the Alabama state line.

Thousands of people come to South Pittsburg for the **National Cornbread Festival** (www.nationalcornbread.com), which takes place over the last weekend of April. A $3 admission gets you inside the festival, which features Cornbread Alley, corn-bread cook-offs, buttermilk-chugging and ice-cream-eating contests, arts-and-crafts shows, a quilt exhibit, and tours of the local Lodge Foundry Plant, where cast-iron skillets are manufactured. Winning recipes tend to shy away from straight-up corn bread—the 2008 cook-off winner made Ancho Shrimp on Smoked Gouda Corncakes—but there is plenty of unadulterated corn bread around too.

South Pittsburg is near I-24, and so there are several mainstream hotels nearby. **Comfort Inn** (exit 152, 423/837-2479, $75–85) and **Holiday Inn Express** (exit 152, 423/837-1500, $76–115) are two choices.

CHATTANOOGA AND THE OVERHILL COUNTRY

Nicknamed the Scenic City, Chattanooga, the smallest of Tennessee's four main cities, is its most livable. Perched on the bank of the Tennessee River, surrounded by mountains, Chattanooga was once an industrial powerhouse. Now it is a model for urban redevelopment. City parks, a pedestrian bridge, free downtown buses, and an abundance of nearby recreation have brought people back downtown. Its arts district is anchored by a museum with one of the best collections of American art in the South. The University of Tennessee has a downtown Chattanooga campus, which lends an additional youthful flourish to the city.

Chattanooga is one of the best destinations for families in Tennessee. Perhaps with the exception of the Great Smoky Mountains, no other part of Tennessee has as much to offer its pint-sized visitors. The Tennessee Aquarium is its flagship attraction, but there is also a downtown IMAX theater, the Chattanooga Zoo, and railroad excursions. On Lookout Mountain, families will enjoy riding the Incline Railroad, going beneath the earth to see Ruby Falls, or exploring the rock gardens at Rock City. On top of this are downtown parks, the local AA baseball team, and nearby Lake Winnepesauka, an amusement park.

The Overhill Region in southeastern Tennessee is a region of natural beauty and rich heritage. Five rivers wind down the mountains and through the valleys here, with names—Hiwassee, Ocoee, Tellico, Conasauga and Tennessee—that trace back to the Overhill Cherokee people. The Ocoee's white-water

PHOTO COURTESY OF TENNESSEE DEPARTMENT OF TOURIST DEVELOPMENT

HIGHLIGHTS

⟨ Tennessee Aquarium: One of the best aquariums in the United States is a great place to see freshwater and ocean creatures up close (page 304).

⟨ Lookout Mountain: A narrow finger of the Cumberland Plateau overlooks Chattanooga and the Eastern Valley in dramatic fashion; this is the site of Rocky City, Ruby Falls, and the setting of a Civil War battle (page 306).

⟨ Rafting the Ocoee: High-velocity rapids keep even the bravest rafters at the edge of their seats on a journey down the Ocoee River (page 323).

⟨ Ducktown Basin Museum: Learn about the legacy of copper mining in the Copper Basin at this top-notch, yet down-home, museum (page 326).

⟨ Tennessee Valley Railroad Excursions: Hop aboard a scenic railroad through old mining towns and beautiful mountain passes (page 331).

⟨ Fort Loudoun State Historic Area: A re-created 18th-century British fort brings to life the complex dynamics of the Tennessee frontier (page 335).

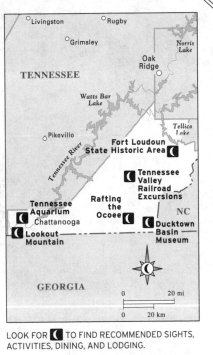

LOOK FOR **⟨** TO FIND RECOMMENDED SIGHTS, ACTIVITIES, DINING, AND LODGING.

rapids attract rafters and kayakers; the calms of the Hiwassee are a refuge for Sandhill crane and other waterfowl.

The foothill country here is dotted with towns and landmarks named in the Cherokee language, and others—like Reliance, Copperhill, and Cleveland—that are linked to lives and industries of more modern settlers. Museums in Ducktown, Etowah, and Englewood preserve the stories of Tennesseans who earned their livelihoods in the mines, on the railroads, and in the textile factories of East Tennessee.

It is the natural beauty of the region that is its greatest calling card, however. The Cherokee National Forest contains hiking trails, bike paths, lakes, and rivers. The landscape invites

you to slow down and enjoy the seasons and the gentle passage of time.

PLANNING YOUR TIME

This region is well suited for a two-pronged vacation: Start with three days in Chattanooga and follow it with three days in the Overhill region. It's a plan that offers a nice balance of urban sophistication and outdoor exploration and can be an ideal family vacation.

If you have only a long weekend, cut your time in Chattanooga to two days and spend your third day at the Ocoee River.

Remember that many attractions in Chattanooga—especially the aquarium—become very crowded during summer weekends.

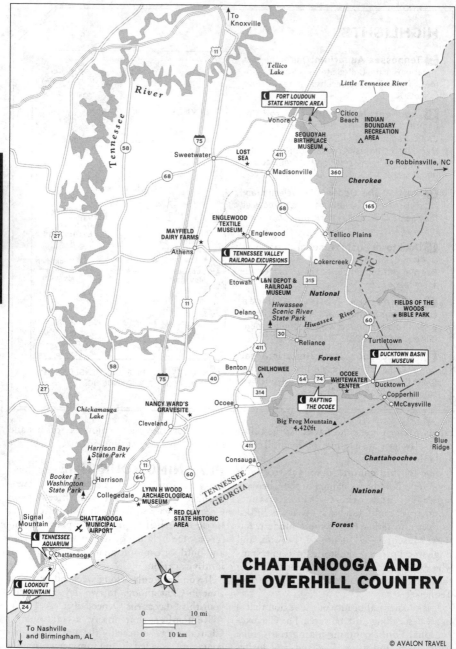

CHATTANOOGA

To Knoxville

Tellico Lake

Little Tennessee River

River

Tennessee

FORT LOUDOUN STATE HISTORIC AREA

Citico Beach

INDIAN BOUNDARY RECREATION AREA

Vonore

SEQUOYAH BIRTHPLACE MUSEUM

To Robbinsville, NC

Sweetwater

LOST SEA

Madisonville

Cherokee

68

360

165

National

MAYFIELD DAIRY FARMS

ENGLEWOOD TEXTILE MUSEUM

Englewood

Tellico Plains

Athens

TENNESSEE VALLEY RAILROAD EXCURSIONS

Cokercreek

Etowah

L&N DEPOT & RAILROAD MUSEUM

315

Hiwassee Scenic River State Park

FIELDS OF THE WOODS BIBLE PARK

Delano

Hiwassee River

30

411

Reliance

Turtletown

DUCKTOWN BASIN MUSEUM

Benton

CHILHOWEE

Forest

60

314

64

74

OCOEE WHITEWATER CENTER

Ducktown

Copperhill

McCaysville

Chickamauga Lake

NANCY WARD'S GRAVESITE

Ocoee

RAFTING THE OCOEE

Big Frog Mountain 4,420ft

Blue Ridge

Cleveland

Harrison Bay State Park

Consauga

411

Chattahoochee

Booker T. Washington State Park

Harrison

Collegedale

LYNN H WOOD ARCHAEOLOGICAL MUSEUM

TENNESSEE
GEORGIA

National

Signal Mountain

CHATTANOOGA MUNICIPAL AIRPORT

RED CLAY STATE HISTORIC AREA

TENNESSEE AQUARIUM

Forest

Chattanooga

LOOKOUT MOUNTAIN

24

To Nashville and Birmingham, AL

CHATTANOOGA AND THE OVERHILL COUNTRY

0   10 mi

0   10 km

© AVALON TRAVEL

Chattanooga

Cradled in a tight bend of the Tennessee River, Chattanooga is a city that has risen from the ashes. Chattanooga's first boom was after the Civil War, when industry and transportation flourished. Expansive warehouses and railway yards bustled with activity, and the city that grew up around them was lively and sophisticated.

Chattanooga's prosperity was not to last, however. By the 1970s and '80s, the Scenic City was dirty, dilapidated, and nearly deserted by all but the most hearty residents.

Chattanooga's turnaround is one of the great stories of the success of urban planning and downtown development. Starting with the flagship Tennessee Aquarium in the early 1990s, Chattanooga has flourished with the addition of new attractions. Planners have also emphasized quality of life for residents; Chattanooga is pedestrian friendly, easy to navigate, and boasts several lovely downtown parks.

HISTORY

Chattanooga's location in the bend of the Tennessee River made it secure, temperate, and fertile. Native Americans are believed to have settled here more than 8,000 years ago. The Cherokees called the area "Chado-na-ugsa," which means "rock that comes to a point," referring to nearby Lookout Mountain.

After the forced removal of the Cherokee, settlers established Ross's Landing, a trading post on the river. In 1839, the town of Chattanooga was incorporated. Eleven years later the first rail line, the Western and Atlantic, arrived in the city.

Chattanooga was called the city where cotton meets corn; it was the gateway to the Deep South. Goods passed through Chattanooga whether by rail or river, giving rise to a massive warehouse and transportation industry. Residents here were sympathetic with the Confederate view, even before the State of

© SUSANNA HENIGHAN POTTER

Chattanooga, as seen from Lookout Mountain

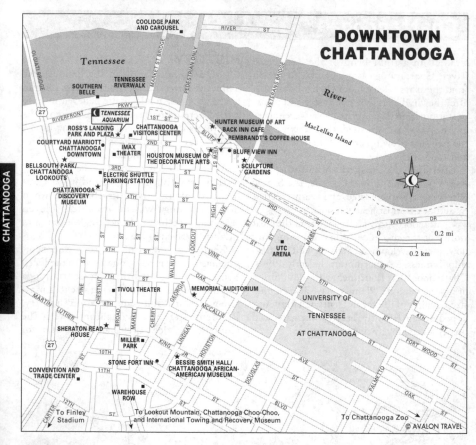

DOWNTOWN CHATTANOOGA

Tennessee

COOLIDGE PARK AND CAROUSEL

RIVER ST

OLGIATI BRIDGE

MARKET ST BRIDGE

PEDESTRIAN ONLY

VETERAN'S BRIDGE

River

MacLellan Island

SOUTHERN BELLE

TENNESSEE RIVERWALK

PKWY

27 RIVERFRONT

TENNESSEE AQUARIUM

1ST ST

HUNTER MUSEUM OF ART

BLUFF VIEW ST

BACK INN CAFE

REMBRANDT'S COFFEE HOUSE

ROSS'S LANDING PARK AND PLAZA

CHATTANOOGA VISITORS CENTER

2ND ST

COURTYARD MARRIOTT CHATTANOOGA DOWNTOWN

IMAX THEATER

HOUSTON MUSEUM OF THE DECORATIVE ARTS

BLUFF VIEW INN

BELLSOUTH PARK/ CHATTANOOGA LOOKOUTS

3RD

ELECTRIC SHUTTLE PARKING/STATION

ST

SCULPTURE GARDENS

CHATTANOOGA DISCOVERY MUSEUM

4TH

ST

3RD

4TH

HIGH

AVE

MABEL

ST

RIVERSIDE DR

5TH

ST

ST

ST

ST

ST

ST

0   0.2 mi

0   0.2 km

LOOKOUT

6TH

VINE

UTC ARENA

ST

PINE

CHESTNUT

WALNUT

OAK

7TH

GEORGIA

5TH

TIVOLI THEATER

MEMORIAL AUDITORIUM

UNIVERSITY OF

8TH

BROAD

MARKET

CHERRY

LINDSAY

MCCALLIE

HOUSTON

ST

TENNESSEE

AT CHATTANOOGA

4TH

ST

FORT WOOD

ST

SHERATON READ HOUSE

27

MILLER PARK

KING

JR

AVE

PALMETTO

OAK

10TH

STONE FORT INN

BESSIE SMITH HALL/ CHATTANOOGA AFRICAN-AMERICAN MUSEUM

DOUGLAS

ST

CONVENTION AND TRADE CENTER

11TH

WAREHOUSE ROW

ST

BLVD

CARTER

12TH

To Finley Stadium

ST

To Lookout Mountain, Chattanooga Choo-Choo, and International Towing and Recovery Museum

To Chattanooga Zoo

© AVALON TRAVEL

MARTIN LUTHER

CHATTANOOGA

Tennessee voted to secede from the Union in 1861.

Chattanooga was of great strategic importance during the Civil War. Confederates moved in to defend her in 1861, and for the first two years of the war Chattanooga was an important supply depot for the Southern states. In the fall of 1863, after the bloody battles of Chickamauga and Chattanooga, the city was in Federal hands. Once again, Chattanooga's infrastructure and strategic position proved useful to its occupiers. Sherman used Chattanooga as a staging point for his march through Georgia and South Carolina, and Union troops built warehouses, stockyards, and hospitals to support the army.

After the Civil War, northern industrialists sought to capitalize on Chattanooga's location, infrastructure, and proximity to natural resources. These industrialists were also the political leaders of the city, and they relied heavily on the political support of newly enfranchised African Americans. During this period, African Americans were elected to local office, established businesses, and pursued education.

Economic woes of the 1890s, combined with the social and political backlash against post-war policies that empowered African

Americans, led to hard times for the city's blacks. Jim Crow arrived in Chattanooga, and would remain until the civil rights movement of the 1950s and '60s.

Chattanooga remained a city based on industry and manufacturing. In 1899 the city secured exclusive bottling rights to Coca-Cola, and the Chattanooga Coca-Cola bottling plant grew into one of the city's largest and most successful businesses. After the Tennessee Valley Authority built dams, increased electricity supply, and eased flooding during the 1930s and 1940s, Chattanooga experienced another boom, further bolstered by World War II. The economic success was not without problems, however. By the late 1960s Chattanooga was one of the most polluted cities in America.

Over the past two decades, Chattanooga has experienced an exciting period of rebirth. Spurred by the success of the Tennessee Aquarium, downtown Chattanooga is once again alive. Pedestrian walkways and good public transportation help make the city a pleasant place to be, while its lovely location on the bank of the Tennessee makes it distinctive.

ORIENTATION

Chattanooga is defined and confined by its geography. The city sits in the bend of the Tennessee River, and is hemmed in by mountains on three sides. Missionary Ridge, which runs along the fourth side, was a barrier for earlier residents but now tunnels pass through it.

The best place to get an understanding of Chattanooga's setting is from atop Lookout Mountain, where you can see the Cumberland Plateau, the Tennessee River, and Missionary Ridge.

Downtown

Market Street and **Broad Street** are the two major north–south thoroughfares downtown. Market Street continues across the river via the Market Street Bridge; Broad Street dead-ends in front of the aquarium. Cross streets from 1st to 9th make navigation simple.

South and east of the aquarium district is the city's business and government center. Here you will find large office buildings, city, state, and federal offices, the University of Tennessee, the city's African-American museum, and Warner Park, home of the Chattanooga Zoo.

Farther south is the Choo Choo, and Chattanooga's old commercial district, centered along **Main Street.** Explore around the Choo Choo and you will see lots of old brick buildings that once housed warehouses, hotels, and manufacturers that needed to be near the railroad. Some of these buildings have been restored and now house new businesses; others still sit empty.

Bluff View is a smattering of elegant old homes located about three blocks east of the aquarium, along the river. The city's art museum is here, along with a collection of outstanding restaurants. You can get to Bluff View on foot either by walking about four blocks along 3rd Street from downtown, along the Riverwalk boardwalk that follows the river, or across the Holmberg pedestrian bridge, a 250-foot lighted glass bridge that connects the south end of Walnut Street to Bluff View.

Across the river from downtown is the **North Shore.** Accessible by car via the Market Street Bridge or by foot along the Walnut Street pedestrian bridge, Northside is a dining, shopping, and entertainment center, with a fresher, more youthful feel than downtown. Coolidge Park along the waterfront is another attraction on this side of the river.

Lookout Mountain

Many of Chattanooga's most famous attractions are on Lookout Mountain, located south of downtown. The best way to get to Lookout Mountain from the city is by driving south on Broad Street. After about two miles, Broad splits into the Ochs Highway (Rte. 58) and the Cummings Highway (Hwys. 42, 72, 11, and 64). Follow Ochs to get to the base of the Incline Railroad or Rock City; follow Cummings to get to Point Park and Ruby Falls. Both roads take you to Lookout Mountain.

You can also get to Lookout Mountain by parking at the bottom and riding the Incline Railroad. When you reach the top, you can walk to Point Park. Other attractions are beyond walking distance, however.

Whenever you are driving on Lookout Mountain, do it with caution. The roads are narrow, windy, heavily trafficked, and—in some places—precarious. Drive slowly and carefully.

SIGHTS
◖ Tennessee Aquarium

The Tennessee Aquarium (1 Broad St., 800/262-0695, www.tnaqua.org, daily 10 A.M.–6 P.M., adults $20, children 3–12 $13) is Chattanooga's landmark attraction. Two huge buildings with angular glass roofs house Ocean Journey and River Journey, salt- and freshwater aquariums with more than 12,000 animals in all. Built in 1992, the aquarium was the first act in Chattanooga's remarkable comeback as a city.

Ocean Journey showcases saltwater creatures, including sharks, rays, and colorful coral reef fish. River Journey follows the watershed from an Appalachian cove forest to a humid Delta swamp, and includes exhibits on the major rivers of the world. Stand-out exhibits include the playful river otters, the boneless beauties—jellyfish, octopus, and cuttlefish—and the American alligator. In between these, there are literally hundreds of captivating and high-quality exhibits of all types of water creatures.

Outside the aquarium there are fountains and a wading pool. Or you can walk over the riverfront and look out at the mighty Tennessee.

In addition to the aquarium itself, there is an IMAX 3-D Theater, which shows nature-related films daily. Tickets may be purchased separately (adults $8, children $6), or as part of a discounted admission package with the aquarium.

The aquarium can get crowded on weekends and during the week during the summer vacation season. Start out early to avoid the worst crowds, and remember that your admission ticket is good all day, so you can take a mid-day break for lunch, and return.

Other Downtown Sights

Chattanooga's African-American history is preserved at the **Bessie Smith Hall and Chattanooga African American Museum** (200 E. Martin Luther King Blvd., 423/266-8658, www.caamhistory.com, Mon.–Fri. 9:30 A.M.–5 P.M., Sat. noon–4 P.M., adults $5, seniors and students $3, children 6–12 $2). The museum is located at the site of the Martin Hotel, once a popular African-American hotel and restaurant. There are hundreds of photographs of black Chattanoogans, with panels that describe the African-American community's contributions in sports, the arts, business, government, and culture. There are pictures of famous black Chattanoogans, including Bessie Smith, Samuel L. Jackson, Valaida Smith, and Roland Hayes. The exhibits include information about African culture, accomplishments, and art.

Just down the hall, in the lobby of the Bessie Smith Hall, is an exhibit dedicated to the legendary blues singer. Smith grew up poor in Chattanooga, having been orphaned at age nine. She developed her singing talent performing for pennies on the streets of Chattanooga. Smith was discovered by Ma Rainey and, later, Columbia Records, and for a period in the 1920s she was the highest-paid American black woman in the entertainment world.

Smith's success did not last. After a bad marriage and personal problems including alcohol abuse, Smith was in the early stages of a comeback when she died in a car accident in North Mississippi in 1937. She was buried in an unmarked grave in Philadelphia. In 1970, rock singer Janis Joplin found out about the grave and bought a headstone, which reads "The greatest blues singer in the world will never stop singing."

Inside the hall you will see photographs of Smith, old concert posters, and a dress she wore in the early days of her singing career.

The **International Towing and Recovery Hall of Fame and Museum** (3315 Broad St., 423/267-3132, www.internationaltowingmuseum.org, Mar.–Oct. Mon.–Sat. 9 A.M.–5 P.M., Nov.–Feb. Mon.–Sat. 10 A.M.–4:30 P.M., year-round Sun. 11 A.M.–5 P.M., adults $8, children 6–18 $4) showcases antique and modern tow trucks and other recovery vehicles. The museum is located in Chattanooga because the first tow truck was fabricated nearby at the Ernest Holmes Company. The museum's Hall of Fame memorializes people who have made significant contributions to the towing and recovery industry. The Wall of the Fallen remembers operators who lost their lives on the job.

The **Chattanooga Zoo** (Warner Park, 1254 E. 3rd St., 423/697-1322, http://zoo.chattanooga.org, daily 9 A.M.–5 P.M., adults $6, seniors $4, children 3–15 $3) is a modest yet fun animal park. The six-acre facility located inside Warner Park houses chimpanzees, red pandas, snow leopards, spider moneys, and jaguars, among others. There is also a petting zoo. A new front entrance to the zoo was constructed in 2008 from Holtzclaw Avenue; this makes it easier to see and find the zoo.

The **Chattanooga Discovery Museum** (321 Chestnut St., 423/756-2738, www.cdmfun.org, Mon.–Sat. 10 A.M.–5 P.M., Sun. noon–5 P.M., $9, under 2 free) is a hands-on museum especially designed for children under 12. Activities include RiverPlay, where kids can pilot a riverboat, and an archaeological dig area. There is a special play area for toddlers too. The Discovery Museum is closed on Wednesday from September through February.

The **Chattanooga History Center** (423/265-3247, www.chattanoogahistory.com) closed its location at 400 Chestnut Street in 2007. The museum will develop and build a new facility, but the expected opening date is not until at least 2010. Call to find out if there are exhibits at a temporary location in the interim.

Bluff View

The bluff overlooking the Tennessee River and downtown Chattanooga is the city's arts center. The foremost attraction here is the **Hunter Museum of American Art** (10 Bluff View, 423/267-0968, www.huntermuseum.org, Mon.–Tues., Fri., and Sat. 10 A.M.–5 P.M., Wed. and Sun. noon–5 P.M., Thurs. 8 A.M.–8 P.M., adults $8, children 3–17 $4). Children under 13 get in free on holidays and weekends. Housed in the former home of

Coca-Cola magnate and philanthropist George Thomas Hunter, the Hunter Museum has one of the most important collections of American art in the Southeast. The permanent collection includes works from the Hudson River School, American Impressionism, Ashcan School, Regionalist, Early Modern, and Contemporary movements. Major touring exhibits are also on display, and visitors enjoy dramatic views of the river below.

On a pleasant day, stroll through the **Bluff View Art District Sculpture Garden,** affiliated with the Hunter Museum but open to the public at no charge.

The **Houston Museum of the Decorative Arts** (201 High St., 423/267-7176, www.thehoustonmuseum.com, Mon.–Fri. 9:30 A.M.–4 P.M., Sat. noon–4 P.M., adults $8, children 4–17 $3.50) houses the decorative arts collection of Anna Safley Houston. Houston was a colorful character who died in relative poverty in 1951, having refused to sell any part of her valuable collection of porcelain and glassware.

Inside the museum you will see parts of Houston's remarkable collection, including antique money banks, steins, face mugs, miniature lamps, and glass baskets, as well as early American furniture and coverlets.

Main Street

South of downtown, at the corner of Main and Market Streets, is the iconic **Chattanooga Choo Choo** (1400 Market St., 423/266-5000, www.choochoo.com), a railroad car. The Choo Choo is located inside the city's old Terminal Station, which is now a Holiday Inn. The terminal was built in 1909 to accommodate the increasing number of passengers who arrived in the city aboard trains including the Chattanooga Choo Choo, which ran from Cincinnati, Ohio, to Chattanooga starting in 1880. The train was made famous in a song by Harry Warren and Mack Gordon, performed in the late 1940s by the Glenn Miller Orchestra. The tune starts with the lines: "Pardon me, boy, Is that that Chattanooga Choo Choo?"

The main sight here is an old wood-burning

engine, which is similar to what would have powered the famous Choo Choo. The engine you see actually came from the Smoky Mountain Railroad, which ran between Knoxville and the Smokies in the 1940s.

There are shops, restaurants, and a small garden around the old railroad engine. Children will enjoy the **Model Railroad Museum** (423/266-5000, daily 10 A.M.–8 P.M., adults $3, children 3–17 $1.50), a miniature world with 3,000 feet of model railroad track, 120 locomotives, and 80 passenger cars.

Better than the Choo Choo, however, is Chattanooga's real, working railroad. The **Tennessee Valley Railroad** (4119 Cromwell Rd., 423/894-8028, www.tvrail.com) offers railroad excursions departing from Grand Junction Station on the other side of Chickamauga Creek and Missionary Ridge. The hour-long ride covers six miles, travels through the Missionary Ridge railroad tunnel, and includes a stop at the East Chattanooga repair shop and turntable.

The Missionary Ridge Local, as the excursion is named, leaves daily March through October, with weekend trips in November and December. Tickets are $14 for adults and $8 for children.

The railroad also offers occasional trips to other destinations in Tennessee and north Georgia.

Lookout Mountain

Lookout Mountain is part of the Cumberland Plateau. It extends 83 miles through Tennessee, Alabama, and Georgia, but the northernmost tip, which overlooks Chattanooga, is its most famous part. No journey to the city is complete without taking a drive up the mountain to enjoy exceptional views and some of the most iconic of Tennessee attractions.

Point Park (1110 E. Brow Rd.) offers the best views off Lookout Mountain. This park is maintained by the National Park Service as part of the Chickamauga and Chattanooga National Military Park and there is a new **visitors center** (423/821-7786, daily 8:30 A.M.–5 P.M.) at the gates of the park. The best thing about the park, however, are the views of the Cumberland Plateau, Chattanooga,

and the Cherokee National Forest in the eastward distance. The Tennessee River winds languidly through the landscape. On a clear day, it is stunning.

Point Park is a fee area; adults 16 years and up will be asked to pay $3 into a turnstile for admittance. Children are free.

Students of the Civil War should visit the **Battles for Chattanooga Electric Map and Museum** (1110 E. Brow Rd., 423/821-2812, www.battlesforchattanooga.com, daily 10 A.M.–5 P.M., adults $7, children 3–12 $5), a private museum that chronicles the several Civil War battles, including the Battle Above the Clouds on Lookout Mountain, that took place in the area. An electric map, which shows 5,000 miniature soldiers and hundreds of lights, is a showpiece of the museum. Hours are extended to 6:30 P.M. during the summer. The museum is located next door to Point Park.

Chattanooga's most famous attraction may well be **Rock City** (1400 Patten Rd., 800/854-0675, www.seerockcity.com, Jan.–Mar. and Nov. daily 8:30 A.M.–5 P.M., Mar.–May and Sept.–Oct. daily 8:30 A.M.–6 P.M., June–Aug. daily 8:30 A.M.–8 P.M., Dec. daily 8:30 A.M.–4 P.M., adults $16, children 3–12 $9). A rock garden with exceptional views, including one that encompasses seven states, Rock City was one of the first tourist attractions in the area. The "See Rock City" billboards painted on barns throughout the South were legendary and iconic; today the gift shop at Rock City overflows with related mementos, including bird houses with the message painted on them.

Visitors to Rock City travel a 4,100-foot trail that winds through ancient rock formations, including a 90-foot waterfall, narrow walkways, and a 1,000-ton balancing rock. Lover's Leap is the viewpoint from which you can see, on a clear day, Georgia, Tennessee, Alabama, North Carolina, South Carolina, Virginia, and Kentucky. Fairyland Caverns and Mother Goose Village are underground collections of folk art, and a 180-foot swinging bridge over the open air is memorable.

Ruby Falls (1720 S. Scenic Hwy., 800/755-7105, daily 8 A.M.–8 P.M., adults $14.95, children

Point Park at Lookout Mountain is part of the Chickamauga and Chattanooga National Military Park.

3–12 $7.95) is an underground waterfall located deep within Lookout Mountain. The traditional entrance to Lookout Mountain Cave was closed in 1905 when the Southern Railway Company sealed it during the construction of a railroad along the side of the mountain. Chemist and entrepreneur Leo Lambert had explored the cave before and believed it would be a lucrative tourist attraction. So in 1928 he started to bore an elevator shaft down into the mountain to the cave. Lambert's unusual plan worked, and by 1930 visitors were touring the cave and the 145-foot waterfall, which Lambert named for his wife, Ruby.

The entrance to Ruby Falls is in a massive limestone building modeled after an Irish castle. It was built out of stone brought up while Lambert was drilling the elevator shaft through the mountain; the top floor was added in 1976.

The tour of Ruby Falls takes about 1.5 hours in total, and involves walking a bit less than a mile on paved underground paths. The climax is seeing and hearing Ruby Falls, as its waters thunder 145 feet to the pool beneath.

The steepest passenger train in the world is the **Incline Railway** (3917 St. Elmo Ave. and 827 E. Brow Rd., 423/821-4224, www.ridetheincline.com, Apr.–May and Sept.–Oct. daily 9 A.M.–6 P.M., June–Aug. daily 8:30 A.M.–9:30 P.M., Nov.–Mar. daily 10 A.M.–6 P.M., adults $13, children 3–12 $7), which climbs from Chattanooga to the top of Lookout Mountain. The railway was built in 1895 and has been ferrying visitors up the mountain ever since.

It takes about 10 minutes to make the journey from the bottom of the mountain to the top, where there are gift shops and restaurants. Point Park is a short walk away, but other Lookout Mountain attractions require a car. Parking is free at the bottom of the mountain, but a fee is charged to park at the top.

On the western edge of Lookout Mountain, in the midst of the upscale residential neighborhood, is **Sunset Rock.** A natural landmark admired for generations, this sheer bluff looks westward and the view at sunset is indeed spectacular. It draws rockclimbers, who rappel down the sheer face of the bluff. The short hike (0.2 mile) down to the rock is steep and rough; wear comfortable shoes and take your time. There is no wall or fence blocking the sheer drop down the face of the rock (which makes for much better pictures). It would not be a good place to bring small children.

On the road up Lookout Mountain you will find the **Chattanooga Nature Center** (400 Garden Rd., 423/821-1160, www.chattanooganaturecenter.org, Mon.–Sat. 9 A.M.–5 P.M., Sun. (summer only) 1–5 P.M., adults $7,

seniors and children 4–11 $4). This is a park, nature preserve, and environmental education facility. Visitors have the opportunity to see 30 different native animal species, including red wolves, bald eagles, bobcats, and raccoons in the Wildlife Wanderland. There is also a 1,400-foot boardwalk that meanders through a seasonal wetland and lowland forest, and takes you to the George S. Bryan Tree House. Gardens include a fragrance garden, organic community garden, and a

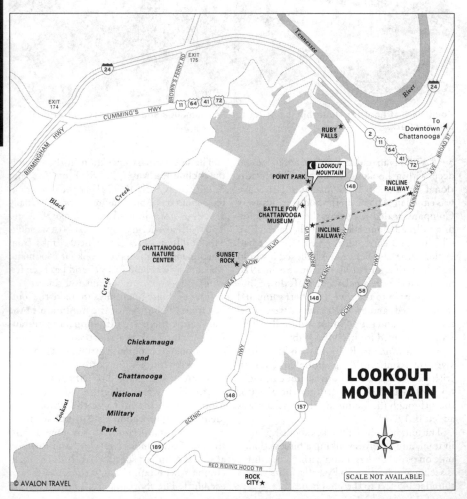

© AVALON TRAVEL

bird and butterfly café. In addition, there are miles of trails for hiking or biking in the adjoining Reflection Riding Arboretum and Botanical Garden. Come on a pleasant day and plan on spending several hours exploring the nature center.

Signal Mountain

Signal Mountain perches on the top of Walden's Ridge about 15 minutes' drive north of Chattanooga. Named because it is believed the Cherokees used it for signal fires, Signal Mountain evolved into an upscale residential community. The Signal Mountain Inn was a popular tourist destination; today it is a retirement home.

Visitors should make the challenging up-hill drive to visit **Signal Point** (Signal Point Rd., 423/821-7786), a park which offers a dramatic view of the Tennessee River below. The site, managed by the National Park Service, is part of the Chickamauga and Chattanooga National Military Park and is the southern terminus of the 300-plus-mile Cumberland Trail.

To get to Signal Mountain, take Highway 127 to Mountain Creek Road.

RECREATION
Parks

Chattanooga's two best city parks are located on the banks of the Tennessee River. **Ross's Landing Park and Plaza,** adjacent to the Tennessee Aquarium at the end of Broad Street, is a sculpted park that uses concrete, glass, stone, and grass to depict the timeline of Chattanooga's history. It is a nice place to stroll, people-watch, or enjoy a picnic.

Over on the other side of the river, **Coolidge Park** is even nicer. This grassy park has paths for walking, benches for sitting, and a glass-enclosed carousel to entertain children and adults. A ride on the merry-go-round is just 50 cents. Come here for lovely views of Chattanooga's downtown.

Outside of town, **Booker T. Washington State Park** (5801 Champion Rd., 423/894-4955) is a day-use park located off Highway 58, on the northeast side of town, whose primary

attraction is Lake Chickamauga. There are several boat launching ramps. Waterskiing, fishing, and pleasure cruising are popular activities. There are also picnic facilities and an Olympic-sized swimming pool.

Farther outside of town, **Harrison Bay State Park** (8411 Harrison Bay Rd., Harrison, 423/344-6214) is also located on Lake Chickamauga. It is named for part of the lake, Harrison Bay, which covers what was once the last Cherokee Indian settlement in this area. The land was inundated in 1940 with the construction and closure of the Chickamauga Dam by the Tennessee Valley Authority.

There are public boat ramps and all types of boats are allowed. In addition, there are picnic facilities, an Olympic-sized pool, and a campground with RV and tent sites. There are also six miles of hiking trails and a bike path.

Biking

There are bike lanes on many downtown streets, and bike-friendly trails along the Chattanooga

Coolidge Park, on the north shore of the Tennessee River, is a pleasant place for a walk.

waterfront, at the Chickamauga Dam, and at the TVA's Raccoon Mountain Reservoir.

With bike-to-work programs and an innovative bike fleet initiative, Chattanooga is well ahead of the curve when it comes to promoting alternative ways of getting around town.

Bike Chattanooga (www.bikechattanooga.org) provides safety courses for bikers, promotes bike-riding, and publishes information about recreational bike riding in the area.

For rentals and other bike-gear needs, contact **River City Bicycles** (122 Tremont St., 423/265-7176) or **Suck Creek Cycle** (501 Cherokee Blvd., 423/266-8883).

River Cruises

Blue Moon Cruises (888/993-2583, www.bluemooncruises.org, $40) offer seasonal cruises down the Tennessee River aboard a 70-foot Skipperliner cruise boat. Blue Moon's cruise down the Tennessee River Gorge lasts about 3.5 hours and departs morning and afternoon from the Chattanooga Pier off of Ross's Landing waterfront park. The naturalist-led cruise emphasizes the animals and plants you see on the riverbanks, as well as the cultural and historical significance of the river over the years.

Spectator Sports

The **Chattanooga Lookouts** (201 Power Alley, 423/267-2208, www.lookouts.com), a farm team for the Cincinnati Reds, play at AT&T Field downtown. The baseball season runs from April to September. General admission to home games is $4 for adults and $2 for children; box seats are $6–8. Contact the box office at 423/267-4849.

Amusement Parks

Just over the state line in Georgia is **Lake Winnepesaukah** (1730 Lakeview Dr., Rossville, GA, 706/866-5681, www.lakewinnie.com, Apr.–Sept. Wed.–Thurs. 10 A.M.–8 P.M., Fri.–Sat. 10 A.M.–10 P.M., Sun. noon–10 P.M.), a family-oriented amusement park operating since 1925. Gate admission is $5 per person; in addition, an unlimited rides pass is $21 per person. Individual ride tickets are also sold. The Cannon Ball is a wooden rollercoaster, and the Boat Chute is the oldest mill chute ride in the United States. There are also modern rides, including the Oh-Zone and Wild Lightning. In addition to rides, Lake Winnepesaukah has a midway and food vendors.

To find Lake Winnepesaukah, drive south on I-75 to the Route 41 exit. Drive on Ringold Road for two miles to McBrien Road. Turn left and the park is two miles ahead on Lakeview Drive.

Hang Gliding

The mountains around Chattanooga are ideal for hang gliding. The **Lookout Mountain Flight Park** (7201 Scenic Hwy., Rising Fawn, GA, 706/398-3541, www.hanglide.com, daily 9 A.M.–6 P.M., closed Wed.) offers tandem glides with a certified instructor and lessons appropriate for all levels. The flight school is the largest hang gliding school in America. A single tandem flight, which lasts about 15 minutes, is $139. A day-long package that includes a tandem flight plus five "bunny hill" low-altitude flights, is $200.

THE ARTS
Venues

The jewel of Chattanooga's arts venues is the **Tivoli Theater** (709 Broad St.), a Beaux Arts–style performance hall that has been restored and equipped with modern amenities. Built in 1921, the Tivoli played films and live dramas to sold-out Chattanooga audiences through the 1950s. But with the advent of television, shopping malls, and the automobile, the downtown theater declined and narrowly escaped demolition in 1961.

After years of consideration and fundraising, the Tivoli was totally restored in the late 1980s and reopened to adoring crowds in 1989. Its domed ceiling, crystal chandeliers, and ornate finishes make this a lovely venue.

Chattanooga's **Memorial Auditorium** (399 McCallie Ave.) is another popular venue for concerts, performances, and special events.

Built in 1924 as a memorial to the soldiers and sailors of World War I, Memorial Auditorium was then the largest space in Chattanooga for concerts other events. It housed boxing matches, roller derbies, tennis matches, banquets, and religious revivals.

Organizations
The **Allied Arts Alliance of Greater Chattanooga** (406 Frazier Ave., www.alliedartschattanooga.org, Mon.–Fri. 8:30 A.M.–5 P.M.) is an umbrella organization that promotes the arts. Contact them for an arts guide to the city or for information about upcoming events.

Chattanooga's **Arts and Education Council** (3069 Broad St., 423/267-1218, www.artsedcouncil.org) organizes a variety of programs, including film festivals and literary conferences.

Film
The **Independent Film Series** (www.artsedcouncil.org) brings award-winning independent films to Chattanooga's downtown Bijou Theatre. The **Back Row Film Series** (www.backrowfilms.com) takes place at the Hunter Museum and features film screenings followed by a related guest speaker.

Visual Arts
The work of local and regional artists is on display at the **Association for Visual Artists Gallery** (30 Frazier Ave., 423/265-4282, www.avartists.org, Tues.–Sat. 11 A.M.–5 P.M.), located on Chattanooga's North Shore.

The **River Gallery** (400 E. 2nd St., 423/265-5033, www.river-gallery.com, Mon.–Sat. 10 A.M.–5 P.M., Sun. 1–5 P.M.) is located in a turn-of-the-century home in the Bluff View Arts District. It exhibits fine arts and crafts from local, regional, and international artists.

Music and Dance
The **Chattanooga Symphony & Opera** (630 Chestnut St., 423/267-8583, www.chattanoogasymphony.org) performs classical, opera, pops, and family concerts every year at the Tivoli Theater.

Ballet Tennessee (3202 Kelly's Ferry Rd., 423/821-2055, www.ballettennessee.org) is Chattanooga's foremost ballet company and school. They perform at the Tivoli Theater and Memorial Auditorium.

Theater
The **Chattanooga Theatre Centre** (400 River Rd., 423/267-8534, www.theatrecentre.com) is a community theater that produces musicals, comedies, and dramas.

EVENTS
Spring
Billed as a writer's conference for readers, the biennial **Conference on Southern Literature** (www.artsedcouncil.org) brings heavyweights in Southern literature to Chattanooga for three days of lectures, discussions, and readings in March. On off years, the Arts and Education Council hosts the **Chattanooga Festival of Writers,** a celebration of the craft of writing.

In April the **4 Bridges Arts Festival** (www.4bridgesartsfestival.org) brings 150 artists to the First Tennessee Pavilion downtown for two days of exhibits, children's activities, and acoustic music. It is a good opportunity to purchase original artwork in a wide variety of formats.

In May, the Chattanooga Bicycle Club and Outdoor Chattanooga host **3 States, 3 Mountains** (www.chattbike.com), a 100-mile bicycle race that originates and ends at Finley Stadium in downtown Chattanooga.

TaleSpin (www.downtownchattanooga.org) is a three-day storytelling festival that includes an evening show at the Tivoli Theatre, daytime telling at Coolidge Park, and ghost stories at night. It usually coincides with Mother's Day, and includes a Sunday-afternoon river cruise with storytelling. Three-day passes cost $45; tickets for individual events are also available.

Summer
Chattanooga's largest annual event is the **Riverbend Festival** (www.riverbendfestival.com). Taking place in mid-June, the

festival stretches for one mile along the city's waterfront and features multiple stages with jazz, blues, rock, pop, country, folk, and classical performers. The festival also includes the Bessie Smith Strut, a street festival along Martin Luther King Boulevard.

On Fridays from May to August, **Rhythm and Noon** provides free midday concerts at Miller Plaza downtown. Performers play classical, folk, rock, jazz, swing, choral music, and blues. The concerts are a warm-up for **Nightfall** (www.downtownchattanooga.org), free Friday-evening concerts held at Miller Plaza from Memorial Day to the last weekend in September. Each concert starts out with a local act and concludes with a headliner. The schedule includes a wide range of genres, from world music to bluegrass.

Fall

On the Friday night of Labor Day weekend, kick off your shoes at **SwingFest** (www.downtownchattanooga.org), an open-air concert featuring local and regional big-band performers.

Every September Chattanooga's **Culture Fest** (www.artsedcouncil.org) turns Coolidge Park into a festival of diverse cultures. International performers, foods from around the world, a merchandise bazaar, and unique arts and crafts are a few of the attractions.

Bluegrass music comes to the waterfront with the **Three Sisters Festival** (www.downtownchattanooga.org), a three-day festival held in early October at Ross's Landing.

SHOPPING
Malls

Hamilton Place (Shallowford Rd.,423/894-7177, www.hamiltonplace.com) is Chattanooga's foremost place for shopping. Located at exit 4A off I-75 northeast of downtown, Hamilton Place has 162 stores including JC Penney, Sears, Dillards, and Belk. It is Tennessee's largest shopping mall.

Books

Chattanooga's best downtown bookstore is **Rock Point Books** (401 Broad St., 423/756-2855). They also offer a regular calendar of open mics, book discussions, and children's story hours.

ACCOMMODATIONS
Under $100

Interstate motels offer good value in the Chattanooga area. In this category, the **Econo Lodge Lookout Mountain** (150 Browns Ferry Rd., 423/821-9000, $65–85) is a good choice for its location convenient to downtown and Lookout Mountain, and for its clean rooms and amenities, including in-room microwaves, refrigerators, and coffeemakers. Guests also enjoy a free continental breakfast.

$100-150

◖ **Bluff View Inn** (Bluff View Art District, 423/265-5033, ext. 2, www.bluffviewartdistrict.com, $105–240) consists of 18 rooms in three different historic properties located in the peaceful Bluff View Art District. Guest rooms in the Maclellen House, Martin House, and Thompson House range from modest-sized quarters with a shower-tub combination to luxurious suites with river views and private balconies and sitting rooms. A full sit-down breakfast is included in room rates, and is served at the Back Inn Café.

If you thought it was a new idea to turn an outmoded train station into a hotel, think again. The Chattanooga Station stopped operating as a train station in 1970 and just three years later it reopened as a tourist attraction. Nineteen years later it was retooled again, this time into the hotel that you see today. The **Chattanooga Choo Choo Holiday Inn** (1400 Market St., 800/872-2529, www.choochoo.com, $120–190) consists of three buildings of hotel rooms, plus distinctive train-car accommodations. The hotel rooms are comfortable and generous in size; they feature amenities such as wireless Internet, in-room coffeemakers, and king-sized beds. Suites are also available, including the spacious and luxurious Glenn Miller Suite.

But what makes the Choo Choo special is its

railcar accommodations. These old sleeper cars have been converted into modern-style rooms, with four-poster beds, desks, and private bathrooms. Each room has a queen-sized bed, and some feature pull-out trundle beds ideal for family accommodations.

In addition to hotel rooms, the Choo Choo has three different restaurants, retail shops, and a railway museum. The lobby and upscale restaurant located in the atrium of the old train station lobby are dramatic and beautiful.

The ◖ **Stone Fort Inn** (120 E. 10th St., 423/267-7866, www.stonefortinn.com, $130–170) is an old-fashioned city hotel with a modern, chic feel. Located about 10 blocks from the aquarium and close to federal and state office buildings, the Stone Fort Inn has 20 guest rooms of varying sizes. All rooms have high-speed Internet connections, oversized whirlpool tubs, luxury bath soaps, claw-footed soaking tubs, TV/VCRs, and cheerful decor. Polished terrazzo floors, marble fireplaces, well-stocked bookshelves, an 1885 grand piano, and a 1920s slate pool table all conjure an atmosphere of cozy elegance in this circa-1909 hotel building. On weekdays there is a continental breakfast and on weekends a gourmet sit-down morning meal. The dining area becomes a public café and restaurant on Wednesday and Thursday evenings, with inviting selections from the bar, live acoustic music, and a menu of inventive small plates. Children under 12 are not permitted at the Old Stone Fort, unless you rent the whole hotel for a special event.

The Chattanoogan (1201 S. Broad St., 423/756-3400, www.chattanoogahotel.com, $119–159) is an upscale hotel and conference center located just south of downtown. The hotel offers 199 guest rooms and suites, many of them with views of Lookout Mountain, and all appointed with modern furnishings, fabrics, and amenities. A dramatic see-through glass fireplace in the lobby is a talking point and attraction in its own right. An on-site spa, conference center, and three restaurants round out the resort's amenities. The Chattanoogan opened in 2001

and underwent extensive renovation in 2007 to keep the decor current and comfortable.

$150-200

Mayor's Mansion Inn (801 Vine St., 423/265-5000, www.mayorsmansioninn.com, $160–295) is a luxury bed-and-breakfast located in an 1889 Victorian mansion built for the mayor of Chattanooga. Mayor's Mansion has 11 guest rooms and is located in the Fort Wood District near the University of Tennessee, less than one mile from downtown Chattanooga. Each guest room is unique, with distinctive fabrics, wallpaper, and antique furniture. Guests may feel like they are bedding down in a home that could just as easily be open for tours. Common areas include a stone terrace, verandahs, and a library. Elegant indulgences include nightly turndown service, a three-course breakfast, and soft cotton robes. Guests may also take advantage of concierge service, Internet access, and other amenities like ironing boards and a video library.

Other downtown Chattanooga hotels include **Courtyard Marriott Chattanooga Downtown** (200 Chestnut St., 423/755-0871, $160–200), located one block from the aquarium and close to other downtown attractions. This 128-room hotel has a handful of riverview rooms (ask for one when making your reservation) and several suites. Amenities include a fitness room, guest laundry, in-room coffeemakers, hair dryers, ironing boards, and refrigerators. There is a restaurant on-site.

Another favorite downtown hotel is the **Sheraton Read House Hotel** (827 Broad St., 800/691-1255, $150–210). Located in a historic redbrick Georgian-style building near the theater district, and about 10 blocks from the aquarium, the Sheraton offers its guests luxury and comfort. Its 219 guest rooms and suites include high-speed Internet, Drexel Heritage furniture, and luxurious beds. There is an indoor zero-edge pool, top-notch workout room, and on-site steakhouse and coffee shop.

Camping

Harrison Bay State Park (8411 Harrison Bay

Rd., Harrison, 423/344-6214), located about 20 minutes drive from downtown, has 134 RV sites and 28 tent-only sites in its lakefront campground. Rates are $12–18.50.

FOOD
Downtown
For good food, casual-yet-polished service, and a convivial atmosphere, go where many Chattanoogans go for a meal out. **212 Market** (212 Market St., 423/265-1212, lunch Mon.–Fri. 11 A.M.–3 P.M., Sat.–Sun. 11:30 A.M.–3 P.M., dinner Mon.–Thurs. 5–9:30 P.M., Fri.–Sat. 5–10 P.M., Sun. 5–9 P.M., lunch $7–14, dinner $15–30) serves upscale daily lunch and dinner specials like ginger-glazed salmon, wild-mushroom ravioli, and Carolina mountain trout. The 212 Pecan Chicken Club is a delectable lunchtime favorite. This was one of the first downtown restaurants to open following the area's rebirth in the early 1990s, and it is still a first choice for dining in the city.

When you give an old-fashioned diner a makeover the result is **The Blue Plate** (191 Chestnut St., Unit B, 423/648-6767, Mon.–Thurs. 11 A.M.–9 P.M., Fri. 11 A.M.–10 P.M., Sat. 9 A.M.–10 P.M., Sun. 9 A.M.–9 P.M., $6–13), a downtown eatery with sleek lines, fresh food, and a home-style heart. You can order breakfast eggs and pancakes all day, or choose a plump, juicy Blue Plate burger. The Blue Plate Chef Salad is piled high with pulled chicken, diced eggs, and mixed cheese, and the entrées include fried-to-order chicken and not-your-mother's baked meatloaf. To prove that this is not your everyday lunch counter, you can also order from a full bar.

Tucked away in the downtown business district is Chattanooga's favorite vegetarian eatery. The **Country Life Vegetarian Restaurant** (809 Market St., 423/634-9925, Mon.–Thurs. 11:30 A.M.–2:30 P.M., Sun. 11:30 A.M.–1:30 P.M., $5–10) serves whole-grain, home-grown, all-vegetarian food. The specials change daily and include things like tofu and brown rice, butternut squash quiche, and veggie fajitas. There is also a well-stocked salad bar.

You might be surprised how good England tastes in Chattanooga. The **English Rose** (1401 Market St., 423/265-5900, Mon.–Sat. 10 A.M.–6 P.M., $5–15) serves authentic British Isles fare, including finger sandwiches, ploughman's lunch, and cottage pie. Come into this welcoming spot for an afternoon tea with scones and sandwiches, or for a meal of steak pies, Dover sole, flounder, or Cornish pasties. The atmosphere is on the refined side, but it's not uptight. The English Rose is a nice change of pace from typical Americana restaurants.

Upscale Southern comfort food is the draw at **Mt. Vernon Restaurant** (3535 Broad St., 423/266-6591, Mon.–Thurs. 11 A.M.–9:30 P.M., Fri. 11 A.M.–10 P.M., Sat. 4:30–10 P.M., $9–16). Located near the base of Lookout Mountain, Mt. Vernon is a favorite among Chattanoogans, who come for its familiar food, generous portions, and hometown feel. Specialties include Southern fried chicken ($13) and Maryland crab cakes ($17). The fried green tomatoes appetizer is always a favorite. At lunchtime you can also order from the under-$10 sandwich menu, with choices like B.L.T., Grouper sandwich, and the Mt. Vernon Club.

Chattanooga's best meat-and-three diner is █ **Zarzour's Cafe** (1627 Rossville Ave., 423/266-0424, Mon.–Fri. 11 A.M.–2 P.M., $5–8), a hole-in-the-wall tucked away in the wrong part of town. Zarzour's was founded by Lebanese immigrant Charles Zarzour in 1913 and the eatery has persisted, through good times and bad, under the family's ownership, for the past nine-plus decades. But it is not Middle Eastern specialties that bring in the regulars; it is some of the best home-cooked Southern food in the city. Flavorful turnip greens, creamy potatoes, comforting baked spaghetti, and hot-from-the-skillet corn bread are among the dishes on the menu. Each day you can choose from one of three main-dish entrées, accompanied by your choice of two side dishes. Or order a hand-patted burger from the grill.

Zarzour's is located a few blocks from the Choo-Choo. To find it, travel east on Main

Street and turn right onto Rossville Pike. About two blocks down on your right, you will see the small grey-brick building with a red awning.

Bluff View

As ubiquitous as the coffee-sandwich-dessert bar is these days, it is still exciting when someone does it well. ☾ **Rembrandt's Coffee House** (204 High St., 423/265-5003, Mon.–Thurs. 7 A.M.–10 P.M., Fri. 7 A.M.–11:30 P.M., Sat. 8 A.M.–11:30 P.M., Sun. 8 A.M.–10 P.M., $5–7) is one such place. Located catty-corner from the Hunter Museum of American Art, Rembrandt's serves excellent hot and cold sandwiches on superb locally baked bread. The menu also offers salads, including a delicious spinach salad with bacon, hard-boiled eggs, and walnuts. The ingredients are fresh and flavorful. For breakfast choose from french-toast panini filled with fruit compote and mascarpone cheese, hot breakfast sandwiches, or lighter options such as bagels, yogurt and fruit, or banana bread. The coffee here is excellent, and you can finish off your meal with a wide array of sweets. Rembrandt's is not without a sense of humor. Step outside and you will see a plate-glass window with a sign reading "Working Artist." He or she will be making hand-dipped chocolate treats you can buy inside.

The setting at ☾ **Back Inn Café** (412 E. 2nd St., 423/265-5033, Mon.–Thurs. 7 A.M.–9 P.M., Fri. 7 A.M.–9 P.M., Sat. 8 A.M.–10 P.M., Sun. 8 A.M.–9 P.M., $14–28) is romantic and relaxing. Located in a stately old home, the Back Inn offers diners the choice of dining in the library, sunroom, or on the terrace overlooking the river. Polished wood floors, elegant Old World finishes, and a lovely view make you feel distinctly at home in this restaurant. The menu features global cuisine with a good wine list.

Lunchtime entrées include Japanese *bento* boxes, penne carbonara, and shrimp and grits. There are also salads and sandwiches. At dinner, choose from entrées such as Thai curry chicken, seafood gratin, and Martin House steak tenderloin. Reservations are recommended.

North Shore

In recent years, the streets across the river from downtown Chattanooga have become popular locations for restaurants.

For a casual meal on this side of the river, head to **Mud Pie Restaurant** (12 Frazier Ave., 423/267-9043, daily 11 A.M.–10 P.M., $5–9). Here you can buy a cup of coffee, sandwich, salad, or soup. But what really makes Mud Pie special is its Cuban menu, which includes classic Cuban sandwiches, Cuban-style steak sandwiches, and side dishes including fried plantains, tamales, and Cuban-style espresso.

Terra Nostra Restaurant and Wine Bar (105 Frazier Ave., 423/634-0238, Mon.–Thurs. 4:30–10 P.M., Fri.–Sat. 4:30–11 P.M., Sun. 4:30–9 P.M., $7–15) is a tapas restaurant with vegetarian, seafood, and meat plates. Come for an afternoon glass of wine to be enjoyed with a plate of cheese and bread. Or come for an exciting dinner; try the handcrafted spinach ravioli, fresh seafood plates, or osso bucco. The restaurant's bold colors and metal sculptures give it a rustic-hip feel. In the tapas tradition, each plate is a small portion, about appetizer size, and you should order several as part of your multicourse meal. In addition to tapas, Terra Nostra has 80 different wines available by the glass, and 90 available by the bottle.

For sushi, many Chattanoogans head to **Sushi Nabe** (110 River St., 423/634-0171, Mon. 4–9 P.M., Tues.–Thurs. and Sun. 11:30 A.M.–2:30 P.M. and 5–9:30 P.M., Fri.–Sat. 11:30 A.M.–2:30 P.M. and 5–10:30 P.M.). Located adjacent to Coolidge Park, this chic eatery offers seating at the sushi bar or at tables. In addition to sushi ($4–7 per roll), you can order stir-fries and other Japanese specialties. There are also convenient dinner combination plates ($15–18).

INFORMATION AND SERVICES
Visitor Information

The **Chattanooga Area Convention and Visitors Bureau** (2 Broad St., 423/756-8687 or 800/322-3344, www.chattanooga-fun.com) provides information online, over the telephone, and in person at its visitors center located right next door to the Tennessee Aquarium at 2 Broad Street.

Media

The *Chattanooga Times Free Press* (www.timesfreepress.com) is the city's daily newspaper. *The Pulse* (www.chattanoogapulse.com) is a free alternative weekly paper with a focus on arts, entertainment, and culture.

Libraries

The **Chattanooga-Hamilton County Bicentennial Library** (1001 Broad St., 423/757-5310, Mon.–Thurs. 9 A.M.–9 P.M., Fri.–Sat. 9 A.M.–6 P.M.) is the city's main downtown library. The entire library is a wireless Internet hot-spot, and there is also free Internet access on library terminals.

Laundry

Gordon's Cleaners (315 N. Market St. and 3546 Broad St., 423/265-5877) has dry cleaning and laundry service downtown.

GETTING THERE

Chattanooga is located along three major interstate highways. I-75 travels north–south from Knoxville in the north to Atlanta in the south. I-24 runs from Nashville to Chattanooga and I-59 runs from Birmingham to Chattanooga.

Chattanooga is about 115 miles from Knoxville, 130 miles from Nashville, 120 miles from Atlanta, and 150 miles from Birmingham.

The **Chattanooga Metropolitan Airport** (CHA, 423/855-2202, www.chattairport.com) is served by a half-dozen airlines providing nonstop service to 10 different U.S. cities: Atlanta, Charlotte, Chicago, Cincinnati, Dallas, Ft. Lauderdale, Memphis, Orlando, Tampa Bay, and Washington, D.C. Airlines are Delta Connection Carriers, U.S. Airways Express, American Eagle, Allegiant Air, Northwest Airlink, and Continental Airlines.

The Chattanooga airport is located about 14 miles east of the city center. To get downtown

from the airport, take Highway 153 south to I-75, and follow the signs to downtown Chattanooga.

GETTING AROUND

Chattanooga is the most pedestrian-friendly Tennessee city. There is plenty of downtown parking and it is easy to get around on foot or by the free public trolleys. You can walk from downtown to Bluff View and even to the north shore via the Walnut Street pedestrian bridge.

You'll need a car to get to Lookout Mountain attractions.

Public Transportation

Chattanooga's public transit service operates a free electric shuttle bus service around downtown. The **CARTA Electric Shuttle** runs from the Chattanooga Choo Choo building on the south side of town to the Tennessee Aquarium along the waterfront. There are stops about every block; if you need to get to a specific place just ask your driver. Maps are posted around the city, and free guides are available at the north parking lot.

The route is convenient to all downtown hotels. There are large parking garages at both ends of the shuttle route. It costs $3 to park by the Choo Choo and $7 to park by the aquarium. Since there is no such thing as free parking anywhere around downtown Chattanooga, parking and riding the shuttle is a very good idea. The shuttle runs approximately every five minutes weekdays 6:30 A.M.–11 P.M., Saturday 9 A.M.–11 P.M., and Sunday 9 A.M.–8:30 P.M.

Parking

All parking around downtown Chattanooga is paid. If you find a metered space along the road, grab it because these are cheapest, at least for short-term parking. There are large lots located across from the Tennessee Aquarium. All-day parking will run you about $7, and evening parking will cost $5. There is a large public lot next to the Choo Choo, where all-day parking is just $3.

The Ocoee

The lands east of Chattanooga are speckled by towns that still bear names bestowed by some of their first settlers. Citico, Chota, Hiwassee, and Tellico were named by Overhill Cherokee, who make the journey over the mountains and into southeastern Tennessee during the 17th century. Red Clay State Historic Park was the site of the last council meeting of the Cherokee before their forced removal in 1838. Today, these lands are part of the southern portion of the Cherokee National Forest, an expanse of 300,000 acres of federal lands that contain rivers, mountains, and rural farmland.

The southern part of the Cherokee National Forest is defined by the powerful Ocoee River, which attracts thrill-seeking rafters and kayakers. Sightseers enjoy scenic drives up Chilhowee Mountain and along the river, past recreation areas and opportunities for hiking and swimming.

Several towns in the southeastern corner of this region have strong mining histories. Ducktown, Copperhill, and Coker Creek are among the quiet towns that now preserve their unique history with museums and historic tours.

The Hiwassee River cuts through the national forest north of the Ocoee, passing the historic town of Reliance, and posing opportunities for laid-back canoe and raft outings.

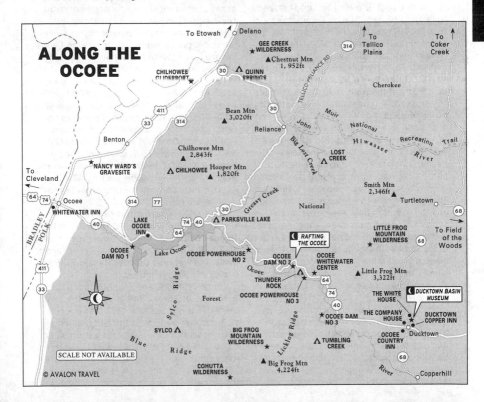

CHATTANOOGA

THE CHEROKEE NATIONAL FOREST

The Cherokee National Forest covers 640,000 acres of land in extreme eastern Tennessee. The southern portion extends from the Georgia state line all the way to the southern boundary of the Great Smoky Mountains National Park, encompassing some 300,000 acres. The northern portion – which covers 327,000 acres – ranges from the northern boundary of the Smokies to the Virginia state line.

The federal government began buying land in East Tennessee around 1912. The government's action was in response to the environmental effects of widespread logging in the southern mountains. Clear cutting, erosion, and wildfires ravaged the environment, and the federal government stepped in to preserve the headwaters of area rivers. In 1920, president Woodrow Wilson declared the lands to be the Cherokee National Forest, and in 1936 the boundaries were redrawn to put the forest entirely within the state of Tennessee (Pisgah and Natahala National Forests were established in North Carolina). During the New Deal, the Civilian Conservation Corps built many of the trails that still exist in the forest and the Tennessee Valley Authority built dams and reservoirs.

National forests differ from national parks in important ways. The motto of the forest service is "Caring for the land and serving the people," a statement which reveals its dual purpose. So while environmental stewardship is one objective of park managers, they are also concerned with encouraging recreation and the use of natural resources. Activities such as off-road mountain biking, hunting, and logging – which are not permitted in the Great Smoky Mountains National Park – are allowed in Cherokee National Forest. Equally significant, commercial and residential development is allowed in certain parts of the national forest.

Some 66,000 acres of the forest is classified as wilderness, a designation that prohibits logging, motorized vehicles, construction, and development. Some 20,000 acres are classified as scenic, a designation that pro-hibits logging and allows only limited vehicle use. Meanwhile, 46,000 acres have been classified as primitive, which opens them up to low-impact recreation in a non-motorized environment. There is a recurring tension between those who want more environmental protection in the forest and those who want to open the lands up to more intensive uses and development.

Despite this, the Cherokee National Forest remains a beautiful, ecologically rich, and – in some parts – wild area. The forest is home to some 120 bird species, including wild turkey, golden eagle, and peregrine falcon; 47 mammal species, including the black bear, red wolf, wild boar, and coyote; and 30 species of reptile, including rattlesnake, copperhead, and salamander. It is home to many endangered species including the northern flying squirrel and two varieties of river mussels.

Hiking, camping, horseback riding, swimming, boating, white-water sports, and biking are just a few of the activities that draw people to the Cherokee National Forest.

The supervisor's office for the entire forest – north and south – is at 2800 North Ocoee Street in Cleveland. Call them at 423/476-9700. The southern forest has two ranger districts and corresponding ranger stations. The **Ocoee/Hiwassee District** (3171 Hwy. 64, 423/338-5201) is located along the Ocoee River near Benton. The **Tellico Ranger Station** (250 Ranger Station Rd., 423/253-2520) is located along the Cherohala Skyway near Tellico Plains.

The northern forest has two ranger stations. The **Nolichucky/Unaka District Ranger Station** (4900 Asheville Hwy., aka SR 70, 423/638-4109) is located near Greeneville. The **Watauga District Ranger Station** (423/735-1500) is in Unicoi.

Ranger stations are generally open daily 8:30 A.M.-4:30 P.M., and they are the best places to buy maps and get other information about recreation in the national forest. You can also visit the online store maintained by the Cradle of Forestry (www.cradleofforestry.com).

CLEVELAND

Cleveland is one gateway to the Cherokee National Forest. The seat of Bradley County, Cleveland is home to Lee University, a four-year Christian college operated by the Church of God, as well as the Church of God Theological Seminary, a graduate school for Christian ministry.

Sights

Find your way to Johnston Park downtown to see the **Cherokee Chieftain,** a large sculpture carved by Peter "Wolf" Toth. The sculpture was presented to the city of Cleveland in 1973, and represents the close association this region has with the Cherokee people.

The **Museum Center at Five Points** (200 Inman St., 423/339-5745, www.museumcenter.org, Tues.–Fri. 9 A.M.–3 P.M., Sat. 10 A.M.–3 P.M., adults $5, children $4) is a history museum dedicated to telling the story of the different groups of people who have lived along the Ocoee River. The museum is located at the end of the Old Copper Trail, the road by which copper traveled from the Copper Basin, through the mountains, and to the railroad at Cleveland.

Accommodations

The **Whitewater Lodge** (2500 Pointe South Rd., 423/479-7811, $30) is a bit far from the action of the Ocoee River, but the price can't be beat. Rooms have a kitchenette with coffeemaker, sink, and stovetop, adding to the bargain. Weekly rates are also available.

COLLEGEDALE

More than 200 ancient artifacts from the Near East are on exhibit at the **Lynn H. Wood Archaeological Museum** (Industrial Dr., Southern Adventist University, 423/236-2030, http://archaeology.southern.edu, Tues.–Thurs. 9–11 A.M. and 1–5 P.M., Fri. 9–11 A.M., Sat.–Sun. 2–5 P.M., free). Museum curators strive to depict life in the Biblical world with artifacts from Egypt, Babylonia, Persia, Syria-Palestine, Greece, Cyprus, and Anatolia. Highlights include a complete series of lamps from the Chalcolitic to early Arabic periods and handwritten cuneiform tablets from Ur.

RED CLAY STATE HISTORIC PARK

Red Clay State Historic Park (1140 Red Clay Park Rd., 423/478-0339, daily 8 A.M.–sunset, $3 per vehicle) was the site of the Cherokee capital from 1832 to 1838. In the years leading up to 1832, the State of Georgia outlawed Cherokee councils, so in 1832 the Cherokee moved their capital from New Echota, Georgia, to Red Clay, Tennessee, just over the state line. As many as 5,000 people attended the 11 council meetings held here until 1838, the year of the Cherokee's forced removal via the Trail of Tears. It was here at Red Clay that many Cherokee first learned of the planned removal.

The park consists of a visitors center (Mon.–Sat. 8 A.M.–4:30 P.M., Sun. 1–4:30 P.M.), re-created Cherokee settlement and council house, and a permanent exhibit on the Cherokee culture. The most prominent natural landmark is the spring, which rises from beneath a limestone ledge to form a deep pool that flows into Mill Creek, a tributary of the Conasauga and Coosa River system. The spring is about 15 feet deep and produces more than 500,000 gallons of water each day.

The park is an official interpretive center on the National Historic Trail of Tears. Cherokee Days of Recognition is held on the first weekend of August each year. It includes authentic Cherokee crafts, food, storytelling, and music.

OCOEE

The town of Ocoee is a smattering of businesses and homes located on Highways 64 and 411.

A few miles north of the intersection, along Highway 411, is the **Gravesite of Nancy Ward,** located atop a small hill. There is a parking area and pathway to the summit. Nancy Ward was born in 1738 at the Cherokee town of Chota and she was named Nanye-hi. Nanye-hi had a queenly appearance and commanding bearing, and she fought alongside her husband and other men in a raid on the Creeks during the 1755 Battle of Taliwa. Ward was

CHATTANOOGA

chosen as Agi-gau-u-e, or "Beloved Woman" of the Cherokee. As such, she sat on the Council of Chiefs, had complete power over prisoners, and led the Women's Council.

In the late 1750s, an English trader named Bryant Ward moved into the area and married Nancy, as she was called by the white settlers, although he already had a wife and family in South Carolina. They had a daughter, Betsy, who joined Five Killer and Catherine, children of Ward's first marriage, as her offspring.

Ward was influential in her tribe, and with the white settlers. She advocated peace between Indians and settlers, and more than once she warned settlers of an impending Indian attack. She spoke at the negotiations held on the Long Island of the Holston and at the Treaty of Hopewell.

With the Hiwassee Purchase of 1819, Ward along with all Cherokee was forced to abandon Chota, their capital city of Overhill Tennessee. She moved south and settled near where her gravesite lies today. Ward died in 1822.

The oldest monument at Ward's gravesite was erected in 1923 by the Nancy Ward Chapter of the Daughters of the American Revolution. Newer exhibits by the Tennessee Overhill Association detail her life.

Accommodations

The **Whitewater Inn** (120 Whitewater Dr., 423/338-1201, www.ocoeewhitewaterinn.com, $60–100) is a standard-issue motel that still has a good deal of polish left. Designed to feel a bit like a mountain lodge, this inn offers comfortable rooms with two queen-sized beds, satellite TV, and telephones. There is free continental breakfast, wireless Internet, and fax and copy service. Apartments with a full kitchen ($150) are also available.

ALONG THE OCOEE

Just past Ocoee on Highway 64, you enter the Cherokee National Forest. The next 26 miles are a winding two-lane blacktop that follows the Ocoee River.

Chilhowee Mountain

For breathtaking views of Parksville Lake,

a picnic ground on Chilhowee Mountain in the southern Cherokee National Forest

© SUSANNA HENIGHAN POTTER

HIKING IN THE SOUTHERN CHEROKEE

If you plan to do much hiking in the southern Cherokee National Forest, you should invest in a good trail map. The best is National Geographic's Trails Illustrated No. 781 *Tellico and Ocoee River Cherokee National Forest.*

There are dozens of hiking trails in the southern Cherokee National Forest. Below are some of the best:

- The **Old Copper Trail** begins at the Ocoee Whitewater Center and is a 2.3-mile (one-way) hike along an old mining road. The Old Copper Trail is the last remaining portion of a road that was built around 1851 to connect the copper-mining towns of Ducktown and Copperhill with Cleveland. It took miners two days to haul the copper by mule the 33 miles to Cleveland. When Highway 64 was built in the 1930s, it followed the old Copper Road route, and subsequent upgrades widened and improved the current highway.

  The present-day hiking trail follows the edge of the river, passing apple trees and stone foundations left by farm families, some of whom were Cherokee Indians, in the early 19th century. You'll also pass a beaver pond and cross four foot bridges, including three timber stringer plank bridges and one heavy timber bridge.

- Other hikes that leave from the Whitewater Center include **Bear Paw Loop** (1.7 miles) and the **Chestnut Mountain Loop** (6 miles).

- One of the most famous trails in the forest is the **Benton MacKaye Trail** (www.bmta. org), a 150-mile trail named for the creator of the Appalachian Trail. When the AT was getting congested, a group of dedicated hikers set out to create a new long-haul hike through the Southern mountains. The Benton MacKaye Trail begins at Spring Mountain, Georgia, as does the AT. It follows a different path, however, and ends at Davenport Gap, North Carolina, in the Great Smoky Mountains National Park. The trail enters the Cherokee National Forest at Big Frog Mountain. Access points are at Forest Service Road 221, Forest Service Road 45, Thunder Rock Campground, and Highway 64 across from Ocoee Powerhouse No. 3.

- **Benton Falls Trail** is an easy 1.5-mile (one-way) trail that leaves from Chilhowee Campground and follows Rock Creek to 65-foot Benton Falls.

- The **John Muir Trail** covers 18.8 miles along the Hiwassee River from Childer's Creek near Reliance to Highway 68 at Farmer. The trail follows a route described by naturalist and writer John Muir in his book *A Thousand Mile Walk to the Gulf.*

- The **Oswald Dome Trail** climbs 3.9 miles up Bean Mountain from the Quinn Springs Campground on Highway 30 near Reliance. The trail ends at an elevation of 3,500 feet near the Oswald Dome fire tower.

- The **Unicoi Turnpike Trail** is a 2.5-mile portion of the historic Unicoi Turnpike, an old road that settlers, hunters, and Indians used to get over the mountains. The trail connects Doc Rogers Fields near Coker Creek with the Unicoi Gap. Along the way you will see a marker for a murdered tollgate keeper and the remnants of Rolling Stone CCC Camp.

CHATTANOOGA

the Ocoee River, and the Great Eastern Valley of Tennessee, take a seven-mile detour up Forest Service Road 77 to the summit of Chilhowee Mountain. There are no fewer than five overlooks on the drive, which terminates at the Cumberland Recreation Area, a day-use facility and campground. There is also a historical marker that recalls the Confederate soldiers who camped in these hills and waged guerilla war on Unionists during the Civil War.

Once at the Cumberland Recreation Area, you can hike 1.5 miles to **Benton Falls,** or take any of the seven other trails in the area. There is also a swimming beach, bathhouses, and picnic tables.

BIKING IN THE SOUTHERN CHEROKEE

Mountain biking is permitted on dozens of trails within Cherokee National Forest, making this a popular destination for off-road bicyclists. The **Chilhowee Mountain Bike Trail System** is centered in the Chilhowee Mountain recreation area, near the town of Ocoee. It includes nine different trails ranging from easy to advanced. The two-mile Azalea Trail is a favorite; the 5.4-mile Clear Creek Trail is challenging with wrenching uphill and screaming downhill segments.

The **Tanasi Mountain Bike Trail System** is located near the Ocoee Whitewater Center and has five trails, including the 11.5-mile advanced Chestnut Mountain-West Fork Loop. The Thunder Rock Express is a 1.5-mile stretch of trail with exciting downhill segments and lots of jumps. The Tanasi system is so revered by mountain bikers that a top-of-the-line titanium-frame mountain bike is named after it.

Elite road bikers head to the **Cherohala Skyway** for endurance rides. The road climbs for 21 miles on the Tennessee side before beginning a 15-mile descent in North Carolina. Steep switchbacks and high elevation make this a challenging ride for even the most experienced bikers. The skyway is the location of the 100-mile **Cherohala Challenge** every June.

The **Tellico Ranger District Trail System** north of the Cherohala Skyway includes the 11-mile Citico Creek and Tellico River Trail, a challenging ride along a gravel road, and the Indian Boundary Loop, a 3.2-mile level track that circles Indian Boundary Lake.

Bike rentals and gear are available from **High Country Adventures** (430 Hwy. 64, 423/261-2310) in Ocoee, and **Trailhead Bicycle Company** (225 1st St. NE, 423/472-9899) offers superior gear and repair services.

Copperhill's **Ocoee Adventure Center** (4654 Hwy. 64, 423/496-4437, www.ocoee-adventurecenter.com) offers guided mountain bike trips and personalized instruction. Rates are $45 per person for a half-day, and $89 per person for a whole day. **Outdoor Adventure Rafting** (629 Welcome Valley Rd., 423/338-5746, www.raft.com) near Benton rents bikes for $15 per hour or $40 per day, and will also customize bike trips for your group.

Parksville Lake

This nearly 2,000-acre lake formed by the Ocoee River is operated as a Forest Service recreation area. There is a swimming beach, campground, picnic area, and boat launches. The lake is popular for fishing, waterskiing, and riding personal watercraft.

Ocoee River Dams

The Tennessee Valley Authority operates three powerhouses along the Ocoee River, which together produce some 70,000 kilowatts of electricity. Ocoee 1, the westernmost facility, pre-dates TVA and forms the Parksville Lake (also called the Ocoee Lake). There is a marker and overlook next to the dam, which was built in 1910.

Ocoee 2 was built in 1913 and consists of a diversion dam, wooden flume, and powerhouse. When the powerhouse is on, the river water is diverted into the flume, which carries it five miles downstream to the Ocoee 2 powerhouse, where it is dropped from a height of 250 feet, creating far more power than it would otherwise. The flume, which is visible as you drive along the river, is on the National Register of Historic Places. Ocoee 3, built in 1942, follows a similar pattern. It has a diversion dam, a tunnel, and a powerhouse.

When the river water is being used to generate electricity, the Ocoee River is just a trickle down a dry riverbed. But TVA releases water for recreation on certain days of the year, according to a published schedule. A one-mile section below Ocoee 3 is the Olympic white-water section and it passes in front of the Ocoee Whitewater Center. A four-mile segment below Ocoee 2 is used by commercial outfitters and water-sports enthusiasts for rafting and kayaking trips.

The Ocoee River was not always recognized as a site for white-water sports. In fact, it was only due to the deterioration of the Ocoee 2 water flume that the river's recreational potential was "discovered." It was around 1976 that years of weathering caused TVA to shut down the flume for repairs, causing river water to flow unimpeded down the Ocoee for the first time in decades.

It did not take long for the first daredevils to discover the rapids; the first river riders rode Navy surplus rafts and discovered the thrill of the unbridled river. The first two outfitters, Ocoee Outdoors and Sunburst Expeditions, opened their doors in 1977.

But TVA was meanwhile repairing the flume, and in 1984 it was ready to again divert the river water away from the riverbed. By this time, however, the rafting industry had blossomed. So in 1984 the Outfitters Association and TVA reached a 35-year agreement where rafting companies would get a minimum of 116 days of rafting water each year, and would pay $2 per customer to compensate TVA for the loss of power generation. It is an agreement which has allowed TVA to continue operation and the rafting industry to flourish.

◖ RAFTING THE OCOEE

White-water rafting is the iconic activity of the southern Cherokee Forest. The four miles between the Ocoee 2 diversion dam and the Ocoee 2 powerhouse are where the fun happens, over 20 different rapids with names like Grumpy, Broken Nose, Double Suck, Slingshot, and Hell's Hole.

The Ocoee River is for experienced or adventurous outdoors people. With Class III–IV rapids, the river can be frightening or dangerous if you're not experienced or confident enough. No one under 12 is permitted to raft anywhere on the Ocoee. Beginners or families with young children should raft down the Hiwassee instead.

Watching as other people make their way down the river is also an enjoyable pastime. Pull-overs and parking areas along the rafting portion of the river are often full of onlookers on summer afternoons and other busy periods.

The Ocoee rafting and floating season runs from March to September. During the spring and fall, outfitters will offer trips on weekends or holidays only. During the summer, there are trips every day. Rafting on the river is dependent on TVA's schedule of water releases. You can pick up a schedule from the Ocoee Whitewater Center.

When you go rafting, do plan to get wet. Don't carry anything with you, like a camera, that can't be submerged. In summer, wear your bathing suit, shorts, a T-shirt, and tennis shoes. During the cooler months, suit up in a wet suit or wear a windbreaker or wool sweater to keep warm. Wool socks and tennis shoes are also nice. Regardless of the season, avoid cotton clothing and bring a change of clothes to put on after your trip.

There are more than 20 companies offering rafting trips down the Ocoee. Some of the best are: Wildwater (Ducktown, 423/496-4904, www.whitewaterexpress.com), Ocoee Rafting (Ducktown, 423/496-3388, www.ocoeerafting.com), Big Frog Expeditions (1278 Welcome Valley, Benton, 423/338-4325, www.ocoeeriver.biz), Nantahala Outdoor Center (13077 U.S. 19, Bryson City, NC, 423/338-5901, www.noc.com), and Ocoee Inn Rafting (2496 U.S. 64, 423/338-2064, www.ocoeeinn.com).

If you want to make a more significant commitment to the sport of kayaking, sign up for a clinic at **Ocoee Adventure Center** (4651 Hwy. 64, 423/496-4437, www.ocoeeadventurecenter.com).

Ocoee Whitewater Center

Built for the 1996 Atlanta Summer Olympics, the Ocoee Whitewater Center (Hwy. 64 W., 423/496-5197, www.fs.fed.us/r8/ocoee, free) is a central source of information about the Ocoee River, and a starting point for several hikes. The center is open April–November daily 9 A.M.–5 P.M., between Thanksgiving and March Friday–Sunday 9 A.M.–5 P.M.

The riverbed in front of the center is pockmarked and rugged; the natural contours of

© SUSANNA HENIGHAN POTTER

the Ocoee Whitewater Center

the river were "improved" in preparation for the Olympics. When the water is low, children and adults will enjoy walking around the pools and streams on the riverbed, or sunning on the rocks. When the water is high, marvel at the power and sound of fast-running water while you watch rafters and kayakers maneuvering down the rapids.

There are rocking chairs and plenty of benches around for relaxing. The Olympic Legacy Bridge spans the river, providing nice views of the water below. During spring and summer, plan to walk through the gardens, which showcase native plants. You can find a guide to the gardens at the visitors center.

Visitors to the center can park for 30 minutes in the lot right next to the center. Long-term users must park below and pay a fee of $3 per vehicle.

Accommodations

The ❰ **Lake Ocoee Inn** (2496 Hwy. 64, 423/338-2064, www.ocoeeinn.com, $55–65) is located about 15 miles west of the Ocoee Whitewater Center and sits on the shore of placid Lake Ocoee (Parksville Lake). This motel opened in 1936 and has nondescript motel rooms, plus four fully equipped cabins. There is also a marina. Generally speaking, Lake Ocoee attracts an outdoorsy crowd. It is also family friendly.

Practicalities

A word about logistics: Gas, food, and lodging are somewhat limited along the Ocoee River. There are gas stations at Ocoee, Ducktown, and at Greasy Creek, about five miles up Highway 30. There are restaurants in Ocoee, Ducktown, and Copper Hill, plus one restaurant along the river. The best way to handle food during a trip to the river is to pack a picnic lunch and enjoy it at one of the many picnic areas in the forest. There are modest groceries in Greasy Creek, Reliance, and Ocoee. There is a larger Piggly Wiggly market in Ducktown.

DUCKTOWN

Ducktown, and its sister city Copperhill, are the heart of the Copper Basin of Tennessee. Here, copper was mined from the 1850s until the 1980s.

CAMPING IN THE SOUTHERN CHEROKEE

There are more than a dozen developed campgrounds in the southern region of the Cherokee National Forest. Campgrounds vary from developed areas with electrical hook-ups for RVs and hot showers to rustic grounds with chemical toilets and no shower facilities at all. Most forest service campgrounds are open from mid-March to December, and most are open on a first-come, first-served basis. Where reservations are available, they must be made through the government's centralized reservation service at www. reserveusa.com or by calling 877/444-6777.

Camping rates range from $10 to $20 depending on the type of site you choose and the popularity of the campground. Below is a list of some of the most popular campgrounds; for a complete list contact the nearest ranger station.

OCOEE/HIWASSEE DISTRICT

The largest campground is **Chilhowee Recreation Area,** located along Forest Service Road 77. There are 86 campsites, warm showers, and flush toilets. You are next door to the McKamy Lake beach and have easy access to 25 miles of hike/bike trails.

Thunder Rock is located near Ocoee Powerhouse No. 3 and is convenient to the Whitewater Center. There are 39 sites, warm showers, and flush toilets. This is a popular campsite for rafters and other water-sports enthusiasts.

Parksville Lake, open April 1–October 31, is located along Rock Creek and has 17 campsites, warm showers, and flush toilets. It is convenient to the white-water section of the Ocoee River and to swimming, boating, and fishing on Parksville Lake.

Lost Creek, located off Highway 30 near Reliance, has 15 sites and is set in a mature hardwood forest next to Big Lost Creek. It is a peaceful and wild area, but the flush toilets and hot showers add a good deal of comfort. RVs are welcome.

TELLICO DISTRICT

Big Oak Cove is an 11-site campground located on the banks of the Tellico River. A retreat for tent campers, the grounds are open from mid-March through December. Hiking, fishing, and wading are available nearby. The fee is $10 per night. There are chemical toilets and cold showers.

Located off the Cherohala Skyway at an elevation of 1,800 feet, **Holly Flats** is an 18-site tent-friendly campsite with limited facilities. There are chemical toilets and cold showers, but little in the way of other comforts. The setting is peaceful and uncrowded.

One of the most popular campgrounds in this part of the forest is **Indian Boundary,** an 88-site campground located on Indian Boundary Lake along the Cherohala Skyway. Four loops offer various levels of comfort, from full RV hook-ups to rustic tent sites. Possible recreation includes hiking or biking around the lake, boating, fishing, and swimming. Reservations are accepted.

In order to fuel the copper smelters, timber was harvested all around. By 1876, all the trees in the area were gone and logs had to be floated in from Fannin County, Georgia. Between 1865 and 1878, 24 million pounds of copper were removed from the earth and 50 square miles of the basin had been stripped of its trees.

The area's mines declined between 1878 and 1890, until a new railroad spur arrived in the area. In 1899 the Tennessee Copper Company opened the Burra Burra Mine in Ducktown and built a new smelter. During this period,

mining companies used an open roasting process to remove copper from the raw ore. This open roasting required lots of timber for fuel and it let off sulfuric acid, which killed vegetation and left the landscape eerily empty. Acid rain fell, polluting the Ocoee River and other nearby bodies of water.

The environmental abuse of more than a century left its mark on Tennessee's Copper Bain. For years, this area was distinctive for its barren orange-red hills and craters, the legacy of many years of deforestation and the open release of sulfuric acid. Residents had mixed feelings about the landscape—it was strangely beautiful, but at the same time it was a constant reminder of environmental damage. There were also concerns about health effects. Early efforts to reforest the old mines date back to the early 20th century, but it was not until the 1970s that scientists figured out a way to successfully introduce trees back into the denuded landscape. Since then, pine trees have grown to cover virtually all of the hills that were once barren.

Copper was mined here until 1987, and the plant at Copperhill still processes sulfur, although the raw materials are trucked in—not mined.

Ducktown was a company town, a fact that is evident as you take a short drive around. Main Street is little more than two blocks with a handful of elegant homes, built by mine owners and bosses. The main residential neighborhood is a collection of modest homes in a slight hollow. The newer parts of town, including gas stations, motels, and a school, are found near the intersection of Highways 64 and 68.

Ducktown Basin Museum

The Ducktown Basin Museum (212 Burra Burra St., 423/496-5778, Mon.–Sat. 10 A.M.–4:30 P.M., adults $4, seniors $3, children $0.50) captures the unique history and culture of Tennessee's Copper Basin. Located in the offices of the old Burra Burra mine, the museum has displays about the historical development of the mines, the culture that developed in the company towns, and the mining business itself. Special topics include mine safety, the railroad, and the history of strikes at the mine. Your visit includes a 15-minute video that tells the story of the entire region, and describes the three periods during which the hills here were mined for copper and other minerals.

At the rear of the museum is one of the only "copper craters" that was not reforested. Although volunteer pine trees are beginning to take root in the red soil, you can still imagine how distinctive the landscape once looked.

Accommodations

Ducktown is close enough to the Ocoee and

the Ducktown Basin Museum

© SUSANNA HENIGHAN POTTER

several outdoor outfitters to make it a popular place for outdoor thrill-seekers. But the additional draw of the mining museum is another reason to make this your home base in the Overhill region.

There are two bed-and-breakfasts in Ducktown, located across the street from one another. **The Company House** (125 Main St., 423/496-5634, www.bbonline.com/tn/companyhouse, $79–89) has six guest rooms, each named for a mine in the area. All rooms have private baths and in-room telephones. **The White House** (104 Main St., 423/496-4166, www.ocoee-whitehousebb.com, $85–95) has three guest rooms, with private baths and free wireless Internet throughout the home.

If motel lodging is more your thing, then there are two options: the **Ducktown Copper Inn** (U.S. 64 and Hwy. 68, 423/496-5541, $55–65) is an aging motel with no-frills accommodation. Rooms have microwaves, refrigerators, and televisions. The **Ocoee Country Inn** (502 Hwy. 64, 423/496-7100, $60–80) is a newer outfit, with many of the same amenities (but less grunge) than its nearby neighbor.

Food
Besides the Hardees and a gas-station convenience store, **The Old Fort** (5075 Hwy. 64, 423/496-5060, Mon.–Sat. 10:30 A.M.–9 P.M., $3–10) is the only game in town. This homey pit stop offers all manner of hamburgers, and dinner plates with entrées like chicken livers, oven-fried chicken breast, and country-style steak. Lighter appetites may want a vegetable plate of your choice of four side dishes, which include creamed corn, mashed potatoes, fried okra, and pinto beans.

COPPERHILL
Copperhill sits on the state line and on the banks of the Ocoee River. On the Georgia side, the town is called McCaysville and the river is called the Toccoa.

There is more going on in Copperhill than Ducktown, due largely to the scenic train excursions that stop here for midday layovers. A pleasant main street district with restaurants and shops make this a nice place to spend an hour or so. Walk up the hillside that faces Ocoee Street for views of the town and the Ocoee/Toccoa River.

Rail Excursions
In addition to the rail excursions offered by the Tennessee Valley Railroad (see *Etowah* later in this chapter), the **Blue Ridge Scenic Railway** (706/632-9833, www.brscenic.com) offers railroad excursions that come to Copperhill. The trip leaves from Blue Ridge, Georgia, and makes a one-hour journey north through the mountains to Copperhill, where you have two hours to eat and shop. Ticket prices for adults range $26–39, depending on the season; prices for the Fall Foliage tours are the most expensive. Children's tickets are about half-price.

Food
Seventy years after its founding, the **New York Restaurant** (95 Ocoee St., 423/496-3855, daily 7 A.M.–3 P.M., $5–6) was remodeled and came under new management in 2007. You can eat at the classic lunch counter, or dine on white tablecloths at a table.

The menu includes plate lunches of hamburger steak, chicken breast and gravy, or chicken salad, and sandwiches including tuna melts and Philly cheesesteaks. There are some modern additions too: hummus in pita and black-bean veggie burgers. You can also order from the breakfast menu all day, and beer is served.

The **Iron Horse Grill** (50 Ocoee St., 423/496-9991, Tues.–Thurs. 11 A.M.–8:30 P.M., Fri.–Sat. 11 A.M.–9:30 P.M., $12–19) is a dimly lit restaurant serving hearty entrées, salads, steaks, and beer on tap.

TURTLETOWN
Drive north from Ducktown on Highway 68 to find more quiet towns and rural countryside.

Just beyond the small community of Turtletown, Highway 294 splits off Highway 68, headed towards North Carolina. About four miles down this road, and about two miles past the state line, there is a remarkable monument to the Christian faith. **Fields of the**

Woods Bible Park (10000 Hwy. 294, Murphy, North Carolina, 828/494-7855, daily sunrise–sunset, free) is a project of the Church of God of Prophecy that contains, among other things, the world's largest cross and the largest representation of the Ten Commandments. The latter is located just inside the park's gates and is laid out on a hillside. Each letter spelling out the commandments is five feet high and four feet wide. This is just the beginning of what Fields of the Woods has to offer. You will also find replicas of Joseph's tomb, where Christ was buried and rose from the dead, and Golgotha, where Jesus offered himself as a sacrifice. There is also a gift shop and café, which are open Monday–Saturday 9 A.M.–5 P.M.

The Hiwassee

Named from the Cherokee word "ayuwasi," which means savannah, or meadow, the Hiwassee River drains fertile agricultural lands and passes through the heartland of the southern Cherokee National Forest.

RELIANCE

The Reliance historic district is located along the Hiwassee River, near where Highways 30 and 315 intersect. The **Hiwassee Union Church** is a two-story board structure built jointly by the local Masonic lodge and the Union Church in 1899. On the north side of the river is the **Higdon Hotel,** also built around 1899.

Your pit stop in Reliance should be the Webb Brothers Texaco, a gas station, post office, general store, river outfitter, and community hub. Inside the shop you'll find a placard with historical information about Reliance.

Reliance is located about 10 miles north of the Ocoee River, along Highway 30. The drive south follows Greasy Creek, a pretty, clear stream that defies its name. You will pass old wood-frame houses and farms that have been in this valley for generations.

HIWASSEE SCENIC RIVER STATE PARK

A 23-mile section of the Hiwassee River has been designated a Tennessee Scenic River. From Highway 411 to the North Carolina state line, the Hiwassee River offers prime opportunities for canoeing, rafting, fishing, hiking, and wildlife-viewing.

Hiwassee Scenic River State Park and the neighboring **Gee Creek Campground** (Spring Creek Rd., Delano, 423/263-0050) are good places to come to explore the river. There are picnic grounds, restrooms, and boat-launch areas. The Gee Creek Campground has 47 tent-friendly campsites, some of which are right next to the river. Campsites are available on a first-come, first-served basis only.

Fishing is popular along the river; anglers frequently catch rainbow and brown trout, large-mouth bass, yellow perch, and catfish.

Unlike the Ocoee River, the Hiwassee is a calm river, with Class I–II (rather than III–IV) rapids. Children six and up are allowed on the Hiwassee.

Because the Hiwassee is calm, most people rent the necessary equipment and make the journey downriver without a guide. Expect to pay $40 and up per day for a six-person raft or $24 per day for a one-person Duckie. Inner tubes and other equipment are also available. Hiwassee outfitters include **Hiwassee Scenic Outfitters, Inc.** (155 Ellis Creek Rd., Reliance, 423/338-8115, www.hiwasseeoutfitters.com) and **Webb Brothers Float Service** (Reliance, 423/338-2373, www.webbbrosfloatservice.com).

DELANO

Located on the edge of the national forest, between Etowah and Benton, the town of Delano is known for **Delano Daylilies** (153 County Rd. 854, 423/263-9323, www.delanodaylilies.com, late May–early June Tues.–Sat. 10 A.M.–5 P.M., free), a noteworthy

SANDHILL CRANES

Located along the Hiwassee River between Dayton and Birchwood, the **Blythe Ferry Unit of the Hiwassee Refuge** (423/614-3018) is a good place for bird-watching. Besides seasonal shorebirds, waders, and common waterfowl such as wintering ducks and geese, the unit has recently become a winter stopover for migrating sandhill and whooping cranes. From just a few birds, the concentration has grown to more than 6,000 at times, making this one of Tennessee's premier wildlife spectacles from November to March. The refuge is closed to the public during the winter, but viewing is possible along the roads and from an observation deck.

To get to the refuge, find the junction between Highways 58 and 60 near Georgetown. Drive 7.8 miles west on Highway 60 and turn right at the wildlife sign.

The best way to get up close to the cranes and other wildlife of the Hiwassee Refuge is aboard **Blue Moon Cruises** (5637 Hwy. 411, Benton, 888/993-2583, www.bluemooncruises.org, $40), which depart from Sale Creek Marina near Soddy-Daisy from December to March. For 3.5 hours you will ply the waters of the Hiwassee on a naturalist-led tour that includes viewing of sandhill cranes.

sandhill cranes at the Blythe Ferry Unit of the Hiwassee Refuge

seasonal attraction and nursery. This nursery raises some 1,300 varieties of colorful daylilies, and from late May to early June every year their garden is busy with area growers shopping for blooms. Casual visitors are also welcome to come and enjoy a stroll throughout the patches of daylilies, but you'll be hard-pressed not to wind up with at least one plant in your possession by the end of your visit. A covered pavilion is a lovely place to sit and relax while your traveling companion chooses lilies. There are also benches throughout the gardens.

Gliding

Gliding is flying without an engine, and you can experience this sublime form of travel at **Chilhowee Glideport** (Hwy. 411, 423/388-2000, www.chilhowee.com) near Benton. A half-hour ride costs $135 and takes you high above the scenic Cherokee National Forest and the Hiwassee and Ocoee Rivers. Chilhowee Glideport also offers lessons and rentals for gliding enthusiasts.

COKER CREEK

Before copper was mined in the Copper Basin, this area was famous for its gold. The Cherokee Indians had known about the gold for years, but whites discovered it around 1825. It didn't take long for a full-fledged gold rush to begin. Trouble was that the gold was on Cherokee land. When the Indians complained to the federal government in 1826, the U.S. army established a garrison here supposedly to enforce the Cherokee's land rights. Even the presence of soldiers did little to keep settlers from tapping into the Cherokee's resources, and the pressure from people such as these was probably one thing that sealed the Cherokee's later fate.

Sights

For the best views of this part of the Cherokee Forest, drive to **Buck Bald,** the site of an old fire tower. The tower was removed in the 1970s, but the site remains a place to enjoy 360-degree views of the surrounding

CHATTANOOGA

landscape. To get there, drive seven miles south of Coker Creek along Highway 68, then turn left onto Buck Bald Road. It is 2.5 miles to the top.

A designated scenic area with four waterfalls and several miles of hiking trails, **Coker Creek Scenic Area and Falls** is a wonderful place for a picnic. The four waterfalls—Upper Coker Creek Falls, Coker Creek Falls, Hiding Place Falls, and Lower Coker Creek Falls—are all located within one-quarter mile of the parking area. There are picnic tables, but no toilets or potable water.

To find the falls, drive south of Coker Creek 3.1 miles along Highway 68. Turn right onto County Road 628 (Ironsburg Road) and travel 0.8 mile. Veer left at the Ironsburg Cemetery onto County Road 626 (Duckett Ridge Road) and travel for three miles. The road will become gravel. Turn left onto Forest Service Road 2138 and travel one mile to the parking area.

Panning for Gold

Although the gold industry petered out at Coker Creek after the Civil War, hobby mining and panning continues. You can buy panning supplies at the **Coker Creek Welcome Center** (Hwy. 68, 423/261-2286, www.cokercreek.org).

It's unlikely that anyone will tell you the best places to pan for gold, but the most popular are easy to find. You can pan at Coker Creek just three tenths of a mile from the welcome center, near Doc Rogers Field. Coker Creek Falls, eight miles south of the welcome center, is also a nice place to pan, although you may soon grow weary of the work and choose to enjoy the falls and swimming hole instead.

Shopping

Coker Creek is home to several art galleries. **Designs by Baerreis** (12203 Hwy. 68, 423/261-2731) is a family-owned gallery showcasing the work of Phil and Martha Baerreis as well as their children. Highlights include Phil's hand-turned wooden boxes and custom-made jewelry by Elisabeth Baerreis. The **Coker Creek**

Gallery (206 Hot Water Rd., 423/261-2157), located just a few hundred yards from Highway 68, has wind chimes, pottery, glass and metal sculptures, jewelry, and more. **Bob Hardin** (135 Hot Water Rd., 423/261-2578) makes knives and leather products in his studio.

Events

Coker Creek's **Autumn Gold Festival** (www.cokercreek.org) is the community's largest event of the year. Taking place during the second full weekend of October—while the autumn leaves are on full display—the festival includes a crafts fair, gold panning, and the crowning of the Autumn Gold Queen.

The town also puts on a **Heritage Festival** (www.cokercreek.org) every May, with live music, Southern food, arts-and-crafts demonstrations, and living history.

ETOWAH

Etowah didn't much exist until 1902, when the Louisville and Nashville Railroad chose the settlement for its new headquarters and rail center. The railroad was planning a new, more direct route between Cincinnati and Atlanta, and it needed a place for crew changes and engine servicing. The passenger station was built first, in 1906. A veritable railroad complex followed: roundhouse, sandhouse, cinder pits, coal bins, oil house, machine shop, blacksmith shop, boiler shop, planing mill, cabinet shop, powerhouse, car repair shop, water tanks, a store, offices, freight depot, and nearly 20 tracks.

The L&N also built houses for its workers, and Etowah was truly a company town where everyone lived, breathed, and worked the railroad. At its peak, more than 2,000 men were employed by the L&N here.

Etowah and its railroad industry flourished until 1928, when the L&N started to replace its wooden railroad carts with steel ones. Two hundred shop men were laid off. In the same year, the L&N closed its headquarters in Etowah, moving them to Knoxville. By 1931, the workforce at Etowah had shrunk to just 80.

Over the succeeding decades, Etowah diversified and people found other work. Passenger trains continued to run until 1968. CSX, the freight train company, still operates a terminal in Etowah.

Sights

Etowah's downtown district faces Highway 411 and the railroad. The historic **Gem Theater** (700 S. Tennessee Ave., aka U.S. 441, www.gemplayers.com), built in 1927, has been renovated and is the home of the Gem Theater Players. For information about upcoming shows, contact the Etowah Arts Commission at 423/263-7608.

You can relive Etowah's railroad history at the **L&N Depot and Railroad Museum** (Tennessee Ave., aka Hwy. 411, 423/263-7840, Mon.–Sat. 10 A.M.–4 P.M., free). The old passenger station is elegant, with high ceilings and delicate wood finishes. It comes alive through old photographs and recollections by area residents, who talk about the hardships and pleasures of a railroad life. The exhibit, entitled "Growing Up with the L&N: Life and Times of a Railroad Town" is more about the social history of Etowah than the railroad itself.

Ask to go upstairs, where you can see more general exhibits about Etowah's history. Sometimes there are local art exhibits on display.

After touring the museum, go outside to see a railroad caboose. There is also a picnic area and a walking trail that follows the railroad tracks.

◖ Tennessee Valley Railroad Excursions

The Tennessee Valley Railroad (423/894-8028, www.tvrail.com), based in Chattanooga, organizes sightseeing tours of the Cherokee National Forest during the summer and fall. The **Hiwassee River Rail Adventure** (adults $32, children $22) is a 3.5-hour, 50-mile journey that follows the path of the Hiwassee River, and includes the breathtaking cork-screw loop around Bald Mountain. The **Copperhill Special** (adults $67, children $40) follows the same route as the Hiwassee journey, but adds an additional 40-mile trip and lunchtime layover in Copperhill.

Passengers on either journey meet at the L&N Depot Museum in Etowah, and are bussed to nearby Gee Creek State Park, where they board the train. Train cars are comfortable with big windows and air-conditioning.

The scenic train excursions are made possible by the combined efforts of the Tennessee Overhill Association and the Tennessee Valley Railroad Museum.

Accommodations

The ◖ **Tennessee Overhill Sleep Inn** (600 Tennessee Ave., 423/263-4343, www.tennesseeoverhillsleepinn.com, $75–105) is a motor inn with comfortable rooms and a good location for exploring this region. There is free high-speed Internet, a hot breakfast, guest laundry, and a fitness room, and in-room amenities such as hair dryers, irons, and voice mail. It is located just a few blocks north of downtown Etowah near several restaurants.

Food

Directly across Tennessee Avenue (otherwise known as Highway 411) from the L&N Depot is **Tony's Italian Restaurant** (718 Tennessee Ave., 423/263-1940, daily 11 A.M.–10 P.M., $5–8), which serves pasta, pizza, calzones, and Italian-style subs. There is a buffet at lunch and dinner that includes lasagna, pizza, salad, and other house specialties.

A short drive north on Tennessee Avenue will take you to **Hah-Hah's Deli** (235 Hwy. 411 N., 423/263-7914, Mon.–Fri. 9 A.M.–3:30 P.M., $5–6), which serves coffee, sandwiches, and Mayfield ice cream.

Information

Contact the **Etowah Area Chamber of Commerce** (727 Tennessee Ave., 423/263-2228, www.etowahcoc.org), located in the L&N building next to the museum, for visitor information. The **Tennessee Overhill Heritage Association** (423/263-7232, www.tennesseeoverhill.com) is a regional tourism agency based in Etowah, with offices in the railroad depot.

The Tellico

The headwaters of the Tellico River are high atop the peaks of the Cherokee Forest. The stream, noted for fishing, flows down the mountain and along the scenic Cherohala Skyway to Tellico Plains, where it flows northward to its confluence with the Little Tennessee. The Tellico Dam impounds the rivers and forms Tellico Lake. Here, near the town of Vonore, are two of the most significant historic attractions in the region: Fort Loudoun State Historic Area and the Sequoyah Birthplace Museum. Both have important ties to Cherokee history.

Towns including Athens, Englewood, and Madisonville are located in the foothills of the mountains, in the Great Valley of East Tennessee. These centers of industry, education, and commerce are still the heartbeat of the Overhill region.

TELLICO PLAINS

Located where the Tellico River emerges from the National Forest, Tellico Plains was once a logging and industrial town. It is now a gateway to the Cherokee National Forest, and the official beginning point of the Cherohala Skyway, a scenic parkway that extends into North Carolina.

The **Cherohala Skyway Visitor Center** (225 Cherohala Skyway, aka Hwy. 165, 423/253-8010, Mar.–Nov. daily 9 A.M.–5 P.M., Dec.–Feb. Fri.–Sun. 9 A.M.–5 P.M.), near the official start of the skyway, has maps and staff who can answer you questions. There is also a large gift shop and bathrooms. Right next door is the **Charles Hall Museum** (229 Cherohala Skyway, 423/253-6767, www.charleshall-museum.com, free), a local history museum packed with antiques, 98 percent of which came from the collection of Tellico-area resident Charles Hall. There are more than 200 guns, an extensive telephone collection, and an impressive coin collection, among others.

Tellico Plains consists of an older "downtown" located on the south side of Highway

165, and several miles of sprawl along Highway 68. The downtown area is home to several real estate offices, building supply companies, local business, restaurants, and shops. **Motorcycle Outfitters** (106 Scott St., 423/253-2088) sells clothes and equipment for bikers, **The Bookshelf** (108 Scott St., 423/253-3183) is a used book store. Galleries including **Castle Art Gallery** cater to visitors looking for local arts and crafts.

For food, head first to **❰ Tellico Grains** (105 Depot St., 423/253-6911, Tues.–Sat. 8 A.M.–4 P.M., $4–8), a bakery and café with its own wood-fired oven. The bread, sandwiches, and pizza are better than you might expect to get in a town this size.

For plate lunches, burgers, and other grilled sandwiches, go to **Town Square Café and Bakery** (Public Sq., 423/253-2200, Mon.–Sat. 6 A.M.–8 P.M., Sun. 6 A.M.–3 P.M., $3–8), a cozy eating house where everyone seems to know each other. The daily lunch special comes with your choice of two sides and bread. They also sell pizza.

Cherohala Skyway

Completed in 1996, this is a two-lane highway that passes through the highest peaks of the southern Unaka Mountains. The 54-mile road, which begins in Tellico Plains, climbs to more than 5,300 feet at its highest level and provides stunning scenic views. It follows the Tellico River for several miles at the beginning, before starting its serious ascent. The road terminates in Robbinsville, North Carolina; about one-third of the road is in Tennessee.

Originally called the Cheoah Parkway and the Overhill Skyway, Tennessee and North Carolina eventually agreed on the Cherohala Skyway, a name which combines the words Cherokee and Nantahala. The highway, which took 34 years and some $100 million to build, replaced narrow, unpaved Forest Service roads that had for many years been the only means of travel over the peaks in this

The Cherohala Skyway connects Tellico Plains and Robbinsville, North Carolina.

part of the forest. Despite predictions to the contrary, the skyway remains relatively uncrowded, providing a pleasant alternative to congested highways through the Great Smoky Mountains National Park.

It will take you about 1.5 hours to drive nonstop from one end of the skyway to the other. Although the road is well maintained and easy to drive, it is windy and you will want to stop frequently to admire the view. Beware of snow and ice during winter.

Sights and stops along the way include **Tellico Ranger Station** (250 Ranger Station Rd., 423/253-2520), a source of information about the forest and the drive. The station is located in a New Deal–era CCC building. **Bald River Falls,** a 100-foot waterfall, is located off the skyway along Forest Service Road 210.

After you pass the ranger station, the road begins to climb. Overlooks on the Tennessee side include **Turkey Creek, Lake View,** and **Brushy Ridge.** There are picnic tables at Turkey Creek and Brushy Ridge. All overlooks are wheelchair-accessible.

The skyway is popular with motorcyclists and serious bicyclists, who enjoy the curves and fresh mountain air.

Indian Boundary

One of the most popular destinations in the southern Cherokee Forest, Indian Boundary (FSR 345, Apr.–Sept.) is a Forest Service campground and recreation area. Located high atop the mountains off the Cherohala Skyway, Indian Boundary is cool in the summer and an ideal place for a camping vacation. Cool off with a swim at the Indian Boundary beach, hike or bike along the three-mile loop that circles the 96-acre Indian Boundary Lake, or go for a boat cruise on the lake. No gasoline engines are allowed in the lake.

The campground has 91 sites, hot showers, and potable water available from spigots around the campground. Several sites have electricity. There is also a camp store (no phone) and picnic area. Despite Indian Boundary's isolation, it is quite popular, especially during the summer. You can reserve a campsite at www.reserveusa.com or by calling 877/444-6777. For information on recreation, contact the Tellico Ranger Station at 423/253-2520.

ENGLEWOOD

A small town located in the foothills of the Appalachian mountains, Englewood is home to the **Englewood Textile Museum** (17 S. Niota St., 423/887-5455, Tues.–Sat. noon–5 P.M., free). The museum remembers the hundreds of area women who worked at textile mills in

Englewood. A hand-painted mural on the outside of the museum depicts a pastoral company town. Inside, you can see some of the clothing that was manufactured here over nearly 100 years. There is an adjacent antiques store.

Food

The **❶ Tellico Junction Cafe** (17 Main St., 423/887-7770, Mon.–Fri. 6 A.M.–4 P.M., Sat. 7 A.M.–4 P.M., Sun. 7 A.M.–noon, $5–12) is a large, open restaurant facing the railroad tracks in downtown Englewood. Dozens of polished wood tables and a wide lunch counter invite you to stop and linger over cups of coffee or plates of grilled sandwiches, plate-lunch specials, or homemade dessert.

ATHENS

The seat of McMinn County, Athens is home to **Tennessee Wesleyan University** (204 E. College St., 423/745-7504, www.twcnet. edu), a Methodist-affiliated four-year university. Chartered in 1857, it is the home of the Old College Harp Singers, a shape-note singing group.

The **McMinn Living History Museum** (522 W. Madison Ave., 423/745-0329, Mon.–Fri. 10 A.M.–5 P.M., Sat. 10 A.M.–4 P.M., adults $5, students and seniors $3) houses 30 different exhibit rooms, including an extensive collection of antique quilts.

One of the Southeast's most distinctive food brands is Mayfield, a maker of milk, dairy, and juice products. Mayfield's largest bottling and processing plant is located just outside of Athens, near where Thomas B. Mayfield Sr., a local dairy farmer, first opened his creamery in 1923. Visitors are welcome at **Mayfield Dairy Farms** (4 Mayfield Ln., 800/629-3435, www.mayfielddairy.com, Mon.–Fri. 9 A.M.–5 P.M., Sat. 9 A.M.–2 P.M., free). The 40-minute tour includes a short video and visits to viewing areas where you can see Mayfield's distinctive yellow milk jugs being made, jugs and other containers being filled, and ice cream being packaged. You also walk by giant vats of milk being pasteurized, and others that are being made into buttermilk. Don't expect to see any cows, though, except for the bronze cow sculpture outside the welcome center. Mayfield buys its raw milk from area dairy farmers; it arrives in giant trucks that enter the dairy gates by the dozens every day.

The tour is free, but be aware that it is awfully hard to pass up the ice cream shop at the end, especially on a hot summer day. It's almost like they planned it that way.

Accommodations

The **Majestic Mansion** (202 E. Washington Ave., 423/746-9041, www.themansionbnb.com, $95–125) is a bed-and-breakfast in downtown residential Athens. Four guest rooms offer classic country decor with elegant touches, such as claw-foot tubs, feather beds, and polished brass fittings. Each room has a private bath, air-conditioning, and television. For breakfast choose between "fitness fare" and "full power breakfast." Spend a quiet afternoon on the screened-in front porch, or relaxing in the sitting room. In-room spa service is available at reasonable prices.

MADISONVILLE

Epicurians should make a beeline to **Benton's Country Hams** (2603 Hwy. 411, 423/442-5003), a family-run ham house where they depend on brown sugar, salt, and a lot of time to cure their hams. Housed in a low-slung inconspicuous cinderblock building on the side of busy Highway 411, Benton's has been a destination for cooks and eaters for generations. Their smoked and unsmoked country hams sell like hotcakes. You can also buy prosciutto, bacon, and luncheon meats that will have you dreaming pig. You know this is the real thing because the scent of hickory smoke clings to your clothes and hair after you depart. My advice: Buy more than you think you'll need. Pork makes a great gift.

SWEETWATER

The Lost Sea (140 Lost Sea Rd., 423/337-6616, www.thelostsea.com, Nov.–Feb. daily 9 A.M.–5 P.M., Mar.–Apr. and Sept.–Oct. daily 9 A.M.–6 P.M., May, June, Aug. daily 9 A.M.–7 P.M., July daily 9 A.M.–8 P.M., adults

$16, children $8) is a cave noted for its four-acre underground lake. Tours include a 0.75-mile guided tour of the caverns, as well as a ride aboard a glass-bottomed boat on the lake. You can even sign up to camp out down in the cave in one of the Lost Sea's so-called "wild tours." This is a memorable experience. The Lost Sea is located at exit 60 off I-75.

While in Sweetwater, satisfy your sweet tooth at **Hunter's Bakery and Cafe** (Main and Morris Sts., Mon.–Thurs. 10 A.M.–5 P.M., Fri.–Sat. 10 A.M.–9 P.M., lunch $5–12, dinner $10–25). This cozy downtown hot-spot has a fox-hunting theme and solidly good food that keeps people coming back again and again. Salads, pasta, and entrées including steak, pork, chicken, and shrimp are offered at lunch and dinner. At the midday meal, you can also pick from signature sandwiches like the tuna melt or the Reuben.

Whatever you do, finish off your meal with one of the café's home-baked big cookies or other confectionaries for the road.

VONORE

Two side by side historical attractions located on Tellico Lake focus on the state's Native American history, but from distinctly different eras and perspectives. Fort Loudoun State Historic Area marks the early era of contact between colonists and Cherokee Indians, while the Sequoyah Birthplace Museum looks in greater detail at the tribe's later interactions with white settlers, including its tragic removal via the Trail of Tears in 1838.

◖ Fort Loudoun State Historic Area

The Fort Loudoun State Historic Area (338 Fort Loudoun Rd., 423/884-6217, daily 8 A.M.–4:30 P.M., free) recalls the British fort that was built in this spot in 1756 to woo the Cherokee Indians during the French and Indian War. The war between the British and the French, and their respective Indian allies, was fought to decide which European power would control the new American colonies. The British built Fort Loudoun in an effort to cement its alliance with the Cherokee, and

therefore strengthen their position to win the war against the French.

Fort Loudoun was located along the Little Tennessee River, and it was the very edge of the American frontier. At first, the British managed to maintain good relations with their Cherokee neighbors. But the uncertain alliance ultimately failed and violence broke out, with each side blaming the other for the problems. After a five-month siege of Fort Loudoun in 1760, the British surrendered. The British negotiated the terms of their surrender with the Cherokee, who agreed to let the 180 men together with 60 women and children retreat to Charleston, South Carolina.

When the British party stopped to camp their first night, their Cherokee guides slipped into the forest and by the next day some 29 of the Fort Loudoun party had been killed, including three women. While the basic facts of the ambush are clear, the motivation of the Cherokee is not. Their actions may have been in retribution for the earlier deaths of some 30 Cherokee at the hands of the British. Or they may have been angry that the British had buried the cannons and destroyed the gunpowder at the fort, contrary to the terms of the surrender.

Whatever the cause, it was a bloody and somber end to the Cherokee-British alliance in the Overhill Tennessee region.

Today, Fort Loudoun sits on the bank of Tellico Lake. The last and most controversial of TVA's dam projects, Tellico Dam was finally closed in 1979 after nearly a decade of debate over its impact on the environment and the loss of historic Cherokee sites.

The park visitors center houses a good museum about the fort, and the film here is one of the best at a Tennessee state park. About 200 yards behind the visitors center is a replica of Fort Loudoun, built according to the archaeological evidence and contemporary accounts from the fort. The simple wooden buildings and the fort walls have been faithfully reconstructed. It is a pleasant place that conjures up the remoteness which would have existed in the 18th century, when the original fort was built.

Every September the **18th Century Trade**

Faire depicts a colonial-era marketplace with merchants, artisans, and entertainers. At Christmas, there are candlelight tours of the fort. In addition, every month there are special programs that include costumed British soldiers and Cherokee Indians.

Fort Loudoun State Historic Area also has a picnic area, five miles of hiking trails, and fishing from a 50-foot pier that projects over Tellico Lake.

Sequoyah Birthplace Museum

Sequoyah was a Cherokee Indian born in about 1776 to Nathanial Gist, a Virginia fur trader, and Wurteh, the daughter of a Cherokee chief. A silversmith by trade, Sequoyah is most famous for creating a written syllabary for the Cherokee language.

It was 1809 when Sequoyah first started to experiment with a written language for the Cherokee. During this period there was extensive interaction between white settlers and the Cherokee, and Sequoyah saw that a written language would allow his people to record their history, write letters, and communicate news.

Sequoyah developed the language independently, and his first student was his young daughter, Ayoka. Together, in 1821, Ayoka and Sequoyah introduced the language to Cherokee elders and within a few months thousands of Cherokee were using the system of 85 symbols. By 1825 much of the Bible and numerous hymns had been translated and in 1828 the *Cherokee Phoenix* became the first national bilingual newspaper.

The story of Sequoyah's accomplishment and the broader legacy of the Cherokee people is preserved at the Sequoyah Birthplace Museum (Hwy. 360, 423/884-6246, www.sequoyah-museum.org, Mon.–Sat. 9 A.M.–5 P.M., Sun. noon–5 P.M., adults $3, seniors $2.50, children 6–12 $1.50), a museum which is managed by the Eastern Band of the Cherokee.

Though dated, the museum provides a thorough and detailed rendering of the Cherokee way of life, the history of the tribe, and the story of Sequoyah himself. At the rear of the museum, at the end of a 100-yard gravel walkway, there is a mound where the remains of 221 Cherokee people are buried. The graves were moved here during the excavation that took place before Tellico Lake was formed.

Every September, the Sequoyah Birthplace Museum hosts a Fall Festival, featuring a Cherokee living-history camp, music, storytelling, Cherokee games, and dance.

Chota and Tanasi Memorials

The towns of Tanasi and Chota were the mother towns of the Overhill Cherokee. It is from the word Tanasi that the name Tennessee is derived. The Cherokee were forced to leave Tanasi, Chota, and other settlements as white settlers moved west into Tennessee, taking more and more Cherokee land.

When Tellico Lake was created in 1979, the sites of these historic Cherokee settlements were flooded. Before the inundation, University of Tennessee archaeologists explored the sites, and found the remains of a great townhouse and the grave of the Cherokee warrior and chief Oconostota, who died in 1783.

After the lake was formed, the Tennessee Historical Commission erected a stone memorial that overlooks the actual site of Tanasi. The pavement in front of the marker is an octagonal slab representing a townhouse and in the center of this is a granite marker engraved with a seven-pointed star, which represents the seven clans of the Cherokee.

One mile north of the Tanasi monument is the parking area for the Chota memorial. It is a quarter-mile walk from the parking area to the memorial, which consists of a full-scale replica of a Cherokee townhouse. The memorial, which stands on a raised surface built above the level of the lake, was erected by the Eastern Band of the Cherokee.

The Tanasi and Chota memorials are located off Bacon Ferry Road. To get there, take Highway 360 to Monroe County Road 455. After about six miles on Route 455 you will see the turnoff for Bacon Ferry Road, and signs to the memorials.

Both sites are also popular places for bird-watching.

KNOXVILLE

Tennessee's most underappreciated city sits on the banks of the Tennessee River, in the foothills of the Appalachian Mountains. Knoxville lacks the identity of other major Tennessee cities—it is not the birthplace of the blues, Music City USA, or the home of the Choo-Choo. Some observers have called Knoxville "Austin without the hype," a moniker more true than not. But Knoxville's viewpoint is ultimately an insular one—this is a city that does not strive to be. It just is.

And what is Knoxville? It is the gateway to the Smokies and the home of the University of Tennessee Volunteers. It is an old industrial city with a rich history. It is a city undergoing a downtown renaissance.

Whatever name you choose to put on Knoxville, take some time to explore it. The city skyline is dominated by the gold-plated Sunsphere, left over from the 1982 World's Fair. Along Gay Street and in the Old City downtown you will find restaurants, bars, and concert halls that are putting Knoxville on the musical map. The University of Tennessee campus is a hotbed of athletic and cultural events. In old suburbs scattered around the city you will find jewels in the rough, like the Knoxville Zoo, Beck Cultural Center, and Ijam's Nature Center.

Knoxville is a city without pretensions. It is a place that gets better the more you get to know it, as long as you give it a chance.

Within a half-hour drive from Knoxville are several communities with their own history and attractions. Oak Ridge is one of three places in the United States that built the components of the atomic bombs used at Hiroshima and Nagasaki, and it continues to

PHOTO COURTESY OF TENNESSEE DEPARTMENT OF TOURIST DEVELOPMENT

HIGHLIGHTS

◖ **East Tennessee History Center:** A brand-new museum about East Tennessee history and settlement, this is a must-see introduction to the region (page 341).

◖ **The Sunsphere:** The gold-plated globe of the Sunsphere defines the Knoxville skyline. Ride to the top for views of Knoxville and the surrounding area (page 346).

◖ **WDVX Blue Plate Special:** How about some music with your lunch? Community radio station WDVX provides a live lunchtime concert every weekday at the Knoxville Visitor Center (page 355).

◖ **Green McAdoo Cultural Center:** The story of the desegregation of Clinton's high school is expertly presented at this multimedia museum (page 365).

◖ **Museum of Appalachia:** This living-history museum pays tribute to the ingenuity, creativity, and tenacity of the mountain folk who settled in the southern Appalachian mountains (page 366).

LOOK FOR ◖ TO FIND RECOMMENDED SIGHTS, ACTIVITIES, DINING, AND LODGING.

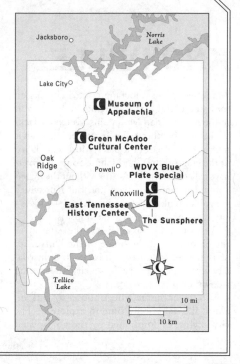

KNOXVILLE

be home to a nuclear facility. In Norris you will find the best museum about the Appalachian way of life, and Clinton is the site of a significant, but underappreciated, scene in the U.S. civil rights movement.

HISTORY

Knoxville's first settler was James White, who in 1786 built a fort where First Creek flows into the Tennessee River and named it after himself. In 1791 governor William Blount chose the fort as capital of the Territory South of the River Ohio, and renamed it after secretary of war Henry Knox.

In the same year the first lots of land were sold, and the town of Knoxville was born. Street names were borrowed from Philadelphia and Baltimore, and four lots

were reserved for Blount College, to be Knoxville's first school. Shortly after the town was laid out, Governor Blount built a frame house overlooking the river, which became the territorial capitol. Knoxville was incorporated in 1815.

During its first 50 years, Knoxville was chiefly a way station for travelers making their way along the Tennessee River or overland on stage roads. The population grew slowly to about 2,000 in 1850 and during the decade before the Civil War the number of residents more than doubled to about 5,000, thanks to the arrival of the East Tennessee and Georgia Railroad.

A majority of Knoxvillians voted to secede from the Union in the June 1861 referendum. But some city residents, and most

East Tennesseans who lived in the rural countryside surrounding Knoxville, supported the Union. Initially Knoxville was occupied by the Confederate Army under Gen. Felix Zollicoffer, whose job was to keep the rail lines open. After East Tennessee Unionists started to harass the Southern troops and burn up railroad bridges, Gen. Zollicoffer launched a campaign of repression against Union supporters in the city and surrounding areas.

Zollicoffer's troops were called south to fight in the fall of 1863, and Federal troops under the command of Gen. Ambrose Burnside quickly took Knoxville. Burnside built a series of forts around the city, which enabled him to easily repulse an attempted attack by Confederates under command of Gen. James Longstreet in November 1863. Knoxville remained under Union control for the duration of the war. Union supporters returned to the city and retaliated against the Confederate sympathizers who had had the upper hand during the early period of the war.

After the Civil War, Knoxville experienced an industrial expansion. Iron and cloth mills, machine shops, apparel and furniture factories, and marble quarries were built. Thanks to the railroad, the city was a major distribution center; in 1896 Knoxville was the third-largest wholesale center in the South, behind Atlanta and New Orleans.

During this time, the first suburbs developed.

West Knoxville, now called Fort Sanders, became the city's premier residential area, with many fine homes and mansions built around the turn of the 20th century. With prosperity came people; by 1900 Knoxville had a population of 32,637.

Knoxville was not without problems, however. Pollution from factories made the city air and water unhealthy. Race relations were poor, and African Americans were stripped of power by political gerrymandering and economic discrimination. As urban problems grew, the city's elite moved into suburbs farther and farther from the city center.

Events in 1919 showed the tensions of the day. In August of that year, a riotous white mob tore down the city jail in search of a mixed-race man who had been charged with murdering a white woman. When the mob did not find the suspect, Maurice Mayes, they headed to the black section of town to cause havoc. When the dust settled, one National Guard officer and one African American had been killed. Some 36 white men were arrested for their actions, but an all-white jury refused to convict. It was a different story for Maurice Mayes, who was convicted and eventually executed for murder.

During the mid-20th century the trend of outward expansion continued in Knoxville. From the 1950s to the 1980s, Knoxville's downtown deteriorated as retail shops closed and people moved to the suburbs. Central Knoxville became a no-man's-land where only downtown office workers dared to venture. In the early 1980s, Knoxville was famously dubbed "a scruffy little city."

Some people trace the present downtown renaissance to the 1982 World's Fair, when the Sunsphere and the World's Fair Park were built and 11 million people came to visit the internationally themed festival event. *Time* magazine uncharitably dubbed the event "Barn Burner in a Backwater" and the *Philadelphia Inquirer* said the grounds were built along a wasted gully of Second Creek, a place that was "like a hole in your sock."

Despite the fears that the World's Fair was overly ambitious, it did break even financially and left Knoxville with a park that the city—some 20 years later—finally decided to use to its full advantage. Over the succeeding years, downtown Knoxville has staged a comeback, with the addition of a downtown art museum, the birth of an entertainment district in the Old City, and, most recently, the rebirth of Gay Street and Market Square as centers for business, commerce, and residential living.

PLANNING YOUR TIME

Knoxville is an ideal destination for a long weekend: Spend two days exploring downtown attractions around Gay Street and the World's Fair Park, and then choose a destination outside of town—such as the Museum of Appalachia, Oak Ridge, or Clinton—for your third day. For the best atmosphere, find a hotel within walking distance of Gay Street and the Old City so you can walk to restaurants and music venues.

Whatever you do, don't plan your trip to coincide with a University of Tennessee home football game unless that's your purpose for coming.

Sights

Knoxville lies on the shore of the Tennessee River, also called Fort Loudoun Lake. The original city and today's downtown center sit atop a bluff overlooking the river. The main thoroughfares through downtown are Gay Street, with its delightful historic storefronts, and Henley Street, which becomes Chapman Highway to the south and Broadway to the

north. The Henley Street and Gay Street bridges are the primary routes over the Tennessee River.

Immediately west of downtown is the **World's Fair Park,** identifiable by the gold-plated Sunsphere. The **University of Tennessee** and one of the city's first suburbs, **Fort Sanders,** lie just west of the World's

Fair park. Cumberland Avenue, also known as "The Strip," is the university's main drag, and it divides UT from Fort Sanders. In recent years, many beautiful old historic homes in Fort Sanders have been torn down for the construction of condominiums.

Cumberland Avenue turns into Kingston Pike, which heads westward from UT, passing suburbs of progressive vintage, beginning with **Sequoyah Hills** and **Bearden.** This land of shopping malls, traffic jams, and sprawl is now called **West Knoxville.**

There are several pleasant historic neighborhoods north and east of the city center. **Fourth and Gill** lies north of town near Emory Place, once a commercial center at the northern end of Gay Street. **Mechanicsville,** north of Western Avenue, developed as housing near Knoxville's old industrial center and is now anchored by Knoxville College. Magnolia Avenue was the primary thoroughfare headed eastward, to neighborhoods including **Park City** and **Holston Hills.**

DOWNTOWN

Downtown Knoxville lies east of Henley Street, and includes the oldest areas of the city plus its modern-day commercial and government center.

◖ East Tennessee History Center

There is an excellent museum about the history of East Tennessee at the East Tennessee History Center (601 S. Gay St., 865/215-8830, www.east-tennessee-history.org, Mon.–Sat. 9 A.M.–4 P.M., Sun. 1–5 P.M., adults $5, seniors $4, children $3). The permanent exhibit, titled "Voices of the Land: The People of East Tennessee," offers a sweeping survey of East Tennessee history, from its early Native American inhabitants to the beginnings of the modern-day tourist trade in the Great Smoky Mountains. In between, you learn about the region's groundbreaking abolitionists, its writers and musicians, and the everyday lives of residents during tumultuous periods like the Civil War and the Civil Rights Movement.

The voices of some 350 people are used to bring the tale to life, as are artifacts such as Davy Crockett's rifle, a ring once belonging to Cherokee "Beloved Woman" Nancy Ward, and the painting *Hauling of Marble* by Lloyd Branson. The underlying message is that East Tennessee's story cannot be lumped into that of the entire state; the region is unique.

The exhibit includes several audio and video presentations and hundreds of panels to read and examine. Plan on spending at least two hours here.

The History Center is located in the city's old customs house, a handsome white marble structure built in 1874. For most of its life, the building housed federal offices and a U.S. post office. Later, it was a headquarters for the Tennessee Valley Authority.

James White Fort

The oldest home in Knoxville is found at James White Fort (205 E. Hill Ave., 865/525-6514, www.discoveret.org/jwf, Apr.–Dec.

The East Tennessee History Center is housed in Knoxville's old customs house.

KNOXVILLE

DOWNTOWN KNOXVILLE

To Knoxville College

To Fountain City

To Knoxville Hostel

OLD CITY

To Mabry-Hazen House, Beck Cultural Exchange Center, Knoxville Zoo, and Chilhowee Park

SUMMIT HILL DR
E CHURCH
HILL AVE
N CENTRAL AVE

KNOXVILLE MARRIOTT

RIVERSIDE DR

CIVIC AUDITORIUM AND COLISEUM

WOMEN'S BASKETBALL HALL OF FAME

JAMES WHITE PKWY

HALL OF FAME DR

JAMES WHITE FORT

158

S CENTRAL
WILLOW
W JACKSON
AVE

JAMES WHITE AVE

STATE AVE
GAY AVE
WALL AVE

REGAL CINEMAS RIVIERA STADIUM

TENNESSEE THEATRE

EAST TENNESSEE HISTORY CENTER

BIJOU THEATRE

BLOUNT MANSION

GAY STREET BRIDGE

THREE RIVERS RAMBLER

33

441

CHAPMAN HWY

FEDERAL COURTHOUSE

VOLUNTEER LANDING

HENLEY ST BRIDGE

FORT AVE

FORT DICKERSON

CRESCENT BEND

25W

WDVX BLUE PLATE SPECIAL

KNOXVILLE VISITORS CENTER

MARKET SQUARE

MARKET
CAFE PL
VINE
UNION
WALNUT
LOCUST

HOTEL ST. OLIVER

KRUTCH PARK

HILTON KNOXVILLE

LAWSON MCGHEE LIBRARY

CITY/COUNTY BUILDING

KNOXVILLE CONVENTION CENTER

MAIN
W HILL AVE
POPLAR

MAPLEHURST INN

Tennessee River

33

441

L&N STATION

KNOXVILLE MUSEUM OF ART

FORT KID

THE SUNSPHERE

World's Fair Park

ESTABROOK RD

MIDDLE WAY DR

LOWER DR

NEYLAND STADIUM

UT DR

McCLUNG MUSEUM

THOMPSON-BOLING ARENA

158

275

10TH
11TH
12TH
13TH
14TH

BRIDGE ST
AGEE ST

JAMES AGEE PARK

FORT SANDERS

LAUREL THEATRE

JAMES AVE
LAUREL AVE
CLINCH AVE

UNIVERSITY CENTER

PHILLIP FULMER DR

WALKWAY

PARK DR

LAKE LOUDON BLVD

CLARENCE BROWN THEATRE

CIRCLE PARK DR

SUMMITT DR

UNIVERSITY   OF   TENNESSEE

75

40

16TH
17TH

GRAND
FOREST
HIGHLAND

WHITE ST
MELROSE AVE

MELROSE PL

PAT HEAD SUMMITT DR

VOLUNTEER BLVD

HOTEL INDIGO KNOXVILLE

FRANCIS ST

20TH ST

ANDY HOLT AVE

CALDONIA AVE

70

11

LAKE AVE

TERRACE AVE

CUMBERLAND AVE

BLVD

62

1

VOLUNTEER

PIKE

KINGSTON

129

Tyson Park

158

0   0.25 mi

0   0.25 km

© AVALON TRAVEL

To South Knoxville

To Knoxville College

THE CRADLE OF COUNTRY MUSIC

Knoxville's place in country music history is not well known, but the roots of several seminal country artists are buried deep in Knoxville history. Several Knoxville institutions are also closely linked with the emergence of country music on the national stage.

The **Andrew Johnson Hotel** (912 S. Gay St.) is now a government office building, but for many years it was Knoxville's landmark hotel. WNOX broadcast the live *Midday Merry-Go-Round* from the hotel, and in 1952, Hank Williams checked in on what would be the final day of his life. It is still a matter of debate whether Williams was alive when his teenage chauffeur put him in the back seat of a Cadillac and drove north for a gig in Canton, Ohio. During a pit stop in Oak Hill, West Virginia, the driver discovered that Williams was dead; he was just 29 years old.

In 1932 the **Tennessee Theatre** (604 S. Gay St.) hosted the first public performance by Union County native Roy Acuff, who performed in a talent contest with his band, Three Rolling Stones.

Knoxville has memorialized its musical history at the **Knoxville Music Monument** (Gay St. and Summit Hill Dr.), which features likenesses of Chet Atkins, an East Tennessee native later known as Mr. Guitar; Archie Campbell, a country music comedian and radio host from nearby Bulls Gap; and Unknown Musicians, representative of jazz, blues, country, and rock 'n' roll artists whose contributions have gone largely unwritten.

It was from a storefront on **Market Square** that Sam Morrison of Bell Sales Company promoted Elvis Presley's "That's All Right (Mama)" by playing it on a loudspeaker outside. Morrison sold hundreds of copies of the single, including two to an RCA talent scout. Several months later, RCA bought Presley's recording contract from Sun Studios in Memphis.

For a detailed tour of Knoxville music history, follow the Cradle of Country Music Walking Tour. A printed guide is available from the Knoxville Visitor Center (301 S. Gay St., 865/523-7263, www.knoxville.org).

Mon.–Sat. 9:30 A.M.–5 P.M., Jan.–Mar. Mon.–Fri. 10 A.M.–4 P.M., adults $5, children 5–17 $2). Gen. James White acquired more than 1,000 acres of land in 1783 under the so-called Land Grab Act passed by the North Carolina legislature. White and his wife, Mary Lawson, moved to the frontier in 1785 and constructed a log cabin near the junction of the French Broad and Holston Rivers, to the west of First Creek. Soon, White built additional log structures and protected them with a stockade; he called the place James White's Fort. Later, William Blount chose the location as the first capital of the Southwest Territory and renamed the fort Knoxville.

White hired Charles McClung to survey his 1,000 acres, and in 1791 he sold lots in the new city of Knoxville for $8 each. White donated lots for a town common, church, and cemetery, and he sold lots for Blount College for a nominal amount.

As Knoxville grew, White's rough-hewn log cabin was threatened by development. In 1906 a local citizen, Isaiah Ford, bought the fort, and carefully moved the structures to a site on Woodland Avenue. In 1960, the fort was moved again to its present location on Hill Avenue. Visitors will learn about White, the establishment of Knoxville, and the rugged way of life on the Tennessee frontier.

Blount Mansion

The Blount Mansion (200 W. Hill Ave., 865/525-2375, www.blountmansion.org, Tues.–Sat. 9:30 A.M.–5 P.M., Sun. 1–5 P.M., adults $5, children 6–17 $2.50) is Knoxville's best historic attraction. First built between 1792 and 1796 by territorial governor William Blount, the "mansion" underwent no less than six periods of construction and alteration during its lifetime. The original structure was the first frame home in Knoxville and one of the first in the whole state. The Cherokee called Blount's home "the House with Many Glass Eyes" because of its large glass windows.

© SUSANNA HENIGHAN POTTER

Blount Mansion

KNOXVILLE

Significant events in Tennessee history took place at Blount Mansion. It is believed that it was here that governor William Blount wrote the first Tennessee constitution. The mansion also served as the second territorial capitol of the soon-to-be state.

Blount Mansion consists today of restored living quarters, office, kitchen, and gardens, as well as a visitors center that houses exhibits about Blount and his home. Guided tours depart at the top of every hour.

Blount Mansion is closed in January.

Market Square

Knoxville's old market square has been given new life thanks to downtown redevelopment over the past 20 years. Once a dirty and depressing corner of the city, Market Square is alive again with commerce. Restaurants, boutiques, and nightclubs populate the square. It is the venue for the city's farmer's market, on Saturday and Wednesday during the summer, and it is a popular location for outdoor events and concerts, like Sundown in the City, a free summer concert series.

Come here to people-watch or to soak up some of Knoxville's youthful downtown vibe.

Find Market Square near the intersection of Market Street and Union Avenue, just a few blocks behind Gay Street. It is within easy walking distance of downtown attractions.

Women's Basketball Hall of Fame

In 1892, one year after James Naismith invented basketball, a woman coach introduced the sport at Smith College. The female sport underwent countless changes during its 100-plus-year history. A few of them: In 1918 bounce passes were legalized, in 1926 the first national women's collegiate championship was held; in 1962 players were permitted to "snatch" the ball from each other; and in 1976 women's basketball made its Olympic debut.

These and other milestones are remembered at the Women's Basketball Hall of Fame (700 Hall of Fame Dr., 865/633-9000, www.wbhof.com, summer Mon.–Fri. 10 A.M.–5 P.M., Sat. 10 A.M.–6 P.M., Sun. 1–5 P.M., Sept.–Apr. Tues.–Fri. 11 A.M.–5 P.M.,

PHOTO COURTESY OF TENNESSEE DEPARTMENT OF TOURIST DEVELOPMENT

the Women's Basketball Hall of Fame

Sat. 10 A.M.–6 P.M., Sun. 1–5 P.M., adults $7.95, seniors and children 6–15 $5.95), a museum dedicated to celebrating women's achievement on the basketball court and to fostering future talent.

The Hall of Fame consists of interactive exhibits that recall the history and development of women's basketball. Visitors will hear women's basketball "inventor" Senda Berenson share her thoughts on the early days of the game. They will sit in a modern-day locker room and hear half-time talks by some of the best coaches in the modern sport. Downstairs are basketball courts where you can test your skill against the sport's best, shoot into baskets from different eras in history, and try on old and new uniforms. In addition, there are exhibits about international women's basketball, the WNBA, and top women's basketball college programs. Finally, visitors can pay tribute to the sport's best at the 91-member Hall of Fame.

The Women's Basketball Hall of Fame is located in an eye-catching building near the eastern end of Knoxville's waterfront. It is home to the world's largest basketball—30 feet tall and 10 tons heavy—which protrudes from the roof.

The Hall of Fame opened in Knoxville in 1999, and there was really no better city for it. The Tennessee Lady Vols are one of the most successful women's basketball teams in the country, and their coach, Pat Head Summitt, is renowned for her style and success.

Volunteer Landing

A one-mile city park sits along the bank of the Tennessee River, providing a nice place to walk or bring the family.

At the eastern end of the park there is a playground and a statue symbolizing the Treaty of the Holston, which took the land on which Knoxville sits away from the Cherokee. This is where Tennessee riverboats depart.

Farther west is another playground and a series of fountains, perfect for romping around in on a hot summer day. At the western end of the park is the ticket booth for the Three Rivers Rambler train.

There are several commercial marinas and restaurants along the park. The best way to get here is to take the pedestrian bridge over Neyland Drive, which departs from the

KNOXVILLE

southwestern corner of the Knoxville City/County Building along Walnut Street.

WORLD'S FAIR PARK

Lying between the University of Tennessee and downtown is the grassy, pleasant grounds of the World's Fair Park. There are several reasons for visitors to head to this area.

◖ The Sunsphere

Knoxville's foremost landmark is the Sunsphere (World's Fair Park, daily 9 A.M.–10 P.M., free). Built for the 1982 World's Fair, the Sunsphere has been a source of pride and consternation for Knoxvillians in years since. The Sunsphere, symbolic of the World's Fair theme "Energy Turns the World," is 266 feet tall. It consists of a five-story golden sphere—which the *New York Times* described as similar to a gold golf ball—perched atop a steel shaft. During the World's Fair, it housed two restaurants.

After the World's Fair ended, Knoxville couldn't decide what to do with the odd monument. Ideas came and went—restaurants, advertising billboard, visitors center—but from 1999 until 2007 the sphere was essentially closed for business all together. Around the 20th anniversary of the World's Fair, the city began to think again about what it could do with this iconic landmark, and five years and $280,000 later, in time for the 25th anniversary of the fair, the city reopened the observation deck to visitors.

The observation deck is located on the 4th floor of the Sunsphere. After a long and clanky elevator ride up, you are deposited in a narrow circular room with a 360-degree view of Knoxville. It is a pretty neat view, and it puts the city in perspective. The Tennessee River sweeps southward; the University of Tennessee sits on the river bluff; and the interstate highways slice this way and that. You look right down on the World's Fair Park, and it's like seeing the world in miniature.

Panels around the observation deck tell about some of Knoxville's attractions and history, and there is a running video with footage from the 1982 World's Fair.

Other floors in the Sunsphere are rented by local businesses.

Knoxville Museum of Art

Located in a building faced dramatically with white marble and designed by New York architect Edward Larabee Barnes, the Knoxville Museum of Art (1050 World's Fair Park Dr., 865/525-6101, www.knoxart.org, Tues.–Thurs. 10 A.M.–5 P.M., Fri. 10 A.M.–8 P.M., Sat. 10 A.M.–5 P.M., Sun. 1–5 P.M., adults $5, 17 and under free) is Knoxville's preeminent visual arts institution. Originally called the Dulin Gallery of Art and located in an early 20th-century mansion, the Knoxville Museum of Art moved to the World's Fair Park after the 1982 World's Fair. The current structure opened in 1990.

The museum has five galleries, an outdoor sculpture garden, gift shop, and exploratory gallery for children. From the rear of the great hall visitors can step outside on the museum balcony for views of the World's Fair Park and downtown Knoxville. The museum's growing permanent collection is bolstered by numerous visiting exhibitions. On Friday evening the museum hosts Alive After Five, with jazz performances.

Admission to the museum is free on Tuesday.

UNIVERSITY OF TENNESSEE

The preeminent public university in Tennessee, the University of Tennessee was founded in 1784 as Blount College. Originally centered at "the hill" on the eastern end of Cumberland Avenue, UT has spread out along the entire length of Cumberland. Its colors—orange and white—were inspired by the orange and white daisies that grow outside on the hill. UT has a student enrollment of some 29,000.

At UT, it is athletics that are truly center stage, or at least so it seems. Take, for example, the fact that in recent years UT has renamed two major roads throughout the campus not after prize-winning scientists or writers, but after Peyton Manning, the UT quarterback who went on to play for the Indianapolis Colts, and Phillip Fulmer, UT football's head coach.

© SUSANNA HENIGHAN POTTER

the Knoxville Museum of Art

Frank H. McClung Museum

The best all-around museum in Knoxville, the Frank H. McClung Museum (1327 Circle Park Dr., 865/974-2144, http://mcclungmuseum.utk. edu, Mon.–Sat. 9 A.M.–5 P.M., Sun. 1–5 P.M., free) houses a wide variety of historical, cultural, and natural history exhibits. Long-standing exhibits explore ancient Egypt, the native peoples of Tennessee, and the Civil War in Knoxville. Other exhibits look at Tennessee's freshwater mussels and decorative arts in Tennessee. There are also special temporary exhibits.

Ewing Gallery

UT's art museum is the Ewing Gallery (1715 Volunteer Blvd., 865/974-3200, www.ewing-gallery.org, Mon.–Fri. 8:30 A.M.–5 P.M., Sun. 1–4 P.M., free). Located on the first floor of the university's Art and Architecture Building, the Ewing Gallery is named for the founder of UT's art program. Student and faculty art shares the 3,000-square-foot exhibition space with visiting shows from other museums.

During UT's summer break, gallery hours are cut back to Monday–Friday 11 A.M.–4 P.M. The gallery closes on university holidays and between exhibits.

Fort Sanders

Knoxville's original suburb, Fort Sanders is a quickly disappearing historic neighborhood that lies between the World's Fair Park and UT. The site of an earthen fort named for Gen. William Sanders who died in the Battle of Knoxville in 1863, Fort Sanders was developed into a residential area beginning in the 1880s. This was home to Knoxville's upper-class merchants, mayors, university professors, and other persons of note. Author James Agee was raised in Fort Sanders.

Because of its vintage and the relative affluence of its residents, Fort Sanders homes are lovely examples of American Victorian and early 20th-century architecture. Towers, broad porches, colorful shutters, and intricate detail work set Fort Sanders homes apart.

As the university grew, Fort Sanders was encroached. By the 1970s, many owners stopped occupying their homes and instead rented them to students. Homes deteriorated. During the 1990s and early years of this century, development has taken a great toll on Fort Sanders. In 1999 alone, 15 historic homes were razed to make room for condominium developments. The destruction caused an outcry, and some of Fort Sanders historic homes are now protected from development.

You can see what is left of Fort Sanders along Highland, Laurel, Forest, and Grand Avenues, between 11th and 17th Streets. **James Agee Park,** at the corner of James Agee Street and Laurel Avenue, is located near the site of Agee's childhood home, where parts of Agee's Pulitzer Prize–winning work *A Death in the Family* are set.

WEST KNOXVILLE

Kingston Pike is the thoroughfare that connects downtown Knoxville with its western suburbs. Immediately past the University of Tennessee, Kingston Pike passes several historic homes. Farther west, you reach the communities of Bearden, West Hills, and Farragut.

Crescent Bend

The Armstrong-Lockett House, more romantically called Crescent Bend (2728 Kingston Pk., 865/637-3163, www.crescentbend.org, Tues.–Sat. 10 A.M.–4 P.M., Sun. 1–4 P.M., $5), was built in 1834 by Drury Paine Armstrong, a local merchant and public official. The brick farmhouse was once the centerpiece of a 600-acre farm. Now it consists of the elegant home and formal Italian gardens facing the Tennessee River.

Visitors who take the guided tour will see a fine collection of china, silver, and other antiques, including wallpaper originally meant for the Hermitage, president Andrew Jackson's home near Nashville.

During March and April Crescent Bend celebrates spring with Tuliptime. This is a delightful time to visit, when more than 20,000 tulips are in bloom. During Tuliptime, the home schedules candlelight dinners, high teas, and other special events.

Crescent Bend is closed in January and February.

Bleak House

Knoxville's Confederate Memorial Hall, better known as Bleak House (3148 Kingston Pk., 865/522-2371, www.knoxvillecmh.org, Wed.–Fri. 1–4 P.M., adults $5, seniors $4) was Gen. James Longstreet's headquarters during the Battle of Fort Sanders and other Civil War battles that took place from November to December 1863. Built in 1858 for Robert Houston and Louisa Armstrong, the Italian villa–style home was named after the popular Charles Dickens novel of the day.

Visitors may be given a tour, which includes the tower where legend has it Confederate sharpshooters were stationed during the Civil War. There is a museum that includes Confederate artifacts.

Girl Scout Museum

East Tennessee's Girl Scout Council operates the Girl Scout Museum at Daisy's Place (1567 Downtown West Blvd., 865/688-9440, www.tanasi.org, Aug.–May Mon. 8:30 A.M.–7:30 P.M., Tues.–Fri. 8:30 A.M.–4:30 P.M., Sat. 9 A.M.–1 P.M., June–July Mon.–Thurs. 8 A.M.–5:30 P.M., Sat. 9 A.M.–1 P.M., free). The museum, one of six such girl scout museums in the United States, features exhibits about the history of girl scouting, Girl Scout cookies, and scouting in East Tennessee. You can see handbooks, songbooks, uniforms, and scrapbooks dating back to 1912.

Farragut Folklife Museum

The first U.S. admiral, David Glasgow Farragut, was born west of Knoxville in an area called Stoney Point. The family moved to New Orleans when Farragut was just five years old. When his mother died of yellow fever, Farragut was adopted by David Porter, and moved to Chester, Pennsylvania. Farragut, who was born James Glasgow Farragut, changed his name to David in honor of his patron and entered the U.S. navy. His naval career was long and proud; Farragut's military service during the Civil War led to his promotion in 1866 to the rank of admiral. It was during an August 1864 battle aboard the USS *Hartford* when Farragut reportedly said, "Damn the torpedoes, full speed ahead," a phrase that lives on today. The town that now exists near Admiral Farragut's birthplace took his name, and now the Farragut City Hall houses a museum dedicated to this mostly unknown Tennessean. The Farragut Folklife Museum (1140 Municipal Center Dr., Farragut, 865/966-7057, www.townoffarragut.org, Mon.–Fri. 10 A.M.–4:30 P.M., free) also houses exhibits about the local marble industry, the Battle of Campbell's Station, and arts, crafts, and other memorabilia from the communities of Farragut and Concord.

Farragut is located near the intersection of Kingston Pike and Campbell Station Road, off I-40 exit 373.

EAST KNOXVILLE

Magnolia Avenue (U.S. 25 W.) and Martin Luther King Boulevard are two thoroughfares that head east from downtown Knoxville. Originally a series of quiet residential neighborhoods, East Knoxville has gradually evolved into a mixture of low-rise office buildings, modest sprawl, and historic homes.

Mabry-Hazen House Museum

The Mabry-Hazen House Museum (1711 Dandridge Ave., 865/522-8661, www.mabryhazen.com, Wed.–Fri. 11 A.M.–5 P.M., Sat. 10 A.M.–3 P.M., adults $5, seniors $4.50, students K–12 $2.50) is located on a pleasant rise in East Knoxville. The handsome home, with green shutters and a wide porch, housed three generations of the same family from 1858 to 1987, and served as headquarters for both Confederate and Union troops during the Civil War. Since 1992 it has been open to the public for tours. The Mabry name comes from Joseph Alexander Mabry Jr., a businessman who donated the land for Market Square and owned the *Knoxville Whig* from 1869 to 1870. The murders of Mabry and his son on Gay Street in 1882 were documented in Mark Twain's work, *Life on the Mississippi*. Mabry's daughter, Alice Mabry, married Rush Strong Hazen, a wealthy businessman. The third generation to live in the house was Evelyn Montgomery Hazen, who helped

author the Harbrace College Handbook, a reference guide for generations of English students.

Beck Cultural Exchange Center

Knoxville's foremost African-American historical and cultural center is the Beck Cultural Exchange Center (1927 Dandridge Ave., 865/524-8461, www.beckcenter.net, Tues.–Sat. 10 A.M.–6 P.M., free). Founded in 1975, Beck is a museum, education center, archive, and community gathering place. In addition to putting on a variety of programs throughout the year, Beck welcomes visitors who want to learn more about Knoxville's African-American history.

Among Beck's permanent exhibits is the William H. Hastie Room, dedicated to preserving the memory of the Knoxville native who became the first black governor of the U.S. Virgin Islands in 1946 and the first African-American federal judge in the United States four years later. Beck also features a gallery with photographs and biographies of prominent African Americans from Knoxville.

The center also preserves the history of the struggle to desegregate Knoxville's public schools, the University of Tennessee, and Maryville College. There is also information about the historic desegregation of schools in Clinton, Tennessee, and the legacy of Austin High School, Knoxville's one-time all-black secondary school.

Alex Haley Square

Pulitzer Prize–winning author Alex Haley has roots in both East and West Tennessee. He grew up in Henning, a sawmill town along the Mississippi River, but he spent a great deal of his adult life in East Tennessee, giving both regions a claim to his legacy.

Haley's preeminence—but also his disarming and loving nature—is evident in a larger-than-life statue of the writer at Alex Haley Square in East Knoxville. In the figure, Haley is reading a book, seeming to invite the viewer to gather round and listen to a story. The statue, park, and playground opened in 1998, six years after Haley's death.

Knoxville Zoo

Children and adults will love the Knoxville Zoo (3500 Knoxville Zoo Dr., 865/637-5331, www.knoxville-zoo.org, summer daily 9:30 A.M.–6 P.M., winter daily 10 A.M.–4:30 P.M., adults $16.95, seniors and children 2–12 $12.95). More than 800 species of animals live at the zoo, in habitats including Grassland Africa, the Red Panda Village, and penguin pool. Giraffes, elephants, camels, giant tortoise, and gorillas are just a few of the iconic animals you will see at the zoo.

The zoo offers special free bird shows every day at 11:30 A.M., 12:30 P.M., and 2:30 P.M. Other attractions include a petting zoo, camel rides ($5), and a colorful carousel ($2).

Surrounding the zoo is Chilhowee Park, with picnic tables, walking paths, and a lake. Parking at the zoo costs an additional $4 per vehicle.

East Tennessee Science Discovery Center

Also located at Chilhowee Park is the East Tennessee Science Discovery Center (Chilhowee Park, 865/594-1494, Mon.–Fri. 9 A.M.–5 P.M., Sat. 10 A.M.–5 P.M., adults $4, seniors and children 5–18 $3, children 3–4 $2), an interactive children's museum. Exhibits include aquariums, whisper dishes, a replica space shuttle, and a liquid-crystal wall. There is also a planetarium; shows are offered most days at 2 and 4 P.M.

SOUTH KNOXVILLE

Chapman Highway (U.S. 441) begins south of the Henley Street Bridge and brings you to South Knoxville.

Ijams Nature Center

Knoxville's best outdoor attraction is Ijams Nature Center (2915 Island Home Ave., 865/577-4717, www.ijams.org, year-round Tues.–Sat. 9 A.M.–5 P.M., Mar.–Oct. Sun. 1–5 P.M., free). The visitors center is a modern earth-friendly construction that houses exhibits about lost animal species and the Ijams family. There is also an enclosure with a red-tail hawk and a turkey vulture, plus native plant and animal species.

The real attraction at Ijams is the 160 acres of protected woodlands and meadows. Come here for a walk through the woods or a stroll along the Tennessee River boardwalk. The grounds also include the Ijams family historic homesite and Mead's Quarry. In total, there are seven miles of walking trails. The grounds are open daily from 8 A.M. to dusk.

Ijams offers a regular schedule of special events: workshops, talks, guided walks, and fairs. Check the website for details.

Fort Dickerson

A Civil War–era earthen fort and three replica cannons are the historical attractions at the Knoxville city park on the south side of the Tennessee River. Panels explain the fort's significance during the battles of Knoxville that took place in the fall of 1863.

Visitors will also enjoy the view (especially during the fall and winter, when the trees have shed their leaves) of the Knoxville skyline, and the view of an old quarry.

Fort Dickerson Park is located three-quarters of a mile south of the Henley Street Bridge on Chapman Highway (U.S. 441). Look for the signs on your right.

Ramsey House Plantation

The home called "the most costly and most admired building in Tennessee" by the 1800 census-taker is open for public tours. Ramsey House Plantation (2614 Thorngrove Pk., 865/546-0745, www.ramseyhouse.org, Tues.–Sat. 10 A.M.–4 P.M., Sun. noon–4 P.M., adults $7, children 6–12 $5) was built between 1795 and 1797 by master carpenter and cabinetmaker Thomas Hope for Col. Francis Alexander Ramsey. Built in the late Georgian style out of pink marble, Ramsey House features intricately carved consoles and other distinctive decorative features. It was said to be the first stone house in Tennessee, as well as the first home in the state with an attached kitchen.

The site of the house is near the fork of the Holston and French Broad Rivers. It was close to a site called Swan Pond, a beaver dam pond well known by hunters and travelers.

Col. Ramsey drained the pond to create pasture and farm land.

Ramsey House was the home of Col. Ramsey's son, James G. M. Ramsey, a doctor, businessman, and author of an authoritative early history of Tennessee, *The Annals of Tennessee to the End of the Eighteenth Century.* James Ramsey and his wife, Margaret Crozier, raised 11 children at the home, then called Mecklenburg. Ramsey supported the Confederate cause during the Civil War, and Mecklenburg was burned by Union troops during the war, destroying a valuable library and collection of early Tennessee antiquities. During the war years and until the early 1870s, Ramsey and his family lived in Atlanta, Savannah, and North Carolina. He returned to East Tennessee in the 1870s, and remained here until his death in 1884.

Ramsey House was purchased in 1952 by the Association for the Preservation of Tennessee Antiquities. It has been fully restored and is open for tours, which include all rooms of the house, the kitchen, and the grounds. Ramsey House has a nice garden, where heirloom vegetables and other plants are grown.

Ramsey House is located off Gov. John Sevier Highway southeast of downtown. The easiest way to get there from downtown is to take Chapman Highway (U.S. 441) south out of town. Turn left onto John Sevier Highway (Hwy. 168). After crossing the Tennessee River, look for Thorngrove Pike on your right, and signs to Ramsey House.

Marble Springs

The early home of Tennessee's first governor, John Sevier, is preserved at Marble Springs (1220 John Sevier Hwy., 865/573-5508, www.discoveret.org/jsma, Tues.–Sun. 10 A.M.–5 P.M., free, tours $4), five miles south of downtown Knoxville. Sevier received 640 acres at the foot of Bays Mountain for his service in the Revolutionary War, and he named the property Marble Springs because there were marble deposits and a large spring. By 1792 Sevier established a farm residence at Marble Springs, although he and his family lived here only periodically. They also had a home in Knoxville.

After Sevier died in 1815, the property changed hands several times until the State of Tennessee bought it in 1941. It remains state-owned, and is operated by the Gov. John Sevier Memorial Association. Over the years, the log home has been restored and several historically accurate outbuildings have been added. Workshops and living-history days are offered year-round.

NORTH KNOXVILLE

Broadway (U.S. 441) travels from downtown Knoxville to Fountain City, an early suburb of the city.

Old Gray Cemetery

Just past Knoxville's scruffy Mission District—past the old 5th Avenue Hotel, a flophouse turned affordable housing project—is the Old Gray Cemetery (543 N. Broadway, 865/522-1425, www.discoveret.org/oldgray). This 13-acre cemetery was established in 1850 and is the final resting place of hundreds of prominent and not-so-prominent city residents. It is a pleasant, wooded, park-like place—nice for a quiet stroll.

Among the buried are William "Parson" Brownlow, minister, journalist, governor and one of Tennessee's most colorful historical characters; feminist Lizzie Crozier French; and C. C. Williams, the father of playwright Tennessee Williams.

Knoxville College

Presbyterian missionaries established a school for freedmen in Knoxville in 1875, and two years later this educational institution was designated as a college. Knoxville College has been educating African Americans since. The campus is an architectural mixed bag—elegant historic structures share space with low-slung modern buildings. Budget challenges have dogged Knoxville College over its modern history, but it has persisted nonetheless in its mission to educate the next generation of black leaders.

Knoxville College is located in Mechanicsville, an old neighborhood found at the intersection of Western Avenue and Middlebrook Pike.

Sports and Recreation

Sports may be Knoxville's single biggest draw. The University of Tennessee Vols play football at Neyland Stadium on the banks of the Tennessee River. The Lady Vols basketball team is the most successful sports team at UT.

But Knoxville is more than just UT sports. There are nice parks, too.

PARKS

Knoxville has more than two dozen city parks. For a complete list of parks and facilities, visit the city website at www.cityofknoxville.org.

World's Fair Park

Knoxville's best city park is the 10-acre World's Fair Park, which connects downtown with UT and brings new life to the site of the 1982 World's Fair. The park consists of walking paths, fountains, a man-made lake, grassy spaces, and a statue of Russian musician and composer Sergei Rachmaninoff, whose last public performance was at UT on February 17, 1943. The fountains are a popular attraction on hot summer days, when families come to romp in the water.

Fort Kid, a massive playground located across the street from the Knoxville Art Museum, adds to the family appeal.

Tyson Park

Located at the western edge of the UT campus along Alcoa Highway, Tyson Park is a venerable city park with playgrounds, picnic tables, walking paths, tennis courts, and a skate park.

Sequoyah Park

Located in West Knoxville, on the banks of the Tennessee River, 87-acre Sequoyah Park is a good place for walking, biking, or relaxing outdoors. There are playgrounds, baseball/softball fields, and lots of open space ideal for a picnic or game of Frisbee.

Sequoyah is located at 1400 Cherokee Boulevard. Get there by driving west on Kingston Pike and turning left onto Cherokee Boulevard.

Chilhowee Park

Chilhowee Park (3301 Magnolia Ave.), located off Magnolia Avenue in East Knoxville, was the city's first major park. The first streetcar line in the city connected downtown with Chilhowee, and on weekends, holidays, and hot summer days throngs would come here for a picnic, a splash in the lake, or to watch baseball games, horse races, or concerts.

Chilhowee is no longer the destination it once was—the mall, the mountains, and the motor car have seen to that—but it is still significant. The 80-acre park has playgrounds, picnic tables, and paths for walking. It also has the Jacob Building, a large exhibit hall used for all manner of gatherings and events.

The Knoxville Zoo, Knox County Fairgrounds, and East Tennessee Science Discovery Center all abut Chilhowee Park for a recreation bonanza.

Greenways

Knoxville has an expanding array of greenways that connect parks and make it possible to get around the city on foot or by bike. Those of special note include the **James White Greenway** that originates at the South Knoxville bridge and follows the Tennessee River to Volunteer Landing downtown. On the other end of Volunteer Landing, you can follow the **Neyland Greenway** to Tyson Park and onwards to the **Third Creek Greenway,** which connects with both the **Bearden Greenway** and the **Sequoyah Greenway.**

On the south side of the river, the **Will Skelton Greenway** begins at Island Home Park, passes through Ijams Nature Center, and follows the shore of the Tennessee to the Forks of the River.

For information about Knoxville greenways, go to www.cityofknoxville.org/greenways or call 865/215-4311 for the Parks and Recreation

Department. The Knox Greenways Coalition (865/215-2807, www.knoxgreenwayscoalition.org) supports the use and development of greenways in the city.

Knoxville Botanical Garden and Arboretum

The Knoxville Botanical Garden and Arboretum (2743 Wimpole St., 865/540-8690, www.knoxarboretum.org, daily sunrise–sunset, free) is a dream that is slowly taking shape. Located on grounds once occupied by a plant nursery, the gardens are an effort by volunteers and family members of the former landowners.

The grounds are leafy and pleasant, though not very manicured. It is a pleasant place to come for a walk. Staff members are generally present on weekdays 8 A.M.–4 P.M.; at other times the garden is unattended.

SPECTATOR SPORTS

Watching sports in Knoxville means one thing: the University of Tennessee Volunteers. Knoxville is the epicenter of Big Orange country and this is a city that is serious about sports. UT is a member of the competitive Southeastern Conference.

Football

UT's biggest spectator sport is football. Neyland Stadium, home of the football team, is awash with bright orange on game days. Named for Gen. Robert Neyland, head coach of the UT football team from 1926 to 1952, Neyland Stadium has a capacity of just over 100,000. Most home games sell out.

The regular college football season runs from September to November. Single tickets go on sale in late July or early August for the upcoming fall season, and cost between $40 and $70. You can buy tickets from the UT box office (1600 Phillip Fulmer Way, 865/656-1200, www.utsports.com). On game days, tickets are sold at Gate 21 at Neyland Stadium beginning four hours before kickoff.

A word to the wise: If you are not coming into town to watch the football game, avoid downtown Knoxville on a game day. The entire city becomes a knot of congestion and Big Orange mania on these days, and if you don't want to be part of it, you'll hate the experience.

More than 100,000 fans pack into Neyland Stadium for UT football games.

Longtime residents who don't particularly fancy college football say that game days are good times to go to the mall, visit the Great Smoky Mountains National Park, or just stay home. Whatever you do, plan ahead.

Basketball

In Knoxville, UT's men's basketball team plays second fiddle to the legendary Lady Vols, eight-time national champions who have been leaders of the women's college basketball pack for a generation. The Lady Vols, under the leadership of coach Pat Head Summitt, play home games at Thompson-Boling Arena from November through March.

Single-game tickets go on sale in October and cost $10–20 depending on your seat. Buy tickets from the UT box office (1600 Phillip Fulmer Way, 865/565-1200, www.utladyvols.com).

Other UT Sports

UT plays a full slate of sports: track and field, baseball, softball, tennis, soccer, rowing, tennis, swimming, golf, and volleyball. The UT women's softball team has performed well in recent years and is developing a reputation as a Southeastern Conference leader. UT tennis and track have good records, and in 2008 the university announced plans for a new golf center to bolster its program in that sport. For a full rundown of UT sports events, contact the athletics box office (1600 Phillip Fulmer Way, 865/565-1200).

Ice Hockey

The **Knoxville Ice Bears** (www.knoxville icebears.com) play at the Knoxville Civic Coliseum. The Ice Bears are a member of the Southern Professional Hockey League and play from October to April.

Entertainment

Knoxville boasts a lively local music scene, plus venues that attract big-name artists. The arts scene also includes professional theater, dance, and music companies.

ARTS VENUES

Knoxville's historic theaters are something special. In 1928 the **Tennessee Theatre** (604 S. Gay St., 865/684-1200, www.tennesseetheatre.com) opened its doors on Gay Street. The theater operated nearly uninterrupted for 50 years as a movie house and concert hall. After being shuttered for a few years, the theater operated during the 1980s and 1990s, although the venue was showing its age. Thankfully, in 2001, plans were announced for a full-fledged restoration that would bring the Tennessee back to its former glory.

Since 2005, when the Tennessee Theatre reopened to praise from concert-goers and performers alike, it has become Knoxville's favorite venue for music, theater, and film. Its interior is awash with ornate detail including plush fabric, intricate details work, and

glistening chandeliers—all reminiscent of the Roaring Twenties when the theater was built. The theater's 1928 original Mighty Wurlitzer pipe organ is also a showstopper.

Check the theater's website for upcoming performances for an opportunity to experience entertainment at its finest. You can also call to request a tour of the theater, if no show is in the offing.

Knoxville's best-sounding concert hall is also located on Gay Street. The **Bijou Theater** (803 S. Gay St., 865/522-0832, www.knoxbijou.com) opened in 1909 as part of the Lamar Hotel. Since then, it has been a venue for concerts and other performances. With a capacity of 700, it is more intimate than the Tennessee Theatre; it is also far less ornate and upscale. The Bijou underwent restoration in 2005, which resulted in a brand-new sound and stage system, better seats, and a new heating and air-conditioning system.

Other Knoxville concert and theater venues include the **Knoxville Civic Auditorium** (500 E. Church Ave., 865/544-5399), which seats 2,500, and the **Thompson-Boling Arena**

(1600 Phillip Fulmer Way, 865/974-0953), with a capacity of almost 25,000.

DANCE AND OPERA

The **Appalachian Ballet Company** (865/982-8463, www.appalachianballet.com) is a regional dance group chartered in 1972. The company puts on three performances each year, including a holiday production of *The Nutcracker.*

Circle Modern Dance (www.circlemoderndance.com) is a grassroots dance group founded in 1990 to provide an alternative to mainstream dance performances. They offer classes and occasional shows.

The **Knoxville Opera** (www.knoxvilleopera.com) offers four performances annually at the Tennessee Theatre in downtown Knoxville. The opera also organizes the Rossini Festival, an Italian street fair, every spring.

THEATER

The University of Tennessee's **Clarence Brown Theater Company** (865/974-5161, http://theatre.utk.edu) presents a wide repertoire of plays featuring nationally and internationally recognized guest artists. The company performs in the 570-seat Clarence Brown Theater (1714 Andy Holt Blvd.) on the UT campus, named for UT alumnus and distinguished film director Clarence Brown. UT is also home to the 400-seat Ula Love Doughty Carousel Theater and a 100-seat black-box theater, which are used for campus productions.

Knoxville's **Carpetbag Theater** (www.carpetbag.org) is a community-based nonprofit professional theater company founded in 1970. It is one of the few tenured African-American professional theater companies in the South. The company produces plays, festivals, youth theater workshops, and other events throughout the year. Their performances often bring to the fore the stories and experiences of people who are otherwise overlooked by history.

The **Tennessee Stage Company** (www.tennesseestage.com) produces Shakespeare in the Square, a free summertime production of Shakespeare's work at Market Square Mall, and the New Play Festival, which brings to life unpublished theatrical works.

MUSIC
◖ WDVX Blue Plate Special

Back in the 1930s and '40s, Knoxville radio station WNOX hosted a lunchtime musical variety show called the *Midday Merry-Go-Round.* Hosted by Lowell Blanchard, the show attracted hundreds of patrons and thousands more who tuned in to listen to the show live on radio. It was a stepping stone to the Grand Ole Opry, and legendary performers like Roy Acuff, Chet Atkins, Kitty Wells, and Bill and Charlie Monroe were among the entertainers.

So when Knoxville radio station WDVX started its own lunchtime live music program back in the 1990s it was following in hallowed footsteps. But it also felt like something quite new and exciting for downtown Knoxville.

Today, the WDVX Blue Plate Special takes place Monday through Friday from noon to 1 P.M. at the Knoxville Visitor Center at 301 South Gay Street (the building also houses the WDVX studios). The performers vary from bluegrass to Americana to rock. It is a wonderful way to pass an hour, since you get to listen to live music and watch a radio show being made at the same time. The atmosphere is intimate, casual, and—at times—electric. A coffee bar serves sandwiches and drinks, but you are welcome to bring your own bag lunch as well.

Knoxville Symphony Orchestra

Established in 1935, the Knoxville Symphony Orchestra (865/291-3310, www.knoxvillesymphony.com) is one of the oldest orchestras in the southeast. The KSO, a professional orchestra since 1973, performs its season from September to May in Knoxville venues including the Civil Auditorium, the Tennessee Theatre, and the Bijou. Special guest conductors and soloists are frequent additions, and seasonal shows include the annual holiday concert.

UT Music

The University of Tennessee's music program (www.music.utk.edu) puts on a full slate of recitals and concerts during the academic year. All events are free and open to the public. They take place in the UT Music Recital Hall (1741 Volunteer Blvd.) and the Alumni Memorial Building (1408 Middle Dr.).

Jubilee Community Arts

One of Knoxville's finest musical institutions is Jubilee Community Arts, which promotes traditional Appalachian music and other folk traditions. Jubilee offers a full slate of concerts and other special events at the **Laurel Theater** (1538 Laurel Ave., 865/522-5851, www.jubileearts.org), a 19th-century church in the Fort Sanders neighborhood that has been converted into a performance hall. The space is intimate, with excellent acoustics and a homey atmosphere. The concert schedule is heavy on regional bluegrass, folk, Americana, and country performers. It also includes Celtic, zydeco, and world music artists. Concerts are scheduled most weeks. The Jubilee Festival in March is a three-day weekend event with a smorgasbord of performances.

When the Laurel Theater is not being used for a concert, various community groups use the space for meetings and other purposes. Several community dance groups have weekly sessions here, as does the Knoxville Writer's Guild. In addition to its live performance schedule, Jubilee Community Arts works with local radio stations to produce programming for the airwaves, including the long-running *Live at Laurel* program, which features recordings of Laurel Theater concerts and is broadcast on WDVX (89.9 FM and 102.9 FM) at noon and 7 P.M. on Sunday.

FILM

First-run movies came back to downtown Knoxville with the opening of Regal Cinemas Riviera Stadium (510 S. Gay St., 865/522-5160), an eight-screen theater in the heart of downtown.

Knoxville's best art-house movie theater is at Downtown West (1640 Downtown West Blvd., 865/693-6327), in the West Hills area near West Town Mall.

NIGHTLIFE

Downtown Knoxville offers plenty of options for entertainment after the sun sets.

The Old City

Near the intersection of Jackson and Depot Streets, a few blocks northeast of Gay Street, is the Old City. Knoxville's former warehouse district, near the train tracks, is now its chief entertainment district. Here you will find **Manhattan's** (101 S. Central St., 865/525-2333), a jazz and blues club with an older clientele. **Patrick Sullivan's** (100 N. Central St., 865/637-4255) is an Irish-inspired restaurant and bar, and a good place to meet for drinks.

Barley's Taproom and Pizzeria (200 E. Jackson St., 865/521-0092, cover varies) is a large tap house with lots of space for mingling and a stage where folk, rock, and country performers can be found just about every night of the week. The 1st-floor bar offers 40 different beers on tap, a full-service restaurant, and a stage. Upstairs are pool tables and dart boards. Outside is a patio where you can witness Knoxville's skyline as you meet and mingle.

Downtown

Downtown nightlife centers on Market Square. Here you can catch up with friends at **Preservation Pub** (28 Market Sq., 865/524-2224, cover varies). In the shadow of its exposed-brick walls decorated with funky art, you just can't help but feel cool. Fabulous drink specials, a hip, youthful attitude, and a steady stream of local rock, folk, and country acts makes Preservation Pub a popular destination. It is also a restaurant.

Also in Market Square, **World Grotto** (16 Market Sq., 865/226-2962, cover varies) is an intriguing subterranean hangout that offers an eclectic array of entertainment—groovy DJs, skateboard movie debuts, and live music of many stripes. Descend into the grotto and be greeted by crystals upon the walls, a springy bamboo dance floor, and Moroccan-style benches on which to hang out with your friends. A bit more urban-world chic than other Knoxville choices.

Located in the Fourth and Gill neighborhood, a few blocks north of downtown, is the cozy and intimate **Sassy Ann's House of Blues** (820 N. 4th Ave., 865/525-5839, cover varies). As the name suggests, Sassy Ann's specializes in the blues—visiting performers, homegrown talent, and open mic–style—but they also book rock and folk artists. Housed in a 100-plus-year-old townhouse with two bars and lots of intimate pockets for seating, Sassy Ann's is a bit like going to a grown-up house party, with live music to boot. Generally speaking, Sassy Ann's has DJ music on Sunday and Thursday nights, with bands on Wednesday, Friday, and Saturday.

The Valarium (1213 Western Ave., 865/522-2820, cover varies) is a 1,000-person standing-only entertainment venue located under the Western Avenue Viaduct, in a seeming wasteland of highway interchanges. Once a venue for cutting-edge bands, then a gay dance hall, this cavernous hall now books performing artists of all types. The bar is outside, allowing the owners to make this an all-ages club.

EVENTS
Spring
Knoxville's stalwart arts festival celebrates its 50th anniversary in 2010. The **Dogwood Arts Festival** (www.dogwoodarts.com) takes place in April to coincide with the springtime blooming of dogwood trees. The core of the festival is the opening of 70 miles of dogwood trails that pass through historic and architecturally significant neighborhoods and by thousands of blooming dogwood trees.

The Dogwood Arts Festival also includes a slate of art shows and other events—workshops, festivals, and concerts—aimed at promoting the arts in the community and in area schools.

In April, the Knoxville Opera organizes the **Rossini Festival** (www.rossinifestival.org), an Italian street fair that takes place on Gay Street and at Market Square Mall in downtown Knoxville. Special wine tastings, opera performances, and European music combines

with a vibrant street fair with a pronounced Mediterranean theme.

Summer
Sundown in the City (www.sundowninthe city.com) is a summer-long free concert series that takes place on Thursday evening at Market Square Mall downtown. These family-friendly events start early in order to catch the after-work downtown crowd. Performers include up-and-coming folk, rock, and Americana artists, as well as local and regional talent.

The **Kuumba Festival** (www.kuumbafest tn.com) is an African-inspired street festival that takes place in June at Market Square downtown and in Chilhowee Park in East Knoxville. The event features parades, music, arts demonstrations, and vendors, all with an African theme.

The end of summer is marked annually with **Boomsday,** a massive fireworks display over the Tennessee River on Labor Day.

SHOPPING
Gay Street
Two of Knoxville's most distinctive stores are found on Gay Street. **Yee Haw Industries** (413 S. Gay St., 865/522-1812) is an upstart letter-press with sass. Its block-lettered posters advertise concerts, shows, and political rallies, and its retail products range from ironic Knoxville-themed calendars to some of the most irresistible notebooks around. Yee Haw's services have been purchased by low-brow and high-brow alike (the *New York Times* once hired them to design their Book Review), but you, too, can get in on the action. The Yee Haw store sits at the entrance to their storefront operation, and they sell posters, T-shirts, calendars, note cards, and more. This is a great place to find a gift you won't see anywhere else.

If Yee Haw Industries is at one end of the Appalachian-country-chic movement, then **Mast General Store** (402 S. Gay St., 865/546-1336) is the other. The first Mast General Store opened in Valle Crucis, North Carolina, in 1883, and it sold everything that folks needed, "from cradles to caskets," as it is said. Mast is now a chain with locations in several Southern mountain cities, including Asheville, North Carolina, and Greenville, South Carolina. Like the others, Knoxville's Mast General Store sells a satisfying variety of sturdy clothing and footwear, classic cookware like cast-iron skillets, old-fashioned candy, and games.

Also on Gay Street, the **East Tennessee Historical Society Gift Shop** (601 S. Gay St., 865/215-8824) has a good collection of books about Tennessee, local arts and crafts, and T-shirts from the 1982 World's Fair.

On Market Square there are two funky fashion stores. **Vagabondia** (27 Market Sq., 865/525-4842) sells sassy trend-setting women's fashions, including lots of dresses and hats. **Reruns** (2 Market Sq., 865/525-9525) is an upmarket thrift store and a downtown institution.

Galleries

Knoxville has an increasingly vibrant gallery scene along Gay Street. Knoxville's Arts & Culture Alliance manages an art gallery in an old furniture store at the **Emporium Center for Arts & Culture** (100 S. Gay St., 865/523-7543, www.knoxalliance.com, Mon.–Fri. 9 A.M.–5 P.M., free). Home to two art galleries, the Emporium puts on 12 different shows annually that showcase local and regional arts.

The Emporium also provides studio space for area artists and office space for arts organizations. The galleries are open until 9 P.M. on the first Friday of each month, and 11 A.M.–3 P.M. on the first Saturday of each month.

Located next door to the Emporium galleries is a downtown satellite of UT's Ewing Gallery. The **University of Tennessee Downtown Gallery** (106 S. Gay St., 865/673-0802, Wed.–Fri. 11 A.M.–6 P.M., Sat. 10 A.M.–3 P.M., free) has a modern, fresh feel. Student and faculty artwork are exhibited alongside shows of regional and national artists.

The Art Market (422 S. Gay St., 865/525-5265) is a stalwart artists' cooperative that traces its roots to the 1982 World's Fair. More than 60 area painters, sculptures, jewelers, weavers, and printmakers display their work at this attractive and welcoming space.

Bookstores

The Book Eddy (2537 Chapman Hwy., 865/573-9959) is an above-average used-book store, with a notable collection of local books and collector's editions. It is located a half-mile south of the Henley Street Bridge in a nondescript shopping plaza.

Another option for used books is **McKay's** (230 Papermill Place Way, 865/588-0331), a warehouse-sized bookstore that is well organized and well loved by readers of all stripes.

The closest new book store to downtown Knoxville is **Barnes and Noble** (8029 Kingston Pk., 865/670-0773), located next to West Town Mall.

TOURS

The **Three Rivers Rambler** (Volunteer Landing, 865/524-9411, www.threeriversrambler.com, adults $19, seniors $17, children 3–12 $11) is an 11-mile scenic railroad excursion that departs from downtown Knoxville. The ride travels along the Tennessee River past Island Home airport to the confluence of the Holston and French Broad Rivers. The journey takes 90 minutes and takes you past farmland and old quarries. The open-air car is a real treat in pleasant weather.

Rambles take place on weekends from May to August, with departures at 2 and 5 P.M. Special seasonal Halloween and Christmas excursions are also offered. You can reserve tickets online or up to 30 minutes before departure at the ticket counter.

To get to the Three Rivers Rambler, take Neyland Drive (Hwy. 158) along the Tennessee River. Look for parking lot C-18 on the shore side of the road, where Rambler guests may park for free.

The **Tennessee Riverboat Company** (300 Neyland Dr., 865/525-7827, www.tnriverboat.com) offers dinner cruises and daytime sightseeing cruises down the Tennessee River on an old-fashioned paddleboat.

Accommodations

On the up side, Knoxville's downtown hotel rooms run a bit cheaper than those in other major Tennessee cities. On the down side, the city has one of the highest combined sales- and room-tax rates in the state: 17.25 percent. Be sure to figure this in when planning your budget.

DOWNTOWN

There is a pleasant array of boutique and chain hotels in downtown Knoxville, many of which are convenient to Gay Street, Market Square, and the riverfront.

$100-150

Knoxville's most unique hotel is a bit hard to find. **(Hotel St. Oliver** (407 Union Ave., 865/521-0050, www.hotelstolivertn.com, $75–200) is located just around the corner from Market Square, but the 1876 townhouse easily blends into its surroundings. Built by German baker Peter Kern in the 19th century, the St. Oliver was converted into a hotel for the 1982 World's Fair. It is not well advertised, but patrons find it nonetheless. Far from the cookie-cutter, Hotel St. Oliver offers superior location, genuinely friendly service, and distinctive accommodation. Its 24 guest rooms have elegant beds, refrigerators, wet bars, and coffee service. Perhaps the best perk is the downstairs library with soft couches and inviting reading nooks that beg you to come in and sit a spell.

Offering an ideal location and intimate, personalized service, the **(Maplehurst Inn** (800 W. Hill Ave., 865/523-7773, www.maplehurstinn.com, $80–150) is worth considering. Each of the 11 guest rooms have a private bath and personalized touches to make you feel like you're at home. Breakfast is served in a cozy dining room overlooking the Tennessee River. Maplehurst dates from the early 20th century, when the townhouse was built for a wealthy merchant. It was converted to a bed-and-breakfast for the 1982 World's Fair, and remains one of the only bed-and-breakfasts in downtown Knoxville.

Located at the north end of downtown, near the Old City and Gay Street, is the **Crowne Plaza Knoxville** (401 W. Summit Hill Dr., 865/522-2600, $110–190). This 197-room high-rise hotel has full business services, an indoor pool and fitness center, 24-hour lounge, and updated guest rooms.

$150-200

Located in a pyramid-shaped building on the Knoxville waterfront, the **(Knoxville Marriott** (500 Hill Ave. SE, 865/637-1234, $150–200) is one of the city's most distinctive landmarks. The unusual design creates a lofty lobby and gives many of the guest rooms impressive river views. In addition to novelty, the Marriott offers its guests a slew of thoughtful amenities especially designed for business travelers. There is an outdoor swimming pool, fitness center, and full-service salon on-site. There are also two restaurants, a gift shop, and lots of meeting space. The Knoxville Marriott is located next door to the Women's Basketball Hall of Fame, and is within walking distance of downtown attractions like Blount Mansion and James White Fort.

The **Hilton Knoxville** (501 W. Church Ave., 865/523-2300, $180–220) is a high-rise hotel located in the midst of downtown office buildings. It is a few blocks from Gay Street and Market Square Mall. The Hilton offers guest rooms, suites, and executive guest rooms with upgraded amenities and the best views of the city. There is a business center, fitness room, pool, cribs and high chairs for children, and on-site ATM, car rental, and café.

Over $200

Feel like part of Knoxville's downtown renaissance at **Cook Loft** (722 S. Gay St., 865/637-8108, www.cookloft.com, $450–500), an urban guesthouse and event venue. Skylights, hardwood floors, high ceilings, exposed-brick walls, large windows, and sleek lines bring the loft concept to life. Two bedrooms and a spacious living room invite you to relax and spread out. The kitchen is well furnished with restaurant-grade appliances, but you probably won't be doing much cooking with all the great restaurants in your backyard. Weekly rates ($2,100) are also available.

UNIVERSITY OF TENNESSEE
$100-150

A timeworn Days Inn on the University of Tennessee campus got a major face-lift, opening in 2009 as **Hotel Indigo Knoxville** (1719 Lake Ave., 865/521-5000, $100–125). Part of a new chain of "upscale value" hotels, Indigo offers an experience apart from the typical hotel room. Guest rooms boast hardwood floors, murals, and spa-like bath fixtures. There is a casual café and coffeehouse on the ground floor, free wireless Internet throughout, and a youthful atmosphere all around. Hotel Indigo's location cannot be beat if you are coming to the university. It would be a hike—or a short trolley ride—to downtown attractions.

Located near the World's Fair Park on the edge of Fort Sanders, the **Cumberland House Hotel** (1109 White Ave., 865/971-4663, $100–150) is a Sheraton. The 130 guest rooms have flat-screen televisions, coffeemakers, hair dryers, and CD players. Suites with kitchenettes and couches are available. The hotel, built in 2005, boasts an on-site restaurant as well as a fitness center. Cumberland House is convenient to UT and to Neyland Stadium.

FOURTH AND GILL
Under $100

The historic residential neighborhood of Fourth and Gill, near the Old City and slightly north of downtown, is home to the **⟨ Knoxville Hostel** (404 Fourth Ave., 865/546-8090, $17). Located in a homey urban cottage with hardwood floors, a generous porch, and small backyard, the Knoxville Hostel offers its guests bunk-bed dorm-style accommodation in sex-segregated bedrooms. Guests can lounge by the TV, use the kitchen, or surf the Internet for free on the hostel computer. Linens are provided, as is a free continental breakfast. All-in-all it's a good deal, even for the budget-conscious. The hostel is within walking distance of the Old City, Gay Street, and the trolley line.

Food

Knoxville dining is impossible to pigeonhole. Downtown eateries cater to the business lunch crowd, college students, and downtown's new young professional residents. Older neighborhoods outside of the city center are home to hole-in-the-wall eateries that defy expectation.

Whatever you do, don't head straight for the familiar chain restaurant. Explore a bit; you'll be richly rewarded.

DOWNTOWN

Gay Street, the Old City, and Market Square have a large concentration of restaurants that cater to all tastes and budgets.

Casual

For coffee, baked treats, and sandwiches, grab a table at **Old City Java** (109 S. Central St., 865/523-9817, Sun.–Thurs. 7:30 A.M.–midnight, Fri.–Sat. 9 A.M.–midnight, $4–9). Hardwood floors, plenty of cozy tables, and wireless Internet make this a popular place to while away a few hours.

Market Square's most celebrated restaurant is **⟨ The Tomato Head** (12 Market Sq., 865/637-4067, Mon. 11 A.M.–3 P.M., Tues.–Thurs. 11 A.M.–9:30 P.M., Fri.–Sat. 11 A.M.–10:30 P.M., Sun. 10 A.M.–9 P.M., $4–9), which opened its doors downtown long before it was cool. Originally a pizza joint, the Tomato Head now serves soup, sandwiches, salads, burritos, and pizza using only the best organic and otherwise pure-at-heart ingredients. The results are way above average. Vegetarians and meat-eaters can rejoice, for options range from a vegetarian sandwich made with meaty and flavorful tofu to a roast beef sandwich heaped with meat. The pizza is still mighty popular, and for good reason. They offer 15 official varieties but you can build your own pie from a list of 45 different toppings (homemade lamb sausage anyone?). The Tomato Head is generally crowded and noisy. You step to the counter, order and pay, and then one of the low-key staff members will bring your order to the table. It's a good meeting place, or also a great place for a quick solo lunch.

The **Downtown Grill & Brewery** (424 S. Gay St., 865/633-8111, Sun.–Thurs. 11 A.M.–midnight, Fri.–Sat. 11 A.M.–3 A.M., $8–18) is as popular for its selection of handcrafted brews as it is for its easy bar-style menu. Mesquite-grilled steak, jumbo pasta plates, pizza, and fajitas all come with a recommendation from the chef for the right beer accompaniment. With outdoor sidewalk seating and a prime location on Gay Street, this is a popular restaurant to meet and mingle.

Pete's Coffee Shop (540 Union Ave., 865/523-2860, Mon.–Fri. 6:30 A.M.–2:30 P.M., Sat. 7 A.M.–noon, $4–10) is the best downtown destination for diner-style breakfast and plate lunches. Located in a storefront a few blocks from Market Square, Pete's attracts a loyal following among downtown office workers and new residents. It is the type of place that offers you a bottomless cup of joe and no-nonsense food like club sandwiches, fried chicken, and omelets.

Japanese

Handcrafted sushi along with cuisine that fuses Japanese, Korean, and Spanish ingredients and styles: That is what **Nama** (135 S. Gay St., 865/633-8539, lunch daily 11:30 A.M.–2:30 P.M., dinner Sun.–Thurs. 4 P.M.–midnight, Fri.–Sat. 4 P.M.–2 A.M., $8–25), a trendy sushi house on Gay Street, offers. The enlightened business set dines here at lunchtime; at night it attracts a youthful, well-heeled crowd. The half-price Maki happy hour from 5 to 7 P.M. is a good deal for the budget diner.

Fusion

La Costa (31 Market Sq., 865/566-0275, Sun.–Thurs. 4–10 P.M., Fri.–Sat. 4–11 P.M., brunch Sun. 10 A.M.–3 P.M., $16–23) offers a surprising fusion of Southern and Latin cuisine in a cozy Market Square storefront. Featuring organic, local, and fair-trade ingredients, La Costa takes care with dishes like the catch of the day served with organic quinoa, jumbo scallops and rice, or the seasonal vegetarian plate. Save space for dessert, which includes sopaipillas, crème brûlée, and sorbet.

English

Who knew that English cuisine would have its day? **The Crown & Goose** (123 S. Central St., 865/524-2100, Tues.–Thurs. 4:30 P.M.–1 A.M., Fri.–Sat. 4:30 P.M.–2 A.M., Sun. 11 A.M.–4 P.M., $12–28) in the Old City is proving that Welsh rarebit, fish-and-chips, and bangers and mash are indeed good food. But to be fair, the Crown & Goose is far more than British Isle pub food. They have adopted the best of the Continent, as well, and put it on display in dishes like spring-vegetable-and-wild-mushroom risotto, San Marzano tomato and Stilton bisque, and the Frenchman's Lunch, a European cheese board served with bread. Best of all, the Crown & Goose has a stylish but unpretentious atmosphere that appreciates good food. This is a nice choice for an unexpectedly good dinner.

Steak

If you are in the mood for a steak, there is really nowhere better to go than **Regas Restaurant** (318 N. Gay St., 865/637-3427, lunch Mon.–Fri. 11 A.M.–2:30 P.M., dinner Mon.–Tues. 5–9 P.M., Wed. 5–9:30 P.M., Thurs.–Sat. 5–10 P.M., $14–40). Opened by Greek immigrants in 1919, Regas has evolved into Knoxville's first choice for fine dining. Choose from no less than six steak options, plus fresh seafood including shrimp and grits and New Zealand lobster tail. At lunch Regas rolls up its sleeves a bit and offers casual business lunches like a shaved prime rib sandwich and lemon chicken with rice pilaf.

UNIVERSITY OF TENNESSEE
Fusion
Knoxville's best restaurant for vegetarians is the **Sunspot** (1909 Cumberland Ave., 865/637-4663, Mon.–Sat. 11 A.M.–10 P.M., Sun. 10:30 A.M.–3 P.M., $8–14), an institution on the UT strip that features eclectic cuisine with strong Southwestern and Latin American influences. For vegetarians there is the baked enchilada, the Tofu Tier (a stack of baked tofu and fried eggplant in a savory miso sauce), and an awesome veggie burger. Carnivores have options like pan-seared tilapia served over cheese grits and Pasta Rustica, chorizo sausage and red peppers served in a spicy tomato sauce. There are dozens of beers on tap and in the bottle.

WEST KNOXVILLE
Fine Dining
For a taste of Knoxville's most elegant food make reservations at **The Orangery** (5412 Kingston Pk., 865/588-2964, lunch Mon.–Fri. 11:30 A.M.–2 P.M., dinner Mon.–Sat. 6–10 P.M., lunch $9–14, dinner $23–44). A French-inspired menu, impeccable wine list, and refined atmosphere make for a luxurious dining experience. Come for lunch for salad Niçoise, roasted-vegetable ravioli, and sautéed shrimp. Dinner specialties include veal porterhouse, prime New York strip, buffalo with caramelized shallots, and elk chop with vegetable puree. What other restaurant can say that?

Italian
The best New York–style pizzas, hand-crafted calzones, and other authentic Italian favorites are offered at **Savelli's** (3055 Sutherland Ave., 865/521-9085, Mon.–Sat. 11 A.M.–9:30 P.M., Sun. 4–9 P.M., $9–19). This homey restaurant is small and often crowded, with good reason: Savelli's serves made-from-scratch Italian food at good prices. Beer is served, but bring your own wine.

SOUTH KNOXVILLE
Steak
Beef lovers rule at **Ye Olde Steak House** (6838 Chapman Hwy., 865/577-9328, Sun.–Thurs. 4:30–9 P.M., Fri.–Sat. 4:30–9:30 P.M., $12–35), where the menu features nearly a dozen different cuts of beef, including a generous hand-patted burger. Seafood and chicken are also served. Ye Olde Steak House is a family-owned steakhouse set in a Tudor-style home (hence the name). It is a funky, family-friendly destination for diners with big appetites.

Beer is served at Ye Olde Steak House, but liquor and wine are not. You may bring your own.

Middle Eastern
For a dining experience like no other, head directly to (**King Tut Grill** (4132 Martin Mill Pk., 865/573-6021, $6–12), a family-owned restaurant in otherwise unremarkable Vestal, a few miles south of the Henley Street bridge. King Tut's has established a loyal following thanks largely to the charisma of its owner, Mo, who serves drinks in flower vases, tells you what to order, and is famous for sending out extra food to his favored customers. Mo and his family offer traditional diner-style meals—hamburgers, meatloaf, baked chicken, and the like—to appease the locals, but the reason to come here is to eat home-style Egyptian fare. The daily menu offers a handful of such favorites, like falafel sandwiches, an Egyptian platter, and the best Greek salad in Knoxville. But it is on Mo's Middle Eastern night that he and his family go all out with stuffed grape leaves, homemade *basboosa*, and the works. Believe what they tell you: This is a restaurant not to be missed.

EAST KNOXVILLE
Barbecue
Set in a slightly scruffy neighborhood, **Dixon Bar-B-Que** (1201 E. Magnolia Ave., 865/525-9305, Thurs.–Sat. 4:30 P.M.–midnight, $6–15) is one of Knoxville's authentic barbecue houses, where the ribs and chicken are smoked the old-fashioned way.

Southern
Arguably Knoxville's best meat-and-three Southern-food house, **Chandlers** (3101 E. Magnolia Ave., 865/595-0212, Mon.–Thurs.

11 A.M.–7:30 P.M., Fri. 11 A.M.–8:30 P.M., Sat. noon–8:30 P.M., Sun. noon–6 P.M., $4–10) is a cafeteria-style restaurant where workingmen and businesspeople rub elbows when the dinner bell rings. The fried chicken is always reliable, and comes with sides like hot rolls, collard greens, fried okra, and stewed apples.

NORTH KNOXVILLE
Sandwiches
Hefty sandwiches on home-baked bread keep them coming to venerable **Steamboat Sandwiches** (2423 N. Central Ave., 865/546-3333, Mon.–Fri. 10 A.M.–3 P.M., Sat. 11 A.M.–2 P.M., $5–8). The "Steamboat" is an oversized sandwich packed with ham, Genoa salami, and Swiss cheese, finished with a mild hot sauce, mayonnaise, mustard, and pickle. Thankfully for those with smaller appetites, you can also order a half-size.

C Litton's (2803 Essary Dr., Fountain City, 865/688-0429, Mon.–Thurs. 11 A.M.–8 P.M., Fri.–Sat. 11 A.M.–10 P.M., $7–17) is a North Knoxville institution, where Knoxvillians go for the city's best burgers, blue-plate lunches, and homemade dessert. Hand-cut fries, jumbo onion rings, red velvet cake, and baked sweet potatoes are some of the things that keep people coming back to Litton's again and again. A family restaurant that began as a humble grocery in 1946, Litton's is worth the drive. To get there, drive north on Broadway (U.S. 441), passing the I-640 overpass. Litton's is located across the street from the Fountain City park.

Information and Services

INFORMATION
For information about Knoxville, contact the **Knoxville Tourism & Sports Corporation** (865/523-7263 or 800/727-8045, www.knoxville.org) for a visitors guide before you come.

Downtown Knoxville (17 Market Sq., 865/246-2654, www.downtownknoxville.org) promotes the city center by publishing maps and guides and maintaining a website.

Visitors Centers
The **Knoxville Visitor Center** (301 S. Gay St., 865/523-7263, Mon.–Fri. 7:45 A.M.–6 P.M., Sat. 9 A.M.–5 P.M., Sun. noon–4 P.M.) is at the corner of Gay Street and Summit Hill Drive. This is the place to pick up information and maps, but it is also a Knoxville gift shop and bookstore, wireless Internet hot-spot, and the venue of the weekday WDVX Blue Plate Special, a midday concert and live radio broadcast. The coffee bar serves hot beverages, basic sandwiches, and sweets.

Newspapers
Knoxville's daily paper is the *Knoxville News* *Sentinel* (www.knoxnews.com). Its alternative weekly, *Metropulse* (www.metropulse.com), is a far better read. Smart commentary, up-to-date entertainment listings, and columns like "Secret History" make it great. Pick yours up free on Wednesdays at local groceries, coffee shops, and restaurants.

Radio
The Knoxville radio dial is crowded with the usual suspects, but a few frequencies are worth seeking out. Chief among them is **WDVX** (89.9 FM and 102.9 FM), a community-supported grassroots radio station that plays a mix of early country, contemporary Americana, and other roots music.

WUOT (91.9 FM) is the university's public radio station. It airs NPR news programs and classical music.

SERVICES
Libraries
Knoxville's main public library is the **Lawson McGhee Library** (500 W. Church Ave., 865/215-8750, Mon.–Thurs.

KNOXVILLE

9 A.M.–8:30 P.M., Fri. 9 A.M.–5:30 P.M., Sat. noon–5 P.M., Sun. 1–5 P.M.). It has public Internet access.

Gay and Lesbian Resources

The **Equality Herald** (www.equalityherald.com) is an online source for gay, lesbian, and transgender news and announcements for East Tennessee, including Knoxville. Gay-owned and gay-friendly businesses are listed on the Knoxville LGBT-friendly business directory (www.knoxbusiness.org).

Another place to network with LGBT people is at the Metropolitan Community Church (7820 Redeemer Ln., 865/531-2539, www.mcc-knoxville.org) in West Knoxville.

Getting There and Around

GETTING THERE
By Air

The **McGhee Tyson Airport** (TYS, www.tys.org) is the Knoxville area's airport. It is located 12 miles south of the city in Blount County.

A half-dozen airlines serve McGhee Tyson with direct flights from 20 U.S. cities, including Orlando, Dallas, Houston, Denver, Memphis, Chicago, Cleveland, St. Paul, New York, Philadelphia, and Washington, D.C. Airlines with service to Knoxville include U.S. Air, United, Delta, American, Continental, Northwest, and Allegiant Air.

Taxis and car rentals are available at the airport. To get to downtown Knoxville from McGhee Tyson, take Alcoa Highway (U.S. 129) north to the city.

By Car

Two major interstate highways cross in Knoxville. I-75 is a north–south highway that connects with Lexington, Kentucky, in the north and Chattanooga to the south. I-40 is an east–west thoroughfare. About 35 miles east of Knoxville I-40 peels off and heads into North Carolina, while I-81 heads to the Tri-Cities and points northeast. I-40 west heads to Nashville and Memphis.

By Bus

Greyhound (www.greyhound.com) serves Knoxville with bus service to Nashville, Chattanooga, Asheville, Atlanta, and many other cities. The Greyhound station is located at 100 E. Magnolia Avenue. The station number is 865/524-0369.

GETTING AROUND
Driving

Knoxville is a city where everyone drives to get where they're going. Sprawling suburbs, shopping malls, and the interstate are evidence of this.

I-640 is a bypass interstate that makes a circle on the northern fringe of Knoxville and allows I-40 through traffic to avoid downtown. Part of I-640 is also I-275.

Until mid-2009, the downtown portion of I-40 is closed for expansion. Highway signs will point you in the direction of the best and closest interstate detour, usually towards I-640 and I-275.

The interstate closure is one reason to get off the highway, but it's not the only one. Visitors should get onto ground level and take thoroughfares like Cumberland/Kingston Pike, Chapman Highway/Henley Street/Broadway, and Central, Magnolia, and Western Avenues to get a better sense of the character and geography of Knoxville. And with the possible exception of Kingston Pike, there's less traffic, too.

PARKING

Drive around downtown searching for a meter, or park in one of the many paid parking lots downtown. No matter what you do, all-day parking in Knoxville will rarely cost you more than $5 per day.

KNOXVILLE

Public Transportation

The Knoxville Trolley Line offers free air-conditioned easy transit throughout downtown Knoxville most weekdays. The Orange Line (weekdays 7 A.M.–6 P.M.) connects UT and the World's Fair Park with downtown, including Gay Street. The Blue Line (weekdays 6 A.M.–6 P.M.) connects Hall of Fame Drive and the Civic Coliseum with Henley Street and downtown. The Green Line (weekdays 7 A.M.–6 P.M.) connects UT with the Fort Sanders neighborhood, and operates only when UT is in session.

In addition, the late-night Purple Line, which operates on Friday and Saturday nights 6 P.M.–3:30 A.M. from August to May, travels from the Old City, along Gay Street, through the World's Fair Park, and to the UT campus.

Most Knoxville Trolleys are red, although sometimes orange Knoxville Transit Authority vans fill in. They stop at locations designated by a trolley sign. For more information, call 865/637-3000 or go online to www.katbus.com.

Around Knoxville

CLINTON

Green McAdoo Cultural Center

In 1955, Green McAdoo School was the segregated primary school for Clinton, a mill town of 4,000 people located about 20 miles northwest of Knoxville. Under the "separate but equal" policy of the segregationist South, graduates of the black primary school were bussed to Knoxville's all-black Austin High School for their secondary education.

Fifty years later, the school building became the Green McAdoo Cultural Center (101 School St., 865/463-6500, www.greenmcadoo.org, Tues.–Sat. 10 A.M.–5 P.M., free), which records and celebrates the remarkable story of the integration of Clinton's high school back in 1956.

Tales of school desegregation in the South normally begin with Little Rock, Arkansas. But they really should begin with Clinton. That's because even before the Little Rock Six entered Little Rock Central High School in the fall of 1958, there were black and white students attending Clinton High School together in rural Tennessee.

In 1951, five black high school students petitioned the Anderson County Board of Education for the right to attend all-white Clinton High School. At this time, black students in Clinton were bussed a long 18 miles into Knoxville to attend the all-black Austin High School.

At first, the students lost their suit. U.S. District Judge Robert Taylor declared that the bussing arrangement met the requirements of separate but equal. However, when the U.S. Supreme Court decided the landmark Brown vs. Board of Education in the spring of 1954, Judge Taylor reversed his earlier ruling and ordered that Clinton High School be integrated at the beginning of the school term in September.

What followed is a remarkable story, recounted at the cultural center through newspaper clippings, video remembrances by the participants, and evocative photographs of the events. Integration went smoothly at first, but as the eyes of the world focused on this trendsetting Tennessee town, tensions began to run high. The National Guard was called in, and the school building was bombed. But the school principal, student body president, local Baptist minister, and other leaders in Clinton took a strong stand in favor of the rule of law—and, therefore, for integration.

One of the most moving displays in the museum is a glass case with letters that were received by Rev. Paul Turner, the white Baptist minister who helped to escort the black students to school and preached against the segregationists. There are anonymous and hateful postcards and letters that decry Rev. Turner, as well as letters of support from unknowns to

© SUSANNA HENIGHAN POTTER

Statues outside the Green McAdoo Cultural Center in Clinton depict the students who desegregated Clinton High School in 1956.

celebrities, including the Rev. Billy Graham and Edward R. Murrow.

Eventually, the world stopped paying a lot of attention to Clinton. New civil rights struggles were taking place all over the South, and the outsider segregationists who fomented the worst of the violence and unrest were gone. Photographers traveled to Clinton to take pictures when Bobby Cain became the first black male to graduate from a desegregated public school in May of 1957, but when Gail Epps followed in his footsteps the following year no one paid any attention.

The events that took place in Clinton were recounted in an hour-long 1957 *See It Now* television program, and its 1960 sequel from CBS Reports, both of which may be seen at the museum. In 2006, the Green McAdoo Cultural Center produced an award-winning documentary about the events titled *Clinton 12,* which was narrated by James Earl Jones.

Outside the museum is a life-sized statue of the Clinton 12, the 12 African American young people who enrolled at Clinton High School in the fall of 1956. When the museum was opened in 2006, 9 of the 12 were on hand to see the statue being unveiled.

The Green McAdoo Cultural Center was funded in part by federal, state, and local funds, as well as through private donations. In 2007, legislation was introduced in Congress that would designate the Green McAdoo Cultural Center as part of the National Park Service.

The old Clinton High School building now houses Clinton Middle School, just a few blocks from the Green McAdoo center.

Get to Clinton by taking Clinton Highway (Hwy. 25 W.) about 15 miles out of Knoxville. Once in Clinton, there are signs directing you to the center.

◖ Museum of Appalachia

There is one place that every visitor to this region should visit if they are the least bit interested in the lifestyles and folk traditions of Appalachia. The **Museum of Appalachia** (2819

GRAINGER COUNTY AGRITOURISM

Grainger County lies northeast of Knoxville. One of the state's most rural counties, Grainger has a rugged landscape, defined by steep ridges and long valleys. The area is perhaps best known for its tomatoes – during the summer it is not uncommon to see farm stands set up around Knoxville with signs touting "Grainger County Tomatoes."

You can get to the source of the abundance by visiting farms in Grainger County yourself. **Ritter Farms** (2999 Hwy. 11-W S., 865/767-2575, www.ritterfarms.com) is one of the largest family-owned farms in the area. They have a commercial kitchen where they prepare jams, jellies, salsas, and other farm-fresh provisions for retail sale. The farm market is open Monday–Saturday year-round; in the spring, summer, and fall you can buy seasonal fresh produce and in winter they specialize in handicrafts, preserves, and baked goods. The country kitchen restaurant serves lunch Wednesday–Friday. Call

ahead to confirm hours. The farm is located between Bean Station and Rutledge.

Tennessee Homegrown Tomatoes (865/828-8316), located near Cherokee Lake on Route 375, about 3.5 miles east of Highway 92, grows all sorts of vegetables – not just tomatoes. They offer farm tours, and host events throughout the growing season.

If you want some wine with your vegetables, you can get some at **Clinch Mountain Winery** (Thorn Hill, 865/767-3600, www.clinchmountainwinery.com, Mon.-Sat. 10 A.M.-8 P.M., Sun. noon-7 P.M.), located on Bullen Valley Road in the Thorn Hill community. Try their most popular varieties, Scooter Trash and Hound Dog Red, at the tasting room.

The crowning event for Grainger County farmers is the **Grainger County Tomato Festival** (www.graingercountytomatofestival. com), which takes place in Rutledge in late July every year.

Farms like this one in Grainger County, northeast of Knoxville, produce fruits, vegetables, and the region's celebrated tomatoes.

KNOXVILLE

Andersonville Hwy., Clinton, 865/494-7680, www.museumofappalachia.org, daily Jan.–Feb. 10 A.M.–4 P.M., Mar. 8 A.M.–5 P.M., Apr.–Labor Day weekdays 8:30 A.M.–6 P.M., weekends 8:30 A.M.–7 P.M., Sept.–Oct. daily 8 A.M.–6 P.M., Nov.–Dec. daily 8 A.M.–5 P.M., adults $12.95, seniors $10, children 6–12 $5) is one-of-a-kind. Its 65 acres contain more of the history of this region than any other place in Tennessee. Its collection includes more than 250,000 artifacts, and more than 100,000 people visit annually.

The museum is a story told in several chapters. Its indoor exhibits include the Appalachian "Hall of Fame," a remarkable collection of things that were made, used, and treasured by the people who came and created a life in the rugged land of the southern Appalachians. There are dolls that were whittled by rugged mountain men; banjos created from food tins; and the remains of a supposed perpetual motion machine. The exhibits are the work of John Rice Irwin, as is the whole museum. Irwin, a mountain man himself, is motivated by his admiration and love for the people who settled the mountains. He believes that the items of everyday life are important, and that through them, we can understand the people who made them. It certainly seems like he's right. Take the time to read the detailed and loving descriptions of each item in the Hall of Fame, and soon you will feel admiration and marvel for the people who made them, in the midst of what we would now consider hard times.

Music fans should not overlook the museum. Its collection of handmade fiddles, guitars, banjos, and mouth harps is unrivaled, and its displays about musicians tell not only who, what, and when, but also why and how. It's not to be missed.

Outside the Hall of Fame, the museum has a collection of mountain buildings. There is a log church, schoolhouse, pioneer homestead, and the log home where Mark Twain's parents lived in Possum Trot, Tennessee. As you explore these old buildings—all of which have been carefully moved from original locations throughout the region—look for members of the museum's menagerie: peacocks, horses, fainting goats, and sheep.

The Museum of Appalachia hosts several events during the year, but none is better-known and loved than its annual **Homecoming** in October. The best musicians, writers, and artists come for the weekend, which offers the most authentic celebration of mountain arts in the region.

In 2008, Irwin announced that he could no longer afford to keep the museum afloat with regular, large personal contributions. The museum would have to consider a few options to balance its books—possibly by cutting back hours in the winter or possibly by seeking corporate and other sponsorships. So while the future of the museum seems certain, be on the lookout for cost-saving changes in the coming years.

NORRIS DAM STATE PARK

TVA's first hydroelectric project was to construct a dam on the Clinch River, in Anderson County north of Knoxville. Construction of the 1,860-foot-long, 265-foot-tall dam started in 1933 and was completed in 1936. It was named for Sen. George Norris of Nebraska, who conceived of and championed the idea of a public power company in the Tennessee Valley.

Hungarian-born architect Roland Wank designed Norris Dam. Wank cared not only about the function of the dam, but its appearance as well. He considered the placement of overlooks on either side of the dam, and designed a visitors center. The dam was proportional; carefully placed window openings and the placement of the formwork boards created texture and pattern.

Today, Norris Dam is part of Norris Dam State Park (125 Village Green Cir.e, Lake City, 865/426-7461 or 800/543-9335). Visitors may see the dam from overlooks on both sides of the lake; U.S. Highway 441—the main thoroughfare in the park—tracks along the top of the dam. It is an impressive sight. The visitors center on the east side of the dam has public restrooms and displays about construction of the dam.

Norris Dam is also home to the **Lenoir Museum** (865/494-9688, Wed.–Sun.

© SUSANNA HENIGHAN POTTER

Norris Dam was the first hydroelectric project built by the Tennessee Valley Authority.

KNOXVILLE

9 A.M.–5 P.M., free), named for Will G. Lenoir, a local resident who amassed a remarkable collection of mountain artifacts during his lifetime. Lenoir traveled the backroads of East Tennessee to purchase housewares, old farm implements, mementos, and other remnants of everyday life of the early 20th century. When Lenoir died, he donated his collection to the State of Tennessee, and eventually the Lenoir museum was built at Norris Dam State Park.

In addition to Lenoir's collection, the museum houses displays about Native Americans and the construction of Norris Dam.

Next to the Lenoir Museum are two authentic structures that were moved to the park during construction of TVA dams and lakes. The **Caleb Crosby Threshing Barn** once sat on the Holston River where the David A. Green Bridge now spans Cherokee Lake on Highway 25 East. Before the lake flooded the farm site, the barn was carefully dismantled and put in storage, where it was kept for 34 years until 1978 when it was reconstructed at Norris Dam.

Next to the threshing barn is the **18th Century Rice Gristmill,** originally constructed in 1798 by James Rice along Lost Creek in Union County. Four generations of the Rice family operated the mill, from 1798 until 1935 when TVA bought the land on which it sat in preparation for flooding of Norris Lake. The Civilian Conservation Corps labeled all the components of the mill, disassembled it, and reassembled it on its present land. During the summer, park staff still operate the mill and have gift items for sale.

Recreation

Despite its rich history, most people come to Norris Dam State Park to relax and enjoy the outdoors. Boating and fishing are popular on the Clinch River and on Norris Lake. There is one licensed commercial marina (865/494-8138) on the lake. There are 15 miles of hiking trails and another 15 miles of multiuse dirt and gravel paths ideal for biking. An Olympic-sized swimming pool is open during the summer daily 10 A.M.–6 P.M.

Cabins and Camping

Norris has 19 rustic cabins ($45–55) and 10 three-bedroom deluxe cabins ($60–95). All cabins are located in a wooded setting, and have kitchens, bathrooms, fireplaces, linens, and outdoor picnic tables and grills. The Norris campground has 75 sites ($20), with electrical and water hook-ups.

OAK RIDGE

America created the atomic bomb—or parts of it, at least—at the Y-12, X-10, and K-25 plants in this city northwest of Knoxville. Today, Oak Ridge and its plants are still an important component in the national defense industry.

History

Oak Ridge did not exist before 1942. When nuclear fission was discovered in the late 1930s, American scientists warned that this technology could be used to create a weapon more powerful than any known to man. As World War II escalated, and the United States joined the conflict in 1941, the U.S. military decided to exploit this technology. Sites in New Mexico, Washington state, and East Tennessee were chosen for the work. The isolated hills in Tennessee were chosen because they were close to roads and rail lines, had ample supply of electricity, and because they would be hard for spies and curiosity-seekers to discover. Before the land was taken over by the government, about 3,000 people lived in homes that were scattered around the hills and valleys. Each homeowner received a letter stating that their land and home was being taken; and how much money they would receive in exchange.

Oak Ridge was built seemingly overnight. Between the spring of 1943 and the fall of 1944, the 59,000-acre tract of land bought for the project was developed into 10,000 homes and apartments, 13,000 dormitory spaces, 5,000 trailers, and more than 16,000 barracks. One of the facilities, **K-25,** where they processed uranium, was at the time the largest

not-so-scenic Oak Ridge, outside the K-25 plant where parts of the atomic bombs dropped on Hiroshima and Nagasaki were made

© SUSANNA HENIGHAN POTTER

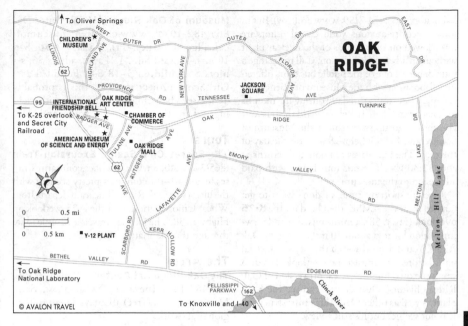

building in the world under one roof. Workers rode bicycles to get from one side of the massive structure to the other.

Tens of thousands of people came to live in Oak Ridge. Housing was in short supply, and African-American and some white workers were housed in drafty, leaky "hutments." Social societies, schools, churches, theaters, barber shops, and much more were developed to entertain and meet the needs of the new residents.

When the United States dropped atomic bombs in Hiroshima and Nagasaki on August 6 and September 2, 1945, many workers at Oak Ridge learned for the first time what they had been doing all this time. Many were proud that they had helped to create the weapons that some believe ended World War II.

The end of the war did not mean the end of Oak Ridge. Y-12 continues to research, develop, and produce weapons for the U.S. military. In 1948 X-10 became the Oak Ridge National Laboratory, a center for science and research managed successively by the University of Chicago, Monsanto Chemical, Union Carbide, and Lockheed Martin corporations. It is now managed by the University of Tennessee and Battelle, and remains a center for scientific research in a wide range of fields.

American Museum of Science and Energy

Oak Ridge's premier attraction is the American Museum of Science and Energy (300 S. Tulane Ave., 865/576-3200, www.amse.org, Mon.– Sat. 9 A.M.–5 P.M., Sun. 1–5 P.M., adults $5, seniors $4, children 6–17 $3). The museum serves double-duty: It houses an exhibit about the development of Oak Ridge, and it is a science museum for young people. The historical exhibit relies on newspaper clippings, original documents, and audio visuals to describe Oak Ridge during World War II. The science museum has features dedicated to types of energy, including nuclear.

Oak Ridge National Laboratory

Before September 11, 2001, visitors were allowed walk-in tours of Y-12/Oak Ridge National

Laboratory (865/574-7199, www.ornl.gov). But in today's security-anxious world, casual visitors are not allowed on the campus of the nuclear plant without an advance reservation. Call to arrange a tour, or get on one of the public bus tours offered in collaboration with the Museum of Science and Energy. These tours run daily during the months of June–September. To get on board the bus tour you must sign up in person at the Museum of Science and Energy before 9 A.M. on the day of the tour. The bus leaves at noon and returns at about 2:30 P.M. The bus tour is free with paid admission to the museum.

If you're short on time, or don't want to get tangled up at the AMSE, then head for the **K-25 overlook** (Hwy. 58), a mini-museum and viewing station located about 10 miles south of Oak Ridge. You'll drive through the city's industrial park before arriving to the overlook. Inside a small enclosed building is a short version of Oak Ridge's history. Outside you can see the K-25 plant as well as other Oak Ridge infrastructure. It is not scenic, but it's still a view.

Other Sights

While most of "old Oak Ridge" has been razed and rebuilt in the ubiquitous modern American style of strip malls and parking lots, parts of the city date back to the 1940s. **Jackson Square** remains largely unchanged since it was built as Oak Ridge's original town center. The low-slung horseshoe-shaped shopping center is home to professional offices, a few cafés, and the Oak Ridge Playhouse. Across Kentucky Street from the square are the remains of the **Alexander Motor Inn,** Oak Ridge's original and only hotel during the war. Above the inn is the **Chapel on the Hill,** a church that served as the place of worship for numerous denominations during the war.

Other attractions in Oak Ridge include the **International Friendship Bell,** located downtown, which is a monument to peace. The **Secret City Commemorative Walk,** also downtown, is a memorial to the 75,000 men and women who built Oak Ridge during the 1940s.

An attraction for children is the **Children's**

Museum of Oak Ridge (416 W. Outer Dr., 865/482-1074, www.childrensmuseumof-oakridge.org, Tues.–Fri. 9 A.M.–5 P.M., Sat. 10 A.M.–4 P.M., Sun. 1–4 P.M., adults $6, seniors $5, children 3–18 $4). Founded as a Girl Scout project in 1973, this is probably Tennessee's best children's museum, with exciting and creative activities for young and old.

Tours

The **Secret City Scenic Excursion Train** (865/241-2140, www.techscribes.com/sarm/srm_scs.htm, $10–15) combines pretty scenery with the history of Oak Ridge. The train departs from Wheat Union Station, near the K-25 overlook on Highway 58. The journey travels a 12-mile route through the Manhattan Project site.

The Arts

The Oak Ridge Art Center (201 Badger Rd., 865/482-1441 Tues.–Fri. 9 A.M.–5 P.M., Sat.–Mon. 1–4 P.M., free) displays local and regional artwork.

Food

For a meal in Oak Ridge head to Jackson Square, where you can join the crowds at **Big Ed's Pizza** (101 Broadway, 865/482-4885, Mon.–Sat. 11 A.M.–11:30 P.M., $8–15), the city's most famous restaurant and a well-loved pizza parlor. Also on Jackson Square is **The Soup Kitchen** (47 E. Tennessee Ave., 865/482-3525, Mon.–Fri. 11 A.M.–7:30 P.M., Sat. 11 A.M.–2 P.M., $5–12), which serves excellent sandwiches, salads, and soups. Dozens of chain restaurants exist along Oak Ridge's main drag.

Information

The **Oak Ridge Welcome Center** (102C Robertsville Rd., 865/482-7821, www.oakridge-visitor.com, year-round Mon.–Fri. 9 A.M.–5 P.M., June–Oct. also open Sat. 9 A.M.–1 P.M.) hands out maps and brochures and helps travelers plan their visit to the city.

MARYVILLE

One of the oldest cities in East Tennessee, Maryville was named for Mary Grainger Blount,

THE RAVEN

The word *colorful* does not do justice to Sam Houston, onetime Tennessee governor and one of the state's most complex and controversial citizens during the first half of the 19th century.

Born in Lexington, Virginia, in 1793, Houston was just 13 when his father died. His mother, Elizabeth, brought Sam and his eight siblings to Blount County, where he went to school for the first time and promptly memorized Pope's translation of Homer's *Iliad*. When his teacher refused to teach Houston Greek and Latin, the teenager disappeared from his family home. Houston traveled the rural mountainsides of East Tennessee, and spent long periods in a Cherokee village. Oo-Loo-Te-Ka, a Cherokee chief, became a surrogate father to Houston, and named him the Raven. Houston learned the language and ways of the Cherokee.

Some years later Houston needed to pay off some debts, and in 1811 he opened a school in Blount County where he charged the then-astronomical fee of $8 per student per year. After about a year, when he was 20 years old and had paid his debts, Houston joined the army and quickly rose to an officer rank. Andrew Jackson noticed Houston's bravery and intelligence at the Battle of Horseshoe Bend during the Creek Wars of 1814. The future president stationed Houston to his regional headquarters in Nashville and the young East Tennessean became part of Jackson's so-called "Tennessee Junto," his political machine.

In 1819 Houston quit the army to study law and shortly after was appointed attorney general for Davidson County. Houston ran successfully for a seat in the U.S. House of Representatives, where he served two terms. In 1827 he was elected governor of Tennessee.

Houston's station at the top of Tennessee politics was not to last. He had a tumultuous private life, fueled by bouts of drinking and depression. While campaigning for his second term as Tennessee governor, Houston married Eliza Allen, the daughter of a prominent Middle Tennessee family. She left him after just 80 days of marriage and Houston resigned the governorship and fled to the Cherokee, now living in Oklahoma.

So began the next chapter for Houston, who went on to marry a Cherokee wife, lead the Texas army against Mexico, and be elected president of the Republic of Texas. Later, in 1840, he married again, this time to Margaret Lea of Alabama, with whom he would have eight children. He worked tirelessly to achieve Texas annexation to the United States, which occurred in 1845. While Houston served as a senator from Texas from 1846 until 1858 he promoted the transcontinental railroad, criticized the army, and supported the Union. In 1859 Houston was elected governor of Texas, where he opposed secession for Texas. He died in 1863.

Tennessee historian and writer Wilma Dykeman described Houston this way: "A strange, interesting combination of scout and scholar, woodsman and humanitarian, Sam Houston balanced Homer with humor and represented a sense of the total community of man."

Sam Houston

the wife of territorial governor William Blount. It is the home of **Maryville College,** a four-year college founded in 1819. Maryville College was among the first southern schools to admit Native Americans, African Americans, and women.

On the northern outskirts of Maryville is Alcoa, established as a company town for the Aluminum Corporation of America in 1914. ALCOA remains an important economic engine for Blount County.

Sights

The **Sam Houston Schoolhouse** (3650 Sam Houston Schoolhouse Rd., 865/983-1550, www.samhoustonhistoricschoolhouse.org, Tues.–Sat. 10 A.M.–5 P.M., Sun. 1–5 P.M., $1) is the one-room schoolhouse where Sam Houston taught for about a year beginning in 1812. Houston, one of early Tennessee's most remarkable citizens, was mostly self-educated. Raised in part by the Cherokee, who named him Raven, Houston went on to be governor of Tennessee, president of the Republic of Texas, and senator and governor of the state of Texas.

The Sam Houston Schoolhouse was built around 1794 by area settlers who wanted a place for their children to be educated. Several different teachers held class in this little one-room schoolhouse until Houston's arrival in 1812. Houston, who took up teaching in order to pay off his debts, stayed for only a year. But his name has remained tied with the institution up to the present day.

Today, the Sam Houston Schoolhouse recreates early schools on the Tennessee frontier. Reenactments can be arranged for groups.

Accommodations and Food

Knoxville's hip-funky eating establishment, the **Tomato Head** (211 W. Broadway, 865/981-1080, Mon. 11 A.M.–3 P.M., Tues.–Thurs. 11 A.M.–9 P.M., Fri.–Sat. 11 A.M.–9:30 P.M.,

PHOTO COURTESY OF TENNESSEE DEPARTMENT OF TOURIST DEVELOPMENT

the Sam Houston Schoolhouse in Maryville

Sun. 10 A.M.–9 P.M., $5–12), has a downtown Maryville location. Come here for pizza by the slice or the pie, sandwiches, salads, and daily specials, all made from scratch from the best ingredients.

Southland Books (601 E. Broadway, 865/984-4847, daily 10 A.M.–1 P.M.) is an excellent used bookstore, popular meeting place, art gallery, and coffee shop. Stop in at any time for a pick-me-up pastry and coffee drink. Owner Lisa Misosky serves a special home-made lunch special every Wednesday.

Located at McGhee Tyson Airport is the **Hilton Knoxville Airport** (2001 Alcoa Hwy., Alcoa, 865/970-4300, www.hiltonknoxvilleairport.com, $150–190). Its 326 guest rooms offer work desks, high-end bedding, coffeemakers, and MP3-player plug-ins.

KNOXVILLE

GREAT SMOKY MOUNTAINS

The Smokies are the most popular national park in the United States, and it is no wonder why. The park's iconic vistas of blue-green mountains topped by the namesake smoky mists are awesome, yet somehow comforting. These are ancient mountains, whose hills and valleys have secrets to keep.

The scenery in the Smokies is unrivaled. Mountaintops such as Clingmans Dome and Mount LeConte offer panoramic vistas of soft-edge mountains. Balds—clearings high up in the mountains—are enchanted places, where wild blueberries and rhododendron grow, and where the sunshine is pure and warm.

Valleys such as Cades Cove are ideal for wildlife-viewing—here you'll see lovely creatures like elk and deer. Mountain streams and rivers offer a kaleidoscope of sights, both under the cold, rushing water and around the water's edge. Within the 800 square miles of parkland, scientists have documented some 10,000 species of plants, animals, and invertebrates, but they believe that as many as 90,000 more live in this remarkably diverse natural wilderness.

You won't be bored in the Smokies. There are some 800 miles of hiking trails within the park, and traveling them brings you face-to-face with wildlife, waterfalls, and breathtaking viewpoints. Once you start hiking the trails of the Smokies, you will never want to stop. Cool mountain streams are ideal for wading and offer some of the best mountain fishing in the country. Visitors also enjoy picnicking and driving along the parks windy, quiet roads.

Some 9.2 million people visit Great Smoky Mountains every year, and they need places to

PHOTO COURTESY OF TENNESSEE DEPARTMENT OF TOURIST DEVELOPMENT

HIGHLIGHTS

◖ **Newfound Gap:** The most prominent mountain pass high in the Smokies, Newfound Gap offers excellent vistas, fresh cool air, and a chance to hike along the famed Appalachian Trail (page 383).

◖ **Cades Cove:** Historic cabins, churches, and farms dot this pastoral mountain cove, ideal for walking, biking, or auto touring (page 384).

◖ **Andrew's Bald:** A high mountain clearing accessible only on foot, Andrew's Bald is one of the Smokies' mysterious bald spots. It is a landscape of wild grasses, rhododendron, and clear air, and the perfect destination for a day hike (page 393).

◖ **Arrowmont:** Established in the early 20th century as a settlement school for mountain folks in Gatlinburg, Arrowmont today is an arts school and gallery with a focus on Appalachian-themed decorative arts (page 401).

◖ **Great Smoky Mountains Arts and Crafts Community:** Drive the back roads near Gatlinburg to find artisans who keep the creativity and ingenuity of mountain crafts alive (page 405).

◖ **Dollywood:** Don't turn up your nose at Dolly Parton's Pigeon Forge theme park. With roller coasters, live music, artisans, and lots more diversions, this place is the definition of good clean fun (page 406).

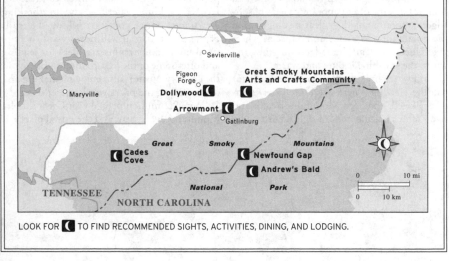

LOOK FOR ◖ TO FIND RECOMMENDED SIGHTS, ACTIVITIES, DINING, AND LODGING.

stay and to eat. The gateway communities in Tennessee—Cosby, Gatlinburg, Pigeon Forge, and Townsend—offer the necessities of life and so much more. If the Smokies soothe the spirit and revive your mind, then Gatlinburg and Pigeon Forge, with theme parks, mini-golf, dinner theaters, and every type of retail store you can imagine, send you crashing right back down to the real world. It's the yin and the yang of East Tennessee. The quieter sides of Cosby and Townsend offer a middle road for those who want it.

HISTORY
Geologic History

The Smoky Mountains are old. They were formed between 200 and 300 million years ago, when the African and North American continental plates collided, causing great peaks to form. Over the succeeding millennia, the

Smoky Mountains weathered away, creating the soft, rounded peaks that now define the mountain range. By comparison, the Himalayas are nearly newborn at 50 million years old.

The park's diverse array of ecosystems, plants, and animals can be traced to the last Ice Age, when glaciers covered large parts of what is now the United States. Animals and plants from northern climes moved southward to escape the ice, and they found refuge in the Smoky Mountains. When the ice receded, many species remained, having adapted to their new home.

Human Settlement

Native Americans lived in the Smokies and their foothills beginning around 7,000 B.C. When the first European explorers traveled through what is now Tennessee, they found the Cherokee Indians, a politically and economically sophisticated tribe of Indians linked to the Iroquois nation.

The first white settlers established homesteads in the Smoky Mountains near Cherokee, North Carolina, in 1795. In 1814 the first families settled in Cataloochee, and seven years later settlers arrived in Cades Cove. Mountain homesteads began to appear in other lowland areas of the Smokies, and along rivers and streams. By 1850 there were 451 residents in Cades Cove, and other large settlements in Cataloochee and Greenbrier.

Life in the mountains was not easy. Families survived off the land, growing crops and raising livestock. Nearly everything they had—tools, clothing, household goods, and games—came from the forests that surrounded them. Corn was the most important crop, and water-powered gristmills were used to grind corn into cornmeal—a staple of life.

The landscape of the Smokies was to change dramatically during the first 30 years of the 20th century. Logging companies, which had previously passed by the mountains owing to their difficult terrain, looked again, inspired by greed and the arrival of railroads in the region. Little River Lumber Company was the first logging company

to arrive in the Smokies in 1903, and the last to leave in 1939, after the creation of the national park. Loggers felled millions of old-growth trees—by the time the last axe struck, only 20 percent of the virgin forest remained. Logging led to forest fires, which sometimes raged for months, and erosion, which polluted rivers and streams.

Logging changed the lifestyle of mountain residents, too. Logging towns appeared seemingly overnight. Logging jobs paid money, and so began the evolution from subsistence to wage living. Residents were also able to sell goods and services to the loggers and logging executives; the very first hotel in Gatlinburg opened to house timber buyers who came to the area.

The environmental toll of such aggressive logging was one of the reasons that folks started to talk about protecting the mountains through a national park.

Establishing a Park

Looking back today, it is remarkable that the Great Smoky Mountains National Park exists at all. It took 17 years, and the combined efforts of Tennessee and North Carolina residents, plus local, state, and federal politicians, to achieve the complicated and daunting job of setting up the park.

The primary challenge was that by the 1920s, when talk of the park began in earnest, the land was in private hands. Some was owned by about 4,000 mountain residents, but the greatest expanses belonged to lumber companies, which had been plundering the mountainsides for timber since the turn of the century.

Early park boosters were businesspeople and politicians from East Tennessee and western North Carolina, who argued that a park would be an economic boon for the region. They foresaw a future when visitors would come in droves to see the park, spending money in the gateway communities on their way. Boosters launched an all-out public relations campaign to promote a park, and in 1926 alone residents pledged $1 million towards the purchase of lands.

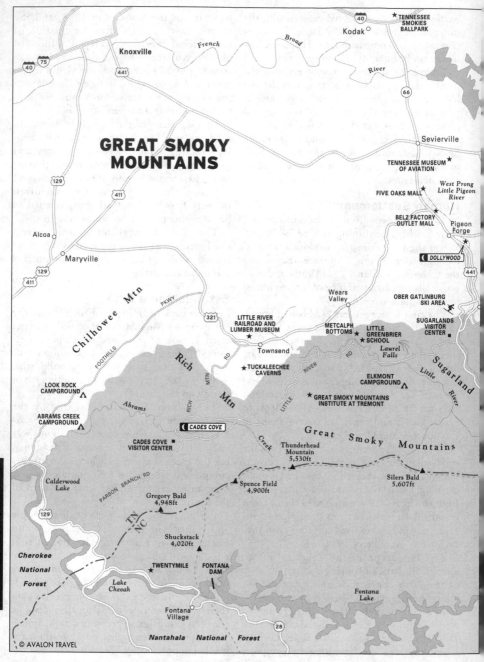

GREAT SMOKY MOUNTAINS

Knoxville

Kodak

TENNESSEE SMOKIES BALLPARK

French Broad River

Sevierville

TENNESSEE MUSEUM OF AVIATION

FIVE OAKS MALL

West Prong Little Pigeon River

BELZ FACTORY OUTLET MALL

Pigeon Forge

DOLLYWOOD

Alcoa

Maryville

Chilhowee Mtn

Wears Valley

OBER GATLINBURG SKI AREA

LITTLE RIVER RAILROAD AND LUMBER MUSEUM

METCALPH BOTTOMS

LITTLE GREENBRIER SCHOOL

SUGARLANDS VISITOR CENTER

Townsend

Laurel Falls

Sugarland

FOOTHILLS PKWY

Rich Mtn

TUCKALEECHEE CAVERNS

LITTLE RIVER

RICH MTN RD

LITTLE RIVER

ELKMONT CAMPGROUND

Little River

LOOK ROCK CAMPGROUND

Abrams

GREAT SMOKY MOUNTAINS INSTITUTE AT TREMONT

ABRAMS CREEK CAMPGROUND

CADES COVE

CADES COVE VISITOR CENTER

Creek

Great Smoky Mountains

Thunderhead Mountain 5,530ft

Silers Bald 5,607ft

Calderwood Lake

PARSON BRANCH RD

Spence Field 4,900ft

Gregory Bald 4,948ft

TN NC

Shuckstack 4,020ft

Cherokee National Forest

TWENTYMILE

FONTANA DAM

Lake Cheoah

Fontana Lake

Fontana Village

Nantahala National Forest

© AVALON TRAVEL

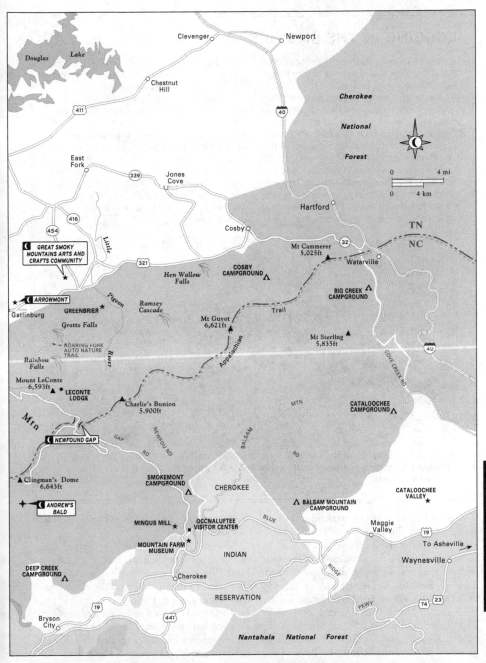

LOGGING IN THE SMOKIES

It comes as a surprise to many visitors today, but at the time that the Great Smoky Mountains National Park was dedicated in 1940, it was largely denuded by logging. Beginning around 1903, timber companies logged the mountains, felling trees to satisfy the growing demand for lumber. It is estimated that 2 billion board feet of lumber came out of the Smokies during this period.

Logging companies built railroads, roads, and towns, the names of which – Elkmont, Tremont, Smokemont, and Proctor – remain as place names in the park today. The environmental effects of logging were devastating. Fires burnt logged areas, leaving the mountainside bare. Streams and rivers swelled with muddy water, caused by erosion and landslides.

Lumber companies fought bitterly against the creation of a park. They took the government to court – one case reached the U.S. Supreme Court – a tactic that was probably aimed mainly at stalling the park long enough to squeeze even more lumber from the mountains. The last timber was extracted from the Smokies in 1939 by Little River Lumber Company in the Tremont area. By 1940, only 20 percent of park lands were covered by old-growth forests.

COURTESY OF LIBRARY OF CONGRESS / JOE MURPHY JR.

A locomotive steams up the Little River circa 1909; before the national park was established, logging companies harvested some 80 percent of the forest in the Smoky Mountains.

The popularity of the park idea among residents drew the attention of state and federal politicians. In 1926 president Calvin Coolidge signed a bill committing the federal government to begin development of a national park in the Great Smokies, as soon as 423,000 acres of land were provided by the states of North Carolina and Tennessee. The states then offered $1 million each for land purchases, and the final $5 million was given by philanthropist John D. Rockefeller Jr. in memory of his mother, Laura Spellman Rockefeller.

Money in hand, states-appointed commissions had the difficult task of purchasing land. The timber companies resisted. First they tried to derail the project itself and later they sought to get the highest possible price for their land—much of which had now been stripped bare of trees. The states took five of the companies to court, a process that depleted funds meant for land purchase and allowed the timber companies time to continue logging in the Smokies.

In part because of the devastating effects of continued logging, support for a park grew even stronger. In 1933 president Franklin D. Roosevelt reversed a previous federal position and earmarked federal money for the purchase of land. By 1940, when the park was dedicated, the U.S. government had contributed more than $2 million.

Perhaps the biggest losers from the park project were the 4,000 people who lived within park boundaries. With no deep pockets like those of the timber companies, they were often stuck taking very little in financial compensation for their homes and farms. Some older residents chose to stay in the park—they sold their property to the government and leased it back for the duration of their lives. But making a livelihood on a land where they were now forbidden to hunt, fish with bait, or cultivate crops was near impossible. Some residents, like the five Walker sisters who lived in a cabin in Little Greenbrier until the 1950s, managed to survive. Others, however, moved to communities outside the park and began new lives.

Great Smoky Mountains National Park was dedicated on September 2, 1940. President Roosevelt came to stand at Newfound Gap and dedicate the Great Smoky Mountains National Park. Among his words were these: "In this park we shall conserve the pine, the redbud, the dogwood, the azalea, the rhododendron, the trout and the thrush for the happiness of the American people. The old frontier that put the hard fiber in the American spirit and the long muscles on the American back, lives and will live in these untamed mountains to give future generations a sense of the land from which their forefathers hewed their homes."

If you watch the short introductory video at park visitors centers, you will see footage of the presidential caravan as it made its way up the mountain to Newfound Gap for the dedication ceremony. The footage of that difficult drive up to the top of the mountain is a powerful symbol of the remarkable efforts and convergence of circumstances that gave rise to this remarkable national park.

ORIENTATION

The crest of the Smokies forms the boundary between Tennessee and North Carolina, bisecting the park from northeast to southwest in an unbroken chain that rises more than 5,000 feet for more than 36 miles. Elevations in the park range from 875 feet to 6,643 feet.

Most people arrive in the park through Gatlinburg, a very touristy hamlet located in the middle of the northern park boundary. To the southwest is Townsend, which has hotels and restaurants but far, far less of both. Cosby, at the eastern side of the Tennessee boundary, is the quietest gateway point of all.

PLANNING YOUR TRIP

As the most-visited national park in the nation, Great Smoky Mountains can seem crowded. Some 9 million people visit the park each year, most of them in their own cars, which clog roadways and fill parking lots. The busiest months are June, July, and August, when some 3.5 million people will visit. The second most popular time is during the peak of the fall foliage show, which generally happens during the last two weeks of October. More than one million people come to the Smokies each October.

There are some effective strategies for avoiding the crowds. First, avoid peak season. If you must come during the summer, or October, visit during the week instead of on weekends. Also, set out early in the day. Most park roads get busy after 10 A.M., and the early mornings can be lovely times to see the sights.

Another good way to avoid the crowds in the Smokies is to get off the beaten track. There is a crowd mentality among most park visitors, which takes them to Sugarlands, Cades Cove, Newfound Gap, and Clingmans Dome, leaving the rest of the park to you. Plan an itinerary that allows you to enter the park through Cosby, Townsend, or another of the secondary gateways and then to explore some of the lesser-known attractions, such as Abrams Creek, Greenbrier, and Cosby.

The final, and single best, way of shedding the crowds is to get out of your car. Among the miles of hiking trails in the Smokies, only a few are highly trafficked. Even the most popular of hiking trails, such as Chimney Tops and Grotto Falls, are downright empty compared to the park's roads. It is well worth the sore muscles and sweat to enjoy some of the park's majesty all alone.

A Word About Driving

Distances to various sites within the park are relatively short; it is 34 miles from Cherokee, North Carolina, to Gatlinburg. But the drives are not quick. National park roads are winding two-lane blacktops. It can take hours to drive from Gatlinburg to Newfound Gap due to traffic congestion and the steep and windy nature of the road. If you are keen on avoiding traffic jams, consider entering the park through either Townsend or Cosby, and start your day early.

Weather

Always check the weather forecast before you come to the Smokies. Temperatures in the park, and especially at the high elevations, can be as much as 30 degrees colder than those in the surrounding area. In summer this is welcome, but in the winter it can be deadly. Rainfall in the park ranges from 55 inches per year in the valleys and 85 inches per year on the peaks, more than is received anywhere else in the United States except the Pacific Northwest.

Seasons

Spring in the Smokies is the season of variable weather; it can be sunny and warm one day and snowy the next. Spring rainfall can cause rivers and streams to swell without warning. Summer is generally hot, with lots of haze and humidity. Afternoon thunderstorms are not uncommon.

Autumn is the park's greatest season. The fall foliage draws thousands of people, and for good reason. The weather is generally cool and crisp, with snow beginning at the high

© SUSANNA HENIGHAN POTTER

The Parkway in Gatlinburg is almost always clogged with foot and vehicle traffic.

elevations in November. Winter is deep in the high elevations; Newfound Gap experiences an average of 69 inches of snowfall per year. In lower elevations only a few inches fall. Many secondary roads are closed during the winter due to frequent snow and ice.

Planning Your Time

If you have only one day in the Smokies, choose between a day hike or a drive to Clingmans Dome. Make the choice based on your own capacity for hiking, the weather (Clingmans Dome is often enveloped in haze), and the season (avoid Clingmans Dome during peak visitation periods).

If you have a few days, go camping. Spend a day hiking, a day driving, and a day exploring Cades Cove. Stout hikers should make reservations at LeConte Lodge and plan a rest day between the hike in and the hike out to enjoy the peace and quiet at the top of the mountain.

Sights

◖ NEWFOUND GAP

This mountain pass located at 5,048 feet is one of the Smokies' greatest attractions. Named because it was not discovered until the 1850s, Newfound Gap is the lowest pass over the mountains. Today's visitors enjoy its refreshing cool air, its views, and the fact that you can straddle the state line between Tennessee and North Carolina. It was here, on September 2, 1940, that President Franklin D. Roosevelt dedicated the Great Smoky Mountains National Park.

There is a large parking lot here, with the best views looking southward into the Oconaluftee River Valley in North Carolina. The Appalachian Trail, which travels the ridge of the mountains through the Smokies, crosses the road here at Newfound Gap. You can hike along the AT in either direction for as long as you like.

Clingmans Dome

Come to Clingmans Dome for the views. Here at the highest point in the park (6,643 feet), you can climb an observation tower that takes you up above the treetops. It is a stunning view and a refreshing experience, and afterwards you can say that you were on the top of Ol' Smoky.

Clingmans Dome is the highest peak in the Smokies, and the third-highest peak in the eastern United States. Once called Smoky Dome, because it is rounded like a dome, it is now called Clingmans after Thomas Lanier Clingman, a North Carolina attorney and politician who was involved in early attempts to measure and catalogue mountain peaks.

The concrete observation tower atop Clingmans Dome dates to the 1960s. Immediately in front of the tower there are two steel-frame towers, a communications tower and a climactic data collection tower. On a clear day, the 360-degree view is truly awesome. Fontana Lake, Mount Mitchell, Knoxville, and Mount LeConte are just a few of the landmarks visible from the tower. Unfortunately, visibility from Clingmans Dome is often limited—often by as much as 80 percent—by air pollution. Park officials blame coal-burning power plants in the Southeastern United States for most of the pollution, which can also pose a health risk for people with breathing difficulties.

Another environmental problem evident at Clingmans Dome is the infestation of mature Fraser fir trees by the balsam wooly adelgid. The dry skeletons of these once-majestic evergreens haunt the mountainsides here. Fraser firs were the iconic champions of the unique spruce-fir forest that exists in the high elevations of the Smokies. But beginning in 1963, the adelgid, an aphid-like insect less than one millimeter long, arrived in the Smokies after coming to the United States from Europe, probably on nursery stock. Without any natural predators, the adelgids thrived on the sap of mature Fraser fir trees. Today, park officials estimate that some 70 percent of mature Fraser fir trees have been killed by the adelgids; the rest are infested. You can identify an infested tree by the white wooly mass covering its bark. Sometimes it causes the tree to look whitewashed.

Park rangers treat a handful of Fraser fir trees with a soap solution to control the adelgids, but it would be too expensive to do this throughout the forest. The park has transplanted some firs to lower elevations in the park, where they can be protected and preserved in the event that scientists discover a way to guard against the microscopic predators.

When planning to visit Clingmans Dome, check the weather first. Remember that it is often much more cold and wet on top of Ol' Smoky than it is in the lowlands. On cloudy or overcast days, there will be no visibility at all.

Clingmans Dome is located at the end of a seven-mile spur road. It is a half-mile walk along a steep, but paved, footpath from the parking area to the base of the observation tower. The road to Clingmans Dome is closed from December 1 through March 31.

Mount LeConte

Mount LeConte seems to keep watch over the Smokies. The 6,593-foot peak stands sentry over the foothills; its size makes it easy to identify, even from a distance. Accessible only by foot, Mount LeConte is a destination for hikers who yearn for a sense of accomplishment. And what an accomplishment it is, with spectacular views and beautiful scenery along the way. The peak is also home to LeConte Lodge, the only indoor accommodation in the park.

ELKMONT

An old logging town that later became a summer resort community, Elkmont is now a campground and the starting point for several day hikes. The park has considered tearing down the deteriorating remains of summer cottages here, but for now they still stand—a reminder of the days before the park existed. Present-day vacationers can lay their heads at the 220-site Elkmont campground.

Elkmont is noted for the appearance here every June of synchronous fireflies. People come in droves to watch the insect show, which normally lasts about two weeks and begins around the second week of June. The park service offers trolley transportation to Elkmont during the firefly show.

Metcalph Bottoms

Metcalph Bottoms is a day-use area popular for picnicking and swimming. From here you can walk one mile to **Little Greenbrier School,** a 19th-century split-log schoolhouse with original furniture.

Just west of Metcalph Bottoms along the Little River Road are two water attractions. **The Sinks** is a waterfall with a pool so deep it once swallowed an entire derailed logging train, or so they say. Swimming here is not recommended, but it is nice to sit and watch the water crash over the falls.

Close to the intersection with Highway 73, which goes to Townsend, is the **Townsend Y,** probably the most popular swimming hole in the park. The river here is relatively wide and smooth, and the grassy bank is perfect for sunbathing.

◖ CADES COVE

Historical and natural attractions lie side-by-side in Cades Cove, a flat mountain valley on the Townsend side of the park. It was a population center before the park was established.

Access to Cades Cove is along an 11-mile one-way loop road. Traffic moves slowly through this pastoral landscape, so plan on spending at least two hours on the loop. Two two-way lanes cross the cove and allow you to shorten or lengthen your drive.

The roads in Cades Cove are closed to vehicular traffic on Wednesday and Saturday mornings until 10 A.M. from May to September. Exploring on foot or bike is a lovely way to experience the cove.

History

There are indications that Cherokee and other native Americans used Cades Cove for hunting and as a way to travel through the rough mountain terrain. But it is believed that whites were the first people to settle permanently in this fertile yet remote place. Early homesteaders came in the 1820s, and by 1850 the population was nearly 700. Families—with names like Jobe, Oliver, Tipton, Shields, Burchfield, Cable, Sparkes, and Gregory—farmed, raised cattle, collected wild chestnuts, and hunted. They built churches, a school, gristmill, and homes. Theirs was the hard yet happy life of the mountains.

In the 1920s and '30s, the government came to buy up Cades Cove land for the park. Some of the remaining 600 residents agreed to the financial settlement and left the cove. Others took less money, but retained the right to live in Cades Cove until they died. One man, John W. Oliver, took Tennessee to court, but he lost and moved out in 1937. During the 1940s, the population of Cades

Cades Cove

Cove dropped quickly. The school closed in 1944 and the post office shuttered in 1947. By the end of the decade it was a ghost town, left to the imaginations of visitors yet to come.

Historic Buildings

Cades Cove is home to more than 70 historic buildings, which makes it the best place in the park to learn about human inhabitation of the Smokies. Along the 11-mile loop you will have the opportunity to explore various homesteads, including the **John Oliver Place,** the **Henry Whitehead Place,** and **Carter Shields Cabin.** Historic churches include the 1902 **Methodist Church,** the 1887 **Primitive Baptist Church,** and the 1915 **Missionary Baptist Church.**

At the extreme western end of the loop is the **Cable Mill** area, which you should explore on foot. The gristmill here is original; it was built by John P. Cable in the 1870s. Outbuildings around the mill were moved here from other parts of the park. They include a cantilever barn, blacksmith shop, smokehouse, and the Gregg-Cable House, believed to be the first frame house built in the cove.

There is a parking lot, visitors center, and restrooms at the Cable Mill.

Wildlife

Deer are a common sight in Cades Cove. You may also see bears, river otters, elk, woodchuck, wild turkeys, rabbits, and squirrels. Elusive animals of the cove include bobcat, raccoons, and gray and red foxes.

Over the years, the park service has debated how to manage the Cades Cove environment. Since it is a "historical district," the objective is not to return the cove to nature but to preserve its open spaces and historic buildings. In the early years, the park service issued grazing permits, built large drainage ditches, and introduced non-native fescue grass. More recently, they have

BLACK BEARS

Black bear attacks are rare, but they have happened. In May 2000 a 50-year-old schoolteacher from Cosby was attacked and killed by two bears in the Elkmont area of the Great Smoky Mountains National Park. In 2006, a six-year-old girl was killed near Benton Falls in the southern Cherokee National Forest; the girl's mother and two-year-old brother were injured in the same attack.

If you ever see a bear in the woods, you should proceed with extreme caution and follow this advice, issued by the National Park Service:

If you see a bear remain watchful. Do not approach it. If your presence causes the bear to change its behavior (stops feeding, changes its travel direction, watches you, etc.) then you're too close. Being too close may promote aggressive behavior from the bear such as running toward you, making loud noises, or swatting the ground. The bear is demanding more space. Don't run, but slowly back away, watching the bear. Try to increase the distance between you and the bear. The bear will probably do the same.

If a bear persistently follows or approaches you, without vocalizing or paw swatting, try changing your direction. If the bear continues to follow you, stand your ground. If the bear gets closer, talk loudly or shout at it. Act aggressively and try to intimidate the bear. Act together as a group if you have companions. Make yourselves look as large as possible (for example, move to higher ground). Throw non-food objects such as rocks at the bear. Use a deterrent such as a stout stick. Don't run and don't turn away from the bear. Don't leave food for the bear; this encourages further problems.

Most injuries from black bear attacks are minor and result from a bear attempting to get at people's food. If the bear's behavior indicates that it is after your food and you're physically attacked, separate yourself from the food and slowly back away.

If the bear shows no interest in your food and you're physically attacked, fight back aggressively with any available object – the bear may consider you as prey! Help protect others by reporting all bear incidents to a park ranger immediately. Above all, keep your distance from bears.

If you see a bear in the woods, proceed with extreme caution.

PHOTO COURTESY OF TENNESSEE DEPARTMENT OF TOURIST DEVELOPMENT

GREAT SMOKY MOUNTAINS

rethought these policies. They are phasing out grazing and haying, resorting instead to prescribed burns to keep the cove open. Native grasses and wildflowers are being reintroduced, and drainage ditches are being plugged so that low-lying areas will return to being wetlands.

Rich Mountain
You can leave Cades Cove (but not enter it) along the one-way Rich Mountain Road, which climbs up and over Rich Mountain and deposits you in Tuckaleechee Cove, near Townsend. The road is steep and curvy, offering lovely views of the cove below. It is closed in winter, from mid-November through mid-March.

Parsons Branch
Another exit from Cades Cove is Parsons Branch Road, a one-way seasonal road that departs the cove near the Cable Mill and heads through unspoiled mountains. After joining with Forge Creek Road, this route ends at Highway 129 and Calderwood Lake. It is 10 miles from Cades Cove to Highway 129.

From 129 you can drive east into North Carolina or west to Chilhowee and the Foothills Parkway in Blount County.

ABRAMS CREEK
Abrams Creek is a lovely and relatively uncrowded corner of the Smokies. Accessible by car only from Happy Valley Road, this is one part of the park you can enjoy without setting foot (or tire) in any of the traditional entry points.

Abrams Creek is the focal point of this recreation area. The creek is deep and wide enough for swimming along the picnic area and campground. It is a good place for fishing, too. From the campground, you can hike four miles to **Abram's Falls**, a 20-foot waterfall. Continue on past the falls another 2.5 miles and you reach Cades Cove.

Foothills Parkway
An 18-mile limited access scenic parkway, the western portion of the Foothills Parkway connects Chilhowee Lake with Townsend. While strictly located outside the bounds of the national park, the parkway offers stunning views of the western reaches of the Smokies. It is lightly traveled and a good alternative to other, more crowded scenic roads.

The parkway follows the ridge of Chilhowee Mountain. There is a campground, picnic area, and observation tower at **Look Rock**.

Seemingly in an effort to confuse visitors, the parkway actually consists of two separate roadways. The eastern section, also called the Foothills Parkway, is a six-mile stretch that connects Cosby with I-40.

Fontana Dam
The tallest dam east of the Rocky Mountains, Fontana was built in 36 short months starting in 1942. Spurred by World War II, crews worked in three shifts 24 hours a day on the construction. Fontana is some 480 feet tall and required a mind-boggling 3 million cubic yards of concrete. Completed, it had a power-generating capacity of 293,600 kilowatts.

The Appalachian Trail passes over the top of the dam, and you can too. It is a mammoth concrete creation—equivalent to a 50-story skyscraper. The **visitors center** (daily 9 A.M.–7 P.M.) is open from May to November, but only when the U.S. Homeland Security threat level is below high (orange). There are picnic tables and an overlook around the dam. Of note to hikers are the restrooms with hot-water showers, dubbed the Fontana Hilton by through-hikers on the Appalachian Trail.

Fontana impounds the Little Tennessee River. The resulting **Fontana Lake** is popular for fishing, boating, and swimming. Fontana Village in North Carolina offers shopping, dining, and lodging options.

GREENBRIER
Greenbrier is a pleasant day-use area located on the banks of the Little Pigeon River.

Greenbrier Cove, located where the Middle Prong runs into the Pigeon River, was a population center before the park was formed. Swimming and fishing are popular pursuits here today.

Greenbrier is accessible from Highway 321, which runs from Cosby to Gatlinburg. It is possible to get here without driving through Pigeon Forge or Gatlinburg, a plus for many visitors. It is a 3.2-mile drive along the Little Pigeon from Highway 321 to Greenbrier Cove. At the cove, the road forks. Turn left along the Middle Prong to find the trailheads for the Old Settlers Trail and the Ramsey Cascades Trail. Turn right for picnic areas and a one-mile trail that leads you to historic homesteads and a cemetery.

COSBY

Here, Cosby refers to the recreation area at the northeast corner of the park, not the town that lies nearby, outside the bounds of the park. This is one of the least-visited areas in the park, offering hiking, waterfalls, camping, and swimming.

The Cosby Creek provides opportunities for swimming and wading. It is a 2.1-mile hike along the Gabes Mountain Trail to **Hen Wallow Falls.** Several other hiking trails pass through Cosby, including the Low Gap Trail that climbs 2.5 miles to the Appalachian Trail.

OCONALUFTEE

This is North Carolina's main gateway to the park. Adjacent to the Oconaluftee Visitor Center is the **Mountain Farm Museum** (828/497-1900, sunrise–sunset, free), a village of original log structures collected from throughout the park. A highlight is seeing a log home built of American Chestnut, before the Chestnut blight. About half a mile north of the Farm Museum is the **Mingus Mill** (mid-March–mid-November daily 9 A.M.–5 P.M., plus Thanksgiving weekend, free), a water-powered gristmill that still operates. Here you can watch as corn is ground into cornmeal.

About three miles north of Oconaluftee is Smokemont. Once a lumber company town, Smokemont is now a recreation area with hiking trails, a picnic area, and a campground.

Located near Bryson City, North Carolina, **Deep Creek** is a recreation area noted for its waterfalls. It is also the location of the Deep Creek and Indian Creek Trails, both of which allow mountain bikes.

A North Carolina attraction of special note is the **Blue Ridge Parkway,** a two-lane scenic blacktop highway that traverses Nantahala and Pisgah National Forests before heading north into Virginia.

CATALOOCHEE

Cataloochee is, in some respects, the other Cades Cove. In other respects, it is quite different. A valley surrounded by mountains, Cataloochee was once the most populous community in what is now the national park. Its name is derived from the Cherokee's word for the area, Gadalutsi, which means "standing up in a row," or "wave upon wave."

Like Cades Cove, Cataloochee is a cove surrounded by wooded mountains. Historic buildings, including a school, churches, a barn, and several homesteads, provide a sense of human inhabitation. In 2001, the park service introduced a herd of elk in Cataloochee; elk are most likely to be seen in the early morning or evenings.

Unlike Cades Cove, Cataloochee is not crowded. The most obvious reason for this is that getting here is a bit of a challenge. The easiest way to get to Cataloochee is to take I-40 east into North Carolina. At exit 20, it's 11 miles along Cove Creek Road to Cataloochee. The last two miles of your journey are along a gravel road, which is fine for standard passenger vehicles but slow going nonetheless.

Those who make the journey to Cataloochee will be rewarded with scenes of an idyllic mountain valley and notable trout fishing, as well as facilities to camp, hike, and picnic.

Driving Tours

Taking a relaxing drive through the park is a great way to see its most prominent attractions. During weekends in the summer and October expect long lines of traffic on the most popular roads. Try to choose a weekday and strike out early to avoid crowds.

The mountain ascents and descents can strain your vehicle. Watch your engine temperature carefully, especially in the summer, and use a low gear when coming down the mountain. Slow-moving vehicles should use pull-outs.

Several park roads are closed in winter. If you plan to visit between November and April, call the park first to confirm closures.

As you drive through the park, you will see signs for **Quiet Walkways.** These trails are designed to encourage you to get out of your car and stroll for a few minutes through the forest. Some of the walkways are short—about half a mile—while others join up with longer trails. Walk as far as you like and then turn back and return to your car the way you came.

NEWFOUND GAP ROAD

Journey through the mountain pass that early settlers used to reach the Tennessee side of the mountains. Newfound Gap Road travels 30 miles from Sugarlands Visitor Center to Oconaluftee in North Carolina. The road climbs some 3,000 feet, traveling through ecosystems including cove hardwood, pine-oak, and northern hardwood forests. At the top of the pass you will find an evergreen spruce-fir forest.

About two miles into your drive, you will find the **Campbell Overlook,** where you can see Mount LeConte and other large peaks. There is also a display that identifies the different types of forest found in the Smokies.

At 4.6 miles is the Chimney Tops Picnic Area, once a common place for bear sightings. If you see a bear remember to keep your distance and do not feed it. Less than a mile past the picnic area is a series of three overlooks giving you views of **Sugarland Mountain** and **Chimney Tops.** From here you can see some of the only virgin spruce forest left in the eastern United States.

After passing along the West Prong of the Little Pigeon River and entering into the harsh northern elevations of the Smokies, you will find **Morton Overlook,** situated at 4,837 feet. Here you can look down on the ribbon of asphalt that you just traveled.

Newfound Gap is located at mile 13.2 on your journey. This mountain pass offers spectacular views. Just two-tenths of a mile beyond Newfound Gap is the entrance to the seven-mile spur road that will take you to Clingmans Dome, the highest point in the park.

From this point, the road descends along the Oconaluftee Valley through the North Carolina side of the park. You will pass several more overlooks and quiet walkways. At mile 29 is the **Mingus Mill,** an old gristmill that operates from early spring through the fall. The drive ends at the **Oconaluftee Visitor Center,** located adjacent to the **Mountain Farm Museum.**

CADES COVE LOOP

Cades Cove is one of the most popular sights in the national park, and a favorite place for auto touring. Traffic along the one-way 11-mile loop road proceeds slowly, and there are frequent opportunities to stop and explore on foot. Beware that during peak visitation, it can take five hours to drive the loop—longer than it would take to walk it. Set out early in the day to have it more to yourself.

The drive begins at the **orientation shelter,** located near the Cades Cove campground and picnic area. If you don't already have one, pick up the detailed guide to Cades Cove here. The first homestead you arrive at is that of John Oliver. If it's crowded, drive on—there are more cabins later in the tour.

You will next pass Cades Cove's three extant churches. These beautiful buildings date from 1887–1915. Opposite the Missionary Baptist Church is Rich Mountain Road, a winding, steep road that goes to Townsend. It is closed during the winter.

At the extreme southwestern corner of the cove is the **Cable Mill** area. Here you will find restrooms and Cades Cove's most substantial visitors center. There is also a collection of historic buildings to explore on foot.

As you drive along the southern side of the cove, you will pass a series of homesteads, including the Dan Lawrence Place, Tipton Place, and the Carter Shields Cabin.

There are two north–south "lanes" that cut through the loop. If you have time, and traffic allows it, drive through one of them to see the broad, flat expanse of the cove more closely.

ROARING FORK AUTO NATURE TRAIL

This six-mile paved road departs from Gatlinburg. To find it, turn left at traffic light No. 8 in Gatlinburg and follow the signs to the park. As you enter the park, roll down your windows to feel the cooler and fresher air of the forest. Sights along the way include the **Noah "Bud" Ogle Place,** where you can get out and walk a short nature trail through the forest. Here you'll see parts of the homestead, including a tubmill and wooden flume.

Just past the Ogle Place, the road becomes one-way and winds for six miles along Roaring Fork, a fast-moving mountain stream. Along the way you will pass more historic structures and the trailhead for Grotto Falls, a popular and relatively easy hike. At the end of the drive is the waterfall **Place of a Thousand Drips,** which runs during wet weather.

Hiking

Hiking is the best way to truly experience the grandeur of the Smoky Mountains. On the trail you will feel the mountain air, see wildflowers and trees, and experience views inaccessible by road. Hiking destinations can be historic structures, crisp waterfalls, or one of the Smokies' seemingly enchanted highland balds. Or you may just wish to walk for walking's sake—to acquire a more intimate understanding of the forest and its inhabitants.

In total the Smokies have a whopping 800 miles of hiking trails. Only Yellowstone and Yosemite have more miles of trails.

PLANNING YOUR HIKE

The Great Smoky Mountains Association publishes the best and most reliable guides to hiking in the Smokies. These guides provide detailed descriptions of hikes, elevations, hazards, and features you will see along the way. They are an investment worth making if you plan to do a lot of hiking. *Hiking Trails of the Smokies* is the authoritative volume. *Day Hikes*

in the Smokies and *History Hikes in the Smokies* offer specialized focus.

You can buy the official NPS trail map for less than a dollar at any visitors center. This map shows trail locations, distances, and the locations of backcountry campsites. The National Geographic/Trail Illustrated map of the Smokies, available at visitors centers and online, is worth the $10 investment, however. It shows much more detail and will hold up to the elements.

Guides and Gear

The best guide service in the Smokies is offered by **A Walk in the Woods** (4413 Scenic Drive E., Gatlinburg, 865/436-8283, www.awalkinthewoods.com), run by husband-and-wife team Erik and Vesna Plakanis, naturalists and mountain enthusiasts. These helpful folks do it all: They lead day hikes and backpacking trips; they offer trip plans for backpackers too busy to do the advance legwork themselves; they shuttle hikers to trailheads or pick them

PHOTO COURTESY OF TENNESSEE DEPARTMENT OF TOURIST DEVELOPMENT

Hiking is the best way to experience the majesty of the Great Smoky Mountains National Park.

up at their destination; and they offer special classes about birds, wildflowers, and medicinal plants of the Smokies. They also rent backpacking and other mountain gear, so you can try it out as a hobby before making an investment in expensive gear.

For last-minute gear purchases visit the folks at **The Happy Hiker** (905 River Rd., Gatlinburg, 865/436-6000). They sell it all, plus books, maps, and other useful stuff.

DAY HIKES

There are as many day hikes in the Smokies as there are days. Below are some of the most highly recommended choices.

Loop Hikes
RICH MOUNTAIN LOOP
(8.5 miles, moderate)
This loop offers lovely views of Cades Cove. In spring you may see mountain laurel and in the fall the colors are spectacular. Park in the large lot at the start of the Cades Cove Loop Road. You will travel along the Rich Mountain

Loop Trail (2.9 miles), Indian Grave Gap Trail (2.5 miles), and the Crooked Arm Ridge Trail (2.2 miles).

CUCUMBER GAP
(5.5 miles, easy)
Cucumber Gap explores the Elkmont area and follows the Little River. Expect beautiful wildflowers in spring. Park near the barricade at the start of Little River Trail above Elkmont campground. You will travel on Little River Trail (2.4 miles) before turning back along the Cucumber Gap Trail (2.4 miles) and Jakes Creek Trail (0.3 mile), which passes Elkmont's abandoned summer cottages. Return to your car along the road.

Waterfall Hikes
LAUREL FALLS
(2.6 miles round-trip, easy)
Laurel Falls may be the most popular hike in the Smokies. The pathway is paved all the way to the falls, and the trailhead is located a short drive east of Sugarlands along the Little River

GREAT SMOKY MOUNTAINS

SAFE HIKING

When planning a day hike in the Smokies, take some time to consider your safety. These common-sense precautions will ensure you have a memorable hike, for the right reasons.

Plan ahead. Using trail maps or guides, determine your route before you set out, and let someone know where you'll be headed and when you expect to be back. Cell phones rarely work on the trail.

Dress the part. Your clothes must protect you from the elements. Layering is always a good choice, since temperatures can vary on the trail and weather conditions can change. Wear sturdy shoes with ankle support. Wear wool or fleece clothing (especially socks), not cotton, which holds water and can make you cold.

Don't overestimate your ability. Be conservative when planning your walk and remember that most people average about 1.5 miles per hour. If you have never hiked before, or if it's been awhile, start with a day hike no longer than 5 miles. Be sure to give yourself enough time to wrap up before sunset, which can be as early as 5:30 P.M. in winter and as late as 9 P.M. in summer.

Eat and drink for energy. Bring water and food, even if you don't think you'll need it. Eat before you're hungry and keep hydrated as you

Planning ahead is the best way to ensure an uneventful and safe hike.

walk. Nuts, dried fruit, and chocolate are good energy foods, as are apples and oranges.

PHOTO COURTESY OF TENNESSEE DEPARTMENT OF TOURIST DEVELOPMENT

Road. If you walk on another 0.75 mile past the falls, you will reach stands of old-growth forest. Parking is limited at the trailhead.

RAMSEY CASCADES
(8 miles round-trip, strenuous)
Ramsey Cascades takes you to a spectacular 100-foot waterfall. The last two miles of the hike are through old-growth forest. The trailhead is located near the Greenbrier day-use area of the park.

HEN WALLOW FALLS
(4.2 miles round-trip, moderate)
Hen Wallow Falls takes you to a 45-foot waterfall. The walk originates near the Cosby picnic area.

Hikes with a View
CHIMNEY TOPS
(4 miles round-trip, strenuous)
This is a difficult but rewarding hike that takes you to the rock formations known as the Chimneys. The trailhead is located almost seven miles south of Sugarlands Visitor Center along the Newfound Gap Road.

ALUM CAVE BLUFF AND
MOUNT LECONTE
(10 miles round-trip, strenuous)
Alum Cave Bluff and Mount LeConte are destinations for seasoned hikers. It is 2.3 miles from the trailhead to Alum Cave Bluffs, and another 2.7 miles to Mount LeConte. (Don't be misled by the relatively short distances; this is a

GREAT SMOKY MOUNTAINS

challenging hike.) Pause for views at Cliff Tops and Myrtle Point. The trailhead for this excursion is located 6.8 miles south of Sugarlands along the Newfound Gap Road.

◖ ANDREW'S BALD
(3.6 miles round-trip, moderate)
Andrew's Bald is one of the Smokies' mysterious highland grassy meadows, called a bald. It is a lovely, magical place, great for relaxing in the sun or even playing a game of Frisbee or catch. The hike departs the Clingmans Dome parking area and travels Forney Ridge Trail.

CHARLIES BUNION
(8 miles round-trip, moderate)
Charlies Bunion follows the Appalachian Trail along the ridge of the mountains. The trail departs Newfound Gap and provides lovely views along the way. It passes through the spruce-fir forest, where you can see evidence of the Fraser fir's demise.

Strolls
GATLINBURG TRAIL
(3.8 miles round-trip, easy)
This trail connects the city of Gatlinburg with Sugarlands Visitor Center and follows the West Prong of the Little Pigeon River. The path is paved. Leashed dogs and bicycles are allowed.

CADES COVE NATURE TRAIL
(0.75 mile round-trip, easy)
Cades Cove Nature Trail takes you through pine and oak forest. The trail departs from near the Henry Whitehead Place, just past the intersection with Parsons Branch Road. A 50-cent trail guide available on-site points out notable plants and other sights.

BACKCOUNTRY CAMPING
Backcountry camping allows you to hike longer and reach more remote sights in the park. Backpackers can plan journeys of one, two, three, or more days, with nights spent at backcountry campsites and shelters. For many people, the self-sufficiency of carrying all that you need on your back is a joy. Twenty-four-hour immersion in the wilderness—sometimes without seeing another person—is equally appealing.

Preparation
Multi-day hiking journeys require planning. Consult reference guides and maps carefully. You can also call the volunteers at the **Backcountry Information Office** (865/436-1297, daily 9 A.M.–noon) for help planning your trip. As you plan your route, remember that five to eight miles is a reasonable distance to cover each day. You'll be carrying a heavy pack, and will need time at the beginning and end of each day to set up and break down camp.

Rules and Regulations
Every backcountry hiker is required to obtain a free permit from the park service. You can obtain these from most visitors centers and campgrounds, including Sugarlands, Cosby Campground Office, Greenbrier Ranger Station, Elkmont Campground, Cades Cove Campground Office, Abrams Creek Ranger Station, and Great Smoky Mountains Institute at Tremont.

All backcountry sites are near sources of water—although sometimes springs or creeks go dry. They have a cleared area for your tent and a cable system for hanging your food out of the reach of bears. Seventeen campsites and all of the Appalachian Trail shelters require advance reservations. These may be made up to a month ahead with the **Backcountry Reservation Office** (865/436-1231, daily 8 A.M.–6 P.M.). Remember, camping is allowed at backcountry sites only.

Several rules apply at backcountry sites: You can stay at any one site for a maximum of three nights, and a maximum of two nights at any backcountry shelter. No more than eight people can camp together at one site. Fires are prohibited, except at designated sites. Neither are you allowed to stake your tent at a shelter site.

Equipment
Certain equipment is essential for backcountry camping. You are advised to bring two

flashlights, water, raingear, comfortable ankle-supporting shoes, high-energy food, and extra clothing. Always carry a map and know how to use it. A camp stove, water-purification tablets, and a spade for burying human waste are also very useful. Of course, you will also need to carry a sleeping bag and tent for the night.

In the higher elevations, you must be prepared for cold, wet weather. Expect snow as early as October and as late as April.

Leave No Trace

As you hike and camp in the backcountry, remember that it is up to you to leave the environment as you met it. Never cut, deface, or take any plant, animal, or historic feature. Don't use soap to wash your dishes or bathe in streams and rivers. Human feces should be buried at least six inches deep at least 100 feet from the nearest water source.

Perhaps the most important rule is that all food should be stored at least 10 feet off the ground and 4 feet from the nearest tree limb. Most all backcountry sites have special cable systems for this purpose. This keeps food out of the reach of bears.

Other Recreation

BIKING

There are no dedicated mountain biking trails in the national park. While you can bike on any park road, many are unsuitable because they are narrow, steep, and clogged with cars. The best biking experience is the 11-mile Cades Cove loop, which is closed to vehicular traffic until 10 A.M. on Wednesday and Saturday mornings from May to September. You can rent bikes ($4) during the summer and fall from the Cades Cove store (865/448-9034), which is open daily 9 A.M.–5 P.M., with a 7 A.M. opening time on Wednesday and Saturday during the biking season.

Bikes are not allowed on park trails, with the exception of the Gatlinburg Trail, Oconaluftee River Trail, and the Deep Creek Trail. Less-traveled park roads that are usually good for biking are Greenbrier and Tremont Roads.

In the state of Tennessee, all children 16 years and younger are required to wear a helmet when they ride a bike. Adults are encouraged to do so as well.

HORSEBACK RIDING

Four concessionaires offer horseback riding trips in the park, starting in mid-March and ending in November. These outfitters will rent you a horse for about $20 an hour. Overnight packages are available.

Tennessee outfitters are **Cades Cove Stables** (Cades Cove, 865/448-6286), **Sugarlands Stables** (865/436-5634), and **Smoky Mountain Stables** (Gatlinburg, 865/436-5634). In North Carolina, **Smokemont Stables** (828/497-2373) is located near Cherokee.

Horses are allowed on certain trails inside the park. The NPS trail map indicates horse trails, as well as backcountry campsites where horses are allowed. In addition, there are five drive-in horse camps that provide access to backcountry horse trails. These camps are located at Cades Cove, Big Creek, Cataloochee, Round Bottom, and Towstring, and are open from April through mid-November. Reservations may be made by calling 877/444-6777 or visiting www.recreation.gov.

FISHING

All streams in the Smokies originate as mountain springs, burbling up along the high mountain ridge. At high elevations they flow quickly over steep, rocky beds. As more streams flow into one another, and the elevation drops, the streams widen and flow more slowly. They are no longer sheltered entirely by the forest canopy, and they become warmer. By the time they reach the park boundaries, they are rivers.

The diversity of the Smokies' streams and

THE RETURN OF THE BROOKIES

The Smokies' greatest fish story of the last decade has been that of the native brook trout. These beautiful fish, also called brookies or speckled trout, were once the only type of trout swimming in the Smokies' waters. They were high-elevation fish, found in fast-moving mountain streams as they dashed down mountainside. But logging and other pressures of the early 20th century nearly wiped out the brook trout. From 1934 to 1974, officials stocked park streams with other types of trout, including rainbow and brown trout, which quickly took over previous brook trout habitats. In 1976 park officials banned fishing for brook trout to protect the disappearing species. They also made a policy decision that stocking fish was contrary to the mission of the park.

But the story does not end there. In 1987, the National Park Service, working alongside other agencies and nonprofits, started to reintroduce the native brook trout, as well as remove rainbow and brown trout from certain streams. Park fisheries managers used a combination of electro-fishing and chemicals to remove non-native trout from stream segments that lie above waterfalls and other barriers that prevent upstream movement of fish.

The result of the reintroduction effort was that beginning in 2006 fishers were able fish for and keep brook trout in all park streams for the first time in nearly 30 years. The population of brook trout is being carefully monitored, and studies have shown that even with fishing, the population remains healthy and self-sustaining. For example, in 2007 officials found that brook trout were the only species of trout in 17 miles of streams, and they were coexisting with other types of trout in 69 additional miles.

Hurdles remain, however, chief among them being the acidification of high-elevation mountain streams due to air pollution. But for now, chalk one up for the brookies.

rivers means a diversity of fish. The fast-moving headwaters at high elevations are the native habitat of brook trout, also called brookies, or speckled trout. As streams reach elevations lower than 3,000 feet, other types of trout begin to appear, such as non-native rainbow and brown trout. Near the park boundaries, where waters are warmer and move more slowly, you will find these plus bass, shiners, minnows, shuckers, and darters.

Fishing in the Smokies is a sport, but it is also an opportunity to view wildlife and experience the rich ecosystem of mountain streams. Anglers, especially those who venture away from roads and into more remote areas of the park, will enjoy the sounds of running water and the sights of salamanders, insects, mammals, and wildflowers.

Guides

Get helpful local knowledge or brush up on your technique with a fishing guide. **Smoky Mountain Anglers** (376 E. Parkway, aka Hwy. 321, Gatlinburg, 865/436-8746, www.smokymountainanger.com) offers full- and half-day guided fishing trips starting at $135. They also sell hand-tied and commercial flies, plus all the other gear an angler would need.

Rules and Regulations

Fishing is governed by rules that have been established to protect species and the environment. It is up to individual anglers to takes these rules to heart so that the fishery remains strong and the surrounding environment remains in balance.

Fishing is allowed in almost all streams and rivers in the park. The park service closes one or two each season due to active brook trout restoration activities; call ahead or check the NPS website to find out which streams are closed.

Anglers must be in possession of a valid Tennessee or North Carolina fishing license, depending on where in the park they are fishing. The park service does not sell these licenses, but they are available online and at outfitters in Townsend, Gatlinburg, Cosby, and other gateway communities.

GREAT SMOKY MOUNTAINS

Live bait may not be used, and only single hooks are allowed. Fishing is allowed 30 minutes after official sunrise and must cease 30 minutes before official sunset. The daily bag limit is five fish, although up to 20 rock bass is allowed. Anglers must stop fishing as soon as they reach their bag limit. Smallmount bass and brook, rainbow, and brown trout must be at least seven inches long to be kept. There is no size limit for rock bass.

As you fish, be a good park citizen. Pick up any trash you may find and don't move or disrupt rocks, which are where many fish lay their eggs.

SWIMMING

There is nothing as refreshing or enlivening as a dip in the icy-cold waters of a mountain stream. The "Y," near the Townsend entrance to the park, is probably the most popular swimming hole in the park. Other good places to swim are at the Abrams Creek campground, the Greenbrier picnic area, and at Cosby.

Because swimming in rocky, fast-moving rivers can be dangerous, the park service officials frown on swimming. Despite this, many people do it. If you swim, remember that there are no lifeguards in the park, and that hidden rocks and ledges lurk beneath the surface of the water. Never dive into streams or rivers.

EVENTS
Spring Wildflower Pilgrimage

Wildflowers in the Smokies are legendary, and every April they are in the spotlight at the Spring Wildflower Pilgrimage (www.springwildflowerpilgrimage.org). This five-day event organized by the Friends of the Great Smoky Mountains National Park consists of wildflower, fauna, and natural history walks, motorcades, photographic tours, art classes, and indoor seminars.

Pilgrimage events are very popular, and advance registration is almost always a must. Registration is $25 per day for an adult, and $10 per day for high school and college students. Children under 12 are free with a registered adult. A detailed schedule is posted online, and reservations are accepted beginning in October the year before.

Townsend Winter Heritage Festival

In 2007, Townsend and the Great Smoky Mountains National Park established a new annual event, the Townsend Winter Heritage Festival (800/525-6834, www.smokiemountains.org). Featuring concerts, lectures, guided hikes, and other special events, the festival focuses on the music, food, history, and culture of people who once lived inside the park. It takes place in early February.

CLASSES
Great Smoky Mountains Institute at Tremont

The Great Smoky Mountains Institute at Tremont (865/448-6709, www.gsmit.org) offers residential environmental education programs year-round. They include naturalist certification and education, photography workshops, hiking weeks, family camping events, and programs for children and teachers.

Accommodations are in large air-conditioned and heated dormitories, and meals are served family-style in a large dining hall. Program fees apply, and reservations are essential.

Smoky Mountain Field School

A partnership between the University of Tennessee and the national park, the Smoky Mountain Field School (865/974-0150, www.ce.utk.edu/smoky) offers workshops, hikes, and hands-on instruction. Programs range from day-long seminars on medicinal plants of the Smokies to a two-day program on fly fishing. Other topics include orienteering, waterfalls of the Smokies, and salamanders in the park. Fees apply to all programs, and advance registration is required.

Ranger-Led Programs

The park service offers lectures, guided walks, and cultural presentations year-round. Check the park service website (www.nps.gov/grsm) for a schedule, or call a visitors center for more information.

Practicalities

CAMPING

There are 10 developed campgrounds in Great Smokies, five on the Tennessee side of the park. None of the campgrounds have showers or hook-ups, and each campground has different size limits for RVs. You can make reservations up to six months in advance for sites at Elmont, Smokemont, Cosby, and Cades Cove by calling 877/444-6777 or online at www.recreation.gov. All other sites are on a first come, first-served basis.

A single campsite may be occupied by no more than six people, in two tents or an RV and one tent.

Townsend Entrance

(**Abram's Creek** (Mar.–Oct., $12) has 16 sites located along Abram's Creek and at the trailhead to Abram's Falls. Accessible only from the extreme western end of the park, this is usually one of the quietest campgrounds.

Located along the Foothills Parkway, which travels from Tellico Lake to Walland, **Look Rock** (May–Oct., $14) is the highest-elevation campground on the Tennessee side of the park. **Cades Cove** (year-round, $17–20) has 159 sites and is located at the head of the Cades Cove loop.

Gatlinburg Entrance

Elkmont (Mar.–Nov., $17–20) is the largest campground in the park. Its 220 sites are situated in a pleasant mountain valley along the Little River.

Cosby Entrance

From Cosby you can easily access two pleasant campgrounds. **Cosby** (Mar.–Oct., $14) has 165 sites along the Cosby Creek. **Big Creek** (Mar.–Oct., $12) is a tents-only campground with 12 sites. It is located just over the North Carolina line along Big Creek.

North Carolina

Other North Carolina sites are **Deep Creek** (Apr.–Oct., $17), located near Bryson City, and **Cataloochee** (Mar.–Oct., $17), on the eastern end of the park. **Smokemont** (Mar.–Dec., $17–20) is located about two-thirds of the way from Newfound Gap to Oconaluftee. **Balsam Mountain** (May–Oct., $14), which at more than 5,300 feet is the highest-elevation campground in the Smokies, is located on the remote Balsam Mountain Road, and is accessible only from the eastern end of the Blue Ridge Parkway.

ACCOMMODATIONS

There is one lodge inside the national park. (**LeConte Lodge** (Mt. LeConte, 865/429-5704, www.leconte-lodge.com, $97 per adult, $76 per child), located at the peak of Mount LeConte, is a rustic inn accessible only by foot. While the amenities are sparse, the lodge is a palace for trail-worn hikers.

Accommodations are in rough-hewn log cabins scattered around the compound. Each guest gets a bunk bed with warm wool blankets. There are flush toilets, but no showers or electricity. Cabins are lighted with kerosene lamps and warmed with kerosene heaters.

The standard cabins sleep four or five people, and are suitable for two couples or a family. LeConte Lodge does not put strangers in cabins together. Larger "lodges" that sleep up to 13 people are also available. Rental rates include breakfast and dinner, and LeConte's meals are famously filling—perfect after a day of fresh air and hiking. If you're a vegetarian, say so when you make your reservation so special arrangements can be made.

LeConte Lodge is open from mid-March through November. Even though you won't be there in the dead of winter, be prepared for cold temperatures and inclement weather. The temperatures here are often 20 or 30 degrees cooler than the lowlands, and it has never gotten above 80 degrees. During spring and fall, there is often snow on the ground and temperatures in the teens.

GREAT SMOKY MOUNTAINS

Reservations are available starting on October 1 for the next year. The lodge is almost always fully booked by November, although you might still find a vacancy for mid-week dates during the spring or fall. If you can't get a room at the inn, there is a park service shelter nearby.

Guests are advised to pack a flashlight and hand towel. You should also pack an extra sweater or coat for the cold weather, plus snacks and water for the trail. Lunch is provided only to guests who are staying more than one night.

FOOD

There are no restaurants or concessions inside the park. The best way to eat is to pack a picnic and enjoy it at one of the many picnic grounds throughout the park. All picnic grounds include tables and fire grates.

HEALTH AND SAFETY

According to the park, motor vehicle accidents and drowning are the leading causes of death in the Smokies. Drive and swim with care. Do not climb on top of waterfalls, and do not go tubing inside the park. If you swim, don't try to show off, and never dive into the water—you cannot see underwater obstructions.

Venomous Snakes

Two species of venomous snakes live inside the park. Northern copperheads and timber rattlesnakes are especially fond of rocky areas, including stone walls and buildings.

Insects

Look out for yellow jackets, a type of wasp with a feisty sting. Yellow jackets build their nests in the ground and get mad when you disturb them. People with allergies should bring epinephrine kits. Remove any rings from your fingers right away if you're stung on the hand.

Medical Care

Sevier County Hospital (865/453-7111) is located 15 miles from Gatlinburg in Sevierville. Blount Memorial Hospital (865/983-7211) is in Maryville, 25 miles from Cades Cove.

INFORMATION

The national park publishes a free quarterly newspaper, *Smokies Guide*, which is available from any NPS-affiliated visitors center. The newspaper includes information about seasonal hazards, road closures, and upcoming events.

To request general park information, contact the park headquarters at 865/436-1200. Campground and other reservations may be made at 877/444-6777. For backcountry campsites call 865/436-1231. You can order maps and guides at 888/898-9102.

A wide selection of brochures, guides, and books are available for purchase at visitors centers or online at www.smokiesinformation.org.

The park website (www.nps.gov/grsm) has a lot of information about attractions, activities, and current conditions. The website offers webcams that show current conditions at Look Rock and Purchase Knob within the park.

Visitors Centers

There are three park visitors centers inside the park, and four outside its boundaries. Each visitors center sells maps, guides, and books. There are volunteers at each center who can help you plan your visit to the park. Information about current weather conditions, road closures, and ranger-led events is also available. All visitors centers are open daily year-round, but close on Christmas Day.

Sugarlands Visitor Center (865/436-1291), located two miles south of Gatlinburg on Highway 441, is the busiest visitors center. In addition to the services described above, there is a museum about the flora and fauna of the park and a free 20-minute video about its history and natural features. Sugarlands is open every day except Christmas Day. The doors open daily at 8 A.M. The center closes at 4:30 P.M. in December, January, and February; at 5 P.M. in March and November; at 6 P.M. in April, May, September, and October; and at 7 P.M.in June, July, and August.

Cades Cove Visitor Center (no phone) is located at the midway point of the 11-mile Cades Cove Loop Road. It opens daily at 9 A.M. and closes at 4:30 P.M. in January and

December; 5 P.M. in February and November; 6 P.M. in March, September, and October; and 7 P.M. from April to August. The Cades Cove Visitor Center is closed on Christmas Day.

On the North Carolina side of the park, the **Oconaluftee Visitor Center** (828/497-1904) is located two miles north of Cherokee, North Carolina. It is open 8:30 A.M.–4:30 P.M. in January, February, March, April, November, and December; 8:30 A.M.–5 P.M. in May; 8 A.M.–6 P.M. June–August; and 8:30 A.M.–6 P.M. in September and October. It is closed on Christmas Day.

In addition to the visitors centers located inside the park, the park service operates centers in gateway communities surrounding the Smokies. All these visitors centers sell maps, guides, and books. They are staffed with people who can answer your questions, and have up-to-date information about weather and roads. They cannot help with reservations or backcountry permits, however.

The **Downtown Gatlinburg Welcome Center** (daily 10 A.M.–6 P.M.) is located at traffic light No. 3 on the Parkway in downtown Gatlinburg.

The **Gatlinburg Welcome Center** (May–Oct. Mon.–Thurs. 8 A.M.–7 P.M., Fri.–Sat. 8 A.M.–9 P.M., Nov.–Apr. daily 8 A.M.–5:30 P.M.) is located on the spur road between Pigeon Forge and Gatlinburg.

The **Sevierville Visitor Center** (3099 Winfield Dunn Pkwy., 865/932-4458, daily 8:30 A.M.–5:30 P.M.) is located on Highway 66 between I-40 and Sevierville.

The **Townsend Visitor Center** is located on Highway 321 in Townsend. It opens daily at 9 A.M. closes at 5 P.M. from November to May. From June–October the center stays open until 6 P.M. The Townsend Visitor Center is closed on Thanksgiving and Christmas Days.

Pets

You may bring your pet to campgrounds and roadsides as long as they are restrained at all times. Pets are not allowed on trails, except for the Gatlinburg and Oconaluftee River Trails.

Communications

Do not count on your cell phone working inside the park. While you are likely to get service in the gateway communities surrounding the park, many parts of the Smokies are outside of cell phone range. Campgrounds and visitors centers have pay phones.

Gateways to the Smokies

The most popular way to get to the Smokies is along the Sevier County corridor, which begins at exit 407 off I-40 and passes through Sevierville, Pigeon Forge, and Gatlinburg. These three communities long ago shed their quiet, rural roots to become pinnacles of hyperactive commercialism. It is hard to imagine a landscape so opposed to the peace and majesty of the national park.

In this land of plenty you will find pancake houses next to outlet malls; monster truck rides next to a Bible museum; and country music dinner theater next to helicopter rides. The "live black bear" attractions seem to have faded into history, but they have been replaced by a rainforest zoo, Christian-themed entertainment complexes, and a theme park owned and operated by Sevier County native Dolly Parton.

The cost of exuberant development is traffic jams, and Sevier County has plenty. It may be a short 15 miles from Sevierville to the park, but it will feel like far more as you stop dozens of times at traffic lights along the way. At least it makes your eventual arrival inside the cool, fresh air of the park that much more welcome.

Is there any good reason to pass through this corner of the world? Sure. There is a time in every person's life for mini-golf, and back-to-school shopping is achieved quickly and inexpensively at outlet malls. Or celebrate your big day with a hot-air balloon ride over the foothills. The most open-minded among us might find themselves pleased at the opportunity to "live the nightmare" at Ripley's Haunted Adventure, or pause, mesmerized, to watch a taffy machine in action.

Or not. If you don't want to join in the fun, then bypass these cities entirely by entering the park through one of the side doors: Townsend or Cosby. It's up to you.

GATLINBURG

Surrounded on three sides by the national park, Gatlinburg is the capital city of the Smokies. Once a quiet mountain hamlet where folks lived off the land, the "Burg" is now a busy tourist trap where anything goes. Anything may be new generations of ever more gargantuan hotels and condominiums, or new attractions that try to giggle, wow, or scare the money out of you. Anything is also the unrelenting commercial machine that peddles pancakes, taffy, T-shirts, and mountain-kitsch goodies to whoever passes by.

Gatlinburg is the Tennessee city closest to the Smokies, but the mountains seem oh so far away. If you came to the Smokies strictly to enjoy nature, stay away from this place. But if you came to have fun, then maybe you'll find it in your heart to spend an afternoon gorging on cotton candy and making funny pictures with your traveling companions.

Ripley's Aquarium of the Smokies

Exactly why you need an aquarium at the doorstep of one of the country's most biologically diverse mountain parks is hard to understand, but too much thought will ruin any trip to Gatlinburg. So if you've grown tired of the environment of the Smoky Mountains, trade it in for exotic ocean seascapes at the Ripley's Aquarium of the Smokies (888/240-1358, www.ripleysaquariumofthesmokies.com, adults $23, children 6–11 $12.25, children 2–5 $6). Here you will see sharks, sting rays, crabs, and lots of colorful tropical fish. There are touch tanks, and daily feeding demonstrations.

GREAT SMOKY MOUNTAINS

© SUSANNA HENIGHAN POTTER

Gatlinburg sits in a mountain valley on the northern edge of the Great Smoky Mountains National Park.

A highlight is walking through an underwater tunnel, where you are surrounded on three sides by aquarium tanks. In 2007, the aquarium unveiled its newest exhibit, "Mars: The Search for Life," which invites you to follow the water in the search for alien life.

(Arrowmont

Gatlinburg has bulldozed over most of its history, but a few remnants remain. One of the best enduring stories is **Arrowmont School of Arts and Crafts** (556 Parkway, 865/436-5860, www.arrowmont.org). Arrowmont began as a settlement school for mountain folks. It opened in 1912 as the Pi Beta Phi Settlement School, named for the Pi Beta Phi fraternity. In addition to providing an education for mountain children, the school promoted local handicrafts. In 1926, Arrowcraft Shop opened in Gatlinburg as a retail outlet for local crafts.

By the mid-1960s Sevier County took over public education, and the settlement school turned its focus to crafts. In 1970 the main studio complex was built. Today, Arrowmont is known for its contemporary arts-and-crafts education. Adults from around the country come here for one- and two-week residential programs in clay, paper, metals, fiber, glass, enamels, weaving, basketry, sculpture, polymer clay, woodturning, and woodworking, among others.

Arrowmont Galleries (free) are open year-round, Monday–Saturday 8:30 A.M.–4:30 P.M. Each year more than 10 juried, invitational, themed, and media-oriented exhibitions are held. The art supply store and bookshop stocks tools, art materials, and other specialty items.

Located next to Arrowmont's retail outlet is the **Ogle Cabin** (556 Parkway). Built of rough-hewn logs around 1807, this cabin was the first homestead in Gatlinburg. The location was chosen by William Ogle, but he died before his family could make the move from South Carolina to the mountains of East Tennessee. His widow, Martha Jane Huskey Ogle, and her seven children, together with her brother Peter Huskey and his family, moved to Gatlinburg—then called White Oak Flats—in 1807. The

Ogle family remained in the cabin until about 1910, and in 1921 it was sold to the Pi Beta Phi fraternity, which converted it into a clinic and later a museum. Ogle and Huskey remain two of the most common names in Gatlinburg.

You can learn more about Gatlinburg's history by picking up a copy of the *Walking and Driving Tour of Historic Gatlinburg,* available at visitors centers.

Attractions

Attractions are Gatlinburg's special variety of fun, so much so that the Attractions Association of Gatlinburg (www.attractions-gatlinburg.com) was formed to help keep them all straight. New attractions open each year, offering a new variation on the theme of mindless, family-friendly, fun activities.

Some attractions that stand out from the rest are the world's largest **Amazing Mirror Maze** (919 Parkway, 865/436-4415, 9 A.M.–midnight, adults and children 10 and up $9, children 3–9 $7) and **Ripley's Believe It or Not Museum** (traffic lights Nos. 7 and 8 on the Parkway, 865/436-5096, Sun.–Thurs. 10 A.M.–9 P.M., Fri.–Sat. 9 A.M.–10 P.M., adults and children 12 and up $15, children 3–11 $8), where you can see some of the strangest and most extreme sights in the world, such as two-headed cows and shrunken heads. **Mysterious Mansion** (River Rd., 865/436-7007, daily 11 A.M.–11 P.M., $9) is a classic haunted house, and **Motion Ride Movie Theater** (Reagan Terrace Mall, 865/430-8985, Sun.–Thurs. 10 A.M.–10 P.M., Fri.–Sat. 10 A.M.–midnight, $10) shows eight different movies where the seats move in tandem with the on-screen action, making you feel like you're really in the cab of an 18-wheeler as it descends, without brakes, down the side of a mountain.

Other attractions in Gatlinburg fall in the category of higher-is-better. The **Space Needle** (115 Historic Nature Trail, 865/436-4629, daily 9 A.M.–10 P.M., adults $7.25, children 5–12 $3) is more than 400 feet tall and offers 360-degree views of Gatlinburg and the surrounding mountains. As if the view were not enough, there is a high-tech arcade, virtual-reality roller coaster, and mini-golf inside at the base of the needle.

The **Gatlinburg Sky Lift** (Traffic Light No. 7, 865/436-4307, www.gatlinburgskylift.com, Apr.–Oct. daily 9 A.M.–10 P.M., Nov.–Mar. daily 9 A.M.–5 P.M. weather permitting, adults $12, children 3–11 $9) is an old-fashioned attraction, dating back to the 1950s. Take a seat in a chairlift and climb gently up 518 feet, enjoying views of Gatlinburg and the mountains along the way. This attraction is as near to a timeless pleasure as you'll find in Gatlinburg.

Skiing

You can drive Ski Mountain Road up to **Ober Gatlinburg** (865/436-5423, www.obergatlinburg.com), but most people prefer to take the aerial tramway (adults $9.50, children 7–11 $6.50) that departs from 1001 Parkway.

Ober Gatlinburg's slopes are not spectacular, but they are good for beginners. In addition to skiing (adults $15–43, seniors and children 7–11 $20–33) you can enjoy year-round ice skating ($8), a black bear habitat ($2), and amusements such as an arcade, go-karts ($6), and mini-golf ($3).

Shopping

The best arts-and-crafts shop in downtown Gatlinburg is **Arrowcraft** (576 Parkway, 865/436-4606), a member of the Southern Highland Craft Guild and affiliate of Arrowmont School of Arts and Crafts. The gallery has a wide selection of crafts, from jewelry to pottery to hand-woven clothing, all made by regional craftspeople.

If you are looking for outdoor equipment and gear, head to the **Happy Hiker** (905 River Rd., 865/436-6000). For fishing gear, go to **Smoky Mountain Angler** (376 E. Parkway, aka Hwy. 321, 865/436-8746), next to the Smoky Mountain Winery.

Events

The **Craftsmen's Fair** (865/436-7479, www.craftsmenfair.com) takes place at the Gatlinburg Convention Center in July and October. For $5 admission, you can watch more than 180 craftspeople from around the country make traditional crafts such as baskets, pottery, brooms, and stained glass.

Accommodations

There are more than 10,000 hotel rooms in and around Gatlinburg. Even at the top of peak season, you will find a place to lay your head. Prices vary according to season; summertime and fall foliage (October) are peak periods, along with Christmas and New Year's.

While there are some high-end hostelries, Gatlinburg specializes in affordable family-friendly lodging.

UNDER $100

Gatlinburg is chockablock with motels, especially along River Road, the road that runs parallel to the Parkway. Some are chain motels and others are independent. The **Riverhouse Motor Lodge** (610 River Rd., 865/436-7821, www.riverhousegatlinburg.com, $60–170) has the most secluded riverfront rooms in town. Rooms have either two queen-sized beds or one king, and many come with fireplaces (gas or wood-burning) and balconies overlooking the river. Rates vary based on your choice of amenities and the season. Continental breakfast is included.

Located right on the Parkway, ◖ **The Gatlinburg Inn** (755 Parkway, 865/436-5133, www.gatlinburginn.com, $58–114) was the third hotel to open in Gatlinburg. Today it holds on to an old-fashioned aura reminiscent of times gone by. The inn was built in 1937 by R. L. Maples Sr. His wife, Wilma Maples, continues to manage the hotel. The inn has 67 rooms and seven suites. There is a swimming pool and tennis courts, and a common sitting area at the front. Lady Bird Johnson, Liberace, Dinah Shore, Tennessee Ernie Ford, and J. C. Penney stayed here, and Boudleaux and Felice Bryant wrote the song "Rocky Top" in room 388. The Gatlinburg Inn is clean and comfortable, but the decor is frozen in the 1970s. The maids wear pink uniforms that went out of style decades ago. All in all, it is a joyful retreat from the Parkway hustle-and-bustle, where the hospitality is still genuine. Its motto is "clean, quiet, and comfortable." What more do you really want? The Gatlinburg Inn is open from April to October. Family suites for up to four people are available for between $94 and $112 per night. Infant cribs are available by request. No motorcycles or motor homes permitted.

$100-150

Located on River Road, **The Edgewater Inn** (402 River Rd., 865/436-4151, www.edgewater-hotel.com, $140–150) is a full-service hotel and conference center ideal for families or business travelers. Guests enjoy free continental breakfast, indoor and outdoor swimming pools, in-room fireplaces, plus free parking and wireless Internet.

Situated in a 1930s home, **Laurel Springs Lodge** (204 Hill St., 865/430-9211, www.laurelspringslodge.com, $95–159) is a bed-and-breakfast with five guest rooms. Each room has a private bath, television, and fine linens. Mini-suites have a DVD/VCR and bathrobes. Breakfast is served each morning at 8:30 A.M., and features fresh, hearty home-style fare, although light options are also available. The inn is located within walking distance of Gatlinburg attractions and restaurants.

Located just a few miles from the Greenbrier area of the Great Smoky Mountains National Park, and five miles from Gatlinburg, **Buckhorn Inn** (2140 Tudor Mountain Rd., 865/436-4668, www.buckhorninn.com, $110–320) is a peaceful and elegant retreat. Situated in the Great Smoky Arts and Crafts Community, on 25 acres of land, the Buckhorn Inn has four types of accommodations. Standard rooms ($115–130) have king-sized beds, private phones, baths, and sitting areas. Premier rooms ($175) add a fireplace, private balcony, whirlpool tub, coffeemaker, and refrigerator. Private cottages ($175) offer the same amenities as a premier room but in a small private cottage. Private guesthouses ($195–320) are two-bedroom guesthouses with full kitchens, fireplaces, living rooms, and ample outdoor spaces. All Buckhorn rooms are furnished in an elegant, yet homey, style.

Comforts abound. Overnight guests enjoy breakfast in the sunny dining room, with views of Mount LeConte in the park. A four-course dinner is served nightly at an additional charge of $30 per person. The food at Buckhorn Inn is superb. You can pass the time walking the nature trail, or strolling in Rachael's Labyrinth. Relax in the library or watch the view from the flagstone terrace. Children under 12 are not permitted at Buckhorn, and on weekends and holidays there is a two-night minimum stay. The innkeepers offers special packages for honeymooners, hikers, fly fishers, and others.

$150-200

Located on a mountainside far above Gatlinburg, **The Lodge at Buckberry Creek** (961 Campbell Lead Rd., 865/430-8030, www.buckberrylodge.com, $180–460) is an all-suite luxury lodge. Modeled after the Adirondack-style mountain lodge, with lots of exposed wood and rustic finishes, Buckberry feels a bit like an elite mountain club that you're lucky to be a member of. Guest suites have king-sized beds, sitting areas, balconies, and kitchens. Fine dinners are served nightly in the restaurant, which wins praises as one of the area's most upscale.

CHALETS AND CABINS

In addition to hotel rooms, Gatlinburg guests can stay in private cabins and "chalets." The term chalet traditionally referred to an A-frame-style vacation home, but it has come to encompass just about every type of vacation apartment. Almost to a rule, chalets and cabins offer amenities like fireplaces, whirlpool tubs, full kitchens, and balconies. They are located on the hillsides and valleys surrounding Gatlinburg.

Rates range $500–1,200 weekly for one- and two-bedroom cabins. Large four- and five-bedroom properties can cost as much as $3,000 per week. Daily rates are often available, and start around $120.

There are dozens of different chalet and cabin developments, and thousands of individual properties. The best way to make a reservation

GREAT SMOKY MOUNTAINS

is to use a reservation service. The friendly folks at **Smoky Mountain Accommodations** (865/436-6943, www.smagatlinburg.com) can recommend a property that fits within your price range and meets your needs, e.g., kid-friendly, close to the park, close to Gatlinburg, etc. On the website you can look at pictures and read a description of each property.

The Chalet Company (865/436-3029, www.thechaletcompany.com) also represents dozens of properties at various prices.

Food

Restaurants in Gatlinburg serve steaks, barbecue, burgers, and other crowd-pleasing country-style food. Snack shops sell sweets, candy, donuts, and other temptations.

The Peddler Restaurant (820 River Rd., 865/436-5794, daily 5–10 P.M., $20–40) is Gatlinburg's best steakhouse, with a super salad bar as well. In addition to New York strip, prime rib, and filet mignon, you can order fresh trout, shrimp, or blackened chicken. The extra-large salad bar comes with dinners, or is available for $13 on its own.

For breakfast all day, the **Pancake Pantry** (628 Parkway, 865/436-4724, June–Oct. daily 7 A.M.–4 P.M., Nov.–May daily 7 A.M.–3 P.M., $6–16) cannot be beat. Its 24 different varieties of pancake share the menu with waffles, eggs, and other traditional hearty breakfast favorites. Beginning at 11:30 A.M. daily, the Pantry offers sandwiches, soups, and salads.

Follow Highway 321 north 1.5 miles to Newman Road to find **❰ Greenbrier Restaurant** (370 Newman Rd., 865/436-6318, Sun.–Thurs. 5–9:30 P.M., Fri.–Sat. 5–10 P.M., $15–30), which serves dinner nightly. Specialties include steak, shrimp, and scrumptious desserts. Vegetarian options include sautéed vegetables with provolone cheese and pasta Alfredo. There is a children's menu ($7–8).

Information

Gatlinburg operates three visitor information centers. The first is located along U.S. Highway 441, before you arrive in the city. This is also a national park visitor information center, and it is a park-and-ride facility for the Gatlinburg Trolley.

The main downtown visitors center is at 811 East Parkway, at traffic light No. 3. The third is located at traffic light No. 5, right next to Ripley's Aquarium.

To request information, contact the **Gatlinburg Chamber of Commerce** (800/588-1817, www.gatlinburg.com).

Services

The **Anna Porter Public Library** (207 Cherokee Orchard Rd., 865/436-5588) has free Internet access and a Smoky Mountain Collection where you can browse history books, guides, and nature reference books.

Wash your clothes at **The Wash Tub** (642 E. Parkway), located about four miles out Highway 321 towards the Arts and Crafts Community.

Gatlinburg's largest food store is **Food City** (865/430-3116), located on Highway 321 opposite the Gatlinburg post office. **Parkway Liquor Store** (286 Parkway, 865/436-9635) sells wine, liquor, and pre-mixed cocktails.

Getting There and Around

Gatlinburg is easy to find, but traffic can be terrible. Vehicles creep slowly along the Parkway, and you feel more like you're cruising than driving. Parking, if you find it, costs around $2 per hour or $8 a day.

The **Gatlinburg Trolleys** are the answer. Free parking is available at the Gatlinburg Welcome Center on the Spur, outside of town, and at the municipal garage located on Highway 321. From either stop you'll pay 50 cents for the trip into town and the trolley will deposit you right in front of the aquarium. From there you can catch rides up River Road (50 cents), out Highway 321 to the Arts and Crafts Community ($1), or into the national park ($2). Exact change is required on all routes. Or you can hoof it—walking distances in Gatlinburg are short.

Trolley route maps are available from visitors centers or by calling the Mass Transit Center at 865/436-3897.

If you are traveling through Gatlinburg only to get to the national park, take the **Gatlinburg By-Pass.** The By-Pass veers off Highway 441 shortly after the Gatlinburg Welcome Center, and climbs the mountainside overlooking Gatlinburg. It deposits you back on Highway 441 inside the national park.

◖ Great Smoky Mountains Arts and Crafts Community

Craft connoisseurs should head to the Great Smoky Mountains Arts and Crafts Community (Light #3A E. Parkway, aka Hwy. 321 N., www.artsandcraftscommunity.com). The community started during the 1930s, when area artisans decided that instead of selling their wares in downtown Gatlinburg, they would invite tourists out to their studios and homes. During the early years, the Arts and Crafts Community featured traditional, local artisans making brooms, furniture, candles, quilts, and more.

Nowadays, the authentic country craftsmen share the stage with modern artisans, who have adopted new styles and media. The community, strung along eight miles of back roads, is home to more than 100 different studios, gift shops, and restaurants.

Ogle's Broom Shop (680 Glades Rd., 865/430-4402) is a third-generation workshop making brooms, walking sticks, and canes. **The Chair Shop** (830 Cantrell Cir., 865/436-7413) sells custom-designed handmade rocking chairs. One of the most remarkable stories of the Arts and Crafts Community is the **Cliff Dwellers Gallery** (668 Glades Rd., 865/436-6921). This chalet-style gallery was built in downtown Gatlinburg in 1933, and served as a gallery and workshop for many years. In 1995, threatened with destruction, the building was moved to Glades Road to form part of the Arts and Crafts Community. It is owned cooperatively by six artists, and carries the work of some 60 more.

The Arts and Crafts Community is located three miles east of downtown Gatlinburg, along East Parkway (Hwy. 321 N.). The route follows Glades Road and Buckhorn Road before running back into Highway 321. The Gatlinburg Trolley travels the route of the arts community. There are also parking areas and public restrooms along the way.

Because of the sheer number of galleries, visitors should think ahead about what they are looking for. Pick up a copy of the Arts and Crafts Community brochure and map, which shows the exact location of each gallery and includes a brief description of what they sell. Or visit the community's website and search for galleries selling the items that you are looking for.

PIGEON FORGE

Nothing can truly prepare you for Pigeon Forge. This long strip of highway that lies between Gatlinburg and Sevierville on the road to the Smokies takes tacky to the tenth degree. You can see the evolution of low-brow consumerism here, where roadside pit stops selling concrete lawn ornaments seem quaint next to the fruits of modern-day developers' machinations. Consider this: In 2008 Pigeon Forge welcomed its newest monstrosity—Belle Island, a massive $110 million Disney World–esque development with 95 retail shops, 126 hotel rooms, and four major restaurants. Located on an actual island, the development boasts the Debbie Reynolds Hollywood Motion Picture Museum, Darrell Waltrip's Racing Experience (named for a famed NASCAR driver and sports commentator), and 3,000 parking spaces.

The bottom line is that bigger is always better in Pigeon Forge, no matter how ugly it is. And what is truly remarkable about Pigeon Forge is that the people love it.

Before you discard Pigeon Forge, consider what it has going for it. The Dollywood theme park is truly something, with its fun rides, mountain craft demonstrations, and musical performances. During the hot summer months, who can resist Dollywood's Splash Country, the crème-de-la-crème of water parks? If shopping is on your list, then try on Pigeon Forge's myriad outlet malls. If you truly let go, then dive right in to all the rest: comedy barns, Elvis museums, indoor skydiving, bungee jumping, car museums, mini-golf, and country music dinner theater. Pigeon Forge is your oyster.

◖ Dollywood

There is no way around it: Dollywood (McCarter Hollow Rd., 800/365-5996, www.dollywood.com, adults $50, seniors 60 and older $47, children 4–11 $40) is just good clean fun. The theme park owned and operated by Sevier County native Dolly Parton, Dollywood combines excellent rides with family-friendly entertainment. Mountain craft demonstrations keep Dolly's childhood alive. The park's wooden roller coaster, the Thunderhead, is thrilling and fun; at River Battle you get to aim and shoot water cannons at fellow riders; and the Blazing Fury takes you through an 1880s frontier town engulfed in flames. Dollywood also has plenty of less thrilling attractions. The county fair has Ferris wheels and other classic amusements. Calico Falls Schoolhouse is a replica of a one-room mountain school, and the Dollywood Express takes you on a five-mile railroad journey through the foothills of the Smokies. There is also a bald eagle sanctuary and the Southern Gospel Music Hall of Fame.

Dollywood also offers live music. Performers on various stages play bluegrass, country, gospel, and oldies. All shows are free with your admission to Dollywood.

Arts-and-crafts demonstrations are also a big part of Dollywood. You can watch glassblowers at work, see lye soap being made, and observe candles being dipped. A blacksmith shop produces metalwork, and a woodcarver makes one-of-a-kind pieces of artwork.

As if this weren't enough, Dollywood puts on several major events each year, when special entertainment is offered. The Festival of Nations, from March to May, includes singers, dancers, and performers from around the world. Barbeque and Bluegrass during September offers special concerts by bluegrass favorites, and Smoky Mountain Christmas in December is a remarkable display of lights. Other events are KidsFest during June, July, and August, and Harvest Celebration in October and November.

For less than the price of two general admission tickets, you can buy a season pass to Dollywood. Many area residents choose this option so they can come back again and again, and so they won't feel compelled to cram everything Dollywood into a single visit.

Dollywood's doors open at 9 A.M. or 10 A.M. and close between 6 and 9 P.M., depending on the season. Call ahead or check the website to find out what time the gates open on any particular day. Dollywood is closed in January, February, and March.

Dollywood's Splash Country (traffic light No. 8, 865/428-9488, daily 10 A.M.–6 P.M., adults $42, seniors 60 and older $39, children 4–11 $36), is a super-duper water park open from mid-May to mid-September. During late June and all of July, the park stays open until 7 P.M.

Splash Country has 23 different rides and slides; some are thrilling white-water adventures and others are placid kid-friendly games. Swiftwater Run takes you round and round a tightening corkscrew until you're sent down the chute. The Cascades is an 8,000-square-foot lagoon-style pool with interactive elements ideal for younger children.

Plan to stay all day to get your money's worth. On top of the admission fee, you'll pay $6 for parking unless you have a gold season pass, or gold super season pass. Guests are not permitted to bring coolers, food, or other picnic goods inside the park, although you can leave the park and return later in the day. Food is available for purchase.

Children under 13 are not allowed in Splash Country without an adult.

Other Sights

Pigeon Forge's city park is **Patriot Park,** located behind the Old Mill. Named for the Patriot Bomber that is on permanent display, the park is the site of festival, fairs, and other events.

You can't help but notice **WonderWorks** (Parkway, 865/868-1800, www.wonderworks-tn.com, daily 9 A.M.–midnight, adults 13 and up $20, children 4–12 $10), whose facade is turned completely upside down. The illusion is merely cosmetic, but it sets the stage for the over-the-top kid-friendly activities inside. WonderWorks includes a disaster zone where you can feel what it would be like to experience a major earthquake or hurricane. There is a gallery of optical illusions, and laser tag ($5 extra). WonderWorks is also home to Hoot N' Holler, a family-friendly dinner theater that is staged several times a day.

Shopping

Pigeon Forge is a destination for outlet shopping. **Belz Factory Outlet Mall** (2655 Teaster Ln., 865/453-7316) houses dozens of name-brand discount stores, such as Bass, Dress Barn, Jockey, and Fossil. Right next door, at the **Shoppes of Pigeon Forge** (161 E. Wears Valley Rd.) you'll find Eddie Bauer, J. Crew, and Harry and David.

The **Factory Outlet Mall of Pigeon Forge** (2850 Parkway) is easily identified by its red roof. Here you'll find Corningware, Pfaltzgraff, plus clothing and shoe outlets.

Though it is technically located inside Sevierville's city limits, the **Five Oaks Mall** (1645 Parkway, Sevierville, 865/453 1053) is Pigeon Forge at heart. Five Oaks is the area's newest and largest outlet mall, with Old Navy, Gap, Van Heusen, Brooks Brothers, and Reebok, among many others.

Most outlet malls open at 10 A.M. during the winter and 9 A.M. during summer. They usually stay open until sunset.

Pigeon Forge Pottery was a Pigeon Forge institution. In 1946, Douglas Ferguson established the business and over the years he formed a reputation for excellent pottery. Visitors enjoyed watching craftspeople work when they visited the shop, and the Pottery's famous black bears were collectors items. Ferguson died in 2000, and the pottery was sold to the Old Mill. Today, **Pigeon River Pottery** (Old Mill Sq., 865/453-1104) sells beautiful handmade pottery in a variety of styles, but you won't find many of the designs that made the pottery famous in the first place. Check the seconds corner for discounted pieces.

Activities

Pigeon Forge leads the United States in far-fetched extreme activities—the type of thing you'll be talking about after you get home.

Case in point: Pigeon Forge was the first U.S. location of Zorb, the New Zealand–invented sport of rolling downhill in an 11-foot inflatable ball. In Zorbit, you are harnessed in and watch as the world spins around you and you roll 600 feet downhill. In Zydro, they throw in a bucket of water and you cascade downhill in a cross between a waterslide and a roller coaster. A ride costs $37–44, but prices decrease if you have a larger group. **Smoky Mountain Zorb** (203 Sugar Hollow Rd., 865/868-1000, www.zorb.com/smoky, daily 11 A.M.–5 P.M.) is located near traffic light No. 1 in Pigeon Forge.

Indoor skydiving is a Pigeon Forge tradition. At **Flyaway** (3106 Parkway, 865/453-7777, www.flyawayindoorskydiving.com, daily 10:45 A.M.–6 P.M.) you can "body fly" in a vertical wind tunnel. For your $30 ticket, you'll get about 20 minutes of instruction, plus the use of a suit, helmet, and other safety gear. Then you'll get about three minutes of flying time inside the tunnel. What fun!

Finally, there is bungee jumping at **The Track** (2575 Parkway, 865/453-4777, www.pigeonforgetrack.com). Jump from a 65-foot platform attached by a harness and elastic bungee cord for just $16. The Track also has bumper cars, go-karts, and an arcade.

Entertainment

Gaudy stage entertainment is another Pigeon Forge hallmark. Massive theater complexes line the parkway, surrounded by even more massive parking lots. **Country Tonite** (129 Showplace Blvd., 865/453-2003, www.countrytonitepf.com, $18–30) is a country music show with patriotic and gospel thrown in. **The Comedy Barn** (865/428-5222, www.comedybarn.com, $25) offers terribly hokey country-style comedy. **The Miracle** (865/428-7469, www.miracletheater.com, $40) tells the story of Jesus Christ. Arrive early to enjoy Noah's Ark Animal Park, where you can have your photograph taken on a camel. **Magic Beyond Belief** (865/428-5600, www.pigeonforgemagic.com, $25) stars Terry Evanswood as magician and exotic animal tamer.

Memories Theatre (2141 Parkway, 865/428-7852, www.memoriestheatre.com, $25) is one of the longest-running shows in town, with perennial Elvis tribute shows plus tributes to other stars such as Dolly Parton and Garth Brooks.

The most famous of dinner theaters is the **Dixie Stampede** (3849 Parkway, 800/356-1676, www.dixiestampede.com, adults $40, children 4–11 $20). Here guests are seated around a circular arena where actors and animals put on a rodeo-inspired dinner show. A four-course barbecue meal is served while you watch.

Food

The **Old Mill** (Old Mill Sq., 865/429-3463) is a favorite for Southern-style dining. Come here for hearty meals all day—the dinner menu offers no less than five different Southern fried specialties: chicken, steak, pork chop, beef liver, and country ham.

Getting Around

Pigeon Forge and Sevierville have joined forces to offer the **Fun Time Trolley** (865/453-6444, www.pigeonforgetrolley.org). The yellow route ($0.50) departs the Sevier County courthouse in Sevierville and travels past outlet malls to the trolley headquarters next to Patriot Park in Pigeon Forge. Purple route ($0.50) begins at Wal-Mart, Governor's Crossing, and Five Oaks Mall and travels along the Pigeon Forge Parkway, stopping at the Apple Barn and the Pigeon Forge Welcome Center before going to the trolley headquarters. The green route ($0.75) travels from the trolley headquarters to the Gatlinburg Welcome Center, where you can catch another trolley into Gatlinburg and on to the national park. Other routes traverse the southern Parkway and Wears Valley Road, and take visitors to Dollywood and Splash Country.

Trolleys run daily from 8:30 A.M. to midnight from early March through October, and 10 A.M.–10 P.M. in November and December.

Exact fare is required, and fare applies each time you get on the trolley. Parkway trolleys run every 20 to 25 minutes, Dollywood trollys every 15 to 20 minutes, Wears Valley trolleys every 40 to 45 minutes, and to the Gatlinburg Welcome Center every 20 to 25 minutes.

SEVIERVILLE

It used to be that the sprawl of malls, oversized theaters, restaurants, and tourist attractions was pretty much contained to Pigeon Forge. Sevierville, the Sevier County seat and first city on the journey from interstate to national park, was a laid-back place. But the lure of tapping into tourist dollars was too much, and Sevierville is beginning to look like a young Pigeon Forge. Even the economic slowdown of 2008 couldn't seem to slow the pace of construction when it comes to mega-developments in Sevierville. Shopping malls, giant flea markets, mini-golf, and hotels now line the entire route along Highways 66 and 441. The old city center of Sevierville is just a blip on the screen.

Sights

Sevier County's elegant Victorian courthouse dominates the Sevierville skyline. Stop here to see a life-sized statue of a willowy young Dolly Parton, Sevier County's hometown girl.

Located at the Sevierville municipal airport, the **Tennessee Museum of Aviation** (135 Air Museum Way, 865/908-0171 or 866/286-8738, www.tnairmuseum.org, Mon.–Sat. 10 A.M.–6 P.M., Sun. 1–6 P.M., adults $12.75, seniors $9.75, children 6–12 $6.75, under 6 free) is an enthusiast's dream. Glass-enclosed cases display memorabilia associated with Tennessee aviation and the heated exhibit hangar houses airworthy planes, including two P-47D Thunderbolts and a Navy TBM Avenger. The aviation museum is located two miles outside of downtown Sevierville along Highway 411. Look for the signs to the airport and aviation museum.

Activities

The Knoxville K-Jays moved east to Sevier County in 2000 and became the **Tennessee Smokies** (Hwy. 66, 865/286-2300, www.smokiesbaseball.com, $6–10). The Smokies, a AA Cubs affiliate, play in a stadium located right next to I-40 at exit 407. The regular season runs from April to August. Smokies games are heavy on between-inning entertainment and promotions. Special no-alcohol seating areas are available. Field-level seats are $9 for adults and $8 for children and seniors; bleacher seats are $7 for adults and $6 for seniors and children. Tickets for the grass berm along the outfield are $6. Reserved-seat tickets are $1 more if you buy them at the gate. Advance tickets are available online and in person at the Smokies box office.

For something totally different, sign up for a hot-air balloon ride with **Smoky Mountain Balloon Adventures** (865/484-0330, www.smokymtnballoons.com). For $229 per adult (less if you agree to join up with another group), you'll get 1–1.5 hours in a hot-air balloon, floating over the foothills of the Smokies. Balloon trips meet up at the Starbucks shop at 646 Winfield Dunn Parkway (Hwy. 66) in Sevierville, and guests are shuttled to the launch site, which varies based on wind and weather conditions. After your flight, you'll enjoy a toast with the captain and you'll get a special certificate as a keepsake. Balloon flights are offered from April to November. Most flights depart early in the morning or late in the afternoon, and reach altitudes of between 1,500 and 2,000 feet above the ground.

Entertainment

Sevier County's only movie theater is **Reel Theatres** (Hwy. 66, 865/453-9055, www.reel-theatres-sevier.com), located one mile north of downtown Sevierville along Highway 66. Its screens show first-run movies daily.

Food

One of Sevierville's most beloved restaurants is the █ **Applewood** (220 Apple Valley Rd., 865/429-8644, daily 8 A.M.–9 P.M., $7–20), a country-cooking institution. Applewood is located next to the Apple Barn, a general store and cider press where you can watch as apple cider and other apple goodies are being made.

Getting Around

Traffic congestion is a problem in Sevierville too. In 2006, officials opened State Route 448, which is supposed to speed up your journey through town. Traffic headed towards Pigeon Forge and the national park should remain on Highway 441 (the Parkway), but traffic headed in the other direction, towards the interstate, should follow the signs to the new Route 448 through town.

An even newer alternate route worth noting is Veteran's Drive, or Highway 449. This four-lane divided highway runs from Highway 411 to Pigeon Forge, bypassing the sprawl and traffic lights. You enter Pigeon Forge near Dollywood.

COSBY

Located on the northeastern side of the Great Smoky Mountains, Cosby is a rural town with services and accommodations for visitors. From the Cosby entrance to the park, you can explore Cosby campground and picnic area, or hike to Henwallow Falls, Mount Cammerer, or join up with the Appalachian Trail.

Historically, Cosby was known as a moonshiner's town. Today, it is home to artists and craftsmen. Near Cosby, the town of Hartford is noted for white-water rafting, and Newport is a center for commerce in the area.

Arts and Crafts

Jean and Lee Schilling make and sell old-time fretted and hammered dulcimers, as well as other traditional musical instruments, at **Mountain Musicrafts and Dulcimers** (Hwy. 32, 423/487-5543). The Schillings are knowledgeable, friendly, and expert craftsmen. The shop is located in a mountain cabin more than 100 years old, which was removed from the Cosby campground area when the national park was created in the 1930s. In addition to musical instruments, they sell audio and video recordings of traditional musicians; this is a great place to stop if you want to bring home the sound of the mountains.

Holloway's Quilts (3892 Cosby Hwy., aka Hwy. 321, 423/487-3866) is a quilter's studio, quilting supply store, and place to purchase finished quilts and other mountain handicrafts. Holloway's is a cozy, welcoming place, jam-packed with goodies of interest to quilters and non-quilters a like. Pop in next door at the studio to see a quilter at work.

Len Landrum makes custom knives out of his machine shop in Cosby. **Landrum Cutlery** (861 Middle Creek Rd., 423/487-5448) is his retail shop, where you can see his latest designs and order or purchase one for yourself. Each knife is hand-forged and, therefore, unique.

Look for the barn board building where the Cosby Highway intersects with Wilton Springs Road to find **Santa Cruz Woodworks** (2776 Cosby Hwy., aka Hwy. 321, 423/623-7856). Bob and Cindy Evans make solid wood cabinets, rocking chairs, birdhouses, trunks, and much more. Browse the shop or put in your custom order.

River Rafting

Near the town of Hartford, the Pigeon River is a popular venue for **white-water rafting.** The Upper Pigeon offers fast-paced class III and IV rapids while the Lower Pigeon is placid and peaceful. Outfitters offer trips on both sections of river, but not every day. Since the Pigeon is a dam-controlled river, trips are offered only when there is water to raft on. Make your reservations in advance.

Outfitters such as **Wildwater Ltd.** (800/451-9972), **Pigeon River Outfitter** (800/776-7238), and the **Nantahala Outdoor Center** (888/905-7238) offer journeys on both parts of the river. All outfitters are located along Old Hartford Road, at exit 477 off I-40.

Llama Trekking

For a truly upscale day hike, or a luxurious backpacking expedition, consider llama trekking. Let the llamas carry your picnic or overnight gear, while you walk comfortably to destinations in the Cherokee National Forest and Nantahala National Forest (since llamas aren't allowed in the Great Smoky Mountains National Park). **English Mountain Llama Treks** (828/622-9686) offers day trips for

between $75 and $100 a person. A two-day trip costs $280 per person, and a three-day trip is $380; all gear and food is provided.

Accommodations

The nine-room **Christopher Place** (1500 Pinnacles Way, Newport, 423/623-6555, www.christopherplace.com, $165–350) is an intimate and elegant bed-and-breakfast. Located near Newport, atop English Mountain, this colonial-style resort is perfect for a romantic getaway with a European atmosphere. Guests may walk the extensive grounds, play tennis, work out in the fitness room, swim in the pool, or relax in the billiards room or library. You may also simply want to retreat to your suite, which is appointed with luxurious furnishings and private bath. Some rooms also have private balconies overlooking the mountains. Christopher Place guests enjoy a full breakfast as part of their room rate. Dinner is served nightly at the Mountain View Dining Room for an additional $35–45 per person. Reservations are required 24 hours in advance.

Not just a place to stay, the **French Broad Outpost Ranch** (461 Old River Rd., Del Rio, 800/005-7678, www.frenchbroadriver.com, $185–230) is a place to go. This dude ranch offers overnight accommodations in the "Rough Cut," a Western-style lodge, and daily horseback riding, ranching, and white-water rafting excursions. Meals are included in the rates, which are $230 per adult per night during the high season and $185 in the low season. Slightly lower prices are offered for children, and weeklong packages are available. Prices include all activities you'll partake in at the ranch. Rooms are rustic, and designed to sleep families or groups. Meals are served family-style, and feature hearty meat-and-potatoes fare.

Food

Carver's Applehouse Restaurant (3460 Cosby Hwy., aka Hwy. 321, 423/487-2710, daily 8 A.M.–8 P.M., $6–16) is country dining the way it ought to be. The dining room overlooks the Carver apple orchard, and the home-style fare is comforting and tasty. Each meal—breakfast, lunch, or dinner—comes with sweet-savory apple fritters and a glass of homemade apple cider. The apple-smoked barbecue is a stand-out, as well as the chicken pot pie. Other choices include steaks, chicken, and fresh mountain trout—grilled or fried. The breakfast menu is extensive, with eggs, pancakes, fried potatoes, and more.

Next door to the restaurant is a farmer's market that sells fresh apples plus other local specialties.

The folks in Cosby know that as strange as it may seem, homemade Mexican food goes well with homegrown mountain music. The **ⓒ Front Porch Mexican Restaurant** (2912 Cosby Hwy., aka Hwy. 321, 423/487-2875, Fri.–Sat. 5–10:30 P.M., Sun. 5–9:30 P.M., $10–20) serves real homemade food—it's not your run-of-the-mill Mexican restaurant. The enchiladas, burritos, and chiles rellenos are made from scratch with fresh ingredients. On Friday and Saturday night at 7 and 9 P.M., local musicians take the stage to play bluegrass and folk music. Overall, it's a dining experience not to be missed. The Front Porch is closed in December and January.

For fine dining, make reservations at least 24 hours in advance at the **Mountain View Restaurant** (1500 Pinnacles Way, 423/623-6555, daily 7–9 P.M., $35–45), the restaurant at upscale Christopher Place resort on English Mountain, near Newport. Dinner is served at 7 P.M., and diners must choose their entrée when they make their reservation the day before. The food is excellent, and the refined ambience perfect for that special occasion. For something decidedly more casual, go to Christopher Place's **Marston's Library Pub** (1500 Pinnacles Way, 423/623-6555, Tues.–Sat. 5:30–8 P.M., $12–15), which serves casual English-style food without advance reservations. Menu options are bangers and mash, fish-and-chips, or a ploughman's lunch of sliced meats, bread, cheese, and mixed greens.

TOWNSEND

Located in the broad flat plain of Tuckaleechee Cove, Townsend is a world apart from Pigeon Forge and Gatlinburg. This park gateway, which provides quick access to Cades Cove

PHOTO COURTESY OF TENNESSEE DEPARTMENT OF TOURIST DEVELOPMENT

fly-fishing near Townsend

GREAT SMOKY MOUNTAINS

and the Little River Road, seems to have the proportions just right: There is still a lot of undisturbed green space surrounding a few hotels, restaurants, and the only heritage center this side of the Smokies. Outfitters rent tubes for floating down the Little River, and Tuckaleechee Caverns are nearby for underground exploring.

Recent archaeological digs found evidence of human settlement in the Tuckaleechee Cove as many as 10,000 years ago. During the early 20th century, Townsend was the end of the railroad line; timber cut from forests inside what is now the national park was floated down the river and loaded onto railcars here in Townsend.

Sights

For an introduction to the history and culture of Townsend and the surrounding park area, visit the **Great Smoky Mountains Heritage Center** (123 Cromwell Dr., 865/448-0044, www.gsmheritagecenter.org, Tues.–Sat. 10 A.M.–5 P.M., Sun. 1–5 P.M., adults $6, seniors $4, children 6–17 $4). Exhibits here describe the remarkable archaeological finds made in Townsend, and explain what scientists have learned from their discoveries. There are interactive exhibits about the lifestyles and culture of Native Americans who lived in the mountains, as well as the white settlers who carved out a life here beginning in the 1700s. Another exhibit, "Tennessee on the Move," describes just how hard it was to get around the mountains before paved roads and advanced automobiles. Outside, you can tour replicas of mountain cabins, a gristmill, cantilever barn, and smokehouse. There is an outdoor amphitheater and indoor auditorium for special events.

The **Little River Railroad and Lumber Museum** (Hwy. 321, 865/448-2211, free) is more than another railroad museum. It is also a place to learn about the extensive logging that took place in the Smokies during the early 20th century. Originally called Tuckaleechee Cove, Townsend got its name from the founder of the Little River Railroad and Lumber Company, Col. W. B. Townsend. Exhibits here include antique railroad equipment and photographs from the era of railroads and logging in the Smokies.

The museum is open June–October weekdays 10 A.M.–2 P.M., Saturday 10 A.M.–5 P.M., and Sunday noon–5 P.M. In April, May, and September the museum is open Saturday 10 A.M.–5 P.M. and Sunday noon–5 P.M. Call for an appointment to visit the museum from November to March.

Tuckaleechee Caverns (825 Cavern Rd., 865/448-2274, Mar. 15–Nov. 15 daily 9 A.M.–6 P.M., adults $14, children 5–11 $7) is the oldest tourist attraction in these parts. The caverns were known to Native Americans and early white settlers, who would travel to the mouth of the caves on hot summer days to cool off. In the early 1950s, local residents W. E. Vananda and Harry Myers invested their savings into making the caves a tourist attraction, because no bank would loan to them. A year after the caverns first opened to the public, its greatest attraction—its underground Big Room—was discovered. The Big Room, part of the one-mile underground tour, is 300 feet by 400 feet, with ceilings of up to 150 feet high. The cave maintains a constant 58-degree temperature, and it's open rain or shine.

Watch dulcimers and other mountain instruments being made at **Wood-n-Strings Dulcimer Shop** (7645 E. Lamar Alexander Pkwy., 865/448-6647, www.clemmerdulcimer.com). This music shop also hosts a free "Pickin' Porch" on Saturdays at 7 P.M. during the summer. Call for a schedule.

Tubing

Tubing may be the lazy man's version of river rafting, but boy is it fun. Plunk your behind down in the middle of an inner tube, and float on down the river. It's that simple.

Tubing is great for the whole family, and the perfect way to cool off on a hot day. Be sure to wear shoes and sunscreen; a pair of sturdy-bottomed shorts are also recommended.

There are several tubing outfitters in Townsend, including **Smoky Mountain River**

Rat (205 Wears Valley Rd., 865/448-8888, www.smokymtnriverrat.com, May–Sept. daily 10 A.M.–5 P.M., $13). Outfitters transport you a mile or so up the river and let you float back down to the starting point.

Events
During the summer and fall, the **Sunset Concert Series** at the Great Smoky Mountains Heritage Center (123 Cromwell Dr., 865/448-0044, www.gsmheritagecenter.org) offers live music in a lovely outdoor amphitheater. The heritage center also puts on the **Spring Heritage Center** in May.

Accommodations
Located right on the main highway in Townsend, **Highland Manor Inn** (7766 E. Lamar Alexander Pkwy., 800/213-9462, www.highlandmanor.com, $49–99) is a respectable motor inn with king- and queen-sized rooms. All rooms have refrigerators, and guests receive free continental breakfast and use of the outdoor swimming pool and playground.

The 10 room **Richmont Inn** (220 Winterberry Ln., 865/448-6751, www.richmontinn.com, $150–250) offers guest rooms and suites, all named for notable Smoky Mountain people and decorated in a tasteful yet rustic style. Guests enjoy a full breakfast featuring homemade breads, plus healthy and hearty options. Evening dessert is served by candlelight with gourmet coffee. Both are served in the inn's dining room with panoramic views of the mountains.

Dancing Bear Lodge (137 Apple Valley Way, 865/448-6000, www.dancingbearlodge.com, $189–279) offers both guest rooms and one- and two-bedroom cabins with a pronounced upscale edge. The lodge has a rustic feel—afforded by lots of wood finishes and botanical artwork—with refined touches like featherbeds and hot tubs. Cabins feature full kitchens, wood-burning fireplaces, and private porches. Guests are invited to a top-notch continental breakfast each morning, and they may make reservations for dinner in the lodge restaurant, which features the only full bar in Townsend. Guests are also invited to lounge in front of the lodge fireplace in the lobby, or on the porch overlooking the mountains.

The Smokies' most luxurious accommodations are, without a doubt, at **Blackberry Farm** (1471 W. Millers Cove Rd., Walland, 865/380-2260, www.blackberryfarm.com, $745–2,000). A 4,200-acre working farm located in unblemished seclusion not far from Townsend, Blackberry Farm is a true upscale resort. A member of the Relais and Chateaux group of resorts and perennial member of the elite circle of top U.S. resorts, Blackberry Farm is a remarkable place to stay. While the refined elegance of meals and atmosphere seems far removed from the rustic, down-home character of the Smokies, the closeness to the land and unspoiled nature of the property brings guests straight to the marvelous beauty of this corner of the world.

Blackberry Farm has 63 guest accommodations, including rooms, suites, cottages, and houses. All rooms are carefully appointed and leave nothing to be desired. Rates include three meals a day, many of which are prepared with organic meats and produce raised right on the farm. The food served at Blackberry Farm is simply unparalleled in these parts, and combines the best of regional ingredients with sophisticated culinary techniques.

Blackberry Farm may not be for most of us, but hats are off to those who can afford this special type of Smoky Mountain luxury.

Food
Coming to **Sister Cats Cafe** (7326 E. Lamar Alexander Pkwy., 865/448-0033, Mon.–Tues. and Thurs.–Sat. 11 A.M.–3 P.M., $9) is a highlight of any trip to Townsend. This casual yet sophisticated restaurant offers refreshingly creative fare. Entrées include smoked chicken salad and an array of paninis—including a vegetarian smoked portabella. A changing daily special may be spinach enchiladas or Italian-sausage lasagna roll. Sides are creative and unexpected: grape salad, mandarin muffins, and corn-bread salad are a few favorites. A unique feature of Sister Cats'

menu is that all lunches cost $9, and include one entrée and one side. Every other Friday evening, Sister Cats puts on a special romantic dinner by reservation only.
Miss Lily's Cafe (122 Depot St., 865/448-1924, Mon.–Fri. 10:30 A.M.–8:30 P.M., Sat. 8 A.M.–8:30 P.M., Sun. 10 A.M.–2 P.M., $11–20) serves Southern food, but with a freshness unknown at many country-cooking-style restaurants. Try the Yankee Pot Roast or Fish and Grits. Salads are fresh and filling. The pulled-pork sandwich is a favorite at lunch or dinner.

Miss Lily's Cafe is next door to the Lily Barn, a venue for weddings and other special events. The barn also sells daylilies, and the gardens are ideal for a picturesque stroll after dinner.

You can catch your own supper at the **Tuckaleechee Trout Farm and Restaurant** (142 Tipton Rd., 865/448-2290). Spring-fed trout ponds teem with fish, which are caught and prepared for dinner. It doesn't get any fresher, or more fun, than this. The trout farm is open afternoons and evenings from April to October; call to confirm.

THE FIRST FRONTIER

The mountains and valleys of Tennessee's northeastern tip were the first frontier of settlement during the 18th century. Old towns and historic sites—including the birthplace of Davy Crockett, the tailor shop of an American president, and Tennessee's first capitol—are the legacy of this rich history. Modern-day cities like Jonesborough and Elizabethton have preserved their historic buildings and are now the best places to soak in the atmosphere of early Tennessee.

The easternmost band of land in Tennessee is the Cherokee National Forest, and it is some of the most beautiful landscape in the state, with rhododendron gardens, cranberry bogs, and high mountain vistas. The Appalachian Trail and other hiking paths are ideal for exploring on foot; winding blacktop roads invite auto touring. Friendly mountain towns like Mountain City, Erwin, and Unicoi provide the essentials for exploring this still-wild part of Tennessee.

West of the mountains lie the Tri-Cities: Bristol, Kingsport, and Johnson City, each with its own unique character. Bristol straddles the state line with Virginia and is known as the place where the first country music stars were discovered. Johnson City is home to East Tennessee State University and a state-of-the-art fossil museum. Kingsport, a leader is downtown revitalization, has a pleasant, walkable downtown district. Together, the Tri-Cities serve as the unofficial capital cities of the rugged mountain region of upper East Tennessee and southwest Virginia.

West of the Tri-Cities the landscape becomes a series of long valleys divided by steep ridges.

PHOTO COURTESY OF TENNESSEE DEPARTMENT OF TOURIST DEVELOPMENT

HIGHLIGHTS

Bristol Motor Speedway: A temple to speed and adrenaline, the Bristol Motor Speedway is part of the NASCAR circuit (page 421).

Gray Fossil Site: Road crews discovered a major fossil site near Johnson City in the early 2000s; now the site is home to an interactive and educational museum of prehistoric Tennessee (page 428).

Roan Mountain: Dramatic mountain peaks, mysterious balds, and the beauty of rhododendron gardens – come to Roan Mountain to experience natural beauty and the majesty of the Southern mountains (page 436).

National Storytelling Festival: Be entertained by the world's best storytellers from the African, European, Native American, and Appalachian traditions (page 443).

Andrew Johnson National Historic Site: The home and tailor shop of Andrew Johnson in Greeneville constitute a memorial to one of the country's most controversial commanders in chief (page 446).

Kyles Ford: A small town on the Clinch River, Kyles Ford is representative of the rural, remote communities of the Appalachian region. But a top-notch country restaurant and eco-village make Kyles Ford a unique destination (page 451).

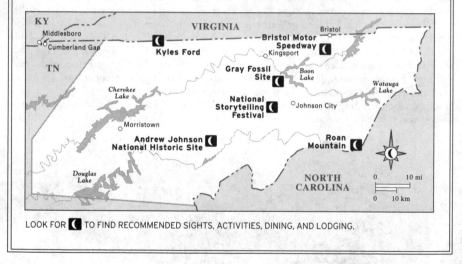

LOOK FOR **(** TO FIND RECOMMENDED SIGHTS, ACTIVITIES, DINING, AND LODGING.

Tucked into this ridge-and-valley landscape is the city of Greeneville, hometown of U.S. president Andrew Johnson. A staunch Unionist in a secessionist state, Johnson's story evinces the complexity of Civil War history in this border state. Rogersville is home to the oldest newspaper press in Tennessee. As you leave the cities and strike out over the countryside of this isolated and enchanting landscape, you realize that Tennessee's first frontier is also quite likely its last.

PLANNING YOUR TIME

If you want to see the whole of northeastern Tennessee, plan on at least a week. This is dense territory: It may look compact on a map, but narrow, windy roads and steep mountains and ridges make travel slow.

If you have less than a week, choose a subregion as your focus. The Tri-Cities offer the greatest diversity of attractions: motor speedways, historic sites, fossils, and live music. If

© AVALON TRAVEL

you enjoy the outdoors, focus on the northern Cherokee National Forest; spend your time auto touring, hiking, and rafting along the Nolichucky River. The remote ridges and valleys in the western area of this region are an ideal destination if you want to leave hustle-and-bustle behind and see some of the most remote territory in the state.

The Tri-Cities

It was an accident of history that three mid-sized cities grew up so close to one another. Bristol and Johnson City were small hamlets until the railroads came through these parts; Kingsport was a quiet river port until it became a planned industrial city at the turn of the 20th century.

The Tri-Cities region has a total population of about 500,000. Johnson City is the largest of the three, closely followed by Bristol and then Kingsport. They are separated by no more than 30 miles each, and form a triangle of urban and suburban sprawl.

Because of their proximity to each other, you can stay in one Tri-City and tour all three. They are also convenient to the northern Cherokee National Forest, Jonesborough, and Elizabethton. If you come for general sightseeing, be sure not to plan your trip to coincide with a major event at Bristol Motor Speedway, when hotels are full and the roads are clogged.

Getting There

Tri-Cities Regional Airport (TRI or TCRA, 2525 Hwy. 75, 423/325-6000, www.tri-flight.com) is located equidistant from each of the Tri-Cities. This small airport offers general aviation services, as well as commercial flights to hub airports in the region.

Four airlines serve the Tri-Cities. Allegiant Air has nonstop service from Orlando and Fort Lauderdale; Delta Connection flies from Atlanta and Cincinnati; Northwest Airlink flies from Memphis and Detroit; and U.S. Airways Express flies from Charlotte to the Tri-Cities.

Getting Around

Getting around the Tri-Cities is easy, if not a little confusing due to the sheer number of roads. I-26 connects Kingsport and Johnson City, and I-81 connects Bristol with points south. U.S. Highway 11E/19W, also called the Bristol Highway, connects Bristol and Johnson City. U.S. Highway 11W connects Kingsport and Bristol.

BRISTOL

Long before the U.S. Congress declared Bristol the birthplace of country music, this city was closely associated with traditional mountain music. It was here in 1927 that a record producer named Ralph Peer came to record local musicians. During these now-famous Bristol Sessions, Peer recorded the Carter Family and Jimmie Rodgers, who have been credited as the first popular country music stars.

Bristol was first called Sapling Grove and from its founding in 1771 until the late 19th century it was nothing more than a rural country hamlet. But then the railroads came to town—Southern Railway and the Norfolk and Western Railroad—and a modern, industrial city was born.

Bristol famously straddles two states, and its main drag, appropriately called State Street, follows the state line between Tennessee and Virginia. South of the city is Bristol's biggest attraction, the Bristol Motor Speedway, which draws a quarter million people on major race days twice each year.

Sights

State Street is a pleasant four-block row of retail shops and professional offices, with a few restaurants and bars along the way. The city's most famous landmark is the **Bristol VA-TENN Sign,** which spans the eastern end of the street. Erected in 1910, the first city slogan

THE TRI-CITIES

to appear was "Push—That's Bristol." In 1921, after a citywide contest was held, the slogan was changed to today's "A Good Place to Live." If you drive down State Street headed east, it is fun to watch the sign come into clearer and clearer focus as you approach.

Another Bristol landmark is the **Country Music Mural,** painted in 1987, which depicts heroes of the city's country music story. The mural features the Carter Family, Jimmie Rodgers, and Ralph Peer, the record producer who orchestrated the 1927 Bristol Sessions. The park at the foot of the mural is a venue for public concerts and the weekly State Street Farmer's Market, which takes place from May to October.

The **Bristol Depot** (corner of E. State St.

and Martin Luther King Blvd.) was built in 1902 for just under $80,000. This handsome brick two-story train station was a busy passenger and freight depot from its construction until the 1970s. It was restored for Bristol's 150th anniversary in 2006. About 12 freight trains continue to pass through each day.

The 1902 redbrick home of Bristol industrialist E. W. King was acquired by the Bristol Historical Association. Following restoration that started in 2008, the association plans to open the home as a museum. The **E. W. King Home** (www.bristolhistoricalassociation.org) is located at the corner of Anderson and 7th Streets.

There is a detailed self-guided walking tour of downtown Bristol available from the

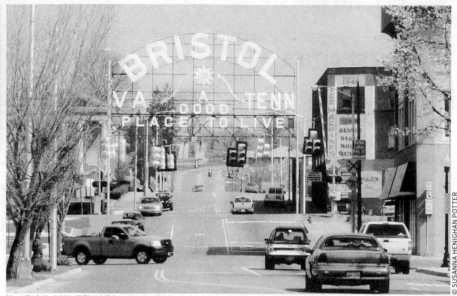

© SUSANNA HENIGHAN POTTER

the Bristol VA-TENN Sign, the city's most famous landmark

Convention and Visitors Bureau. You can also rent an audio version of the tour, or listen to it on the chamber of commerce website.

MOUNTAIN MUSIC MUSEUM

In 1998, Bristol opened its first museum dedicated to the city's place in musical history. The Mountain Music Museum (500 Gate City Hwy., Bristol Mall, 276/645-0035, www.mountainmusicmuseum.org, Mon.–Sat. 10 A.M.–9 P.M., Sun. 1–6 P.M., free) is located in a shopping mall a few miles away from downtown Bristol. There are plans afoot for a brand-new 24,000-square-foot purpose-built museum and heritage center, which will be located at the corner of Cumberland Avenue and Moore Street. But until that is completed, possibly in 2010, the mall museum is the best place to come for a look into Bristol's musical past.

The exhibits include memorabilia from the Carter Family, hometown boy "Tennessee" Ernie Ford, Jimmie Rodgers, Bill Monroe, the Stanley Brothers, Flatt & Scruggs, and several lesser-known Bristol artists and groups. Its gift shop has the best selection in town of traditional, bluegrass, and old-time music CDs.

"TENNESSEE" ERNIE FORD'S HOME

Bristol native Ernest Jennings Ford was a country and gospel star during the 1950s and '60s. Ford got his start as a radio announcer in California after World War II, where he adopted the nickname "Tennessee Ernie" and the country character the Pea Picker. Ford recorded his first album in 1949 and made his Grand Ole Opry debut in 1950. He is known for his gravelly, deep voice, and his rendition of "Sixteen Tons," a song about the hardships of coal mining. The chorus goes like this: "You load 16 tons, and what do you get? Another day older and deeper in debt. St. Peter don't you call me, cause I can't go. I owe my soul to the company store."

Ford was born and grew up in a small white house on Anderson Street, a few blocks away from downtown Bristol. His home was purchased and restored by the Bristol Historical Association (www.bristolhistoricalassociation.org), which now offers tours of the property by appointment.

THE BRISTOL SESSIONS

By the mid-1920s, a genre of music variously called "old-time music," "old Southern tunes," "hill-country tunes," and "hillbilly music" was gaining popularity. The first fiddle record was made in 1922 and the first country vocal record made a year later. Early recording artists like Charley Oaks, Uncle Am Stuart, George Reneau, and Uncle Dave Macon made records that were distributed on a small scale by a Knoxville music promoter named Gus Nennsteil.

Major-label record executives sensed that something was happening down South. Beginning in 1926, record companies began to organize "field sessions" so artists could be recorded without having to make an expensive trip to New York. The sessions that took place in Bristol in July and August 1927 proved that country music – as it eventually came to be called – both sounded good and could be a commercial success.

It was Victor Talking Machine Company talent scout Ralph Peer who ran the Bristol sessions. He chose Bristol because it was the largest urban center in the Appalachian region. Peer, who had run previous field sessions for Victor and other music labels, set up his studio in a hat warehouse on State Street. Advertisements in the newspaper initially generated limited response, but when news emerged that artists were being paid up to $100 in cash on the spot and could earn more in royalties, Peer had to schedule night sessions to accommodate everyone.

By the end of the sessions, Peer had recorded 19 performers and 76 songs, including A. P., Sara, and Maybelle Carter singing "Bury Me Under the Weeping Willow," "Little Log Cabin By the Sea," "The Storms Are on the Ocean," "Single Girl, Married Girl," and "The Wandering Boy." Jimmie Rodgers, who heard about the sessions only because he was staying in a boardinghouse in town, recorded "The Soldier's Sweetheart" and "Sleep, Baby, Sleep." Other artists included a gospel quartet from Alcoa, Bristol's Tenneva Ramblers string band, and a Kentucky holiness preacher and his congregation.

As a result of the Bristol sessions, Jimmie Rodgers and the Carter Family became overnight commercial successes. Musicologists who look back on the sessions also note that Peer made little attempt to coach or influence the artists who came to record in 1927, so the entire session is a valuable portrayal of traditional American music of the period. In addition, the business model that Peer established, where performers were paid cash up-front for recording and then earned royalties for each record sold, formed the basis of the modern recording industry.

Record labels continued to schedule field sessions around Tennessee in the succeeding years, hoping to replicate the success of Bristol in 1927. Victor returned to Bristol in 1928 and went to Nashville the same year; Columbia had sessions in Johnson City and Memphis in 1929, and Vocalion recorded in Knoxville in 1929 and 1930. The sessions led to a rich trove of recordings by diverse Tennessee artists.

The Great Depression and other economic and social forces put a close on field sessions by the early 1930s. But the genre that had been born in Bristol in 1927 was established, and music has never been the same.

If you go, you will see furnishings from the period of Ford's childhood and memorabilia from his recording career. Ford died in 1991 of liver disease, but the musician knew about plans to restore his home and was pleased by the effort.

◖ BRISTOL MOTOR SPEEDWAY
The Bristol Motor Speedway (Hwy. 11E/19, 423/989-6942, www.bristolmotorspeedway.com)

looks like a spaceship that has landed on the countryside southeast of Bristol. The speedway is a massive building—arguably the largest arena in the United States. It seats 160,000 people, and on major race days as many as 100,000 more crowd the grounds around the track to tailgate.

Bristol's race track was first developed in the early 1960s, and it would have been in nearby Piney Flats if the town hadn't banned alcohol sales on Sundays. The first race was the Volunteer 500, run in July of 1961. Nearly 50 years later, Bristol is one of NASCAR's most beloved tracks, renowned for its 36-degree banking on both ends. It was sold to its current owner, Bruton Smith, for $26 million in 1996.

Going to the races is one of the most popular, and iconic, things to do while in Bristol. The track's main events take place in the spring and late summer, and attract a quarter-million race fans. These events are a major commitment, and they sell out in a matter of days. Ticket prices start at $100, and you'll also need a place to stay. The best accommodations are in your own RV or trailer at one of the campgrounds immediately around the track. You can also get a hotel room around Bristol and fight the traffic to and from the track every day.

If you can't make it to one of the major events, check out the schedule at the Bristol Dragway, also called **Thunder Valley.** There are weekend events here from March to September, and most will set you back a mere $5. Events include street fights, drag-bike events, and the NHRA-rated Thunder Valley Nationals, usually in May. For a current schedule contact the Dragway at 423/764-DRAG (423/764-3724) or www.bristoldragway.com.

If you can't make a race event, take a tour of the massive racetrack. Even non-race fans will enjoy seeing such a major racetrack up close. During the hour-long tour of the facility, you will see the area where drivers stay when they come to Bristol, take a cruise down the drag strip, and circle the track itself. You'll also get a bird's-eye view of the track from track owner Bruton Smith's own suite. Tours begin at the souvenir shop in the Bruton Smith building, a large white building next to the track. They depart every hour on the hour. Tours are offered Monday–Saturday with the first tour at 9 A.M. and the last starting at 4 P.M. On Sunday, the tours start at noon and end at 4 P.M. No tours are given during the week preceding a major race event. Call 423/989-6960 for tour information.

A tour will run an adult $5, much less than the $100 or $200 required for a seat at the main events.

APPALACHIAN CAVERNS
Tour a cave and learn about the people who used it during the settlement period and the Civil War at Appalachian Caverns (420 Cave Hill Rd., Blountville, 423/323-2337, www.appacaverns.com, Mon.–Sat. 9 A.M.–6 P.M., Sun. 1–5 P.M., adults $9, seniors $7.50, children 4–11 $6). The hour-long regular tour is good for all audiences. Wild tours, where you get dirty, are also available, and cost more than the regular admission.

Entertainment
PICKIN' PORCH
The Appalachian Cultural Music Association puts on free concerts most Thursday evenings 7–9 P.M. at the Pickin' Porch in the Bristol Mall. For a schedule, contact them at 276/645-0035.

THE ARTS
Bristol's historic **Paramount Center for the Arts** (518 State St., 423/274-8920, www.theparamountcenter.com) is city's first venue for theater and concerts. Built in 1931 and restored in 1991, the Paramount is an historic site and a great venue for entertainment.

NIGHTLIFE
O'Mainnin's Pub and Grille (712 State St., 423/844-0049) has open-mic nights on Wednesday, and live entertainment on weekends. **State Line Bar and Grill** (423/652-0792) has happy hour, ladies' nights, and DJ music for the dance floor.

SPECTATOR SPORTS
The **Bristol White Sox** (1501 Euclid Ave., 276/669-6859, www.bristolsox.com), a Chicago White Sox farm team, play at DeVault Memorial Stadium from June to August.

EVENTS
Bristol's headline event of the year is the **Rhythm and Roots Reunion** (www.bristolrhythm.com)

IN THE FOLD

While it's located across the state line in Virginia, it's impossible to talk about this part of the state without mentioning **The Carter Family Memorial Music Center** (A. P. Carter Hwy., Hiltons, VA, 276/386-6054, www.carterfamilyfold.org). Established in the 1970s by Janette Carter, a daughter of A. P. and Sara Carter, the center's mission is to preserve old-time music.

The Carter Fold is in Poor Valley, north of Clinch Mountain in southwest Virginia. This humble yet lovely corner of the world is where Carters have lived for generations. The music center consists of the Carter Family Museum, which houses exhibits about the first family of country music; the one-room log cabin where A. P. Carter was born; and an outdoor amphitheater where live concerts are held on Saturday nights.

Action at the Carter Fold revolves around the Saturday-night concerts. You may not hear big names, but you will hear big sounds. This is mountain music the way it really is, without interference from record producers and music executives. There is lots of room up front for dancing, and no alcohol is allowed; these are family-friendly affairs. Tickets are $5-10 for adults and $1 for children 6-11. Come early to tour the museum and the A. P. Carter Cabin.

Camping is allowed on the grounds of the music center. The closest hotels are in Bristol and Kingsport.

The Carter Fold is located only a few miles over the state line, but getting there involves a 20-minute drive over winding back roads. To get there, go to Gate City and then head east on Highway 58. Follow the green highway signs to the Carter Fold.

---

held in late September. Stages are set up along State Street, inside the Paramount Center, and in other venues downtown for the three-day weekend festival. Musical styles include alternative country, bluegrass, roots, and blues. Recent headliners have been Ralph Stanley, Sam Bush, Doc Watson, and the Carolina Chocolate Drops. A three-day pass costs about $40.

Reserve your hotel room early since this is an increasingly popular event. Organizers offer shuttle buses to and from area hotels.

The **State Street Farmer's Market** (www.statestreetfarmersmarket.com) convenes in front of the Country Music Mural in downtown Bristol on Saturday mornings from May to October, and on Saturdays and Wednesdays from June to September. In addition to local produce, you will usually find live music.

Accommodations

Bristol is the land of chain motels. Partly because I-81 passes right through town, and partly because of the demand for rooms caused by the Bristol Motor Speedway, Bristol seems to have more than its share of standard-issue motels.

Be aware that while room rates around Bristol are generally low, during the weekends of the big race events, in March and August, hotels hike their prices by as much as 1,000 percent. On a recent trip, a nondescript Econo Lodge that was charging $38 on other days raised its price to more than $350 per night.

The **Holiday Inn** (3005 Linden Dr., 276/466-4100, $95–120) is located at the Bristol Convention Center and offers more amenities than most Bristol motels, including a fitness room, business center, and airport shuttle. Nearby is the **Courtyard by Marriott** (3169 Linden Dr., 276/591-4400, $110–200), whose guests enjoy an indoor pool, on-site restaurant, fitness and business centers, and airport shuttle.

Over on the Tennessee side of the state line, **Hampton Inn** (3299 W. State St., 423/764-3600, $110–200) is located along Highway 11W, near the Bristol Regional Medical Center.

Food

Bristol's finest restaurant is **The Troutdale Dining Room** (412 6th St., 423/968-9099,

Tues.–Sat. 5 P.M.–close, $25–60). Located in an 1850 Victorian townhouse, the Troutdale has a superb menu that changes with the seasons. Dishes like veal scallopini and pan-seared Hawaiian sea bass are impressive and well executed. The restaurant offers an array of trout dishes, made with seafood from the Troutdale's own 600-gallon fish tank. There's no batter-fried fish here, though—it's more in the vein of trout roulade and Akashi poached trout. There are daily and monthly specials, as well as a glorious six-course tasting menu ($100-plus) that is like heaven for your taste buds. Other features you can expect: exquisite service, a superior wine list, delectable desserts, and an unquestionable upscale atmosphere.

There are several restaurants downtown. Pick up a cup of coffee or a sandwich from **Java J's** (501 State St., 276/466-8882, Mon.–Thurs. 7 A.M.–10 P.M., Fri. 7 A.M.–11 P.M., Sat. 8 A.M.–11 P.M., Sun. 11 A.M.–5 P.M., $5–9), a relaxing and comfortable place for a pick-me-up. Paninis and designer salads, plus hot, cold, or blended coffee beverages, are on offer.

Just a few steps from State Street you can dine in an authentic burger bar, straight from the 1950s. **Burger Bar** (8 Piedmont Ave., 276/466-6200, Mon.–Fri. 6:30 A.M.–5 P.M., Sat. 7:30 A.M.–2 P.M., $3–8) may be where Hank Williams passed up his last meal (so the story goes), but you won't go hungry here. Burgers are what they're famous for, but their plate lunches and homemade desserts are also worth the trip. This is the type of place that has long faded from most urban areas in the state.

For Italian food, choose **Valentino's** (1501 King College Rd., 423/968-7655, Mon.–Thurs. 10:30 A.M.–10:30 P.M., Fri.–Sat. 10:30 A.M.–11 P.M., Sun. 11 A.M.–10 P.M., $6–16), which serves pasta, pizza, calzones, subs, gyros, and salads.

For Southern-style cooking, go to **Mother's Restaurant** (1500 Euclid Ave., 276/466-2531, Mon.–Sat. 7 A.M.–7:45 P.M., $3–7) on the Virginia side of town. This is the type of place where everyone seems to know each other, and where the dinner rolls and corn bread (the best in Bristol) are made from scratch.

If you're up for an adventure, or if barbecue is your calling, then make a detour to ☾ **Ridgewood Barbeque** (900 Elizabethton Hwy., aka Old 19E, 423/538-7543, Mon.–Thurs. 11 A.M.–7:30 P.M., Fri.–Sat. 11 A.M.–2:30 P.M. and 4:30–8:30 P.M., $7–12). Here the beef and pork barbecue is made the old-fashioned way—slowly—and the result is the most sublime barbecue within at least 100 miles. At the Ridgewood, there's no pork shoulder, only hams, which are smoked over hickory embers for nine hours before being cooled, thin-sliced, and then heated on the grill and sauced with the Ridgewood's own sweet and tangy barbecue sauce. Pork and beef (barbecue aficionados scoff at beef) platters come smothered with hand-cut, home-fried French fries. Sandwiches are served on white-bread sandwich buns. Side dishes of tangy coleslaw and smoky baked beans are advisable, although not because you need added sustenance. Portion control is not something that is practiced at the Ridgewood.

Even though the Ridgewood is well off the beaten track, it is popular. So expect to wait if you arrive at mealtime. Seating is also limited. To find the Ridgewood, drive southeast from Bristol towards Blountville and Bluff City. From Bluff City, take Highway 19E/37 towards Elizabethton. Shortly after crossing the railroad tracks, look on your right for the nondescript two-lane Elizabethton Highway, also called Old 19E. It's easy to miss. Once you're on the Elizabethon Highway, the Ridgewood is located on your right in a low-slung strip mall with a red awning. Look for the cars in the parking lot.

Information

The **Bristol Convention and Visitors Bureau** (20 Volunteer Parkway, 423/989-4850, www.bristolchamber.org) publishes maps, guides, and a walking tour of the downtown. The office serves as a visitors center and is open Monday–Friday 8:30 A.M.–5:30 P.M.

The **Birthplace of Country Music Alliance** (www.birthplaceofcountrymusic.org) is the driving force behind a lot of the good things that are happening in Bristol. This organization is working on the establishment of a downtown museum, and they promote local musical events. In addition, they are an excellent resource for information about Bristol's musical heritage.

JOHNSON CITY

The largest city in Washington County, Johnson City was once an industrial city. It was founded in 1856 by Henry Johnson as a railroad depot called Johnson's Station. After the Civil War, iron ore furnaces here processed ore from the Cranberry Mines in North Carolina. Three railroads—including the Carolina, Clinchfield, and Ohio—passed through the city.

In 1903 a U.S. Veterans Administration rest home was built in Johnson City for Union Civil War veterans, and 10 years later a normal school was established. The Quillen College of Medicine, named for State Representative James Quillen, was founded in 1974.

Downtown Johnson City still has a gritty, post-industrial feel, with lots of boarded-up buildings and empty streets. The city is enlivened by the presence of East Tennessee State University, a state school with total enrollment of about 14,000. It includes the Quillen College of Medicine and also a College of Pharmacy that opened in 2007. ETSU's Appalachian Studies program is also of note. Its journal *Now and Then* is a biannual magazine devoted to the history and culture of Appalachia. The university campus lies southwest of the city center, and provides several attractions for visitors.

East Tennessee State University

The **Carroll Reece Museum** (ETSU, 423/439-4392, www.etsu.edu/reece, Tues., Wed., and Fri. 9 A.M.–4 P.M., Thurs. 9 A.M.–7 P.M., free) is a regional art and history museum. Named for the late congressman B. Carroll Reece, the museum's permanent exhibit includes a feature on music of the Tri-Cities. An interactive computer kiosk allows you to see archival video footage of early performances by stars such as Jimmie Rodgers and the Carter Family. Other exhibit halls feature student work and changing exhibits.

Congressman James Quillen hailed from

SUDDEN SERVICE

For once, it is not the Golden Arches that define fast food. In the Tri-Cities, look for the large, turquoise, and garishly decorated fast-food chain known locally simply as **Pal's.**

Fred "Pal" Barger opened his first fast-food restaurant in Kingsport in 1956, after meeting Ray Kroc of McDonald's fame at a restaurant convention. The second Pal's opened in 1958. The chain expanded again in the 1990s and at the same time adopted its present slogan, "Great Food in a Flash." Now there are 20 Pal's from Morristown to Lebanon, Virginia. Many are drive-ins only.

Don't worry about missing Pal's: the restaurants are painted a blinding shade of blue and come with a humongous weiner, drink, French fries, and burger as outdoor decorations. Pal's is beloved for its quart-sized sweetened iced tea, called the Big Tea, as well as for its fast and accurate service. The sauceburger, chipped ham, and Frenchie fries are also well loved. In 2002, president George W. Bush gave Pal's Sudden Service the Baldridge National Quality Award.

---

upper East Tennessee and he represented the area for more than 30 years in Congress. A noted conservative, Quillen introduced the first law outlawing desecration of the U.S. flag in 1968. The late congressman's papers and memorabilia are housed on the 4th floor of the Sherrod Library. The **Quillen Gallery** (Lake St. and Seehorn Rd., 423/439-1000, Mon.–Fri. 8 A.M.–4:30 P.M., free) includes dozens of cases of photographs, plaques, and other memorabilia of the Republican's career in politics, including his collection of elephant statues. There is a room which has been furnished to look like the congressman's Washington office.

Also on the 4th floor of the library is the **Archives of Appalachia** (423/439-4338), a project of the Appalachian Studies Department. While not much to see, the archives are an important depository of documents and primary source material related to the culture, economics, and history of the Appalachian region.

ETSU has an arboretum, and you can take a tour of its giant trees, including a 200-year-old white oak in front of Sherrod Library. Collect a map of the giant trees from the Reese Museum, or contact the ETSU Arboretum (www.etsu.edu/arboretum).

If you visit ETSU, stop at the public safety office at the main entrance for a visitor's parking pass.

Quillen Veterans Administration Medical Center

The massive medical school and health center located adjacent to ETSU has an interesting history. In 1903, it was established as a residential home for ailing Union Army veterans. It evolved into a facility for all veterans of war. At the time of the writing of the 1939 WPA Guide to Tennessee, Mountain Home, as the facility came to be known, was home to 3,500 patients, including 400 hospital cases and 2,000 permanently disabled residents. Mountain Home had its own post office, theater, and chapel, and residents here were trained in handicrafts.

In the 1960s, civic leaders in upper East Tennessee first started to discuss the need for a regional health center in the area. It took almost 20 years to make this dream a reality, and in 1978 the first class of students at the Quillen College of Medicine began courses. Today, the university's medical school is a leading healthcare provider in the region.

Tipton-Haynes Historic Site

The Tipton-Haynes Historic Site (2620 S. Roan St., 423/926-3631, Apr.–Nov. Mon.–Sat. 9 A.M.–3 P.M., adults $4, children 12 and under $2) consists of 11 historic buildings, a cave, and a wooded area. It represents several areas of early Tennessee history. Woodland Indians and Cherokee hunted buffalo that were drawn to the spring here. Later, the buffalo trail became an early stage road, and long hunters camped in the cave.

The home on the property began in 1784 when John Tipton, a Maryland native, built a log cabin here. Tipton is remembered in history because he was an outspoken opponent of the State of Franklin, the unofficial state established by overmountain settlers in 1783. When North Carolina authorities seized some of State of Franklin proponent John Sevier's slaves in 1788, they took them to Tipton's home. When Sevier tried to recover his slaves, a skirmish erupted. This so-called Battle of the Lost State of Franklin marked the end of the State of Franklin movement.

In 1837 the property changed hands from the Tipton to the Haynes family. Landon Carter Haynes, who added a Greek Revival portico, was a farmer, lawyer, newspaper editor, and a three-term member of the Tennessee General Assembly. Haynes was also a secessionist who departed to West Tennessee after the Civil War.

The Tipton-Haynes property was conveyed to the state in 1944–1945. It is maintained by the Tipton-Haynes Historical Association. Call ahead to arrange an appointment during the winter.

Hands On! Regional Museum

Travelers with children should take note of the Hands On! Regional Museum (315 E. Main St., 423/434-4263, www.handsonmuseum.org, Tues.–Fri. 9 A.M.–5 P.M., Sat. 10 A.M.–5 P.M., Sun. 1–5 P.M., adults and children 3 years and up $8). This is an interactive museum of arts and sciences where children can fly an airplane, visit a coal mine, and walk through an ancient ark filled with exotic animals from around the world. In addition to its regular opening hours, the museum is also open on Mondays in June, July, and August.

Entertainment

There are two live-music venues that you should know about in Johnson City. The first, the **Down Home** (300 W. Main St., 423/929-9822, www.downhome.com), is this region's best venue for rock, folk, blues, and other roots-style music. Founded in 1976, the Down

Home has now nurtured at least two generations of music lovers in upper East Tennessee. The inside is polished wood on the floor and walls. There are about 160 seats—most of them in straight-back wooden chairs—so the atmosphere is intimate and live. There are shows here most every Thursday through Sunday night, and open mics on Wednesday. The kitchen serves bar food and Tex-Mex on Thursday through Sunday nights.

The Down Home is located on a nondescript block a short drive from downtown. A small marquee is about all you'll see from the road, so look good or you'll miss it.

The second venue for live music in Johnson City is the **Acoustic Coffeehouse** (415 W. Walnut St., 423/434-9872, www.acoustic-coffeehouse.com), which has live acts most nights of the week. The patio out front is a popular place to sit in nice weather, and this is also a good place to grab a cup of joe during the day or night.

Accommodations

Carnegie Hotel (1216 W. State of Franklin Rd., 423/979-6400, www.carnegiehotel.com, $180-350) is Johnson City's finest hotel. Located next door to ETSU, the hotel offers standard amenities plus special high-end touches like separate soaking tubs, daily newspapers, bathroom scales, and dry-cleaning service. An on-site restaurant, spa, and fitness room mean you may not ever have to leave. The Carnegie first opened in the 1890s and reopened in 2000. It is a good choice for business travelers.

Food

Quite possibly the most popular restaurant in Johnson City, **The Firehouse** (627 W. Walnut St., 423/929-7377, Mon.–Thurs. 11 A.M.–9:30 P.M., Fri.–Sat. 11 A.M.–10 P.M., $7–18) serves hickory-smoked barbecue with traditional accompaniments like corn bread, coleslaw, and baked beans. You can also order non-barbecue items such as fish, steaks, and sandwiches.

A popular choice for good Italian food is **Alta Cucina** (1200 N. Roan St., 423/928-2092, Mon.–Thurs. 11 A.M.–9:30 P.M., Fri. 11 A.M.–10 P.M., Sat. noon–10 P.M., Sun. noon–9 P.M., lunch $6–13, dinner $12–30). The lunch menu includes hot and cold sandwiches, salads, pasta, pizza, calzone, stromboli, and other Italian favorites. Dinner specialties include fresh grilled seafood and steak, plus pastas. There is a full bar, and take-out is available.

Indian specialties such as tandoori chicken and paneer sag are on the menu at **Sitar Indian Cuisine** (2102 N. Roan St., 423/926-7799, Mon.–Fri. 11 A.M.–2:30 P.M. and 5–10 P.M., Sat.–Sun. 11:30 A.M.–3:30 P.M. and 5–10:30 P.M., $6–14). The inside of the restaurant is dark and cool, the service is efficient, and the food is respectable.

Information

The **Johnson City Chamber of Commerce** (603 E. Market St., 423/461-8000, www.johnsoncitytnchamber.com) provides visitor information.

AROUND JOHNSON CITY
Rocky Mount

The first territorial capitol of Tennessee sits about five miles outside of Johnson City, on the road to Bristol. **Rocky Mount** (Hwy. 19W, Piney Flats, 423/538-7396, www.rockymountmuseum.com, Tues.–Sat. 11 A.M.–5 P.M., adults $6, seniors $5, children 5–18 $4) is open from March through mid-December and at other times by appointment. It was in this frontier homestead—the home of land surveyor William Cobb—that the governor of the Southwest Territory, William Blount, lived from October 1790 to March 1792. In a spare office here Blount organized the territory's first census and elections. In 1792 he moved to Blount Mansion in Knoxville, and the capitol moved with him.

Although the home seems rustic to us today, it was luxurious by the standards of the early Tennessee frontier. Glass windows, abundant provisions, and feather beds were some of the comforts Blount enjoyed at Rocky Mount.

Today, the home is primarily a living-history museum. Staff dress in period costumes and play Mr. and Mrs. Cobb, Governor Blount, and other members of the Cobb household and extended family. You may also see them tending to farm animals, raising the kitchen garden, or performing other daily tasks of frontier life. Inside, there is a museum and video that discuss frontier life and the early political history of Tennessee.

◖ Gray Fossil Site

Crews cutting a new road near Gray, Tennessee, in 2000 discovered fossilized animal bones, setting off a sequence of events that led to the opening in 2007 of the **Natural History Museum at the Gray Fossil Site** (1212 Suncrest Dr., 866/202-6223, www.grayfossilmuseum.org, daily 8:30 A.M.–5 P.M., adults $5, seniors $4, children 5–12 $3). The fossil

find spawned the creation of a paleontology program at East Tennessee State University, which now leads the scientific investigation of the Gray site. So far, two new ancient animal species, a red panda and badger, have been discovered.

The Gray site is over five acres and the best estimate is that it will take more than 100 years to fully excavate and study the fossils that lie here. It is so rich in fossil remains because some 4.5 to 7 million years ago it was a water hole, where beasts large and small came to drink and, in some cases, die.

The museum and outdoor displays are designed for children, but adults will enjoy them as well. The museum describes the animal and plant life that surrounded the water hole. It also takes visitors through the tedious yet exciting process of discovery and analysis that scientists follow. Overall, the exhibits are captivating and creative.

Upstairs, you join a guide who takes you out

Visitors to the Gray Fossil Site can watch as archaeologists work.

© SUSANNA HENIGHAN POTTER

to the site itself. Inside, you can peer into the laboratory where each bone fragment that is found is carefully clean, analyzed, preserved, and stored.

KINGSPORT

A city with industrial roots and a unique history, Kingsport is the most culturally sophisticated of the Tri-Cities. Located on the Holston River, Kingsport was an important shipping port for years before the city was born. The Long Island of the Holston, a large island that lies in the Holston River, was a site of political and spiritual importance to Cherokee Indians.

Downtown Kingsport is being revived, and it is a pleasant place to walk around. Attractions around the city include historic homes and one of the largest city parks in the state.

History

Kingsport is located along the route of a historic trail used by Indians, hunters, and early settlers. The Long Island of the Holston, a 3,000-plus-acre island in the Holston River, was important to Cherokee Indians and it served as a neutral meeting ground for Indians and settlers. The Long Island of the Holston Treaty was negotiated here in 1777. By 1809 Cherokee had ceded the island and nearby lands to settlers, and the settlement on the Holston became known as Ross's Landing. The city of Kingsport was first chartered in 1822.

Kingsport was destined to remain a quiet river community until the early 20th century, when industrialists and city planners joined to establish a new, model city. This self-proclaimed "All-American City" was born around 1915 with the establishment of the Kingsport Improvement Corporation. The corporation, founded by the owners of the Carolina, Clinchfield & Ohio Railway, had the job of planning and building a new industrial city.

Different experts were hired to plan the city, design housing, make landscape designs, develop a school system, and install sewerage and sanitation facilities. Corporation lawyers drew up articles of incorporation in 1917.

But what really made Kingsport a success was the industry that it attracted. Tennessee Eastman was and is Kingsport's largest employer. Over the years, Eastman has produced photographic chemicals, war explosives, acetate yarn, polypropylene for outdoor signs, and polyester plastic for use in beverage bottles, among many other things. During World War II and beyond, Eastman was responsible for managing the Y-12 National Security Complex at Oak Ridge.

Like other small and midsized American cities, Kingsport has wrangled with problems like sprawl and the decline of its downtown.

Sights

Central Kingsport is the city that was laid out by town planners and industrialists in the early 20th century. The oldest attractions in Kingsport are located slightly west of downtown, along the Holston River. A nine-mile greenway connects the Holston River area with Historic Exchange Place on the east side of town.

HISTORIC DOWNTOWN

The planned nature of Kingsport is evident downtown. Broad Street is a wide, divided two-lane road with four blocks of storefronts, many of which still sport notable art deco architecture. The old depots for the Carolina, Clinchfield & Ohio railway stand along Main Street; the passenger depot is now a bank and the freight depot houses the visitors bureau. At the other end of Broad Street is the **Church Circle,** a traffic circle that houses four churches. At the corner of Center and Commerce Streets is a mural that represents Kingsport's history. Students of architecture should follow the 1.8-mile walking tour developed by the Downtown Kingsport Association.

It has taken a lot of effort to bring Kingsport's downtown to what it is today. Like other towns of its size in Tennessee, Kingsport suffered during the 1970s and '80s as businesses moved out of downtown and economic activity spread to the outlying areas, starting with the first shopping malls. But in 1974 a downtown association was formed, and over the past 30-plus years they have led the way in Kingsport's resurgence. They have been involved with projects ranging from the improvement of sidewalks to annual arts events.

THE BOATYARD

The oldest part of Kingsport is the Boatyard, located along the Holston River on the west side of town. The **Netherland Inn** (2144 Netherland Inn Rd., 423/246-7982, www.netherlandinn.com, May–Oct. Sat.–Sun. 2–4 P.M., adults $4, children under 7 $1) was a stagecoach stop, inn, and boatyard catering to travelers who came through this country by land or river. The inn, first built between 1802 and 1808 by William King, is named after Richard Netherland, who bought the property in 1818 and expanded it. Group tours may be arranged by appointment.

At the rear of the inn are several log homes, including a Daniel Boone cabin, which was moved here in order to preserve it. This is the symbolic beginning of the Daniel Boone Heritage Trail, which celebrates the wilderness trail that Boone and thousands of other early settlers used to enter the Tennessee frontier.

Across the road from the Netherland Inn is one end of Kingsport's greenway system. You can walk or bike nine miles from here all the way to Exchange Place, on the other side of town.

The greenway passes the **Long Island of the Holston.** A site of political and spiritual importance to the Cherokee, and a place for meetings between the Cherokee and white settlers, the Long Island is now home to **Heritage Park,** which has walking trails, picnic tables, and historical markers. Parts of the island are residential, while a coal gasification plant belonging to Tennessee Eastman sits on the southern end of the island.

EXCHANGE PLACE

This 1850s homestead is a living-history museum and center for workshops, festivals, and other special events that celebrate traditional arts, crafts, and ways of life. Exchange Place (4812 Orebank Rd., 423/288-6071, www.exchangeplace.info, Apr.–Sept. Thurs.–Fri. 10 A.M.–2 P.M., Sat.–Sun. 2–4:30 P.M., free) consists of about a dozen period buildings, most of them original to the property. They include the "saddlebag"-style log house, kitchen, spring house, schoolroom, blacksmith shop, and barn. Across the road is an early 20th-century home that serves as the visitors center. Exchange Place got its name because its owner, John Preston, exchanged money for travelers who passed by on the stagecoach road from Virginia into Tennessee. He also exchanged goods.

Exchange Place is operated by a private nonprofit organization. Some of the funds needed to maintain the old buildings come from the proceeds of selling works completed by the Exchange Place Quilters and Overmountain Weavers, volunteers who weave and quilt.

Several special events are held here every year. They include the Spring Garden Fair at the end of April, the Fall Folk Arts Festival at the end of September, and Christmas activities in December.

Parks

Kingsport has an extraordinary city park. **Bays Mountain Park** (853 Bays Mountain Park Rd., 423/229-9447, www.baysmountain.com, June–Aug. Mon.–Sat. 8:30 A.M.–8 P.M., Sun. 1–8 P.M., Sept.–May Mon.–Fri. 8:30 A.M.–5 P.M., Sat. 8:30 A.M.–8 P.M., Sun. 1–8 P.M., $3 per car) is a 3,300-acre nature preserve that lies between Bays Mountain and the Holston River Mountain, southwest of downtown Kingsport. It takes about 15 minutes to drive to Bays Mountain from downtown. The park's attractions include a nature center (Mon.–Fri. 8:30 A.M.–5 P.M., Sat.–Sun. 1–8 P.M.) with exhibits on plants, weather, space, and animals; a planetarium with regularly scheduled shows; star observatory; deer, wolf, bobcat, otter, and raptor habitats;

farmstead cabin; and 25 miles of hiking trails. There are also service roads open to mountain bikers after they have paid a $2 registration fee. A barge cruises the Bays Mountain Reservoir on weekends year-round and daily from June to August. Bays Mountain offers special naturalist-led programs nearly every day, ranging from wolf-howls to moonlight barge rides. Check their website for current programs and schedules.

Warrior's Path State Park (Hemlock Rd., 423/239-8531) is located on the shores of Fort Patrick Henry Lake, as the Holston River is called south of the Fort Patrick Henry Dam. There are 12 miles of hiking trails, mountain bike paths, an Olympic-sized swimming pool, an 18-hole golf course, and a 22-hole disc golf course. Boaters enjoy cruising and fishing on the lake; paddle and fishing boats are available for rent from the marina office. In addition, there is a 135-site campground with modern hot-water bathhouses and water and electrical hook-ups. Warrior's Path State Park is located southeast of downtown Kingsport, about 15 minutes' drive from the city.

Events

The **Spring Garden Fair** (www.exchangeplace. info) kicks off the season in April at Exchange Place, a working farm and living-history museum. The Garden Fair features local and regional craftspersons, food, and music. The bookend to the spring fair is the **Fall Folk Arts Festival** in September, also held at Exchange Place.

In July, Kingsport celebrates **Fun Fest** (www.funfest.net), a weeklong series of concerts, sports competitions, fireworks, and a hot-air balloon rally.

Accommodations

Located near the civic auditorium and close to downtown Kingsport, **Fox Manor B&B** (1612 Watauga St., 423/378-3844, www.foxmanor.com, $110–150) is a 19th-century townhome that has been converted into a luxurious bed-and-breakfast. The five guest rooms are decorated with rich fabrics, deep woods, and top-notch furnishings. High-quality linens, fireplaces, ceiling fans, and private baths add to the appeal. Breakfast is served in an elegant dining room. Other common rooms include the library with an English-style bar and the cozy verandah.

Arcadia Manor (4368 Bloomingdale Pk., 423/288-8533, www.arcadiamanor.com, $125) is a country estate located about seven miles from downtown Kingsport and built in the 1870s. Four guest rooms in the house have private bathrooms. Outside two log cabins offer privacy and rustic-style accommodations, but with modern-day comforts like air-conditioning, TV, coffeemakers, microwaves, telephones, and refrigerators. Full breakfast is included.

Chain hotels in Kingsport include the **Days Inn Kingsport** (805 Lynn Garden Dr., 423/246-7126, $70–80), located very close to downtown. There is free continental breakfast, in-room coffeemakers, hair dryers, microwaves, and refrigerators. There is an outdoor pool.

Located about midway between downtown and Exchange Place is a **Comfort Inn** (100 Indian Center Court, 423/378-4418, $80–90), a 122-room hotel with standard amenities and an above-average hot breakfast bar. There is an outdoor pool.

Food

The **Café N'Orleans** (316 Cumberland St., 423/245-5400, Mon.–Fri. 11 A.M.–2 P.M., Tues. 5–8 P.M., $5–11) downtown offers gumbo, jambalaya, po' boys, and other Louisiana favorites.

Jan Mar Restaurant (114 Broad St., 423/245-0731, Mon.–Fri. 6 A.M.–3:30 P.M., Sat. 6 A.M.–2:30 P.M., $5–9) is a cozy, comfortable place for breakfast or lunch. Biscuits and gravy are the morning favorite, and at lunch choose between a hearty burger or one of the daily plate-lunch specials.

Sandwiches are the specialty at **Deli Sandwich Factory** (1308 E. Stone Dr., 423/246-3354, Mon.–Sat. 10 A.M.–8:30 P.M., $3–7). The house specialty is the Kitchen Sink Sandwich that features ham, smoked turkey, salami, corned beef, roast beef, and Swiss cheese.

For home-style Southern fare, head to **Mama's House Buffet** (2608 N. John B. Dennis Hwy., 423/247-5691, Wed. and Sat. 8–10:30 A.M., Mon.–Thurs. 11 A.M.–8:30 P.M., Fri.–Sat. 11 A.M.–9 P.M., Sun. 11 A.M.–7 P.M., $6–10), which offers lunch and dinner daily and breakfast on Wednesday and Saturday. The buffet features different meats and sides daily, but expect choices like sweet potatoes, meatloaf, bread dressing, pork loin, sliced ham, brown beans, and spaghetti and meatballs.

One of Kingsport's most popular barbecue joints has downtown and east-side locations. **Broad Street BBQ** (2921 E. Center St., 423/247-8646, Mon.–Fri. 11 A.M.–6 P.M., Sat. 11 A.M.–3 P.M., $5–7; 115 Broad St., 423/245-7382, Mon.–Wed. 11 A.M.–3 P.M., Thurs.–Fri. 11 A.M.–7 P.M., Sat. 11 A.M.–3 P.M., $5–7) offers a full menu of barbecue choices, including hickory-smoked ribs, pulled pork, and barbecue chicken.

Another option for barbecue is **12 Bones** (242 E. Main St., 423/239-7225, daily 11 A.M.–9 P.M., $5–15), which offers pulled chicken and pulled pork, as well as chopped brisket, among other favorites.

Kingsport's best seafood restaurant is **Riverfront Seafood Company** (1777 Netherland Inn Rd., 423/245-3474, $7–20). Casual food here includes oyster, shrimp, white fish, and smoked turkey po' boys. At least a dozen types of fish are available fried, grilled, or prepared specially according to house recipes. Crab legs and Maine lobster are also on the menu.

Information

Downtown Kingsport (140 W. Main St., 423/246-6550) promotes the city center and publishes a walking tour to historic sites. The **Kingsport Convention and Visitors Bureau** (151 E. Main St., 423/392-8820, www.visitkingsport.com) has maps and brochures and can help you organize tours and group events.

Northern Cherokee National Forest

The northern Cherokee National Forest covers 327,000 acres from the northern boundary of the Great Smoky Mountains National Park to the Virginia state line. It encompasses wilderness regions, state parks, and towns. Because it is a national forest, and not a national park, commercial enterprises, including logging, are allowed.

The Appalachian Trail passes through this part of the Cherokee National Forest, and there are abundant opportunities for hiking, biking, camping, and other outdoor pursuits. The Nolichucky River is popular with whitewater rafters and the Watauga Lake offers boating and fishing prospects.

Sights include Roan Mountain's rhododendron gardens, Shady Valley's cranberry bogs, and dramatic Backbone Rock. Thanks to the smattering of towns, including Erwin and Mountain City, there is enough "civilization" to make this countryside accessible and easy

to explore. While it's outside of the bounds of the national forest, Elizabethton shares the characteristics of the region, and offers a quaint downtown experience with shopping, restaurants, and historic homes.

Information

For information about the northern Cherokee Forest, visit one of two ranger stations. The **Watauga Ranger District** (4400 Unicoi Dr., 423/735-1500, Mon.–Fri. 8 A.M.–4:30 P.M.) is in the town of Unicoi and is the headquarters for the northernmost portion of the forest. The **Unaka/Nolichucky Ranger District** (4900 Asheville Hwy., aka Hwy. 70, Greeneville, 423/683-4109, Mon.–Fri. 8 A.M.–4:30 P.M.) is headquartered outside of the bounds of the forest, in Greeneville. Both ranger stations offer maps, guides, and other helpful information about the forest.

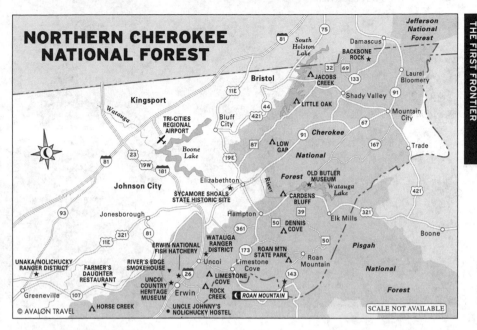

NORTHERN CHEROKEE NATIONAL FOREST

LAUREL BLOOMERY

Laurel Bloomery is located in the extreme northeastern corner of Tennessee, the first town you will meet after crossing over the Virginia state line. Named for the mountain laurel that grows here and the iron smelters, or bloomers, which once raged here, Laurel Bloomery is now a peaceful mountain village. Every August, on the weekend before Labor Day, the town hosts an **Old Time Fiddlers' Convention** (423/727-9595) at the Old Mill Music Park on Highway 91. The tradition of an annual music convention began here back in 1925, and this is one of the best places to come to hear real old-time music. The music usually gets started around 6 P.M. and keeps rolling well into the night. Many conventioneers set up camp along the river for the weekend.

Gentry Creek Falls

Chain-effect waterfalls—one 30 and one 40 feet high—are located along Gentry Creek near Laurel Bloomery. It is a 2.5-mile hike to the falls from the trailhead, which is located on Gentry Creek Road a short ways off Highway 91. To get there, turn on Gentry Creek Road and drive for 0.7 mile. Turn right, following Gentry Creek Road, for another 1.8 miles. At this point the road becomes unpaved. Drive for 0.2 mile and turn right again, and follow the road another 1.8 miles to the trailhead. There is limited parking. For information, contact the Watauga Ranger District of the Cherokee National Forest at 423/735-1500.

BACKBONE ROCK

A remarkable natural and man-made landmark west of Laurel Bloomery, on the road between Damascas, Virginia, and Shady Valley, Tennessee, Backbone Rock is a rock formation that developed where the Beaverdam Creek flows past a spur of Holston Mountain. The rock is nearly 100 feet tall in places and about 50 feet thick; it is called Backbone Rock because it resembles a spine. In 1901 a tunnel was drilled through the rock to make way for the railroad. Today, the road passes through

© SUSANNA HENIGHAN POTTER

Backbone Rock

this gap, known locally as the shortest tunnel in the world.

Get out of your car and hike the short path up and over the rock. The trail is steep and rocky, and children should be closely supervised along it. Another hike takes you to Backbone Falls.

There is a lovely creekside picnic area here, and the Beaverdam Creek invites you to wade or swim in its clear waters.

Facilities include a picnic area and a primitive campground.

SHADY VALLEY

Located at 2,800 feet and surrounded by mountains is Shady Valley, a high-mountain cove that is best known for its wetlands. Bogs and white pine/hemlock forests once covered most of the valley; they flourished here due to the higher elevation and the influence of the last Ice Age. With human settlement, many of the bogs were drained to make way for agriculture.

Today, Shady Valley is a quiet collection of old and new homes on rolling farmland. The winding rural roads leading to the valley attract motorcyclists. The four-way intersection of highways constitutes the commercial center—there are three gas station/delis but little else. The town has erected an information board near the intersection, and here you'll find a map to at least four of Shady Grove's cranberry bogs. The easiest one to find is **Schoolyard Springs,** located a few hundred yards from the Shady Valley Elementary School. Local residents have built a boardwalk over and around the bog. Here you can watch the bog bubble up from below and listen to a symphony of birdsongs. The effort to preserve Shady Valley's bogs has been led by the Nature Conservancy.

Shady Valley celebrates its cranberry bogs and much more with the annual **Cranberry Festival** (423/739-2131) held during the second full weekend in October. You could not imagine a more picturesque setting, what with the glorious fall leaves surrounding the valley like a giant-sized stadium. The festival includes various cranberry-themed events, plus an arts-and-crafts auction and other amusements.

MOUNTAIN CITY

This small town of about 3,000 is the seat of Johnson County and a commercial hub for the northernmost mountains in Tennessee. The **Johnson County Welcome Center and Museum** (716 S. Shady St., aka Hwy. 421, 423/727-5800, www.johnsoncountychamber.org, Mon.–Sat. 9 A.M.–5 P.M.) is a good stop for information and orientation. The museum houses local historical relics, and there are brochures, maps, and helpful people to offer assistance.

Golf

Redtail Mountain is a high-end residential development near Mountain City. Its 18-hole, par-72 golf course is open to nonresidents. Greens fees are $55 on weekdays and $70 on weekends. To reserve a tee time call the pro shop at 423/727-7931.

Accommodations

The **Prospect Hill B&B Inn** (801 W. Main St., aka Hwy. 67, 423/727-0139, www.prospect-hill.com, $100–180) is a five-room inn housed in an 1889 brick Victorian-shingle home. Fully renovated and carefully restored, the inn's guest rooms have special features like whirlpool tubs, private balconies, and private entrances. All guests enjoy the mountain views from the porch and a hearty homemade breakfast. Rooms are furnished in a classic, tasteful style, with original artwork hanging in many of them. If you're looking for a getaway, this is a good choice.

Food

For a cup of coffee, light lunch, or slice of homemade cheesecake, come by **Craig's Coffee House** (122 Murphy St., 423/727-0567, Mon.–Wed. 7 A.M.–3 P.M., Thurs.–Fri. 7 A.M.–2 P.M. and 5–8 P.M., Sat. 8 A.M.–2 P.M., $4–15). Serving fresh-roasted coffee, daily lunch specials, and home-cooked dinners twice a week, Craig's is a popular meeting place for the denizens of Mountain City. It is located in a cozy white building opposite the Mountain City Primary School.

If you're in the mood for Italian cooking,

you're in luck. **Angelo's Main Street Cafe** (310 W. Main St., 423/72704600, Tues.–Sat. 8 A.M.–9 P.M., Sun. 8 A.M.–3 P.M., $8–10) serves pasta dishes like fettuccini Alfredo, eggplant parmesan, and spaghetti and meatballs. The café also has breakfast all day plus home-cooked favorites like chicken and dumplings and meatloaf.

TRADE

Considered the oldest community in Tennessee, this mountain hamlet is located within spitting distance of the North Carolina state line. Named Trade because it was where settlers and Indians once met to trade, the town is now a quiet, rural settlement with lovely scenery all around. Highway 421, which connects Trade with Mountain City, is a winding, scenic route through the mountains. It is said that North Carolina fugitive Tom Dula, made famous by the folk song Tom Dooley, hid out in Trade until a posse found him and arrested him for murdering his fiancée.

For a bite of food in Trade stop at **Sharpie's Restaurant** (Hwy 421, 423/727 0079, Mon.–Thurs. 6 A.M.–8 P.M., Fri. 6 A.M.–9 P.M., Sat. 6 A.M.–8 P.M., $5–12). This friendly little diner-style restaurant has burgers, steaks, roasted chicken, and sandwiches.

WATAUGA LAKE

The Tennessee Valley Authority was at work in this part of Tennessee too. In 1949, TVA completed the Watauga Dam and created Watauga Lake, the highest-elevation lake in Tennessee. Even today, it is surprising to find a placid lake amid the Unaka mountain peaks in this landscape. The lake is picturesque, with clear, cool waters ideal for swimming and fishing.

Pontoon boats, fishing boats, and sailboats are available for rent from **Fish Springs Marina** (191 Fish Springs Rd., Hampton, 423/768-2336). An all-day rental will cost $150–180, plus fuel. Reservations are recommended, especially on weekends.

When the lake was formed, the town of Butler was inundated. "Old Butler" lies at the bottom

CAMPING IN THE NORTHERN CHEROKEE FOREST

Campgrounds are located throughout the Unaka and Watauga Districts of the Cherokee National Forest. All forest service campgrounds are available on a first-come, first-served basis only. They have potable water and toilets; some have warm-water showers.

- **Backbone Rock Recreation Area** is located near the Virginia state line. Its 11 campsites accommodate tents or trailers – but not RVs. There are flush toilets and drinking water, but no showers or electrical hook-ups.

- **Cardens Bluff Campground** is a 43-site campground on Watauga Lake, which can accommodate tent and trailer campers. Amenities include showers, drinking water, and flush toilets. There are no electrical hook-ups.

- **Jacobs Creek Recreation Area** is located near the Virginia state line on the banks of South Holston Lake. Its 29 sites can accommodate tents or RVs. There are showers, drinking water, and flush toilets.

- **Little Oak Campground,** also located on South Holston Lake, is a large campground with 72 tent and RV sites. It has showers, flush toilets, and drinking water.

- **Rock Creek Recreation Area** near Erwin sits at the foot of Unaka Mountain. It has 36 campsites, 14 with electrical hook-ups. Day-use facilities include a swimming pool, bike trail, hiking paths, and picnic tables. Fees are $10 for sites with electricity and $5 for sites without. To find Rock Creek, take Rock Creek Road from Main Street in Erwin. It is three miles to the campground.

- **Limestone Cove Campground** near Erwin has 18 tent-friendly campsites near Indian Creek. Sites have a tent pad, lantern post, grill, and vault toilets.

- **Dennis Cove Campground** near Hampton has 18 campsites, flush toilets, no hook-ups, and no showers. It is along Laurel Fork Creek, making it popular among anglers. To get here, take U.S. Highway 19E through Hampton and turn right onto Dennis Cove Road. Drive up the mountain 4.5 miles; the campground is on your right.

---

of the lake, but "New Butler" remains on the shore of the water. The **Old Butler Museum** (Hwy. 67, 423/768-2432, Sat.–Sun. 1–4 P.M. and other times by appointment, free) houses community artifacts taken from the post office, barber shop, and people's homes before it was flooded, and it records the way of life of more than 400 families in the Watauga River valley who were forced to move when the lake was made.

Downstream from Watauga Lake is Wilbur Lake, also called Horseshoe Lake. Wilbur Lake was created in 1912 when the Watauga Power Company dammed the Watauga River. Since 1945 the dam has been owned by TVA.

There are public canoe launches on Wilbur Lake, but no commercial recreation facilities. Because the water is very cold, only rainbow and brown trout are found in the waters. Both are stocked.

Accommodations

You can rent your own cabin overlooking the lake from **Cherokee Forest Mountain Cabins** (789 Grindstaff Rd., Butler, www.cabin-4me.com, $170–210). These fully furnished homes away from home have fireplaces, hot tubs, full kitchens, and plenty of space to relax and unwind. Weekly rates are available.

Iron Mountain Inn (138 Moreland Dr., Butler, 423/768-2446, www.ironmountaininn.com, $130–250) is a four-room bed-and-breakfast located in a log cabin. The innkeepers offer a variety of special packages that focus on pastimes including hiking, golf, fishing, and biking. There are also romantic getaways, holiday specials, and special midweek or off-season rates.

◖ ROAN MOUNTAIN

Quite possibly the most lovely natural site in northeastern Tennessee, Roan Mountain is a high mountain ridge noted for its open balds and rhododendron gardens. Part of the Cherokee National Forest, Roan Mountain is a five-mile stretch of ridge that straddles the North Carolina–Tennessee state line and ranges from 6,286 feet at its peak to 5,500 feet at Carver's Gap. The 10-mile stretch of the Appalachian Trail that follows the crest of Roan Mountain is believed by some to be the most beautiful of the entire trail. Treeless mountain balds, including Jane's Bald, Grassy Bald, and Round Bald, open up sweeping views of the Blue Ridge mountains. During June, the tall, bushy Catawba rhododendron bloom, creating a blanket of pink, white, and yellow flowers.

Visitors to the top of Roan Mountain can stop at the National Park Service information cabin for maps and directions. From the cabin you can take an easy, short walk along a paved track through the rhododendron gardens to an overlook. The Cloudland Trail is a 1.2-mile moderate hike to the Roan High Bluff Overlook.

Also nearby is **Miller's Homestead,** a 1909 farmhouse that has been restored to show traditional mountain life. The homestead is open from Memorial Day to Labor Day, and on summer weekends special storytelling, music, and arts-and-crafts programs keep it alive.

If you wish to make Roan Mountain your destination, then there is no better home base than **Roan Mountain State Park** (1015 Hwy. 143, 423/772-0190), located eight miles down the mountain. Park facilities include a museum, cabins, campground, swimming pool, and tennis courts. Even if you don't stay at the park the **museum** (daily 8 A.M.–4:30 P.M., free) is well worth a stop for its detailed look at the natural and human history of the nearby mountains.

The 30 fully equipped cabins ($65–100) are open year-round and provide kitchens, wood stoves, and outdoor grills. A campground ($14.50–17.50) has 107 sites, including 87 with RV water/electricity hook-ups.

ELIZABETHTON

The seat of Carter County, Elizabethton is one of the oldest incorporated towns in Tennessee. Its downtown is vibrant, and the important

historic site of Sycamore Shoals is on the outskirts of town. The Doe River, which passes through the city, makes it a scenic spot.

Historic Downtown

Spanning the Doe River in downtown Elizabethton is the **Doe River Covered Bridge,** which crosses the Doe River at Hattie Avenue. This 1882 wooden bridge spans some 134 feet and rests on earth and limestone abutments. It was high enough to withstand floods, including the Great May Flood of 1901. It is now closed to vehicular traffic—a new concrete bridge spans the river at Elk Avenue—but remains open to foot and bike traffic. There is a pleasant park on the east bank of the river from which you can enjoy views of the bridge.

On the west bank, you can see a piece of early Tennessee history. It was in the early 1770s that the very first overmountain settlers began to establish farms in what is now northeastern Tennessee. The wilderness still belonged to the Cherokee Indians, but the settlers could not resist the promise that it represented. By 1772, an estimated 80 farms were located along the Holston and Watauga Rivers.

The settlers soon realized they needed some form of local government. They were outside the bounds of the closest state—North Carolina—and far away from the nearest courthouse. In 1772 the settlers formed the Watauga Association, which allowed them to prosecute criminals and settle disputes. A part of the sycamore tree under which this association was formed is on display a few steps from the Doe River Covered Bridge.

Elizabethton has a number of historic homes, old businesses, and landmarks, including the tallest Fraser fir in the state of Tennessee. Get a copy of the brochure *Elizabethton Walking Tour* from the visitors bureau or the public library to explore further.

Carter Mansion

One of the first settlers in this area was John Carter, a trader who first moved into modern-day Tennessee in 1770. In 1772 he

© SUSANNA HENIGHAN POTTER

The Carter Mansion was one of the finest homes on the Tennessee frontier.

moved near the Watauga River, in present-day Elizabethton. John Carter was one of the signers of the Watauga Association agreement. John Carter's son, Landon, was also a political leader and businessman. Landon Carter's wife, Elizabeth, was Elizabethton's namesake, and Carter County was named for him. The family home has been preserved and is now called the Carter Mansion (1651 W. Elk Ave., 423/543-6140 or 423/543-5808, free). The simple white frame home may look homely, but it was luxury on the frontier. Its hand-carved crown molding, chair rail, and mantels are evidence of this.

Tours of the home are offered daily at 2 P.M. from May to August, and at other times by appointment. The home is managed by the Sycamore Shoals State Historic Site.

Port Rayon

As you drive into Elizabethton from the west you cannot miss the large factory that sits along the banks of the Watauga River.

This is the remains of the **Bemberg and Glanzstoff rayon factories,** which opened in the 1920s. In their heyday, these factories had their own rail depot, called Port Rayon, which brought members of their workforce to the factory every day. The factories experienced ups and downs throughout the Great Depression, World War II, and during the post-war years. At their peak in 1949, the factories employed some 6,000 people. Economic fluctuations, the cost of new environmental protection measures, and changing corporate structures caused the factories to downsize during the 1970s, '80s, and '90s. By 1998, there were just 250 people employed at the factory, now called North American Rayon Corporation. A massive fire broke out at North American Rayon in 2000. It took firefighters a week to fully put out the blaze, which led to the final closure and demolition of the factory.

Sycamore Shoals

Many of the most important events in early Tennessee history took place in the area of **Sycamore Shoals State Historic Site** (1651 Elk Ave., 423/543-5808) along the Watauga River, just a few miles outside of Elizabethton. It was near here in 1775 that the Cherokee agreed to sell 20 million acres of land to Richard Henderson in what is now known as the Transylvania Purchase. Fort Watauga, built as a defensive fort for early settlers along the Watauga River, was near here. And in an open glade next to the river, hundreds of overmountain men mustered in 1780 as they began their march to King's Mountain to fight the British during the Revolutionary War.

The historic site consists of a replica of Fort Watauga and a walking trail that takes you along the Watauga River to the areas where some of these momentous events are believed to have taken place. Inside the visitors center (Mon.–Fri. 8 A.M.–4:30 P.M., Sun. 1–4:30 P.M., free) there is a museum and video.

Annual events at Sycamore Shoals include the staging of *The Wataugans* in July, the

© SUSANNA HENIGHAN POTTER

Sycamore Shoals was the place where hundreds of overmountain men mustered for the march to King's Mountain during the American Revolution.

Muster at Fort Watauga in May, the Native American Festival in June, the Overmountain Victory Trail Celebration in September, and the Fort Watauga Knap-In in October.

Accommodations

Old Main Manor (708 N. Main St., 423/542-8277, www.oldmainmanor.com, $65–85) is a redbrick townhouse with two guest rooms. Hardwood floors, super-stuffed couches, and luxurious bedding are among the touches you can expect. Breakfast is served in the dining room or on a tray delivered straight to you.

The Doe River Inn (217 Academy St., 423/292-2848, $75–125) is set in an 1894 home, near where early settlers forded the Doe River. There are two guest rooms in the house, or you can rent the two-bedroom cottage or one-bedroom carriage house, also on the property.

Food

The Coffee Company (444 E. Elk Ave., 423/542-3438, Mon.–Sat. 11 A.M.–2:30 P.M.) is a coffee shop and bakery that also offers the best salads and sandwiches in town. Sandwiches include a grilled panini with meat or veggies, French dip, or pesto turkey. Salads feature fruit, meat, and vegetables.

Fine dining is on the menu at **Carter at Main** (829 E. Elk Ave., 423/543-4212, Tues.–Sat. 11 A.M.–9 P.M., Sun. 11:30 A.M.–3 P.M., lunch $8–10, dinner $12–40). In an elegant Victorian mansion, now painted coral-red, Carter at Main offers streamlined upscale lunches and relaxed dinners to remember. The lunch menu features sandwiches, soups, and salads, like the Carter Club, Dilly Cucumber, and the chicken salad plate. Dinner features choices of fresh pasta, seafood, or steak specialties. Pecan chicken, Carolina stuffed trout, and Smoky Mountain pork chop are among the favorites. Because Carter on Main is set in an old home, seating may be in one of several dining rooms, including an outdoor patio and gazebo.

Information

The best guide to Elizabethton is the walking tour, a substantial brochure available from the local tourism council and some downtown businesses. Pick up a copy at the **Elizabethton-Carter County Chamber of Commerce and Tourism Council** (500 19E Bypass, 423/547-3850, www.tourelizabethton.com) or the **Elizabethton Public Library** (201 N. Sycamore St., 423/547-6360).

ERWIN

Gateway to the Cherokee wilderness and commercial center for largely rural Unicoi County, Erwin is a friendly but unpretentious town. Located along both I-26 and an active railroad line, Erwin is a place where things and people are on the move. A smattering of restaurants, hotels, and the only bona fide hostel in these parts make it a good home base for exploring the forest.

Erwin had a succession of names during its early history. First known as Unaka, it was changed to Longmire in 1840. Then it became Vanderbilt. In 1879 town officials agreed to name the city after D. J. N. Ervin, who donated 15 acres of land to establish a county seat. Unfortunately for Mr. Ervin, a mistake by post office officials caused the name to be recorded as Erwin. Finally, a name stuck.

Unlikely industries keep Erwin afloat: State and federal fish hatcheries produce broodstock and fish and National Fuel Services prepares enriched uranium for nuclear-powered navy ships. CSX Rail also has a depot and car repair center in Erwin.

For 40 years starting in 1917, Erwin was home to one of America's largest and most well-known manufacturers of hand-painted pottery. Southern Pottery, located a few miles outside of town, created dinnerware that was sold under the name Blue Ridge. Men shaped, finished, and fired the dishes while a decorating department of more than 500 area women painted designs on by hand. Blue Ridge pottery is now highly collectable.

The appeal of Blue Ridge pottery is the individual flair left behind by the painters. While the women worked from patterns, they painted by hand, and so each plate turned out just a little different from the next.

Sights

Erwin is home to two fish hatcheries, one operated by the state and one by the federal government. The **Erwin National Fish Hatchery** (423/743-4712, Mon.–Fri. 7 A.M.–3:30 P.M., free) produces between 10 million and 12 million rainbow trout eggs annually, which are shipped to federal, state, and tribal fish hatcheries around the country. It is one of two federal rainbow trout broodstock facilities in the country. There is a small exhibit and display raceway for visitors. If you visit outside of working hours, there is an outdoor kiosk next to the display raceway.

The **Erwin State Trout Hatchery** (475 Banner Springs Rd., 423/743-4842, Mon.–Fri. 7:30 A.M.–4:30 P.M.) is one of the facilities that receives Erwin's trout eggs. This hatchery keeps the trout until they are big enough to be released into area streams and lakes. Visitors can walk up and down the raceways and look at the fish.

On the grounds of the Erwin National Fish Hatchery, in a building that once housed the fishery superintendent, is the **Unicoi County Heritage Museum** (423/743-9449, daily 1–5 P.M., free), which is open from May through October. The museum houses exhibits about Erwin and Unicoi County; it has a nice collection of Blue Ridge Pottery from the old Southern Pottery plant in Erwin and displays about the Clinchfield Railroad, which is closely tied to the history of Erwin. At the rear of the museum is a 30-minute nature trail with marked trees and other plants.

The heritage museum is housed in a white Victorian farmhouse built in 1903 as accommodation for the fish hatchery superintendent.

In 1982, instead of demolishing the old house as ordered by the federal government, the local chamber of commerce petitioned for the old building to be saved and turned into a local history museum.

Erwin is surrounded by good **apple-growing country.** Farms in this area produce sweet, crisp apples that are sold in the fall. The **Unicoi County Chamber of Commerce** (100 Main St., 423/743-9584, www.unicoicounty.org) can provide you with a list of area farms that are open to the public.

Recreation

The Nolichucky River makes for an exciting, beautiful, and unpredictable rafting trip. River outfitters in Erwin offer trips along the Upper and Lower Nolichucky. With class II–IV rapids, the river trip is exciting. It also offers a lovely journey down an otherwise inaccessible 3,000-foot river gorge. Due to the rapids, no one under 12 years is allowed on the river. On average, a full-day river trip costs $60–80 per person.

Erwin-based outfitters include **Cherokee Adventures** (2000 Jonesborough Rd., 423/743-7733, www.cherokeeadventures.com) and **USA Raft** (1005 Jones Branch Rd., 423/743-3221, www.usaraft.com), also known as Mountain Adventure Guides.

Events

The **Unicoi County Apple Festival** (www.unicoicounty.org) takes place in October and includes a gospel music showcase, apple contests, a show of Blue Ridge pottery, and free shuttle buses to the Unicoi County Heritage Museum.

Shopping

Alan Stegall keeps the tradition of pottery alive in Erwin. His shop, **Stegall's Pottery** (200 Nolichucky Ave., 423/743-3227), across from the public library, produces beautiful mugs, platters, and other stoneware.

Accommodations

Hikers and budget travelers love **⟨ Uncle**

Johnny's Nolichucky Hostel (151 River Rd., 423/735-0548, www.unclejohnnys.net, $17.50–40). Located two miles outside of Erwin along the Nolichucky River, the hostel is about 60 feet from the Appalachian Trail. Through-hikers fill up the hostel during the early spring months, but outdoor folks with lesser ambitions love it year-round. Guests at Uncle Johnny's choose from accommodations ranging from private cabins to communal bunkhouses. Rooms are heated, and there is a bathhouse with hot water, showers, and a sink for washing dishes. There is a definite outdoors feel here; the front desk sells just about every piece of gear a hiker might need, and the accommodations are rustic. But for a hiker, especially one who is trying to complete the 2,170-mile Appalachian Trail, the digs are downright palatial.

There is a bike path into town and a fleet of bikes available to borrow from. Uncle Johnny will also shuttle you into town. Most hikers head first for food—Erwin has its share of chain restaurants—and then to do a load of laundry and check their email at the local library. The Nolichucky Hostel is a good base even if you are not hiking the whole Appalachian Trail. Section hikers use it as a base, and others fashion great day hikes that end at the doorstep. Talk to Uncle Johnny for help planning your itinerary.

In addition to the hostel, there is a **Holiday Inn Express** (2002 Temple Hill Rd., 423/743-4100, $80–100) and a **Super 8** (1101 N. Buffalo St., 423/743-0200, $50–70).

Food

J. D.'s Market (1313 Jackson Love Hwy., 423/743-4035, daily 6 A.M.–11 P.M., $5–9), a low-slung circular building that is also a gas station, is a popular pit stop for a working-man's breakfast of eggs, toast, hash browns, and coffee. At lunch, grilled sandwiches, burgers, and hot dogs are on the menu, along with specials—burrito casserole, for example. Sit at the lunch counter or at a booth in the small dining room.

Erwin's most memorable meals are served at the **☾ River's Edge Smoke House** (2004 Jonesborough Rd., 423/743-3713, Thurs.–Sun. 11:30 A.M.–8:30 P.M., $5–15). Located on the bank of the Nolichucky River, River's Edge serves barbecued beef, pork, and turkey, plus hand-tossed pizzas. Smoked prime rib is the house specialty, but the landfill barbecue platter (ribs, turkey, beef, and pork) is also popular. Smaller appetites can choose a barbecue or fried catfish sandwich. There is also a lunch buffet on weekdays and Sundays. The large wood-paneled dining room has high ceilings and commanding views of the river and nearby woods. Look for the giant knife and fork on the road to know you have arrived.

Located on Highway 107, midway between Erwin and Greeneville, is **☾ The Farmer's Daughter Restaurant** (7700 Erwin Hwy., aka Hwy. 107, 423/257-4650, Fri.–Sat. 11:30 A.M.–8:30 P.M., Sun. 11:30 A.M.–5 P.M., $12). This wood-paneled eatery is well worth the drive, especially for those who relish home-style country cooking. The menu features a changing selection of main entrées, which are served with a smorgasbord of family-style side dishes: mashed potatoes, cornbread salad, carrot soufflé, fried okra, creamed corn, and coleslaw. Entrées include dishes like fried chicken livers, fried chicken, chicken and dumplings, barbecue ribs, and country ham. Adult plates are $12 and plates for children (6–11 years) are $6. Children five years and younger eat free. Each table gets to choose two main dish entrées. The day's vegetables come with the meal, along with drinks.

Ridges and Valleys

West of the Cherokee National Forest, the high mountains are replaced with a series of ridges and valleys. These ridges run parallel to the mountains—at a northeasterly keel—and cause roads and railways to follow a similar slantways track.

Some of these valleys are home to relatively large towns and busy roads. But as you head westward, and push north towards the Kentucky state line, you enter into countryside that remains largely unblemished by widespread development.

JONESBOROUGH

If this region of Tennessee is the state's first frontier, then Jonesborough is its first town. Established in 1779 while the frontier was still part of North Carolina, Jonesborough was named for Willie Jones, a North Carolina legislator who supported westward expansion. Jonesborough was the capital of the erstwhile State of Franklin and an important commercial and political hub in the years before Tennessee became a state. Other interesting historical connections are that Andrew Jackson practiced law in Jonesborough for several months in 1788, and that the first regularly published abolitionist newspaper was published in Jonesborough by Quaker Elihu Embree starting in 1820.

The best thing about Jonesborough today is that its history has been preserved. Way back in the 1970s, when other cities were building strip malls and highways, Jonesborough started to preserve its historic downtown. It was the first downtown district in Tennessee to be placed on the National Register of Historic Places. In 1973, the first National Storytelling Festival was held, and after more than 30 years it continues to be one of Tennessee's most popular annual events.

Today, historic Jonesborough is one of the most vibrant small towns in the region for shopping and dining. Its downtown district is inviting and a pleasant place for a stroll. And since the National Storytelling Center opened here in 2002, visitors who miss the storytelling festival may still hear some great tales.

Sights

The **Historic Jonesborough Visitors Center** and the **Jonesborough-Washington**

County History Museum (117 Boone St., 423/753-1015, Mon.–Fri. 8 A.M.–5 P.M., Sat.–Sun. 10 A.M.–5 P.M., free) share a building about one block from Main Street. Together, they make a good first stop for visitors to the town. The visitors center has maps and other information, while the museum houses artifacts and memorabilia about Tennessee's oldest town, including the oldest known photo of Jonesborough, which dates to 1850.

HISTORIC DOWNTOWN
Jonesborough's oldest frame building is the **Chester Inn** (116 W. Main St.). The Chester Inn was constructed in the late 1790s by William Chester, a medical doctor who capitalized on the new stage road that passed through town. Now owned by the state, the Chester Inn houses the offices of the National Storytelling Festival.

The **Christopher Taylor House** (124 W. Main St.) appears a bit out of place among Jonesborough's handsome frame and brick buildings. This log cabin, which once housed Andrew Jackson, was moved to Main Street and restored. It was built around 1778.

National Storytelling Festival
The National Storytelling Festival (800/952-8392, www.storytellingcenter.net) is Jonesborough's premier event. Taking place over the first weekend in October, the festival features multiple tents with storytellers from a diverse range of traditions and styles. Traditional mountain tellers share the stage with world performers from Africa, Asia, Europe, and South America. Native American, Irish, and African-American storytelling traditions are showcased. Indeed, if you thought that storytelling was a dying art, you will be pleasantly surprised by the depth and relevance of the artists who perform at the festival.

The storytelling festival began in 1973 and today it attracts some 10,000 people each year. Weekend passes cost $135–155 for adults and $115–135 for children; single-day passes are also available. Registered attendees receive a detailed schedule for each tent, and you can simply choose which tellers you want to hear. Food is served in a food court and at area restaurants, or you can pack a picnic. The storytelling festival is a good experience for people of just about every walk of life, and considered

PHOTO COURTESY OF TENNESSEE DEPARTMENT OF TOURIST DEVELOPMENT

National Storytelling Festival

to be one of Tennessee's best and most unique events.

Book a room very, very early if you hope to stay in Jonesborough proper during the festival (and be prepared to pay premium rates). The closest motel accommodations are in Johnson City. Erwin and Greeneville are not far away, and camping is available at Davy Crockett State Park.

If you can't make it to the national festival, you can still hear stories in Jonesborough. From June to October, on Tuesdays through Saturdays, the **National Storytelling Center** (116 W. Main St., 423/753-2171, www.storytellingcenter.net, Tues.–Sat. 10 A.M.–5 P.M.) offers free storytelling from the storyteller in residence. While it lacks the electricity and excitement of the large-scale festival, it is still a wonderful way to pass some time and rediscover this classic art form. During the rest of the year, the center houses exhibits about storytelling. It also has a nice gift shop.

Recreation

For something a little different, take the family to **The Wetlands** (123 Boone St., 423/753-1553, May–Aug. Mon.–Fri. 10 A.M.–6 P.M., Sat. 10 A.M.–6 P.M., Sun. 10 A.M.–6 P.M., Aug.–Sept. weekends only, adults $11, children 4–12 $9, seniors $8), a water park that includes flume rides, boardwalks, a wave pool, and much more. Check for exact opening dates, which normally coincide with local school calendars.

Accommodations

There are bed-and-breakfast-style inns and guesthouses in Jonesborough. On the highways leading to town you will find major chain motels.

The historic ☾ **Eureka Hotel** (127 W. Main St., 423/913-6100 or 877/734-6100, www.eurekajonesborough.com, $109–129) is your best choice for accommodations in Jonesborough. Built in 1797 and expanded 100 years later, this handsome hotel offers 16 guest rooms that blend old-fashioned atmosphere with modern comforts. Amenities include soundproof insulation, voice mail and data ports, private

telephone lines, individual climate control, and cable TV. Private baths, high-speed wireless Internet, and a continental breakfast round out the offerings. The Eureka Inn is centrally located and guests will enjoy use of the back garden plus off-street private parking.

Many of Jonesborough's other bed-and-breakfasts are located in historic homes that line quiet side streets in town. Distinctive bed-and-breakfast-style accommodations are found at the **Blair-Moore House** (201 W. Main St, 423/753-0044, www.blairmoorehouse.com, $125–160). This Greek Revival–style brick home has been fully restored and an English-style garden built in the rear. The two guest rooms and one suite have high ceilings, four-poster beds, and fine linens. Rooms also each have a private balcony and bathroom, with antique claw-foot tubs. The suite also has a walk-in shower. The homemade breakfast prepared by hostess Tami Moore is a real winner.

The **Mohler Guest House** (509 W. Main St., 423/913-3000, www.mohlerguesthouseofjonesborough.com, $85–150) is an 1885-era home with guest accommodations featuring private baths, central heat and air-conditioning, cable TV, Internet, full breakfast, and fireplaces. Rooms are furnished with wrought-iron bed frames, and guests will enjoy relaxing on the rear deck.

The **Fidder's Glen Bed 'n' Breakfast** (104 S. Third Ave., 423/913-3259, www.fiddlersglenbnb.com, $120–130) is an 1854 Carpenter Gothic home with two guest rooms, friendly cats, and a hostess who plays the fiddle. The music room holds a large collection of musical instruments, and the library upstairs will keep you occupied if Jonesborough fails to. Rooms have private bathrooms, and guests will enjoy a filling breakfast in the morning.

Housed in an elegant 1832 home on four acres, the **Febuary Hill Bed and Breakfast** (102 W. College St., 423/737-6501, www.bbonline.com/tn/febuaryhill, $150–200) is named for a local family, not the month. This large and upscale home sits just a block from Main Street atop a hill overlooking the town. Each room has a private bathroom.

Food

Jonesborough has a pleasing array of eateries. Located a few blocks from the historic downtown, the **Olde Town Pancake House** (142 Boone St., 423/913-8111, Mon.–Thurs. 7 A.M.–2 P.M., Fri. 7 A.M.–8 P.M., Sat. 7 A.M.–2 P.M., $3.25–12) is a classic breakfast eatery. There are dozens of varieties of pancakes, including buttermilk, buckwheat, and apple stack. In addition, choose from omelets, biscuits and gravy, or classic breakfasts of eggs, toast, and bacon. At lunch you can also order grilled sandwiches, burgers, or dinner specials like fried catfish and rib-eye steak.

Jonesborough's "it" restaurant is **The Bistro** (105 E. Main St., 423/788-0244, Mon.–Sat. 11 A.M.–4 P.M. and 5–9 P.M., Sun. 11 A.M.–2 P.M., $9–30), which serves dishes like pecan-encrusted salmon, filet mignon, and even a Black Angus hot dog.

For a cup of coffee, a plate of the daily lunch special, or a bowl of soup beans and corn bread, head to **Cranberry Thistle** (107 E. Main St., 423/753-0090, Tues.–Fri. 8 A.M.–7 P.M., Sat. 9 A.M.–7 P.M., $3–10). Midday diners are treated to live music in the dining room, or sit out front with the locals who meet here to keep up-to-date on the latest news. Breakfasts are economical and filling, and the fresh-baked cakes and pies are heavenly. After 7 P.M., when the kitchen closes, Cranberry Thistle remains open serving desserts and coffee until about 10 P.M., or whenever the crowd starts to head home.

Information

The **Historic Jonesborough Visitors Center** (117 Boone St., 866/401-4223, www.jonesboroughtn.org, Mon.–Fri. 8 A.M.–5 P.M., Sat.–Sun. 10 A.M.–5 P.M.) is open daily and provides free

THE LOST STATE OF FRANKLIN

For about five years in the 1780s, settlers in what is now upper East Tennessee tried to establish a new American state called Franklin. The movement was spurred mostly by the feeling among many of these overmountain families that they were too far away from the government of North Carolina, and that North Carolina was not providing the law and order that they needed.

The State of Franklin movement met with opposition in North Carolina, which viewed it as an act of rebellion. More important, however, was the fact that many wealthy North Carolina land speculators held title to land over the mountains, and that existence of a separate state could invalidate their claims.

Despite the opposition from North Carolina, and a few local settlers as well, the State of Franklin enjoyed some success. In December 1784 a convention met in Jonesborough that agreed that the North Carolina constitution would form the basis of Franklin's government, with a few minor alterations. A second convention a year later led to the adoption of the Holston Constitution, which provided for a unicameral legislature. At a third convention

in March 1786, John Sevier was elected the governor of Franklin.

North Carolina continued to oppose the statehood movement in its western territories. Overmountain settlers themselves had mixed feelings about Franklin. North Carolina improved its government services in the frontier as conciliation, so some settlers no longer saw the need for a separate state government. But in the area south of the French Broad, the frontier of the day, residents appreciated the strong anti-Indian stance taken by Sevier and the Franklin government.

Support for the State of Franklin dwindled by early 1789. By this time the Cherokee had been pushed south of the Little Tennessee River, providing, at least for now, peace. John Sevier became a member of the North Carolina legislature from Greene County, and retreated as an outspoken proponent of separate statehood.

No leader emerged to succeed Sevier, and the movement faded into history. And indeed it would be less than 10 years later that the lands over the mountain, now called Tennessee, would be admitted as the 16th state.

maps, a walking tour, and other information about the town.

GREENEVILLE

Founded in 1783 and named after Nathanial Greene, a Revolutionary War hero, Greeneville is the seat of Greene County. Two American heroes, Davy Crockett and U.S. president Andrew Johnson, are affiliated with the city and the county.

◖ Andrew Johnson National Historic Site

America's 17th president called Greeneville home. Andrew Johnson was born in Raleigh, North Carolina, in 1808, but he spent the better part of his life in this Tennessee city. It was here that Johnson, a self-educated tailor, first showed promise as a debater and political leader. Three Johnson buildings remain in Greeneville and together they comprise the Andrew Johnson National Historic Site (121 Monument Ave., 423/638-3551, www.nps.gov/anjo, daily 9 A.M.–5 P.M., free). Johnson's Early Home is where he and his wife, Eliza McCardle, lived during the early years of their marriage. Next door is Johnson's old Tailor Shop, fully enclosed by the present-day visitors center, where Tailor sewed clothes and debated local politics with his customers and friends. About three blocks away is the Johnson Homestead, the grander home to which the Johnsons moved in 1851, and where they returned in 1869 after his term as president.

Inside the Early Home are displays about Johnson's early life and family. The visitors center contains a museum about Johnson's political career, and inside the Tailor Shop you can see some of the tools Johnson would have used to sew clothes. Guided tours of the Homestead include several family bedrooms and the parlor, arranged as it would have been during Johnson's post-presidential years. As evidence of the unpopularity of Johnson's pro-Union views, the tour includes a section of unflattering graffiti on an interior wall, just some of what the Johnsons found upon their return to Greeneville in 1869.

In addition to these buildings, there is also a replica of the Raleigh, North Carolina, building where Johnson was born. This is located across the street from the Early Home, and was erected in 1999. On a hill overlooking the town is Johnson's grave, over which are the words, "His Faith In the People Never Wavered."

The visitors center is open daily except holidays. Tours of the Homestead are offered hourly on the half-hour; tickets for this free tour must be obtained from the visitors center in advance.

Other Sights

Greene County is named for Nathanial Greene, a Revolutionary War hero. The local history museum also bears his name. Come to the **Nathanial Greene Museum** (101 W. McKee St., 423/636-1558, Tues.–Sat. 10 A.M.–4 P.M., free) for a closer look at the town's history, its notable buildings, and its hometown hero, Andrew Johnson.

Greeneville's most prominent home was built between 1815 and 1821 by Irish and enslaved African artisans. The **Dickson-Williams Mansion** (108 N. Irish St.) was owned first by William Dickson, a wealthy landowner, merchant, and Greeneville's first postmaster. His daughter, Catherine Dickson Williams, was well known for entertaining esteemed guests including the Marquis de Lafayette, Davy Crockett, and three presidents: Andrew Johnson, Andrew Jackson, and James K. Polk. Tours of the home are given daily at 1 P.M. and cost $10 for adults and $5 for children 6 to 18 years. For reservations and information, contact Main Street Tours at 423/787-0500.

Tours

Main Street Tours (310 S. Main St., 423/787-0500) offers a guided walking tour of Greeneville, which stops at historically and architecturally significant buildings, the oldest jail in Tennessee, and sites important to Andrew Johnson's history. The tours are offered April through October Monday through Saturday at 9:30 A.M. Tickets, which cost $5, may be purchased at the General Morgan Inn.

In addition to these guided tours, local

officials have developed two self-guided tours for visitors. One, titled "A Walk with the President," is a walking tour of Greeneville. The second includes 40 different auto tours of Greene County. Copies of either are available from Greene County Partnership (115 Academy St., 423/638-4111, www.greenecountypartnership.com).

Recreation

Kinser Park (710 Kinser Park Ln., 423/639-5912, Apr.–Oct. Mon.–Thurs. 8 A.M.–8 P.M., Fri.–Sat. 8 A.M.–10 P.M., Sun. 8 A.M.–8 P.M., www.kinserpark.com) is a public park with a swimming pool, water slide, putt-putt golf course, 18-hole golf course, volleyball, basketball, tennis, and other ball fields, and a 157-site campground.

Food

The denizens of Greeneville meet for lunch over club sandwiches and chicken salad at the **Tannery Downtown** (117 E. Depot St., 423/638-2772, Mon.–Fri. 10:30 A.M.–2 P.M., $5–6), located a few doors down from the Andrew Johnson visitors center.

For something more elegant, choose **Brumley's** (111 N. Main St., 423/787-1000, Mon.–Sat. 7 A.M.–9 P.M., Sun. 10 A.M.–2 P.M., lunch $7–10, dinner $18–30) in the General Morgan Inn. The weekday soup and salad bar is popular with lunchtime diners, along with the smothered black beans and rice, roasted pork, and crab cakes. Dinner offers elegant choices such as baked sea bass and filet mignon.

Accommodations

Named for the Confederate outlaw and hero General John Hunt Morgan, nicknamed "The Thunderbolt of the Confederacy," who was killed in Greeneville, the **[General Morgan Inn** (111 N. Main St., www.generalmorgan-inn.com, $107–120) is Greeneville's most distinctive hotel. First opened as the Grand Central Hotel in 1884, the General Morgan was restored and reopened in 1996. Its lobby has a high ceiling and elegant chandeliers; the refinement continues in the 52 guest rooms and suites where you'll find luxury linens, marble vanities, wireless Internet, and iPod-compatible radios. Guests can also take advantage of business services and passes to a local gym.

Information

The **Greene County Partnership Tourism Council** (115 Academy St., 423/638-4111, www.greenecountypartnership.com) has maps and other guides to Greeneville and the rest of Greene County.

AROUND GREENEVILLE
Tusculum

About 10 miles east of Greeneville is Tusculum, a small college town. Tusculum was chartered in 1794 and is the oldest college in Tennessee. In 1872 it admitted women, making it one of the first coeducational colleges in the United States. Nine buildings on the Tusculum campus have been placed on the National Register of Historic Places, including the **Andrew Johnson Presidential Library and Museum** (Tusculum College, 423/636-7348, www.tusculum.edu/johnson, Mon.–Fri. 9 A.M.–5 P.M., free). This is the official museum and library dedicated to Johnson, a Tusculum trustee, as designated by Congress. The museum houses political memorabilia, artifacts, and photographs emphasizing the daily life of the Johnson family, including the bed in which he died. His papers are also here, and are used by researchers and historians.

The **Samuel Doak Museum** (Tusculum College, 423/636-8554, www.tusculum.edu/museum/doak, Mon.–Fri. 9 A.M.–5 P.M., adults $2), owned by the college, is the home that Reverend Samuel Witherspoon Doak built beginning in 1818 for his father, Dr. Samuel Doak. Dr. Doak had been one of the first ministers on the Tennessee frontier. He preached to the over-mountain men before they left on their journey to Kings Mountain in 1780. Dr. Doak moved to Washington County and established Salem Church and school in the early 1780s. The school became Washington College, a day and boarding school for young men. Boys from far and near traveled for the opportunity to learn Latin, mathematics, and other subjects.

The Samuel Doak House is where both Samuel Doaks lived from 1818 until 1829, when Dr. Doak died. The museum features a few articles of furniture original to the Doak home. The handsome redbrick building was lived in by members of the Doak family until the 1950s. There is also a replica of Doak's original schoolhouse on the property.

For food in this area, head to **Tusculum Eatery** (905 Erwin Hwy., 423/638-9210, Mon.–Fri. 10:30 A.M.–2:30 P.M., $4–7), a pleasant place to pass the time while you munch on fresh-made sandwiches, salads, and daily specials like lasagna and chicken pot pie. Artwork by local artists adorns the walls.

Limestone

Davy Crockett was not born on a mountaintop in Tennessee; he was born in the rolling foot-hills, near where the Limestone River flows into the Nolichucky. His birthplace is near the present-day settlement of Limestone, about 15 minutes' drive from Greeneville. The cabin where Crockett was born is long gone, but a replica sits on the banks of the Nolichucky at the **Davy Crockett Birthplace State Park** (1245 Davy Crockett Park Rd., 423/257-2167), also home to a museum about this most famous Tennessean.

Crockett lived on the banks of the river with his parents for 10 years before the family decamped to Morristown to open a tavern. After he became a man, Crockett continued to move gradually westward, seemingly following the ever-migrating frontier of America. He is known to have lived in Greene, Hamblen, Lincoln, Franklin, Lawrence, and Obion Counties in Tennessee before he moved to Texas, where he was killed at the Alamo.

Crockett's folksy language and boasting stories turned him into one of the most enduring symbols of the frontiersman. A museum at the state park includes copies of all the known portraits of Crockett, memorabilia he inspired, plus information about what is known about this remarkable man. Crockett's most famous sayings include, "Let your tongue speak what your heart thinks," and "Be always sure you're right, then go ahead."

HUNTING FOR QUILTS

As you drive through upper East Tennessee, look for colorful quilt squares on the sides of barns and other buildings. These are no spontaneous displays of artwork; they are part of the Appalachian Quilt Trail, a program designed to encourage visitors to some of Tennessee's most rural and isolated landscapes.

It began in 2004 when the first quilt panel was hung on a barn in Grainger County. Over the succeeding years, some 200 panels representing heirloom quilt patterns have been hung in 19 counties and along 300 miles of rural driving routes. The southernmost quilt is in Englewood; the northernmost is in Kyles Ford, near the Virginia state line. New squares are going up all the time, and there are efforts afoot to expand the trail farther south.

You can download a map of the entire trail at www.vacationaqt.com. Looking for the quilt squares makes a fun car game as you travel through this part of Tennessee.

the Appalachian Quilt Trail

© RICHARD HENIGHAN

In addition to the sights related to Crockett, the state park has a campground with 88 sites, which are available on a first-come, first-served basis; about 2.5 miles of hiking trails; and a swimming pool, which is open from Memorial Day to Labor Day.

ROGERSVILLE

A town of many firsts, Rogersville is a worthwhile destination. Tennessee's first newspaper was published here, and the city is home of the oldest courthouse, inn, and post office still in operation in Tennessee.

Rogersville was settled in about 1775. According to legend, some of those early settlers were Davy Crockett's grandparents. It was named after Joseph Rogers, an Irishman who received the land on which Rogersville sits as a wedding present from his father-in-law, Col. Thomas Amis.

Rogersville was on the Wilderness Road, the route that traveled from Bean Station to Cumberland Gap and into Kentucky. Beginning in the 1840s, the city was a transportation hub for native pink and red marble, which was used in construction of the Washington Monument in Washington, D.C., the South Carolina State Capitol, and the municipal buildings in Baltimore.

Today, Rogersville is a quiet yet relatively happening place. A handful of unique attractions, an inviting downtown district, and the nearby countryside, which is beautiful and rural, make this a small town worth remembering.

Historic Downtown

Take a few minutes to explore Rogersville's historic district. The **Hawkins County Courthouse** is the oldest original courthouse still in use in Tennessee. It was built in 1836 and was fashioned after Independence Hall in Philadelphia. Across the road from the courthouse is **Overton Lodge,** the oldest Masonic Lodge in continuous operation in Tennessee. The lodge was chartered in 1805. The present building was constructed in 1839 as the first branch of the Bank of the State of Tennessee. Also on the town square is the **Hale Street Inn** (110 W. Main St.). Built in 1824 it is the oldest continually operating inn in Tennessee.

A few blocks north is the **Swift College Campus** (200 N. Depot St.). Swift College was a Northern Presbyterian college for African Americans and operated from 1883 to 1955. It was founded by Dr. William Henderson Franklin of Knoxville, who was the first black graduate of Maryville College. From 1955 to 1963 it was Hawkins County's African-American high school. After integration, the lovely administration building was torn down. Remaining buildings are used by the Hawkins County Department of Education.

Price Public School is a community center that was once Rogersville's African-American school. Established in 1868, Price Public School educated blacks from 1870 until desegregation. The present building was constructed in 1922. Hours vary; if you are able to go inside you can view a room dedicated to Swift College and Price Public School.

A printed guide to historic Rogersville is available from the Rogersville Heritage Association (415 S. Depot St.) and the Rogersville–Hawkins County Chamber of Commerce (107 E. Main St.).

Tennessee Newspaper and Printing Museum

The *Knoxville Gazette* was first published in Rogersville in November 1791, before it was moved to Knoxville. George Roulstone and Robert Ferguson arrived in Rogersville on the invitation of governor William Blount, and they named their newspaper in anticipation of the establishment of the new city to the south. But while Knoxville was getting off the ground, Roulstone and Ferguson published for about one year from Rogersville. When the time came to move, they moved the presses to Knoxville on a flatboat down the Holston River.

Rogersville's first newspaper is recalled at the **Tennessee Newspaper and Printing Museum** (415 S. Depot St., 423/272-1961, free), located in the town's old train depot. Its advertised opening hours are Monday–Saturday

10 A.M.–4 P.M., but experience says it is best to call ahead and confirm.

The museum contains a re-created 19th-century print shop, original copies of more than two dozen newspapers that were printed here, and artifacts from the Pressman's Home. You can also see the last linotype machine used to set type for a Tennessee newspaper; the machine was used by the *Rogersville Review* until 1982.

Pressman's Home

Located about 12 miles north of Rogersville are the abandoned remains of Pressman's Home, a once thriving community affiliated with the 125,000-member International Printing Pressmen and Assistants' Union (IPPAU). Rogersville native George Berry headed the union from 1907 until 1948, and it was due to his efforts that the substantial facility was built in remote upper East Tennessee.

Pressman's Home covered 2,700 acres. It had its own phone and electrical system, post office, and farm. In addition to being the administrative headquarters of the IPPAU, Pressman's Home was a retirement home, sanatorium, and printing trade school. For a time, Pressman's Home was the largest training school of its kind in the world. New and experienced pressmen came here to learn offset printing methods. They also offered a correspondence school.

Pressman's Home operated from 1911 until 1966, when union officials decided they needed to return to a more cosmopolitan place. In 1967 the IPPAU headquarters moved to Washington, D.C. Not 10 years later the IPPAU merged with another union and disappeared from the union registry.

Today, Pressman's Home is abandoned and the community has been renamed Camelot. It is not a very inviting place. A former country club and golf course on the property failed, and plans to turn it into a state prison and an

THE MELUNGEON MYSTERY

Hancock County was one of the first parts of Tennessee to be settled by Europeans. A 1673 letter by early explorer Abraham Wood described his visit to the area: "Eight dayes jorny down this river lives a white people which have long beards and whiskers and weares clothing . . ." These white people were also described by John Sevier in 1784, who reported that they seemed to have been living in the area for some time.

The word that came to be used to describe these mysterious early settlers was "melungeon." Even the origin of the word is unclear; it was initially thought to have derived from the French word *mélange*, meaning mixture. Other research suggests it may be an Afro-Portuguese word meaning "white person," and still other scholars believe it is from the Turkish language and means "cursed soul."

When Anglo-European settlers arrived in the area, they conveniently decided that the Melungeons, who had olive complexions and dark hair, were people of color, and promptly took their land. Discrimination and prejudice caused Melungeons and their descendants to retreat to some of the most rural and remote territory of the county.

Despite ongoing efforts to determine exactly how and when Melungeons arrived in Appalachia, there are still many questions about the origins of these very early Tennesseans. In the 1990s, a 30-member panel put together by Clinch Valley College of the University of Virginia spent four years researching Melungeons. The consensus, by no means definitive, was that they are of Middle Eastern or Mediterranean heritage. It is still debated how they came to Appalachia and whether they intermarried with Native Americans.

Despite the passage of time and increasing interest in Melungeon heritage, the story of the Melungeons remains one that is often told in whispers. A good source of information about the Melungeon story is the Melungeon Heritage Association (www.melungeon.org).

environmental education center did not reach fruition. In 2008, fire destroyed what was left of the hotel. But if you drive north on Highway 70, and then turn left on Highway 94, you will soon see the still-imposing edifices of the remaining buildings.

Shopping

The **Local Artists Gallery** (124 E. Main St., 423/921-7656) has a wide selection of arts and crafts, including paintings and prints, woodwork, pottery, textiles, and candles.

Accommodations

The **Hale Springs Inn** (110 E. Main St., 423/272-5171) was built in 1824 and is set to reopen in 2009 following extensive renovations. The inn balances modern comfort with ambiance befitting such a historic structure. This should be your first choice for accommodations in Rogersville.

Food

Rogersville has several casual coffee shops that double as cafés. **Miss Bea's** (109 S. Church St., 423/272-6555, Mon.–Thurs. 7 A.M.–3 P.M., Fri. 7 A.M.–5 P.M., Sat. 8 A.M.–5 P.M., $4–5) has a wide repertoire of sandwiches, paninis, wraps, and soups. Each day, they offer two soups and sandwiches to choose from. Popular favorites are the turkey and artichoke panini, chicken-and-grape-salad sandwich, and the stuffed-pepper soup. For breakfast, Miss Bea offers stratas and biscuits, plus a variety of pastries. They also serve fresh-brewed specialty coffees.

Offering lunch-counter fare, daily lunch specials, and hearty breakfast platters, **Oh Henry's** (201 E. Main St., 423/272-0980, Mon.–Sat. 6 A.M.–11 P.M., $4–12) is an institution in Rogersville. It's a down-home, no-frill, friendly type of place.

If you want to mingle with youthful and progressive-minded folks, then head to the **Community Cup** (114 E. Main St., 423/272-7656), a coffee shop, book store, and hang-out spot. The Cup opens Monday–Saturday at 9 A.M., and is usually open until about 8 P.M. It is family friendly.

Information

The **Rogersville Heritage Association** (415 S. Depot St., 423/272-1961, www.rogersvilleheritage.org) does an admirable job of promoting the town and sharing its history with the world. You can also contact the **Rogersville-Hawkins County Chamber of Commerce** (107 E. Main St., 423/272-2186, www.rogersville-tn.com).

KYLES FORD

The countryside north of Rogersville, in Hawkins and Hancock Counties, is some of the most rural and isolated in this region. If the northeastern tip of Tennessee is its first frontier, then this is the last.

It is the rugged landscape that keeps this area from changing. Long, steep valleys lie between Clinch and Powell Mountains. The Clinch River flows unimpeded from Virginia, cutting a wide valley, which is prone to flood. And narrow, two-land roads wind around hills and over mountains. This is beautiful countryside, but only if you're willing to slow down and enjoy it.

As for a destination, head north along Highway 70 to Kyles Ford, a small settlement along the Clinch just a few miles from Virginia. In 2007, an exciting development project led by the Clinch River RC&D, a rural development organization serving Claiborne, Grainger, Hancock, Hawkins, and Union Counties, gave visitors a good reason to make the trip.

River Place (2788 Hwy. 70, 423/733-4400, Mon.–Sat. 6:30 A.M.–8 P.M., $4–9), a general store and restaurant, is the cornerstone of the development project. This handsome riverfront building is a small grocery and the best restaurant in these parts. The food here is truly made from scratch; homemade biscuits, comfort casseroles, and sides like real mashed potatoes will please your palate. The matter-of-fact friendliness of the folks here will please your spirit. The slogan is: "Nothing fancy. Just food you want to eat."

Behind the café are **River Place Cabins** (423/733-4400, www.clinchriverecotourism.com, $80–95 or $575 per week), four vacation cabins and a 1800s cottage now restored for guests. The vacation cabins are brand-new in 2007, but look like they've been settled into the hillside for years. Interior wood paneling, quilts, and simple decor ease your mind and invite relaxation. The cabins overlook the Clinch River and have fully functioning kitchens, telephone, and central heat and air. There's no cell phone service, and you have to drive to the local library to check your email.

A few hundred yards down the road, on the other side of the river, the **Clinch River Conservation and Retreat Center** (3225 Hwy. 70, 423/733-9341) is an old farmhouse has been restored and renovated to become an environmental retreat center and venue for reunions, meetings, and other gatherings.

SNEEDVILLE

A small town deep in the rural landscape, Sneedville suffers from an unfairly unflattering name. It is named for Knoxville lawyer W. H. Sneed, who represented Hancock County in its 1840s struggle to become a county. Sneedville is the commercial and government center for a mostly rural and largely undeveloped part of the state.

Sneedville is the headquarters of a regional artisan's cooperative. **Clinch Appalachian Artisans Cooperative** (Jubilee Center, 197 N. Jockey St., 423/733-4195, www.clinchartists.com) appears at area festivals and art shows. Inside their Sneedville gift shop you'll find locally made jewelry, woodwork, brooms, stained glass, gourd art, and much more.

Located in the same building as the artisan's cooperative is a retail outlet of **Clinch-Powell Community Kitchens** (423/733-4007), an innovative project that allows farmers use of a commercial kitchen to bottle or package their goods. The retail outlet is an excellent place to stock up on locally produced jams, salsas, vegetable preserves, and other goods that support local farmers and the local economy.

BACKGROUND

The Land

Tennessee is a long, narrow state. Shaped roughly like a parallelogram, it is 500 miles from east to west, and 110 miles from north to south. Partly due to its unusual shape, Tennessee, along with Missouri, borders more states than any other in the country. Its neighbors are North Carolina, Virginia, Kentucky, Missouri, Arkansas, Mississippi, Alabama, and Georgia. Tennessee is the thirty-sixth largest state in the United States, with a land mass of 44,169 square miles.

Like the rest of the United States, some 500 million years ago Tennessee was covered by a large shallow sea. As the sea dried up, the land that is now Tennessee turned swampy and eventually dry. The sea creatures that once lived in the sea died, their skeletons forming limestone. The plants and animals that lived in the swampy landscape died, eventually forming coal.

Beginning about 600 million years ago, the Appalachian Mountains were formed through plate movement. Once sharp and rocky, the Appalachians have been worn down over million of years to the gentle, rounded slopes that now characterize the range.

GEOGRAPHY

If you ask a Tennessean where they are from, the answer is never as simple as "Tennessee." Tennessee is divided by the Tennessee River into

PHOTO COURTESY OF TENNESSEE DEPARTMENT OF TOURIST DEVELOPMENT

three "Grand Divisions": East Tennessee, Middle Tennessee, and West Tennessee. These three regions are set apart by more than geography; they have unique histories, politics, and identities.

East Tennessee

East Tennessee is defined by the Appalachian Mountains and their foothills. The culture in this region was historically that of small farms, isolated mountain communities, and Scotch-Irish heritage. East Tennessee is the least racially diverse part of the state. It opposed secession during the Civil War and votes overwhelmingly Republican.

Within East Tennessee are two geographic regions. The Unaka Mountains are part of the Appalachian Mountain chain, which peak along the state's border with North Carolina. This zone includes the Great Smoky Mountains National Park. It is also where you will find Clingmans Dome, which at 6,643 feet above sea level is the highest point in Tennessee.

West of the Unaka Mountains is the Great Valley of East Tennessee, home to Knoxville and Chattanooga. This region is characterized by picturesque low ridges and a wide, fertile valley.

Middle Tennessee

Middle Tennessee is home to Tennessee's capital city, Nashville, and some of its most fertile farmland. Before the Civil War, great plantation mansions dotted the countryside south of Nashville. Today, Tennessee Walking Horse farms, new industries, and the economic success of Nashville continue to make Middle Tennessee prosperous.

Geographically, Middle Tennessee begins with the Cumberland Plateau, which rises to about 2,000 feet above sea level and lies west of East Tennessee's Great Valley. Despite its name, the plateau is not flat; there are a number of steep valleys in the plateau, the largest being the Sequatchie Valley.

The Highland Rim is a region of hills, valleys, and fertile farmland that lies west of the plateau. The largest physical region of Tennessee, the Highland Rim contains some 10,650 square miles of land, or almost 25 percent of the state. Almost entirely surrounded by the Highland Rim is the Central Basin, a low, flat, and fertile region in north-central Tennessee. Nashville is located in the Central Basin.

© SUSANNA HENIGHAN POTTER

cotton ready for harvest, still a common sight in parts of West Tennessee

West Tennessee

West Tennessee is more like the Deep South than any other part of the state. Mostly flat and rural, this was the epicenter of the state's cotton industry both before and after the Civil War. The Gulf Coastal Plain, an area of 9,000 square miles, is drained by the Mississippi River and its tributaries. Memphis lies in the southwestern corner of this area.

RIVERS AND LAKES

The largest river in Tennessee is the Mississippi River, which forms the western border of the state. The Hatchie River is among the smaller tributaries that drain West Tennessee and flow into the Mississippi.

The state's two most important rivers are the Cumberland and Tennessee Rivers. The Cumberland River flows through Nashville and along the north-central portion of the state. The Tennessee River flows in a U-shape, first flowing south through East Tennessee, through Knoxville and Chattanooga, and then northward, defining the boundary between Middle and West Tennessee. Both the Cumberland and the Tennessee Rivers empty into the Ohio River, which flows to the Mississippi.

All but one of Tennessee's major lakes are man made, having been created by the Tennessee Valley Authority during the last century. The lone exception to this is Reelfoot Lake in northeastern Tennessee, which was formed from the 1811 New Madrid earthquake when the mouth of what had been Reelfoot Creek was closed off and the creek's water spread out to cover the surrounding land.

CLIMATE

Tennessee has a mild climate. The average temperature is 58 degrees; in winter temperatures generally hover between 30 and 40 degrees, and temperatures are between 70 and 80 degrees in summer. Summer days can feel very hot, however, especially in Middle and West Tennessee. Of the state's three major cities, Memphis temperatures rise slightly higher than the others during the summer, and the

city stays warmest in winter. Knoxville is the coolest city.

The state receives an average of 50 inches of rain per year, and only a few places in the Appalachian Mountains receive more than 10 inches of snow per year. Most parts of Tennessee receive little, if any, snow or ice precipitation annually.

Heavy rains associated with tropical weather systems can sometimes affect the state, and winter weather can close roads in the higher elevations along the Cumberland Plateau and the Smoky Mountains.

A historic drought in the summer of 2007 raised concerns about water supply throughout Tennessee.

Tornadoes

The Mid-South, including western and central Tennessee, is prone to tornadoes. The tornado season runs from November to April. The danger of tornadoes is compounded by the fact that they may strike after dark and that in many areas of the state, visibility is limited by hills and trees.

On Super Tuesday, February 5, 2008, a series of tornadoes struck Tennessee, killing 32 people, most of them in Sumner and Macon Counties north of Nashville. Of those who died, 20 were in mobile homes when the storm struck. The event, one of the most deadly natural disasters in Tennessee history, led to calls for better education and awareness.

The best way to avoid injury in a tornado is to monitor weather radio and to move quickly to a cellar, basement, or windowless interior room if a tornado is on the way.

FLORA AND FAUNA

Encyclopedias are written about Tennessee's rich and diverse menagerie of animals and plants. The eastern mountains are one of the most biologically diverse areas in the United States, and whole volumes are devoted to their flora and fauna.

Middle and West Tennessee share the more typical plants and animals of the Deep South. Western Tennessee's cypress swamps are rich

TENNESSEE PEARLS

The fast-running rivers of Tennessee are home to freshwater mussels, and these mussels sometimes create beautiful pearls.

Native Americans were the first to discover Tennessee's pearls; Indians harvested mussels for food and used the pearls in jewelry. Tennessee history knows many stories of simple folks who stumbled upon a pearl, getting an unexpected payday in the process. In one such story, Charles Bradford and James Johnson were looking for bait to go fishing in the Caney Fork River in the early 1880s. They had pulled up several mussels and inside one found a large white pearl. The boys sent the pearl to Tiffany's in New York and received a check for $83.

Stories such as this one fueled the Tennessee pearl industry for many years. The industry peaked between 1882 and 1914, when special musseling boats would ply the Tennessee and other rivers, dragging a "brail" (resembling an underwater rake) that captured river mussels. In more modern times, diving is the most popular way to harvest wild mussels from the watery depths.

Tennessee pearls were a variety of colors and shapes, and the mother-of-pearl from the mussel shells was used in button manufacturing during the early part of the 20th century, before plastic buttons became common.

Tennessee pearls declined following the establishment of the Tennessee Valley Authority and the damming of many rivers in the state. Dams caused rivers to flow more slowly, eliminating the fast-moving water habitat required by freshwater mussels. Pollution also hurt wild mussels, as did overfishing and the rise of pearl cultivation in Asia.

The Tennessee River Pearl Farm near Camden, Tennessee, still harvests pearls from the river, although they are cultivated. Some of the pearls harvested here are fashioned into jewelry, but most are exported to Asia where they are used in the cultivation of high-grade pearls.

The pearl was named the Tennessee state gem in 1979.

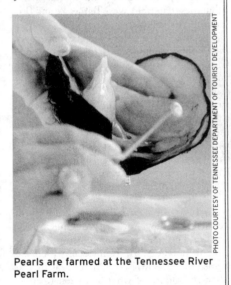

PHOTO COURTESY OF TENNESSEE DEPARTMENT OF TOURIST DEVELOPMENT

Pearls are farmed at the Tennessee River Pearl Farm.

depositories of plant and animal life, while the plains are important for agriculture.

Wildflowers

In the spring and summer, wildflowers spring up along roadsides, mountain streams, and pastures. Look for the small yellow blooms of **St. Johnswort** and the bushy purple crowns of **ironweed.** Delicate purple **bluebells** and white, pink, or purple **phlox** blanket cool stream banks and coves. Placid lakes and ponds come alive with the white-pink blooms of **water lily.**

Fields and gardens are decorated with the bracing yellow blooms of **sunflowers** and the bright-orange colors of **butterfly weed.** Cultivated lawns and gardens showcase delicate **roses** and elegant **irises,** the state flower of Tennessee.

Trees

Tennessee's official state tree is the **tulip poplar,** a fast-growing tree often used for timber. It blooms in May. **Flowering dogwoods** are celebrated with a springtime festival in Knoxville. The dogwood's vibrant flowers are actually white-colored leaves that surround a tight cluster of flowers in the center. Some dogwood "blooms" are pink. Throughout the state you will see **magnolia** trees, notable for their thick, heavy green leaves and large white blooms.

In West Tennessee's wetlands and at Reelfoot Lake, look for **cypress** trees, easily identifiable by their rough, bumpy knees.

Birds

Little birds are somehow the most charming. Field, swamp, house, chipping, and song **sparrows,** as they flit about and perch on tree limbs, are ubiquitous and somehow comforting. Look for the red **cardinal,** the black-and-white **junco,** and the yellow **goldfinch.**

The **Carolina chickadee** puffs out its breast in winter and the **blue jay** patrols bird-feeders. The **mockingbird** is Tennessee's state bird; it mimics the calls of other birds and has a grey body and dark wings.

Unless you are unusually patient or light of foot, you're unlikely to see the nocturnal **Eastern screech-owl** or its cousins, the Great Horned Owl and Barred Owl, in the wild. Keep your eyes pinned on the sky for **hawks,** red-tailed, sharp-skinned, and Cooper's. **Bald eagles** winter at Reelfoot Lake and other protected locations in the state.

Wild turkeys are making a comeback; groups may be seen patrolling many state parks and natural areas. Look for the male's impressive feathers. Listen for the knocking of the **woodpeckers**—hairy, red-headed, downy, and pileated varieties.

Bodies of water are some of the best places to seek feathered friends. **Sandhill cranes** winter on the Hiwassee River in East Tennessee. Float down a river and you may see a statuesque **great blue heron** hunting for food. **Wood ducks** and **mallards,** whose males have a striking green head, live around ponds and lakes.

Big Animals

Many of the large, wild creatures of Tennessee are threatened. **Elk** and **bison,** which ranged here before settlement by Europeans, have been reintroduced at Land Between the Lakes and the Great Smoky Mountains National Park. Scruffy **feral pigs** live in scattered populations in East Tennessee. **Black bears,** the icon of the Smoky Mountains, have a shaggy black coat and sharp sense of smell. They can run and climb trees. **Coyotes** and **red fox** are lovely, quick, and adaptable. **Bobcats** are stealthy and elusive hunters that prefer the hours right before sunrise and right after sunset.

Small Animals

Raccoons, with their bandit's mask and striped tail, are adorable until one has ruined your bird-feeder or gotten into your garbage (or even bitten you, which has been known to happen). **Eastern cottontail** is the most common type of rabbit, and they prefer grasslands and cultivated areas. Look for the white of their stubby tail. **Eastern chipmunks** are small creatures that scurry along forest floors, pastureland, and city parks. **Eastern gray**

The raccoon is Tennessee's state animal.

HEMLOCKS UNDER THREAT

First the American Chestnut, then Fraser firs, and now the hemlocks. Non-native insects have taken a terrible toll on the native trees of the Smokies. The dead trees visible throughout the spruce-fir forests at high elevations are testament to the loss of Fraser firs. Now, park scientists and others are racing against time to protect hemlock trees.

The hemlock wooly adelgid is the culprit. Native to Asia, the adelgid feeds at the base of the hemlock needles, disrupting nutrient flow and eventually causing the tree to starve to death. Hemlock wooly adelgids were first discovered near Richmond, Virginia, in the 1950s. To date, they have spread through the eastern regions of the hemlock's native range.

Hemlocks are beautiful, big trees. They can live to be more than 600 years old and can grow to heights of more than 165 feet. Hemlock trees grow in a variety of habitats, and serve myriad purposes in the Smokies' ecosystem. By blocking out the sunlight, hemlocks keep mountain streams cool. Migratory birds such as the Blackburnian Warbler and the Wood Thrush shelter in hemlock groves. Loss of hemlocks will have a negative effect on rivers and streams. Already, scientists are seeing higher acidity in some streams where dead hemlock trees have fallen.

Scientists are using insecticidal soap to spray infested trees, but this method is labor intensive and works only for trees that are near roadsides or otherwise easily accessible. Insecticides applied around the soil of the trees is also an effective method, but prohibitively expensive for a park with millions of hemlock trees to protect.

Biological control – the introduction of a natural predator beetle to the wooly adelgid – is the most promising long-term method of control. Scientists have pinned their hopes on a poppy seed-sized predator beetle that, in its native Japan, eats only hemlock adelgids. Since 2002 the park has been releasing the predator beetle in the Smokies, and more than 350,000 have been released to date. The predator program got a boost in 2004 when the University of Tennessee opened a new beetle rearing facility. However, the cost and limited supply of the beetles is the greatest hurdle.

A large number of hemlocks have already been lost, and park officials warn that the consequences of their deaths are only beginning to show. In addition to efforts to stop the spread of the adelgid, scientists are intent on saving enough hemlocks at different elevations in the park in order to save a representative gene pool, which could be used to repopulate the forest if the adelgid threat is ever fully contained.

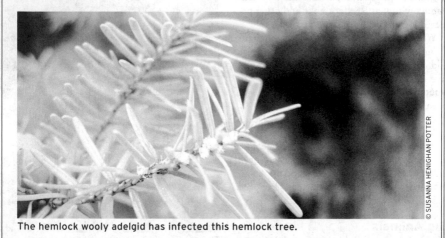

© SUSANNA HENIGHAN POTTER

The hemlock wooly adelgid has infected this hemlock tree.

squirrels are easier to see—they are larger and more ubiquitous.

Amphibians and Reptiles

Listen for the "harumph" of the **bullfrog** or the night song of the **Cope's gray tree frog** near water. Salamanders and newts flourish in the damp, cool forests of the eastern mountains: look for the lizardlike **Eastern newt** and the **spotted salamander,** which can grow up to 10 inches. The largest of the salamanders is the **Eastern tiger salamander,** which comes in a rainbow of colors and patterns best left to your imagination. They grow up to 13 inches.

Snapping turtles live in rivers and streams, rarely coming on land. The **Eastern box turtle** prefers moist forests and grasslands. Most Tennessee snakes are harmless. The **garter snake** is the most common. It prefers areas that are cool and moist. **Green snakes** like bushes and low-hanging branches near the water.

ENVIRONMENTAL ISSUES
Forestry

Beginning in the 1980s, the number of paper and wood chip mills in Tennessee grew dramatically. With no legislation regulating the clearing of forested land, some parts of Tennessee experienced widespread clear-cutting of old forests. Over the years, local environmental groups have fought for an overarching law that would insist on responsible forestry practices. While no such law has been passed, some stopgap measures have been put in place.

Strip Mining

Strip mines have a devastating environmental impact. In a strip mine, the surface of the earth above a seam of coal is removed, leaving scarred and bare earth. The most devastating type of strip mining is mountaintop removal, when the whole mountain is destroyed by explosives to get to the coal, which can lie as many as 800 feet below the surface.

Mountaintop removal and other types of strip mining have terrible consequences for drinking-water quality, animal and plant life, and the native culture of places that are affected. Dumping of debris from the removal process buries streams and fills valleys. When the coal companies are done, they pile dirt back up on the exposed mountains and drop exotic grass seed from above. In this way, they say, the mountain is restored. But while they may be able to approximate the shape of the old mountain, they cannot re-create the intricate web of life that once existed there.

Strip mining is most common in parts of Virginia, West Virginia, and Kentucky, but it takes place in Tennessee, too. Mining operations exist in Scott, Campbell, and Claiborne Counties in the northern Cumberland Plateau region. Residents and environmental activists fought to prevent mountaintop removal at Zeb Mountain in Scott and Campbell Counties, but were unsuccessful.

In 2004, the last year for which statistics are available, Tennessee had 43 coal mines and produced 2.8 million short tons of coal.

Air Pollution

Car emissions, industrial pollution, and other activities cause air pollution. In Tennessee, exhaust from cars and trucks, plus the toxic emissions from coal-fired generating plants, are the biggest contributors to air pollution.

The American Lung Association has ranked each of the state's four main cities, Memphis, Nashville, Knoxville, and Chattanooga, as among the nation's 30 most polluted cities.

As a result, Clean Air Tennessee, a state-sponsored agency, monitors air quality in seven locations in the state: Memphis, Nashville, Knoxville, the Tri-Cities, Clarksville, Chattanooga, and the Great Smoky Mountains National Park. You can check air-quality forecasts and historical air-quality data on their website, www.cleanairtn.org. On this website you can sign up to receive alerts when air-quality levels reach dangerous levels in your area.

The air quality in the Great Smoky Mountains National Park is a serious concern for scientists. According to the park, the average visibility is 25 miles, compared to the national average of 93 miles. Some days, haze causes visibility to diminish to less than one mile. Some days, the level of ground-level ozone exceeds what is recommended for human exposure.

Air quality is usually worst during the hot summer months of July and August.

Land Use

According to the Tennessee Environmental Council, the state has the seventh-highest rate of development in the United States. Some 80,000 acres of rural land are developed in Tennessee each year. The areas around Nashville and Knoxville have seen the greatest sprawl.

Urban and suburban sprawl leads to long driving times, increased air pollution, strain on scarce water resources, and the elimination of farmland, rural landscapes, and natural habitats. Smart growth policies, zoning issues, and better transportation solutions are some of the biggest challenges facing Tennessee at the moment.

Water Pollution

The cleanliness of Tennessee's rivers, lakes, and streams is monitored according to the standards of the Clean Water Act. The Tennessee Department of Environment and Conservation monitors the health of the state's rivers, and publishes an annual list that divides bodies of water into categories one through five, where category one is the cleanest and five the dirtiest. In its last report, the agency reported that some 25 percent of the state's river miles were category one and 31 percent were in the dirtiest category. As for lakes and reservoirs, 21 percent of lake acres were classified as "impaired."

Most water pollution is caused by sedimentation and silt run-off from construction and agriculture. Habitat alternation, pathogens found in wastewater, and nutrients from fertilizers are also problems. Some pollution can be readily cleaned up, but so-called "legacy pollutants," such as PCBs and chlordane from old industrial sites, can remain present for years and can poison fish and other marine animals.

According to the state government, some 41 percent of pollution in streams and rivers in 2006 came from agriculture; 19 percent from hydrologic modification; and 18 percent from municipal sources. For lakes, some 72 percent of contaminants were legacy pollutants.

The state is supposed to post a warning when a river or stream is deemed too polluted for fishing, swimming, or other forms of use. For a listing of such bodies of water, contact the Water Pollution Control division of the Department of Environment and Conservation (615/532-0625).

History

THE FIRST TENNESSEANS

The first humans settled in what is now Tennessee 15,000–12,000 years ago. Descended from people who crossed into North America at the last Ice Age, these Paleoindians were nomads who hunted large game animals including mammoths, mastodons, and caribou. Remains of these extinct mammals have been found in West Tennessee, and the Indians' arrowheads and spear points have been found all over the state. The Ice Age hunters camped in caves and under rock shelters, but remained predominantly nomadic.

About 10,000 years ago, the climate and vegetation of the region changed. The deciduous forest that still covers large parts of the state replaced the evergreen forest of the fading Ice Age. Large game animals disappeared, and deer and elk arrived, attracted by the forests of hickory, chestnut, and beech. Descendants of the Paleoindians gradually abandoned the nomadic lifestyle of their ancestors and established settlements, often near rivers. They hunted deer, bear, and turkey; gathered nuts and wild fruit; and harvested freshwater fish and mussels. They also took a few tentative steps towards cultivation by growing squash and gourds.

This Archaic Period was replaced by the Woodland Period about 3,000 years ago. The Woodland Indians adopted the bow and arrow for hunting, and—at the end of their predominance—began cultivating maize and beans as staple crops. Ceramic pottery appeared, and ritualism took on a greater importance in the society. Pinson Mounds, burial mounds near Jackson in West Tennessee, date from this period, as does the wrongly named Old Stone Fort near Manchester, believed to have been built and used for ceremonies by the Woodland Indians of the area.

The development of a more complex culture continued, and at about A.D. 900 the Woodland culture gave way to the Mississippian Period, an era marked by population growth, an increase in trade and warfare, the rise of the chieftain, and cultural accomplishments. The Mississippian era is best known for the impressive large pyramid mounds that were left behind in places such as Etowah and Toqua in Tennessee and Moundville in Alabama. Mississippian Indians also created beautiful ornaments and symbolic objects including combs, pipes, and jewelry.

Europeans Arrive

Having conquered Peru, the Spanish nobleman Hernando de Soto embarked on a search for gold in the American southeast in 1539. De Soto's band wandered through Florida, Georgia, and the Carolinas before crossing into what is now Tennessee, probably in June 1540. His exact route is a source of controversy, but historians believe he made his way through parts of East Tennessee before heading back into Georgia. The popular myth that he camped on the Chickasaw Bluff—the site of Memphis today—in 1541 remains unproven.

It was more than 100 years until another European is reported in the Tennessee wilderness, although life for the natives was already changing. De Soto and his men brought firearms and disease, and there was news of other whites living to the east. Disease and warfare led to a decline in population for Tennessee's Indians during the pre-settlement period. As a result, Indian communities formed new tribes with each other: the Creek Confederacy and Choctaws were among the tribes that were formed. In Tennessee, the Shawnee moved south into the Cumberland River country— land previously claimed as hunting ground by the Chickasaw Nation. Also at this time, a new tribe came over the Smoky Mountains from North Carolina, possibly to escape encroachment of European settlers, to form what would become the most important Indian group in modern Tennessee: the Overhill Cherokees.

In 1673 European scouts entered Tennessee at its eastern and western ends. Englishmen James Needham, Gabriel Arthur, and eight hired Indian guides were the first European party to enter East Tennessee. Needham did not last long; he was killed by his Indian guides early in the outing. Arthur won over his traveling companions and joined them on war trips and hunts before returning to Virginia in 1674. Meanwhile, on the western end of the state, French explorers Father Jacques Marquette and trader Louis Joliet came down the Mississippi River and claimed the surrounding valley for the French.

Nine years later, Robert Cavelier de La Salle paused at the Chickasaw Bluff near present-day Memphis and built Fort Prudhomme as a temporary base. The fort was short-lived, but the site would be used by the French in years to come in their war against the Chickasaws and later in the French and Indian War.

The Long Hunters

The first Europeans to carve out a foothold in the unknown frontier of Tennessee were traders who made journeys into Indian territory to hunt and trade. These men disappeared for months at a time into the wilderness, and were therefore known as long hunters. They left with European-made goods and returned with animal skins. They led pack-trains of horses and donkeys over narrow, steep, and crooked mountain trails and through sometimes-hostile territory. It was a lonely, hard life, full of uncertainty. Some of the long hunters were no better than crooks; others were respected by both the Indians and Europeans.

The long hunters included men like Elisha Walden, Kasper Mansker, and Abraham Bledsoe. Daniel Boone, born in North

Carolina, was in present-day Washington County in northeastern Tennessee when, in 1760, he carved on a beech tree that he had "cilled" a "bar" nearby. Thomas Sharp Spencer became known as Big Foot and is said to have spent the winter in a hollowed-out sycamore tree. Another trader, a Scotch-Irish man named James Adair, traded with the Indians for years and eventually wrote *A History of the American Indian,* published in London in 1775 and one of the first such accounts.

The animal skins and furs that were the aim of these men's exploits were eventually sold in Charleston and exported to Europe. In 1748 alone, South Carolina merchants exported more than 160,000 skins worth $250,000. The trade was profitable for merchants and, to a lesser extent, the traders themselves. But it was rarely profitable for the Indians, and it helped to wipe out much of Tennessee's native animal life.

The French and Indian War

In 1754 the contest between the French and the British for control of the New World boiled over into war. Indian alliances were seen as critical to success, and so the British set out to win the support of the Cherokee. They did this by agreeing to build a fort in the land over the mountain from North Carolina—territory which came to be known as the Overhill country. The Cherokee wanted the fort to protect their women and children from French or hostile Indian attack while the men were away. The fort was begun in 1756 near the fork of the Little Tennessee and Tellico Rivers and it was named Fort Loudoun after the commander of British forces in America. Twelve cannons were transported over the rough mountain terrain by horse to defend the fort from enemy attack.

The construction of Fort Loudoun did not prove to be the glue to hold the Cherokee and British together. In fact, it was not long before relations deteriorated to the point where the Cherokee chief Standing Turkey directed an attack on the fort. A siege ensued. Reinforcements were called for and dispatched, but the British colonel and 1,300 men turned back before reaching the fort. The English inside the fort

were weakened by lack of food, and surrendered. On August 9, 1760, 180 men, 60 women, and a few children marched out of Fort Loudoun, the first steps of a 140-mile journey to the nearest British fort. The group had been promised to be allowed to retreat peacefully, but on the first night of the journey the group was ambushed: killed were 3 officers, 23 privates, 3 women. The rest were taken prisoner. The Indians said they were inspired to violence upon finding that the British had failed to surrender all of their firepower as promised.

The Cherokee's action was soon avenged. A year later, Col. James Grant led a party into the Lower Cherokee territory, where they destroyed villages, burnt homes, and cut down fields of corn.

The French and Indian War ended in 1763, and in the Treaty of Paris the French withdrew any claims to lands east of the Mississippi. This result emboldened European settlers and land speculators, who were drawn to the land of the Overhill country. The fact that the land still belonged to the Indians did not stop the movement west.

EARLY SETTLERS
The First Settlements

With the issue of French possession resolved, settlers began to filter into the Overhill country. Early settlers included William Bean on the Holston River; Evan Shelby at Sapling Grove (later Bristol); John Carter in the Carter Valley; and Jacob Brown on the Nolichucky River. By 1771 the settlers at Watauga and Nolichucky won a lease from the Cherokee, and the next year, they formed the Watauga Association, a quasi-government and the first such in Tennessee territory.

The settlers' success in obtaining land concessions from the Indians was eclipsed in 1775, when the Transylvania Company, led by Richard Henderson of North Carolina, traded £10,000 of goods for 20 million acres of land in Kentucky and Tennessee. The agreement, negotiated at a treaty conference at Sycamore Shoals, was opposed by the Cherokee Indian chief Dragging Canoe, who warned that the Cherokee were

© SUSANNA HENIGHAN POTTER

Fort Nashborough, the first settlement in Nashville, was founded on Christmas Day, 1779. A re-creation of the original fort remains on the riverfront in Nashville.

paving the way for their own extinction. Despite his warning, the treaty was signed.

Dragging Canoe remained the leader of the Cherokee's resistance to European settlement. In 1776 he orchestrated assaults on the white settlements of Watauga, Nolichucky, Long Island, and Carter's Valley. The offensive, called by some the Cherokee War, had limited success at first, but ended in defeat for the natives. In 1777 the Cherokee signed a peace treaty with the settlers that ceded more land to the Europeans.

Dragging Canoe and others did not accept the treaty, and left the Cherokee as a result. He and his followers moved south, near Chickamauga Creek, where they became known as the Chickamauga tribe. Over time, this tribe attracted other Indians whose common purpose was opposition to white settlement.

The Indians could not, however, overpower the increasing tide of European settlers, who brought superior firepower and greater numbers. Pressure on political leaders to free up more and more land for settlement made relations with the Indians and land agreements with them one of the most important features of political life on the frontier.

In the end, these leaders delivered. Europeans obtained Indian land in Tennessee through a series of treaties and purchases, beginning with the Sycamore Shoals purchase in 1775 and continuing until 1818 when the Chickasaw ceded all control to land west of the Mississippi. Negotiating on behalf of the settlers were leaders including William Blount, the territorial governor, and Andrew Jackson, the first U.S. president from Tennessee.

Indian Removal

Contact with Europeans had a significant impact on the Cherokee's way of life. Christian missionaries introduced education, and in the 1820s Sequoyah developed a Cherokee alphabet, allowing the Indians to read and write in their own language. The Cherokee adopted some of the European's farming practices, as well as some of their social practices, including slavery. Adoption of the European lifestyle was most common among the significant number of mixed-race Cherokee. In 1827 the Cherokee Nation was established, complete with a constitutional system of government and a capital in New Echota, Georgia. From 1828 until 1832, its newspaper, the *Cherokee Phoenix,* was published in both English and Cherokee.

The census of 1828 counted 15,000 Cherokee remaining in Tennessee. They owned 1,000 slaves, 22,400 head of cattle, 7,600 horses, 1,800 spinning wheels, 700 looms, 12 sawmills, 55 blacksmith shops, and 6 cotton gins.

Despite these beginnings of assimilation, or because of them, the Cherokee were not welcome to remain in the new territory. Settlers pushed for a strong policy that would lead to the Cherokee's removal, and they looked over the border to Georgia to see that it could be done. There, in 1832, authorities surveyed lands owned by Cherokees and disposed of them by lottery. Laws were passed to prohibit Indian assemblies and bar Indians from bringing suit in the state. The majority of Tennessee settlers, as well as Georgia officials, pushed for similar measures to be adopted in Tennessee.

The Cherokee were divided in their response: Some felt that moving west represented the best future for their tribe, others wanted to stay and fight for their land and the Cherokee Nation. In the end, the Cherokee leaders lost hope of remaining and on December 29, 1835, they signed the removal treaty. Under the agreement, the Cherokee were paid $5 million for all their lands east of the Mississippi and they were required to move west within two years. When that time expired in 1838 and only a small number of the Cherokee had moved, the U.S. army evicted the rest by force.

Thousands of Cherokee died along the ensuing Trail of Tears, which followed four different routes through Tennessee and eventually into Oklahoma. A southern route extended from Chattanooga to Memphis; two northern routes headed into Kentucky and Missouri before turning southward into Oklahoma; the fourth was a water route along the Tennessee and Mississippi Rivers. Harsh weather, food shortages, and the brutality of the journey cost thousands of Cherokee lives. In the end, out of the estimated 14,000 Cherokee who began the journey, more than 4,000 are believed to have died along the way.

Some Cherokee remained by hiding deep in the Great Smoky Mountains. Later, they were given land which became the Cherokee Reservation in North Carolina.

STATEHOOD

Almost as soon as settlers began living on the Tennessee frontier there were movements to form government. Dissatisfied with the protection offered by North Carolina's distant government, settlers drew up their own governments as early as the 1780s. The Watauga Association and Cumberland Compact were early forms of government. In 1785, settlers in northeastern Tennessee seceded from North Carolina and established the State of Franklin. The experiment was short-lived, but foretold that in the future the lands west of the Smoky Mountains would be their own state.

Before Tennessee could become a state, however, it was a territory of the United States. In 1789 North Carolina ratified its own constitution and in doing so ceded its western lands, the Tennessee country, to the U.S. government. These lands eventually became known as the Southwest Territory and in 1790 president George Washington appointed William Blount its territorial governor.

Blount was a 41-year-old land speculator and businessman who had campaigned actively for the position. A veteran of the War for Independence, Blount knew George Washington and was one of the signers of the U.S. Constitution in 1787.

At the time of its establishment, the Southwest Territory was some 43,000 square miles in area. The population of 35,000 was centered in two main areas: the northeastern corner and the Cumberland settlements near present-day Nashville.

Governor Blount moved quickly to establish a territorial government. In October 1790 he arrived in Washington County and established the state's first capitol in the home of William Cobb. This simple wood frame house known as Rocky Mount would be the territory's capital for the next 18 months before it moved to James White's Fort in Knoxville.

The territory's first election was held in 1793 and the resulting Council met a year later. They established the town of Knoxville, created a tax rate, and chartered Greeneville and Blount Colleges. They also ordered a census in 1795, which showed a population of more than 77,000 people and support for statehood.

The territory had met the federal requirements for statehood, and so Blount and other territorial leaders set out to make Tennessee a state. They called a constitutional convention, and delegates spent three weeks writing Tennessee's first constitution. The first statewide poll elected John Sevier governor of the new state. Meanwhile Tennessee's request to become a state was being debated in Washington, where finally, on June 1, 1796, President Washington signed the statehood bill and Tennessee became the 16th state in the Union.

Frontier Life

The new state of Tennessee attracted settlers who were drawn by cheap land and the opportunity it represented. Between 1790 and 1800 the state's population tripled, and by 1810 Tennessee's population had grown to 250,000. The expansion caused a shift in power as the middle and western parts of the state became more populated. The capital moved from Knoxville to Nashville in 1812.

Life during the early 19th century in Tennessee was largely rural. For the subsistence farmers who made up the majority of the state's population, life was a relentless cycle of hard work. Many families lived in one- or two-room cabins and spent their days growing food and the fibers needed to make their own clothes; raising animals that supplied farm power, meat, and hides; building or repairing buildings and tools; and cutting firewood in prodigious quantities.

Small-hold farmers often owned no slaves. Those who did only owned one or two and worked alongside them.

Children provided valuable labor on the Tennessee farm. Boys often plowed their first furrow at age nine, and girls of that age were expected to mind younger children, help cook, and learn the skills of midwifery, sewing, and gardening. While women's time was often consumed with child-rearing, cooking, and sewing, the housewife worked in the field alongside her husband when she was needed.

Education and Religion

There were no public schools on the frontier and the few private schools that existed were not accessible to the farming class. Religious missionaries were often the only people who could read and write in a community, and the first schools were established by churches. Presbyterian, Methodist, and Baptist ministers were the first to reach many settlements in Tennessee.

Settlements were spread out and few had established churches. As a result, the camp meeting became entrenched in Tennessee culture. The homegrown spirituality of the camp meeting appealed to Tennesseans' independent spirit, which looked suspiciously at official religion and embraced the informal and deeply personal religion of the camp meeting.

The meetings were major events drawing between a few hundred and thousands of people. Wilma Dykeman writes: "From distances as far as 40, 50 and more miles, they came in wagons, carriages, a wide array of vehicles, and raised their tents . . . They spent the summer days and nights surrounded by seemingly endless expanse of green forest, supplied with a bounty of cold pure water, breathing that acrid blue wood smoke from rows of campfires and the rich smells of food cooking over glowing red coals, listening to the greetings of old friends, the voices of children playing, crying, growing drowsy, a stamping of the horses, and the bedlam of the meeting itself once the services had begun."

Camp services were passionate and emotional, reaching a feverish pitch as men and women were overtaken by the spirit. Many camp meetings attracted both black and white participants.

The War of 1812

Tennesseans were among the "War Hawks" in Congress who advocated for war with Great Britain in 1812. The conflict was seen by many as an opportunity to rid their borders once and for all of all Indians. The government asked for 2,800 volunteers and 30,000 Tennesseans offered to enlist. This is when Tennessee's nickname as the Volunteer State was born.

Nashville lawyer, politician, and businessman Andrew Jackson was chosen as the leader of the Tennessee volunteers. Despite their shortage of supplies and lack of support from the War Department, Jackson's militia prevailed in a series of lopsided victories. Given command of the southern military district, Andrew Jackson led U.S. forces at the Battle of New Orleans on January 8, 1815. The ragtag group inflicted a crushing defeat on the British, and despite having occurred after the signing of the peace treaty with Great Britain, the battle was a victory that launched Jackson onto the road to the presidency.

Growth of Slavery

The state's first settlers planted the seed of slavery in Tennessee, and the state's westward expansion cemented the institution. In 1791 there were 3,400 blacks in Tennessee—about 10 percent of the general population. By 1810, blacks were more than 20 percent of Tennessee's people. The invention of the cotton gin and subsequent rise of King Cotton after the turn of the 19th century also caused a rapid expansion of slavery.

Slavery was most important in West Tennessee; eastern Tennessee, with its mountainous landscape and small farms, had the fewest slaves. In Middle Tennessee the slave population was concentrated in the central basin, in the counties of Davidson, Maury, Rutherford, and Williamson. By 1860, 40 percent of the state's slave population was in West Tennessee, with the greatest concentration in Shelby, Fayette, and Haywood Counties, where cotton was grown on plantations somewhat similar to those of the Deep South.

As slavery grew, slave markets were established in Nashville and Memphis. The ban on the interstate sale of slaves was virtually ignored.

From 1790, when the state was founded, until 1831 Tennessee's slave code was relatively lenient. The law recognized a slave as both a chattel and a person, and slaves were entitled to expect protection against the elements and other people. Owners could free their slaves for any reason, and many did, causing growth in Tennessee's free black population in the first half of the 1800s. These free blacks concentrated in eastern and Middle Tennessee and particularly the cities of Nashville, Memphis, and Knoxville, where they worked as laborers and artisans.

There were vocal opponents to slavery in Tennessee, especially in the eastern part of the state. The first newspaper in the United States devoted to emancipation was established in 1819 in Jonesboro by Elihu Embree. Charles Osborne, a Quaker minister, preached against slavery shortly after the turn of the century in Tennessee. Emancipationists formed societies in counties including Washington, Sullivan, Blount, Grainger, and Cocke. Many of these early abolitionists opposed slavery on religious grounds, arguing that it was incompatible with the spirit of Christianity.

These abolitionists often argued for the gradual end of slavery, and sometimes advocated for the removal of freed slaves to Africa.

Slave Experiences

There was no single slave experience for Tennessee's slaves. On the farm, a slave's experience depended on the size of the farm and type of crops that were grown. The number of slaves on the farm also influenced the slave experience.

Most Tennessee slaves lived on small- or medium-sized farms. The 1860 census showed that only one person in the state owned more than 300 slaves, and 47 owned more than 100. More than 75 percent of all slave-owners had fewer than 10 slaves. Work assignments varied, but almost all slaves were expected to contribute to their own subsistence by keeping a vegetable garden. Slaves with special skills in areas like carpentry, masonry, blacksmithing, or weaving were hired out.

Urban slaves were domestics, coachmen, housepainters, laundresses, and midwives. In cities, many families owned just one or two slaves, and it was common for slaves to be hired out to others in order to provide a source of income for the slave-owner. It became customary in some cities for a market day on New Year's Day, where slaves and employers bargained for slave labor over the coming year.

Slaves sought to overcome their circumstances by building close-knit communities. These communities acted as surrogate families for slaves whose own spouse, parents, siblings, and children were often sold, causing lifelong separation.

Religion also served as a survival mechanism for Tennessee's slaves. Methodist and Baptist churches opened their doors to slaves, providing a space were slaves could be together. The musical tradition that resulted is today's gospel music. Religion also provided a vehicle for some slaves to learn how to read and write.

THE CIVIL WAR

In the 1830s, Tennessee's position on slavery hardened. The Virginia slave uprising led by Nat Turner frightened slave owners, who instituted patrols to search for runaway slaves and tightened codes on slave conduct. In 1834, the state constitution was amended to bar free blacks from voting, a sign of whites' increasing fear of the black people living in their midst.

The division between East and West Tennessee widened as many in the east were sympathetic with the anti-slavery forces that were growing in Northern states. In the west, the support for slavery was unrelenting.

Despite several strident secessionists, including Tennessee's governor Isham Harris, Tennessee remained uncertain about secession. In February 1861, the state voted against a convention on secession. But with the attack on Fort Sumter two months later, followed by president Abraham Lincoln's call for volunteers to coerce the seceded states back to the Union, public opinion shifted. On June 8, 1861, Tennesseans voted 105,000 to 47,000 to secede.

A Border State

Tennessee was of great strategic importance during the Civil War. It sent an estimated 186,000 men to fight for the Confederacy, more than any other state. Another 31,000 are credited with having joined the Union army.

Tennessee had resources which both Union and Confederacy deemed important for victory, including agricultural and manufacturing industries, railroads, and rivers. And its geographic position as a long-border state made it nearly unavoidable.

Tennessee Battles

Some 454 battles and skirmishes were fought in Tennessee during the war. Most were small, but several key battles took place on Tennessee soil.

The first of these was the Union victory at Forts Henry and Donelson in January 1862. Gen. Ulysses S. Grant and 15,000 Union troops steamed up the Tennessee River and quickly captured Fort Henry. They then marched overland to Fort Donelson, and, 10 days later, this Confederate fort fell as well. The battle of Fort Donelson is where U.S. Grant earned his sobriquet: He was asked by the Confederate general the terms of capitulation and he replied, "unconditional surrender."

The Battle of Shiloh was the bloodiest and largest to take place in Tennessee. The battle took place near Pittsburgh Landing (the Federal name for the struggle) on the Mississippi River about 20 miles north of the Mississippi state line. More than 100,000 men took part in this battle and there were more than 24,000 casualties.

The battle began with a surprise Confederate attack at dawn on April 6, 1862, a Sunday. For several hours, victory seemed in reach for the Southern troops, but the Union rallied, and held. They built a strong defensive line covering Pittsburgh Landing, and on April 7 they took the offensive and swept the Confederates from the field. The Confederates' loss was devastating, and Shiloh represents a harbinger of the future bloodletting between Blue and Gray.

Another important Tennessee battle was at Stone's River, near Murfreesboro, on December 31, 1862. Like at Shiloh, the early momentum here was with the Confederates, but victory belonged to the Union. The Battle of Chickamauga Creek, fought a few miles over the state line in Georgia, was a rare Confederate victory. It did not come cheaply, however, with 21,000 members of the Army of Tennessee killed.

Federal forces retreated and dug in near Chattanooga, while Confederates occupied the heights above the town. Union reinforcements led by General Grant drove the Confederates back into Georgia at Battle of Lookout Mountain, also known as the "Battle Above the Clouds," on November 25, 1863.

Wartime Occupation

Battles were only part of the wartime experience in Tennessee. The Civil War caused hardship for ordinary residents on a scale that many had never before seen. There was famine and poverty. Schools and churches were closed. Harassment and recrimination plagued the state, and fear was widespread.

In February 1863, one observer described the population of Memphis as "11,000 original whites, 5,000 slaves, and 19,000 newcomers of all kinds, including traders, fugitives, hangers-on, and negroes."

Memphis fell to the Union on June 6, 1862, and it was occupied for the remainder of the war. The city's experience during this wartime occupation reversed decades of growth, and left a city that would struggle for years to come back.

Those who could, fled the city. Many of those who remained stopped doing business (some of these because they refused to pledge allegiance to the Union and were not permitted). Northern traders entered the city and took over many industries, while blacks who abandoned nearby plantations flooded into the city.

While the military focused on punishing Confederate sympathizers, conditions in Memphis deteriorated. Crime and disorder abounded and guerrilla bands developed to fight the Union occupation. The Federal commander responsible for the city was Major Gen. William T. Sherman, and he adopted a policy of collective responsibility, which held civilians responsible for guerrilla attacks in their neighborhoods. Sherman destroyed hundreds of homes, farms, and towns in the exercise of this policy.

The war was equally damaging in other parts of Tennessee. In Middle Tennessee, retreating Confederate soldiers after the fall of Fort Donelson demolished railroads and burned bridges so as not to leave them for the Union. Union troops also destroyed and appropriated the region's resources. Federals took horses, pigs, cows, corn, hay, cotton, fence rails, firearms, and tools. Sometimes this was carried out through official requisitions, but at other times it amounted to little more than pillaging.

Criminals took advantage of the loss of public order, and bands of thieves and bandits began roaming the countryside.

The experience in East Tennessee was different. Because of the region's widespread Union sympathies, it was the Confederacy that first occupied the eastern territory. During this time hundreds of alleged Unionists were charged with treason and jailed. When the Confederates began conscripting men into military service in 1862, tensions in East Tennessee grew. Many East Tennesseans fled to Kentucky, and distrust, bitterness, and violence escalated. In September 1863 the tables turned, however, and the Confederates were replaced by the Federals, whose victories elsewhere enabled them to now focus on occupying friendly East Tennessee.

The Effects of the War

Tennessee lost most of a generation of young men to the Civil War. Infrastructure was destroyed, and thousands of farms, homes, and other properties were razed. The state's reputation on the national stage had been tarnished, and it would be decades until Tennessee had the political power that it enjoyed during the Age of Jackson. But while the war caused tremendous hardships for the state, it also led to the freeing of some 275,000 black Tennesseans from slavery.

RECONSTRUCTION

Tennessee was no less divided during the years following the Civil War than it was during the conflict. The end to the war ushered in a period where former Unionists—now allied with the Radical Republicans in Congress—disenfranchised and otherwise marginalized former Confederates and others who had been sympathetic with the Southern cause.

They also pushed through laws that extended voting and other rights to the newly freed blacks, changes which led to a powerful backlash and the establishment of such shadowy groups as the Ku Klux Klan.

William G. "Parson" Brownlow of Knoxville, a vocal supporter of the Union, was elected governor of Tennessee in 1865. During the same year, the voters approved a constitutional amendment abolishing slavery, making Tennessee the only seceded state to abolish slavery by its own act. Brownlow and his supporters bent laws and manipulated loyalties in order to secure ratification of the 14th and 15th Amendments to the constitution, paving the way for Tennessee to be admitted back to the Union, the first Southern state to be readmitted following the war. Brownlow's success ensured that Tennessee would not experience the Congressionally mandated Reconstruction that other former Confederate states did.

Recognizing that the unpopularity of his positions among Tennessee's numerous former Confederates placed his political future in jeopardy, Brownlow and his supporters extended the right to vote to thousands of freedmen in February 1867. During the statewide vote a few months later, Brownlow and his followers were swept to victory, largely due to the support of black voters.

The quick rise to power of former enemies and the social changes caused by the end of slavery led some former Confederates to bitterness and frustration. In the summer of 1867, the Ku Klux Klan emerged as a political and

terrorist movement to keep freedmen in their traditional place. Klan members initially concerned themselves principally with supporting former Confederates and their families, but they were soon known more for their attacks on black men and women. The KKK was strongest in Middle and West Tennessee, except for a small pocket near Bristol in East Tennessee.

Governor Brownlow responded strongly to the KKK's activities, and in 1869 he declared martial law in nine counties where the organization was most active. But when Brownlow left Tennessee shortly thereafter to fill a seat in the U.S. Senate, the KKK's Grand Wizard, former Confederate Gen. Nathan Bedford Forrest, declared the group's mission accomplished and encouraged members to burn their robes. The KKK's influence quickly faded, only to reemerge some 50 years later at Stone Mountain, Georgia.

Brownlow was replaced by Senate Speaker Dewitt C. Senter, who quickly struck a more moderate position than his predecessor by setting aside the law that had barred Confederate veterans from voting.

The greatest legacy of the Civil War was the emancipation of Tennessee's slaves. Following the war, many freed blacks left the countryside and moved to cities, including Memphis, Nashville, Chattanooga, and Knoxville, where they worked as skilled laborers, domestics, and more. Other blacks remained in the countryside, working as wage laborers on farms or share-cropping in exchange for occupancy on part of a former large-scale plantation.

The Freedmen's Bureau worked in Tennessee for a short period after the end of the war, and it succeeded in establishing schools for blacks. During this period the state's first black colleges were established: Fisk, Tennessee Central, LeMoyne, Roger Williams, Lane, and Knoxville.

As in other states, blacks in Tennessee enjoyed short-lived political power during Reconstruction. The right to vote and the concentration of blacks in certain urban areas paved the way for blacks to be elected to the

Tennessee House of Representatives, beginning with Sampson Keeble of Nashville in 1872. In all, 13 blacks were elected as representatives between 1872 and 1887, including James C. Napier, Edward Shaw, and William Yardley, who also ran for governor.

Initially, these pioneers met mild acceptance from whites, but as time progressed whites became uncomfortable sharing political power with black people. By the 1890s, racist Jim Crow policies of segregation, poll taxes, secret ballots, literacy tests, and intimidation prevented blacks from holding elected office—and in many cases, voting—in Tennessee again until after the civil rights movement of the 1960s.

The Republican Party saw the end of its influence with the end of the Brownlow governorship. Democrats rejected the divisive policies of the Radical Republicans, sought to protect the racial order that set blacks at a disadvantage to whites, and were less concerned about the state's mounting debt than the Republicans.

Economic Recovery

The social and political upheaval caused by the Civil War was matched or exceeded by the economic catastrophe that it represented for the state. Farms and industry were damaged or destroyed; public infrastructure was razed; schools were closed; and the system of slavery that underpinned most of the state's economy was gone.

The economic setback was seen as an opportunity by those proponents of the "New South," who advocated for an industrial and economic revival that would catapult the South to prosperity impossible under the agrarian and slavery-based antebellum economy. The New South movement was personified by carpetbagging Northern capitalists moved to Tennessee and set up industries that would benefit from cheap labor and abundant natural resources. Many Tennesseans welcomed these newcomers, and advocated for their fellow Tennesseans to put aside regional differences and welcome the Northern investors.

The result was an array of industries that were chartered during the years following the Civil War. Mining, foundries, machine shops, manufacturing, sawmills, gristmills, furniture factories, and textile industries were established. Knoxville and Chattanooga improved quickly. Over the 10-year period from 1860 to 1870, Chattanooga's industrial works grew from employing 214 men to more than 2,000.

Memphis and Nashville also worked to attract industries. Memphis was on the cusp of a commercial and industrial boom in 1873 when yellow fever hit the city; the epidemic caused widespread death and hurt Memphis's economic recovery. In Nashville, new distilleries, sawmills, paper mills, stove factories, and an oil refinery led the way to industrialization.

Industry also settled in the small towns and countryside. The coal-rich region of the Cumberland Mountains were the site of major coal mining operations. Copper mines were opened in Cleveland, flouring mills in Jackson, and textile factories in Tullahoma and other parts of the state.

Agriculture

A revolution was brewing in agriculture too. Civil War veterans returned to small farms all over the state and resumed farming with implements largely unchanged for hundreds of years. Every task was achieved by hand, with the lone help of one or two farm animals.

But farm technology was beginning to change. Thirty years after the war, new labor-saving devices began to be put to use. These included early cotton pickers, reapers, and planters. Seed cleaners, corn-shellers, and improved plows were made available. In 1871 the state formed the Bureau of Agriculture, whose employees prepared soil maps and studied the state's climate, population, and the prices of land. New methods such as crop diversification, crop rotation, cover crops, and the use of commercial fertilizers were introduced and farmers were encouraged to use them.

Meanwhile, farmers themselves established a strong grassroots movement in the state. The Patrons of Husbandry, or the Grange, was organized shortly after the war to encourage members to improve farming methods and enhance their economic influence. Government encouraged county fair associations, which organized fairs where farmers could be awarded for their crops and encouraged to use new farming methods. The Farmers' Alliance and the Agricultural Wheel, both national organizations, grew in prominence in the 1880s and advocated currency reform, empowerment of farmers, and control of communication and transportation systems. The Alliance gave low-interest loans to farmers and encouraged cooperative selling.

While the Alliance and the Wheel were not political organizations as such, they supported candidates who adopted their views on agricultural matters. In 1890 the Alliance supported the Democrat, John P. Buchanan, for governor, and he was successful. For their part, political elites did not take the farming movement or its leaders very seriously, ridiculing them as "hayseeds," "clodhoppers," and "wool-hat boys." In other places, rural and small-town residents resisted the Wheel and the Alliance, in part because they feared challenge of the status quo. As the Alliance became more radical in its views, the support in Tennessee dwindled and by 1892 it had faded in many parts of the state.

While some blacks remained on farms as wage laborers or sharecroppers, many left for the cities, causing a labor shortage. Attempts to attract foreign or Northern immigrants to the state were unsuccessful. Tennessee's poor whites filled this labor shortage, now able to own or rent land for the first time.

Education
Despite popular attempts and pleas by some politicians for a sound education system, Tennessee lagged behind in public education during the post-war years. In 1873 the legislature passed a school law that set up a basic framework of school administration, but the state's debt and financial problems crippled the new system. Private funds stepped in—the Peabody Fund contributed to Tennessee's schools, including the old University of Nashville, renamed Peabody after its benefactor. Meanwhile, teachers' institutes were established during the 1880s in order to raise the level of instruction at Tennessee's public schools.

THE 20TH AND 21ST CENTURIES
Prohibition
Prohibition was the first major issue to face Tennesseans in the new century. An 1877 law that forbade the sale of alcohol within four miles of a rural school had been used to great effect by Prohibitionists to restrict the sale and traffic of alcohol in towns all over the countryside. As the century turned, pressure mounted to extend the law, and public opinion in support of temperance grew, although it was never without contest from the powerful distillery industry. Finally, in 1909, the legislature passed the Manufacturer's Bill, which would halt the production of intoxicants in the state, and overrode Governor Patterson's veto. When the United States followed suit with the 18th Amendment in 1920, Prohibition was old news in Tennessee.

World War I
True to its nickname, Tennessee sent a large number of troops to fight in World War I. Most became part of the Thirtieth "Old Hickory" Division, which entered the war on August 17, 1918. The most famous Tennessee veteran of World War I was Alvin C. York, a farm boy from the Cumberland Mountains who staged a one-man offensive against the German army after becoming separated from his own detachment. Reports say that York killed 20 German soldiers and persuaded 131 more to surrender.

Women's Suffrage
The movement for women's suffrage had been established in Tennessee prior to the turn of the 20th century, and it gained influence as the century progressed. The Southern Woman Suffrage Conference was held in Memphis in 1906, and a statewide suffrage organization was

established. State bills to give women the right to vote failed in 1913 and 1917, but support was gradually growing. In the summer of 1920, the 19th Amendment had been ratified by 35 states and one more ratification was needed to make it law. Tennessee was one of five states yet to vote on the measure, and on August 9, Governor Roberts called a special sitting of the legislature to consider the amendment.

Furious campaigning and public debate led up to the special sitting. The Senate easily ratified the amendment 25 to 4, but in the House of Representatives the vote was much closer: 49 to 47. Governor Roberts certified the result and notified the secretary of state: Tennessee had cast the deciding vote for women's suffrage.

Peay

The 1920s were years of growth and development in Tennessee, thanks in part to the able leadership of Austin Peay, elected governor in 1922. He reformed the state government, cut waste, and set out to improve the state's roads and schools. The improvements won Peay support from the state's rural residents, who benefited from better transportation and education. Spending on schools doubled during Peay's three terms as governor, and the school term increased from 127 to 155 days per year.

Peay also saw the importance of establishing parks: Reelfoot Lake State Park was established during his third term, finally ending fears of development in the area. Peay also supported establishment of the Great Smoky Mountains National Park, and raised $1.5 million in a bond issue as the state's part toward the purchase of the land. Peay was dead by the time the park was opened in 1940, but it is largely to his credit that it was created.

The Depression

The progress and hope of the 1920s was soon forgotten with the Great Depression. Tennessee's economic hard times started before the 1929 stock market crash. Farming in the state was hobbled by low prices and low returns during the 1920s. Farmers and laborers displaced by this trend sought work in

new industries like the Dupont plant in Old Hickory, Eastman-Kodak in Kingsport, or the Aluminum Company of America in Blount County. But others, including many African Americans, left Tennessee for northern cities such as Chicago.

The Depression made bad things worse. Farmers tried to survive, turning to subsistence farming. In cities unemployed workers lined up for relief. Major bank failures in 1930 brought most financial business in the state to a halt.

President Roosevelt's New Deal provided some relief for Tennesseans. The Civilian Conservation Corps, Public Works Administration, and Civil Works Administration were established in Tennessee. Through the CCC, more than 7,000 Tennesseans planted millions of pine seedlings, developed parks, and built fire towers. Through the PWA more than 500 projects were undertaken, including bridges, housing, water systems, and roads. Hundreds of Tennesseans were employed by the CWA to clean public buildings, landscape roads, and do other work.

But no New Deal institution had more impact on Tennessee then the Tennessee Valley Authority. Architects of TVA saw it as a way to improve agriculture along the Tennessee River, alleviate poverty, and produce electrical power. The dam system would also improve navigation along what was then an often dangerous river. The law establishing TVA was introduced by Sen. George W. Norris of Nebraska and passed in 1933. Soon after, dams were under construction and trade on the river increased due to improved navigability. Even more importantly, electric power was now so cheap that even Tennesseans in remote parts of the state could afford it. By 1945, TVA was the largest electrical utility in the nation and new industries were attracted by cheap energy and improved transportation. Tourists also came to enjoy the so-called Great Lakes of the South.

The TVA story is not without its losers, however. TVA purchased or condemned more than one million acres of land and flooded

300,000 acres more, forcing 14,000 families to be displaced.

The Crump Machine

The 1930s in Tennessee was the age of Ed Crump, Memphis's longtime mayor and political boss. The son of a former Confederate, Crump was born in Mississippi in 1874 and moved to Memphis when he was 17 years old. First elected in 1909 as a city councilman, Crump was a genius of human nature and organization. Able to assure statewide candidates the support of influential Shelby County, Crump's power extended beyond Memphis. His political power often required corruptions, patronage, and the loss of individual freedoms. To get ahead you had to pay homage to Boss Crump. He was particularly popular during the Depression, when constituents and others looked to Crump for much-needed relief.

Crump manipulated the votes in his home Shelby County by paying the $2 poll tax for cooperative voters. He allied with black leaders such as Robert Church Jr. to win support in the black community of Memphis.

World War II

Tennessee, like the rest of the country, was changed by World War II. The war effort changed the state's economy and led to a migration to the cities unprecedented in Tennessee's history. The tiny mountain town of Oak Ridge became the state's fifth-largest city almost overnight, and is synonymous with the atomic bomb that was dropped on Hiroshima at the final stage of the war.

More than 300,000 Tennesseans served in World War II and just under 6,000 died. During the war, Camps Forrest, Campbell, and Tyson served as prisoner-of-war camps. Several hundred war refugees settled in Tennessee, many in the Nashville area.

The war also sped up Tennessee's industrialization. Industrial centers in Memphis, Chattanooga, and Knoxville converted to war production, while new industries were established in smaller cities such as Kingsport. Agriculture was no longer Tennessee's most important economic activity. The industrial growth was a catalyst for urbanization. Nashville's population grew by 25 percent during the war, and Shelby County's by 35 percent. The war also finally saw the end to the Great Depression.

The war also brought women into the workplace in numbers that were then unprecedented; approximately one-third of the state's workers were female by the end of the war.

Tennesseans supported the war not only by volunteering, but on the home front as well. Families planted victory gardens, invested in war bonds, and supported soldiers.

Tennesseans served with distinction during the war. Cordell Hull, a native of Pickett County, was U.S. secretary of state for 12 years and is known as the "Father of the United Nations" for his role in drawing up the foundation of that institution.

Oak Ridge

No community was more transformed the by the war than Oak Ridge. A remote area of countryside west of Knoxville in East Tennessee, Oak Ridge was home to some 4,000 people, most of them farmers. The army was searching for a place to build the facilities to construct an atom bomb, and this 52,000-acre area fit the bill. In 1942 residents of Oak Ridge began to receive notices that they would have to leave because the government was taking their land. Clinton Laboratories, named after the nearest town, was built seemingly overnight. Housing was provided in dormitories, trailers, and "victory cottages." Scientists, engineers, and researchers moved in, together with blue-collar workers who were needed to labor at the facility, later named Oak Ridge National Laboratory.

Work proceeded on schedule inside the laboratory and on August 6, 1945, shortly after 9 A.M., the first atomic bomb was dropped over Hiroshima. Three days later the second bomb exploded over Nagasaki, and on August 14, Japan surrendered.

Oak Ridge remains today a key part of the United States' nuclear system. While some degree of integration has taken place, Oak Ridge still has a different feel than most Tennessee towns, due in large part to the thousands of scientists and professionals who live there. The Oak Ridge facility also remains a source of controversy, uncertainty, and shame for many Tennesseans who object to the weaponry that was and still is manufactured on their soil.

Post-War Tennessee

Tennessee's industrialization continued after the war. By 1960 there were more city dwellers then rural dwellers in the state and Tennessee was ranked the 16th most industrialized state in the United States. Industry that had developed during the war transformed to peacetime operation.

Ex-servicemen were not content with the political machines that had controlled Tennessee politics for decades. In 1948 congressman Estes Kefauver won a U.S. Senate seat, defeating the candidate chosen by Memphis mayor Ed Crump. The defeat signaled an end to Crump's substantial influence in statewide elections. In 1953 Tennessee repealed the state poll tax, again limiting politicians' ability to manipulate the vote. The tide of change also swept in Sen. Albert Gore Sr. and governor Frank Clement in 1952. Kefauver, Gore, and Clement were moderate Democrats of the New South.

Civil Rights in Tennessee

The early gains for blacks during Reconstruction were lost during the decades that followed. Segregation, the threat of violence, poll taxes, and literacy tests discriminated against blacks in all spheres of life: economic, social, political, and educational. The fight to right these wrongs was waged by many brave Tennesseans.

Early civil rights victories in Tennessee included the 1905 successful boycott of Nashville's segregated streetcars, and the creation of a competing black-owned streetcar company. In the 1920s in Chattanooga, blacks successfully defeated the Ku Klux Klan at the polls. Black institutions of learning persevered in educating young African Americans and developing a generation of leaders.

Following World War II, there was new-found energy in the fight for civil rights. Returning black servicemen who had fought for their country demanded greater equality, and the economic opportunities of the age raised the stakes of economic equality. In 1946, racially based violence targeted at a returned black serviceman in Columbia brought national attention to violence against black citizens and raised awareness of the need to protect blacks' civil rights.

The Highlander Folk School, founded in Grundy County and later moved to Cocke County, was an important training center for community activists and civil rights leaders in the 1950s. Founder Miles Horton believed in popular education and sought to bring black and white activists together to share experiences. Many leaders in the national civil rights movement, including Rev. Martin Luther King and Rosa Parks, attended the folk school.

In the 1950s, the first steps toward public school desegregation took place in Tennessee. Following a lawsuit filed by black parents, Clinton desegregated its schools in 1956 on order of a federal court judge. The integration began peacefully, but outside agitators arrived to organize resistance and in the end Governor Clement was forced to call in 600 National Guardsman to diffuse the violent atmosphere. But the first black students were allowed to stay, and in May 1957 Bobby Cain became the first African American to graduate from an integrated public high school in the South.

In the fall of 1957 Nashville's public schools were desegregated. As many as half of the white students stayed home in protest and one integrated school, Hattie Cotton School, was dynamited and partially destroyed. Other Tennessee cities desegregated at a slower pace and by 1960 only 169 of Tennessee's almost 150,000 black children of school age attended integrated schools.

The Nashville lunch counter sit-ins of 1960 were an important milestone in both the local and national civil rights movements. Led by students from the city's black universities, the sit-ins eventually forced an end to racial segregation of the city's public services. Over two months hundreds of black students were arrested for sitting at white-only downtown lunch counters. Black consumers' boycott of downtown stores put additional pressure on the business community. On April 19 thousands of protesters marched in silence to the courthouse to confront city officials and the next day Rev. Martin Luther King Jr. addressed Fisk University. On May 10, 1960, several downtown stores integrated their lunch counters and Nashville became the first major city in the South to begin desegregating its public facilities.

As the civil rights movement continued Tennesseans played an important part. Tennesseans were involved with organizing the Student Nonviolent Coordinating Committee, and participated in the Freedom Rides, which sought to integrate buses across the south. In 1965 A. W. Willis Jr. of Memphis became the first African American representative elected to the state's General Assembly in more than 60 years. Three years later, Memphis's sanitation workers went on strike to protest discriminatory pay and work rules. Dr. King came to Memphis to support the striking workers.

On April 4, 1968, King was assassinated by a sniper as he stood on the balcony of the Lorraine Motel in downtown Memphis.

Modern Tennessee

The industrialization that began during World War II has continued in modern-day Tennessee. In 1980 Nissan built what was then the largest truck assembly plant in the world at Smyrna, Tennessee. In 1987 Saturn Corporation chose Spring Hill as the site for its $2.1 billion automobile plant.

At the same time, however, the state's older industries—including textiles and manufacturing—have suffered losses over the past three decades, due in part to the movement of industry outside of the United States.

During the 1950s and beyond, Tennessee developed a reputation as a hotbed of musical talent. Memphis's Elvis Presley may have invented rock 'n' roll, and his Graceland mansion remains one of the state's most enduring tourist attractions. The Grand Ole Opry in Nashville was representative of a second musical genre that came to call Tennessee home: country music.

Government and Economy

GOVERNMENT

Tennessee is governed by its constitution, unchanged since 1870 when it was revised in light of emancipation, the Civil War, and reconstruction.

Tennessee has a governor who is elected to four-year terms, a legislature, and court system. The Lieutenant Governor is not elected statewide; he or she is chosen by the Senate and also serves as its Speaker.

The legislature, or General Assembly, is made up of the 99-member House of Representatives and the 33-member Senate. The Tennessee State Supreme Court is made of five members, no two of whom can be from the same Grand Division. The Supreme Court chooses the state's attorney general.

The executive branch consists of 21 cabinet-level departments, which employ some 39,000 state workers. Departments are led by a commissioner, who is appointed by the governor and serves as a member of his cabinet.

Tennessee has 95 counties; the largest is Shelby County, which contains Memphis. The smallest county by size is Trausdale, with 113 square miles; the smallest population is in Pickett County.

The state has 11 electoral college votes in U.S. presidential elections.

Modern Politics

Like other Southern states, Tennessee has seen a gradual shift to the political right since the 1960s. The shift began in 1966 with Howard

Baker's election to the U.S. Senate, and continued with Tennessee's support for Republican presidential candidate Richard Nixon in 1968 and 1972. Despite a few exceptions, the shift has continued into the 21st century, although Nashville, Memphis, and other parts of Middle and West Tennessee remain Democratic territory.

East Tennessee holds the distinction as one of a handful of Southern territories that has consistently supported the Republican Party since the Civil War. Today, Republicans outpoll Democrats in this region by as much as three to one.

The statewide trend towards the Republican party continued in 2008, with Tennessee being one of only a handful of states where Democrat Barack Obama received a lesser proportion of votes than did Senator John Kerry four years earlier. State Republicans also succeeded in gaining control of both houses of the state legislature. The lone Democrat on the scene is Phil Bredeson, who will finish his second four-year term as governor in 2010.

Andrew Jackson may still be the most prominent Tennessean in American political history, but Tennessee politicians continue to play a role on the national stage. Albert Gore Jr., elected to the U.S. House of Representatives in 1976, served as vice president under president Bill Clinton from 1992 until 2000, and lost the highly contested 2000 presidential contest to George W. Bush. Gore famously lost his home state to Bush, further evidence of Tennessee's move to the right. Gore went on to champion global climate change and win the Nobel Peace Prize.

Lamar Alexander, a former governor of Tennessee, was appointed secretary of education by the first President Bush in 1990. Alexander—famous for his flannel shirts—ran unsuccessfully for president and was later elected senator from Tennessee. Bill Frist, a doctor, was also elected senator and rose to be the Republican majority leader during the presidency of George W. Bush, before quitting politics for medical philanthropy.

The most recent Tennessean to seek the Oval Office was former senator and *Law and Order* star Fred Thompson, from Lewisburg in Middle Tennessee.

One of the most persistent political issues for Tennesseans in modern times has been the state's tax structure. The state first established a 2 percent sales tax in 1947, and it was increased incrementally over the years, eventually reaching 7 percent today. With local options, it is one of the highest sales tax rates in the country. (The state sales tax on food is 5.5 percent.) At the same time, the state has failed on more than one occasion—most recently during the second term of Republican governor Donald Sundquist in the late 1990s—to establish an income tax that would provide greater stability to the state's revenues.

In 2008 Tennessee faced a serious budget crunch that led to the elimination of thousands of state jobs, cutbacks at state-funded universities, and the scaling back of the state health insurance program.

ECONOMY

Tennessee has the 18th-largest economy in the United States. Important industries include health care, education, farming, electrical power, and tourism. In the past few years, most job growth has been recorded in the areas of leisure, hospitality, education, and health care. Manufacturing, mining, and construction jobs have declined. Despite the overall decline in manufacturing, there was good news in 2008, when Volkswagen announced that it chose Chattanooga as home for a new, $1 billion plant, expected to bring some 2,000 jobs to the state in the coming years.

Tennessee's unemployment rate fluctuates, but generally sits a half-point above the national average. In 2008, the jobless rate was about 5.2 percent.

About 12.4 percent of Tennessee families live in poverty, more than the 10 percent nationwide average. The median household income in 2006 was $40,315—83 percent of the U.S. median income.

All of Tennessee's cities have poverty rates higher than the state or national average. Memphis' poverty rate is the state's highest: 19 percent of Memphis families are poor. Knoxville's family poverty rate is 16.7 percent.

Agriculture

Farming accounts for 11 percent, or $44.2 billion, of the Tennessee economy. More than 43 percent of the state's land is used in farming; 60 percent of this is cropland.

Soybeans, tobacco, corn, and hay are among Tennessee's most important agricultural crops. Cattle and calf production, chicken farming, and cotton cultivation are also important parts of the farm economy.

Greene County in northeastern Tennessee is the leading county for all types of cow farming; Giles and Lincoln Counties in the south-central part of the state rank second and third. The leading cotton producer is Haywood County, followed by Crockett and Tipton, all three of which are located in West Tennessee. Other counties where agriculture figures largely into the economy are Obion, Henry, Rutherford, and Robertson.

Tennessee ranks second among U.S. states for equine production, and walking or quarter horses account for more than half of the state's estimated 210,000 head of equine. The state ranks fifth for tomatoes, sixth for tobacco, and ninth for cotton.

Some farmers have begun converting to corn production in anticipation of a biofuel boom.

Tourism

According to the state department that promotes tourism, the industry generated some $13.4 billion in economic activity in 2006. More than 181,000 Tennessee jobs are linked to tourism. The state counted some 49.75 million overnight and day-trip visitors in 2006, and credited the industry with generating more than $1 billion in state and local tax revenue.

People and Culture

DEMOGRAPHICS

Tennessee is home to 6.2 million people. Almost one-quarter of these are 18 years and younger; about 13 percent are older than 65. Tennessee is 80 percent white and 17 percent black. Three-quarters of Tennesseans have a high school diploma and 20 percent have at least a bachelor's degree.

Memphis counts 674,000 residents and is the state's largest city. More than 63 percent of Memphians are African-American, a greater proportion than is found in any other American city. Memphis has the youngest average age of the four major Tennessee cities.

Nashville's population is 591,000. Some 64 percent of these are white, 29 percent are African-American, and 7 percent are Latino or Hispanic. Nashville's foreign-born population tripled during the decade between 1990 and 2000, and the city is now 11 percent foreign-born. This includes large populations from Mexico, Vietnam, Laos, and Somalia. Nashville is also home to more than 11,000 Iraqi Kurds.

Knoxville, Tennessee's third largest city, has a population of about 183,000. Some 170,000 people live in Chattanooga.

RELIGION

Tennessee is unquestionably part of the U.S. Bible Belt; the conservative Christian faith is both prevalent and prominent all over the state. Eighty-three percent of Tennesseans call themselves Christians and more than half of these identify as Baptist. The second-largest Christian denomination is Methodist. Nashville is the headquarters of the Southern Baptist Convention, the National Baptist Convention, and the United Methodist Church. Memphis is the headquarters of the mostly African-American Church of God in Christ.

While Tennessee's urban centers are the home of church headquarters, religious fervor is strongest in the rural communities. Pentecostal churches have been known for rites such as speaking in tongues and snake-handling, although these activities are not as widespread as they once were.

Non-Christians will feel most comfortable in urban areas, where religious minorities have grown in recent years and where the influence of the local churches is not as great.

One practical effect of Tennessee's Christian bent is that many counties and even some cities are totally dry, while most bar the sale of alcohol on Sundays.

LANGUAGE

Tennesseans speak English, of a kind. The Tennessee drawl varies from the language of the Upper South, spoken in East Tennessee and closely associated with the region's Scotch-Irish roots, and the language of West Tennessee, more akin to that of Mississippi and the Lower South.

Little in Tennesseans' speech is distinct to the state itself. Speech patterns heard in Tennessee are also heard in other states in the region.

Speech patterns that have been documented throughout the state, but which may be more prevalent in the east, include the following, outlined by Michael Montgomery of the University of South Carolina in the *Tennessee Encyclopedia of History and Culture.* Montgomery writes that Tennesseans tend to pronounce vowels in the words *pen* and *hem* as *pin* and *him;* they shift the accent to the beginning of words, so *Tennessee* becomes *TIN-isee;* they clip or reduce the vowel in words like *ride* so it sounds more like *rad;* and vowels in other words are stretched, so that a single syllable word like *bed* becomes *bay-ud.*

Tennessee speech patterns are not limited to word pronunciation. Tennesseans also speak with folksy and down-home language. Speakers often use colorful metaphors, and greater value is placed on the quality of expression than the perfection of grammar.

ARTS
Crafts

Many Tennessee craft traditions have their roots in the handmade housewares that rural families had to make for themselves, including things like quilts, baskets, coverlets, candles, and furniture. These items were fashioned out of materials that could be raised or harvested nearby, and colors were derived from natural dyes such as walnut hulls and indigo.

Many of the same crafts were produced by African Americans, who developed their own craft traditions, often with even fewer raw materials than their white counterparts. For example, African-American quilts often used patterns and colors reflective of African culture. Blacksmiths were often African-American, and these skilled artisans developed both practical and decorative pieces for white and black households.

As the lifestyles of Tennesseans changed, and more household items were available in stores and by mail-order, crafts were produced for sale. In 1929, the Southern Highland Handicraft Guild was formed and held its first meeting in Knoxville. In 1950 the Guild merged with Southern Highlanders Inc., an organization established by the Tennessee Valley Authority, and the group's marketing and promotion efforts pushed westward towards the Cumberland Plateau and Nashville.

Today, artists from around the United States have settled in Tennessee to practice modern forms of traditional crafts of quilting, weaving, pottery, furniture-making, and basket-making, among others. While market forces have promoted a certain false folksiness among some artists, a great many of today's practicing artisans remain true to the mountain heritage that gave birth to the craft tradition in the first place.

Music

Tennessee may be more famous for its music than for anything else. The blues was born on Beale Street; the Grand Ole Opry popularized old-time mountain music; and the Fisk Jubilee singers of Nashville introduced African-American spirituals to the world. Rock 'n' roll traces its roots to Elvis Presley,

Carl Perkins, Jerry Lee Lewis, and the city of Memphis.

The blues became popular in cities from New Orleans to St. Louis at the turn of the 20th century. But thanks in large part to composer and performer W. C. Handy, the musical form will be forever associated with Memphis and Beale Street. Early blues greats like Walter "Furry" Lewis, Booker T. Washington "Bukka" White, "Little Laura" Dukes, and Ma Rainey started in Memphis.

Sun Records in the 1950s recorded some of the first commercial blues records, but the label is most famous for discovering Elvis Presley. Stax Records created a new sound, soul, in the late 1950s and early 1960s.

Country music was born in Bristol, Tennessee, where the earliest recordings of Jimmie Rodgers and the Carter Family were made in the 1920s. In the decades that followed, Nashville became the capital of country music, beginning thanks to radio station WSM and dozens of rural musicians who trekked to town to play on the radio. America was hungry for a type of music to call its own, and country music was it. First called "hillbilly music," country was popularized by barn-dance radio shows, including the Grand Ole Opry. Over the years, country music mellowed out, adopting the Nashville Sound that softened its edges and made it palatable to a wider audience. Today, the city is second only to New York as a center for recorded music, and many country music stars still live in and around the city.

Dance

Clogging, or buck dancing, is a style of folk dance that originated with the Scotch-Irish settlers in the eastern mountains of Tennessee. Characterized by an erect upper body and a fast-paced toe-heel movement with the feet, traditional clogging is improvisational. Performers move at a very fast pace to the music of string bands.

Clogging was popularized during the 1940s and 1950s on television and radio shows that showcased country music. Modern clogging is often choreographed and performed with a partner.

Clogging can trace influences from Native American and African-American styles of dance, as well as the traditional dance of the British Isles.

Literature

The first literature inspired by Tennessee is not well known. *The Tennessean; A Novel, Founded on Facts* is a melodramatic novel, published in 1827 and written by Anne Newport Royall. Its plot brings readers along on a three-day journey from Nashville to Knoxville, and is the first novel set in Tennessee. The first novel written by a Tennessean was *Woodville; or, The Anchoret Reclaimed. A Descriptive Tale,* published in Knoxville in 1832 and written by Charles W. Todd.

Later Tennessee literature is better known. English novelist Frances Hodgson Burnett

A statue of writer Alex Haley sits in Knoxville.

lived in New Market and then Knoxville in the 1860s and 1870s. While best known for her tales *Little Lord Fauntleroy* and *The Secret Garden,* Burnett penned several works set in Tennessee. In the 1920s, a group of writers at Vanderbilt University emerged under the leadership of John Crowe Ransom. The group's magazine *The Fugitive* was published 1922–1925. The Fugitives were succeeded by the Agrarians, who published their manifesto, *I'll Take My Stand,* in 1930. Writer Robert Penn Warren was a member of both the Fugitives and the Agrarians, and he went on to win the Pulitzer Prize for *All the King's Men,* about governor Huey Long of Louisiana. Warren's novels *The Cave, Flood,* and *Meet Me in the Green Glen* are set in Tennessee.

Another award-winning Tennessee writer is Peter Taylor, who studied at Rhodes College and Vanderbilt University before moving to North Carolina and writing the Pulitzer Prize–winning *A Summons to Memphis* in 1986, and *In Tennessee Country* in 1994.

James Agee is another Pulitzer Prize–winner. Raised in Knoxville, Agee wrote poetry, journalism, and screenplays before his winning *A Death in the Family* was published. Agee is also known for his singular work *Let Us Now Praise Famous Men,* with photographer Walker Evans, which documented the lives of poor whites during the Great Depression.

Few people knew Memphis-born writer and historian Shelby Foote until Ken Burns's landmark Civil War documentary. In addition to his seminal trilogy on the war, Foote wrote the novel *Shiloh* in 1952.

Women have also excelled as writers in Tennessee. Anne Armstrong published *The Seas of God* in 1915 and *This Day and Time* in 1930, both of which were set in her native East Tennessee. Evelyn Scott wrote *The Wave,* set during the Civil War, as well as an autobiography, *Escapade,* depicting the six years she and her common-law husband spent living in Brazil.

Perhaps the best-known female Tennessee writer is Nikki Giovanni, of Knoxville, who established herself as a poet of international importance with her 1968 *Black Feeling, Black Talk.*

No Tennessee writer is better known or more widely acclaimed than Alex Haley, whose *Roots* won the Pulitzer Prize and inspired a landmark film and television series. Haley's other works include *Queen,* which is based on the story of his grandmother, who worked and lived in Savannah, Tennessee, on the Tennessee River.

Knoxville native Cormac McCarthy is widely known for his works, including *All the Pretty Horses* and *The Road,* which were both made into films. But McCarthy had started out writing about his native East Tennessee in works such as *The Orchard Keeper* and *Suttree.*

ESSENTIALS

Getting There and Around

Most visitors to and around Tennessee drive their own cars. The highways are good, distances are manageable, and most destinations in the state are not accessible by public transportation.

If you're coming into Nashville or Memphis for a weekend getaway or a conference, you can manage without a car. Otherwise, you will need your own wheels to get around.

AIR

International airports in Tennessee include Nashville International Airport (BNA) and Memphis International Airport (MEM). McGhee Tyson Airport (TYS) in Knoxville, Chattanooga Metropolitan Airport (CHA), and the Tri-Cities Regional Airport (TRI) offer domestic service to hubs in the eastern United States.

RAIL

Only western Tennessee is easily accessible by rail. Amtrak runs from Chicago to New Orleans, with stops in Memphis, Newbern-Dyersburg in West Tennessee, and Fulton on the border with Kentucky. The route, called The City of New Orleans, runs daily.

PHOTO COURTESY OF TENNESSEE DEPARTMENT OF TOURIST DEVELOPMENT

BUS

Greyhound fully serves Tennessee, with daily routes that criss-cross the state in nearly every direction.

CAR

Tennessee is within one day's drive of 75 percent of the U.S. population, and most visitors to the state get here in their own cars. There are seven interstates that run into the state, from just about every direction you might want to come.

While urban centers, pit-stop motels, and population centers are all found along or very near interstates, some of Tennessee's most lovely landscapes are far from the stretches of multi-lane pavement.

Road Rules

Tennessee recognizes other states' driver's licenses and learner's permits. New residents are required to obtain a Tennessee license within 30 days of establishing residency, however.

Speed limits vary. On interstates limits range from 55 to 75 miles per hour. Limits on primary and secondary routes vary based on local conditions. Travelers should pay special attention to slow zones around schools; speeding tickets in these areas often attract high penalties.

It is required by law that all drivers and passengers in a moving vehicle wear their seatbelts. Infants less than one year old must be restrained in a rear-facing car seat; children 1–3 years must be restrained in a front-facing car seat. A child between four and eight years

who is less than four feet, nine inches tall must have a booster seat.

Drunk driving is dangerous and against the law. It is illegal to drive in Tennessee with a blood alcohol concentration of 0.08 percent or more.

Car Rentals

Rental cars are widely available throughout Tennessee. The greatest concentration of rental agencies are found at major airports, but neighborhood and downtown locations can also be found. Most rental agencies require the renter to be at least 24 years old; some have an even higher age requirement.

Before renting a car, call you credit card company and primary car insurance provider to find out what kind of insurance you have on a rental. You can likely forego the expensive insurance packages offered by rental companies.

For the best rates on car rentals, book early. Most companies allow you to reserve a car in advance without paying a deposit.

Taxis

Taxis are available in major cities, including Memphis, Nashville, Knoxville, Chattanooga, and Clarksville. Taxi service in other parts of the state will be spotty and expensive.

Taxi stands are found in just a few locations, including airports and major tourist sites, such as Beale Street in Memphis. Otherwise you will have to call to summon a taxi.

Traffic Reports

For current traffic and road reports, including weather-related closures, construction closures,

TENNESSEE DRIVING DISTANCES

© AVALON TRAVEL

and traffic jams, dial 511 from any mobile or land line. You can also log on to www.tn511.com.

RECREATIONAL VEHICLE

Recreational vehicles are an increasingly popular way to see Tennessee due to the prevalence of good campgrounds and the beautiful landscape of the state.

All state park campgrounds welcome RVs and provide utilities such as water, electricity, and a dump station. For people who enjoy the outdoors but do not want to forgo the basic comforts of home, RVs provide some real advantages. RVs range from little trailers that pop up to provide space for sleeping to monstrous homes-on-wheels. Gas mileage ranges from 7 to 13 miles per gallon, depending on the size and age of the RV.

All RVers should have mercy on other drivers and pull over from time to time so that traffic can pass, especially on mountain roads that are steep and difficult for RVs to climb.

RV Rentals

You can rent an RV for a one-way or local trip from **Cruise America** (www.cruiseamerica. com), which has locations in Knoxville (1543 Downtown West Blvd., 865/560-9229), Nashville (201 Donelson Pk., 615/885-4281), and Memphis (10230 Highway 70, Lakeland, 901/867-0039). Renters should be 25 years or older. Rental rates vary depending on the size of the vehicle and other factors. They also charge for mileage, and you can buy kits that include sheets, towels, dishes, and other basic necessities.

Get RV (888/438-7844, www.getRV.com) is an agency that hooks you up with RV owners who want to rent their vehicle when it's not in use.

Recreation

NATIONAL PARKS

Tennessee's most significant national park is the Great Smoky Mountains National Park, the most visited national park in the United States. This is the crown jewel of the state's natural areas, and a major draw for visitors.

Other federal lands are more wild and less visited. The Big South Fork and Land Between the Lakes are uncrowded recreation areas along the northern border with Kentucky. The Cherokee National Forest flanks the Smokies on the north and south, creating an uninterrupted buffer of federally protected lands along the entire eastern mountain range.

STATE PARKS

Tennessee's state parks are truly glorious. The state has 54 parks and 77 state natural areas, stretching from the Appalachian Mountains in the east to the banks of the Mississippi River in the west. State parks and natural areas encompass 185,000 acres throughout the state. In 2007, Tennessee's parks were judged the best in the nation by the National Recreation and Park Association. The commendation came after a long and bitter fight over user fees and state budget woes that led to the closure of 14 parks and the imposition of user fees at 23 parks between 2002 and 2006. The fight over the future of the state parks illustrated how valuable they are indeed.

Each state park includes basic amenities such as picnic facilities and day-use areas with public restrooms, water, and a park office of some kind. Most parks also have campgrounds, hiking trails, playgrounds, and facilities for sports such as volleyball, basketball, and baseball. A number of parks have swimming beaches, bicycle trails, areas for fishing or hunting, and backcountry campsites.

The park system includes six parks with inns, twelve with golf courses, eight with restaurants, and four with marinas. A number of parks also have cabins, ideal for families or other groups.

For travelers who enjoy the out-of-doors, the state parks are some of the best places in the state to visit. Despite persistent budget problems, the parks are generally well maintained. Accommodations are not luxurious, but they are clean and comfortable, and the natural beauty that exists in many of the parks is unparalleled. Camping in a state park sure beats the KOA any day.

Detailed information about fees, amenities, and services may be found on the state park website (http://state.tn.us/environment/parks). You can also request a published map and brochure. Enthusiasts may also want to subscribe to the *Tennessee Conservationist,* a magazine published by the State Department of Environment and Conservation.

HIKING

Opportunities to hike are abundant in Tennessee. State parks, national forests, national parks, and wildlife refuges are just a few of the areas where you will find places for a walk in the woods.

High-profile hiking trails such as the Appalachian Trail in the eastern mountains are indeed special. But lesser-known walks are often equally spectacular, and the best hike may well be the one closest to where you are right now.

Day hikes require just a few pieces of gear: comfortable and sturdy shoes; a day pack with water, food, and a map; and several layers of clothing, especially during volatile spring and fall months. In the winter, it's a good idea to bring a change of socks and extra layers of warm clothes.

Other gear is optional: A walking stick makes rough or steep terrain a bit easier and a camera is always a nice idea.

Whenever you go hiking, be sure to tell someone where you're going and when you expect to be back. Cell phones many not work on the trail.

Many state parks and the national parks in the eastern mountains welcome overnight hikers. Backpackers must carry lightweight tents, sleeping bags, food, and extra gear on their backs. They must also register in advance. You can sometimes reserve backcountry campsites. These campsites offer little more than a clearing for your tent and a ring of stones for your fire. Some are built near sources of water. Some trails have overnight shelters, especially nice in winter.

Hiking is probably the single best way to experience Tennessee's nature, and there are few better ways to spend a day or two.

BICYLING

Bicycling is an increasingly popular pastime in Tennessee. Only in a handful of urban areas, and on some college campuses, is bicycling a form of regular transportation. But mountain and road-biking is popular for staying fit and having fun.

Of course you can bicycle just about anywhere (but not on the interstates). Cities such as Nashville, Knoxville, and Murfreesboro have greenways especially for bikers (and walkers). Dedicated mountain bike trails are popping up in parks across the state, including at Montgomery Bell State Park, Big Ridge State Park, and Meeman-Shelby Forest State Park. City parks in Memphis and Nashville also welcome bikers.

The Tennessee Bicycle Racing Association (www.tbra.org) promotes biking and is an umbrella organization for several local bike groups. The Tennessee Mountain Biking Alliance (http://mtb-tn.blogspot.com) promotes mountain biking and can put you in touch with mountain bikers in your neck of the woods. Local bike shops are also a good place to find out about good bike routes, local safety issues, and upcoming events.

FISHING

Fishing is tremendously popular in Tennessee. The lakes created by the Tennessee Valley Authority produced many opportunities to fish. Smaller rivers and streams in all parts of the state are also good for fishing.

Some of the most common types of fish caught in Tennessee rivers and lakes are bass, trout, crappie, perch, pike, catfish, and carp. Various rivers and lakes are stocked regularly with fish.

Subject to a few exceptions, everyone who is 13 and older and who attempts to take fish from a body of water should have a valid Tennessee fishing license. License fees vary by type and duration: A one-day fishing license for a Tennessee state resident is $5.50; an annual fish-hunt license for a state resident is $28.

Out-of-staters pay more: An annual license for all types of fish costs $81.

Annual licenses go on sale every year on February 18, and are good until the last day of February the next year.

You can buy a fishing license from county clerks, sporting good stores, boat docks, and offices of the Tennessee Wildlife Resources Agency. You can buy a license online at www.tnwildlife.org; licenses processed online are subject to a $3.25 processing fee. You can also buy licenses by mail or over the phone by calling 888/814-8972.

Rules about limits, minimum sizes, and seasons are detailed and depend on the lake or stream. The Tennessee Wildlife Resources Agency publishes a comprehensive guide to fishing regulations every year. This guide includes fish stocking schedules, dam release timetables, detailed information about limits, and warnings about contaminates in certain types of Tennessee fish. You can request a copy of the guide from any TWRA office, or download a copy online from www.tnwildlife.org.

TWRA offices are located in Crossville (931/484-9571), Nashville (Ellington Agricultural Center, 615/781-6500), Morristown (423/587-7037), and Jackson (731/423-5725).

Accommodations

Accommodations in Tennessee fall into three main categories, with little grey area in between.

HOTELS AND MOTELS

Chain motels are ubiquitous, particularly along interstates. These properties are entirely predictable; their amenities depend on the price tag and location. Most motel chains allow you to make reservations in advance by telephone or on the Internet. Most motels require a credit card number at the time of reservation, but they don't usually charge your card until you arrive. Always ask about the cancellation policy to avoid paying for a room that you do not ultimately need or use.

Savvy shoppers can save money on their hotel room. Shop around, and pay attention to price differentials based on location; if you're willing to be a few miles up the interstate from the city, you'll realize some significant savings. You may also be amazed by the power of the words "That rate seems high to me. Do you have anything better?" Employed regularly, this approach will usually save you a few bucks each night, at least.

Chain motels do not offer unique accommodations and only the rarest among them is situated somewhere more charming than an asphalt parking lot. But for travelers who are looking for flexibility, familiarity, and a good deal, chain motels can fit the bill.

Independent motels and hotels range from no-brand roadside motels to upscale boutique hotels in urban centers. By their very nature, these properties are each a little different. Boutique hotels tend to be more expensive than chain hotels, but they also allow you to feel as if you are staying in a place with a history and character of its own. They may also offer personalized service that is not available at cookie-cutter motels.

BED-AND-BREAKFASTS

Bed-and-breakfasts are about as far from a chain motel as one can get. Usually located in small towns, rural areas, and quiet residential neighborhoods of major cities, bed-and-breakfasts are independent guest houses. The quality of the offering depends entirely on the hosts, and the entire bed-and-breakfast experience often takes on the character and tone of the person in whose home you are sleeping. Good bed-and-breakfast hosts can sense the line between being welcoming and overly chatty, but some seem to struggle with this.

Bed-and-breakfasts offer a number of

advantages over the typical motel. Their locations are often superior; the guest rooms have lots of character and charm; and a full and often homemade breakfast is included. Some bed-and-breakfasts are located in historic buildings, and many are furnished with antiques.

Reservations for bed-and-breakfasts are not as flexible as most motels. Many bed-and-breakfasts require a deposit, and many require payment in full before you arrive. Making payments can be a challenge too; while some are equipped with credit card facilities, others accept only checks and cash. Cancellation policies are also more stringent than most motels. All of this can make it hard for travelers who like to be flexible and leave things till the last minute. But if your travel plans are certain and you just can't bear another night in a bland hotel room, a bed-and-breakfast is the ideal alternative.

Bed-and-breakfast rates vary, but generally range $90–150 per night based on double occupancy.

Bed and Breakfast Inns Online (www.bbonline.com) is a national listing service that includes hundreds of Tennessee bed-and-breakfasts.

HOSTELS

At this writing, there are youth hostels in Nashville, Knoxville, and upper East Tennessee. Hostels provide dormitory-style accommodations at a fraction of the cost of a standard motel room. Bathroom and kitchen facilities are usually shared, and there are common rooms with couches, televisions, and Internet access. Hostels are usually favored by young and international travelers, and they are a good place to meet people.

Food

Throughout Tennessee, you will find restaurants that specialize in local and regional dishes. In urban centers, there is a wide variety of dining available, from ethnic eateries to fine-dining restaurants.

Chain restaurants, including fast-food joints, are all over the state. But travelers owe it to themselves to eat in local restaurants for a taste of something more authentic.

PLATE-LUNCH DINERS

Plate-lunch diners, also called meat-and-threes, are found throughout Tennessee, with the greatest concentration in Memphis and Nashville. These humble eateries serve the type of food that Tennesseans cook (or once cooked) at home: main dish meats like baked chicken, meatloaf, fried catfish, and chicken and dumplings; side dishes (also called "vegetables") including macaroni and cheese, mashed potatoes, greens, creamed corn, squash, and fried okra; breads, including corn bread, biscuits, and yeast rolls; and desserts like peach cobbler, Jello, and cream pies. Hands down, these diners are the best places to become acquainted, or renew your relationship, with Southern home cooking.

Plate-lunch diners focus on the midday meal. Most offer a different menu of meats and sides daily. Large restaurants may have as many as eight different main dishes to choose from; smaller diners may offer two or three. Some are set up cafeteria-style and others employ waiters. All offer a good value for money and generally speedy food service.

Plate-lunch diners exist in rural and urban communities, although in the countryside there's less fuss attached. They are simply where people go to eat.

The food served in these restaurants is generally hearty; health-conscious eaters should be careful. Vegetarians should also note that even some vegetable dishes, like greens, are often cooked with meat.

REGIONAL SPECIALTIES
Barbecue

Memphis is the epicenter of Tennessee's barbecue culture. Here they host an annual festival dedicated to barbecue, and bona fide barbecue pits burn daily. In Memphis, they'll douse anything with barbecue sauce, hence the city's specialty: barbecue spaghetti.

Barbecue restaurants are usually humble places by appearances, with characters behind the counter and in the kitchen. Most swear by their own special barbecue recipe and guard it jealously. Nearly all good barbecue, however, requires time and patience, as the meat—usually pork—is smoked for hours and sometimes days over a fire. After the meat is cooked, it is tender and juicy and doused with barbecue sauce, which is tangy and sweet.

Pork barbecue is the most common, and it's often served pulled next to soft white bread. Barbecue chicken, turkey, ribs, bologna, and beef can also be found on many menus.

The Southern Foodways Alliance, part of the University of Mississippi's Center for the Study of Southern Culture, conducted an oral history project about Memphis and West Tennessee barbecue in the early 2000s. You can read transcripts of the interviews and see photos on the SFA website at www.southernfoodways.com.

Catfish

Fried catfish is a food tradition that started along Tennessee's rivers, where river catfish are caught. Today, fried catfish served in restaurants is just as likely to come from a catfish farm. For real river catfish, look for restaurants located near rivers and lakes, such as those near Reelfoot Lake in northwestern Tennessee, or the City Fish Market in Brownsville.

Fried catfish (it's rarely served any way besides fried) is normally coated with a thin dusting of cornmeal, seasonings, and flour. On its own, the fish is relatively bland. Tangy tartar sauce, vinegar-based hot sauce, and traditional sides like coleslaw and baked beans enliven the flavor. Hush puppies are the traditional accompaniment.

Farmer's Markets

Farmer's markets are popping up in more and more Tennessee communities. Knoxville, Nashville, and Memphis have large markets every Saturday (Nashville's operates daily). Dozens of small towns have their own weekly, seasonal markets.

There is a great deal of variety when it comes to the types of markets that exist. Some markets take place under tents, provide entertainment, and invite artisans to sell arts and crafts as well as food products. Other markets consist of little more than a bunch of farmers who have arranged the week's harvest on the back of their tailgates.

Regardless of the style, farmer's markets are a great place to meet people and buy wholesome food.

The State Department of Agriculture (www.agriculture.state.tn) maintains a listing of all registered farmer's markets, including locations and contact information.

Tips for Travelers

OPPORTUNITIES FOR STUDY

Tennessee is home to almost 50 colleges and universities, plus 13 public community colleges. The University of Tennessee, with campuses in Knoxville, Chattanooga, and Martin, is the largest. Other public colleges and universities include East Tennessee State University in Johnson City, Middle Tennessee State University in Murfreesboro, Tennessee State University in Nashville, and the University of Memphis. Private colleges include the historically black Fisk University in Nashville and Lemoyne-Owen College in Memphis; the University of the South at Sewanee, which is affiliated with the Episcopal Church; Memphis College of Art and Rhodes College in Memphis; and Vanderbilt University in Nashville. Each of these, plus the 31 other private institutions of higher learning, offer myriad short- and long-term education programs in fields as various as religious studies and medicine.

Several institutions of note offer workshops in arts and crafts. **The Appalachian Center for**

Craft (Smithville, 931/372-3051, www.tntech. edu/craftcenter) is an affiliate of Tennessee Tech University and specializes in instruction in decorative arts and crafts. Full-time students can pursue a bachelor's degree in fine arts or a certificate in clay, fiber, glass, metal, or woodwork. The center also offers more than 100 different workshops each year. The school is set in scenic countryside on the Cumberland Plateau.

Perhaps one of the best-known craft schools in the entire United States, Gatlinburg's **Arrowmont** (865/436-5860, www.arrowmont. org) offers dozens of short courses and weekend workshops annually. Arrowmont began as a settlement school for mountain folks, but today it is a center that combines traditional crafts with modern techniques and themes.

WOMEN TRAVELING ALONE

Women traveling alone in Tennessee may encounter a few people who don't understand, but most people will simply leave you alone. Solo women might find themselves the object of unwanted attention, especially at bars and restaurants at night. But usually a firm "I'm not interested" will do the trick.

Anyone—man or woman—traveling alone in the outdoors should take special precautions. Backpackers and campers should always tell someone where they will be and when they expect to be back. Ideally, establish a check-in routine with someone back home, and beware of overly-friendly strangers on the trail.

GAY AND LESBIAN TRAVELERS

Tennessee's gay, lesbian, bisexual, and transgender people have a mixed bag. On one hand, this is the Bible belt, a state where not long ago a bill was introduced that would have banned teachers from even saying the word "gay" in the classroom. On the other hand, there has been no better time to be gay in Tennessee. More and more social, civic, and political organizations are waking up to the gay community, and there are vibrant gay scenes in many Tennessee cities.

For gay travelers, this means that the experience on the road can vary tremendously. You may not be able to expect a warm welcome at the mom-and-pop diner out in the country, but you can find good gay nightlife and gay-friendly lodging in many cities.

The decision about how out to be on the road is entirely up to you, but be prepared for some harassment if you are open everywhere you go. The farther off the beaten track you travel, the less likely it is that the people you encounter have had many opportunities to get to know openly gay people. Some may be downright mean, but others have such stunted gaydar they probably won't even notice.

Several specific guidebooks and websites give helpful listings of gay-friendly hotels, restaurants, and bars. The Damron guides (www.damron. com) offer Tennessee listings; the International Gay and Lesbian Travel Association (IGLTA, www.iglta.org) is a trade organization with listings of gay-friendly hotels, tour operators, and much more. San Francisco–based Now, Voyager (www.nowvoyager.com) is a gay-owned and -operated travel agency that specializes in gay tours, vacation packages, and cruises.

You should also check out local gay and lesbian organizations and newspapers.

Nashville

Three different publications cover the gay, lesbian, bisexual, and transgender community in Nashville. The *Church Street Freedom Press* (www.churchstreetfreedompress.com) and *InsideOut Nashville* (www.insideoutnashville. com) are free weeklies; *Out and About* (www. outandaboutnewspaper.com) is a free monthly newsmagazine.

To meet other gay people and find out about events, stop by the Outloud Café and Bookstore (1703 Church St., 615/340-0034, www.outloudonline.com).

In Nashville, the **Doubletree Downtown** welcomes lesbian and gay guests. They also offer commitment ceremonies. International Travel Inc. (4004 Hillsboro Rd., 615/385-1222) is a Nashville-based gay-friendly travel agency.

Memphis

The **Memphis Gay and Lesbian Community**

Center (892 S. Cooper St., 901/278-4297, www. mglcc.org) is a clearinghouse of information for the gay and lesbian community. They have a directory of gay-friendly businesses, host social events, and promote tolerance and equality.

Mid-South Pride (www.midsouthpride.org) organizes Memphis Pride in June. The *Memphis Triangle Journal* is a free weekly paper available at local bookstores, libraries, and other locations.

SENIOR TRAVELERS

Elderhostel (800/454-5768, www.elderhostel. org), which organizes educational tours for people over 55, offers tours in Memphis and Nashville.

For discounts and help with trip planning, try the **AARP** (800/687-2777, www.aarp.org), which offers a full-service travel agency, trip insurance, a motor club, and AARP Passport program, which provides you with senior discounts for hotels, car rentals, and other things.

Persons over 55 should always check for a senior citizen discount. Most attractions and some hotels and restaurants have special pricing for senior citizens.

TRAVELERS WITH DISABILITIES

More people with disabilities are traveling than ever before. The Americans with Disabilities Act requires most public buildings to make provisions for disabled people, although in practice accessibility may be spotty.

When you make your hotel reservations, always check that the hotel is prepared to accommodate you. Airlines will also make special arrangements for you if you request help in advance. To reduce stress, try to travel during off-peak times.

Several national organizations have information and advice about traveling with disabilities. The Society for Accessible Travel and Hospitality (www.sath.org) publishes links to major airlines' accessibility policies and publishes travel tips for people with all types of disabilities, including blindness, deafness, mobility disorders, diabetes, kidney disease, and arthritis. The Society publishes *Open World*, a magazine about accessible travel.

Wheelchair Getaways (800/642-2042, www.wheelchairgetaways.com) is a national chain specializing in renting vans that are wheelchair accessible or otherwise designed for disabled drivers and travelers. Wheelchair Getaways has locations in Memphis (901/795-6533) and Knoxville (865/717-3997), and they will deliver to Nashville and other locations in the state.

Avis offers **Avis Access,** a program for travelers with disabilities. Call the dedicated 24-hour toll-free number 800/879-4273 for help renting a car with features such as transfer boards, hand controls, spinner knobs, and swivel seats.

TRAVELING WITH CHILDREN

It is hard to imagine a state better for family vacations than Tennessee. The state parks provide numerous places to camp, hike, swim, fish, and explore and cities have attractions like zoos, children's museums, aquariums, and trains.

Many hotels and inns offer special discounts for families, and casual restaurants almost always have a children's menu with lower-priced, kid-friendly choices.

FOREIGN TRAVELERS

Tennessee attracts a fair number of foreign visitors. Elvis, the international popularity of blues and country music, and the beauty of the eastern mountains bring people to the state from all over the globe.

Communication

Foreign travelers will find a warm welcome. Those in the tourist trade are used to dealing with all sorts of people, and will be pleased that you have come from so far away to visit their home. If you are not a native English speaker, it may be difficult to understand the local accent at first. Just smile and ask the person to say it again, a bit slower. Good humor and a positive attitude will help at all times.

Visas and Officialdom

Most citizens of a foreign country require a visa to enter the United States. There are many types of visas, issued according to the purpose of your visit. Business and pleasure travelers apply for B-1 and B-2 visas respectively. When you apply for your visa, you will be required to prove that the purpose of you trip is business, pleasure, or for medical treatment; that you plan to remain in the U.S. for a limited period; and that you have a place of residence outside the United States. Apply for your visa at the nearest U.S. embassy. For more information, contact the U.S. Citizenship and Immigration Service (www.uscis.gov).

Nationals of 27 countries may be able to use the Visa Waiver Program, operated by Customs and Border Protection. Presently, these 27 countries are: Andorra, Australia, Austria, Belgium, Brunei, Denmark, Finland, France, Germany, Iceland, Ireland, Italy, Japan, Liechtenstein, Luxemburg, Monaco, the Netherlands, New Zealand, Norway, Portugal, San Marino, Singapore, Slovenia, Spain, Sweden, Switzerland, and the United Kingdom.

Take note that in recent years the United States has begun to require visa-waiver participants to have upgraded passports, with digital photographs and machine-readable information. They have also introduced requirements that even visa-waiver citizens register in advance before arriving in the United States. For more information about the Visa Waiver Program, contact the Customs and Border Protection Agency (www.travel.state.gov).

All foreign travelers are now required to participate in U.S. Visit, a program operated by the Department of Homeland Security. Under the program, your fingerprints and photograph are taken—digitally and without ink—as you are being screened by the immigration officer.

Arrival

Nashville and Memphis are international airports, with daily international flights. At the Nashville International Airport, you can exchange currency at SunTrust Bank near A/B concourse, or at the Business Service Center (Wright Travel, 615/275-2660) near C/D concourse.

The Memphis airport is well equipped for foreign travelers. The lone international airline, Northwest/KLM Royal Dutch Airlines, provides interpreters for the Customs Clearance Facility and the boarding areas for international flights. They can accommodate Dutch, German, Arabic, Spanish, and French-speaking passengers.

International travel services are provided at the Business Service Center (Ticket Lobby B, 901/922-8090, Mon.–Fri. 7 A.M.–7:30 P.M., Sat. 7:30 A.M.–7:30 P.M., Sun. 11 A.M.–7:30 P.M.). Here you can exchange currency, buy travel insurance, make telephone calls and send faxes, wire money, and buy travelers checks. An additional kiosk is located in Concourse B near the international gates (gate B-36). Here you can buy travel insurance and exchange currency. The hours are daily 4:30–7:30 P.M.

Memphis International Airport is a "Transit Without Visa" port of entry. This means that foreign travelers whose flight will connect through Memphis on the way to another foreign destination beyond the United States no longer need a U.S. transit visa just to connect.

Health and Safety

DISEASES
West Nile Virus

West Nile virus was first recorded in humans in the United States in the early 2000s, and by 2007 nearly every state, including Tennessee, had reported confirmed cases of the disease. West Nile is spread by mosquitoes.

Summer is mosquito season in Tennessee. You can prevent mosquito breeding by eliminating standing water around your property. You can prevent mosquito bites by wearing an insect repellant containing 30–50 percent DEET. Picaridin is available in 7 and 15 percent concentrations and would need to be applied more frequently. Wearing long-sleeved pants and shirts and avoiding being outdoors during dusk and dawn are also ways to avoid exposure to mosquitoes.

Fever, chills, weakness, drowsiness, and fatigue are some of the symptoms of West Nile virus.

Lyme Disease

Lyme disease is a bacterial infection spread by deer ticks. The first indication you might have Lyme disease is the appearance of a red rash where you have been bitten by a tick. Following that, symptoms are flu-like. During late-stage Lyme disease, neurological effects are reported.

Ticks are external parasites that attach themselves to warm-blooded creatures like dogs, deer, and humans. Ticks suck blood from their host.

Tick bites are unpleasant enough, even if there is no infection of Lyme disease. After coming in from the woods, especially if you were walking off-trail, carefully inspect your body for ticks. If one has attached itself to you, remove it by carefully "unscrewing" it from your body with tweezers.

You can avoid ticks by wearing long sleeves and pants, tucking in your shirt, and wearing a hat. You can minimize your exposure to ticks by staying on trails and walking paths where you don't brush up against trees and branches.

POISON IVY

If there is one plant that you should learn to identify, it is poison ivy. This woody vine grows in woods all around Tennessee. Touching it can leave you with a painful and terribly uncomfortable reaction.

Poison ivy is green and the leaves grow in clusters of three. There are no thorns. Its berries are a grey-white color, and if the vine is climbing you will notice root "hairs" on the vine. The following mnemonic might help: "Leaves of three let it be; berries white, danger in sight."

An estimated 15–35 percent of people are not allergic to poison ivy. But after repeated exposure this protection is worn down. People who are allergic will experience more and more severe reactions with each episode of exposure.

Poison ivy is easily spread over your body by your hands, or from person to person through skin-to-skin contact. Never touch your eyes or face if you think you may have touched poison ivy, and always wash yourself with hot soapy water if you think you may have come into contact with the vine.

Treat poison ivy rashes with over-the-counter itch creams. In severe cases, you may need to go to the doctor.

VENOMOUS SNAKES

The vast majority of snakes in Tennessee are nonvenomous. Only four species of venomous snakes exist here: Copperheads (northern and southern) live throughout the state, along with the timber rattlesnake. The pygmy rattlesnake lives in the Kentucky Lake region and the cottonmouth water moccasin is found in wet areas in the western part of the state.

Venomous snakes of Tennessee can usually by identified by their elliptical (cat-eye) shaped pupils. Most also have thick bodies, blunt tails, and triangular-shaped heads.

MEDICAL SERVICES

Hospitals, medical centers, and doctors offices are located throughout the state. Walk-in medical centers may be found in the yellow pages and are the best bet for minor needs while you're on vacation. In an emergency, proceed to the closest hospital or call 911.

The single most important thing you can have if you get sick while traveling is health insurance. Before you leave, check with your insurance provider about in-network doctors and medical facilities in the area where you'll be traveling.

Prescriptions

Always travel with your prescription drugs in their original container and with a copy of the prescription issued by your doctor. If you can, get refills before you leave.

DRUGS

Tennessee's greatest drug problem is with methamphetamine, a highly addictive stimulant sometimes called "speed," "crank," and "ice," among other names. During the 1990s and 2000s, meth use spread quickly through rural America, including Tennessee. In 2004, Tennessee passed comprehensive legislation to combat meth. A year later, some 60 percent of Tennessee counties reported that meth remained their most serious drug problem.

The state's anti-meth strategy has been to aggressively seek out illegal meth labs, increase public education about meth use, and promote recovery programs. Despite the efforts, it is still difficult to eliminate meth use, partly because meth is relatively easy to manufacture in so-called "labs," which can be built in homes, hotel rooms, trailers, and even vehicles.

Meth is a dangerous and highly addictive drug. It takes a terrible toll on the health of users, creates myriad family and social problems, and is among one of the most addictive drugs out there.

Other drugs such as cocaine and marijuana are also used and can be just as damaging to families and communities.

CRIME
Crime is a part of life anywhere, and travelers should take precautions to avoid being a victim of crime. Leave valuables at home and secure your hotel room and car at all times. Always be aware of your surroundings, and don't allow yourself to be drawn into conversations with strangers in deserted, dark, or otherwise sketchy circumstances. Single travelers, especially women, should take special care to stay in well-lit and highly populated areas, especially at night.

Information and Services

MONEY
Banks
Dozens of local and regional banks are found throughout Tennessee. Most banks will cash travelers checks, exchange currency, and send wire transfers. Banks are generally open weekdays 9 A.M.–4 P.M., although some are open later and on Saturdays. Automatic Teller Machines (ATMs) are ubiquitous, and many are compatible with bank cards bearing the Plus or Cirrus icons. Between fees charged by your own bank and the bank that owns the ATM you are using, expect to pay $2–5 extra to get cash from an ATM that does not belong to your own bank.

Sales Tax
Sales tax is charged on all goods, including food and groceries.

The sales tax you pay is split between the state and local governments. Tennessee's sales tax is 5.5 percent on food and groceries, and 7 percent on all other goods. Cities and towns add an additional "local use tax," usually between 1.5 percent and 2.75 percent.

Hotel Tax
There is no statewide tax on hotel rooms, but 45 different cities have established their own hotel tax, ranging from 5 to 7 percent.

Cost
Tennessee routinely ranks favorably on cost-of-living indexes. Visitors can comfortably eat their fill in casual restaurants and coffee shops for $30 a day, although it is possible to spend much more if you prefer to eat in upscale restaurants.

The cost of accommodations varies widely, depending on the area you are visiting, the type of accommodations you are seeking, and when you are traveling. The most expensive hotel rooms are in urban centers. Rates go up during major events, on weekends, and during peak travel months in the summer. Cheaper accommodations will be found on the outskirts of town and along rural interstate routes. Budget travelers should consider camping.

If you are not coming in your own car, one of your most substantial expenses will be a rental car. Most rentals bottom out at $30 a day, and rates can be much higher if you don't reserve in advance or if you are renting only for a day or two.

Discounts
Most historic sites, museums, and attractions

offer special discounts for senior citizens and children under 12. Some attractions also have discounts for students and servicemen and -women. Even if you don't see any discount posted, it is worth asking if one exists.

Many chain hotels offer discounts for AAA members.

Bargaining

Consumer Reports magazine reported that you can often get a better hotel rate simply by asking for one. If the rate you are quoted sounds a little high, simply say that it is more than you were planning to spend and ask if they can offer a better rate. Many times, especially if it is out of season, the answer will be yes. Your negotiations will be more successful if you are willing to walk away if the answer is no.

Tipping

You should tip waiters and waitresses between 15 and 20 percent in a "sit-down" restaurant. You can tip 5 to 10 percent in a cafeteria or restaurant where you collect your own food from the counter.

Tip a bell hop or bag handler $1 per bag, or more if they went out of their way to help you.

TOURIST INFORMATION

The Tennessee Department of Tourism Development (615/741-2158, www.tnvacation. com) is a source of visitor information about Tennessee. They publish an annual guide that contains hotel and attraction listings. The website has lots of links to local attractions and chambers of commerce.

Many cities have their own tourist organizations: Memphis, Nashville, Knoxville, Chattanooga, and Clarksville are among the Tennessee cities with a visitors bureau. In some rural areas, counties have teamed up to develop visitor information for the region. Other organizations, such as the National Park Service, Army Corps of Engineers, and the Tennessee State Parks, publish visitor information for certain attractions. Specific listings for visitor information are found throughout this book.

Several regional tourism organizations provide useful information and publications.

In West Tennessee there is the **Southwest Tennessee Tourism Association** (www.tast. tn.org) and the **Northwest Tennessee Tourism Association** (www.reelfootlakeoutdoors.com).

Middle Tennessee has the **Middle Tennessee Tourism Council** (www.middletennesseetourism.com), which covers the counties around Nashville; the **Upper Cumberland Tourism Association** (www.uppercumberland.org), which promotes the region surrounding the Cumberland River and the northern plateau; and the **South Central Tennessee Tourism Association** (www.sctta.net).

East Tennessee has several regional organizations. In southeast Tennessee, contact the **Tennessee Overhill Heritage Association** (www.tennesseeoverhill.com) or the **Southeast Tennessee Tourism Association** (www. southeasttennessee.com). Northeast Tennessee is represented by the **Northeast Tennessee Tourism Association** (www.netta.com). The area surrounding Knoxville and including the Smoky Mountains is served by the **Middle East Tennessee Tourism Council** (www.vacationeasttennessee.org).

If all else fails, contact the chamber of commerce for the county you will be visiting. Chambers of commerce will willingly mail you a sheaf of brochures and any visitor information that may exist. If you are already in town, stop by in person. You are sure to find someone who will be glad to help you.

Maps

Rand McNally publishes the best maps of Tennessee. In addition to the statewide map, Rand McNally publishes maps of Memphis, Nashville, Knoxville, Chattanooga, the Great Smoky Mountains National Park, Clarksville, Murfreesboro-Smyrna, and Gatlinburg–Pigeon Forge. You can buy Rand McNally maps from bookstores and through online sales outlets like Amazon.com. Rand McNally also sells downloadable PDF maps that you can view on your computer or print out.

For trail maps or topographical maps of

TENNESSEE AREA CODES

© AVALON TRAVEL

parks and other natural areas, look for National Geographic's Trails Illustrated series.

The State Department of Transportation updates its official transportation map annually. Request a free copy at www.tdot.state.tn.us, or by calling 615/741-2508. The official map is also available from many Tennessee welcome centers, chambers of commerce, and other tourism-related offices.

The State also creates maps of dozens of Tennessee cities and towns. All these maps are available for free download from the Department of Transportation website.

Hubbard Scientific (www.amep.com) produces beautiful raised-relief maps of Tennessee, the Great Smoky Mountains National Park, and other regions of the state. Found on display in some visitors centers, these maps make great wall art. They are also useful reference, especially for the eastern parts of Tennessee where the landscape is mountainous.

COMMUNICATION
Area Codes

At this writing, Tennessee has six different area codes. Memphis and vicinity use 901; the western plains are 731. The Heartland, including Clarksville, uses 931, while Nashville and the counties immediately north of the city are in 615.

East Tennessee uses 423, except for Knoxville and eight surrounding counties, which are in 865.

Cell Phones

Cell phone signals are powerful and reliable in cities and along the interstates. In rural parts of the state you should not count on your cell phone, and in mountainous areas such as the Cumberland Plateau and the Great Smoky Mountains National Park, forget about it altogether.

TIME ZONES

The eastern third of Tennessee lies in the Eastern Time Zone; Middle and West Tennessee are in Central Time Zone, one hour earlier. The time zone line runs a slanted course from Signal Mountain in the south to the Big South Fork National River and Recreation Area in the north. The time zone line falls at milemarker 340 along I-40, just west of Rockwood and a few miles east of Crossville. Chattanooga, Dayton, Rockwood, Crossville, Rugby, Fall Creek Falls State Park, the Catoosa Wildlife Management Area, and Big South Fork lie close to or on the time zone line, and visitors to these areas should take special care to ensure they are on the right clock.

RESOURCES

Suggested Reading

PHOTOGRAPHY AND ART

Escott, Colin. *The Grand Ole Opry: The Making of an American Icon.* Nashville: Center Street, 2006. An authorized (and somewhat sanitized) look at the Grand Ole Opry. Lots of pictures, reminiscences, and short sidebars make it an attractive coffee-table book.

McGuire, Jim. *Nashville Portraits: Legends of Country Music.* Guilford, CT: The Lyons Press, 2007. Sixty stunning photographs of country music legends including Johnny Cash, Waylon Jennings, Doc Watson, and Dolly Parton. The companion book to an eponymous exhibit that debuted in 2007.

Sherraden, Jim, Paul Kingsbury, and Elek Horvath. *Hatch Show Print: The History of a Great American Poster Shop.* San Francisco: Chronicle Books, 2001. A fully illustrated, beautiful book about Hatch Show Print, the Nashville advertising and letter press founded in 1897.

GUIDES

Brandt, Robert. *Touring the Middle Tennessee Backroads.* Winston-Salem, NC: John F. Blair Publisher, 1995. Robert Brandt is a Nashville judge and self-professed "zealot" for Middle Tennessee. His guidebook details 15 driving tours through backroads in the Heartland of Tennessee. Brandt's knowledge of local history and architecture cannot be surpassed, and his enthusiasm for his subject shines through the prose. While some of the entries are now dated, the guide remains an invaluable source of information about small towns in the region.

Hiking Trails of the Smokies. Gatlinburg, TN: Great Smoky Mountains Natural History Association, 2001. The most comprehensive guide to hiking trails of the Smokies is small enough to fit in the glove compartment of your car. Descriptions give details of elevation, distance, and difficulty. They also describe the natural and historical features along the trail. The same publishers produce related guides of day hikes and history hikes.

Van West, Carroll. *Tennessee's Historical Landscapes: A Traveler's Guide.* Knoxville: University of Tennessee Press, 1995. The editor of the *Tennessee Historical Quarterly* and a professor of history at Middle Tennessee State University, Carroll Van West guides readers along highways and byways pointing out historical structures and other signs of history along the way. A good traveling companion, especially for students of architecture and landscape.

The WPA Guide to Tennessee. Knoxville: The University of Tennessee Press, 1986. The Works Progress Administration guide to Tennessee, written in 1939 and originally published by Viking Press, is a fascinating portrait of Depression-era Tennessee. Published as part of a New Deal project to employ writers and document the culture and character of the nation, the guide contains visitor information, historical sketches, and profiles of the state's literature, culture, agriculture, industry, and more. The guide, republished as part of Tennessee's "Homecoming '86," is a delightful traveling companion.

GENERAL HISTORY

Bergeron, Paul H. *Paths of the Past: Tennessee, 1770–1970*. Knoxville: University of Tennessee Press, 1979. This is a concise, straight-up history of Tennessee, with a few illustrations and maps.

Corlew, Robert E. *Tennessee: A Short History*. Knoxville: The University of Tennessee Press, 1990. The definitive survey of Tennessee history, this text was first written in 1969 and has been updated several times by writers including Stanley J. Folmsbee and Enoch Mitchell. This is a useful reference guide for a serious reader.

Dykeman, Wilma. *Tennessee*. New York: W. W. Norton & Company, and the American Association for State and Local History, 1984. Novelist and essayist Wilma Dykeman says more about the people of Tennessee and the events that shaped the modern state in this slim and highly readable volume than you would find in the most detailed and plodding historical account. It becomes a companion, and a means through which to understand the Tennessee spirit and character.

SPECIALIZED HISTORY

Arnow, Harriet Simpson. *Seedtime on the Cumberland*. Lincoln, NE: Bison Books, 1995. Originally published in 1961, this is the classic narrative of the settlement of southern Kentucky and Middle Tennessee. A classic of Tennessee history, Southern culture, and the act of settlement, this is truly a must-read for those seeking to understand rural life.

Beifuss, Joan Turner. *At the River I Stand*. Brooklyn, NY: Carlson Pub., 1985. This account of the Memphis garbagemen's strike of 1968 is told from the ground up. It places the assassination of Dr. Martin Luther King in its immediate, if not historical, context.

Bond, Beverley G., and Janann Sherman. *Memphis: In Black and White*. Mount Pleasant, SC: Arcadia Publishing, 2003. This lively history of Memphis pays special attention to the dynamics of race and class. The slim and easy-to-read volume contains interesting anecdotes, and lots of illustrations. It is an excellent introduction to the city.

Branch, Taylor. *Parting the Waters: America in the King Years 1954–63*. New York: Simon and Schuster, 1989. The most authoritative account of the Civil rights movement, told through the life of Dr. Martin Luther King. The first in a three-volume account of the movement, *Parting the Waters* includes descriptions of the Nashville Sit-Ins of 1960. The final volume, *At Canaan's Edge,* includes King's assassination in Memphis.

Callahan, North. *TVA: Bridge Over Troubled Waters*. South Brunswick, NJ: A. S. Barnes & Co., 1980. A history of the Tennessee Valley Authority.

Crosby, Molly Caldwell. *The American Plague*. New York: Berkley Books, 2006. A portrait of "the epidemic that shaped our history": the yellow fever epidemic of 1878 that wiped out New Orleans and Memphis.

Egerton, John. *Speak Now Against the Day: The Generation Before the Civil Rights Movement in the South*. Chapel Hill: University of North Carolina Press, 1995. Nashville native John Egerton tells the relatively unacknowledged story of Southerners, white and black, who stood up against segregation and racial hatred during the years before the Civil rights movement.

Egerton, John. *Visions of Utopia*. Knoxville: The University of Tennessee Press, 1977. An accessible and fascinating portrait of three intentional Tennessee communities: Ruskin in Middle Tennessee, Nashoba in West Tennessee, and Rugby in East Tennessee. Egerton's usual sterling prose and sensitive observations make this volume well worth reading.

Honey, Michael. *Going Down Jericho Road: The Memphis Strike, Martin Luther King's Last Campaign*. New York: W. W. Norton & Co., 2007. Labor historian Michael Honey depicts with academic detail and novelistic drama the Memphis Sanitation Strike of 1968. He documents Memphis of the late 1960s, and the quest for economic justice which brought Dr. King to the city. King's assassination and its aftermath are depicted in devastating detail.

Potter, Jerry O. *Sultana Tragedy: America's Greatest Maritime Disaster*. Gretna, LA: Pelican Publishing Company, Inc., 1992. The definitive account of American's worst maritime disaster. The end of the Civil War and the assassination of Abraham Lincoln grabbed the headlines in April 1864, so much so that the sinking of the *Sultana* and the death of more than 1,800 men in the Mississippi River near Memphis went almost unnoticed. This book tells a tale more poignant and moving than the loss of the *Titanic*.

Sword, Wiley. *The Confederacy's Last Hurrah: Spring Hill, Franklin and Nashville*. Lawrence: University Press of Kansas, 2004. This is a well-written and devastating account of John Bell Hood's disastrous campaign through Middle Tennessee during the waning months of the Confederacy. It was a campaign that cost the South more than 23,000 men. With unflinching honesty, Sword describes the opportunities lost and poor decisions made by Gen. Hood.

BIOGRAPHY

James, Marquis. *The Raven: A Biography of Sam Houston*. Indianapolis: The Bobbs-Merrill Company, 1929. Possibly the most remarkable Tennessean in history, Sam Houston was raised by the Cherokee, memorized Homer's *Iliad*, and was twice elected governor of Tennessee before he headed west to the new American frontier to become president of the Texas Republic.

Leeming, David. *Amazing Grace: A Life of Beauford Delaney*. New York: Oxford University Press (USA), 1998. Beauford Delaney was a brilliant but often overlooked modernist painter who was born in Knoxville in 1901. African-American and gay, Delaney later moved to New York where he worked as an artist and moved in circles that included James Baldwin and Henry Miller.

Moore, Carmen. *Somebody's Angel Child: The Story of Bessie Smith*. New York: Thomas Cromwell Company, 1969. The illustrated story of Chattanooga native Bessie Smith's remarkable rise to, then fall from, the top of the music world.

MUSIC

Carlin, Richard. *Country Music*. New York: Black Dog and Leventhal Publishers, 2006. This is a highly illustrated, well-written, and useful reference for fans of country music. It profiles the people, places, and events that contributed to country's evolution. With lots of graphic elements and photographs, it is a good book to dip into.

Gordon, Robert. *It Came From Memphis*. Boston: Faber and Faber, 1994. Memphis resident Robert Gordon takes the backroads to tell the remarkable musical story that emerged from Memphis during the 1950s and '60s. He paints a textured picture of the milieu from which rock 'n' roll eventually rose.

Guralnick, Peter. *Careless Love: The Unmaking of Elvis Presley*. Boston: Little, Brown and Company, 1999. Volume two of Peter Guralnick's definitive biography of Elvis Presley. Guralnick writes in the introduction that he "knows of no sadder story" than Presley's life from 1958 until his death in 1977. The book unflinchingly examines the gradual unraveling of America's greatest pop star.

Guralnick, Peter. *Last Train to Memphis: The Rise of Elvis Presley*. Boston: Little, Brown and Company, 1994. Quite possibly the definitive biography of the King. In volume one, Guralick re-creates Presley's first 24 years, including his childhood in Mississippi and Tennessee, his remarkable rise to fame, and the pivotal events of 1958, when he was drafted into the army and buried his beloved mother.

Handy, W. C. *Father of the Blues*. New York: The Macmillan Company, 1941. This memoir by Memphis's most famous blues man depicts the city during the first quarter of the 20th century. It is an entertaining and endearing read.

Kingsbury, Paul (ed.). *Will the Circle Be Unbroken: Country Music in America*. London: DK Adult, 2006. An illustrated collection of articles by 43 writers, including several performing artists, this book is a useful reference on the genre's development from 1920 until the present.

Kossner, Michael. *How Nashville Became Music City: 50 Years of Music Row*. Milwaukee: Hal Leonard, 2006. Forget about the stars and the singers, this profile of country music focuses on the people you've never heard of: the executives, songwriters, and behind-the-scenes technicians who really make the music happen. An interesting read for fans who don't mind seeing how the sausage is made; a good introduction for people aspiring to be a part of it.

Raichelson, Richard M. *Beale Street Talks: A Walking Tour Down the Home of the Blues*. Memphis: Arcadia Records, 1999. A slim, well-written tome that describes Beale Street as it was, and Beale Street as it is. This is a handy companion for exploring the street.

Sharp, Tim. *Memphis Music: Before the Blues*. Mount Pleasant, SC: Arcadia Publishing, 2007. Part of the Images of America series, this work includes rare and evocative photographs of Memphis people. The result is a painting of the backdrop on which the Memphis blues were born in the early 20th century.

Wolfe, Charles K. *Tennessee Strings*. Knoxville: University of Tennessee Press, 1977. The definitive survey of Tennessee musical history. This slim volume is easy to read.

Zimmerman, Peter Coats. *Tennessee Music: Its People and Places*. San Francisco: Miller Freeman Books, 1998. Tries, and succeeds, to do the impossible: tell the varied stories of Tennessee music all the way from Bristol to Memphis. Nicely illustrated.

REFERENCE

Abramson, Rudy, and Jean Haskell, eds. *Encyclopedia of Appalachia*. Knoxville: University of Tennessee Press, 2006. From language to food to history, this tome has 2,000 entries that will force readers to expand their conception of just what "Appalachia" is.

Montgomery, Michael, and Joseph Hall. *Dictionary of Smoky Mountain English*. Knoxville: University of Tennessee Press, 2004. Have you ever wanted to know what "cumfluttered" means, or know the term for "a designated person in a mountain community who kept boards in order to construct a coffin at short notice"? This is the reference book for you.

Van West, Carroll, ed. *The Tennessee Encyclopedia of History and Culture*. Nashville: Tennessee Historical Society and Rutledge Hill Press, 1998. Perhaps the most valuable tome on Tennessee, this 1,200-page encyclopedia covers the people, places, events, and movements that defined Tennessee history and the culture of its people. Dip in frequently and you will be all the wiser.

FICTION

Agee, James. *A Death in the Family.* New York: Vintage, 1998. First published in 1958, this is the story of a Knoxville family whose domestic happiness is disrupted by the sudden death of the father. The story is largely autobiographical, and features evocative descriptions of Knoxville in 1915. Winner of the Pulitzer Prize for fiction.

Burton, Linda, ed. *Stories from Tennessee.* Knoxville: University of Tennessee Press, 1983. An anthology of Tennessee literature, the volume begins with a story by David Crockett on hunting in Tennessee and concludes with works by 20th-century authors such as Shelby Foote, Cormac McCarthy, and Robert Drake.

Cawood, Chris. *Tennessee's Coal Creek War: Another Fight for Freedom.* Kingston, TN: Magnolia Hill Press, 1995. For 10 months in the late 19th century, the National Guard occupied Coal Creek, now known as Lake City, to prevent labor unrest among coal miners. This historical novel is set during this so-called "coal war" of 1891.

Grisham, John. *The Firm.* Boston: G. K. Hall, 1992. Probably the most celebrated Memphis-set novel in recent years, especially following the success of the eponymous film. Mitchell McDeere takes on corrupt and criminal mob lawyers. It includes references to many city landmarks.

Haun, Mildred. *The Hawk's Done Gone and Other Stories.* Nashville: Vanderbilt University Press, 1968. A collection of stories set in the Smoky Mountains and told using dialect. This volume comes closer than any other to capturing the authentic language, culture, and way of life of East Tennessee's mountain residents during the early 20th century.

Marshall, Catherine. *Christy.* New York: McGraw Hill, 1967. The fictional story of a young teacher, Christy Huddleston, who moves to the Smoky Mountains in 1912 to teach. The story is based on Catherine Marshall's own experience in the mountains. It was adapted into a drama and spawned a television mini-series.

McCarthy, Cormac. *Suttree.* New York: Random House, 1979. Cornelius Suttree is a fisherman who lives in a houseboat in Knoxville during the 1950s. This novel possesses McCarthy's typically clear language, robust characters, and tells a tale punctuated by violence and shocking events.

Neely, Jack. *From the Shadow Side and Other Stories of Knoxville.* Oak Ridge, TN: Tellico Books, 2003. Columnist for the Knoxville *Metropulse,* historian, and master storyteller Jack Neely has done more to preserve Knoxville history than any other. His most recent work builds on his previous volumes: *Secret History* and *Secret History II,* both of which are also worth seeking out.

Taylor, Peter. *Summons to Memphis.* New York: Knopf Publishing Group, 1986. Celebrated and award-winning Tennessee writer Peter Taylor won the Pulitzer Prize for fiction for this novel in 1986. Phillip Carver returns home to Tennessee at the request of his three older sisters to talk his father out of remarrying. In so doing, he is forced to confront a troubling family history. This is a classic of American literature, set in a South that is fading away.

Wright, Richard. *Black Boy.* New York: Chelsea House, 2006. The 1945 memoir of African-American writer Richard Wright recounts several years of residency in Memphis. His portrayal of segregation and racism in Memphis and Mississippi are powerful still today.

FOOD

Lewis, Edna, and Scott Peacock. *The Gift of Southern Cooking: Recipes and Revelations from Two Great American Cooks.* New York: Knopf Publishing Group, 2003. Grande dame of Southern food Edna Lewis and son-of-the-soil chef Scott Peacock joined forces on this seminal text of Southern cuisine. It demystifies, documents, and inspires. Ideal for those who really care about Southern foodways.

Lundy, Ronnie, ed. *Cornbread Nation 3.* Chapel Hill: University of North Carolina Press, 2006. The third in a series of collections on Southern food and cooking. Published in collaboration with the Southern Foodways Alliance, which is dedicated to preserving and celebrating Southern food traditions, the Cornbread Nation collection is an ode to food traditions large and small. Topics include paw-paws, corn, and pork. *Cornbread Nation 2* focused on barbecue. *Cornbread Nation 1* was edited by restaurateur and Southern food celebrant John Egerton.

Stern, Jane and Michael. *Southern Country Cooking from the Loveless Cafe: Biscuits, Hams, and Jams from Nashville's Favorite Café.* Nashville: Rutledge Hill Press, 2005. Road-food aficionados wrote the cookbook on Nashville's most famous pit stop: the Loveless Cafe. Located at the northern terminus of the Natchez Trace Parkway, the Loveless is quintessential Southern cooking: delectable biscuits, country ham, and homemade preserves. Now you can take some of that down-home flavor home with you.

Internet Resources

Tennessee State Parks
www.state.tn.us/environment/parks

An online directory of all Tennessee state parks, this site provides useful details, including campground descriptions, cabin rental information, and the low-down on activities.

Tennessee Department of Tourism Development
www.tnvacation.com

On Tennessee's official tourism website you can request a visitors guide, search for upcoming events, or look up details about hundreds of attractions, hotels, and restaurants.

Tennessee Encyclopedia of History and Culture
www.tennesseeencyclopedia.net

The online edition of an excellent reference book, this website should be your first stop for information on all topics Tennessee. Articles about people, places, and events are written by hundreds of different experts. Online entries are updated regularly.

Nashville Convention and Visitors Bureau
www.visitmusiccity.com

The official tourism website for Nashville, this site offers concert listings, hotel booking services, and useful visitor information. You can also order a visitors guide and money-saving coupons.

Memphis Convention and Visitors Bureau
www.memphistravel.com

The official travel website for Memphis, come here for listings of hotels, attractions, and events. Download coupons, request a visitors guide, or book hotels.

Knoxville Tourism & Sports Corporation
www.knoxville.org

The official travel website for Knoxville, here you can read current news, get a calendar of events, or request visitor information. Also links to the live stream of radio station WDVX, East Tennessee's finest.

The Tennessean
www.tennessean.com

Nashville's major newspaper posts news, entertainment, sports, and business stories online. Sign up for a daily newsletter of headlines from Music City, or search the archives.

The Nashville Scene
www.nashvillescene.com

Nashville's alternative weekly has a great website. The dining guide is fabulous, the stories interesting and archived, and the entertainment calendar is the best in town. Go to "Our Critics' Picks" for a run-down on the best shows in town. The annual manual, reader's choice awards, and other special editions are useful for newcomers and old-timers alike.

The Memphis Flyer
www.memphisflyer.com

Memphis's alternative weekly newspaper publishes entertainment listings and article archives on its website.

Metropulse
www.metropulse.com

The finest alternative weekly in the state, Knoxville's *Metropulse* offers the usual entertainment listings, restaurant reviews, and political analysis, plus special features like Jack Neely's Secret History column.

Memphis Magazine
www.memphismagazine.com

Good restaurant reviews and useful event listings. Subscriptions available online ($15 annual).

502

Index

A

Aaron Douglas Gallery: 145
Abraham Lincoln Museum: 265
Abrams Creek: 387
accommodations: 485-486; see also specific place
Actors Bridge Ensemble: 156
Adams: 196
Adamsville: 116
Ada's Unusual Country Store: 110
Adventure Science Center: 140
African American heritage: Aaron Douglas Gallery 145; Africa in April 53-54; Alex Haley House Museum 82-83; Beale Street 29, 32-33; Beale Street Music Festival 54; Beck Cultural Exchange Center 349; Belle Meade Plantation 137; Bessie Smith Hall and Chattanooga African American Museum 304; Bradley Academy 258; Civil Rights Room at the Nashville Public Library 130-131; Edmondson, William 138; First Baptist Beale Street Church 33; Fisk University 142-143, 145; Fortress Rosencrans 256; Green McAdoo Cultural Center 365-366; Hadley Park 145; Heritage Tours Memphis 47; Highlander Folk School 474; Jubilee Singers 144; Kemet Jubilee 54; Knoxville College 351; Kuumba Festival 357; McKissack and McKissack Architects 136; McLemore House 208-209; Meharry Medical College 145; Music City Jazz and Blues Festival 160; Nashville Black Heritage Tours 147; National Civil Rights Museum 15; Slavehaven Underground Railroad Museum 36-37; Stax Museum of American Soul Music 41; Tennessee State University 145; Tom Lee Park 57; W. C. Handy Home and Museum 29-30
Agricultural Wheel: 471
agriculture: 477
agritourism: 367
Airpark Trail: 89
air pollution: 459-460
airports: Chattanooga Metropolitan Airport (CHA) 316; McGhee Tyson Airport (TYS) 364; Memphis International Airport (MEM) 73; Nashville International Airport (BNA) 185; Tri-Cities Regional Airport (TRI) 418
air travel: 481
Alamo: 85
Alexander Motor Inn: 372

Alex Haley House Museum: 82-83
Alex Haley Square: 349
Allied Arts Alliance of Greater Chattanooga: 311
Alum Cave Bluff: 392-393
Alumni Memorial Building: 356
Alvin C. York State Historic Area: 272
Amazing Mirror Maze: 401
American Museum of Science and Energy: 371
Amish country: 228-229
amphibians: 459
amusement/theme parks: Dollywood 406; Lake Winnepesaukah 310; Wetlands, The 444; WonderWorks 406-407
Anderson Road Fitness Trail: 164
Andrew Johnson Hotel: 343
Andrew Johnson National Historic Site: 446
Andrew Johnson Presidential Library and Museum: 447
Andrew's Bald: 393
Antiques Week: 157
Appalachian Ballet Company: 355
Appalachian Center for Craft: 286, 487-488
apples: 441
Arcade (Nashville): 131
Archaeofest: 110
Archives of Appalachia: 425-426
area codes: 494
Arnold Engineering Development Center: 247
Arrowmont: 401, 488
art galleries: see specific gallery
Artists' Cooperative Theatre: 156
Art Museum of the University of Memphis: 46
arts and crafts: 478-480; see also specific place
Arts and Education Council: 311
A. Schwab: 30-31, 33
Association for Visual Artists Gallery: 311
Athenaeum Rectory: 223
Athens: 334
Audubon Park: 58
auto racing: Bristol Motor Speedway 421-422; Memphis Motorsports Park 60; Nashville Superspeedway 167; Thunder Valley 422
Autumn Gold Festival: 330
Awesome April: 157-158

B

Backbone Rock: 433-434
backcountry camping: 393-394
ballet: 53, 157, 311, 355

Ballet Memphis: 53
Ballet Tennessee: 311
banks: 492
barbecue: 54, 207, 245, 486-487
bargaining: 493
Barton Creek Recreational Area: 249-250
baseball: 60, 167-168, 310, 408-409, 422
basketball: 59-60, 354
Battle of Shiloh: 467
Battles for Chattanooga Electric Map and
    Museum: 306
Bays Mountain Park: 430-431
Beechcraft Heritage Museum: 247
Beale Street: 29, 32-33
Beale Street Music Festival: 54
Beale Street Zydeco Music Festival: 55
Bearden Greenway: 352
Bear Paw Loop: 321
Bearwaller Gap Trail: 201
Bear Wheels Mountain Bike Trail: 201
bed-and-breakfasts: 485-486
Bell, Madison Smartt: 155
Bell Buckle: 236-238
Belle Meade Plantation: 137
Belmont Mansion: 133, 136
Belmont University: 137
Belvidere: 253-254
Belz Museum of Asian and Judaic Art: 35
Bemberg rayon factory: 438
Bemis Mill Village Museum: 107
Benton Falls Trail: 321
Benton MacKaye Trail: 321
Benton's Country Hams: 334
Bessie Smith Hall and Chattanooga African
    American Museum: 304
Bethel Springs: 110
Bicentennial Mall: 142
bicycling: general discussion 484; Big South
    Fork 269; Chattanooga 309-310; Fall Creek
    Falls 288; Great Smoky Mountains 394;
    Memphis 58; Montgomery Bell State Park
    206; Nashville 165-166; Reelfoot Lake 89;
    southern Cherokee National Forest 322;
    Tims Ford State Park 254
Big Hill Pond State Park: 118
Big South Fork National River and Recreation
    Area: 268-270
Bijou Theater: 354
birds/bird-watching: 457
bison: 457
Black Bayou Trail: 89
black bears: 386, 457
Blair School of Music: 157

Bledsoe Creek State Park: 199
Blount, William: 464-465
Blount Mansion: 343-344
Bluebird Cafe: 150
Bluebird on the Mountain: 153
Bluegrass Along the Harpeth: 211
Bluegrass Nights at the Ryman: 153
Blue Heron Mining Community: 269
Blue Ridge Parkway: 388
blues: Memphis 48-49; Nashville 151-152
Bluff View: 305
Bluff View Art District Sculpture Garden: 305
boating: Dale Hollow Lake 273; Fall Creek Lake
    288; Land Between the Lakes 104; Pickwick
    Landing 115; Reelfoot Lake 88-89; Tims Ford
    State Park 254-255
Boatyard, The: 430
bobcats: 457
Boiler Room Theatre: 210-211
Bon Aqua: 207
Bond, Julian: 155
Bonnaroo: 250-251
Booker T. Washington State Park: 309
books/bookstores: general discussion
    479-480; Chattanooga 312; Dyersburg 85;
    Halls 86; Knoxville 358; Memphis 55-56;
    Nashville 160, 162; Oak Ridge 374
Boomsday: 357
botanical gardens and arboretums:
    Cheekwood 138; ETSU Arboretum 426;
    Knoxville Botanical Garden and Arboretum
    353; Memphis Botanical Garden 45
Bradley Academy Museum and Cultural Center:
    257-258
Breckenridge Hatter's Shop: 225
bridges: Cordell Hull Bridge 200; Doe
    River Covered Bridge 437; Shelby Street
    Pedestrian Bridge 126; Stone Bridge 242
Bristol: 418-425
Bristol Motor Speedway: 421-422
Bristol Sessions: 421
Bristol VA-TENN sign: 418-419
Bristol White Sox: 422
Broadway (Nashville): 124-127
brook trout: 395
Brown-Daly-Horne Home: 239
Brownlow, William G.: 469-470
Brownsville: 79-82
Brownsville Blues Fall Festival: 81
Brushy Ridge: 333
Bryan College: 289
Bryon Symphony Orchestra: 275
Buck Bald: 329-330

Buffalo River: 227
bungee jumping: 407
bus travel: 482
Buzzard's Roost: 288

C

Cable Mill: 385, 390
Cable Trail: 288
Cades Cove: 384-385, 387
Cades Cove Loop: 389-390
Cades Cove Nature Trail: 393
Cades Cove Visitor Center: 398-399
Caleb Crosby Threshing Barn: 369
Camden: 93-94
Campbell Overlook: 389
Campground Trail: 89
camping: see specific place
Canal Loop Trails: 103
Cannon Center for the Performing Arts: 53
Cannonsburgh Village: 258
canoeing and kayaking: Big South Fork 269;
   Buffalo River 227; Elk River 243; Harpeth
   River State Park 204
Carl Van Vechten Gallery: 143, 145
Carnival Memphis: 54
Carnton Plantation: 209
Carpetbag Theater: 355
Carroll Reece Museum: 425
Carter Fold Family Memorial Music Center: 423
Carter Mansion: 437-438
Carthage: 200-201
car travel: 482
Castalian Springs: 200
Cataloochee: 388
catfish: 487
caves/caverns: Appalachian Caverns 422; Bell
   Witch Cave 196; Cumberland Caverns 291;
   Dunbar Cave 193-194; Lost Sea 334-335;
   Tuckaleechee Caverns 412
Celebration of Cultures: 160
celebrities, Nashville: 155
cell phones: 494
Centennial Park: 163
Centennial Park Concert Series: 157
Center Furnace: 103
Center Hill Lake: 285
Center Shields Cabin: 385
Chair Shop: 405
Chapel on the Hill: 372
Charles Hall Museum: 332
Charlie's Bunion: 393
Chattanooga: 301-316; accommodations
   312-314; arts 310-311; events 311-312; food
314-315; information and services 315-316;
   recreation 309-310; shopping 312; sights
   304-309; transportation 316
Chattanooga Discovery Museum: 305
Chattanooga Festival of Writers: 311
Chattanooga History Center: 305
Chattanooga Lookouts: 310
Chattanooga Nature Center: 308-309
Chattanooga Symphony & Opera: 311
Chattanooga Theatre Centre: 311
Cheekwood: 138-139
Cherohala Challenge: 322
Cherohala Skyway: 322, 332-333
Cherokee and Davy Crockett Museum: 229
Cherokee Chieftain: 319
Cherokee National Forest: 317-328, 432-442
Cherry Mansion: 111
Chester Inn: 443
Chestnut Mountain Loop: 321
Chickasaw Nation: 461
Chickasaw State Park: 118
children, traveling with: 489
Children's Holocaust Memorial: 296-297
Children's Museum of Memphis: 46
Children's Museum of Oak Ridge: 372
children's theater: 156
Chilhowee Mountain: 320-321
Chilhowee Mountain Bike System: 322
Chilhowee Park: 352
Chimney Tops: 389, 392
Christ Church Episcopal (Rugby): 267
Christ Episcopal Church (Brownsville): 80
Christmas in Lynchburg: 245
Christopher Taylor House: 443
Chucalissa: 45
Church Circle: 429
Church of the Full Gospel Tabernacle: 44-45
Church Park: 33
cinemas: Memphis 53; Nashville 157; see also
   specific place
Circle Modern Dance: 355
Circle Players: 156
City Cemetery (Nashville): 139-140
civil rights: 474-475
Civil Rights Room at the Nashville Public
   Library: 130-131
Civil War: general discussion 467-469; Battle
   of Nashville 141; Bleak House 348; Carnton
   Plantation 209; Carter House 210; Cherry
   Mansion 111; Confederate Park 57; Dover
   Hotel 98; Elmwood Cemetery 44; Fort
   Dickerson 350; Fort Donelson National
   Battlefield 98; Fort Granger 209-210; Fort

Negley 139; Fort Pillow 83; Franklin 220–221; Johnsonville State Historic Area 96; Mabry-Hazen House 349; Oaklands 256–257; Point Park 306; Sam Davis Home and Museum 259–260; Shiloh National Military Park 113–114; Signal Point 309; Spring Hill 219, 220; Stones River National Battlefield 256, 257
Clarence Brown Theater Company: 355
Clarkrange: 274
Clarksville: 190–196
Cleveland: 319
Cliff Dwellers Gallery: 405
Clifton: 111
climate: 455
Clinch Appalachian Artisans Cooperative: 452
Clinch-Powell Community Kitchens: 452
Clingmans Dome: 383–384
Clinton: 365–366, 368
Coal Miner's Daughter Museum: 92
Coker Creek: 329–330
Collegedale: 319
college sports: 59–60, 168
Columbia: 222–225
communication: 494
Confederate Park: 57
Conference on Southern Literature: 311
Cookeville: 274–275
Cookeville Children's Museum: 275
Cookeville Drama Center: 275
Cookeville History Museum: 275
Coolidge Park: 309
Cooper-Young Festival: 54
Cooter's: 145–146
Copperhill: 327
copper mining: 321, 324–326, 327
Cordell Hull Birthplace State Historic Area: 273–274
Cordell Hull Lake: 201
Cordell Hull Lock and Dam: 201
Cornersville: 241
Cornstalk Heights: 279
Cosby: 388, 409–411
costs: 492–493
Cotton Museum: 35
Counce: 115
country music: *see specific place*
Country Music Association Music Festival: 159
Country Music Hall of Fame: 124–125, 150
Country Music Marathon: 158
Country Music Mural: 419
Country Music Television Music Awards: 158
Court Square: 57
Cowan: 255–256

Cowboy Church: 149
coyotes: 457
crafts: 478
Craftsmen's Fair: 402
Cragfont: 200
Cranberry Festival: 434
Crescent Bend: 348
crime: 492
Crossville: 281–283
Crump, Ed: 473
Cucumber Gap: 391
Culture Fest: 312
Cumberland Art Society Backdoor Gallery: 275
Cumberland County Courthouse: 282
Cumberland County Playhouse: 282–283
Cumberland Gap: 264–265
Cumberland Gap National Historic Park: 264
Cumberland Homesteads: 279–281
Cumberland Mountain General Store: 274
Cumberland Mountain State Park: 281
Cumberland Plateau: 261–297
Cumberland River Center: 191–192
Cumberland Trail: 276
currency exchange: 490
Customs House: 126
Customs House Museum and Cultural Center: 193
Cyclemo's Motorcycle Museum: 202
Cypress Grove Nature Park: 107

D
Daisy Theater: 33
Dale Hollow Lake: 272–273
Dale Hollow National Fish Hatchery 273
dance: 53, 157, 311, 355, 479
Danny Thomas ALSAC Pavilion: 37
Davy Crockett Birthplace State Park: 448–449
Davy Crockett Days: 231
Davy Crockett Museum: 229
Davy Crockett State Park: 230–231
daylilies: 328–329
Dayton: 289, 291
Defeated Creek: 201
Delano: 328–329
demographics: 477
Dickens of a Christmas (Franklin): 212
Dickson: 206–207
Dickson-Williams Mansion: 446
disabilities, travelers with: 489
discounts: 492–493
diseases: 490–491
distilleries: George Dickel Distillery 248–249; Jack Daniel's Distillery 244; Prichard's Distillery 243

District, The (Nashville): 124-127
Dixon, The: 45
Dogwood Arts Festival: 357
Dogwood Park and Performance Pavilion: 275
Dollywood: 406
Dover: 98-100
Down Home: 426-427
Downtown Presbyterian Church: 131
Dragging Canoe: 462-463
drugs: 491-492
Ducktown: 324-327
Ducktown Basin Museum: 326
Dunlap: 292
Dunlap Coke Oven Park: 292
Dyer Observatory: 153
Dyersburg: 85

E

earthquakes: 90
East Knoxville: 349-350
East Nashville Tomato Art Festival: 159
East Tennessee History Center: 341
East Tennessee Science Discovery Center: 350
East Tennessee State University: 425-426
ecological reserves and wildlife refuges:
    Big Cypress Tree State Natural Area 86;
    Burgess Falls State Natural Area 285-286;
    Chickasaw National Wildlife Refuge 85-86;
    Cross Creeks National Wildlife Refuge 100;
    Frozen Head State Natural Area 277-278;
    Ghost River State Natural Area 117-118;
    Hatchie River National Wildlife Area 81;
    Ozone Falls State Natural Area 279; Radnor
    Lake State Natural Area 163-164; Reelfoot
    Lake National Wildlife Refuge 88; Savage
    Gulf State Natural Area 291-292; Short
    Springs Natural Area 250; Tennessee
    National Wildlife Refuge 96; Virgin Falls
    State Natural Area 284-285
economy: 476-477
Edgar Evins State Park: 285
Edmondson, William: 138
Edwin and Percy Warner Parks: 164
18th Century Rice Gristmill: 369
18th Century Trade Faire: 335-336
Electro Chalybeate Well: 107
Elephant Sanctuary: 226
Elizabethton: 437-440
elk: 457
Elk and Bison Prairie: 102
Elkmont: 384
Elmwood Cemetery: 44
Elvis Birthday Celebration: 55

Elvis Presley Plaza: 33
Elvis Week: 54
Englewood: 333-334
Englewood Textile Museum: 333-334
environmental issues: 459-460
Ernest Tubb Midnite Jamboree: 149
Erwin: 440-442
Erwin National Fish Hatchery: 440
Erwin State Trout Hatchery: 440
Estill Springs: 253
Ethridge: 228-229
Etowah: 330-331
European settlement: 461-464
Ewing Gallery: 347
E. W. King Home: 419
Exchange Place: 430
expenses: 492-493

F

Fall Creek Falls State Park: 287-289
Fall Fest: 159
Fall Folk Arts Festival: 431
Falls Mill: 253-254
Fan Fair: 158
Farm, The: 228
Farmers' Alliance: 471
farmer's markets: 487
Farragut Folklife Museum: 348-349
fauna: 457, 459
Fayetteville: 242-243
Fayetteville Lincoln County Museum: 242
Feile Franklin Festival: 211
Festival of British and Appalachian Culture:
    267
festivals and events: best 23; Memphis 53-55;
    Nashville 157-160; *see also specific event;
    place*
Fields of the Woods Bible Park: 327-328
Fiery Gizzard Trail: 293
Fire Museum of Memphis: 37
First Baptist Beale Street Church: 33
fishing and hunting: general discussion
    484-485; Big South Fork 269; Franklin
    State Forest 253; Great Smoky Mountains
    394-396; Harpeth River State Park 204;
    Land Between the Lakes 104; Long Hunter
    State Park 260; Montgomery Bell State Park
    206; Pickwick Landing 115; Reelfoot Lake 89;
    Tims Ford State Park 254-255
Fisk Little Theatre: 143
Fisk University: 142-143, 145
flintknapping: 252
flora: 455-457

Fontana Dam: 387
Fontana Lake: 387
food and drink: 486-487
football: 166-167, 353-354
Foothills Parkway: 387
foreign travelers: 489-490
Forrest, Nathan Bedford: 95
Forrest Park: 57-58
Fort Campbell: 196
Fort Donelson: 98, 99, 467
Fort Henry Trails: 103
Fort Kid: 352
Fort Loudoun: 462
Fort Loudoun State Historic Area: 335-336
Fort Nashborough: 126
Fort Negley Park: 139
Fort Pillow massacre: 84
Fort Pillow State Historic Park: 83
Fort Sanders: 347-348
4 Bridges Arts Festival: 311
Frank H. McClung Museum: 347
Franklin: 207-215
Franklin Jazz Festival: 211
Franklin on the Fourth: 211
Franklin Post Office: 207-208
Franklin Rodeo: 211
Franklin State Forest: 253
French and Indian War: 462
Frist Center for the Visual Arts: 127
Frontier Days (Lynchburg): 245
Frozen Head Trail: 276
Fun Fest: 431

G

Gallina Building: 33
Gatlinburg: 400-405
Gatlinburg Sky Lift: 402
Gatlinburg Trail: 393
Gatlinburg Welcome Center: 399
gay and lesbian travelers: 488-489
Gay Street: 340, 341
Gem Theater: 331
General Motors Plant (Spring Hill): 222
geography: 453-455
George Dickel Distillery: 248-249
Gibson Guitar Factory: 31, 34
Gibson Showcase: 149
Giles County Courthouse: 238-239
Gilliam, "Jefferson Street" Joe: 155
Girl Scout Museum: 348
Glanzstoff rayon factory: 438
gliding: 329
Goats, Music, and More Festival: 232

Golden Pond Visitor Center and Planetarium: 102-103
gold panning: 330
golf: Clarksville 194; Crossville 282; Fall Creek Falls 288; Franklin 210; Memphis 58-59; Montgomery Bell State Park 205; Mountain City 435; Nashville 165; Old Stone Fort State Archaeological Park 252; Pickwick Landing 115; Tims Ford State Rustic Park 254
Gore, Al, Jr.: 155
Gorge Overlook Trail: 288
Gospel Music Association Dove Awards: 158
government: 475-476
Graceland: 41-44
Grainger County: 367
Grainger County Tomato Festival: 367
Grand Junction: 118
Grand Ole Opry: 146, 147, 148, 149
Grand Ole Opry Museum: 146
Grassy Cove: 279
Grassy Cove Community House: 279
Grassy Cove Methodist Church and Cemetery: 279
Grassy Cove Trail: 276
Grassy Island Auto Tour: 88
Grassy Island Hiking Trail: 89
Gray Fossil Site: 428-429
Greater Memphis Arts Council: 53
Great Smoky Mountains: 376-414; accommodations 397-398; camping 393-394, 397; driving tours 389-390; food 398; gateways 399-414; health and safety 398; hiking 390-394; information 398-399; orientation 381; pets 399; recreation 394-396; sights 383-385, 387-388
Great Smoky Mountains Arts and Crafts Community: 405
Great Smoky Mountains Heritage Center: 412
Great Smoky Mountains Institute at Tremont: 396
Great Western Iron Furnace: 101
Greek Festival: 159
Greenbrier: 387-388
Greeneville: 446-447
Green Frog Village: 85
greenways: 352-353
Grooms, Red: 155
Grundy Lakes State Park: 292-293
Guenther's Sorghum Mill: 276
gyms: 59, 166

H

Haley Memorial: 112

Halls: 86
Hamilton Creek Park: 164, 165
Hands On! Regional Museum: 426
Handy, W. C.: 29-30, 31
Handy Awards: 54
Handy Park: 33, 57
hang gliding: 310
Harpeth River State Park: 204-205
Harriman: 278-279
Harriman Heritage Museum: 279
Harrison Bay State Park: 309
Harrogate: 265
Hatchie Fall Festival: 81
Haywood County Museum: 80
Hazard Cave: 271
health and safety: 490-492
hemlocks: 458
Hendersonville: 199-200
Henning: 82-83
Henry Horton State Park: 232
Henry Whitehead Place: 385
Heritage Festival (Coker Creek): 330
Heritage Park (Kingsport): 430
Hermitage, The: 197-198
Hidden Passage Trail: 271
Higdon Hotel: 328
Highlander Folk School: 474
hiking: general discussion 484; Big South Fork
    269; Cumberland Mountain State Park 281;
    Fall Creek Falls 288; Franklin State Forest
    253; Great Smoky Mountains 390-394;
    Grundy Lakes 293; Harpeth River State
    Park 204-205; Land Between the Lakes 103;
    Leiper's Fork 217; Long Hunter State Park
    260; Montgomery Bell State Park 206; Old
    Stone Fort State Archaeological Park 252;
    Pickett State Park 271; Pickwick Landing 115;
    Reelfoot Lake 89; safety tips 392; Savage
    Gulf State Natural Area 292; southern
    Cherokee National Forest 321; Tims Ford
    State Park 254-255
Hiram Masonic Lodge: 207
Historic Clarksville: 192-193
Historic Collinsville: 196
Historic Downtown Franklin: 207-208
Historic Rugby: 266-267
Hiwassee River: 328-331
Hiwassee River State Park: 328
Hiwassee Union Church: 328
Hohenwald: 226-228
Homeplace, The: 102
Homestead House Museum: 280
Honker Lake Loop Trail: 103

horses/horseback riding: Big South Fork 269;
    Fall Creek Falls 288; Great Smoky Mountains
    394; Harlinsdale Farm 210; Natchez Trace
    State Park 93; Tennessee Walking Horse
    Museum 245; Tennessee Walking Horse
    National Celebration 233-234; Tennessee
    Walking Horse Show 245; Wartrace
    235-236; Waterfall Farms 232-233
hostels: 486
Host of Christmas Past: 242
hot-air balloons: 409
hotels: 485
hotel tax: 492
Houston, Sam: 373
Houston Museum of the Decorative Arts: 305
Hughes Public Library: 267
Humboldt: 83
Hume Fogg: 127
Hundred Oaks Castle: 253
Hunter Museum of American Art: 305
hunting: see fishing and hunting
Hurricane Mills: 91-93

I

ice hockey: 60, 168, 354
Ijams Nature Center: 350
Independence Day (Nashville): 159
Indian Boundary: 333
Indian Rock House: 271
indoor skydiving: 407
insects: 398
International Friendship Bell: 372
International Rock-a-Billy Festival: 107
International Rock-a-Billy Hall of Fame: 107
International Towing and Recovery Hall of
    Fame and Museum: 304-305
itinerary suggestions: 14-24

J

Jack Daniel's Distillery: 244
Jack Daniel's World Champion Invitational
    Barbeque: 245
Jackson: 105-107, 109-110
Jackson, Andrew: 198-199, 466
Jackson Square (Oak Ridge): 372
Jail House Museum (Winchester): 253
James Agee Park: 348
James D. Vaughan Museum: 229-230
Jamestown: 271-272
James White Fort: 341, 343
James White Greenway: 352
jazz: 49, 151-152
Jazz on the Lawn (Clarksville): 194

Jazz on the Lawn (Nashville): 153
Jean Derryberry Gallery: 275
Jenkins-Bradburn House: 225
Jim Warren Park: 210
John Merritt Classic: 159-160
John Muir Trail: 321
John Oliver Place: 385
John Ruhm-Graham Home: 225
Johnson City: 425-427
Johnson City Welcome Center and Museum: 435
Johnsonville State Historic Area: 96
Johnston, Albert Sidney: 112
Jones, Bobby: 155
Jones, Casey: 108
Jonesborough: 442-446
Jonesborough-Washington County History
    Museum: 442-443
J. Percy Priest Lake: 164-165, 260
Jubilee Community Arts: 356
Jubilee Hall: 143
juke joints: 50-51
Justin P. Wilson Cumberland Trail State Park: 276

K

kayaking: see canoeing and kayaking
Kelso: 243
Kemet Jubilee: 54
Kentucky Lake: 91-94, 96-100
Keystone Trail: 89
King, Rev. Martin Luther, Jr.: 475
Kingsport: 429-432
Kingston: 278-279
Kinser Park: 447
Knoxville: 337-365; accommodations 359-360;
    entertainment 354-358; food 360-363;
    information and services 363-364; shopping
    357-358; sights 340-351; sports and
    recreation 352-354; transportation 364-365
Knoxville Civic Auditorium: 354
Knoxville Ice Bears: 354
Knoxville Museum of Art: 346
Knoxville Music Monument: 343
Knoxville Opera: 355
Knoxville Symphony Orchestra: 355
K-25 Overlook: 372
Ku Klux Klan: 240, 469, 474
Kuumba Festival: 357
Kyles Ford: 451-452

L

Ladies' Rest Room: 231
La Grange: 116-118
Lake Acorn: 206

lakes: 455
Land Between the Lakes: 100-105
land use: 460
language: 478
Lauderdale County Tomato Festival: 86
Lauderdale Courts: 38, 40
Laurel Bloomery: 433
Laurel Falls Loop: 292
Laurel-Snow Trail: 276
Laurel Theater: 356
Lawn Chair Theatre: 217
Lawrenceburg: 229-230
Leiper's Fork: 216-218
Lenoir Museum: 368-369
lesbian and gay travelers: 488-489
Lewisburg: 231-232
Lichterman Nature Center: 46-47
Limestone: 448-449
Lincoln County Bluegrass and Crafts Festival:
    242
Lincoln County Fair: 242
literature: 479-480
Little Congress Bicycle Museum: 264
Little Greenbrier School: 384
llama trekking: 410
logging: 380
Lone Rock Trail: 293
longest yard sale: 203
Long Hungry Creek Farm: 202
long hunters: 461-462
Long Hunter State Park: 164, 260
Lookout Mountain: 306-309
Look Rock: 387
Loretta Doll and Fan Museum: 92
Lyme disease: 491
Lynchburg: 243-246
Lynn H. Wood Archaeological Museum: 319
Lynnville: 241-242

M

Mabry-Hazen House Museum: 349
Madisonville: 334
Magevney House: 40-41
Main Street Festival (Franklin): 211
Main Street Jazzfest (Murfreesboro): 258
Mallory-Neely House: 40-41
Manchester: 251
Manor Hall: 225
map information: 493-494
Marble Plains Trail: 254
Marble Springs: 351
Marionette Shows at the Nashville Public
    Library: 156

Market Square (Knoxville): 343, 344
Markham's Department Store: 201
Mark Twain Spring Park: 272
Marshall County Community Theater: 231-232
Maryville: 372, 374
Maryville College: 374
Mason: 86
Mayfield Dairy Farms: 334
McLemore House: 208-209
McMinn Living History Museum: 334
McMinnville: 291
McNairy County Historical Museum: 116
medical services: 491
Meeman-Shelby Forest State Park: 58
Melungeons: 450
Memorial Auditorium (Chattanooga): 310-311
Memphis: 25-75; accommodations 61-64;
   entertainment 48-49, 50-51, 52-55; food
   64-71; information and services 72-73;
   orientation 28-29; shopping 55-57; sights
   29-48; sports and recreation 57-60;
   transportation 73-75
Memphis Brooks Museum of Art: 41
Memphis Grizzlies: 59
Memphis in May: 54
Memphis International Festival: 54
Memphis Music and Heritage Festival: 54
Memphis Redbirds: 60
Memphis Rock 'n' Soul Museum: 31
Memphis Symphony Orchestra: 53
Mennonites: 285
Meriwether Lewis Gravesite and Memorial: 227
Metcalph Bottoms: 384
Methodist Church (Cades Cove): 385
Middle Tennessee State University: 256
Mid-South Fair: 54
Miller's Homestead: 437
Millikan's Overlook: 288
Mind Field: 80-81
Miner's Hall: 292
Mingus Mill: 388, 389
Missionary Baptist Church (Cades Cove): 385
Mississippi River Museum: 36
Mississippi River Trail: 58
Mitchell Museum: 247
money: 492-493
Monteagle: 294-295
Monterey: 275-277
Montgomery Bell State Park: 205-207
Moore County Jail: 244-245
Morton Overlook: 389
Mountain City: 435
Mountain Farm Museum: 388, 389

Mountain Music Museum: 420
Mount LeConte: 384, 392-393
Mount Pleasant: 225-226
Mount Pleasant/Maury County Phosphate
   Museum: 225
Mousetail Landing State Park: 93
Mud Island: 36, 37
Mule Day: 223-224
Murfreesboro: 256-260
Murfreesboro Courthouse: 256
Murfreesboro/Rutherford County Center for
   the Arts: 258
Museum Center at Five Points: 319
Museum of Appalachia: 366, 368
museums: *see specific museum;* railroads and
   trains
music: 478-479; itinerary suggestions 21-24
Musica: 132
Music City Bowl: 160
Music City Brewer's Festival: 159
Music City Jazz and Blues Festival (JAMS):
   160
Music on the Mountain: 153
Music Row: 131-132
Music Valley: 145-147
Music Valley Wax Museum of the Stars: 146
Mysterious Mansion: 401

N
Narrows of the Harpeth: 204
Nashville: 119-186; accommodations 168-174;
   entertainment 147-163; food 174-182;
   information and services 183-184;
   orientation 122-124; shopping 160-163;
   sights 124-147; sports and recreation
   163-168; transportation 185-186
Nashville Ballet: 157
Nashville Chamber Orchestra: 157
Nashville Children's Theatre: 156
Nashville Dream: 167
Nashville Film Festival: 158
Nashville Kangaroos: 167
Nashville Metros: 168
Nashville Predators: 168
Nashville Pride Festival: 159
Nashville Public Library: 130-131, 156
Nashville Sounds: 167-168
Nashville Symphony Orchestra: 156-157
Natchez Trace: 216-231
Natchez Trace Parkway: 165
Natchez Trace State Park and Forest: 93
Nathan Bedford Forrest State Park: 94
Nathaniel Greene Museum: 446

National Bird Dog Museum: 118
National Cemetery: 98
National Civil Rights Museum: 34-35
National Cornbread Festival: 297
National Ornamental Metal Museum: 45
national parks: 483
National Storytelling Center: 444
National Storytelling Festival: 443-444
Native American heritage: Castalian Springs 200; Cherokee and Davy Crockett Museum 229; Chota Memorial 336; Fort Loudoun State Historic Area 335-336; Gravesite of Nancy Ward 319-320; history 460-464; Long Island of the Holston 430; Ocoee 319-320; Old Copper Trail 321; Old Stone Fort State Archaeological Park 251-252; Pinson Mounds State Archaeological Park 110; Red Clay State Historic Park 319; Sequoyah Birthplace Museum 336; Shiloh Indian Mounds 114; Sycamore Shoals 438-439; Tanasi Memorial 336
Natural Bridge: 227
Natural History Museum at the Gray Fossil Site: 428-429
Netherland Inn: 430
New Ballet Ensemble: 53
New Daisy Theater: 33
Newfound Gap: 383-384
Newfound Gap Road: 389
New Madrid Quake: 90
Neyland Greenway: 352
Nightfall: 312
nightlife: Bristol 422; Franklin 211; Knoxville 356-357; Memphis 48-49, 50-51, 52-53; Murfreesboro 258; Nashville 147, 149-155
Nissan North America: 260
Noah "Bud" Ogle Place: 390
Normandy: 248-249
Normandy Lake: 249-251
Norris Dam State Park: 368-370
North Chickamauga Trail: 276
northern Cherokee National Forest: 432-442
North Knoxville: 351
Northside Clocks: 251
North-South Trail: 103
Nutbush: 82

O

Oaklands: 256-257
Oaklands Victorian Fair: 258
Oak Ridge: 370-372, 473-474
Oak Ridge Art Center: 372
Oak Ridge National Laboratory: 371-372

Obed River Trail: 276
Obed Wild and Scenic River: 277
Ober Gatlinburg: 402
Ocoee: 319-320
Ocoee River Dams: 322-323
Ocoee Whitewater Center: 323-324
Oconaluftee: 388
Oconaluftee Visitor Center: 399
off-highway vehicles (OHV): 103
Ogle Cabin: 401
Ogle's Broom Shop: 405
Oktoberfest (Clarksville): 194
Oktoberfest (Nashville): 160
Old Copper Trail: 321
Old Gray Cemetery: 351
Old Hickory: 197-199
Old Hickory Lake: 198-199
Old Stone Fort State Archaeological Park: 251-252
Old Time Fiddlers' Convention: 433
Old Time Music Fest: 107
Oneida: 265
opera: 53, 157, 311, 355
Opry Month: 153
Orpheum Theatre: 32, 53
Oswald Dome Trail: 321
Overhill country: 462
Overton Park: 57

P

packing: 13
Palace Theatre (Crossville): 282
Paleoindians: 460
Paramount Center for the Arts: 422
Paris: 96-97
Paris Landing State Park: 97-98
parks: best 18; Memphis 57-58; Nashville 163-165; see also specific park; place
Parksville Lake: 322
Parsons Branch: 387
Parthenon, The: 132-133
Patriot Park: 406
Patsy Cline Memorial: 93-94
Paw Paw Trail: 288
Peabody Hotel Memphis: 35-36
Pearl, Minnie: 205
pearls: 456
Peay, Austin: 472
People's Branch Theatre: 156
performing arts: Chattanooga 310-311; Knoxville 354-356; Memphis 53; Nashville 156-157; see also specific place
Pickett State Park: 271

Pickin' Porch: 422
Pickwick Landing State Park: 114-115
Pigeon Forge: 405-408
Piggly Wiggly: 68
pigs, feral: 457
Piney River Trail: 276
Pinkerton Park: 210
Pink Palace: 45-46
Pinnacle Overlook: 264
Pinson Mounds State Archaeological Park: 110
Pioneer Hall Museum: 283
plants: 455-457
plate-lunch diners: 486
Playhouse on the Square: 53
Pleasant Hill: 283
poison ivy: 491
politics: 475-476
Polk, James K., home of: 222-223
pollution: 459-460
Port Rayon: 438
Port Royal State Historic Area: 195-196
Pratt Museum: 196
prescriptions: 491
Pressman's Home: 450-451
Price-Jackson House: 225
Price Public School: 449
Primitive Baptist Church: 385
Prohibition: 471
Project Motion: 53
Puckett's Grocery: 217
Pulaski: 238-241
Pull-Tight Players: 211
Pyramid, The: 38

QR

Quillen Gallery: 425
Quillen Veterans Administration Medical
    Center: 426
quilts: 448
rafting: Big South Fork 269; Nolichucky River
    441; Ocoee River 323-324; Pigeon River 410
railroads and trains: Big South Fork Scenic
    Railroad 269; Blue Ridge Scenic Railway
    327; Bristol Depot 419; Casey Jones Home
    and Railroad Museum 105-106; Chattanooga
    Choo Choo 305-306; Cookeville Depot
    Museum 275; Copperhill Special 331;
    Cowan Railroad Museum 255; Crossville
    Depot 282; Hiwassee River Rail Adventure
    331; Incline Railway 307; L&N Depot and
    Railroad Museum 331; Little River Railroad
    and Lumber Museum 412; Lynnville Depot
    Museum and Train Station 241; Model

Railroad Museum 306; N.C. & St. Louis
    Depot and Railroad Museum 106-107; New
    River Scenic Railway 268; Secret City Scenic
    Excursion Train 372; Tennessee Central
    Railway Museum 140, 147; Tennessee Valley
    Railroad 306
rail transportation: 481
Ramsey House Plantation: 350-351
Rattle and Snap: 225-226
RC and Moon Pie Festival: 237
RCA Studio B: 132
Real Life Players: 156
Reconstruction: 469-470
recreation: general discussion 483-485; see
    also specific activity; place
recreational vehicles: 483
Red Boiling Springs: 201-204
Red Clay State Historic Park: 319
Reelfoot Lake: 86-91
Reelfoot Lake State Park Visitor Center: 88
Reliance: 328
religion: 477-478
Renaissance Center (Dickson): 206
reptiles: 459
restaurants: see specific place
Rhea County Courthouse: 289
Rhythm and Noon: 312
Rhythm and Roots Reunion: 422-423
Rich Mountain: 387
Rich Mountain Loop: 391
Ripley: 86
Ripley's Believe It or Not Museum: 401
Rippavilla: 219-221
Ritter Farms: 367
Riverbend Festival: 311-312
Riverfest: 194
River Gallery: 311
Riverkings: 60
river rafting: see rafting
rivers: 455
RiverWalk (Clarksville): 191-192
River Walk (Memphis): 36
Roane County Courthouse: 278
Roane County Museum of History: 278
Roan Mountain: 436-437
Roan Mountain State Park: 437
Roaring Fork Auto Nature Trail: 390
Rock City: 306
Rock Creek Trail: 271
Rock House Shrine: 284
Rock Island State Park: 285
Rocky Mount: 427-428
Rogersville: 449-451

Rossini Festival: 357
Ross's Landing Park and Plaza: 309
Roxy Regional Theatre: 194
Ruby Falls: 306-307
Rudolph, Wilma: 192
Rugby: 265-268
Running of the Iroquois Steeplechase: 159
Ryman Auditorium: 125-126, 150

S

sales tax: 492
Sam Davis Home and Museum: 259-260
Sam Houston Schoolhouse: 374
Samuel Doak Museum: 447-448
sandhill cranes: 329
Sarratt Gallery: 137
Savage Day Loop: 292
Savannah: 111-113
Schoolyard Springs: 434
Scopes Monkey Trial: 290, 291
Secret City Commemorative Walk: 372
Selmer: 116
senior travelers: 489
Sequoyah Birthplace Museum: 336
Sequoyah Greenway: 352
Sequoyah Park: 352
Sevierville: 408-409
Sevierville Visitor Center: 399
Sewanee: 295-296
Sewanee Natural Bridge: 296
Shady Valley: 434
Shakespeare in the Park (Cookeville): 275
Shannon Street Blues and Heritage Festival: 107
Sharpe Planetarium: 46
Shelby Farms: 58
Shelbyville: 232-235
Sheriff Buford Pusser Home and Museum: 116
Shiloh: 114
Shiloh National Cemetery: 114
Shiloh National Military Park: 113-114
shopping: see specific place
Shoreline Trail: 254
Signal Mountain: 309
skiing: 402
Slavehaven Underground Railroad Museum: 36-37
slavery: 466-467
"Sleepy" John Estes Home: 79
Smith County Courthouse: 200
Smith County Heritage Museum: 201
Smith-Trahern Mansion: 193
Smithville: 286

Smithville Fiddler's Jamboree: 286
Smoky Mountain Field School: 396
Smoky Mountain Trail: 276
Smyrna: 259-260
snakes: 398, 491
Sneedville: 452
soccer: 168
Soulsville: 42
South Bison Range: 102
South Cumberland State Park: 294
southern Cherokee National Forest: 317-328
Southern Festival of Books: 160
South Knoxville: 350-351
South Pittsburg: 297
Space Needle: 401-402
Sparta: 283-284
spectator sports: Bristol 422; Chattanooga 310; Jackson 107; Knoxville 353-354; Memphis 59-60; Nashville 166-168; Sevierville 408-409
Spotted Saddle Horse Show: 245
Spring Garden Fair: 431
Spring Heritage Center: 413
Spring Hill: 218-222
Spring in the Hollow: 245
Spring Wildflower Pilgrimage: 396
Standing Stone State Park: 274
statehood: 464-465
State of Franklin: 445
state parks: 483-484
State Street Farmer's Market: 423
Stax Museum of American Soul Music: 41
Stieglitz Collection: 143
Stinging Fork Trail: 276
St. Jude Children's Research Hospital: 37
Stone Door: 292
storytelling: 443-444
Streeter, Vannoy: 234
strip mining: 459
study opportunities: 487-488
Sugarland Mountain: 389
Sugarlands Visitor Center: 398
Summertown Bluegrass Reunion: 230
Sundown in the City: 357
Sunset Concert Series (Townsend): 413
Sunset Rock: 307
Sunsphere: 346
Sun Studio: 38
Sweetwater: 334-335
swimming: see specific place
Swingfest: 312
Sycamore Shoals: 438-439
Symphony in the Park (Cookeville): 275

T

TaleSpin: 311
Tanasi Mountain Bike Trail System: 322
taxes: 492
taxi service: 482
Tellico Plains: 332-333
Tellico Ranger District Trail System: 322
Tellico River: 332-336
Temple of Adas Israel: 80
Tennessee Agricultural Museum: 141-142
Tennessee Aquarium: 304
Tennessee Crafts Fair: 158-159
Tennessee delta: 79-86
"Tennessee" Ernie Ford's Home: 420-421
Tennessee Hometown Tomatoes: 367
Tennessee Military Museum: 130
Tennessee Miller Coliseum: 258
Tennessee Museum of Aviation: 408
Tennessee Museum of Early Farm Life: 221-222
Tennessee Newspaper and Printing Museum:
    449-450
Tennessee Renaissance Festival: 159
Tennessee Repertory Theatre: 156
Tennessee River Folklife Center: 94
Tennessee River Freshwater Pearl Museum and
    Farm: 94
Tennessee River Gorge Trail: 276
Tennessee River Museum: 111
Tennessee Smokies: 408-409
Tennessee Sports Hall of Fame: 126
Tennessee Stage Company: 355
Tennessee State Capitol: 127
Tennessee State Library and Archives: 127
Tennessee State Museum: 127, 130
Tennessee Supreme Court: 127
Tennessee Tech University: 274
Tennessee Theatre: 343, 354
Tennessee Titans: 166-167
Tennessee Valley Authority (TVA): 472-473
Tennessee Walking Horse Museum: 245
Tennessee Walking Horse National Celebration:
    233-234
Tennessee Walking Horse Parkway: 231
Tennessee Walking Horse Show: 245
Tennessee War Memorial: 127
Tennessee Wesleyan University: 334
tennis: 59, 166
Texas Troubadour Theatre: 149
theater: Bristol 422; Chattanooga 310-311;
    Clarksville 194; Cookeville 275; Crossville
    282-283; Etowah 331; Franklin 210-211;
    Knoxville 355; Lewisburg 231-232; Memphis
    53; Murfreesboro 258; Nashville 156

Theatre Memphis: 53
TheatreWorks: 53
Third Creek Greenway: 352
Thomas Martin House: 239
Thompson-Boling Arena: 354-355
Three Hickories Nature Trail: 164
Three Sisters Festival: 312
3 States, 3 Mountains: 311
time zones: 494
Tims Ford State Park: 254-255
Tin Pan South: 158
tipping: 493
Tipton-Haynes Historic Site: 426
Tivoli Theater: 310
T. O. Fuller State Park: 58
Tom Lee Park: 57
tornadoes: 455
tourism: 477
tourist information: 493-494
Town and Country Tour of Homes: 211
Townsend: 411-414
Townsend Visitor Center: 399
Townsend Winter Heritage Festival: 396
Townsend Y: 384
Tracy City: 292-293
trade: 435
Trail of Tears: 464
train transportation: 481; see also railroads
    and trains
transportation: general discussion 13,
    481-483; see also specific place
Travellers Rest Plantation and Museum: 140-141
trees: 456-457
Tri-Cities: 418-432
Trinity Music City U.S.A.: 199-200
Tripp Home: 80
T. S. Stribling Museum: 111
tubing: 412-413
Tullahoma: 246-248
Tullahoma Fine Arts Center: 247
Turkey Creek Lake View: 333
Turkey Creek Nature Trail: 201
Turtletown: 327-328
Tusculum: 447-448
Twin Forks Horse Trail: 164
Tyson Park: 352

U

Uncle Dave Macon Days Festival: 258
Unicoi County Apple Festival: 441
Unicoi County Heritage Museum: 440
Unicoi Turnpike Trail: 321
University of Memphis Tigers: 59-60

University of Tennessee: 346–348
University of the South: 295–296
Upper Cumberland Arts Alliance Gallery: 275
Upper Cumberland Military Museum: 282
Upper Room, The: 132
UT Music Recital Hall: 356

V

Vanderbilt Fine Arts Gallery: 137
Vanderbilt University: 136–137
Victorian Village: 40–41
visas, travel: 489–490
Volunteer Landing: 345–346
Vonore: 335–336

WXYZ

Walking Horse Country: 231–238
Walling: 285
Walnut Grove: 225
War of 1812: 466
Warrior's Path State Park: 431
Wartrace: 235–236
Wartrace Creek: 201
Watauga Lake: 435–436
waterfalls: Abram's Falls 387; Bald River
   Falls 333; Benton Falls 321; Burgess Falls
   285–286; Cane Creek Cascade 287; Cane
   Creek Falls 287; Coker Creek 330; Deep
   Creek 388, Fall Creek Falls 287–288; Foster
   Falls 293; Gentry Creek Falls 433; Hen
   Wallow Falls 388, 392; Laurel Falls 391–392;
   Old Stone Fort State Archaeological Park
   252; Ozone Falls 279; Piney Falls 287; Place
   of a Thousand Drips 390; Ramsey Cascades
   392; Ruby Falls 306–307; Rutledge Falls 251;
   Sinks, The 384; Virgin Falls 284–285
water pollution: 460
Watts Bar Belle: 278
W. C. Handy Home and Museum: 29–30
WDVX Blue Plate Special: 355
weather: 455
Webb School: 236–237
Webb School Arts and Crafts Festival: 237

West Knoxville: 348–349
West Nile virus: 490–491
West Tennessee Delta Heritage Center: 79–80
West Tennessee Diamond Jacks: 107
West Tennessee Regional Art Center: 83
West Tennessee State Fair: 107
West Tennessee Strawberry Festival: 83
White Bluff: 207
white-water rafting: *see* rafting
Whitwell: 296–297
Wild Bill's: 51
wildflowers: 456
wildlife: 385, 386, 387, 457, 459
Williamson County Fair: 211
Willie Nelson and Friends Museum: 146
Will Skelton Greenway: 352
Winchester: 252–253
wine/wineries: Beachaven Vineyards and
   Winery 194; Beans Creek Winery 251; Clinch
   Mountain Winery 367; Highland Manor
   Winery 272; Tri-Star Vineyards and Winery
   233
Winfrey, Oprah: 155
Wolf River Monument: 117
Women's Basketball Hall of Fame: 344–345
women's suffrage: 471–472
women travelers: 488
Woodlands Nature Station: 103
Woodland Trail: 288
Woodruff-Fontaine House: 40
World Championship Barbeque Cooking
   Contest: 54
World's Biggest Fish Fry: 97
World's Fair Park: 346, 352
Wynneworld: 200
yard sale, longest: 203
Ye Olde Jail Museum (Jamestown): 272
zoos and aquariums: Chattanooga Zoo
   305; Knoxville Zoo 350; Memphis Zoo 41;
   Nashville Zoo at Grassmere 140; Ripley's
   Aquarium of the Smokies 400–401;
   Tennessee Aquarium 304; Tennessee Safari
   Park at Hillcrest 85

Map Index

Along the Ocoee: 317
Chattanooga, Downtown: 302
Chattanooga and the Overhill Country: 300
Clarksville: 190
Cumberland Plateau: 263
Downtown and the Delta: Memphis and West
    Tennessee: 14
First Frontier, The: 417
Franklin: 208
From the Smokies to Scenic City: East
    Tennessee: 19
Great Smoky Mountains: 378-379
Heartland, The: 189
Into the Heartland: Nashville and Middle
    Tennessee: 16
Jackson: 106
Kentucky Lake: 92
Knoxville: 339

Knoxville, Downtown: 342
Lookout Mountain: 308
Memphis: 27
Memphis, Downtown: 30
Memphis, Midtown: 39
Music Valley (Nashville): 146
Nashville: 121
Nashville, Downtown: 128-129
Nashville, Midtown, and the West End: 134-135
Nashville, South: 139
Northern Cherokee National Forest: 433
Oak Ridge: 371
Reelfoot Lake: 87
Tennessee: east side 4-5; west side 2-3
Tennessee Area Codes: 494
Tennessee Driving Distances: 482
Tri-Cities, The: 419
Western Plains: 78

Acknowledgments

It has been a joy getting to know my home state in such detail over the past few years. Tennessee may have been flowing through my veins, but I had a lot to learn. Many people helped me along the way.

Thanks to Tad Pierson of American Dream Safari and Sherman Willmott of Shangri-La Projects for showing me the Memphis they love, and to Jackie Reed of the Memphis Convention and Visitors Bureau for pointing me in the right directions.

In Nashville, I am grateful for the warm welcome and hospitality of Phil and Dikkie Schoggen, old friends who became new ones. Thanks also to Ed Hamlett for sharing his thoughts on what makes his city special.

In East Tennessee, I am thankful for the suggestions provided by so many family friends, who shared their own favorite places and pit stops.

I would also like to thank the staff of Avalon Travel for believing that I was the right person for this job, and for making this a better book.

Friends and family in Tennessee, the Virgin Islands, and beyond encouraged me during this project. I could not have written this book without the support of my husband, Amarro, who forgave my absences and tolerated my preoccupation with all things Tennessee, including country music.

But above all, I am grateful for the help and support of my parents, Lucy and Rich Henighan, who first instilled in me my love of exploration and understanding. Lucy and Rich listened patiently to my progress reports and believed I could get the project done. They were my traveling companions and helpers, and this book is dedicated to them.

www.moon.com

DESTINATIONS | ACTIVITIES | BLOGS | MAPS | BOOKS

MOON.COM is ready to help plan your next trip! Filled with fresh trip ideas and strategies, author interviews, informative travel blogs, a detailed map library, and descriptions of all the Moon guidebooks, Moon.com is all you need to get out and explore the world—or even places in your own backyard. While at Moon.com, sign up for our monthly e-newsletter for updates on new releases, travel tips, and expert advice from our on-the-go Moon authors. As always, when you travel with Moon, expect an experience that is uncommon and truly unique.

MOON IS ON FACEBOOK—BECOME A FAN!
JOIN THE MOON PHOTO GROUP ON FLICKR

MAP SYMBOLS

▰▰▰ Expressway	**C** Highlight	✕ Airfield	⌁ Golf Course
▰▰▰ Primary Road	○ City/Town	✈ Airport	**P** Parking Area
▰▰▰ Secondary Road	◉ State Capital	▲ Mountain	▰ Archaeological Site
▭▭▭ Unpaved Road	⊛ National Capital	✦ Unique Natural Feature	▮ Church
- - - - Trail	★ Point of Interest		
·········· Ferry	• Accommodation	⋙ Waterfall	▦ Gas Station
▬▬▬ Railroad	▼ Restaurant/Bar	▲ Park	Glacier
▨▨▨ Pedestrian Walkway	■ Other Location	▣ Trailhead	Mangrove
▥▥▥ Stairs	⋀ Campground	⛷ Skiing Area	Reef
			Swamp

CONVERSION TABLES

°C = (°F - 32) / 1.8
°F = (°C x 1.8) + 32
1 inch = 2.54 centimeters (cm)
1 foot = 0.304 meters (m)
1 yard = 0.914 meters
1 mile = 1.6093 kilometers (km)
1 km = 0.6214 miles
1 fathom = 1.8288 m
1 chain = 20.1168 m
1 furlong = 201.168 m
1 acre = 0.4047 hectares
1 sq km = 100 hectares
1 sq mile = 2.59 square km
1 ounce = 28.35 grams
1 pound = 0.4536 kilograms
1 short ton = 0.90718 metric ton
1 short ton = 2,000 pounds
1 long ton = 1.016 metric tons
1 long ton = 2,240 pounds
1 metric ton = 1,000 kilograms
1 quart = 0.94635 liters
1 US gallon = 3.7854 liters
1 Imperial gallon = 4.5459 liters
1 nautical mile = 1.852 km

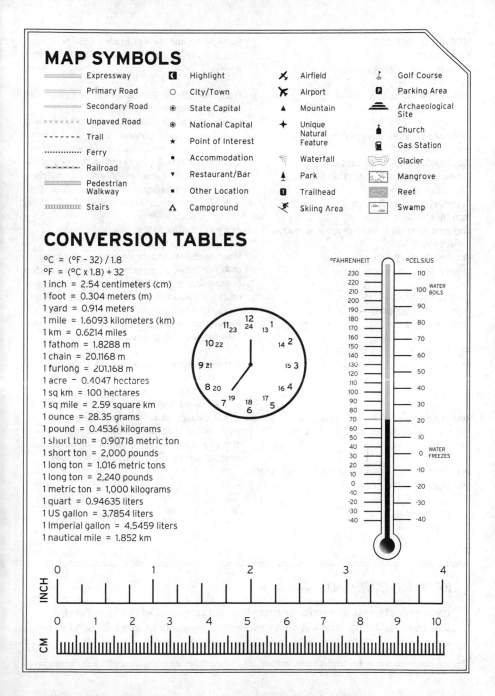

MOON TENNESSEE

Avalon Travel
a member of the Perseus Books Group
1700 Fourth Street
Berkeley, CA 94710, USA
www.moon.com

Editor and Series Manager: Kathryn Ettinger
Copy Editor: Amy Scott
Graphics Coordinator: Tabitha Lahr
Production Coordinators: Tabitha Lahr,
   Christine DeLorenzo
Cover Designer: Tabitha Lahr
Map Editor: Albert Angulo
Cartographers: Chris Markiewicz, Jon Niemczyk,
   Kat Bennett
Proofreader: Kia Wang
Indexer: Greg Jewett

ISBN-10: 1-59880-114-7
ISBN-13: 978-1-59880-114-9
ISSN: 1091-3343

Printing History
1st Edition – 1997
5th Edition – April 2009
5 4 3 2

Text © 2009 by Susanna Henighan Potter.
Maps © 2009 by Avalon Travel.
All rights reserved.

Publisher's Note: Jeff Bradley wrote four editions of
Moon Handbooks Tennessee.

Some photos and illustrations are used by permission and are the property of the original copyright owners.

Front cover photo: Tennessee forest and mountains at dusk © Ron and Patty Thomas/Getty Images
Interior photos: Courtesy of Tennessee Department of Tourist Development, pages 1, 9 (both), 10, 11, 12, 13, 17 (downtown Nashville), 18 (both), 19 (Gay Street), 20, 21, 23 (both); Courtesy of the Memphis Convention and Visitors Bureau, page 7; © Susanna Henighan Potter, pages 6, 8, 14, 15, 16, 17 (Cheekwood), 19 (Sunsphere), 22, 24

Printed in the United States by RR Donnelley

KEEPING CURRENT

If you have a favorite gem you'd like to see included in the next edition, or see anything that needs updating, clarification, or correction, please drop us a line. Send your comments via email to feedback@moon.com, or use the address above.